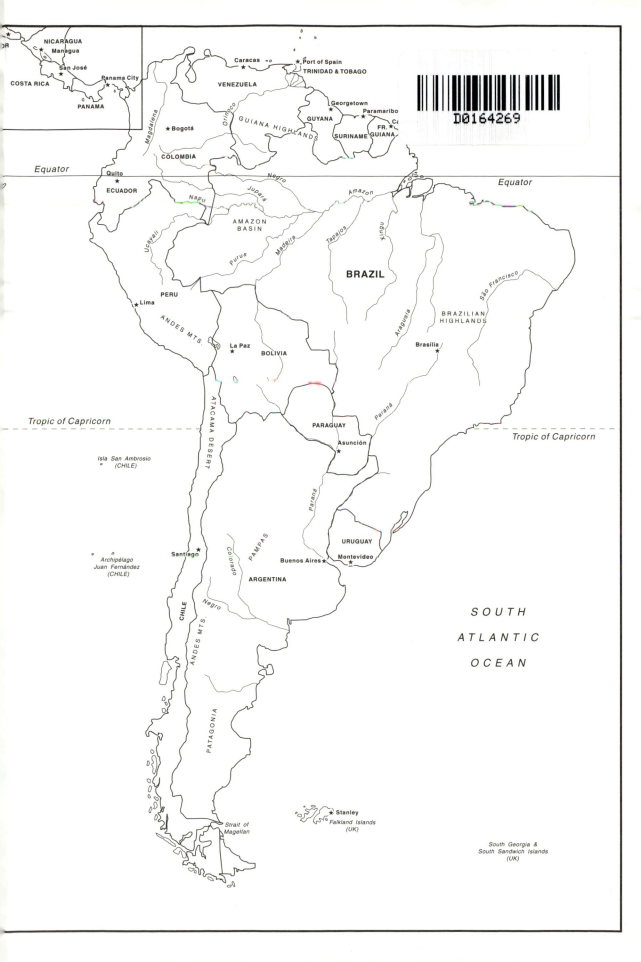

NICARAGUA
★ Managua
★ San José
COSTA RICA
Panama City ★
PANAMA

Caracas ★ □ ○
VENEZUELA
★ Bogotá
COLOMBIA

Port of Spain ★
TRINIDAD & TOBAGO

Georgetown ★
Paramaribo
GUYANA ★
GUIANA HIGHLANDS
SURINAME
FR.
GUIANA

D0164269

Equator
Quito ★
ECUADOR

Napo
Jupará
Negro
Amazon
Equator

Orinoco
Magdalena

AMAZON
BASIN

Ucayali
Purus
Madeira
Tapajos
Xingu

PERU
★ Lima

ANDES MTS.

São Francisco

BRAZIL

BRAZILIAN
HIGHLANDS

La Paz ★
BOLIVIA
Araguaia
★ Brasília

Tropic of Capricorn

Isla San Ambrosio
○ (CHILE)

ATACAMA DESERT

Paraná
PARAGUAY
Asunción ★

Tropic of Capricorn

Archipélago
Juan Fernández
(CHILE)

Santiago ★
Colorado
PAMPAS
Buenos Aires ★

Paraná
URUGUAY
Montevideo ★

CHILE
Negro
ARGENTINA

ANDES MTS.

SOUTH

ATLANTIC

OCEAN

PATAGONIA

★ Stanley
Falkland Islands
(UK)

Strait of
Magellan

South Georgia &
South Sandwich Islands
(UK)

THE GREENWOOD

Women'

WORLD

Editor-in-Chief

Lynn Walter
University of Wisconsin, Green Bay

Volume Editor

Amy Lind
Arizona State University, Tempe

Contributors

Irma T. Alonso
Florida International University, Miami

Florence E. Babb
University of Iowa, Iowa City

Elida Guardia Bonet
Austin, Texas

Elizabeth L. Borland
University of Arizona, Tucson

María Molinas Cabrera
Asunción, Paraguay

Lisa-Marí Centeno
Tempe, Arizona

Jane Clough-Riquelme
University of California, San Diego

Julie Cupples
University of Canterbury, Christchurch, New Zealand

Kalowatie Deonandan
University of Saskatchewan, Saskatoon, Canada

Elisabeth Jay Friedman
Barnard College, New York, New York

Gioconda Herrera
FLACSO, Quito, Ecuador

Nathalie Lebon
Randolph-Macon College, Ashland, Virginia

Ilse Agshagen Leitinger
Evergreen, Colorado

Emi McLaughlin
Arizona State University, Tempe

Kelley Ready
Brandeis University, Waltham, Massachusetts

Susana Rostagnol
Universidad de la República, Montevideo, Uruguay

Juana Suárez
University of North Carolina, Greensboro

Alvaro Vergara-Mery
Western Kentucky University, Bowling Green

Vanessa von Struensee
Arlington, Virginia

Diana H. Yoon
New York University, New York, New York

THE GREENWOOD ENCYCLOPEDIA OF
Women's Issues
WORLDWIDE

CENTRAL AND SOUTH AMERICA

Editor-in-Chief
Lynn Walter

Volume Editor
Amy Lind

GREENWOOD PRESS
Westport, Connecticut • London

Library of Congress Cataloging-in-Publication Data

The Greenwood encyclopedia of women's issues worldwide : Central and South America /
   Lynn Walter, editor-in-chief, Amy Lind, volume editor.
      p.   cm.
   Includes bibliographical references and index.
   ISBN 0–313–32787–4 (set : alk. paper) — ISBN 0–313–32129–9 (alk. paper)
   1. Women — Central America — History.   2. Women — South America —
History.   I. Title: Encyclopedia of women's issues worldwide.   II. Walter, Lynn,
1945–   III. Lind, Amy.
   HQ1467.G74   2003
   305.4'09728 — dc21   2003040826

British Library Cataloguing in Publication Data is available.

Library of Congress Catalog Card Number: 2003040826
ISBN: 0–313–32787–4 (set code)
         0–313–32087–X (Asia and Oceania)
         0–313–32129–9 (Central and South America)
         0–313–31855–7 (Europe)
         0–313–31888–3 (The Middle East and North Africa)
         0–313–31852–2 (North America and the Caribbean)
         0–313–32145–0 (Sub-Saharan Africa)

First published in 2003

Greenwood Press, 88 Post Road West, Westport, CT 06881
An imprint of Greenwood Publishing Group, Inc.
www.greenwood.com

Printed in the United States of America

The paper used in this book complies with the
Permanent Paper Standard issued by the National
Information Standards Organization (Z39.48–1984).

10 9 8 7 6 5 4 3 2 1

Volume map cartography by Mapcraft.com. Country map cartography by Bookcomp, Inc.

CONTENTS

CONTENTS

*The Six-Volume Comprehensive Index begins on
page 569 of the final volume, Sub-Saharan Africa*

SET FOREWORD

The Greenwood Encyclopedia of Women's Issues Worldwide is a six-volume set presenting authoritative, comprehensive, and current data on a broad range of contemporary women's issues in more than 130 countries around the world. Each volume covers a major populated world region: Asia and Oceania, Central and South America, Europe, the Middle East and North Africa, North America and the Caribbean, and Sub-Saharan Africa. Volumes are organized by chapters, with each focusing on a specific country or group of countries or islands, following a broad outline of topics—education, employment and the economy, family and sexuality, health, politics and law, religion and spirituality, and violence. Under these topics, contributors were asked to consider a range of contemporary issues from illiteracy and wage discrepancies to unequal familial roles and political participation and to highlight issues of special concern to women in the country. In this way, the set provides a global perspective on women's issues, ensures breadth and depth of issue coverage, and facilitates cross-national comparison.

Along with locating women's agenda in specific national and historical contexts, each chapter looks at the cultural differences among women as well as the significance of class, religion, sexuality, and race on their lives. And, as women's movements and their non-governmental organizations (NGOs) are among the most worldwide forms of civic participation, their effectiveness in addressing women's issues is also examined. In addition to focusing on national and local organizations, many authors also highlight the major role the United Nations has played in addressing women's issues nationally and in supporting women's networks globally and point to the importance of its 1979 Convention on the Elimination of All Forms of Discrimination Against Women (CEDAW), which is still the most comprehensive international agreement on the rights of women.

Contributors were chosen for their expertise on women's issues in the country or area about which they write. Each contributor provides an authoritative resource guide with suggested reading, web sites, films/videos, and organizations as well as a selected bibliography and extensive references. The chapters and resource guides are designed for students, scholars, and engaged citizens to study contemporary women's issues in depth in specific countries and from a global perspective.

This ambitious project has been made possible by the work of many scholars who contributed their knowledge and commitment. I want to thank all of them and especially the other volume editors, Manisha Desai, Cheryl Toronto Kalny, Amy Lind, Bahira Sherif-Trask, and Aili Mari Tripp. Thanks also to Christine Marra of Marrathon Productions and Wendi Schnaufer of Greenwood Publishing Group for their editorial assistance.

As I read the many chapters of this series what struck me most was the sheer force and determination of the many women and men who are seeking solutions to the problems of inequality and poverty, discrimination, and injustice that lie at the root of women's experiences worldwide. I hope this series will further their vision.

Lynn Walter, Editor-in-Chief

USER'S GUIDE

The Greenwood Encyclopedia of Women's Issues Worldwide is a six-volume set covering the world's most populated regions:

Asia and Oceania

Central and South America

Europe

The Middle East and North Africa

North America and the Caribbean

Sub-Saharan Africa

All volumes contain an introduction from the editor in chief that overviews women's issues today around the world and introduces the set. Each volume editor broadly characterizes contemporary women's issues in the particular region(s). The volumes are divided into chapters, ordered alphabetically by country name. A few chapters treat several countries (e.g., Tajikistan, Kazakhstan, Turkmenistan, and Kyrgyzstan, which are grouped together as Central Asia) or a group of islands (e.g., the Netherland Antilles).

The comprehensive coverage facilitates comparisons between nations and among regions. The following is an outline showing the sections of each chapter. In rare instances where information was not available or applicable for a particular country, sections were omitted. Variations in a few subheads may have been appropriate in some volumes.

Profile of [the Nation]

A paragraph on the land, people(s), form of government, economy, and demographic statistics on female/male population, infant mortality, maternal mortality, total fertility, and life expectancy.

Overview of Women's Issues

A brief introduction to the major issues to be covered, giving the reader a sense of the state of women's lives in the country.

Education

Opportunities

Literacy

Employment and Economics

Job/Career Opportunities

    Unemployment

Pay

Working Conditions

    Sexual Harassment

Support for Mothers/Caretakers

    Maternal Leave

    Daycare

    Family and Medical Leave

Inheritance and Property Rights

Social/Government Programs

    Sustainable Development

    Welfare and Welfare Reform or Social Welfare and Social Welfare Reform

Family and Sexuality

Gender Roles

Marriage

    Sexuality

Reproduction

    Sex Education

    Contraception and Abortion or Contraception and Reproductive Health

    Teen Pregnancy

Health

Health Care Access

Diseases and Disorders

    AIDS

    Body Image

    Eating Disorders

    Cancer

A regional map is in the inside cover of each volume. Additionally, each chapter has an accompanying country or mini-region map. Each volume has an index consisting of subject and person entries; a comprehensive set index is included at the end of the Sub-Saharan Africa volume.

INTRODUCTION

Women in the twenty countries in Central and South America have played important roles in their communities and nations as community leaders, politicians, agricultural laborers, indigenous leaders, informal sector workers, domestic servants, mothers, religious and educational reformers, human rights activists, and more. From the indigenous cultures, or original inhabitants, that thrived in the region before the colonial period, to the colonial influences of Spain, Portugal, the Netherlands, France, and England to the present, women of all socioeconomic classes, cultures, and ethnic backgrounds have contributed to the growth and diversity of a region with mixed blessings and contradictions. Now, often viewed as existing "in the shadows" of their wealthy neighbors to the north (especially the United States), impoverished Central and South American countries have developed their own cultural and national traditions and identities. Although historically women's participation in public life has been scantily addressed, there is now a vast amount of literature that documents how a diversity of women from indigenous, African, European, Creole, Jewish, Indian, Chinese, Japanese and mestiza (mixed race) backgrounds have influenced regional development and made their voices heard. Particularly in the twentieth and twenty-first centuries, women have participated actively in human rights, workers' indigenous, and antipoverty movements, and have created their own gender-based movements as well. Indeed, the world has much to learn from the rich history of Central and South American women.

OVERVIEW OF WOMEN'S ISSUES

Although many advances have been made for women, much has to be addressed to provide many women of Central and South America with basic needs, legal protection, and cultural respect. As in other regions, it is difficult to generalize about the lives of women, since they come from a range of socioeconomic, ethnic, racial, and religious backgrounds. Today, almost half of the region's population live under their countries' established poverty lines, and a much higher percentage live in substandard conditions.[1] Poor women are disproportionately affected by poverty because they perform multiple roles in household and paid labor, and many must survive economically as single parents. In the twentieth century, many women gained entry into the workplace, but they continue to be paid less than men. Furthermore, many women work in the "informal sector" of the economy: as street vendors, domestic servants, artisans, or agricultural producers. There, while it is easier to take care of children and work simultaneously, they receive no benefits and less pay, in addition to working long hours.

Women and men of this region experience the highest income inequalities in the world.[2] While in theory all women could—and should—have access to basic resources in the areas of health, reproductive care, and education, many do not. The total population of this region has more than tripled since 1950.[3] Women now constitute just over 50 percent of the region's population, up from approximately 49.7 percent in 1950. In the early 1990s, the average fertility rate was 3.1 percent in Latin American countries, a sharp decline from the rate of 5.9 percent in 1950–1955.[4] In general, fertility rates are higher in rural areas. The average life expectancy of women ranges from 64 years in Bolivia to 78 years in Uruguay and Chile.[5]

Most of the countries in this region are considered part of Latin America: Guatemala, El Salvador, Honduras, Nicaragua, Costa Rica, Panama, Venezuela, Colombia, Ecuador, Peru, Chile, Argentina, Bolivia, Paraguay, Uruguay, and Brazil. In these countries, most women are from indigenous or mestiza backgrounds. In 1990, indigenous people comprised 71 percent of Bolivia's total population (4.9 million), and in Guatemala indigenous people accounted for 66 percent of the total population of 5.3 million.[6] Bolivia, Guatemala, Peru, and Ecuador—the four countries in this region with the largest indigenous populations—are home to approximately 23 million indigenous people. Countries with large European populations, such as Costa Rica, Argentina, and Uruguay, include only 1–2 percent indigenous people.

Throughout the region, a small but significant percentage of the population are of European descent, a group now typically part of the ruling classes. In addition, many people of African descent (Afro-Latin Americans, or *afro-latinoamericanos*) reside throughout the region, direct descendents of West African slaves brought by European conquerors. Interestingly, some are descendents of escaped slaves, as is true of many Afro-Ecuadorians, whose ancestors escaped from a ship headed toward what is now Peru and developed their own communities. Women of Chinese, Japanese, Jewish, and Middle Eastern descent have also contributed to the cultural development of Latin America. In addition, there are enormous differences among rural and urban women. Rapid urbanization has taken place throughout the region since the 1960s, as rural peasant families have sought employment and a better life in urban centers. Now more than 40 percent of the population in all countries reside in urban areas; in Argentina, Chile, and Uruguay, more than 85 percent reside in cities. Montevideo, Uruguay, for example, is home to over 90 percent of the nation's total population.[7]

In addition, many Central and South Americans have immigrated to wealthier countries such as the United States, fleeing from economic poverty and political persecution. In Central America, a region torn by ethnic and military conflict, many people have fled to Mexico or the United States. El Salvador's principal source of national income is remittances sent home by Salvadoreans who reside in North America. Increasingly, South Americans have also left home in search of a better life. The third largest urban population of Ecuadoreans resides in New York City: only Guayaquil and Quito have larger populations. Some countries allow nonresidents to vote, and conduct their political campaigns at home as well as in U.S. cities such as Los Angeles, Chicago, San Francisco, and New York. People's daily lives are now greatly influenced by these migration patterns as well as by global communication.

Central America, a thin strip of land linking North and South America, has been influenced by Spanish as well as Creole (African or African/indigenous) and indigenous traditions; in this way, these countries share identities with the Caribbean as well as Latin America. Perhaps known best throughout the world for the Panama Canal and for a history of inequalities, including ethnic violence, oligarchic landownership, military coups, and revolutions, this region is rich in resources and contradictions. The Pacific coast of Central America is primarily Spanish/indigenous influenced; there, Spanish is spoken. The Atlantic coast is home to Creole speakers, whose cultural practices are distinct from those of the majority Spanish population. Belize, a small country located on the Atlantic coast of Central America, is populated primarily by Creoles, indigenous people, and Europeans. There, unlike the rest of Central America, English is the official language, although other languages are spoken as well.

In northern South America, three small countries have distinct histories: Guyana (formerly known as British Guiana), French Guiana, and Suriname (formerly known as Dutch Guiana). This area, which is primarily tropical and perhaps has more in common with Caribbean countries than with Latin America, has a rich variety of resources and boasts the highest standards of living in the region. At the same time, these countries are the least understood in terms of academic scholarship, and many women continue to struggle to survive economically and to gain political visibility. Women from these countries speak a range of languages, including Dutch (Suriname), English/Creole (Guyana), French (French Guiana), South and Southeast Asian languages, and several native languages. In contrast to

Latin America, Suriname gained its independence in 1975; Guyana gained its independence in 1966; and French Guiana continues to be an overseas department of France.

In general, South America is rich in natural resources, thanks to a wide range of geographical areas, including the striking Andes Mountains; the Amazon rain forest; the pampas (plains) of Argentina; Ecuador's Galápagos Islands; the archipelago of the southernmost tip; and subtropical coastal zones. During the twentieth century, women's lives changed dramatically, as the region transformed from primarily agricultural-based societies to, in some cases, industrialized developing nations. During the early part of the century, governments established welfare states, following the European and North American models, in an attempt to address the needs of the poor and disenfranchised. Today, countries struggle over the notion of welfare, and most governments have made major cuts in social spending to meet their economic debt obligations. Poor and indigenous women, in particular, have suffered from this, since they must continually fend for their own survival in increasingly harsh economic conditions. On the other hand, to the extent that they can afford the new commodities on the market brought by industrialization, middle-class and upper-class women have benefited greatly from the region's modernization process. It is important to keep in mind, though, that the middle and upper classes are very small sectors. Most women have not benefited as much, and some have even experienced declines in their standards of living since the early 1960s.

Religion has played an important role in shaping women's lives and experiences. Catholicism is the largest religion in all countries except Guyana and Suriname. Other denominations of Christianity also have played important roles historically. In the second half of the twentieth century, some evangelical Christian sects mobilized women into their ranks, particularly women residing in poor urban sectors. Native indigenous rituals and forms of spirituality are also very important. Today, for example, in most Catholic processions, participants mix indigenous and Catholic rituals and symbolism, and even the most orthodox Catholics have incorporated elements of indigenous belief systems into their practices. A small but significant percentage of the regional population practices Judaism, and still others practice Hinduism, Islam, and Buddhism. This diversity of political and cultural backgrounds shapes women's lives in many important ways. Women's roles, identities, and experiences can be understood only at the intersection of these historical, cultural, economic, and political processes.

It is important to point out that important debates have taken place about how European societies have interpreted non-European women's experiences. Some scholars, for example, have taken for granted that men's and women's roles, and the inequalities that feminists criticize in Western countries, exist throughout the world. Others argue that this is a Western bias, and not all indigenous cultures necessarily hierarchize women and men in this way.[8] Still others argue that women from indigenous cultures did not experience sexism until European colonizers arrived. According to this view, sexism was introduced by Europeans and imposed upon native communities.[9] In indigenous cultures in the Andean region (Peru, Ecuador, Chile, Bolivia, Colombia, and Venezuela), for example, some scholars of women's issues point out that indigenous women and men played complementary, rather than conflictive or unequal, roles in domestic and agricultural labor.[10] In earlier agriculture-based societies, women and men may have played different roles but were viewed as equal in terms of their importance in economic, political, and cultural life. Regardless of one's view on this debate, what scholars can agree upon is that it is difficult to assess what happened historically, since many written narratives about women's lives prior to colonial contact are told from the perspectives of men or not told at all. This continues today, as scholars from outside the region assess indigenous traditions through their own lens, rather than through the lens of the culture being examined.[11]

WOMEN'S ROLES AND POSITIONS IN THE ECONOMY

Today, women in Central and South America are among the poorest in the world. Though the region is home to a wide variety of resources necessary for the entire planet's survival, including the largest remaining rain forest in the world (the Amazon rain forest) and large deposits of oil (especially in Venezuela), wealth continues to be concentrated in the hands of a few. In the 1990s, following a period of intensive economic crisis that began in the early 1980s, the gap between rich and poor became significantly wider than ever before in contemporary history. In countries such as Peru, Bolivia, and El Salvador, around 50 percent of the total population was living under their countries' established poverty lines. As elsewhere, women of this region tend to experience higher rates of poverty than men, a result of what scholars and United Nations policymakers refer to as the "global feminization of poverty."[12] The global feminization of poverty is due in part to women's multiple roles as mothers, caretakers, economic providers (sometimes as single parents), and "community managers,"[13] a term that refers to women's voluntary roles in community-based survival. In Peru, for example, thousands of women have participated on a volunteer basis in locally organized communal kitchens (*cocinas comunales*), a strategy developed to assist people at the neighborhood level during the economic crisis. While these types of strategies often are viewed as "temporary" by the women involved in them, many communal kitchens and local women's organizations continue to serve their communities 20 years later because the economic crisis has grown deeper.

A primary reason for the ongoing crisis concerns the foreign debts of

Central and South American countries. During the 1970s many governments took out large loans that accrued interest. In the early 1980s, when governments lost money through lowering costs of oil exports and other economic factors, they were unable to meet their debt obligations—a growing problem in many developing countries throughout the world. While Mexico was the first country, in 1982, to claim that it could not meet its debt payments, other countries soon followed suit (see the chapter on Mexico in the volume on North America and the Caribbean).

Most recently, countries including Argentina, Uruguay, Brazil, and Ecuador have experienced severe financial crises in which major banks have been forced into bankruptcy. Hundreds of thousands of citizens lost their entire savings in one fell swoop as banks ran out of cash reserves. Entire generations now face their senior years without retirement funding except what is provided by their family members, many of whom are unemployed or underemployed due to the economic situation. El Salvador and Ecuador have "dollarized" their economies, replacing their national currencies with the U.S. dollar in order to stabilize economic development. Other countries are considering this strategy as a way to acquire stronger positions in the global marketplace. Historically marginalized communities remain on the fringe of the core of national development and prosperity. Women's work in their households and communities has increased, rather than decreased, contrary to what international development experts had predicted and hoped for in previous decades.[14]

Many grassroots women's organizations were established during the 1980s to respond to the economic crisis. Some were organized by local women themselves, others were organized by the Catholic Church, political parties, or a national government. Because women, in their roles as mothers and household managers, understood the daily consequences of the increasingly high cost of living, they were the first to organize around this issue in their rural and urban communities. Governments and international charities recognized the potential of women to volunteer in community development projects. Most positively, this meant that governments funded projects that women had participated in and/or created. On the other hand, some also took advantage of the fact that women would participate with little compensation, thus creating a gap between the value placed on men's and women's contributions to the ongoing development process. There are a range of perspectives on how many women's organizations existed during this period. One regional study claims that in 1991, 14,851 women's base organizations existed in Peru; this estimate includes communal kitchens and the Municipality of Lima's Glass of Milk Committees.[15] Other studies give lower estimates, although in general it is difficult to assess because most organizations do not register with the city or national government.

MOTHERS, FEMINISTS, AND POLITICIANS: WOMEN'S CONTRIBUTIONS TO POLITICS

Women have made enormous contributions to politics throughout the region. Suffragist movements existed as early as the late eighteenth century, in some cases decades earlier than in the United States. Suffragists in Chile, Argentina, Uruguay, and Peru organized regional conferences and networks to address the issue of women's right to vote in the Americas. In 1910, the First International Women's Congress of Argentina (Primer Congreso Femenino Internacional de Argentina) was organized. The Panamerican Congress of Women was held in Chile (1922) and Peru (1924). These events marked a turning point in women's consciousness throughout the region, much of it based on early feminist, anarchist, socialist, and liberal writings from Europe.[16] In 1929, Ecuador became the first country to grant (literate) women the right to vote. In 1961, Paraguay became the last country to grant women the right to vote. Brazil, Uruguay, and Cuba extended voting rights to women in the 1930s; Guatemala, Panama, Argentina, Venezuela, Suriname, Costa Rica, Chile, and El Salvador, in the 1940s; Bolivia, Colombia, Guyana, Honduras, Peru and Nicaragua, in the 1950s.

Women's activism during the suffrage period was limited primarily to voting rights and to addressing the needs of literate, primarily upper-class women. In Ecuador and elsewhere, illiterate people, especially indigenous people who spoke Spanish as a second language, did not gain the right to vote until much later, when many governments redrafted their constitutions in response to demands from indigenous and agrarian sectors to reform the concentration of land rights and political power in the oligarchic sector, a system put into place during the colonial period. Thus, indigenous women's right to vote came much later.

Eleven states in the region are bicameral (two legislative chambers; senate and house of representatives, for example); eight states are unicameral (single chamber). French Guiana has one national representative who sits in the French legislature. Most constitutions reflect a mix of European, English, and/or U.S. traditions of government. The first woman elected as a cabinet minister was a Justice Minister in Chile in 1952. Several women have filled ministry positions since then, although they still remain a political minority. With a few exceptions, women's participation in the formal political process, including their entry into national political positions, has become more common and accepted in recent decades, although important female leaders did exist in precolonial indigenous cultures, independence movements, and the early twentieth century. In 1989, Violeta Chamorro was the first female elected President of Nicaragua (1989–1997); only two other women served as presidents before Chamorro, although neither was actually elected and both administrations were abruptly ended by military coups (María Estela Martínez, widow of Juan Perón, in Argentina, 1974–

1976; Lidia Gueiler, Tejada, Bolivia, 1979–1980). The first female to be elected to a legislative seat was Senator Carlota Queiroz, elected in Brazil in 1932. Since then, an increasing number of women have been elected as national representatives and senators. More women are elected to municipal and provincial/departmental positions than to national positions: this reflects the global trend in female leadership. Indigenous women have been elected to the legislature in some countries, such as Bolivia, in recent years.

In the 1990s, several countries adopted legislation to establish a female quota system, a type of affirmative action in the election process. Argentina, the first country to establish a quota system, requires that 30 percent of all party candidates be female. Proponents of this system agree that a quota system is necessary for advancing women's status in formal politics. Opponents contend that the quotas have not helped, since political parties are not required to back their own candidates evenly, and in many cases they back their male candidates more than their female candidates. As a result, few female candidates are actually elected.[17] In addition, electing female politicians does not necessarily mean that women's issues will actually be addressed: some female politicians do not adhere to feminist principles, for example. Regardless of one's views on the new quotas, it is clear that women's presence in formal politics is growing stronger, although there is much that could be done to change social and cultural values related to women's abilities to serve as public leaders in their countries.

The U.N. Decade for the Advancement of Women (1975–1985) set the stage for governmental reform in the region: following the decade, several governments adopted the Convention to Eliminate Discrimination Against Women, a legal victory for supporters of women's rights. Today, most countries have state agencies designed specifically to address women's roles in national development, many of which focus their attention on the needs of poor women. Peru is one of the few countries that has an entire ministry dedicated to the issue: the Ministry of Women and Social Development. Most other countries house agencies within larger ministries that oversee women and development policies, plans, and projects throughout the country. Many activists from civic women's groups, particularly from nongovernmental organizations (NGOs) have served as political leaders in these state agencies. In practice, it is difficult to distinguish between women who work in the formal arena of the government and women who work in private (for profit and nonprofit) organizations, since many women have experience in both sectors.

In addition to women's formal political participation, a vibrant, widespread women's movement exists throughout the region. The "second wave" women's movement emerged primarily in the 1970s, following women's active involvement in several social movements during that period. As women participated in antiauthoritarian, human rights, student, labor, antipoverty, and popular education movements, they gained important political advocacy skills, yet continued to be viewed as "secondary" participants in the movements and in society in general. Frustrated by sexism within social movements, women decided to create their own organizations to address gender issues. What were once small, grassroots women's groups in the 1970s, many modeled after feminist consciousness-raising groups in Europe and the United States, became large, productive NGOs that have played key roles in shaping national policies, development plans, and political reforms. Today, thousands of women's NGOs address an array of issues: domestic violence, education, health care, reproductive rights, political reform, human rights abuses, lesbian rights, political violence, poverty, religion, and women's legal rights.

"Mothers' movements" are perhaps the best-known example of women's activism in the region. The Mothers of Plaza de Mayo placed motherhood on the global map as they marched in front of Argentina's governmental palace to protest their children's having been murdered, tortured, or "disappeared" by the Argentine military during the period of military rule in the country (1976–1983). During this period, tens of thousands of people were "disappeared," a term that refers to the military strategy of taking people from their homes, placing them in hidden camps or prisons, and eventually assassinating them. The Mothers of Plaza de Mayo were women who were not politically active in any sense of the word. They became active because they lost their sons, daughters, and/or grandchildren during Argentina's "Dirty War." Acting as mothers, they marched around the Plaza de Mayo with their children's names written on handmade bandanas they wore on their heads. Many wore house dresses or aprons to publicly display their roles as mothers in challenging the nation to return their "disappeared" children to them. Because they were seen as mothers, they were viewed as apolitical; thus, while most Argentines risked their lives if they gathered in a public space, the Mothers initially were allowed to march.[18] Since the Mothers first took to the streets in 1977, women have organized their own human rights groups throughout the region. Because many countries were under military rule during the 1970s and/or 1980s, women have been among the first to protest this systematic violence.

OUTLOOK FOR THE TWENTY-FIRST CENTURY

Though Latin American women have learned from early suffragist and "second wave" feminist movements in Europe and the United States, it is important to point out that they have successfully created their own movements and visions from which we can all learn. Many women have been important visionaries in the twentieth and twenty-first centuries. The winner of the 1992 Nobel Peace Prize, Guatemalan Rigoberta Menchú, continues to be an important figure. Her effort to work for peace in Guatemala shows us how indigenous women have made strides in public life in their own countries and globally.[19] Since the early 1970s, Domitila Barrios de Chungara, a Bolivian woman born into a tin-mining family, has fought endlessly for the rights of poor, indigenous women and men.[20] Benedita da Silva, an Afro-Brazilian woman born and raised in a shantytown (*favela*), is the first black woman senator in Brazil and an outspoken advocate for racial and gender justice.[21] Numerous individuals have lost their lives in their struggles to create more just societies. Professional women have reached new heights in business, the arts, media, and politics, despite the "glass ceilings" that women continue to face in the workplace. While the region's colonial legacy has dramatically altered the economic landscape, it can be said that Central and South America are blessed with a rich diversity of cultural, intellectual, and political traditions that make it unique in the world. While women face many challenges, they have made important strides in achieving legal and social justice for many women of the region. The challenge is to maintain these advances while facing a dire economic future.

NOTES

1. Poverty lines established by national governments often tend to be low and out-of-date. As a result, most statistics of populations living under the poverty line are low estimates of the actual number of people living in substandard conditions. Most poverty lines are based on the cost of living in relation to employment levels. Cost of living may include housing, transportation, education, child care, food and other basic items needed for survival. Unemployment rates are extremely difficult to obtain because many people work in the informal sector (e.g., street vending, domestic service), especially women.

2. Teresa Valdés et al., *Mujeros latinoamericanos en cifras: Tomo comparativo* (Santiago de Chile: Instituto de la Mujer, Ministerio de Asuntos Sociales de España and Facultad Latinoamericana de Ciencias Sociales, 1995).

3. Ibid.

4. Ibid.

5. World Bank, http://genderstats.worldbank.org.

6. Valdés et al., 1995, 51.

7. See chapters on Argentina, Chile, and Uruguay in this volume.

8. Chandra Mohanty, "Under Western Eyes: Feminist Scholarship and Colonial Discourses," in *Third World Women and the Politics of Feminism*, eds. Chandra Mohanty, Ann Russo, and Lourdes Torres (Bloomington: Indiana University Press, 1991), 1–50.

9. See Irene Silverblatt, *Moon, Sun, and Witches* (Princeton, NJ: Princeton University Press, 1987).

10. See Harris, 1978.

11. Mohanty, 1991.

12. Noeleen Heyser, ed., *A Commitment to the World's Women* (New York: U.N. Development Fund for Women, 1995).

13. Caroline Moser, *Gender, Planning and Development* (New York: Routledge, 1993).

14. Lourdes Benería, "The Mexican Debt-Crisis," in *Unequal Burden*, eds. Lourdes Benería and Shelley Feldman (Boulder, CO: Westview Press, 1992), 83–104.

15. Valdés et al., 1995, 179.

16. Valdés et al., 1995.

17. María Lourdes Zabala, *Mujeres, cuotas y ciudadania en Bolivia* (La Paz: Coordinadora de la Mujer and UNICEF, 1999).

18. Later the military government began to perceive the Mothers as a threat, and they, too, became targets of repression. In December 1977, the military infiltrated the Mothers' organization and kidnapped and disappeared twelve women, including the Mothers' leader, Azucena de Vicenti. Despite this setback, the Mothers continued to march, and many still fill the Plaza on Thursday afternoons.

19. Elisabeth Burgos-Debray, ed., *I, Rigoberta Menchú* (New York: Verso, 1984).

20. Domitila Barrios de Chungara, with Moema Viezzer, *Let Me Speak!* (New York: Monthly Review Press, 1978).

21. See Medea Benjamin and Maisa Mendonea, eds., *Benedita da Silva* (Oakland, CA: Food First, 1997).

BIBLIOGRAPHY

Barrios de Chungara, Domitila, with Moema Viezzer. *Let Me Speak! Testimony of Domitila, a Woman of the Bolivian Mines*. New York: Monthly Review Press, 1978.

Benería, Lourdes. "The Mexican Debt Crisis: Restructuring the Economy and the Household." In *Unequal Burden*, edited by Lourdes Benería and Shelley Feldman, 83–104. Boulder: Westview Press, 1992.

Benjamin, Medea, and Maisa Mendonca, eds. *Benedita da Silva: An Afro-Brazilian Woman's Story of Politics and Love*. Oakland, CA: Food First, 1997.

Burgos-Debray, Elisabeth, ed. *I, Rigoberta Menchú: An Indian Woman in Guatemala*. New York: Verso, 1984.

Harris, Olivia. "Complementarity and Conflict: An Andean View of Women and Men." In *Sex and Age as Principles of Social Differentiation*, edited by J. S. La-Fontaine, 21–40. London: Academic Press, 1978.

Heyser, Noeleen, ed. *A Commitment to the World's Women: Beijing and Beyond*. New York: U.N. Development Fund for Women, 1995.

Mohanty, Chandra. "Under Western Eyes: Feminist Scholarship and Colonial Discourses." In *Third World Women and the Politics of Feminism*, edited by Chandra Talpade Mohanty, Ann Russo, and Lourdes Torres, 1–50. Bloomington: Indiana University Press, 1991.

Moser, Caroline. *Gender Planning and Development*. New York: Routledge, 1993.

Silverblatt, Irene. *Moon, Sun, and Witches: Gender Ideologies and Class in Inca and Colonial Peru*. Princeton, NJ: Princeton University Press, 1987.

Valdés, Teresa, et al. *Mujeres latinoamericanas en cifras: Tomo comparativo*. Santiago de Chile: Instituto de la Mujer, Ministerio de Asuntos Sociales de España and Facultad Latinoamericana de Ciencias Sociales, 1995.

World Bank. *Gender Statistics on Latin America*, 2002. http://genderstats.worldbank.org.

Zabala, María Lourdes. *Mujeres, cuotas y ciudadania en Bolivia*. La Paz: Coordinadora de la Mujer and UNICEF, 1999.

I

ARGENTINA

Elizabeth L. Borland

PROFILE OF ARGENTINA

Argentina occupies most of the Southern Cone, the southern portion of South America, directly to the east of Chile. It is the country with the eighth largest landmass in the world, with over a million square miles. Its diverse geography includes the mountainous western Andes, the tropical and subtropical lowland north, the Patagonian alpine steppes of the south, and the pampas, a region of level plains stretching southwest from the Atlantic coast and the Rio de la Plata. About 90 percent of its inhabitants live in urban areas, principally in the pampas region, where the capital city of Buenos Aires and the second city of Córdoba are located.[1] Argentina was colonized by the Spanish Crown in the sixteenth century and gained its independence in the 1820s. After a period of national consolidation, it established a constitutional democracy and, by the 1890s, was one of the wealthiest and most prosperous nations in the world. However, this prosperity was short-lived, and the latter twentieth century was frequently shattered by dictatorship, most notably in the repressive period of the "Dirty War" (1976–1983), in which as many as 30,000 Argentines were "disappeared" or kidnapped (then usually detained, tortured, and murdered) by special military forces.[2] Democracy was restored in 1983, when free elections were held and military leaders were ousted. Since then, Argentines have focused on the consolidation of democracy and economic restructuring via neoliberal policies favoring deregulation and privatization for free-market capital-

ism, a process that has recently culminated in political crises and a severe recession unparalleled in Argentine history.

According to the 2001 census, Argentina's population is about 36 million, 52 percent of whom are women.[3] The small indigenous population is mostly located in the northern regions of Argentina, near the Bolivian border, while the population of the metropolitan capital and other urban areas is mainly of European and mestizo descent. Most Argentines of European background trace their roots to waves of immigration in the late nineteenth and early twentieth centuries from Spain and Italy, and (less so) from other nations of western Europe. About 90 percent of the population are nominally Roman Catholic, although the number of practicing Catholics is smaller.[4] On average, women live longer than men; current life expectancy is about 76 years for women and 68 years for men.[5] The maternal mortality rate is 46.3 and the infant mortality rate is 22.2. The average number of births per woman (total fertility) is 2.6. The population is relatively young, with 31 percent below age 15.[6] While Argentina has historically been one of the more prosperous nations in Latin America, recent economic crises have rapidly enlarged the ranks of the poor; more than half of Argentines are living in poverty.[7]

OVERVIEW OF WOMEN'S ISSUES

The decades of redemocratization, the approval of a new constitution, liberalization, and the resulting growth of unemployment have changed life in Argentina in many ways. Women have been both positively and negatively affected by these changes. Women have seized educational opportunities, and more women are working in the paid labor force. Even so, there is a high degree of sex segregation and discrimination, and fields dominated by women have lower occupational status and pay. Unemployment, brought on in part by economic policies that privatized many state enterprises, has disproportionately affected women. Attitudes about sexuality and reproduction have become more progressive, but gender norms still confine the behavior of Argentine women and men. Democratic reforms and human rights issues have been championed by women's organizations, and some campaigns have gained widespread public attention. A new political quota system, which supports women candidates, has increased female representation in legislative bodies both nationally and in provincial governments, but feminist claims have often been left out. The influence of the Catholic Church on political leaders is an obstacle to progressive social change in areas of sexual and reproductive rights. Though their influence has been limited, a growing number of women's and feminist groups have organized to demand equal rights.

EDUCATION

Opportunities

In the latter half of the nineteenth century, educational reforms emphasized secular coeducation, particularly through the work of Doming Sarmiento, an influential intellectual and president of Argentina (1868–1874). Sarmiento opened up teaching careers for women, calling pedagogy a patriotic duty in the fight against illiteracy and "backwardness." Female teachers helped to overcome a national shortage, and (due to a lack of other options) were willing to teach for lower wages. By the turn of the century, literacy rates for men and women were similar. The increased educational opportunities for girls and women not only created generations of literate women; they also led to an increase in the number of professional, educated, and politically savvy women.[8]

Today, there are three levels of education in the Argentine system, all of which are available at free public or private (mainly Catholic) schools. The educational system has recently undergone a series of reforms, implementing a longer primary school requirement and a shorter term for secondary school. In the new primary level, schooling is compulsory for all nine years. Students then enter a three-year secondary program called General Basic Education (EGB). After the EGB, continuing students may choose vocational or university training.

Literacy

Overall, women have somewhat higher educational levels than men, though there are similar rates of completion for women and men at all educational levels. Literacy rates are the same for men and women: 98 percent. About 32 percent of both sexes complete the primary educational level, and 12 percent the secondary (EGB) level. Women are slightly more likely to complete post-EGB training—7 percent of women versus 5 percent of men. In 1998, 20 percent of all Argentines had attended or completed university, 55 percent had attended or completed secondary school, 87 percent had completed primary school, and 14 percent had not completed primary school.[9]

Despite the similar rates for men's and women's educational completion and literacy in Argentina, vocational segregation persists at both the EGB and the university levels. Women are less likely to attend vocational programs in agriculture (they are 32 percent of all agriculture students). They are even less likely to train in technical programs (women are 21 percent of all technical students). Women in vocational or technical programs tend to train in fields where women concentrate, such as personal services, light industries, and health care. Women are also more likely to study in pre-university programs to teach primary school. These trends contribute to the lower average salaries earned by female workers, since the vocations studied by women tend to be lower-paying.

At the university level, 49 percent of all students are women, but they are not equally represented in all areas of study.[10] In 1998, women were overrepresented in teacher training (80 percent), humanities and fine arts (74 percent), natural sciences and medicine (61 percent in each), and law (55 percent). There were fewer women in business administration (46 percent). Women were severely underrepresented in engineering, where they made up just 19 percent of all students.[11] As with vocational training, the differences in the fields of university study chosen by men and women are important because women are overrepresented in lower-paying fields.

EMPLOYMENT AND ECONOMICS

Since the beginning of the 1990s, the Argentine government has pursued financial policies that have privatized many sectors of the economy. President Carlos Menem (1991–1999) implemented these economic policies in the Convertibility Plan (Plan de Convertibilidad) of April 1991. To counter hyperinflation, which was at 200 percent when Menem took office, the Argentine peso was pegged to the U.S. dollar.[12] The government reduced the size of the federal bureaucracy (including social and public health care services) and rapidly privatized the state sector, including two television stations, the national telephone company, the electric utility, parts of the petroleum company, and the national airline, Aerolíneas Argentinas.

Making pastries in a bakery in Tucumán. Digital Press Photos/ NewsCom.

Foreign investors purchased many of these companies. Although Argentine state bureaucracy is less bloated today than before Menem's reforms, the following decade was marked by a sharp decline in real wages, increased unemployment, a decrease in union bargaining power, increased worker uncertainty, and a widening gap between rich and poor. Disadvantaged by gender inequality, women are more vulnerable to economic problems. Women are also disadvantaged by occupational segregation, a substantial sex gap in pay, and sexual harassment in the workplace.

Job/Career Opportunities

Women's participation in the labor force has slowly grown since the turn of the twentieth century. By the turn of the century, a legion of female workers had entered factories in Argentina's major cities. By 1914, a fifth of the employed working class consisted of women and children.[13] As large factories with standardized equipment came to predominate, working-class women and girls became an even more attractive labor source for industrialists. The food, tobacco, garment, and textile industries were particularly dependent on female labor. Factory owners hired women because they would work for lower salaries (sometimes half or a third of those paid to men) and were considered highly productive, agile workers. Many women preferred factory work to the other major option: domestic service.[14] Although women composed about 20 percent of the Argentine workforce for the first half of the century, in the 1960s this pattern began to shift as women entered middle-class service occupations such as public administration, retail, banking, and insurance. Increased consumerism and public consumption of Argentine products swelled the ranks of the middle classes, and contributed to the increased number of female salaried workers in the service sector. By 1970, 26 percent of all women were economically active. This figure continued to rise, from 32 percent in 1980 to the 2000 high of 40 percent.[15]

While men's level of participation in the labor force has not changed since the early 1990s, women's economic activity has increased. Most women in the labor force are between 20 and 39 years old, but levels of labor force participation are similar for men and women between the ages of 20 and 59. Women are also overrepresented in the informal sector, particularly domestic service.[16]

Despite legislative measures designed to prevent some forms of discrimination in the workplace, it remains legal and common to select employees on the basis of sex,[17] and the Argentine job market is marked by occupational sex segregation. There is near parity for professional occupations and for jobs requiring university qualifications; but half of working women are in the unskilled labor force, compared with 30 percent of men.[18] Women are overrepresented in service jobs (68 percent); particularly teaching (79 percent), social and health services (66 percent), and domestic service (93 percent). About 20 percent of all Argentine women work in domestic service, a field with low pay, high turnover, low social status, and little or no state oversight. Women are underrepresented in construction and industrial jobs, and account for less than 20 percent of workers in the metal industry, construction, electricity, gas and water, and transportation sectors. Occupational segregation by sex contributes to the considerably lower salaries earned by Argentine women. Furthermore, within occupations, women tend to occupy the lower-paying, less prestigious jobs.

Women are also disadvantaged as entrepreneurs. They are less likely to own their own businesses; only 19 percent of employers are female, and these women generally have small establishments, with between two and five employees.[19] Legislation enacted in 1997 sought to promote equal opportunity in entrepreneurship, but the recent economic crisis makes the current climate risky for aspiring female entrepreneurs.

Unemployment

Unemployment intensely hurts both women and men in contemporary Argentina, but women are overrepresented in the growing number of unemployed and underemployed Argentines. The unemployment rate has increased drastically since the early 1990s, going from about 6 percent at the beginning of the decade to a high of 21.5 percent in May 2002. Unemployment rates are higher for women, unskilled workers, and youth. Women between the ages of 20 and 49 are more likely to be personally affected by unemployment than their male counterparts. Divorced and widowed women are more likely to be unemployed than married women. Young women are more likely than young men to have trouble finding their first jobs; in 1998, 17 percent of new female workers were unemployed, compared to 9 percent of new male workers. Women's spells of unemployment, on average, last longer than men's: in 1998, 73 percent of men found a new job within six months of unemployment, while only 53 percent of women did so.[20] Furthermore, unemployed women are more educated than unemployed men.[21]

Women are also disproportionately affected by underemployment (officially defined as less than 35 hours a week) — they are more than twice as likely to be underemployed as their male counterparts. An estimated 24 percent of working women are classified as underemployed.[22]

Pay

There has long been a substantial gap in pay between men and women in Argentina. During the first half of the twentieth century, women factory workers earned 30 to 50 percent of what men earned, a practice supported by industrialists and male-dominated labor unions, who saw women's labor as less valuable.[23] Even though laws were passed in the 1990s requiring equal pay for equal work, there is substantial evidence that Argentine women are continually disadvantaged due to pay discrimination. Women are trained in less lucrative fields and they tend to work in lower-paying sectors. Men are more likely to advance in their careers. Women are also more likely than men to be salaried workers, but are less likely to receive full benefits, including health care. In 1999, women earned 67 cents for every dollar earned by men in Argentina, with an average monthly salary of $462 for women and $691 for men.[24] The greatest wage gap appears among older women, while there is more wage parity for young people.

The wage gap between divorced, separated, or widowed women and men is even greater—these women earn 60 percent of the pay earned by men with similar marital status. The wage gap is also high for women with education beyond high school: these women earn 60 cents for every dollar earned by men. There is less of a wage gap for less educated workers.

The female labor force is more educated than the male labor force (about half of all women had completed secondary school), but women are paid less—evidence that educational requirements are more stringent for women than for their male peers but their investment in education has a lesser return than men's. Women need a significantly greater level of education than men to access the same pay; it is estimated that, on average, they must study four more years to obtain the same salary as a similar man. And although the educational attainment of working women rose during the 1990s, employment opportunities have not followed suit.[25]

Despite the implementation of reforms for pay equity, programs have not been fully carried out in public or private workplaces. Not surprisingly, unemployment contributed to income inequality in the 1990s and workers seeking wage increases are at a disadvantage due to the tight job market. In the current economic crisis, concerns about gender inequality are likely to get short shrift.

Working Conditions

Women in Argentina have long been treated differently in the workplace. Argentine women have traditionally been seen as secondary or supplemental income earners for their families, an idea that contributes to pay discrimination and working conditions that devalue women's contributions. Women workers are often seen as a distinct group from their male peers, one in need of protection.

Differential treatment for women workers has long been present in political discourse; concern about bad working conditions and long hours for women and girls led to the establishment of labor legislation in 1908. The Socialist Party and Catholic groups supported this legislation, arguing that work for poor women was a "necessary evil" and that these groups needed to be protected.[26] Labor unions successfully demanded that women be restricted from certain jobs, and from nighttime labor. The central concerns leading to these reforms were that working conditions for women workers would affect their ability to reproduce and care for children. More recently, legislation has addressed the mandatory provision of child care for women workers (ignoring that fathers may also need child care and that not all women are mothers).

Sexual Harassment

In addition to being treated as a secondary labor source, female workers are often subjected to sexual harassment. There have been few studies of sexual harassment in Argentina, but two studies suggest that the rates are high. The International Work Organization (Organización Internacional del Trabajo) found that 16.6 percent of Argentine women who work said that they had received a demand for sexual favors from a superior.[27] There have been demands for action against sexual harassment in the workplace since soon after the restoration of democracy, but workers are still not protected in most cases.[28] Even though polls suggest that almost half of all working women say that they have been sexually harassed, there are no broad legal measures that protect all workers—except for national public employees and public employees in the city of Buenos Aires. Private employees are not protected, and neither are public employees in many of the provincial governments. Under the existing policy, drafted in 1993, sexual harassment is defined as "an act by an official who, in carrying out his or her duties, takes advantage of a superior relationship and compels the other party to agree to sexual requests." These policies focus on quid pro quo sexual harassment (where the threat is explicit), but do not protect workers from sexual harassment by peers or from acts which create an uncomfortable working environment. Moreover, the law exempts high-ranking public officials, such as ministers and secretaries in the executive branch, diplomats, security and police personnel, and even official clergy.

Public awareness about sexual harassment is increasing. The first media campaign to discourage harassing behavior was launched in October 2000, with national radio ads, TV notices in the subway system in Buenos Aires, and posters put up around the city. These campaigns increased demands for labor unions and political parties to take up the issue legislatively, but no laws have yet been passed. And in an economic setting with high unemployment, where workers are hesitant to risk losing their jobs, women are likely to be more vulnerable to the advances of their superiors.

Support for Mothers/Caretakers

Working women are faced with dilemmas about how to care for their children when they are at work. The contradiction between an Argentine woman's ascribed role as mother and her need and desire for waged labor has been a difficult issue to resolve, particularly for working class women. As early as the 1930s, some businesses in Argentina installed nurseries so that working women could leave their children under the care of other women during their shifts. In large factories, this practice became common in the 1940s, partly due to the rise in power of Argentine labor unions.[29] As part of a series of popular reforms, in 1946 President Juan Perón instituted maternity leave for female workers. More recent reforms have attempted to protect both male and female workers with family responsibilities.

Even so, protective legislation can be a double-edged sword for Argentine women. For instance, current laws state that employers must provide nurseries if they employ over 50 women. This leads to a situation where the burden for child care is ascribed solely to mothers, and it makes women workers seem more expensive for employers, which may lead to employment discrimination and contribute to women's unemployment.[30] Reforms to make these policies gender-neutral have been presented in Congress for a decade, but have not been approved. Critics have pointed out that the apathy of employers and unions has also prevented the implementation of better policies. For instance, multinational corporations that offer family-friendly policies in their home countries have not offered these same options to employees in Argentina. Labor unions—traditionally dominated by males—have not embraced demands for day-care centers for workers' children.[31]

Inheritance and Property Rights

Argentine women's right to own and manage property was restricted in laws stemming from the colonial period. The 1878 Civil Code treated women as minors when they married. They could not enter into contracts without a husband's signature, they could not act as witnesses, and they could not administer property. This law was reformed in 1926, when women became able to administer property and sign contracts. Today, women have equal property and inheritance rights.

Social/Government Programs

Sustainable Development

Like many other Latin American economies, Argentina continues to feel the effects of having massive debt. Plans for economic development have focused on economic liberalization to promote international investment, but they place Argentina in a precarious position in terms of sustainable development, as evidenced by the current crisis. The investment rate is low, and the decrease in public spending that was part of market-led reforms has contributed to the worsening of environmental problems, particularly those related to a deterioration of the infrastructure in urban areas (for example, water and sewage services). Environmental considerations played little role in reforms, and there is little regulation of private industry. Sustainable development and environmental preservation have not been policy priorities.

Social Welfare

Retirement policies in Argentina treat men and women differently. Men are more likely to be covered by Social Security, although benefits received by all retired persons have declined dramatically as a result of austerity measures. In 1993, retirement law was reformed, raising the age of retirement to 65 for men and to 60 for women. For public employees, retirement benefits are calculated by using the average salary earned during the final ten years of employment. Some have argued that this system disadvantages women, since they have not accumulated as much seniority when they retire at 60 than men have at 65, even if they were constantly in the workforce (and many women leave the workforce to raise children). Women are also disadvantaged in the private sector, but for different reasons. Retirement benefits for workers employed by the private sector are calculated with a formula that takes into account living expenses and life expectancy. Since women, on average, live longer, benefits are smaller for retired females. Feminists and others concerned with retirement policy have proposed raising the retirement age for women, but unions have come out against these proposals, arguing that women are both at the job and at home, and thus are too tired to work through their sixties. Furthermore, the male and female informal sectors grew throughout the 1980s, and informal workers could not access pension plans or most other programs.

Social Welfare Reform

Public sector welfare programs were limited in Argentina until 1944, when Juan Perón became president. He embraced the idea of the welfare state and instituted social insurance and public pension programs that remained largely in place until the 1990s. Prior to 1944, workers had to provide for themselves, sometimes through mutual aid societies, and the poor turned to charitable organizations that received occasional state contributions. Perón's 1954 policies expanded coverage from commercial, industrial, and public employees to the self-employed and rural workers. The state took responsibility for uncovered elderly persons without employed family members. Even after the fall of Perón, military governments kept these policies in place because they were seen as necessary to maintain a cooperative and efficient workforce, though there were more funds for military and police personnel than other employees.[32] Despite the fact that welfare policies remained in place under the dictatorship and into the early democratic period, the real value of welfare benefits declined due to inflation. At the same time, fewer Argentines were covered, both due to reforms and changes in the structure of the workforce. For instance, the age of retirement was raised in 1993. Retirement benefits have not kept place with inflation and are increasingly unreliable, leading to deprivation and organized protest by retirees.

FAMILY AND SEXUALITY

Gender Roles

Catholic teachings lend support to the belief that different roles for men and women are natural and important for the functioning of Argentine society. According to these religious ideals, a healthy society is built upon happy households, and this requires men and women to strictly adhere to gender roles: a good father uses his authority to protect and sustain his family and its honor; a mother must sacrifice for her children, showing infinite tenderness. One example of this comes from the popular practice of making a pilgrimage to a remote stretch of desert in the province of San Juan to visit the sanctuary of the Correa, a symbol of motherhood and hope. According to legend, Correa was a devoted mother who died while attempting to walk through the desert to be with her husband; miraculously, her infant son survived by nursing from his dead mother. Her story provides Argentines an example of the ultimate sacrifice that a good mother might make for her husband and children.

Traditional roles have long been touted by leaders in Argentina as the root of the nation's values, a discourse that is marked by the idea that Catholic values are at the core of an Argentine identity.[33] For instance, during the last era of military dictatorship in Argentina (1966–1983), military leaders lauded the sanctity of the home, pledging their status as protectors of the family, marriage, and traditional Catholic values. Central to this ideology is the notion that a woman's most noble role is in the home, being a mother and supporting her worker-husband. One historian noted that "the role of a good woman was to marry and bear future generations."[34] Good women are not sexual, but maternal. Men, on the other hand, have roles defined by machismo—a social system in which manhood depends on one's ability to dominate others (especially women) and to protect one's honor, even by means of sexual aggression or violence.

While gender roles have become less rigid since the 1970s, traditional norms still are strong in many sectors of society, and this negatively affects women and girls in many different ways. Despite a trend toward smaller families and an increase in women's labor force participation, women continue to be the primary caretakers of children, and motherhood continues to be an important role and responsibility for women. Gender norms demand that women bear the brunt of the responsibility for raising children; as in many other nations, employed Argentine mothers work a double shift. While fathers are more likely to help with child care than in the past, domestic chores like cooking, washing, ironing, and cleaning are still generally considered a woman's responsibility. Gender roles also affect Argentine girls. The idea that motherhood is the most important and desired role for women partly explains why poor Argentine teens engage in unprotected sex and risk pregnancy.[35]

Gender norms regarding sexuality also limit the acceptable options available to girls and women. Very few Argentines self-identify as gay or lesbian and many homosexuals remain in the closet, even in cosmopolitan areas like Buenos Aires. There is evidence from surveys which suggests that there is greater social acceptance of gays (55 percent) than lesbians (10 percent) in the general public.[36] (While several groups have formed to promote lesbian visibility and rights, and there are several magazines produced by the gay and lesbian community, homosexuality is largely hidden and often informally sanctioned by the public.)

Marriage

The institution of marriage, governed by civil codes based on Catholic doctrine and Spanish colonial policies, was gradually reformed in the twentieth century. The 1870 Civil Code denied married women the right to enter into contracts or to have control over their children; married women were considered minors under the guardianship of their husbands. In 1888 marriage became a civil institution, making a civil ceremony mandatory and a religious ceremony optional. Divorce was permitted, but one could not remarry after divorce. In 1926 further reforms enlarged economic opportunities for women; they could have a profession, keep their wages, sign contracts, and manage property. Civil divorce was recognized in 1954, though it was abolished during the dictatorship and not reinstated and reformed until 1987, enabling divorced Argentines to remarry. Yet today in Argentina, husbands still represent households as sole administrators of conjugal society. This policy is attributed to fears about the stability of the institution of the family should women get recognized as co-heads of households.

Patterns of family life have undergone several shifts since the 1970s. Changes have been attributed to women's increased education and labor force participation, legalization of divorce, shifting sexual norms, and a decline in the fertility rate. In the 1980s, most Argentine couples with children had a male breadwinner and a female homemaker (75 percent), but contemporary female labor force participation has altered this pattern. According to a 2001 study of families in the greater Buenos Aires metropolitan area, 45 percent of households have at least one woman contributing to the family income.[37] Married women with children leave their homes to work in order to replace the loss of buying power caused by deteriorating wages; their earnings enable families to maintain their customary level of consumption in a time of widespread economic constraint, although this is becoming more difficult as prices continue to rise.

Another interesting trend in Argentine society is for women to be more educated than their mates. In 1980, 24 percent of wives were less educated than their husbands; today this figure is only 18 percent. In contrast, 34 percent of wives are more educated than their husbands, and 48 percent have an equal level of education.

The legalization of divorce has had a great impact on family patterns. Although divorce was debated in Congress as early as 1902, it was not fully legalized until 1987 despite dramatic antidivorce demonstrations orchestrated by the Catholic Church.[38] In the 1990s, there was an increase in divorce and separation. In 1999, half of the Argentine population was single, a little less than a third was married, 8 percent lived with a partner,

3.5 percent was divorced or separated, and 9 percent was widowed.[39] Women are more likely than men to be single, widowed, or divorced. Women are less likely than men to remarry after being divorced or widowed, a situation that contributed to an overall increase in female-headed households in the 1990s.

Although nuclear families make up 56 percent of all households, there has been an increase in other types of households. For instance, more Argentines are living in blended ("step") families (15.4 percent of all households) and as unmarried couples (8 percent of all adults).[40] Couples are increasingly likely not to have children, and the average number of children per household has declined. Finally, 25 percent of urban households are headed by women. Female-headed households are economically disadvantaged. Women are less likely to earn a living wage, and thus are saddled with an extra burden when they are raising children alone.

Reproduction

Sex Education and Contraception

Reproductive decision-making for women is tied to social norms about motherhood. Argentina has one of the lowest birthrates in Latin America; it experienced a demographic decline that began in the end of the 1880s and accelerated in the post–World War I period. The demographic shift during this period was alarming to political leaders and to society more generally because it challenged the ideal of motherhood, as well as the ethnic demography of the nation. For most of the twentieth century Argentine leaders continued to demand that women stay home and raise children, but clearly couples were using family planning to control fertility. As women's involvement in the workforce expanded, conservative groups argued that the woman's place was in the home. Despite widespread entry of women into the workforce in the 1970s, the government of the first and only female president of Argentina, Isabel Perón (1974–1976), passed legislation to encourage the growth of families and to eliminate the public provision of birth control, including contraception and sterilization. The law also called for an intensive health education campaign to emphasize the "risks" involved with practicing contraception.[41] Although the government discouraged them, contraceptives were available in the private sector and were used by Argentines of all classes. However, contraceptives were less accessible to lower-class Argentines and those living in rural areas because these sectors of the population relied (and continue to rely) on public health services. The laws did not succeed in their goal and the population growth rate continued to drop.

These restrictive policies continued until 1986, when the newly democratized government promoted legislation to increase reproductive rights. The government issued a decree that called on the Ministry of Health and

Social Action to create and implement programs for the improvement of maternal and child health. In 1988, this measure was strengthened when Congress introduced a reproductive health program to provide women of "high reproductive risk" with family planning services and information. According to the U.N. Department of Economic and Social Development, the Argentine government's view of the current fertility level is that it is satisfactory and requires no intervention. The fertility rate in 1998 was low for Latin America, at 2.6 births per woman; however, many experts feel that there should be better access to contraceptives and sex education in order to prevent unwanted pregnancies and increase reproductive choice.[42]

Contraceptive policy changes have made family planning services more accessible throughout Argentina. In metropolitan Buenos Aires, reforms have made sex education, information about family planning, and contraceptives available in the public hospitals and not just through the private sector. Yet access is still limited in poor communities. In 1990, the Investigation of Poverty in Argentina (Investigación de la Pobreza en la Argentina) discovered that 39.9 percent of all women did not use any contraceptives. However, while 35.6 percent above the poverty line used contraceptives, 80.2 percent of women below the poverty line did not practice birth control.[43] Poor women who practice birth control are likely to do so sporadically, leading to the spread of sexually transmitted diseases and pregnancies that may result in illegal abortion.

Abortion

Abortion is almost entirely illegal in Argentina. The Penal Code considers it a "crime against life and person." Today, abortion may be performed by a licensed physician, with a woman's consent, in only two situations: (1) in the case of grave risk to the mother's life or health, when danger cannot be averted by any other measure, or (2) in the case of the rape of a retarded or mentally ill woman, when legal proceedings have been initiated. The first exception suggests that the law could be widely interpreted to allow for the protection of psychological or physical health. The second implies that women would have to prove they have been raped, which can be quite difficult. Yet, these kinds of conditional provisions are seldom used by women in Latin America because "the legal maneuvers necessary to gain access to legal abortion services may be frustrating, complicated, and time consuming." In fact, "the process may be so lengthy and cumbersome that a woman's request remains pending after she has given birth."[44] Even though abortion is illegal, it is a common practice in Argentina. In fact, the World Health Organization estimates 365,000 abortions per year, and other agencies have estimated up to 400,000.[45] This figure implies an estimated abortion ratio of as high as 500 abortions per 1000 live births. Women who can afford safe and sanitary abortions performed by trained doctors are able to access this service in clinics similar to those in the United States or Europe. But poorer women are not so lucky, and often resort to risky abortive measures. For this reason, the majority of women who are killed or hurt by abortion are poor. The consequences of these clandestine abortions are an estimated 300 to 400 deaths each year. This figure places Argentina on the World Health Organization's list of nations with high maternal mortality rates. In fact, abortion is the leading cause of maternal mortality; about 30 percent of maternal deaths result from illegal abortions, and death rates are higher in the more isolated provinces of Argentina.

Although the position of the Catholic Church is very strict, the Argentine population is in favor of legalizing abortion in certain circumstances. Several surveys show that the majority (anywhere from 57 to 81 percent) of people in Buenos Aires believe that abortion should be legalized in at least some cases, such as rape and risk of maternal mortality.[46] Despite attitudes favoring the relaxation of laws on abortion, political leaders have been hesitant to address the problems caused by illegal abortion. Feminists point out that it is easy for Argentina's elites to ignore abortion's consequences, since they can afford contraceptives and, if necessary, easily gain entry to clinics where abortions are performed safely, albeit clandestinely.

Teen Pregnancy

A lack of sex education contributes to teen pregnancy in Argentina. There is no national-level program for sex education, and official policy dictates that it is a parent's responsibility to educate rather than the responsibility of the state. Adolescent fertility in Argentine is relatively high compared with the general fertility rate: 30 births per 1000 girls under age 20. Rates are substantially higher in the northern provinces (107.6 in Misiones and 106.9 in Chaco).[47] Experts have attributed these high levels to a lack of sex education and reproductive services, increasingly young age at first sexual intercourse, lack of job opportunities for teens, and gender roles emphasizing women's motherhood. Teen pregnancy puts girls and their babies physically at risk, and contributes to the cycle of poverty faced by girls with few economic opportunities.

HEALTH

Health Care Access

Economic policies put into place in the 1990s in Argentina included a series of measures to privatize health services; these reforms have adversely affected the large segments of the population that depend on public health services.[48] The public health care system in Argentina offered widespread coverage through social security programs for public workers since the 1950s. Before the 1991 Convertibility Plan, 70 percent of all health care was provided through social security programs. However the health care system began to deteriorate, and less government money was spent on health care. Today, public health expenditures account for less than 3 percent of the total national budget. The current system is divided among three sectors: the private sector, the public sector, and the Social Security provided to workers in the state sector. The public sector provides health care for approximately 30 percent of the population. The government also undertakes preventative health measures, such as immunization programs, prevention of infectious diseases, and "responsible parenthood" campaigns.[49] Residents of Buenos Aires have better access to medical care than people in other areas, particular rural zones. However, the current constraints on government spending caused by the economic recession have led to a shortage of medical supplies and medicines, a problem that disproportionately affects the poor.

Reproductive health services are available to many women, but there are several problematic trends. In 1994, the federal government instituted a program in support of maternal and child health, and access to prenatal care has increased. In most cases, delivery occurs in hospitals (97 percent).[50] Of these institutional deliveries, 23.5 percent are by cesarean section; a high rate, particularly in the developing world.[51] This figure is alarming because cesarean deliveries carry a greater risk for women's health. Access to health care for adolescent girls can also be problematic, since it is hard for teens to get services without parental consent. There are few or no programs targeting adolescent reproductive health, or the prevention of sexually transmitted illnesses and unwanted pregnancies. However, in some provinces, prenatal care is available free of charge to teen mothers. For instance, in Catamarca, a law was passed in 1992 to offer free prenatal care and nutritional supplements, and to cover the cost of delivery.

Diseases and Disorders

On the whole, Argentine women are healthier than their male counterparts. They live longer; current life expectancy is about 76 years for women and 68 years for men.[52] In 1999, the leading causes of death for Argentine women were heart and circulatory illness (36.3 percent), cancer (18.9 percent, almost 20 percent of which was breast cancer), and respiratory illness (12.6 percent). Accidents account for 3.7 percent of all female mortality. Maternal mortality is relatively high in Argentina. The maternal morality rate fell from a high of about 52 (per 100,000) in 1990 to 46 in 2000.[53] Many of the deaths reported in these figures are preventable, since 36 percent of maternal deaths are from abortion, 11 percent from hemorrhages, and 16 percent from toxemia.

AIDS

There is a lack of firm statistics on the transmission of HIV and the spread of AIDS in Argentina, although there is public attention to the problem. Those statistics which are available do not differentiate by sex. However, recent research suggests that predominant risk factors have shifted from gay contact to drug use and heterosexual contact. For women, impoverished young mothers are the group most at risk. The government has created a series of widespread ad campaigns encouraging condom use to stop the spread of AIDS.

Eating Disorders

Argentina is estimated to have the highest rates of anorexia and bulimia in the world, with rates over three times those of the United States. These disorders are characterized by a fear of gaining weight, a distortion of one's body image, and excessive dieting or binge-purge behaviors; young women are the vast majority of the affected. A 1996 study by the Argentine Association to Fight Bulimia and Anorexia estimated that one in ten Argentine girls between the ages of 14 and 18 is clinically anorexic or bulimic. Health experts attribute this phenomenon to a cultural obsession with thinness and fashion which exceeds that in other countries.[54]

The eating disorder epidemic has recently gotten the attention of Argentine lawmakers. Some charged that Argentina's clothing industry exacerbates the problem by producing clothing in arbitrary small, medium and large sizes that bear only minor resemblance to international standards.[55] In June 2000, after receiving a petition signed by 100,000 people, the Senate passed a bill to require that Argentine clothing manufacturers produce exact numeric sizes.

POLITICS AND LAW

Suffrage

Women were granted the right to vote in 1947 in a campaign led by charismatic first lady Eva Duarte de Perón, known familiarly as Evita. Although previous suffrage movements had been unsuccessful at achieving the support of political parties, Evita and her husband, President Juan Perón, had little trouble gaining election reforms. They were eager to capture the support of working-class Argentine women for Perón's party, the Peronistas. Following this gain, the Peronistas founded a women's branch (the Rama *Feminina*) with the charismatic Evita at the helm. The Rama Feminina advanced women's issues to national prominence and successfully supported female candidates for office.[56] For instance, in 1955, 21.6 percent of the Chamber of Deputies was female. Yet, political parties have continued a tradition of viewing women as a "sector" rather than as central.[57]

Political Participation

Women's representation remained low throughout most of the twentieth century, though gains were made. The greatest strides came from the

Quota Law (*Ley de Cupos*), which was introduced in 1991 and took effect in 1993. It is the world's first established quota law for women as national legislators. An attempt to compensate for the absence of women in elected office, the Quota Law requires that a minimum of 30 percent of political party candidates in all electoral districts must be female, and that they must be placed in "electable" positions on party lists. The law has substantially increased female representation in the Chamber of Deputies (from 3.9 percent in 1985 and 5.8 percent in 1991, to 27.6 percent in 1997). The results have not been as striking in the Senate, where women representatives were 6.5 percent in 1986 and 8.7 percent in 1989, and are today 27 percent. Further, the number of women elected is smaller than the number nominated as candidates. Critics have charged that the law has not been incorporated by most parties, and that men manipulate the quotas by deciding which women occupy electable positions on the lists; these women are often the men's wives, lovers, sisters, or friends.[58] The current economic and political crises have led to calls for political reform, and it remains to be seen how such changes would affect the Quota Law.

The Restoration of Democracy

Women's participation in politics was notable during the fight to end the military dictatorship and the subsequent period of democratic consolidation. During the repressive period of Argentine dictatorship in the late 1970s, groups demanding human rights began to appear, led by the Mothers of the Plaza de Mayo (*Madres de Plaza de Mayo*). This organization, comprised of mothers whose grown children were disappeared ones (*desaparecidos*), was the first to confront the military government in 1977. They demonstrated silently by circling the central plaza, the Plaza de Mayo, each week, carrying photos of their missing children and wearing white diapers or scarves embroidered with their son's and daughter's names on their heads as a powerful symbol of their motherhood. The Madres were important because they were the first organization to gain international attention to pressure the Argentine government about human rights abuses. Although a few Madres were targeted for disappearance by the repressive regime, most were able to continue their activism. Many have suggested that this is due to the fact that the Madres were able to use societal expectations about motherhood as a tool of resistance and as a protective shield; after all, they were just following societal dictates to look after their children. "They were the first to demonstrate publicly against the dictatorship, thus opening up a political space for popular mobilization, at a moment when this was nonexistent due to the political repression. Because of these mobilizations women and their problems gained visibility and political importance, which was further developed during the political opening."[59]

Argentine society faced many transformations during the early democratic period. The junta continued to deny the accusations of the Madres and their supporters, but in December 1983, a constitutional government headed by Radical Civic Union leader Raúl Alfonsín democratically replaced the junta by winning 52 percent of the vote. In the period immediately following the restoration of democracy, Argentines were wary after so many years of violence and repression. In order to strengthen and protect human rights, the government focused on controlling the military and preventing future coups. Also of central importance were discussions of human rights, the demands of the Madres to find out the truth about their children's and grandchildren's disappearances,[60] and the resulting investigations and trials.

When democracy was restored by elections in 1983, many changes came swiftly to the Argentine way of life. In addition to an end to campaigns of terror, social movements coalesced to demand not only accountability for the "Dirty War," but also to call for greater protection of individual civil liberties. Among the many movements were feminist organizations and individuals who demanded legalization of divorce and an end to the "power of the fatherland" (*patria potestad*)—a law that gave full custody of children to their fathers. In addition, the Catholic Church hierarchy, which was heavily criticized by human rights organizations as a sympathizer of the military during the dictatorship, found its long-standing constitutional privileges were being questioned. The church's legitimacy as the moral voice of Argentina—along with its long-standing ideas about women and work, sexual behavior, contraception, reproduction, and marriage—was under attack.

Women's Rights

The reformed Argentine Constitution (1994), Article 75, includes provisions for equal rights for men and women and a convention for the elimination of all forms of discrimination against women in keeping with the U.N. Convention on the Elimination of All Forms of Discrimination Against Women. Under the constitutional provision of equal pay for equal work, women and men must be compensated equally for their work. Article 37 guarantees equal opportunities for elective office and equal access to political parties.

Women's rights have also been guaranteed in civil, family, and criminal law. For instance, laws passed in 1985 gave mothers and fathers equal custody over their children. Laws and policies were developed throughout the 1990s to address domestic violence and sexual assault, although it is hard to gauge their effectiveness due to underreporting of intimate crime. Law reforms in 1999 defined rape more generally than in the past, allowing for male or female victims and perpetrators, and included non-penile/vaginal penetration as a form of rape.

In 1991, the National Women's Advisory (Consejo Nacional de la Mujer;

CNM), was created as a part of the executive branch to promote and monitor antidiscrimination measures. CNM was charged with strengthening programs for women's issues, monitoring equality in elections, and overseeing the implementation of workplace equal opportunity laws. Later measures created a federal board with representation from provincial governments in 1996. The political nature of the CNM and its proximity to controversial issues has led to a great deal of variation in the policies adopted and the degree to which they are enforced. Changes of regime have plagued the CNM. For instance, in the late 1990s, a feminist head of CNM was pressured to quit after she made statements in support of reproductive rights and sex education.

Feminist Movements

Argentine feminism began in Buenos Aires at the turn of the twentieth century, when individual women thought and wrote about the discrimination against women. However, it was not until the 1920s that women organized to defend their rights, inspired by the suffragettes of the United States, Britain, and France. It was during this period that Julieta Lanteri formed the National Feminist Party (Partido Feminista Nacional) to insist that women were not fit solely for motherhood, but should have civil, political, and economic rights. After gaining suffrage, the women's movement continued to evolve in the 1960s and early 1970s, with influences from global feminism.

However, all of this ended when women's organizations were targeted, threatened, and finally banned in 1976 by the military government. The silence and fear of the Dirty War kept women's groups and other associations from openly protesting or organizing until the dramatic presence of the Madres de Plaza de Mayo in 1977.[61] Even so, many groups continued to meet clandestinely or informally as self-help groups or consciousness-raising parties during the dictatorship. This aided in the resuscitation of the feminist movement after democracy was restored.

The current wave of feminism, which includes the feminist movement in Argentina, originated in Buenos Aires in 1981. At this time, groups assembled to campaign against *patria potestad*. Demands coalesced in 1983, when democracy was reestablished, opening opportunities for social movement groups and resulting in a wave of new women's initiatives. The Women's Multisectorial (Multisectoral de la Mujer) was formed as an umbrella group to unite women's groups, politicians, labor organizations, human rights activists, housewives, and individual feminists. The traditional *patria potestad* law gave fathers the absolute right over their children. The women fought until 1985, when the law was changed so that parental authority rested equally on both parents. Campaigns also succeeded in reforming laws to equalize the status of children born out of wedlock, and decriminalize birth control. Before 1983, speaking about feminism meant challenging the established order so much that even the most progressive sectors of Argentina would not consider including feminist demands in their reforms.[62] Moreover, many women's organizations that provided services and activities for women did not claim to be feminist. For example, one activist in the early 1980s believed that "it was simply too dangerous to use the word [feminism] and still reach the community."[63] However, the organizations that had formed to fight *patria potestad* did emphasize feminism, and after winning their campaign, they continued and branched out to embrace other women's rights issues. The movement includes centers for research and the development of feminist theory, such as Center for Women's Studies (CEM/Centro de Estudios de la Mujer) and Center for Studies of State and Society (CEDES/Centro de Estudios de Estado y Sociedad), as well as social movement organizations that address sexual and reproductive rights, domestic violence, pay equity, eating disorders, and other issues.

Women's organizations in Argentina sometimes join together in campaigns or meetings, but they are also divided by ideological and tactical differences. Since 1981, there has been an annual national women's conference (the Encuentro Nacional de Mujeres) each winter that has drawn as many as 150,000 women from diverse organizations and perspectives. Women's organizations also work together in a variety of umbrella groups, such as Women Called Together for Freedom of Choice (Mujeres Autoconvocadas para Decidir en Libertad). But divisions between "independent" or "autonomous" feminists and those who work with the government or with nongovernmental organizations (NGOs) sometimes stand in the way of cooperation between women's groups. "Autonomous" feminists in Argentina charge that women who work in NGOs or governmental institutions have been co-opted. This divisive phenomenon has been noted elsewhere in Latin America, and some have argued that "NGO-ification"—women's incorporation into parties and official institutions and NGOs—led to a demobilization of feminist movements throughout Latin America in the 1990s.

Feminist organizations in Argentina have embraced a wide variety of tactics and activities to frame their fight against patriarchy. Some engage in traditional political lobbying for legislative reforms; others focus on research or advocacy of issues like teen pregnancy, abortion and domestic violence. Groups hold workshops on contraception or self-defense, or offer leadership training for women. Still others focus on media diffusion, taking out ads or networking with journalists to increase the visibility of feminist concerns in the news media. There are also groups that regularly engage in street drama, protest, and other forms of public demonstration to get their feminist messages across. Many groups use a combination of two or more of these strategies.

Overall, elite allies are not readily accessible to those advocating feminist concerns. The political parties and coalitions—even on the left—have not embraced feminist issues in their platforms. In 1999, only one congress-woman, Graciela Fernández Meijide, was involved in collective action (as a human rights activists) prior to her election, and she denied the importance of social movements in postdictatorship politics. The media have been somewhat more open to coverage of feminist issues, though sporadically. Few organizations—both NGOs and other social movement organizations—have been willing to ally themselves with the reproductive rights movement, for instance, by signing open letters placed in newspapers by feminist groups and individuals.

Lesbian Rights

Lesbians and gay men have gained visibility in Argentina in recent years, particularly in the capital city of Buenos Aires. In December 2002, Buenos Aires passed legislation supporting a Civil Union Register which is open to same-sex couples.[64] There is a diverse lesbian movement composed of at least eight organizations that vary from support and reflection groups to activist-oriented organizations, like Lesbians in Sight (Lesbianas a la Vista) that engage in public demonstrations, street drama, and other campaigns for lesbian visibility. While some lesbian groups cooperate extensively with gay men's organizations and other groups in the homosexual/bisexual/transgender community, many lesbian organizations are reluctant to do so. The have accused gay men's groups of machismo and misogyny, and prefer to work independently.

RELIGION AND SPIRITUALITY

The Roman Catholic Church

The influence of the Roman Catholic Church in Argentina extends from what gets taught in schools, to sexual norms, to the traditional division of labor in the family, and to the roles of women and men. In Argentina the church has held special privileges since colonial times; today these include recognition in the Constitution and direct funding from the government. Since 90 percent of Argentines identify as Catholic, women's roles as religious leaders are minimal because women are not permitted to become priests in the Catholic Church. The influence of the Catholic Church in the political sphere should not be underestimated, and it presents a central obstacle to Argentine feminists.

The women's movement has often been embroiled in conflict with the Catholic Church. The battle over reproductive and sexual rights is one key example. Feminist organizations were active when the abortion debate surfaced in the politics surrounding the Constitutional Convention of 1994. This process evoked debate about abortion, contraceptive distribution by the state and by NGOs, and sex education in the face of high abortion rates and the AIDS epidemic. Even the minor provisions for legal abortion came under attack from the hierarchy of the Catholic Church. The Catholic bishops, under the leadership of the bishop of Buenos Aires, launched an offensive to include a clause defending life after conception, which would have prohibited abortion completely.[65] Despite the fact that abortion was not on the list of items to be examined for reform that had been drafted in the Pact of San José (an agreement that stipulated what would be in the new constitution of 1994), the Church hierarchy wanted delegates to change the laws. The bishops were so strongly opposed to abortion that they pressured the government and rallied antiabortion activists so the members of the Convention would further limit access to abortion. For example, each delegate to the Constitutional Convention received a letter signed by all of the Argentine bishops that contained the antiabortion text approved by the church hierarchy, photographs of fetuses, and a petition with 100,000 signatures against allowing legal abortion in any circumstance. This attempt failed, however, and the conditions for legal abortion remained as stipulated.

Another example of the strong connection between church and state occurred during the 1995 U.N. World Conference on Women in Beijing, which produced the "strongest documents in gender equality, empowerment and justice ever produced and agreed to by the world's governments."[66] Beijing was most successful in passing legislation to legitimize sex education and sexual health, despite threats unleashed against the final document by the Vatican and its allies.[67] Though most other Latin American nations opposed the Vatican's population policies for the first time, Argentina maintained the church's antiabortion stand. Argentina and the other pro-Vatican countries, along with fundamentalist Islamic nations, made sure that the most controversial issues were related to reproductive rights. Despite heated debate, the Platform for Action reaffirmed "the right to decide the number and spacing of children and to attain the highest standard of sexual and reproductive health."[68] Although the conference also declared that the human rights of women "include the right to have control over and to decide freely and responsibly on matters related to their sexuality, including sexual and reproductive health, free of coercion, discrimination and violence,"[69] over 30 governments, including Argentina, and the Holy See, reserved this paragraph.

Spirituality

Although the importance of the Catholic Church has declined since the 1980s, women continue to be more active church attendees than their male counterparts. Rural women are more religious than urban women, though there is a trend toward evangelical Protestantism in urban areas that has found converts among poor women. In addition, nontraditional forms of spirituality have risen since democracy, with an increase in the popularity of "New Age" practices like meditation, yoga, and other spiritual activities.

VIOLENCE

Domestic Violence

There is a lack of data measuring violence against women in Argentina. Statistics from the judicial branch state that the number of court cases related to family violence averaged between 1,600 and 2,000 each year from 1996 to 2000. However, regional centers that aid victims of family violence report much higher numbers; for instance, around 5,000 people sought help from the Argentine Association for the Prevention of Family Violence in 1998 alone, and the domestic violence crisis hot line in Buenos Aires receives over 25,000 calls a year.[70]

Both governmental and nongovernmental agencies provide support for victims of domestic violence. The most extensive law addressing domestic violence in Argentine history was passed in 1994: the National Law for Protection Against Family Violence. It created information and counseling centers for physical and psychological violence, and requires mediation hearings for victims and their abusers. Various types of public services are offered to victims of domestic violence by NGOs in Argentina. There are prevention and assistance programs for battered women throughout the country, some of which are run by the Argentine Association for the Prevention of Family Violence. Many groups are run by feminists, and include both violence prevention and advocacy, as well as counseling and crisis support services.

Rape/Sexual Assault

An estimated 5,000 to 7,000 cases of rape are reported in Argentina each year, but the number of persons convicted for these crimes ranges from 400 to 500 per year.[71] The vast majority of the victims of rape and sexual assaults are female: women and girls constitute 87 percent of all reporting victims. Girls are particularly vulnerable; in 76 percent of all sexual crimes reported, the victim was under the age of 21.[72] There is a national network of institutional resources for women who have been sexually assaulted. It includes over 40 groups that provide support for the victims of rape and sexual assault throughout urban areas in the nation, and in some rural ones as well.

Trafficking in Women and Children

After an extensive history of thriving in Argentina, particularly in Buenos Aires, prostitution was legalized, publicly controlled, and monitored in the

1940s.[73] Prostitution was prohibited during the military dictatorship and continues to be illegal, but it has maintained its status as a major illegal business. In the city of Buenos Aires alone, there are estimated to be 10,000 women prostitutes, 30 percent working in the street and 70 percent within brothels.[74] A great majority of prostitutes are exploited by pimps or other third parties. The recent economic crisis has driven more women into prostitution, and a recent television exposé documented how desperate elderly women have turned to selling their bodies in Buenos Aires.[75]

Estimates suggest that child and teen prostitution of both girls and boys has risen notably since the 1990s. Organizations that work with prostitutes have been increasingly concerned about the trafficking of women (particularly girls or very young women) in Argentina. Traffickers bring poor girls from the Dominican Republic, Central America, and Paraguay and force them to work in Argentina.[76]

OUTLOOK FOR THE TWENTY-FIRST CENTURY

The present situation of women in Argentina gives reason for both optimism and pessimism. The short-term forecast is bleak; economic recession has dashed the hopes of Argentines and has plunged much of the country into poverty. Yet from a long-term perspective, women are becoming more and more educated, and they have made strides in the labor force and in political representation with the passage of the Quota Law. Even so, women face a substantial pay gap, and discrimination in the workplace. Women have been disproportionately affected by the rising unemployment that has paralyzed the Argentine economy. They continue to be denied access to a full range of reproductive options, and they are victimized by domestic violence, sexual assault, and prostitution. In addition, there is a notable disparity between the standard of living for urban and rural women; 10 percent of the total population is rural, and has the highest rates of poverty, maternal mortality, teen pregnancy, and illiteracy, and the least access to reproductive services, education, and health care. The small but dedicated feminist movement has its work cut out as it seeks to transform the social practices that restrain gender equality throughout Argentina.

NOTES

1. Instituto Nacional de Estadística y Censos (INDEC), *Censo nacional de población y vivienda* (Buenos Aires: Republica Argentina, 2001).

2. *Nunca más*, the official report commissioned in 1986 by civilian president Raúl Alfonsín, listed 9,000 *desaparecidos* (disappeared ones), but some estimates are over three times greater. As the "Dirty War" progressed, more people were disappeared, regardless of their activities. The *desaparecidos* often had no political involvement whatsoever. Many were merely involved in labor unions, student organizations,

or charitable work with the poor; others were disappeared after witnessing a disappearance or being implicated by others—all it took was suspicion. Silence and secrecy reigned.

3. INDEC, 2002.

4. *Catholic Almanac* (Paterson, NJ: St. Anthony's Guild, 1999).

5. Subsecretaria de la Mujer, *Mujeres en Argentina* (Buenos Aires: República Argentina, 1999).

6. INDEC, *Encuesta de desarrollo social* (Buenos Aires: República Argentina, 2000).

7. INDEC, 2002.

8. Mark Szuchman, "Childhood Education and Politics in Nineteenth Century Argentina: The Case of Buenos Aires," *Hispanic American Historical Review* 70, no. 1 (1990): 109–38; Carlos Newland, "La educación elemental en Hispanoamerica: Desde la independencia hasta la centralización de los sistemas educativos nacionales," *Hispanic American Historical Review* 71, no. 2 (1991): 335–64.

9. INDEC, *Encuesta permanente de hogares* (Buenos Aires: República Argentina, 1998).

10. Subsecretaria de la Mujer, *Mujeres en Argentina*, 1999.

11. UNESCO, 1999. Statistical yearbook (New York: UNESCO, 1999).

12. In January 2002, Argentina defaulted on international loans and the peso was depegged from the dollar as a means of easing the economic crisis and stimulating foreign investments. While long-term effects remain to be seen, the value of the peso has declined to below 70 percent its former rate.

13. David Rock, *Argentina, 1516–1987* (Berkeley: University of California Press, 1987 [1985]).

14. Fernando Rocchi, "Concentración de capital, concentración de mujeres," in *Historia de las mujeres en la Argentina, siglo XX*, eds. Fernanda Gil Lozano, Vaeria Silvina Pita, and Maria Gabriela Ini (Buenos Aires: Taurus, 2000), 223–44.

15. INDEC, 2000.

16. María José Lubertino, *Perón y la iglesia (1943–1955)* (Buenos Aires: Centro Editor de América Latina, 1987).

17. For instance, help wanted ads often specify the sex of the job applicants being sought.

18. Subsecretaria de la Mujer, *Mujeres en el mercado laboral en Argentina*, Serie Enlace (Buenos Aires: Subsecretaria de la Mujer, 1999).

19. Ibid.

20. Ibid.

21. INDEC, 2000.

22. Subsecretaria de la Mujer, *Mujeres en el mercado laboral* (1999).

23. Mirta Zaida Lobato, "Lenguaje laboral y de género: Primera mitad del siglo XX," in *Historia de las mujeres en la Argentina, siglo XX*, eds. Fernanda Gil Lozano, Vaeria Silvina Pita, and Maria Gabriela Ini (Buenos Aires: Taurus, 2000), 95–116.

24. Recent inflation has meant that workers' paychecks do not go as far as they used to. June 2002 consumer prices were up 28 percent compared to a year before.

25. Maria José Lubertino, *Mujeres trabajando* (Buenos Aires: Instituto Social y Político de la Mujer, 2000), www.ispm.org.as/documentos/mujerestrabajando.htm.

26. Rocchi, 2000.

27. Mariana Carabajal, "Argentina: Por primera vez lanzan una campaña contra el acoso sexual laboral," *Página 12* (October 25, 2000).

28. Marysa Navarro, "Hidden, Silent and Anonymous: Women Workers in the

Argentine Trade Union Movement," in *The World of Women's Trade Unionism*, ed. N. Soldon (Westport, CT: Greenwood Press, 1985), 165–98.

29. Lobato, 2000.

30. Nikki Craske, *Women and Politics in Latin America* (New Brunswick, NJ: Rutgers University Press, 1999).

31. Lubertino, 2000.

32. Peter Lloyd-Sherlock, "Models of Public Sector Intervention: Providing for the Elderly in Argentina (c. 1890–1994)," *Journal of Latin American Studies* 29 (1997): 1–21.

33. María Alicia Gutiérrez, "Parirás con dolor," in *Nuestros cuerpos, nuestras vidas* (Buenos Aires: Foro por los Derechos Reproductivos, 1998), 75–94.

34. Donna Guy, *Sex and Danger in Buenos Aires* (Lincoln: University of Nebraska Press, 1990).

35. Rosa Geldstein and Edith Pantelides. "Double Subordination, Double Risk: Class, Gender and Sexuality in Adolescent Women in Argentina," *Reproductive Health Matters* 9 (1997): 121–31.

36. Ana Lía Kornblit, Mario Pecheny, and Jorge Vujosevich, *Gays y lesbianas: Formación de la identidad y derechos humanos* (Buenos Aires: La Colmena, 1998).

37. Catalina Wainerman, *Familia y trabajo* (New York: United Nations, 2001).

38. Subsecretaria de la Mujer, *Mujeres en el mercado laboral* (1999).

39. Ibid.

40. Subsecretaria de la Mujer, *Mujeres en Argentina* (1999).

41. Sylvina Ramos and Anahi Viladrich, "Aborto en América Latina: ¿Cómo seguir?," paper presented at the meeting of ISIS Internacional in Santiago, Chile, 1991; Horacio D. Gregoratti and Carlos Luzzetti, "Argentina," in *Population Policy in Developed Countries*, ed. Bernard Berelson, chapter 7 (New York: McGraw Hill, 1974).

42. INDEC, 1998.

43. Susana Checa and Martha I. Rosenberg, *Aborto hospitalizado* (Buenos Aires: Ediciones El Cielo por Asalto, 1996).

44. John M. Paxman, Alberto Rizo, Laura Brown, and Janie Benson, "The Clandestine Epidemic: The Practice of Unsafe Abortion in Latin America," *Studies in Family Planning* 24, no. 4 (1993): 205–26.

45. Because of the illegality of abortion and the Argentine government's population policies, there have been few wide-ranging or long-term studies on the incidence of abortion in Argentina. Furthermore, there are many difficulties in collecting and ascertaining whether abortion data is correct in an illegal and secretive environment. In nations where abortion is illegal, the only way to approximate these figures is to use hospital registers, death certificates, and retrospective surveys (Ramos and Viladrich, 1991). According to Ramos, mortality rates are the only continuous registers regarding abortion in Argentina (Ramos, 1988, 49).

46. Sylvina Ramos, "¿Aborto?," *Ciencia Hoy* 1, no. 1 (1988): 50; Dalia Szulik and Mónica Patracci, "Public Opinion and Abortion in Argentina," paper presented at the meetings of the American Sociological Association, 1988.

47. Mónica Gogna, "Una inconsistente defensa de la vida," *Conciencia latinoamericana* 6, no. 3 (1994): 4–8.

48. Mabel Bellucci, "El feminismo en estos tiempos neoliberales," *Feminaria* 8, no. 3 (1995).

49. Checa and Rosenberg, 1996.

50. Ministerio de Salud y Acción Social, *Estadísticas vitales. Información básica—1995*

(Buenos Aires: Dirección de Estadísticas de Salud, Programa Nacional de Estadísticas de Salud, 1996).

51. Galimberti, as cited in Martha Rosenberg, with Theresa Durand, "Diagnóstico de la ciudad de Buenos Aires" (Proyecto "Desarollo de Estrategias de Seguimiento de los Documentos de la Conferencia del Cairo, Copenhagen and Beijing," 1998), unpublished report.

52. Subsecretaria de la Mujer, *Mujeres en Argentina* (1999).

53. INDEC, 2000.

54. Mabel Burin, "Salud mental," in *Tribunal Permanente por los Derechos de las Mujeres a la Salud, Jornada preparatoria* (Buenos Aires: Foro Permanente por los Derechos de las Mujeres, 1997).

55. Ibid.

56. Rock, 1987 [1985].

57. Craske, 1999.

58. Jacqueline Jiménez-Polanco, "Women's Political Representation in the Chambers of Deputies of Argentina, Brazil, Chile, Mexico, and the Dominican Republic," paper presented at the XXI International Congress of the Latin American Studies Association, Chicago, 1998.

59. Mónica Flori, "Argentine Women's Organizations During the Transition to Democracy," *Feminist Issues* (1988): 53–66.

60. The Abuelas [Grandmothers] de Plaza de Mayo were founded in 1977, using similar tactics to demand the return of their kidnapped grandchildren, who were disappeared with their parents or were born in detention and adopted by military officers. See Rita Arditti, *Searching for Life* (Berkeley: University of California Press, 1999).

61. Marguerite Guzman Bouvard, *Revolutionizing Motherhood* (Wilmington, DE: Scholarly Resources, 1994).

62. Bellucci, 1995.

63. Nancy Sternbach, "Argentine Feminism: Gaining Speed." *off our backs* 14, no. 3 (1984): 9.

64. IGLHRC, 2003.

65. Gogna, 1994.

66. Women's Environment and Development Organization (WEDO), "A Brief Analysis of UN Fourth World Conference on Women Beijing Declaration and Platform for Action" (New York: WEDO, 1995), 1.

67. Cristina Grela, "Una 'S' para el 2000," *La muralla y el laberinto* (Buenos Aires: Comité de América Latina y el Caribe para la Defensa de los Derechos de la Mujer, 1996), 75–76.

68. WEDO, 1995, 10.

69. Ibid.

70. Silvia Chejter, *Argentina* (New York: United Nations Development Programme, 2001), www.undp.org/rblac/gender/argentina.htm.

71. Ibid.

72. Ibid.

73. Guy, 1990.

74. Transvestite prostitution is also extensive in Argentina, although data on the number of transvestite prostitutes are nonexistent.

75. TV America, 2002

76. Chejter, 2001.

RESOURCE GUIDE

Suggested Reading

Flori, Mónica. "Argentine Women's Organizations During the Transition to Democracy." *Feminist Issues* 8, no. 3 (1988): 53–66. An overview of women's organizations in Argentina during the consolidation of democracy.

Geldstein, Rosa, and Edith Pantelides. "Double Subordination, Double Risk: Class, Gender and Sexuality in Adolescent Women in Argentina." *Reproductive Health Matters* 9 (1997): 121–31. Argentine sociologists write on the problems facing poor teen girls in Argentina as they negotiate sexual and gender norms.

Guzman Bouvard, Marguerite. *Revolutionizing Motherhood*. Wilmington, DE: Scholarly Resources, 1994. A highly readable and moving history of the Madres de la Plaza de Mayo based on intensive participant observation and interviews by Guzman Bouvard.

Ramos, Sylvina. "¿Aborto?" *Ciencia Hoy* 1, no. 1 (December 1988/January 1989): 45–52. An article on reproductive rights in Argentina by an Argentine sociologist, and the expert on abortion in Argentina.

Subsecretaría de la Mujer, República Argentina. *Mujeres en Argentina: Estado de situación a cinco años de Beijing*. Buenos Aires: Subsecretaría de la Mujer, Ministerio de Relaciones Exteriores, Comercio Internacional y Culto, 1999. An extensive report on the status of women in Argentina in the five years after the U.N. Conference on Women in Beijing. Statistics on education, employment, health, and social status.

Waylen, Georgina. "Gender and Democratic Politics: A Comparative Analysis of Consolidation in Argentina and Chile." *Journal of Latin American Studies* 32 (2000): 765–93. Political science article on the Quota Law and the obstacles facing women seeking political power in Argentina and Chile.

Film

Las Madres: The Mothers of Plaza De Mayo. 1985. 64 mins. Directed by Susana Muñoz and Lourdes Portillo. Distributed by Women Make Movies.

Web Sites

Lesbianas a la Vista, lesbianasalavista.com.ar.
An activist organization dedicated to promoting sexual rights and lesbian visibility, and strengthening the lesbian community based in Buenos Aires. Contains a calendar of events, photos of campaigns, and message boards.

Mothers (*Madres*) of the Plaza de Mayo, www.madres.org.
A social movement for human rights composed of the mothers of *desaparecidos*. Extensive content on human rights issues in English.

National Institute for Statistics and the Census (Instituto Nacional de Estadísticas y Censos; INDEC), www.indec.gov.ar.
Demographic data and social statistics, many of which are available in English.

National Women's Advisory (Consejo Nacional de la Mujer), www.cnm.gov.ar.
Contains information on federal programs, statistics, and documents on women in Argentina, in Spanish.

Women's Social and Political Institute (Instituto Social y Político de la Mujer), www.ispm.org.ar.
The Institute is a nonprofit association that promotes women's rights and political participation, and does social, political, and economic research. Some English content.

Organizations

ATEM
Salta 1064
Capital Federal 1074, Argentina
Phone: (54 11) 4374 0389
Email: atem@atem.wamani.apc.org

A group of independent feminists active in Buenos Aires since the 1980s. They produce a feminist magazine, titled *Brujas*.

Equal Rights for Argentine Women (Derechos Iguales para la Mujer Argentina; DIMA)
Avenida Libertador 5460
Capital Federal 1426, Argentina
Email: srioja@movi.com.ar
Web site: www.dima.s5.com

A nonprofit organization that engages in lobbying and research on equal rights in Argentina.

Foundation for the Equality of Women (Fundación Mujeres en Igualdad)
Urquiza 1835
Buenos Aires 1602, Argentina
Phone/fax: (54 11) 4791 0821
Email: mei@mei.com.ar
Web site: www.mei.com.ar

A nonprofit, private foundation that focuses on coalition-building between women's organizations and leadership development for women.

Foundation for the Study and Research of Women (Fundación para Estudio e Investigación de la Mujer)
Paraná 135—Piso 3, 13
Buenos Aires 1017, Argentina
Phone/fax: (54 11) 4372 2763
Email: feim@ciudad.com.ar

Research and publications on women and health, education, employment, and the media.

SELECTED BIBLIOGRAPHY

Arditti, Rita. *Searching for Life: The Grandmothers of the Plaza de Mayo and the Disappeared Children of Argentina*. Berkeley: University of California Press, 1999.

Burdick, Michael A. *For God and the Fatherland: Religion and Politics in Argentina*. Albany: State University of New York Press, 1995.

Center for Reproductive Law and Policy (CRLP). *Women of the World: Laws and Policies Affecting Their Reproductive Lives—Latin America and the Caribbean*. New York: Center for Reproductive Law and Policy, 1997.

Chejter, Silvia. *Argentina*. New York: United Nations Development Programme. 2001. www.undp.org/rblac/gender/argentina.htm.

Chisari, Omar O., José María Fanelli, and Roberto Frenkel. "Argentina: Growth Resumption, Sustainability, and Environment." *World Development* 24, no. 2 (1996): 227–40.

Craske, Nikki. *Women and Politics in Latin America*. New Brunswick, NJ: Rutgers University Press, 1999.

Deere, Carmen Diana, and Magdalena León. *Empowering Women: Land and Property Rights in Latin America*. Pittsburgh, PA: University of Pittsburgh Press, 2001.

Dunlop, Joan, Rachel Kyte, and Mia McDonald. "Women Redrawing the Map: The World After the Beijing and Cairo Conferences." *SAIS Review* 16, no. 1 (1996): 153–65.

Flori, Mónica. "Argentine Women's Organizations During the Transition to Democracy." *Feminist Issues* (1988): 53–66.

Geldstein, Rosa, and Edith Pantelides. "Double Subordination, Double Risk: Class, Gender and Sexuality in Adolescent Women in Argentina." *Reproductive Health Matters* 9 (1997): 121–31.

González, Martín, and Alicia Menéndez. *The Effect of Unemployment on Labor Earnings Inequality: Argentina in the Nineties*. Princeton, NJ: Research Program in Development Studies, Princeton University, 2000. www.wws.princeton.edu/~rpds/unefinal.pdf.

Gregoratti, Horatio D., and Carlos Luzzetti. "Argentina." In *Population Policy in Developed Countries*, edited by Bernard Berelson, chapter 7. New York: McGraw Hill, 1974.

Guy, Donna. *Sex and Danger in Buenos Aires: Prostitution, Family, and Nation in Argentina*. Lincoln: University of Nebraska Press, 1990.

Guzman Bouvard, Marguerite. *Revolutionizing Motherhood*. Wilmington, DE: Scholarly Resources, 1994.

Hodges, Donald C. *Argentina 1943–1987*. Albuquerque: University of New Mexico Press, 1988.

Jiménez-Polanco, Jacqueline. "Women's Political Representation in the Chambers of Deputies of Argentina, Brazil, Chile, Mexico, and the Dominican Republic." Paper presented at the XXI International Congress of the Latin American Studies Association, Chicago, 1998.

Lavrin, Asunción. *Women, Feminism, and Social Change*. Lincoln: University of Nebraska Press, 1995.

Lloyd-Sherlock, Peter. "Models of Public Sector Intervention: Providing for the Elderly in Argentina (c. 1890–1994)." *Journal of Latin American Studies* 29 (1997): 1–21.

Love, Elizabeth. "Prisoners of Perfection: Countless Argentine Women Suffer from

Eating Disorders, and the Psyche of Youth Is Battered by a Cultural Obsession with Appearance." Chronicle Foreign Service, 2000.

Navarro, Marysa. "Hidden, Silent and Anonymous: Women Workers in the Argentine Trade Union Movement." In *The World of Women's Trade Unionism*, edited by N. Soldon, 165–98. Westport, CT: Greenwood Press.

———. "Argentina: The Long Road to Women's Rights." In *Women's Rights: A Global View*, Chapter 1, edited by Lynn Walter. Westport, CT: Greenwood Press, 2001.

Paxman, John M., Alberto Rizo, Laura Brown, and Janie Benson. "The Clandestine Epidemic: The Practice of Unsafe Abortion in Latin America." *Studies in Family Planning* 24, no. 4 (1993): 205–26.

Rock, David. *Argentina, 1516–1987*. Berkeley: University of California Press, 1987 [1985].

Sternbach, Nancy. "Argentine Feminism: Gaining Speed." *off our backs* 14, no. 3 (1984): 9.

Szuchman, Mark. "Childhood Education and Politics in Nineteenth Century Argentina: The Case of Buenos Aires." *Hispanic American Historical Review* 70, no. 1 (1990): 109–38.

Szulik, Dalia, and Mónica Patracci. "Public Opinion and Abortion in Argentina." Paper presented at the meetings of the American Sociological Association, 2001.

United Nations Department of Economic and Social Development (UNDESD). *World Abortion Policies 1994*. New York: UNDESD, 1994.

United Nations Educational, Scientific and Cultural Organization (UNESCO). *Statistical Yearbook*. New York: UNESCO, 1999.

Waylen, Georgina. "Gender and Democratic Politics: A Comparative Analysis of Consolidation in Argentina and Chile." *Journal of Latin American Studies* 32 (2000): 765–93.

Women's Environment and Development Organization (WEDO). "A Brief Analysis of the UN Fourth World Conference on Women, Beijing. Declaration and Platform for Action." New York: WEDO, 1995.

Spanish Bibliography

Bellucci, Mabel. "El feminismo en estos tiempos neoliberales." *Feminaria* 8, no. 3 (1995).

Burin, Mabel. "Salud mental." In *Tribunal permanente por los derechos de las mujeres a la salud, Jornada preparatoria*. Buenos Aires: Foro Permanente por los Derechos de las Mujeres, 1997.

Carabajal, Mariana. "Argentina: Por primera vez lanzan una campaña contra el acoso sexual laboral." *Página* 12 (October 25, 2000).

Catholic Almanac. Paterson, NJ: St. Anthony's Guild, 1999.

Checa, Susana and Martha I. Rosenberg. *Aborto hospitalizado*. Buenos Aires: Ediciones El Cielo por Asalto, 1996.

Gogna, Mónica. *El embarazo adolescente: Diagnóstico de situación y lineamientos para la intervención*. Buenos Aires: Secretaria de Desarrollo Social, Presidencia de la Nación Argentina, 1996.

———. "Una inconsistente defensa de la vida." *Conciencia latinoamericana* 6, no. 3 (1994): 4–8.

Grela, Cristina. "Una 'S' para el 2000." In *La muralla y el laberinto*, 75–76. Buenos Aires: Comité de América Latina y el Caribe para la Defensa de los Derechos de la Mujer, 1996.

Gutiérrez, María Alicia. "Parirás con dolor." In *Nuestros cuerpos, nuestras vidas: Propuestas para la promoción de los derechos sexuales y reproductivos*, edited by Foro por los Derechos Reproductivos, 75–94. Buenos Aires: Foro por los Derechos Reproductivos, 1998.

Instituto Nacional de Estadística y Censos (INDEC). *Censo nacional de población y vivienda*. Buenos Aires: República Argentina, 2001.

————. *Empleo y desempleo*. República Argentina. www.indec.gov.ar. Accessed January 15, 2003.

————. *Encuesta permanente de hogares*. Buenos Aires: República Argentina, 1998.

————. *Encuesta de desarrollo social*. Buenos Aires: República Argentina, 2000.

Kornblit, Ana Lía, Mario Pecheny, and Jorge Vujosevich. *Gays y lesbianas: Formación de la identidad y derechos humanos*. Buenos Aires: La Colmena, 1998.

Lobato, Mirta Zaida. "Lenguaje laboral y de género: Primera mitad del siglo XX." In *Historia de las mujeres en la Argentina, siglo XX*, edited by Fernanda Gil Lozano, Vaeria Silvina Pita and Maria Gabriela Ini, 95–116. Buenos Aires: Taurus, 2000.

Lubertino, María José. *Perón y la iglesia (1943–1955)*. Buenos Aires: Centro Editor de América Latina, 1987.

————. *Mujeres trabajando*. Buenos Aires: Instituto Social y Político de la Mujer, 2000. www.ispm.org.ar/documentos/mujerestrabajando.htm. Accessed Dec. 5, 2001.

Ministerio de Salud y Acción Social (MSAC). 1996. *Estadísticas vitales. Información básica—1995*. Buenos Aires: Dirección de Estadísticas de Salud, Programa Nacional de Estadísticas de Salud, 1996.

Newland, Carlos. "La educación elemental en Hispanoamerica: Desde la independencia hasta la centralización de los sistemas educativos nacionales." *Hispanic American Historical Review* 71, no. 2 (1991): 335–64.

Palma, Zulema. "El ejercicio de los derechos sexuales y reproductivos como ejercicio de ciudadanía y sus implicancias con la salud." Unpublished paper.

"¿Prostitución en la Tercera Edad. doc?" Buenos Aires: TV America. Episode 148. Aired July 7, 2002.

Ramos, Sylvina. 1988. "¿Aborto?" *Ciencia Hoy* 1, no. 1 (1988): 45–52.

Ramos, Sylvina, and Anahi Viladrich. "Aborto en América Latina: ¿Como seguir?" Paper presented at the meeting of ISIS Internacional in Santiago, Chile, 1991.

Rocchi, Fernando. "Concentración de capital, concentración de mujeres." In *Historia de las mujeres en la Argentina, siglo XX*, edited by Fernanda Gil Lozano, Vaeria Silvina Pita and Maria Gabriela Ini, 223–44. Buenos Aires: Taurus, 2000.

Rosenberg, Martha, with Theresa Durand. "Diagnóstico de la ciudad de Buenos Aires." Proyecto "Desarrollo de Estrategias de Seguimiento de los Documentos de la Conferencia del Cairo, Copenhagen y Beijing." 1998. Unpublished report.

Subsecretaria de la Mujer, República Argentina. *Mujeres en Argentina: Estado de situación a cinco años de Beijing*. Buenos Aires: Subsecretaria de la Mujer, 1999a.

————. *Mujeres en el mercado laboral en Argentina*. Serie Enlace. Buenos Aires: Subsecretaria de la Mujer, 1999b.

Wainerman, Catalina. *Familia y trabajo: Recreando relaciones de género*. New York: United Nations, 2001.

Wainerman, Catalina, and Zulma Recchini de Lattes. *El trabajo femenino en el banquillo de los acusados: La medición censal en América Latina*. Mexico City: Terranova, 1981.

2

BELIZE

Irma T. Alonso

PROFILE OF BELIZE

Belize, formerly known as British Honduras, is located in Central America, on the Caribbean Sea, between Guatemala and Mexico. The country is different from other Central American countries in that it is not related to the Spanish culture. Instead, Belize maintains close ties with the United Kingdom as a member of the Commonwealth, and to the English-speaking Caribbean as a member of the Caribbean Community and Common Market. Belize became independent from the United Kingdom in 1981, and the queen of England is the (mainly ceremonial) head of the state, represented by a governor-general. Since 1981 local elections have been disputed between two political parties, the People's United Party and the United Democratic Party. The government is a parliamentary democracy, and the economy is based on private enterprise. The country is multicultural and multiethnic, but most of the population speaks English. However, Spanish and dialects including Mayan are also spoken. The various ethnic groups are descended from the Mayan Indians, Spanish explorers, and African slaves.[1]

Belize's total landmass is almost 23,000 square kilometers.[2]

The terrain is flat, with low mountains in the south, and is roughly 60 percent forested. Natural resources include arable land, timber, fish, and hydropower. It is estimated that in 2001, the total population was 256,062, 50.9 percent male and 49.1 percent females. The average annual population growth rate was estimated at 2.7 percent.[3] The population has been transformed since thousands of Asians and Central American refugees arrived in Belize in the 1980s, while at the same time Belizeans were looking for a better life in the United States. At present, almost half of the population live in Belize City.[4]

The population is relatively young, with a median age of nineteen years, as a result of both the high fertility rate and migration patterns. Forty-two percent of the population is younger than 14 years, 54 percent in the age group 15–64, and only 4 percent are 65 years old or above. In 2001 the estimated birthrate was 31.69 per 1,000, and the death rate was 4.7 per 1,000. The total fertility rate was extremely high, estimated at 4.05 children born per woman, while the infant mortality rate, one of the highest in the Caribbean, was estimated at 25.14 per 1,000 live births. Overall, average life expectancy was estimated at 71.1 years: for males, 68.9 years, and that for females, 73.6 years.[5]

OVERVIEW OF WOMEN'S ISSUES

The Belize government created the Department of Women's Affairs, under the Ministry of Human Development, Women, and Civil Society, and in 1990 signed and ratified the Convention on the Elimination of All Forms of Discrimination Against Women. Despite these advances, there are substantial issues affecting women. Some of the main problems are related to extreme poverty, severe health problems due to AIDS/HIV, insufficient programs to deal with the high fertility rate as a result of lack of access to family planning, widespread domestic violence, and discrimination in the labor market.

EDUCATION

Opportunities

Education is compulsory for children between the ages of 5 and 14. Nevertheless, only 75 percent of those children attend school, and only 42 percent of the potential students between the ages of 15 and 19 years old are enrolled in school. To make matters worse, most of the schools are located in urban areas, the majority of which are concentrated in Belize City. As a result the educational situation in other urban areas and in rural areas are even more deplorable than the national averages indicate.

At the primary level, 70 percent of the teachers are female, but only half of them are fully trained. At the secondary level only 46 percent of the teachers are university graduates, and only 60 percent of these graduates have a professional teaching qualification. An additional problem is that only 35 percent of the male and 53 percent of the female students progress to the secondary level, as the programs offered at the secondary level only have space for half of the primary school graduates.[6] There is a 10 percent repetition rate at all levels, and the teacher-pupil ratio is below 20:1, given the few children attending school.

Literacy

The literacy rate is only vaguely defined, and any person 15 years or older who has completed some type of schooling is classified as being able to read and write. According to this definition, the literacy rate is estimated at 75.5 percent.[7] More optimistic estimates indicate that only 6.8 percent of adult males and 7.2 percent of adult females are illiterate.[8]

EMPLOYMENT AND ECONOMICS

Job/Career Opportunities

The economy of Belize is an open economy with an adverse trade balance. Its main trade partners are the United States and the United Kingdom, and to a lesser extent, Mexico, as well as other Central American and CARICOM countries. Belize depends primarily on agriculture, in particular bananas, sugar, citrus fruits, and fish. More recently the economy has been diversified into tourism and other services.[9] Sugar is the main crop and accounts for nearly half of exports, while the banana sector is the largest employer. Ecotourism has become important particularly, given the abundance of rain forests and a variety of archeological sites.

In the year 2000, Belize's total GDP (gross domestic product) was estimated at $790 million, or $3,200 in per capita.[10] Forty-six percent of the population is classified as poor (unable to meet expenses on basic food and nonfood items). It is estimated that rural areas have a higher poverty rate (42.5 percent) than urban areas (20.6 percent). Female-

Woman working in an outdoor Belize grocery store. Photo © TRIP/D. Hoey.

headed households have a higher proportion of families falling below the poverty line (30.6 percent) than those headed by males (23.6 percent).[11]

Economic output is from the following sectors: agriculture (18 percent); industry (24 percent), mainly food processing; and services (58 percent), mainly government activities, trade, banking, and tourism. The labor force, estimated at 71,000, is 74 percent male and 26 percent female.[12] Unemployment is reported at 12.8 percent, but unofficial estimates place it as high as 35 percent. The unemployment rate for women is twice that of men, and in rural areas unemployment is even higher than in urban areas. Furthermore, women constituted two-thirds of those jobless for more than a year.[13]

The labor market in Belize is deficient in terms of skilled labor and there are severe shortages of all types of technical personnel.[14] In 1998 the educational level of the labor force was as follows: 25 percent of all employees had no formal education, 45 percent had only an elementary education, 15 percent were educated through the secondary level, and only 3.5 percent were university graduates.[15] Jobs in the agricultural sector dominate the market, and these jobs are low paying because they require only minimal skills. The breakdown for the labor force is agriculture, 37 percent male, 6 percent female; industry, 19 percent male, 12 percent female; services, 44 percent male, 81 percent female.

Pay

Although Belize's constitution stipulates equal pay for equal work, men are paid more than women and hold higher positions even in those occupations in which women are more numerous. In addition, men dominate the high-paying jobs and occupy 94 percent of all managerial positions, while women occupy two-thirds of all clerical positions.[16] Most women in Belize are concentrated in traditional female low status, poorly paid occupations, such as manufacturing, tourism, and domestic work. Another important concern is that women have a harder time obtaining loans for business and agricultural ventures. Gender bias continues to be a glaring feature of the labor market.

Support for Mothers/Caretakers

Maternal, Family, and Medical Leave

In Belize, maternity benefits are stipulated in the social insurance system by a law enacted in 1979. This law also specifies old age, disability, and death benefits, as well as work-related injury and sickness benefits. The maternity allowance covers 80 percent of the average insurable earnings and is payable for up to twelve weeks. There is also a maternity grant of B$100 (US$50) per child.

Daycare

There is a scarcity of child care services in both rural and urban areas, since the government does not support or subsidize child care facilities.

Social/Government Programs

The main economic activities in Belize are based on natural resources, and the country consequently faces some major environmental problems. These environmental problems are related to the country's poverty, the inability to enforce legislation, and the vulnerability of the country to hurricanes. The World Bank has financed projects to support poverty reduction by increasing poorer communities' access to small-scale basic social and economic infrastructure, and also by the construction of drainage infrastructure to reduce flooding caused by hurricanes.

FAMILY AND SEXUALITY

At the beginning of the twenty-first century the average household size is 4.5 persons, down from more than five persons in 1991.[17] In terms of families, three trends now predominate in Belize. First, most of the families have a much younger head of the household than in the 1980s; second, both spouses are working outside the home; and third, because of emigration, there has been a rise in the number of abandoned or street children. The breakdown and the disappearance of the family unit underlies the high crime rate, child abuse, and many other social problems. Almost 60 percent of children are born out of wedlock.[18]

Gender Roles

Women's values in Belize are the result of the gender-specific socialization of children. This process limits women's social and economic mobility to a much greater degree than that of men. Women's values come primarily from their roles as wives and mothers and they are judged on how many children they have and what kind of mother they are. These traditional gender roles are emphasized by the books used in the schools.

Reproduction and Sex Education

The total fertility rate in Belize is one of the highest in the Caribbean because the use of contraceptives is very limited. It is calculated that only one-third of women in union use family planning.[19] The government does not have an official population policy, although it supports the provision of family planning by other agencies. However, there is active opposition to family planning from the Catholic Church, and the population of Belize is more than 60 percent Catholic. The Belize Family Life Association, founded in 1985, is the sole organization in Belize dedicated primarily to offering family planning. It also offers Pap smears, pregnancy testing, contraceptives, and health education. This organization has taken the lead in presenting school programs and organizes teen awareness workshops. It also works with the National AIDS Task Force.

Contraception and Abortion

The Catholic Church opposes sex education. Nonetheless some family life education is offered at the primary school level. The use of contraceptives and other issues of family planning have been neglected in Belize. Family planning has been largely controlled by private physicians and NGOs, but only about 10 percent of the population use private health services.[20]

In Belize, abortion is illegal unless the pregnancy constitutes a risk to the life or to the physical or mental health of the woman or of her other children. Both abortionists and women who have abortions can face 14 years in prison. Nevertheless, abortions are performed. These illegal abortions are the leading cause of deaths among women in the country. In addition, the high rates of cervical cancer and infertility among Belizean women have also been linked to the high rates of illegal abortions.[21]

Teen Pregnancy

With half of the population under the age of 19, teenage pregnancy and children born to single mothers are serious problems in Belize. Teenage pregnancy causes many girls to drop out of high school. Most high schools expel pregnant girls, who frequently cannot continue their education.[22]

HEALTH

Health Care Access

The health system in Belize has been classified as deficient not only because of the limited budget, but also because it is overcentralized and lacks reliable information regarding the health status of the population. The availability of private health services is very limited; health care is provided by the government through eight hospitals (at least one hospital in each of the six districts of the country). The problem is that these hospitals only provide primary care and are located only in urban areas. Rural areas are served by small-scale health centers or posts and mobile clinics. The urban population with access to health services has been estimated at 51.2 percent, while only 46.4 percent of the rural population has access to these services.

Diseases and Disorders

The principal reasons for hospitalization include heart disease, accidents, cancer, pneumonia, and infectious diseases.[23] It has been reported that more than 40 percent of women attending prenatal clinics are anemic. In particular, women in rural areas do not receive adequate care.

Access to safe water is 100 percent in urban areas, but only 69 percent in the rural areas, for an average of 85 percent for the entire country. Sanitation coverage has been even more limited, with 59 percent of the population being served in urban areas, but only 21.4 percent in rural areas, for a national average of 40 percent.[24]

AIDS

Since 1992, Belize has ranked second in Central America (after Honduras) in AIDS incidence, and has the highest rate of HIV infection in Central America. Estimates for 1999 indicated that 2,400 persons were living with AIDS, and the adult prevalent rate was 2.01 percent (compared with 0.2 percent in Nicaragua).[25] The main modes of transmission have been heterosexual contact (68 percent) and bisexual contact (16 percent). Since the 1990s there has been an increase in the incidence of AIDS among women, mainly as a result of sexual exploitation. Infected persons have very little access to public health care. In Belize the public health system does not provide even the most basic treatment, such as cell counts and viral load testing.

POLITICS AND LAW

Suffrage

There is universal suffrage for all citizens 18 years of age and over. Women did not acquire the right to vote or to run for office until 1954.

Political Participation

Women have been underrepresented in the political arena, but their participation is increasing. Between 1975 and 1993 only three women served as heads of government departments. By 1998, two women were elected to the 29-seat House of Representatives, and both the appointed speaker of the House and the president of the Senate were women. Women also occupy four of nine Senate seats and one cabinet position, and three are permanent secretaries in ministries. The position of chief elections officer is also occupied by a woman.

RELIGION AND SPIRITUALITY

Almost two-thirds of Belizeans are Roman Catholics. The Catholic Church plays an important role because it influences issues affecting women, in particular those related to family planning, sex education, and abortion. The church has been active in discouraging sex education, on the assumption that it will increase promiscuity.

VIOLENCE

Domestic Violence

Violence against women is a chronic problem, as researchers have documented for a Mayan community in Belize.[26] In terms of domestic violence, it is estimated that there are about 1,000 domestic violence cases during the year, and 90 percent of these violent crimes against women are perpetrated by the partner or spouse. However, there is no punishment related to these crimes because they are considered private or family matters. There is just one shelter, located in Belize City, for battered women; it is set up only for short stays.

Rape/Sexual Assault

In Belize rape and sexual harassment are illegal, but offenders are rarely punished. In cases of rape, a decision to pursue charges entails onerous legal obstacles for the woman. Marital rape did not become illegal until 1999.

Trafficking in Women

Prostitution has flourished as a result of the British military presence along the border with Guatemala. The booming tourist industry, mass labor migration, and poverty resulting from the high unemployment rates also have contributed to the growth of prostitution. No one statute specifically prohibits prostitution or the exploitation of prostitutes. Prostitution is a petty offense, and only the prostitutes are punished.

There have been violations of human rights where women are brought into the country under the guise of being offered jobs as dancers, waitresses, or housekeepers. Upon arrival in Belize, however, they are forced to engage in prostitution. Despite police investigations, no arrests have been made.[27] In addition, the trafficking in and exploitation of women have contributed to the epidemic of HIV/AIDS.

OUTLOOK FOR THE TWENTY-FIRST CENTURY

The future of women in Belize is not promising. The main problem identified is that the powerful Catholic Church opposes the important issue of family planning.[28] At the same time, the government of Belize is trying to implement the Beijing Platform within the context of the CARICOM Regional Plan for Action.[29] The Belize government's plan has identified education, health, violence against women, power, decision-making, poverty, and unemployment as the priorities for action in implementing the Beijing Platform. However, the government has not allocated additional resources to overcome the issues affecting women, has not set time limits, and has not even set benchmarks for measuring progress in the areas identified. Women involved in the NGOs in Belize will have a difficult time trying to urge the government to become involved in these issues so there can be progress in resolving the main problems affecting women.

NOTES

1. U.S. Department of State, Central Intelligence Agency (CIA), *2001 World Factbook* (2002), www.cia.gov/cia/publications/factbook/index.html.

2. One square kilometer equals 0.39 square mile.

3. CIA, 2002.

4. International Planned Parenthood Federation (IPPF), *Belize: Country Profile* (2002), http://ippfnet.ippf.org/pub/IPPF_CountryProfile.asp?ISOCode=BZ.

5. CIA, 2002.

6. International Women's Rights Action Watch (IWRAW), *IWRAW Country Report. Belize: First and Second Periodic Report, Dated 1 November 1996* (CEDAW/C/BLZ/1–2) (1996), www.igc.org/iwraw/publications/countries/belize.html.

7. CIA, 2002; IWRAW, 1996.

8. World Bank Group, *Belize: Country Brief* (2002), http://lnweb18.worldbank.org/Extrnal/lac.

9. Ibid.; Economist Intelligence Unit (EIU), *Country Profile: Jamaica, Belize, Organization of Eastern Caribbean States* (London: EIU, 2002).

10. CIA, 2002.

11. World Bank Group, 2002.

12. IPPF, 2002.

13. IWRAW, 1996.

14. CIA, 2002.

15. Government of Belize, *National Human Development Report 1998: Placing People at the Centre of Our Development* (1999), www.belize.gov.bz/library/humandevelopment/welcome.html.

16. Ibid.

17. Pan American Health Organization, *Belize: Basic Health Profiles, Summaries 1999.* Data updated for 2001. Document available at www.paho.org/english/sha/prflbel.htm.

18. United Nations High Commissioner for Human Rights (UNHCHR), *Concluding Observations of the CEDAW: Belize*, Document A/54/38, (01/07/99), paragraphs 31–69. Document accessed August 15, 2002, at www.unhchr.ch/tbs/doc.nsf/(Symbol)/A.54.38,paras.31-69.En?Opendocument.

19. IPPF, 2002.

20. Ibid.

21. Tom Barry, *Inside Belize* (Albuquerque, NM: Inter-Hemispheric Education Resource Center, 1992); IWRAW, 2002.

22. UNHCHR, 1999.

23. Government of Belize, *National Human Development Report 1998* (1999).

24. Government of Belize, 1999.

25. CIA, 2002; Brenner Brown, "Gaps in HIV Care in Central America," *International Family Panning Perspectives* 27, no. 44 (2001): 163.

26. McClusky, 2001.

27. U.S. Department of State, Bureau of Democracy, Human Rights, and Labor, *Belize Country Report on Human Rights Practices for 1999* (Washington, DC: Bureau of Democracy, Human Rights, and Labor, 2000), document accessed on June 17, 2002, at www.state.gov/www/global/human_rights/1999_hrp_report/belize.html.

28. UNHCHR, 1999.

29. Women's Environment and Development Organization (WEDO), *Mapping Progress: Assessing Implementation of the Beijing Platform 1998* (1998; Detroit: Gale Group, 2002).

RESOURCE GUIDE

Suggested Reading

Barry, Tom. *Inside Belize*. Albuquerque, NM: Inter-Hemispheric Education Resource Center, 1992.

Brown, Brenner. "Gaps in HIV Care in Central America." *International Family Panning Perspectives*, 27, no. 44 (2001): 163.

McClaurin, Irma. *Women of Belize: Gender and Change in Central America*. New Brunswick, NJ: Rutgers University Press, 1996.

McClusky, Laura J. *"Here, Our Culture Is Hard": Stories of Domestic Violence from a Mayan Community in Belize*. Austin: University of Texas Press, 2001.

Peedle, Ian. *Belize: A Guide to the People, Politics, and Culture*. New York: Interlink Books, 1999.

Premdas, Ralph R., ed. *Identity, Ethnicity and Culture in the Caribbean*. St. Augustine, Trinidad and Tobago: University of the West Indies, School of Continuing Studies, 1999.

Web Sites and Organizations

Belize Family Life Association (BFLA)
Executive Director: Mrs. Jewel Quallo Rosberg
127 Barracks Road, P.O. Box 529
Belize City, Belize, CA
Phone: (501) 2-31-018
Fax: (501) 2-32-667

Founded in 1985, it is the only organization in Belize dedicated primarily to family planning.

Belize Organization for Women and Development (BOWAD)
38 Freetown Road, P.O. Box 1243

Belize City, Belize, CA
Phone: (501) 2-34-460
Fax: (501) 2-34-491
Email: bowad@btl.net

National Women's Commission of Belize
26 Albert Street, P.O. Box 846
Belize City, Belize, CA
Phone: (501) 2-72-831
Fax: (501) 2-71-275
Email: womenscom@btl.net
Web site: www.belizeweb.com/womenscom

Established in 1982 to serve as an advisory board to the government on issues relating
to women.

Women's Affairs Department in the Ministry of Human Development, Women, and
Civil Society
Director: Ms. Anita Zetina
26 Albert Street
Belize City, Belize, CA
Phone: (501) 2-77-397/73-888
Fax: (501) 2-71-275
Web site: www.belize.gov.bz/cabinet/d_balderamos_garcia/welcome/

SELECTED BIBLIOGRAPHY

Economist Intelligence Unit (EIU). *Country Profile: Jamaica, Belize, Organization of
Eastern Caribbean States*. London: EIU, 2002.

Government of Belize. *National Human Development Report 1998: Placing People at the
Centre of Our Development*. 1999. Document accessed June 17, 2002, at www.
belize.gov.bz/library/humandevelopment/welcome.html.

———. *About Belize*. 2002. Document accessed on June 19, 2002, at www.belize.gov.
bz/belize/welcome.html.

International Planned Parenthood Federation (IPPF). *Country Fact Sheets. Family Planning in the Western Hemisphere: Belize*. 1996. Detroit: Gale Group, 2002.

———. *Belize: Country Profile*. 2002. Document accessed on June 17, 2002, at http://
ippfnet.ippf.org/pub/IPPF_CountryProfile.asp?ISOCode=BZ.

International Women's Rights Action Watch (IWRAW). *IWRAW Country Report.
Belize: First and Second Periodic Report, Dated 1 November 1996* (CEDAW/C/BLZ/
1–2). 1996. Document accessed on June 17, 2002, at www.igc.org/iwraw/
publications/countries/belize.html.

Pan American Health Organization (PAHO) and World Health Organization
(WHO). *Belize: Basic Country Health Profiles*. Belize City: PAHO/WHO, 2001.

T. C. Williams School of Law, University of Richmond. *Constitution Finder*. 2002.
Document accessed on June 18, 2002, at http://confinder.richmond.edu/.

United Nations High Commissioner for Human Rights (UNHCHR). *Concluding Observations of the CEDAW: Belize*. 01/07/99. Document A/54/38, paragraphs 31–
69. Document accessed on August 15, 2002, at www.unhchr.ch/tbs/doc.nsf/
(Symbol)/A.54.38,paras.31-69.En?Opendocument.

U.S. Department of State, Bureau of Democracy, Human Rights, and Labor. *Belize
Country Report on Human Rights Practices for 1999*. Washington, DC: Bureau of

Democracy, Human Rights, and Labor, 2002. Document accessed on June 17, 2002, at http://www.state.gov/www/global/human_rights/1999_hrp_report/belize.html.

U.S. Department of State, Central Intelligence Agency (CIA). *2001 World Factbook*. 2002. Document accessed on June 16, 2002, at www.cia.gov/cia/publications/factbook/index.html.

U.S. Social Security Administration (SSA). *Social Security Programs Throughout the World, 1999*. 1999. Document accessed on June 19, 2002, at www.ssa.gov/statistics/ssptw/1999/English/belize.pdf.

Women's Environment and Development Organization (WEDO). *Mapping Progress: Assessing Implementation of the Beijing Platform 1998*. Detroit: Gale Group, 2002.

World Bank. *Gender Profile: Belize*. 2002. Document accessed on June 18, 2002, at http://genderstats.worldbank.org/SummaryGender.asp?

World Bank Group. *Belize: Country Brief*. Document accessed on June 18, 2002, at http://lnweb18.worldbank.org/Extrnal/lac.

3

BOLIVIA

Vanessa von Struensee

PROFILE OF BOLIVIA

Bolivia is a landlocked country located in the center of South America. Its geography includes the Andes Mountains, grasslands, and the Amazon River basin. La Paz, the political capital, is located in a deep valley in the Andes, surrounded by the Altiplano, a high, cold, wind-swept plain. Most Bolivians (70 percent) live on the Altiplano. The remainder live in the Amazon, the Andes, or the subtropics. Bolivia is bordered by Peru and Chile on the west, Brazil on the northeast, and Argentina and Paraguay to the South. While rich in history, culture, and natural beauty, Bolivia is the most impoverished country in South America and the second most impoverished country in the Western Hemisphere, next to Haiti.

Bolivia's precolonial societies greatly shaped the lives of women and men today. The Tiahuanacu, one of the largest civilizations, existed in Bolivia during the period A.D. 500–1200. The Incan civilization, A.D. 1200–1531, is legendary for its accomplishments and highly structured empire. The Incas were conquered by Spain in 1531; much of their empire was destroyed in two years. The Spanish discovery of silver in Po-

tosí made it the mining capital of South America, and transformed it into the largest city in the Western Hemisphere at that time. In 1809, South America's first independence movement began in Sucre, Bolivia, against the Spanish. Simón Bolívar was victorious against the Spanish, winning independence in 1824 for Peru (which then included Bolivia). During the twentieth century, economic crises, military dictatorships, interventionist superpowers, and an international drug war have all played crucial roles in the long history of political instability and poverty in Bolivia. Comparatively democratic civilian rule was established in the 1980s, but leaders have faced difficult problems of deep-seated poverty, social unrest, and drug production.

Today, Bolivia has the largest indigenous population in the region. Of a total population of over 8 million, approximately 60–70 percent are indigenous: 30 percent Quechua, 25 percent Aymara, and 5–10 percent from various ethnic communities in Bolivia's Amazon region.[1] The largest of the approximately three dozen indigenous groups in the country are the Aymara, Quechua, and Guaraní. The remaining population is identified as mestizo (mixed race) and white (of Spanish/European backgrounds, 10 percent). The official languages are Spanish, Aymara, and Quechua. Bolivia has two capital cities: La Paz (the seat of government) and Sucre (the seat of the judiciary system). The government is a unicameral, parliamentary democracy. Seventy-five percent of the population is literate and 80 percent of the population lives below the poverty line. In 2000, 63 percent of the Bolivian population lived in urban areas and 37 percent lived in rural areas.[2]

The population is relatively young, with 40 percent under the age of 15.[3] Women account for just over 50 percent of the population. In 2000, the overall fertility rate was 3.9 children per woman.[4] In 1995, the maternal mortality rate was 550 per 100,000 live births. In 1998, the infant mortality rate was 60 per 100,000 live births.[5] During the same year, life expectancy was approximately 64.3 years for women and 60.9 years for men.[6]

OVERVIEW OF WOMEN'S ISSUES

Because they are from diverse ethnic, racial, socioeconomic and geographic backgrounds, it is difficult to generalize about the lives of Bolivian women. Women in rural areas often rely upon subsistence agriculture. Poor women in La Paz and El Alto face the challenging circumstances of a persistent economic crisis and high unemployment rates. Over the years, middle- to upper-class women have made some gains professionally and politically yet still face gender barriers. In legal terms, women's status has improved since the 1960s, but most Bolivian women have not benefited from the advances. Since the early 1980s, women's economic situation has actually deteriorated, and more people are living in poverty than before then. Most women work in Bolivia's informal sector, and those who work in the formal sector still face gender discrimination in the workplace. Indigenous women and new urban settlers in La Paz, Cochabamba, and Santa Cruz experience major racial, gender and class-based discrimination.

Bolivian women have organized to address these issues, contributing to a fragmented but strong cross-

Two traditionally dressed Quechua women chat in the streets on Potosí. Photo © TRIP/M. Jelliffe.

section of women's groups, networks, and federations throughout the country. Perhaps more than anywhere else in Latin America, Bolivian peasant and indigenous women have organized nationwide associations to address their needs and to challenge the law. Middle-class, urban women have developed nongovernmental organizations (NGOs) and contributed to national policymaking and legislation. At the same time, inequalities among rich and poor women greatly divide their experiences of the country's modernization process.

EDUCATION

Opportunities

The right to education for all Bolivians is recognized in the Constitution and in the Education Reform Law that amended the Bolivian Education Code in 1994. The law states that education is a right and a duty of all Bolivians; that it must be intercultural and bilingual; and that it must promote justice, solidarity, and social equity. One of the purposes of the law is to promote gender equality in education, and thus increase women's active participation in society. Despite the inclusive nature of the law, gender equality in secondary school enrollment has not yet occurred.

Literacy

In 2000, the illiteracy rate for adult women was 20.7 percent, compared to 8.0 percent for men.[7] Women's higher illiteracy rates can be attributed to the social, cultural, and economic barriers they face. Women who speak Spanish as a second language, in particular, face additional obstacles as they attempt to enter the educational system. Some reforms have been made in an attempt to make education accessible to all Bolivians. Teachers have been offered incentives to live and teach in rural areas where Quechua, Aymara, or other native languages are spoken. Despite these reforms, it remains difficult to find enough teachers willing to go to rural areas to work. Additionally, many poor families send their boys to school but not their girls, due to cultural gender stereotypes. Some women's NGOs and community organizations have addressed women's literacy. They offer basic literacy classes to women in poor neighborhoods. This, too, has been an important alternative form of education, particularly for older women.

EMPLOYMENT AND ECONOMICS

Bolivia is rich in natural resources, including silver and other minerals, natural gas, petroleum, and agricultural products such as soybeans, cotton, potatoes, corn, sugarcane, rice, wheat, coffee, beef, barley, and quinine. Major exports include natural gas, tin, zinc, coffee, silver, tungsten, wood, gold, jewelry, and soybeans.[8]

About two-thirds of Bolivians, many of whom are subsistence farmers, live in poverty. Living conditions of the indigenous peoples, who constitute most of the population, have always been substandard, although some indigenous communities have become quite prosperous. Agriculture accounts for roughly 15 percent of Bolivia's gross national product (GNP). The extraction of minerals and hydrocarbons accounts for another 10 percent, while manufacturing represents less than 17 percent of the GNP.[9] For better or for worse, the illegal drug trade has fueled a lot of money into Bolivia's economy and has provided an important economic cushion. In particular, the production of coca has served both to turn a small drug-dealing elite into multimillionaires and to provide income for local farmers who produce coca and sell to middlemen.

Bolivia's foreign debt surpassed $6 billion in 2001. Although the government has received several loans, few Bolivians have seen improvements in their standards of living. As elsewhere, Bolivian women tend to have higher poverty rates than men, a result of the "feminization of poverty," in which many women are paid lower wages than men and/or become single heads of household. Women's economic opportunities vary according to region as well as socioeconomic status. Women in rural areas like the Chapare, where the majority of coca is produced, have no comparable economic opportunities to make a living that are not related to coca cultivation.

Job/Career Opportunities

In 2000, women accounted for 38 percent of the total labor force.[10] In 1999, almost 46 percent of employed "adults" (10 years old and over) in urban areas were women. They worked mainly as salespersons, teachers, health care providers, and domestics in private homes.[11] Most women in urban areas work in the informal economy and the services and trade sectors, including domestic service and small business, whereas in rural areas the vast majority of economically active women are employed in agriculture.[12] In 1990–1997, most women could be categorized as self-employed.[13] Many women, for example, are vendors in the busy streets of the cities; others work at agricultural markets or flea markets; still others are employed as domestic servants.

Pay

Although the minimum wage law treats men and women equally, women generally earn less than men for doing the same job. However, the gender gap in wages has become smaller in some economic sectors. In 1997, in the industry and services sectors, women made 75 percent of what men did, compared to 65 percent in 1980.[14]

Working Conditions

All Bolivians have the constitutional right to gainful employment. According to labor laws, women are not allowed to work night shifts or jobs that require lifting 20 kilos (about 45 pounds) or more continually or 25 kilos (about 55 pounds) occasionally.[15] Because most women work in the informal sector, they are largely unprotected by law. One law provides that domestic servants are allowed to work no more than 16-hour days—a very long day by most standards.[16]

Sexual Harassment

The new Code of Criminal Procedures states that sexual harassment is a civil crime.[17] Educational institutions also address it under a regulation regarding misdemeanors and disciplinary measures for teachers and administrative teaching staff, which theoretically considers sexual harassment to be a very serious offense.[18] Regulations for Bolivia's university system also provide for disciplinary measures and internal administrative hearings for sexual harassment within the system. Despite these laws, most cases of sexual harassment go unreported. Many women face harassment in isolation and, since they are not familiar with the laws, do not recognize the situation as a potential legal case, and/or do not trust the legal system to support them if they come forward.

Support for Mothers/Caretakers

Maternal Leave and Daycare

According to Bolivian law, women are prohibited from working at their place of employment 45 days before and 45 days after giving birth. Working mothers are allowed one hour daily to breast-feed their infants. Businesses with 50 or more employees are required to have daycare centers where working mothers can leave their children.[19]

Inheritance and Property Rights

Women and men have equal rights to inheritance in Bolivia. Only blood relatives or married individuals are allowed to inherit property, however, making it impossible for same-sex partners to inherit legally.

Social/Government Programs

Bolivian governments have a long history of providing welfare to marginalized sectors. In the twentieth century, the 1952 revolution marked a significant shift in governmental focus. During that year, indigenous communities and women were extended citizenship rights for the first time, and the government redrafted the Constitution to reflect these newly acquired civil rights. An important aspect of this revolution was the redistribution of land. Most of Bolivia's land had been owned by a very small Spanish elite, but in 1952 many peasant communities were given parcels of land. While this by no means resolved the issue—land struggles continue today—it did represent a shift in the state's attitude toward poor sectors.

Since 1952, several governments have created national development plans that include proposals to promote sustainable development, social welfare services, and economic reform. Particularly since the 1970s, when the governments began to address them, women's and gender issues became important components in some of these plans.

Sustainable Development

Sustainable development is central to Bolivia's national development agenda. Various state agencies address women's roles in sustainable development and their agricultural participation. Most recently, as part of the government's effort to eradicate coca, a plant that many indigenous Bolivians utilize for cultural and social purposes, new sustainable development projects have been promoted to replace the production of coca with other agricultural products. "Alternative development," the name given to this strategy, focuses on crop substitution in the coca-producing regions of the country. Despite this and other rural development policies, Bolivian women and men have not gained higher incomes or better livelihoods. In fact, many rural Bolivians continue to migrate to urban areas in search of employment and a better life, only to end up homeless and jobless.

Welfare Reform

In general, the Bolivian government is not able to provide much support to those in need. Although conceived as a welfare state in the first half of the twentieth century, today the state has undergone an intense process of restructuring and privatization. One important consequence is the cutting of social spending (already an extremely small portion of government spending) and the call for the private sector—including companies, non-profits, and individual families—to provide their own welfare services.

Because women are involved in child rearing and community work, many of them have played important roles in providing welfare for their communities, especially in poor sectors. Some have participated in government-sponsored food distribution schemes, including glass-of-milk and food-for-work programs. Through this process, Bolivian governments have helped to catalyze women's organizations as well as co-opt them. Many women have been recruited as volunteers in government food distribution programs.

General Hugo Banzer, a dictator in Bolivia during the 1970s and later a democratically elected president (1997–2001), created mothers' clubs (*clubes de madres*) in which hundreds of women were recruited to participate. Through the process, many women became aware of their various roles and of the discrimination they faced. At the same time, their interests were co-opted by a government that was more concerned with gaining political support than with the needs and rights of women.[20] The government also has recruited women to participate in community projects, including the Municipality of El Alto's food-for-work program in the 1990s, in which many women worked on local projects in exchange for food for themselves and their families.[21]

FAMILY AND SEXUALITY

Gender Roles

Women's and men's gender roles in Bolivia are influenced by religion, education, culture, economics, and politics. In indigenous communities, the gender division of labor is not always seen as unequal, as in Westernized societies. Rather, women's and men's roles in their relationships, households, and workplaces are viewed as complementary rather than conflictive.[22] In mestizo sectors, women's and men's roles may be seen in more Western terms and tend to be influenced by Catholic norms. Many people in these sectors may believe that women's primary role is in the household, as a mother and caretaker, whereas men's role is as the primary breadwinner. Critics of this idea about Western versus non-Western women's gender roles claim that while the notion of equality may originate in Europe, this does not preclude gender inequalities from taking place in indigenous communities. For example, indigenous women experience domestic violence just as mestiza women do. Despite these traditional stereotypes of women's gender roles, most Bolivian women work both inside and outside the household. Women who challenge these traditional roles, including unmarried women, single mothers, and lesbians, may experience more freedom in some ways yet still face social stigmas.

Marriage

It is difficult to estimate the number of married women in Bolivia, since many women and men marry under common law. In general, married women and men have the same rights under the law, although a husband has the right to forbid his wife to work in certain professions for "reasons of morality" or when she is not completing her responsibilities in the household. This law, however, is rarely utilized or upheld.

Reproduction

Much could be done to improve women's reproductive rights in Bolivia, a country in which health care is inaccessible to many people and women's health education is lacking. Many women are unable to get care for childbirth, so maternal morality rates are among the highest in South America.[23] The maternal mortality ratio was 390 per 100,000 live births for 1990–1998. Almost half of deliveries were attended by skilled health personnel in 1995–1998.[24] Specialized programs for sexual and reproductive health include the comprehensive Women's Health Services Program, the National Program for Sexual and Reproductive Health, and the Comprehensive Schoolchildren and Adolescent Health Care Program. Women's organizations also are addressing women's health and reproductive rights, although they are often met with resistance by conservative members of the medical, religious, and other professional communities.

In 1999, the National Forum on Sexual and Reproductive Health was established. It is a strategic alliance of major civil society organizations, including NGOs and international development agencies, that is developing plans and activities related to sexual and reproductive health.[25]

Sex Education

The Bolivian government places sexual education activities within the framework of the National Program of Comprehensive Health Care for Adolescents. Some studies show that sex education for adolescents comes largely from the mass media, not unlike other countries throughout the world.[26]

An estimated 44.9 percent of women nationwide access family planning services during the prenatal period. Of this number, 4.3 percent of patients use the public sector, leaving NGOs providing care to 53 percent, Social Security to 36 percent, and the private sector to 6.2 percent.[27] This indicates the important role that nonprofit NGOs play in providing support for and education to women of childbearing age. A 1998 study reported that 50 percent of public sector health providers could not define reproductive rights, and that, unlike the private sector, public centers did not offer counseling on contraceptive methods.[28]

The 1999–2002 government-based National Program for Sexual and Reproductive Health has guidelines for sexual and reproductive rights. This program provides family planning education for the entire population, including adolescents, pregnant and nonpregnant women, and special groups. Approximately 73 percent of Bolivian women know how to use some method of family planning, but only 66 percent know how to obtain a method.[29]

Contraception and Abortion

Contraception is regulated by the standards set out in the 1996 Health Code and the Law on Medication. The pill and the IUD continue to be popular contraceptive methods in Bolivia. Almost 80 percent of women of childbearing age and 72 percent of men are familiar with these methods. While there is a high rate of knowledge about contraceptive methods in general, data from 1998 showed that the number of persons of childbearing age who actually used contraception was considerably lower. Of people in relationships, only 48.3 percent of women and 52 percent of men did so.[30] Forty-five percent of women in marriages, including common-law marriages, use some form of contraception. Of this number, only 18 percent use a modern method of contraception.[31]

Abortion in Bolivia is a criminal offense, but is not punished when the mother's life is in danger or when the pregnancy is the result of rape, incest, or abduction for sexual purposes not followed by marriage. Nonetheless, judges tend not to authorize even legal abortions promptly. Despite their illegality, many women seek abortions. Criminalizing abortion causes women to experience a lack of information, education, and reproductive health services.

Teen Pregnancy

The national average adolescent fertility rate is 14 percent, and 52 percent for adolescents who have received little or no formal schooling. While 92 percent of female adolescents between the ages of 15 and 19 state that they know of a contraceptive method, only 30.7 percent of adolescents in relationships use a method.[32] In contrast, among adolescent women who are not in a stable partnership but have an active sex life, 63.5 percent use some form of contraception. In 1999, the government approved the National Program of Comprehensive Health Care for Adolescents. The program is a tool to direct policy and program initiatives in the health care sector toward more comprehensive health services for this segment of the population.[33]

HEALTH

Health Care Access

Health care is guaranteed to all Bolivians, but access, especially in rural areas, is not a reality. One study shows that approximately 40 percent of the population use public health services; another 10 percent use private organizations; 9–11 percent rely upon self-treatment; and the rest use traditional medicine.[34]

The Ministry of Health and Social Planning is the government body in charge of designing, implementing, and regulating health-related services. It is also responsible for supervising, evaluating, and coordinating the National Health System. The Strategic Health Plan, approved in 1998, contains the main guidelines for administrative and technical management, funding, care delivery, cross-sector activities, social management, and legal issues for the health system.[35]

Diseases and Disorders

AIDS

In 1999, approximately 4,200 people in Bolivia were living with HIV/AIDS. Of this number, 4,100 were adults between the ages of 15 and 49 and 680 of those were women.[36] The largest segment of the population that is contracting the virus is heterosexual men, followed by heterosexual women. Only recently has the Bolivian government addressed HIV/AIDS. As elsewhere, gay and lesbian NGOs were among the first to address the growing pandemic as it affected women and men in Bolivia. HIV/AIDS prevention policies primarily target popular awareness and the promotion of condom use. AIDS patients do not receive economic assistance from the government.

Cancer

Little research has been conducted to evaluate the incidence and types of cancer among Bolivian women. Particularly in rural and urban poor areas, many women may die from cancer because they cannot afford medical treatment. In addition, for a variety of reasons the cause of their illness or death may not be reported, which contributes to the underreporting.

Depression

Studies of women's depression are rare in Bolivia, as in the rest of the region. Women's depression arises from a wide variety of social, environmental, and physical circumstances. Women with severe depression may attribute their mental health to issues within their families (e.g., sexual abuse, drug abuse, abandonment, dysfunctionality) as well as to broader social inequalities (e.g., racism, poverty, classism, institutionalized heterosexuality, and political violence).

POLITICS AND LAW

Suffrage

Bolivian women gained the right to vote in 1952, a direct result of the government reforms that took place following the country's revolution. Unlike other Latin American countries, where suffrage came about because of a women's suffrage movement, Bolivian women acquired voting rights through a much broader societal revolution that addressed land rights, massive reforms in the countryside, and racial/ethnic rights.

Political Participation

Women have a rich history of political participation, beginning with the suffragist movements of the early twentieth century, the 1952 revolution, the antimilitary and human rights movements of the 1970s, and the feminist movement that emerged in the 1980s. Women from various socioeconomic sectors have created their own organizations to address gender discrimination and women's rights. The strength of women's organizations can be attributed to several historical factors: women's resistance, international pressures and support, and governmental reforms. In 1990, Bolivia finally ratified the United Nations Convention on the Elimination of All Forms of Discrimination Against Women (CEDAW).

In Bolivia women can legally vote or hold political office, but they are underrepresented in government and politics. Bolivia boasts one of the few female presidents in South America: Lidia Gueiler Tejada (1979–1980), who led the transition government for eight months, only to be ousted by a military coup. Historically, very few women have held high-ranking ministerial positions. The first female state minister in Bolivia headed the Ministry of Labor in 1968. In 1993, 1 of 27 national senators was a woman (3.7 percent) and 10 of 130 representatives were women (7.7 percent).[37] Most female elected officials are concentrated in the provincial, municipal, and city council positions. Remedios Loza, a candidate of the populist party, Conscience of the Country (Conciencia del Patria/CONDEPA), was the first indigenous woman to be elected to Congress in the early 1990s. She also was CONDEPA's unsuccessful presidential candidate in the 1997 election.

In 1997, political parties finally acceded to demands from women activists by approving a law that every third candidate on party lists must be a woman. In addition, municipal election ballots must list candidates in alternating gender order.[38] The objective was for women to hold at least 30 percent of parliamentary seats. This newly established female quota system is seen as necessary and important by some, and as ineffective by others. Proponents believe that this type of affirmative action model will help women enter the traditional political arena. Opponents have shown that since its establishment in the late 1990s, fewer women have been elected than before the quota took affect.[39]

In 1994, the government of President Gonzalo Sánchez de Losada (1993–1997, 2002–present) initiated social reforms to accompany the government's rigid economic restructuring measures. Three types of legislation were introduced: the Law of Popular Participation, and decentralization and education reform measures. Bolivia's Law of Popular Participation contributed to the establishment of over 300 new municipalities throughout the country and to a total restructuring of local political leadership and democratic procedures. Some women policymakers and politicians were hopeful that this process would help integrate more women into the local political structures. The Law of Popular Participation recognizes the legal status of grassroots indigenous and rural organizations as part of the official political system, at the same time allowing an educational reform permitting both boys and girls to pursue studies in their native languages. Critics of the law, however, claim that gender disparities still exist in local municipalities and that while some women have been elected to the new positions, others have lost out.[40]

Women's Rights

Feminist Movements

Bolivian women gained few rights until the 1952 revolution. The extent to which women had any legal rights during the early twentieth century depended largely upon their socioeconomic and racial-ethnic status; for instance, upper-class women were granted certain rights as part of a social class. The 1952 revolution brought significant changes for women, peasants, and the poor. Since the early 1970s, Bolivian governments have established state committees or agencies to address women's contributions to national development. Today, women's issues are housed in the Ministry of Gender, Inter-Generational and Family Affairs. The vice minister of gender affairs is directly responsible for overseeing this policy and research area.

Since the 1970s, women at all levels of society have worked together in numerous organizations to further their causes. For many, popular protest has been more effective than formal parliamentary participation. According to one study, 40 percent of all Bolivians believe that democracy is a sham.[41] Many Bolivian women who are involved in feminist movements came of age as young leftist activists, mostly middle-class intellectuals and university students, who risked their lives fighting for democracy and political-economic equality during the 1970s and early 1980s. Some later formed or joined NGOs, which became a major channel for expressing political ideas and actions: their efforts to provide alternative health, welfare, and education services to marginal sectors of the population were often construed as being in clear opposition to military dictatorships and as the uneven results of capitalist development.

Bolivian women's peasant networks are among the strongest in the world. The Bartolina Sisa Peasant Women's Federation, for example, has existed since the 1970s. The well-known tin-mining wives' movements began in the early 1980s, when the Bolivian state began to privatize the mining industry and displace over 20,000 workers.[42] Many wives of miners fought back by organizing their own committees to address human rights violations and their dire economic situations. At the time, the country was experiencing inflation rates up to 20,000 percent, and those workers who still received pay carried the bills home in large flour sacks. Domitila Barrios de Chungara was an important leader in this movement.[43] Indigenous women have organized to address their specific needs and demands as members of the most oppressed group in the country.

More recently, women have played important roles in the coca-producers movement (*cocaleros*) movement and in the protest against water privatization in Cochabamba (2001). Small coca producers are, in a sense, caught in the cross fire of the coca eradication campaign and their need to survive on a daily basis. Since most of the coca has been eradicated and there has been much civil unrest in the Chapare region, many farmers have been forced to move to urban areas such as Cochabamba. Today, Cochabamba, the third largest city in Bolivia, has an unprecedented rate of homelessness because of this crisis.

Women coca producers have learned from men and organized their own organizations. In September 2000, farmers unions blocked one of Bolivia's major highways for twenty-seven days, demanding a halt to the zero coca goal. Two months later women farmers formed unions resembling the men's, holding demonstrations and blockades to protest government repression and the obliteration of their crops. Women have also responded to the repression that has resulted from this process. Bolivia has a separate set of laws for drug-related crimes, based on the U.S. D.E.A. model, under which farmers with relatively small quantities of coca can be arrested. It is important to note that coca is not a drug, but an ingredient used in the production of cocaine. However, in this context, coca has become viewed as a drug according to the new laws. Women have protested these laws, which typically assume guilt until one proves his/her innocence, as well as protesting the conditions of thousands of Bolivians who are imprisoned while awaiting trial for up to five years. To protest conditions in women's prisons, the women have organized demonstrations, one of which involved ten women who tied their hands and feet to iron bars on a balcony and crucified themselves for up to nine days without food, while the inmate population supported them with a hunger strike.[44]

Lesbian Rights

The Bolivian penal code is silent on the issue of homosexuality, but lesbians, gay men, bisexuals, and transgendered people (anyone who appears to be homosexual) are not free from illicit police actions that have the effect of controlling their behavior. Bolivian police officers operate largely outside of the formal law, idiosyncratically dispensing a rough-and-ready—and often self-serving—form of street justice. Raids of gay bars are fairly common. As elsewhere, impoverished LGBT people are the most affected by these forms of social control. Thus, suspected lesbians and gay men may be detained for questioning on any number of trumped-up charges, such as theft or drug possession. In these cases, both parties understand that the "real crime" at issue his/her homosexuality, and that the suspect is expected to compensate the arresting officers in return for their silence about this matter.[45] More men are arrested for these trumped-up crimes than are women, although there are some important exceptions. Most recently, Bolivia's radical women's group, Mujeres Creando, was repressed by the police while they were filming a video in downtown La Paz. One of its founders was in jail for several days, and the press took advantage of this occurrence by stigmatizing the group in national newspapers.[46]

There are few lesbian organizations in Bolivia, with the notable exception of Mujeres Creando, which includes "out" lesbians as well heterosexual women from various socioeconomic levels. The first formal gay organization in Bolivia, Dignidad, was founded in Cochabamba in the late 1980s. In 1994, a gay support group known as Unidos en la Lucha por la Dignidad y la Salud was formed, and the country's first Gay Day celebration was held.[47] Despite the newness of LGBT NGOs and groups, lesbians have played important roles in women's movements and in professional, political, and cultural spheres of society.

RELIGION AND SPIRITUALITY

Rituals and Religious Practices

Most Bolivians (97 percent) are Roman Catholic, although in reality most practice a mix of Catholic customs imported from Europe and indigenous traditions. Aymara and Quechua communities believe that the surrounding land, mountains, rivers, and plains are central to human existence. Pachamama, or Mother Earth, holds a privileged status in many indigenous communities and is central to their forms of spirituality and ways of life. Traditionally, in some indigenous communities women have held high status in their communities as healers and many indigenous women adhere to indigenous traditions even today. Like elsewhere, the Catholic Church is patriarchal in Bolivia and women tend to hold low-ranking positions in the institution. A minority of women belong to other Christian denominations. A small but significant portion of the population practice Judaism, although many European Jews who migrated to Bolivia have now moved to other countries in the hemisphere.[48]

VIOLENCE

Bolivia has approved the Inter-American Convention for the Prevention, Punishment and Eradication of Violence against Women, which requires that states "take integrated measures to prevent and eliminate violence against women" and "study the causes and consequences of violence against women and the effectiveness of prevention measures."[49] According to the Convention, the state is responsible for acts of violence perpetrated against women directly, through its agents, and indirectly, by private individuals. This responsibility extends not only to actions (concrete acts of violence) but also to omissions (not taking measures to avoid occurrence of violence). Despite this legislation, many Bolivian women have been victims of domestic, random, or political violence.

Domestic Violence

As elsewhere, violence against women in Bolivia is pervasive. According to one study, in 1998 almost 60 percent of reported assaults were against women.[50] In 1998, 17 percent of women had been assaulted by their intimate partner during the previous 12 months and 62 percent of women reported experiencing some kind of domestic violence or abuse at least once in their lifetime.[51]

The Law Against Domestic and Family Violence and the Law to Protect Victims of Crimes Against Sexual Freedom were passed in the 1990s. The Law Against Family and Domestic Violence provides for legal and psychological counseling for the victims as well as what are called Women and Family Protection Brigades. It mandates temporary shelters for victims of violence and institutions to rehabilitate their assailants. The Ministry of Sustainable Development and Planning is the responsible body to implement programs for the prevention, detection and handling of family violence, via the Deputy Ministry of Gender, Inter-Generational and Family Affairs.

Educational campaigns concerning domestic violence also exist. The state regulates the dissemination of education materials in the fields of education and health care. Charges of domestic violence can be brought under family law or criminal law. In addition, several women's organizations systematically address domestic violence in specific communities. For example, some organizations provide temporary shelters, legal support, psychological services, and educational materials for women and their families and communities.

Rape/Sexual Assault

Rape is a crime punishable by law. It is classified in the Penal Code under the chapter on Crimes Against Sexual Freedom. Most rapes are unreported, however, since there is a lack of support for female victims in the legal and criminal systems. Women's NGOs have addressed this problem more than the government has, although much needs to be done to improve this situation. Some women are raped by police officers or soldiers; those who are not may fear further problems if they tell authorities what happened to them.

War and Military Repression

Bolivia's history of military repression has contributed to the growth of resistance movements throughout the country. Women have been affected by military repression in gender-specific ways, including the ways in which they are captured, tortured, and otherwise treated as prisoners—a trend seen historically in militarized countries throughout Latin America.[52] Although Bolivian military governments were not among the harshest in the region, women leftists, students, peasants, indigenous women, and labor activists still suffered during these periods.

Most recently, women have been victims of violence in the "war on drugs." This is true particularly in the subtropical Chapare region, an area that provided much of the world's cocaine supply until the introduction of the eradication plan. Women and men have experienced discrimination both as coca producers and in the prison system, which is now full of people arrested on drug offenses and awaiting trial. Law 1008 is the best-known of these new laws. Associated with Law 1008 is the Dignity Plan (Plan Dignidad), the five-year plan introduced by President Hugo Banzer Suárez (1997–2001) in 1997 to eradicate the cultivation of all illegal coca by 2002. Under Law 1008 the eradication of coca was to be accomplished gradually, through voluntary eradication in exchange for compensation and crop substitution. Under the plan, the goal is to move from individual to community compensation, with the complete elimination of compensation within five years. Most debated, however, is the prevalent use of violence as a means of meeting the zero coca goal. In 2000, Plan Dignidad "reduced coca cultivation by 33 percent nationwide—and by over 90 percent in the Chapare" region.[53] The success in eradication has come about at the expense of human rights and by militarization of the region. Human rights abuses have disproportionately affected the female population.[54] In addition to economic deprivation, women suffer aggression from troops who control the population through beating, raping, and abusing them. Systemic factors conducive to the impunity of the forces include an established pattern of abusive conduct by the police against the poorer sectors of society, an inability of victims of abuse to make detailed complaints, fear of retaliation, and lack of a public entity with sufficient resources to investigate reports of abuse and to bring abusers to justice.

OUTLOOK FOR THE TWENTY-FIRST CENTURY

Bolivian women face a series of contradictions in the twenty-first century. On the one hand, women have gained important legal and political victories since the 1952 revolution. On the other hand, many of these newly acquired rights are not accessible to the majority of Bolivia's women, who are among the poorest in the Western Hemisphere. While many women have played protagonist roles in social movements, thereby earning respect, much could be done to address the country's colonial legacy and enormous structural inequalities faced by Bolivian women and men.

NOTES

1. World Health Organization (WHO), Violence Against Women Information Pack (2000), available at www.who.int.

2. United Nations Statistics Division (UNSTATS), *Indicators 2000, at Human Settlements* (2002), available at www.un.org/Depts/unsd/social.htm.

3. Center for Reproductive Law and Policy (CRLP) and Estudio para la Defensa de los Derechos de la Mujer (DEMUS), *Women of the World: Bolivia* (New York: Center for Reproductive Law and Policy, 2001).

4. World Bank, *Gender Statistics: Bolivia*, available at http://genderstats.worldbank.org.

5. CRLP, 2001.

6. World Bank, 2002.

7. Ibid.

8. U.S. Department of State, Central Intelligence Agency (CIA), *World Factbook 2001* (2002). www.cia.gov/cia/publications/factbook/index.html.

9. Facultad Latinoamericano de Ciencias Sociales (FLACSO). *Mujeres en Bolivia*

(2002), www.eurosur.org/FLACSO/mujeres/bolivia/m-pais.htm; United States Department of State (USDS), *Country Reports: Bolivia 2000* (2001), www.state.gov.

10. World Bank, 2002.

11. International Labor Organization (ILO), *World of Work* (2001), available at www.ilo.org/public/english/bureau/inf/magazine/41/traffic.htm.

12. USDS, 2001.

13. UNSTATS, 2002.

14. USDS, 2001.

15. Teresa Valdés et al., *Mujeres latinoamericanas en cifras: Tomo comparativo* (Santiago de Chile: Instituto de la Mujer, Ministerio de Asuntos Sociales de España and Facultad Latinoamericana de Ciencias Sociales [FLACSO-Chile], 1995), 152.

16. Ibid.

17. *De Beijing a Bolivia: ¿Cuánto hemos avanzado las mujeres en Bolivia? Informe a 5 años de la Conferencia Mundial Sobre la Mujer, Beijing 1995* (La Paz, 2000); USDS, 2001.

18. *Reglamento de faltas y sanciones del magisterio y personal docente administrativo*, R.S. no. 21441 (Apr. 21, 1993), art. 11.

19. Valdés et al., 1995.

20. Amy Lind, "Making Feminist Sense of Neoliberalism: The Institutionalization of Women's Struggles for Survival in Ecuador and Bolivia," *Journal of Developing Societies* 18, no. 2/3 (2002): 228–258; S. Salinas Mulder et al., *Una protesta sin propuesta: Situación de la mujer en Bolivia, 1976–1994* (La Paz, 1994).

21. A. Ochsendorf, "Constructing Power Through Food-for-Work Projects in El Alto, Bolivia" (undergraduate honors thesis, Wellesley College, 1998).

22. Olivia Harris, "Complementarity and Conflict: An Andean View of Women and Men," in *Sex and Age as Principles of Social Differentiation*, ed. J. LaFontaine (London: Academic Press, 1978).

23. Engenderhealth (2002), www.engenderhealth.org/ia/cbc/bolivia.html.

24. UNSTATS, 2002.

25. CRLP, 2001.

26. Javier Rodríguez Morales et al., *Adolescentes: Diagnóstico de la educación sexual en la ciudad de Sucre 1997–1998*, available at www.fhi.org/sp/bolivias/bolass24.html.

27. National Health System (NHS), *La crisis del sector salud y la reforma del sector*, available at www.sns.gov.bo/pilares8.html.

28. Micaela Parras et al., *Manejo de la perspectiva de género en servicios de salud sexual y reproductiva: Análisis comparativo en centros públicos y privados 1997–1998*, available at www.fhi.org/sp/bolivias/bolasbss25.html.

29. UNDP, 2000.

30. Instituto Nacional de Estadística (INE) et al., *Encuesta nacional de Demografía y Salud 1998* (La Paz: INE, 1998), 3.

31. United Nations Population Fund (UNFPA), *The State of World Population 2000* (2000), 5, available at www.unfpa.org/swp/2000/english/indicators/indicators1.html.

32. INE, 1998.

33. Ministry of Health and Social Provision (MHSP), *Programa nacional de atención integral a la salud de los (las) adolescentes: Documento Programático MSPS-Bolivia 1998–2002*, approved April 26, 1999.

34. NHS, 2002.

35. CRLP, 2001.

36. UNAIDS and WHO, *Report on the Global HIV/AIDS Epidemic* (2000), available at www.unaids.org/epidemic_update/report/table_E.htm.

37. Valdés et al. (1995).

38. María Lourdes Zabala, *Mujeres, cuotas y ciudadania* (La Paz: Coordinadora de la Mujer/UNICEF, 1999).

39. Ibid.

40. Ibid.

41. Atilio A. Boron, *State, Capitalism, and Democracy in Latin America* (Boulder, CO: Lynne Rienner, 1995).

42. W. McFarren, "The Politics of Bolivia's Economic Crisis: Survival Strategies of Displaced Tin-Mining Households," in *Unequal Burden*, eds. L. Benería and S. Feldman (Boulder, CO: Westview Press, 1992), 131–58.

43. Domitila Barrios de Chungara with Moema Viezzer, *Let Me Speak!: Testimony of Domitila, a Woman of the Bolivian Mines* (New York: Monthly Review Press, 1978).

44. Solimar Santos, "Unintended Consequences of United States' Foreign Drug Policy in Bolivia," *University of Miami Inter-American Law Review* 33 (Spring 2002): 127.

45. Richard Wright, "Bolivia," in *Sociolegal Control of Homosexuality*, eds. Donald J. West and Richard Green (New York: Plenum Press, 1997).

46. International Gay and Lesbian Human Rights Commission (IGLHRC), "Video Crew Assaulted, Jailed" (2002), available at www.iglhrc.org/world/southamerica/Bolivia2002sap.html.

47. Wright, 1997.

48. Leo Spitzer, *Hotel Bolivia: The Culture of Memory in a Refuge from Nazism* (New York: Hill and Wang, 1998).

49. *Words and Deeds: Holding Governments Accountable in the Beijing +5 Review Process* (July 1999), www.equalitynow.org/action_eng_16_4.html.

50. USDS, 2001.

51. USDS, 2001.

52. Ximena Bunster, "Surviving Beyond Fear: Women and Torture in Latin America," in *Surviving Beyond Fear: Women, Children, and Human Rights in Latin America* ed. Marjorie Agosin (Fredonia, NY: White Pine Press, 1993), 98–125.

53. Washington Office on Latin America (WOLA), "U.S.-Funded Security Forces in Bolivia Committing Serious Human Rights Abuses: Members of Congress Send Letter Asking Administration to Cut off Aid," press release (March 14, 2002); and *Annual Drug Certification Process—Time for a Change* (on file with author), available at www.wola.org.

54. Maia Szalavitz, "War on Drugs, War on Women," reprinted in Lindesmith—Drug Policy Foundation Online Library (1999), at www.lindesmith.org/library/szalavitz2.html.

RESOURCE GUIDE

Suggested Reading

Barrios de Chungara, Domitila, with Moema Viezzer. *Let Me Speak!: Testimony of Domitila, a Woman of the Bolivian Mines*. New York: Monthly Review Press, 1978. In this autobiography, Domitila Barrios de Chungara speaks from the heart as she tells her story of growing up in a Bolivian tin-mining town, then becoming a peasant leader and candidate for the vice presidency of the country.

Harris, Olivia. "Complementarity and Conflict: An Andean View of Women and Men." In *Sex and Age as Principles of Social Differentiation*, edited by J. La-Fontaine. London: Academic Press, 1978. This classic and important article discusses Western and Andean views on gender relations.

Harris, Olivia. *To Make the Earth Bear Fruit: Ethnographic Essays on Fertility, Work and Gender in Highland Bolivia*. London: Institute of Latin American Studies, University of London, 2000. In this collection of essays, anthropologist Olivia Harris addresses a range of issues that shed light on the experiences of indigenous women in Bolivia's highlands.

Lind, Amy. "Making Feminist Sense of Neoliberalism: Women's Struggles for Survival in Ecuador and Bolivia." *Journal of Developing Societies* 18, no. 2/3 (2002): 228–58. Social scientist Amy Lind addresses the creative ways in which women have collectively organized to address poverty and political violence in Bolivia and Ecuador.

McFarren, W. "The Politics of Bolivia's Economic Crisis: Survival Strategies of Displaced Tin-Mining Households." In *Unequal Burden*, edited by L. Benería and S. Feldman, 131–58. Boulder, CO: Westview Press, 1992. This article discusses how migrant women in El Alto, many of them displaced by Bolivia's privatization of the mining sector, have coped with the harsh economic reality of their new urban environments.

Paulson, Susan, and Pamela Calla. "Gender and Ethnicity in Bolivian Politics: Transformation or Paternalism?" *Journal of Latin American Anthropology* 5, no. 2 (2000): 112–49. The authors, both anthropologists, address how the Bolivian state has addressed gender and ethnic relations in the country.

Stephenson, Marcia. *Gender and Modernity in Andean Bolivia*. Austin: University of Texas Press, 1999. This book provides an excellent analysis of gender relations and cultural politics in Bolivian history, as told through the disciplines of history and literature.

Wright, Timothy. "Gay Organizations, NGOs, and the Globalization of Sexual Identity: The Case of Bolivia." *Journal of Latin American Anthropology* 5, no. 2 (2000): 89–111. Wright addresses the important roles gay and lesbian organizations have played in Santa Cruz, Bolivia. He illustrates the contradictions that Bolivian activists and policymakers face as they rely upon external funding for their survival as an organization and movement.

Videos

Hell to Pay. 1988. 52 mins. VHS. Directed by Alexandra Anderson and Anne Cottringer. An analysis of the international debt crisis as told from the perspective of Aymara and Quechua women in Bolivia. Although peasant women are assumed not to understand the global economy, this video shows that Bolivian women comprehend the burden of foreign debt better than trained "experts," since they are among those who have suffered the most.

Web Sites

Engenderhealth, www.engenderhealth.org/ia/cbc/bolivia.html.

Human Rights Watch, www.hrw.org/spanish/informes/1995/bolivia.html.

Organizations

Casa de la Mujer (House of Women)
Avenida Hernando Sanabria y Tercer Anillo

Santa Cruz, Bolivia
Phone: (591) 3-521803
Fax: (591) 3-521451
Email: ksamujer@roble.scz.entelnet.bo

An autonomous space for women to address the intersecting issues of class, ethnicity, and gender. Current areas of interest include gender and environmental education, women's citizen education and political participation, and law and violence.

Centro de Información y Desarrollo de la Mujer (CIDEM/Women's Development and Information Center)
Avenida 6 de Agosto
Edificio Centenario, Piso 1, Oficina B1
La Paz, Bolivia
Phone: (591) 2-444794, (591) 2-444795
Email: cidem@caoba.entelnet.bo

CIDEM addresses women's legal and political rights, and provides support and education to women. CIDEM houses the largest women's studies library in the country. Visitors can have access to the library holdings for a small fee.

Centro de Promoción de la Mujer "Gregoria Apaza" (Gregoria Apaza Center for the Promotion of Women)
Calle Eulet No. 215, Av. 16 de Julio
El Alto, Bolivia
Phone: (591) 2-840351

This women's NGO focuses primarily on the needs of Aymara and other women living in El Alto, a city comprised primarily of poor migrants. It addresses issues of poverty, economic and political empowerment, and sexual and reproductive rights.

Colectivo Rebeldía (Rebellion Collective)
Avenida Irala 167, Primero Piso
Santa Cruz, Bolivia
Phone: 03-368101
Email: core@mail.cotas.com.bo
Contact person: Madela Saínz Meschwitz

The Rebellion Collective addresses a broad range of social justice issues that affect poor and marginalized women in Santa Cruz. The Collective has a radio program, "Women's Word" ("Palabra de Mujer") and utilizes both direct and indirect forms of political action to bring awareness to Bolivian politicians and society members about the oppression of women. It offers programming primarily in the area of women's popular education and communication.

Coordinadora de la Mujer (Women's Network)
Avenida 20 de Octubre 2151
Edificio La Paz, Mezanine 1 y 2
Casilla 9136
La Paz, Bolivia
Phone: (591) 2-356291, 339124, 335471
Email: fpc@coordinadoramujer.com
Web site: www.coordinadoramujer.org

The Women's Network is a national umbrella organization that addresses women's roles in economic development and the political process. In recent years, this NGO has focused much attention on women's political rights and has provided support for female politicians throughout the country. The Spanish-language web site includes data on Bolivian women's political and economic participation, publications, and current projects.

Fundación La Paz (La Paz Foundation)
Villa Copacabana
La Paz, Bolivia
Phone: (591) 232276
Fax: (591) 232233
Email: fudepka@kolla.net
Contact person: Maritza Jiménez Bullain, Director of the Women's Program

An NGO that addresses women's integration into local grassroots and municipal political processes in the La Paz metropolitan area. The organization is dedicated to providing resources for poor women and their families, and to helping women organize to address issues of urban poverty, violence, and economic development.

Grupo de Trabajo Sobre Embarazo No Deseado y Aborto (Working Group on Unwanted Pregnancy and Abortion)
Avenida Arce 2595
Casilla 9
La Paz, Bolivia
Phone: (591) 2-430281
Email: cddbol@ceibo.entelnet.bo

This group address women's sexual and reproductive rights.

Instituto Femenino para la Formación Integral (IFFI; Feminine Institute for Integral Formation)
Jordan 732
Cochabamba, Bolivia
Phone: (591) 222112, 251303
Email: iffi@albatros.cnb.net
Contact person: Katia Uriona Gamarra

IFFI promotes the integration of women into the political process through educational programs, training workshops, political pressure, and research. The NGO addresses women's participation in neighborhood movements, local municipalities and the provincial administration.

Mujeres Creando (Women Creating)
Casilla 12860
La Paz, Bolivia
Email: creando@ceibo.entelnet.bo

Mujeres Creando, a feminist collective composed of lesbian and heterosexual women from various social sectors, is one of the most visible women's activist groups in the country and has been internationally recognized for their radical stance on gender, racial, class, and sexual rights. See the photographic essay depicting *Mujeres Creando*'s famous public graffiti in the web article, "Mujeres Creando Paints Bolivia," written by Thomas Kruze: www.americas.org/news/Features/199906_Gay_Rights/bolivias_mujeres_creando.htm.

Oficina Jurídica de la Mujer (Women's Juridical Office)
Cochabamba, Bolivia
Email: cendocojon@bo.com

One of Cochabamba's most important women's NGOs, it addresses women's legal and political rights.

Organización de Mujeres Aymaras de Kollasuyo (OMAK; Kollasuyo Aymara Women's Organization)
Calle 7, Esquina 4, Número 65
Barrio Petrolero
El Alto, Bolivia
Phone: 806890
Email: omak@latinwide.com
Contact person: Andrea Flores Tonconi

OMAK works to bring awareness to Aymara indigenous women in Bolivia through promoting their active participation at various levels of community, regional, and national politics. The organization's goal is to end poverty amongst and discrimination against Aymara women.

SELECTED BIBLIOGRAPHY

Albro, Robert. "Hazarding Popular Spirits: Metaforces of Political Culture and Cultural Politicking in Quillacollo, Bolivia." Department of Anthropology, University of Chicago, 1999.
———. "Introduction: A New Time and Place for Bolivian Popular Politics." Ethnology 37, no. 2: (1998): 99–116.
———. "Virtual Patriliny: Image Mutability and Populist Politics in Quillacollo, Bolivia." Political and Legal Anthropology Review 20, no. 1 (1997): 73–92.
Andean Information Network. Law 1008. Cochabamba: Andean Information Network. 2002. At www.scbbs-bo.com/ain/ain/details/dlaw1008.htm.
Bolivian Health Regulations ND.SNS-02-96 for the Care of Women and Newborns at Health Posts, Health Centers and District Hospitals. Canadian International Development Agency (CIDA).
Boron, Atilio A. State, Capitalism, and Democracy in Latin America. Boulder, CO: Lynne Rienner, 1995.
Bunster, Ximena. "Surviving Beyond Fear: Women and Torture in Latin America." In Surviving Beyond Fear: Women, Children, and Human Rights in Latin America, edited by Marjorie Agosín, 98–125. Fredonia, NY: White Pine Press, 1993.
Center for Reproductive Law and Policy (CRLP) and Estudio para la Defensa de los Derechos de la Mujer (DEMUS). Women of the World: Bolivia. New York: Center for Reproductive Law and Policy, 2001.
Dubberly, David E. "Commentary on the Ley del Regimen de la Coca y Sustancias Controladas," American Bar Association: Inter-American Legal Materials 6 (1995): 278, available at www.natlaw.com/pubs/spbocs1.htm.

Information Please. *Countries of the World: Bolivia.* Available at www.infoplease.com/ipa/a0107345.htm.

International Gay and Lesbian Human Rights Commission (IGLHRC). "Video Crew Assaulted, Jailed: Defend the Right to Freedom of Expression," Emergency Action Alert, August 20, 2002. www.iglhrc.org/world/southamerica/Bolivia2002sep.html, 2003.

International Labor Organization (ILO). *World of Work.* 2001. Available at www.ilo.org/public/english/bureau/inf/magazine/41/traffic.htm.

International Lesbian and Gay Association (ILGA). "World Legal Survey: Bolivia." www.ilga.org/Information/legal_survey/americas/bolivia.htm.

Lind, Amy. "Making Feminist Sense of Neoliberalism: The Institutionalization of Women's Struggles for Survival in Ecuador and Bolivia." *Journal of Developing Societies* 2/3 (2002).

McFarren, W. "The Politics of Bolivia's Economic Crisis: Survival Strategies of Displaced Tin-Mining Households." In *Unequal Burden*, edited by L. Benería and S. Feldman, 131–58. Boulder, CO: Westview Press, 1992.

Ministry of Health and Social Planning (MHSP), Personal Care Unit. 1999–2002 National Program for Sexual and Reproductive Health. Approved by Ministerial Decree No. 0134, March 31, 1999.

———. Violence Against Women and Girls Project. La Paz: MHSP.

National Health System. *Family Planning.* Available at www.sns.gov.bo/presatm-plafa8.htm.

Ochsendorf, A. "Constructing Power Through Food-for-Work Projects in El Alto Bolivia." Undergraduate honors thesis, Wellesley College, 1998.

Pan-American Health Organization. Program for Prevention of Violence in Schools.

Roncken, Theo. *Bolivia: Impunity and the Control of Corruption in the Fight Against Drugs, Democracy, Human Rights, and Militarism in the War on Drugs in Latin America.* 1997. www.tni.org/drugs/folder1/roncken.htm.

Santos, Solimar. "Unintended Consequences of United States' Foreign Drug Policy in Bolivia." *University of Miami Inter-American Law Review* 33 (spring 2000): 127.

Spitzer, Leo. *Hotel Bolivia: The Culture of Memory in a Refuge from Nazism.* New York: Hill and Wang, 1998.

Stephenson, Marcia. *Gender and Modernity in Andean Bolivia.* Austin: University of Texas Press, 1999.

Szalavitz, Maia. "War on Drugs, War on Women." Reprinted in Lindesmith—Drug Policy Foundation Online Library (1999), at www.lindesmith.org/library/szalavitz2.html.

UNAIDS and World Health Organization (WHO). *Report on the Global HIV/AIDS Epidemic 2000.* 2000. Available at www.unaids.org/epidemic_update/report/table_E.htm.

United Nations. *For the Record 2002: The UN Human Rights System.* www/hri.ca/fortherecord2002/vol4/boliviarr.htm.

United Nations Population Fund (UNFPA). *The State of World Population 2000* (2000). Available at www.unfpa.org/swp/2000/english/indicators/indicators1.html.

United Nations Statistics Division (UNSTATS). *Indicators 2000, at Human Settlements.* 2000. Available at www.un.org/Depts/unsd/social.htm.

U.S. Department of State. Background Note, Bolivia. April 2001. Available at www.state.gov.

———. *Country Reports: Bolivia 2000.* 2001. www.state.gov.

U.S. Department of State, Central Intelligence Agency (CIA). *2001 World Factbook.* www.cia.gov/cia/publications/factbook/index.html.

Washington Office on Latin America (WOLA). *Annual Drug Certification Process— Time for a Change.* On file with author. Available at www.wola.org.

———. "Failing to Make the Grade: The Case Against U.S. Drug Certification Policy." Washington, DC: WOLA, 1999. Available at www/wola.org/drugpolfailing.html.

———. "U.S.-Funded Security Forces in Bolivia Committing Serious Human Rights Abuses: Members of Congress Send Letter Asking Administration to Cut off Aid." Press release, March 14, 2002. www.wola.org.

Williams, Jacqueline. "Waging the War on Drugs in Bolivia." In *Drugs & Democracy: Related Links and Documentation,* TNI. www.tni.org/drugs/links/boldrg.htm.

Words and Deeds: Holding Governments Accountable in the Beijing + 5 Review Process. July 2000. www.equalitynow.org/action_eng_16_4.html.

World Bank. *Gender Statistics: Bolivia.* 2002. http://genderstats.worldbank.org.

———. *World Development Indicators 2000,* 90. 2000.

World Health Organization (WHO). Violence Against Women Information Pack. 2000. Available at www.who.int.

Wright, Richard. "Bolivia." In *Sociolegal Control of Homosexuality,* edited by Donald J. West and Richard Green. New York: Plenum Press, 1997.

Spanish Bibliography

De Beijing a Bolivia: ¿Cuánto hemos avanzado las mujeres en Bolivia? Informe a 5 años de la Conferencia Mundial Sobre la Mujer, Beijing 1995. La Paz.

Facultad Latinoamericano de Ciencias Sociales (FLACSO). 2002. *Mujeres en Bolivia.* www.eurosur.org/FLACSO/mujeres/bolivia/m-pais.htm.

Human Rights Watch. *Abusos fuera del Chapare, violaciones a los derechos humanos y la guerra anti-drogas.* New York: Human Rights Watch. Available at www.hrw.org/spanish/informes/1995/bolivia4.html. (Last visited September 24, 2001.)

———. *Resumen y recomendaciones: Violaciones a los derechos humanos y la guerra anti-drogas.* New York: Human Rights Watch, 1995. Available at www.hrw.org/spanish/informes/1995/bolivia.html.

Instituto Nacional de Estadística (INE) et al. *Encuesta nacional de demografía y salud 1998,* 3. La Paz: INE, 1998.

Medina, Javier. *Etnicidad, género y participación popular.* La Paz: SNPP, 1995.

Ministry of Health and Social Planning. *Programa nacional de atención integral a la salud de los (las) adolescentes.* Documento Programático MSPS-Bolivia 1998–2002 (1999). Approved by Ministerial Resolution No. 0170, April 26, 1999.

Montaño, Julieta. "Mujeres del mundo: Leyes y políticas que afectan sus vidas reproductivas. América Latina y el Caribe." Unpublished report, Cochabamba: Oficina Juridica de la Mujer.

National Health System. *La crisis del sector salud y la reforma del sector.* 2002. Available at www.sns.gov.bo/pilares8.html.

Parras, Micaela, et al., *Manejo de la perspectiva de género en servicios de salud sexual y reproductiva: Análisis comparativo en centros públicos y privados 1997–1998.* Available at www.fhi.org/sp/bolivias/bolasbss25.html.

Reglamento de faltas y sanciones del magisterio y personal docente administrativo, art. 11. R.S. No. 21441, April 21, 1993.

Rodriguez Morales, Javier, et al. *Adolescentes: Diagnóstico de la educación sexual en la ciudad de Sucre 1997–1998*. 2002. Available at www.fhi.org/sp/bolivias/bolass24. html.

Salinas Mulder, S., et al. *Una protesta sin propuesta: Situación de la mujer en Bolivia, 1976–1994*. La Paz: n.p., 1994.

Subsecretaría de Asuntos de Género (SAG). *Cambiar es cosa de dos*. La Paz: Ministerio de Desarrollo Humano, 1995.

———. *Construyendo la equidad*. La Paz: Artes Gráficas Latinas, 1997.

Valdés, Teresa, et al. *Mujeres latinoamericanas en cifras: Tomo comparativo*. Santiago de Chile: Instituto de la Mujer, Ministerio de Asuntos Sociales de Espana and Facultad Latinoamericana de Ciencias Sociales, 1995.

Zabala, María Lourdes. *Mujeres, cuotas y ciudadania en Bolivia*. La Paz: Coordinadora de la Mujer and UNICEF, 1999.

4

BRAZIL

Nathalie Lebon

PROFILE OF BRAZIL

Brazil is by many standards a giant. It is as large as the contiguous United States (without Alaska), and thus the largest country in South America, bordering all countries of the region except Ecuador and Chile. It is home to the world's mightiest river, the Amazon, which gives its name to the world's largest remaining rain forest area, but it also has a varied physical environment: from the humid Amazon lowlands to the arid semi-desert of the Northeast, the eastern highlands, and the southern pampas (plains). Unlike much of the rest of the Americas, there are no major mountain ranges in Brazil.

Brazil is the fifth largest nation-state in the world in terms of population, with 169 million, most of whom reside less than 100 miles from the coast. Women constitute 51 percent of the population. At the time of conquest by the Portuguese in the fifteenth century, an estimated 2.5 million indigenous people lived in Brazil.[1] Today an estimated 236,000–300,000 (0.2 percent of the population) are members of 206 distinct peoples, speaking 170 languages.[2] The Portuguese co-

lonial system of plantations and mines rested on the exploitation of the labor of enslaved Africans. As a result, almost half of Brazil's population today is of at least partial African descent, which places Brazil second only to Nigeria in this regard. Brazil gained independence from Portugal in 1822 and proclaimed itself a republic in 1889, a year after the abolition of slavery. What had been trickle of migrant labor became a tidal wave of Portuguese, Italians, and Spaniards (75 percent of those who migrated), as well as Germans, Poles, Japanese, and Middle Easterners. The migration of Japanese and Lebanese generated ambiguous reactions, given Brazilian elites' wishes to whiten the country through this migration.[3] Today there are about 250,000 people of Japanese descent in Brazil, the largest such group outside Japan.

Brazil is a federation of 26 states, with a president elected by universal suffrage since 1985. Despite its rank as the ninth largest economy worldwide, a GDP of $711,000 billion in 1996, and a GDP of $800,000 billion in 1998 (according to the Brazil Embassy).[4] "Belindia" is an epithet often used to describe Brazil: it highlights the highly dichotomized socioeconomic characteristics of its population, referring to Belgium, a small, wealthy, industrialized European nation, and India, which is noted for the poor conditions under which large numbers of its people live. The divide cuts many ways, urban versus rural (75.6 percent of the population lived in cities in 1991), European versus African or Native American descent, male versus female, as well as along class of origin and region of residence. This means that any general social indicator masks considerable internal differences. For example, life expectancy was 64.8 years for men and 71.2 years for women in 1999, but since the 1940s, the life expectancy of people of African descent (browns and blacks) has been about seven years less than of people of European descent.[5] Perhaps worse, despite the remarkable decline in the general infant mortality rate since World War II, racially disaggregated data reveals that in 1993, 37 white mothers out of 1,000 saw their newborn baby die, versus almost twice as many mothers of color (62/1,000).[6] Similarly great disparities also exist regionally for infant mortality, from 22/1,000 in the industrial South and Southeast to more than twice as many (56/1,000) in the impoverished Northeast.[7] The general rate of maternal mortality is estimated at 114 per 1,000 live births, a rate similar to that of some of the poorest Latin American countries, and the total fertility rate was 2.52 in 1995.[8]

OVERVIEW OF WOMEN'S ISSUES

It is difficult to make broad generalizations about women's issues in Brazil. A few might withstand the test: Some of the most blatant forms of male domination, such as seclusion or clitoridectomy, are absent from Brazilian culture. A vibrant second-wave feminist movement was able, especially during the period of transition from the military dictatorship to formal democracy (mid-1970s–late 1980s), to foster tremendous changes in the lives of Brazilian women: legislating working women's rights (such as a 120-day paid maternity leave); bringing attention to women's health issues, as well as sexual and reproductive rights; providing services such as abortions in the restricted cases in which they are allowed by law; bringing changes in the law with regard to "crimes of passion"; and, in the political arena, the creation of a national women's rights council.[9] Many of these achievements were enshrined in the 1988 Constitution.

Nevertheless, a double standard is still the rule in terms of gender issues. Women have an extremely low level of representation in Congress and public office in general; the majority of women are still confined to poorly paid jobs with difficult working conditions, as domestic workers or in the informal sector; an inordinate number of women are dying of treatable and preventable diseases, or simply from being pregnant. They also die at the hands of violent partners, who often remain unpunished. Brazilian culture is one of machismo; of low tolerance for female—and perhaps to a lesser extent, male—homosexuality; of commodification of women's bodies that has led, among other things, to a booming plastic surgery industry. Some of the greatest difficulties Brazilian women of the working and working-poor classes (i.e., the majority) face at this time are the cutbacks in state health, education, and social services in general, as well as governmental policies meant to facilitate the repayment of the external debt that have eroded family incomes and increased inequalities.

EDUCATION

Opportunities and Literacy

Until the mid-to-late nineteenth century, education for girls focused on "the needle," on other domestic skills, and on learning to read just enough to understand prayer books. Normal schools, which were coeducational teacher-training schools, provided one of the few opportunities for women of the well-to-do classes to continue their education. It took until 1879, with much determination on the part of early advocates of women's emancipation, to see the doors of Brazilian institutions of higher learning finally open to upper-class, mostly urban, white women—while the rest of the female population remained illiterate. According to the 1872 census for example, 19.8 percent of the total male population and 11.5 percent of the total female population was literate, although rates of literacy were much higher in the cities, where the gap between white men and women was narrower. Options for slave girls' education were nonexistent.[10]

Currently the literacy rates of men and women are similar in the population at large. In fact, young women (ages 15 to 25) show a considerably lower illiteracy rate (5.7 percent) than young men (9.2 percent), and the level of education of women is now greater than that of men.[11] From 1992 to 1997, the percentage of men with a middle school education rose from 15.9 percent to 19.4 percent, while for women the numbers were 22.4 percent and 28.3 percent.[12] There are few differences in the mean years of schooling of girls and boys in different regions of the country. However, racially disaggregated data show that the illiteracy rate among blacks was 16.5 percent, versus 9 percent among whites, in 1999. The differential is even greater among younger generations: 4.5 percent of whites between the ages of 15 and 25, and 13.4 percent among black youth.[13]

This is also true among women. In 1960, Afro-Brazilian women were three times as likely as white working women to have no formal schooling. Women of African descent were also less likely than whites to have completed middle or high school.[14] The racial gap has been reduced, with the number of women of color entering university growing faster than that of white women. Nevertheless, 22 percent of white women have 11 or more years of schooling, compared with only 9.3 percent of dark-skinned and 10.6 percent of brown-skinned women.[15]

Scholars working in this area note that it is not so much in the access to education that discrimination takes place today—although quality education depends on how much you can afford—but in the shaping of gender and racial roles, in the reinforcing of different expectations and opportunities for men and women, for blacks and whites . . . what is called the hidden curriculum.[16] Indeed, the fact that Brazilian women have a slight advantage in education has not translated into their holding better-paid and more prestigious jobs than men. Afro-Brazilian women are the most likely to see their educational achievement nullified in terms of what jobs they get, as will become amply clear in the following section on employment.

EMPLOYMENT AND ECONOMICS

Jobs/Career Opportunities

According to colonial travel accounts, most planter-class Brazilian women lived secluded in their homes, their health suffering from a lack of activity because they were waited on by house slaves. Female slaves and free women from the working classes, on the other hand, were overworked, heavily involved in agricultural work, domestic service, and dressmaking: 63 percent of women—including large numbers of slave women—were employed in domestic service in Rio in 1872, and others worked as seamstresses.[17]

In fact, it was only at the end of the nineteenth century that the only alternative to domestic service for women from the middle class became available to these women: teaching primary school. Of course women teachers received lower pay than the men they replaced. By 1906, women in Rio de Janeiro accounted for more than two-thirds of the city's teachers.[18] These early beginnings of the racial and gender division of labor have left their mark on the current job opportunities for women, though these opportunities have also been molded by more recent restructuring of the division of labor.

By 1960, the large majority of Afro-Brazilian women were still employed as domestic workers (68 percent of them versus a nonnegligible 28 percent of white women), while at the other end of the labor market 48 percent of white women were employed in professional and clerical jobs, versus only 12 percent of Afro-Brazilian women.[19] Over the next two decades, as the economy grew and modernized, women shifted into white-collar work. Afro-Brazilian women registered the largest absolute gain due to their very modest starting point (34 percent of urban Afro-Brazilian employed women were working in professional and technical activities by 1980). Still, they lagged considerably behind white women (63 percent) in this type of employment.[20]

Women's participation rate in the labor force rose slowly, reaching 20 percent of the economically active population in the early 1970s; but by 1997 it had reached 42.2 percent.[21] This trend is both the fruit of and an important reason behind the considerable changes in gender roles since about 1975. Nevertheless, studies from the 1990s show that women's traditional social reproduction role is still shaping their entry into the labor force. In this regard, "about 40 percent of women in the labor force find themselves in situations of greater vulnerability than men vis-à-vis the type of employment they enjoy, their remuneration, social protection or working conditions. These are traditionally female occupations such as domestic work, unpaid activities and activities of production for home use, besides female niches such as nursing and schoolteaching."[22] Indeed, women, and especially women of color, are still overrepresented[23] in informal sector activities that offer low wages, no benefits, and no stability. In rural areas, female labor on the family farms is still invisible, and large numbers of women work as *boias frias* (literally, cold lunch box), or as day laborers. In the cities, they are self-employed street vendors, laundresses, or seamstresses in sweatshops or at home, subcontracting from well-known multinational companies. Stable blue-collar jobs in the formal sector are still a men's preserve.

In terms of participation in the three main economic sectors, a large majority of economically active women are employed in the mostly low-paid service sector, which includes domestic service (72.6 percent, versus 41.6 percent of men); in 1988 a mere 12.7 percent of women worked in industry (29 percent of men) and 14.7 percent in agriculture (versus 29.4 percent of men).[24]

On the bright side, women have started to make inroads in male-dominated occupational citadels such as architecture, medicine, and law. A recent study shows that, nationally, women constitute 37.9 percent of medical doctors, 53.5 percent of architects, 11.6 percent of engineers, and

25.5 percent of judges and prosecutors.[25] Given the racial hierarchy of the job market in Brazil, white women have benefited from these new opportunities to a greater extent than women of color: the 1991 census data regarding the industrial sector shows that 42 percent of white women, versus only 25 percent of brown and 16.3 percent of black women, were employed in professional occupations.[26]

Pay

In 1999 Brazil trailed only Sierra Leone in terms of inequity in income distribution.[27] Even though the Constitution prohibits discrimination in wages and hiring on the basis of sex or race, statistics validate the claim that not only do glaring inequalities persist, but that "labor market inequalities between whites and Afro-Brazilians and between women and men have actually increased with economic growth and modernization in Brazil."[28] The situation is further complicated by significant discrepancies between regions and between urban and rural areas. Nevertheless, gender and race are extremely salient in the overall picture.

If the 1960–1980 period saw large numbers of women shift to better-paid white-collar work, the gap between women's and men's earnings still remained, and in fact increased: in 1960 white women's wages in white-collar positions were 55 percent of white men's, compared with only 49 percent in 1980. Similarly, Afro-Brazilian women made 61 percent of Afro-Brazilian men's wages in 1960 versus 57 percent in 1980. Gains were made only in the lowest categories of unskilled manual labor, mostly because women were starting from such an unfavorable position.[29] This means that the discrepancy between the wages of white and black women workers also increased.[30]

By 1991, despite serious difficulties, the Brazilian economy had grown, and so had employment opportunities for women and men. Census data from that year show a slow reduction in the wage gap, at least in some parts of the country; women now made about 60 percent of men's earnings in their own race, and Afro-Brazilians made about 60 percent of white earnings in São Paulo.[31] Such discrepancies also hold for professionals in medicine, law, and engineering, where women earn less than their male colleagues.[32] However, almost the entire wage gap between white women and white men (99 percent of it), at least in São Paulo, can be explained not by differences in schooling or job experience, but as a result of discrimination. For Afro-Brazilian women, who earn even less than white women, 51 percent of the wage gap with white men is due to discrimination, while the rest is due to differences in human capital (i.e., schooling and the like—which are linked to the constraints and opportunities of race in Brazilian society).[33]

How do we explain such counterintuitive increases in discriminatory practices? Researchers argue that the greater opportunities and upward mobility in an expanded economy have generated greater competition, especially for the highest-paying jobs, which in turn has favored the strengthening of the color and gender lines as a means to maintain privileged access.[34] In this regard it is interesting to note that although white women make more money than black men in urban areas, the reverse is true for the less "modernized" rural areas: white men make on average 2.5 minimum wages (about $250 per month); white women, 0.9; black men, 1.4; and black women, 0.7.[35]

Working Conditions

Sexual Harassment

Until recently there was very little national discussion of sexual harassment. In fact, sexual harassment was not considered seriously. Change has been occurring since research conducted by the Women's Secretariat of the trade union Força Sindical showed that harassment and sexual violence were the second most important concerns of working women. This led to a bill that was approved in April of 2001 by the Senate. The new law criminalizes sexual harassment as a crime against custom (*crime contra os costumes*) and against sexual freedom. Such an act can carry one to two years in jail for the perpetrator. It will be interesting to see to what extent women will feel they have the social support they need to come forward with complaints.

Support for Mothers/Caretakers

Maternal Leave

The cult of domesticity—the idea that a woman's proper place is with her children—shaped normative women's roles throughout the colonial period and up until the 1970s. Yet, it has rarely been a real option for the large majority of Brazilian women, especially women of color, whose families rely on their labor. As a result, women have had to rely mostly on each other to meet competing demands on their time by work and family. Yet, contemporary Brazilian laws are much more cognizant of the requirements of social reproduction than the equivalent U.S. legislation. Known as the "lipstick lobby," feminist activists were very successful at enshrining such concerns in the new Constitution, drafted in 1988: they ensured that working mothers were entitled to a paid maternal leave of 120 days after giving birth. They also made sure that a paternal leave of five days was guaranteed by the Constitution. (Their main argument was that the birth of a child should mean at least as much to fathers as watching the soccer World Cup matches, which always keeps them away from work for several days).[36] The Constitution also guarantees employment to pregnant women until five months after the birth of their child. Further legislation provides the right to two special breaks a day to nurse an infant child, and requires that firms employing more than 30 women provide the physical space for such activity. It even allows for a two-week "rest" period for women who have undergone a legal abortion (allowed in cases of threat to the health of the mother and of rape).

One problem is that since about half of the Brazilian population works in the informal sector, and therefore does not contribute to the Social Security system, many do not benefit from these provisions. This is all the more true for women, and particularly women of color, who are concentrated in that sector (in 1988, 51.7 percent of women and 48 percent of men were active in the informal sector).[37] The second issue is an unintended consequence of the incredible victory that the Constitution represented for women workers: large numbers of employers requested a certificate of sterilization before hiring any woman worker.

Daycare

The 1988 Constitution not only declares a worker's right to "assistance free of charge to children and dependents from birth until six years of age in daycare and preschool centers";[38] it also includes the right of the child to receive such benefits from the state. Brazilian legislation in fact has been broad enough since the 1970s to acknowledge a right to free daycare for all women, not just working mothers. These important constitutional rights were the fruit of a strong daycare movement (*movimento por creches*), born from the interaction between neighborhood movements and the feminist movement in the 1970s/early 1980s, and the children's rights movement in the 1980s.

In reality, a large number of mothers entrust their children to the care of a female neighbor or family member. The number of state-funded daycare centers and preschools is limited, and so is state support of private daycare centers—these are almost always located in middle-to-upper-class neighborhoods. However, low-income neighborhood women's struggles have led to innovative solutions, such as state support of community-organized centers or of individual women who take care of others' children, by providing them with food and the services of daycare professionals-in-training. In most cases, however, severe difficulties remain in terms of gravely inadequate facilities, poor quality of services, and overcrowding.

Family and Medical Leave

There is no provision for family leave besides leave for marriage or death of a close relative. On the other hand, the Social Security system will pay for a medical leave to anyone who misses more than 15 days of work due to illness. This is available only to those who are registered in the Social Security system.

Inheritance and Property Rights

Most pre-1980s Latin American civil codes, Brazil's included, allocated the administration of marital property to the husband in his role of head of household. This has changed since the 1988 Constitution, which states explicitly that men and women have equal rights to own land, independent of their marital status. Such provisions are particularly crucial for rural women. So are the agrarian reform efforts under way that provide for joint land titling for couples if they so choose. In this regard Brazil lags behind countries such as Guatemala and Nicaragua, where all titling of land to couples is joint. Moreover, Brazil's land reform agency has proved to be quite resistant to titling couples.[39]

As far as inheritance is concerned, the 1988 Constitution establishes that unless the couple has decided for the separation of property, the surviving spouse is entitled to half of the inheritance. The other half is distributed in the following order: children and grandchildren, parents and grandparents, surviving spouse.

Social/Government Programs

The populist government of Getúlio Vargas in the 1930s–1940s had started setting up a Social Security system for Brazilian workers. Many of these provisions found their way in the most recent Constitution. The latter ensures the right of all men and women who contributed to the system to benefits such as retirement pensions, long-term and short-term disability leave, workers compensation, pensions for those who depend on a registered worker who died (important for women homemakers), and aid for registered workers with dependent children under 14 years of age.

A major improvement of the 1988 Constitution is that it allows street vendors, domestic workers, women working on family farms, day laborers, and all those in the informal sector of the economy to contribute and be covered. Unfortunately, large numbers of workers in the informal sector are unable to contribute. Similarly, all registered workers, except domestic workers—a large number of whom are women of color—are entitled to unemployment benefits for a maximum of four months and in the miserly amount of one minimum wage (about U.S.$150).[40] Again, few are registered and therefore receive these benefits.

In fact, the segment of the population in the informal sector has been increasing as people are pushed out of the formal sector by waves of economic recessions. It is estimated that it now represents 55 percent of the labor force nationally.[41] Since the 1980s, macroeconomic policies have geared the country's economy toward repaying Brazil's external and internal debt and confronting the vagaries of the world economy. The economic adjustment policies pursued by President Fernando Collor de Mello, and his successors Itamar Franco and Fernando H. Cardoso, have meant dwindling public funding and privatization of social programs. Women have been especially affected by these hardships: they bore most of the negative consequences of structural adjustment programs that cut public services linked to areas of social reproduction (such as health and education), for which women have traditionally been responsible. In other words, economic policies have run counter to the political choices expressed in the Constitution and other documents, which suggest an essential role for the state in social welfare.

The late 1990s saw, amid tremendous political battles, an effort by the Brazilian government to reform the Social Security system, in particular the pension system, which allows men to retire after 35 years of work and women after 30. The system offers generous packages to certain categories, such as judges, journalists, and teachers. As the population ages, and the ratio of contributors to collectors of Social Security is shrinking, some action is indeed required.[42] It is however not clear what measures will finally be voted on and how women will be differently affected from men.

FAMILY AND SEXUALITY

Gender Roles

Like most cultures in the region, Brazil's gender roles have been structured around the originally Mediterranean *marianismo*/machismo tandem, which attributes to women a central role in the family as mothers, a strong moral sense, and infinite selflessness despite (or maybe because of) the husband's demonstrations of dominance and strength based on violence, feminine conquests, and success in the public sphere. This model has been tempered, however, by influences from the greater female autonomy found in West African gender systems and in their survival in Afro-Brazilian communities.

The apparatus of the state, and of industrialists, put all its weight behind the "woman the homemaker" role, pushing in the 1920s and 1930s to delegitimize the woman worker and turn her into a model housewife.[43] This ideology explains the low participation of women in the formal labor force until the 1970s and is responsible for the stereotype of woman as complementary wage earner, which in turn is used to justify her lower wages. Contemporary roles do include woman's work outside the home, although often as a "help" to her husband's efforts at bringing in income for the family. But gender roles are no doubt changing. According to the Brazilian Institute of Statistics, the number of Brazilians living in a household consisting of one man and his children, without the mother, although still small, has almost tripled over since the 1980s.[44]

Race and gender ideology are very much intertwined. The construction of gender and race in Brazil is evident through the marketing of the slim, blond, blue-eyed television megastar Xuxa. Her success is due to the fact that, on the one hand, she embodies the reconciliation of two contradictory ideals of woman: the sexpot woman and the docile, nurturing mother. On another level, she extols the beauty and superiority of whiteness, in a country where most are brown- or dark-skinned, while propping up the façade of the myth of racial democracy, notably through the long, highly mediatized relationship she had with the famous black soccer player Pélé.[45] Xuxa's success also makes sense when we listen to women of African descent recount how their men, especially if they do well in the world, turn away from them to marry white women. There is a contrast of the stereotypes of black, *mulatta*, and white women in Brazilian literature. The *preta* or black woman is viewed as "dirty, greasy and grimy." She is a "workhorse," while the *mulatta* is the symbol of Brazil itself—the tropical mulatto land—but simultaneously she is perceived as shrewd, lazy, the quintessential sex symbol: "carefree, fun-loving, popular, volatile like all mixed-blood women."[46] The light-skinned woman is preferred to these two women for marriage and to provide lighter offspring, in an effort to "purify the blood."

Marriage

Anchored in the reality of colonial Brazil, where legal marriage was rare among the racially mixed lower classes and served mostly as a marker of social differentiation, race and class still shape the conjugal status of Brazilian women.[47] Research on the demographics of the black population between 1940 and 1980 identified more unmarried black men and women, lower levels of legally married black and brown women, and more mixed couples consisting of black men and white women (rather than the reverse).[48] Today, there are a considerable number of nonlegally sanctioned unions among the middle classes, too, as young couples often now live together before getting married, and because of changes in separation/divorce patterns. As a result, half as many heterosexual marriages are celebrated than in the 1970s (4.6/1000 inhabitants in 1999) (compared to 8.9/1000 in the United States).[49] New legislation is taking these changes into account, attempting to give stable unions that are not legally sanctioned some of the rights so far reserved for legal unions. This is especially important for women because among those legally married, at least in Rio, there are 52.5 percent men versus 47.5 percent women. Women marry earlier, but remain separated and live longer than men.[50] It is particularly important with regard to alimony—compensating the woman for leaving the labor market and providing domestic work—which currently is severely restricted in consensual unions.[51]

Divorce was legalized in 1977, replacing the older system of legal separation.[52] The number of divorces and legal separations is on the increase, and doubled between 1981 and 1988 (13/100 marriage in 1988).[53] As a result, the number of female-headed households has been on the increase. It went from 13 percent of families in 1970 to 20.1 percent in 1989, and to approximately 26 percent in 1998.[54] As in other countries in the region, these households are often among the poorest, given their head's limited job opportunities and remuneration. Women of color are overrepresented among them, a pattern that the earlier discussion regarding marriage partially explains.

In Brazil, as elsewhere in the region, economic difficulties, such as the ones encountered throughout the 1980s and 1990s, have prevented many men from fulfilling their role of family provider, so far the linchpin of masculine identity. Under the pressure, many have chosen to abandon their families.[55] The lower number of unions may also reflect women's unwillingness to stay in abusive relationships and their greater ability to leave, given the greater financial independence their involvement in the job market affords them. Some also may feel free to live their homosexuality more openly.

Be it in consensual or official heterosexual unions, the double standard still holds, affording freedom or at least understanding for the man who cheats on his wife but requiring strict monogamy on the part of women. Research for the Health Department showed that in 1999, 20 percent of men versus 4 percent of women simultaneously maintained one stable relationship and one or more casual relationships.[56] The AIDS epidemic has brought such issues to the fore with a vengeance, as we will see as we begin our discussion of reproductive and health issues.

Reproduction

Women's health and reproductive rights issues have been at the forefront of the second wave of the Brazilian women's movement since its inception in the 1970s. It is the area where the largest array of groups and organizations can be found, including a national network, the National Feminist Network for Health and Reproductive Rights (hereafter referred to as RedeSaúde). It is also of interest to the nation as a whole: contraception/fertility/fecundity was the topic with greatest coverage by the four major dailies between May and August 1998.[57]

Sex Education

Sex education remains a scarce commodity in Brazil; research has found that Brazilians have little knowledge of biology, and in particular of the fertile period. Medical doctors offer little support—for example, they have been found to refrain from explaining to women with sexually transmitted diseases how they contracted them. Yet, here again, change is happening. In 2001, a feminist nongovernmental organization (ECOS), working in partnership with a private foundation and a private-sector company (Schering), provided the conceptual content for a series of videos and educational kits to be distributed in the public school networks in four south-eastern states. The 20 videos are also being televised, thus allowing a much greater dissemination of new concepts on sexuality, not only to promote safer sexual practices but also to stimulate discussion and greater equity in male/female relationships.[58]

Contraception and Abortion

The fertility rate has declined very rapidly in Brazil since the 1980s, with a total fertility rate now at 2.52 children per woman. Yet, the fact that women have fewer children does not liberate more resources for those who do, or for other women's health issues. Brazilian women have fewer children partly as a result of a high sterilization rate, despite the illegality of the procedure. Lack of information and availability of other contraception methods is leaving women with little choice, and sterilization is increasingly common, including among young women and especially among poor women. The oral contraceptive is the other widely used contraception method in Brazil. High-dose pills are still common. Pills are relatively expensive, but since they are available over the counter, many women self-prescribe, which leads to serious side effects, including strokes. In São Paulo, use of the pill is slightly more common than sterilization (respectively, 38.6 percent and 36.1 percent among women who used contraception in 1992). As recently as 1996, a political candidate was brought to justice for having offered free sterilization procedures in exchange for votes.[59] In the mostly Afro-Brazilian Northeast, these figures are reversed (62.9 percent use sterilization and 23.0 percent use the pill).[60] Due to these regional differences, as well as to racial inequality in living standards and, at times, to barely veiled racist leanings on the part of public authorities, a disproportionate number of Afro-Brazilian women are being sterilized. This, of course, has been an important struggle for Afro-Brazilian women's groups. Hoping to broaden the contraceptive options of women, public health services launched an initiative in 1999 to ensure greater availability of reversible contraception methods, including condoms, in the public health system and in private clinics. The state is thus making some small steps toward the 1988 Constitution provisions which state that "family planning is based on a couple's free choices, without coercion, with the State obliged to provide the resources necessary for the exercise of this right."[61]

Astronomical rates of cesarean sections have finally been addressed as a public health issue. The problem was so pressing that target percentages were established to bring the number of cesareans done in public hospitals gradually to 30 percent by 2000.[62] This is still much higher than the 10 percent in western Europe, but a great improvement over the 90 percent C-sections registered in numerous hospitals before the campaign. The reasons for this trend of epidemic proportion are to be found in the desire of doctors to control their time and increase their monetary income, as well as, at least for some, the satisfaction they get from literally bringing a child into the world. For the woman, other issues come into play besides the need to control her time schedule, such as the desire to facilitate a sterilization procedure she requested, the cultural capital and self-valorization gained in adopting what may be seen as a sophisticated and "modern" mode of delivery, rejecting one's association with nature, and the belief by women that they need an undamaged vagina to be able to provide sexual satisfaction for their husband/partner.

Abortion has been legal in Brazil in case of threat to the life of the mother and of rape/incest since the late 1940s. In all other cases, abortion is a crime. Unfortunately, women who could not afford an intervention in a private clinic had to wait until 1989 for the first public hospital to perform abortions in these legal cases. Reliable data are difficult to obtain, but it is estimated that as many as 1.4 million unsafe illegal abortions are performed in Brazil each year, leaving many dead or gravely impaired in the process.[63] A number of proposals to decriminalize abortion have been pushed through Congress, and intense political struggles have ensued since the mid-90s. A few advances have been made, such as the passing in 1997 of a bill that required the public health system to universally implement abortion services to comply with the law. There are now 14 such services throughout the country. The penal code today also allows abortions in cases of mortal fetal anomaly and of threats to the health of the mother (as opposed to threats to her life).

Teen Pregnancy

Although overall fertility rates in Brazil have steadily declined since the 1980s, census data show that the fertility rate among women between 15 and 19 years of age has experienced a 20 percent increase between 1970 and 1991. Other national-level research shows that almost 14 percent of women below the age of 15 had at least one child in 1996. This indicator experienced a 20 percent increase between 1993 and 1997.[64] Young women from rural areas and with no access to education are especially likely to become mothers early. These numbers are also clearly related to the low rate of use of contraception among these age groups (86 percent of women 15–19, and 58 percent of women age 20–24, do not use any contraceptive methods).

Brazil has a high rate of abortion among teenagers (32 per 1000, but still lower than the U.S. rate, 36 per 1000). These mostly unsafe abortions are responsible for 16 percent of maternal deaths of women 15–19 years of age in the poorest regions of Brazil. Moreover, the number of abortions among young women is increasing: from 1993 to 1997, the curettages provided by the public health system for teenagers after botched abortions went from 19 percent to 22 percent of the total of such operations.[65]

HEALTH

Health Care Access

Although boasting the ninth largest economy in terms of gross national product, Brazil was ranked 125th by the World Health Organization in terms of health and health care conditions in 2000. A privileged section of Brazilians enjoys a quality of life and of health care similar to that of industrialized nations and suffers from the same diseases, whereas the less well-off majority is still struggling with unsanitary living conditions, and suffers from gastrointestinal and pulmonary infections, as well as increasingly from cardiovascular and other noncommunicable diseases. This dichotomous national scenario can be traced back to the sharp inequalities resulting from Brazil's colonial slave-based society and the subsequent exclusion of nonelite sectors from access to state services, such as sanitation, water supply, and medical services.

The Brazilian Constitution of 1988 meant to remedy this situation: it states that health is a right for everyone and that it is the state's duty to maintain and improve the population's health, providing services including those for women's reproductive health and contraception. Yet, a mere 25 percent of the Brazilian population have access to health insurance plans, either through their formal-sector job or through individual policies, and they absorbed 88 percent of the total Health Ministry annual budget in 1994. The other 75 percent of the population rely solely on the free public health system, and hence on the meager remainder of the Health Ministry budget.[66] A long period of neglect of prevention and of basic health services, to the benefit of curative services, is only slowly being redressed, notably through an effort, since 1994, to implement primary health programs.[67] Altogether the lack of public investment has led to a deterioration of the health care system in general since the 1970s. Structural adjustment measures forced the federal government cut its health spending from $11.3 to $7.5 billion between 1989 and 1993. The numbers were to be back up to about U.S.$80 billion (191 R$) per capita in 1998,[68] after a drastic temporary tax on financial activities. Most state and municipal governments have also been reducing their spending on health, severe consequences for women's health.

PAISM, the Comprehensive Women's Health Program, was defined as early as 1984 by the Health Department as its national policy. PAISM is based largely on the work and recommendations of the women's health movement, and gained prominence thanks to its effective lobbying. It is meant to offer state support for women's health in all stages of their life cycle. In most cases, however, in part as a result of lack of political will but mostly of the financial difficulties described above, it became dead letter. Between 1994 and 1998, as a result of the massive participation of Brazilian women's health activists in the processes surrounding the United

Nations 1995 Conference on Women and the 1994 Conference on Population and Development, and their clever use of the international instruments signed by their government as leverage for implementation at the national level, PAISM was revived. This has meant that many health administrators have been sensitized to the fact that reproductive health involves more than maternal health. One serious shortcoming of PAISM is that it does not require the race of a woman to be recorded or be considered in public policy, even though the living conditions of black women put them at greater risk for a number of health risks, probably in terms of maternal health.

Diseases and Disorders

AIDS

Brazil, in the late 1980s, was one of the countries with the largest number of cases of AIDS worldwide. Since then the disease has evolved from an urban issue affecting mostly upwardly mobile populations to one spread throughout the national territory, disproportionately affecting the country's low-income, and therefore darker-skinned, population. On the bright side, since 1996, retroviral drugs have been provided universally and free of charge, and deaths due to AIDS were reduced by 50 percent between 1995 and 1999. Unfortunately, the reduction in the number of deaths among women (37.3 percent) has been a little over half that for men (71 percent).[69] This is most likely because of later diagnosis and of the trajectory of the disease, for which heterosexual sex has become an essential vehicle of transmission. Indeed, there has been a "feminization" of the disease. In 1986, there were 16 men with HIV for each woman with the disease, while in 1998 the ratio was two men for each woman aged 25 and above. In fact, in the state of São Paulo, AIDS has been the first cause of death among women aged 20 to 44 since 1994.[70] Among those aged 15–24, however, the ratio already was of one young man for each young HIV-positive woman.[71] The main cause of infection of young women is heterosexual relations (for 72 percent of them), while among young men, the main cause is the use of contaminated needles for drugs (43 percent of them).[72] Research among young marginalized people of color in the United States has shown the impact of social structure on their perception of what constitutes risky behavior, and therefore on their adoption of safe sex practices. There is no reason to believe that such processes are not at work among Brazilian marginalized populations as well. In the population at large, Brazilian women in stable relationships are particularly at risk due to the social acceptance of extramarital affairs for married men and the difficulty of negotiating any sort of safe sex practices within the ties of matrimony.

Body Image

Issues related to body image do not seem to be expressed through eating disorders as in cultures/nations of the global north. They seem to be expressed instead through a frenzied recourse to plastic surgery, involving mostly liposuction of the belly and thighs, as well as reduction of the breasts—which reminds us to what extent the "beautiful" body is culturally constructed. The success of television mega-star Xuxa, discussed earlier, also reveals to what extent in Brazil the beautiful body is the light-skinned, blond, blue-eyed body. Such "Europeanizing aesthetic ideals" seem to permeate all the way through to new magazines such as *Raça Negra*, which target the black middle class and in which lighter-skinned women of mixed ancestry seem to set the standard. While in the mainstream the brown-skinned *mulata* with her flowing, wavy hair may be admired, almost revered, she does not command respect but is generally turned into a stereotypical figure of tropical lust and sensuality.

Cancer

Reproductive tract cancers, which are responsible for 30 percent of all cancer deaths in Brazil, are an important reproductive health problem faced by Brazilian women. Many such deaths are easily preventable, but, for example, the rates of Pap smear exams for the detection of cervical cancer are very low: even in São Paulo, only 4 percent of women get a Pap smear.[73] Women's health groups have battled for years to obtain expanded gynecological cancer screening services in public health facilities. The public health services finally launched a major national program against cervical cancer in 1998. During its most intensive phase, in just three months, 3 million women were examined.[74]

Obviously, women's health should not be limited to their reproductive health, but it is the area that receives the most attention from the authorities. The bleak picture provided in earlier pages gives an idea of how neglected other women's health issues, such as mental health or menopause issues might be. AIDS provides us with another example.

POLITICS AND LAW

It was not until 1962 and the Statute of the Married Woman that women were no longer considered as perpetual minors and married women gained the right to "engage in commerce, alienate their immovable property by sale or gift, or even administer that property without their husbands' consent."[75] The 1988 Constitution finally defined the family as "a group constituted either by marriage or by stable unions, with equal rights granted to men and women within those families and to all children whether born in wedlock or not."[76] In early 2001, a new Civil Code was finally voted by

Members of women's labor unions and organizations participate in an International Women's Day march dressed as witches
to protest President Fernando Henrique Cardoso's economic
policy and discrimination against women in the workplace, Rio
de Janeiro, March 1999. AP/Wide World Photos.

Congress, after 26 years of deliberation (the last code dated from
1916). It still needs to be approved
by the president. This new code incorporates the advances made in the
1988 Constitution and most of the
recommendations made by feminist
activists who had pushed for a
"Civil Statute of Women" in 1981.
Among other things, the new code
does away with the concept of
"male head of household" and calls
for "shared leadership" in the family; husbands no longer have the
right to ask for the annulment of
marriage because their wife was not
a virgin when they married; and
men can take their wives' names.
Nevertheless, the new code contains
remnants of patriarchal ideology, such as the article that allows either of
the spouses to initiate separation as a result of "dishonorable conduct."
Feminist lawyers have pointed out that even though the language sounds
gender-neutral, most articles relative to honor and honesty in Brazilian civil
legislation have been traditionally aimed at women's sexuality.[77] The code
also fails to legislate on artificial insemination, in-vitro fertilization and
other new reproductive technologies.

Suffrage and Political Participation

In 1932 the Brazilian women's suffrage movement, led by biologist Bertha Lutz, obtained the right to vote for women with the same literacy
requirements imposed on men at the time. This right was confirmed in
the 1934 Constitution. Illiterate Brazilians, both men and women, had to
wait for the return of formal democracy in the mid-1980s before they could
vote.

In the two decades preceding women's gaining the right to vote, a few
well-educated, upper-middle-class women were able to compete for, and
win, important public positions. Many of them were members of distinguished families, often with a father or a husband involved in politics. This
was the case of the first Brazilian woman mayor in 1929 and of the first
woman elected to Congress in 1933. It was not until the 1935 elections and
efforts to encourage and educate women about the vote that a substantial
number of women (ten of them), including leading feminist figures, were
elected to the legislatures. Two feminists, including Lutz, were members

of the committee of the Constituent Assembly charged with drafting the new constitution. They pushed for and secured the inclusion of numerous legal changes, such as equal pay for equal work, social welfare measures for pregnant women and mothers, equal political rights and citizenship and equal nationality rights for women (a Brazilian woman marrying a foreign national could now keep her Brazilian nationality). Unfortunately, most of these gains were lost as early as 1937 as the authoritarian regime of Getúlio Vargas, known as the Estado Novo, took power. It lasted until the end of World War II. Even those areas of government service that had been open to a few women professionals were now closed to them, even after the number of men available to fill these posts dwindled because of the war effort. Vargas's new regime, unfriendly to the idea of women's equality, promoted strongly differentiated gender roles.

The years of democratic rule (1946–1964), the year of the military coup, and 21 years of dictatorship saw only two women elected to the national Congress and none in the 1946 Constituent Assembly. Although women were active in political parties, they were usually relegated to social activities. Seldom were women part of the decision-making bodies of parties. When the military loosened its grip on the political system in the late 1970s/early 1980s, eight women were among the 479 elected members of the Chamber of Deputies, and one woman was elected to the Senate in 1982. Twenty-six women made it to the Constituent Assembly in 1986. Among them was a remarkable woman, Benedita da Silva, a black resident of Rio's slums, member of the newly formed left-wing Workers' Party. She was the only black woman elected to this Assembly, and the first black woman ever to be elected to Congress. In 1994, she became the first black woman senator.

Today, women's representation in formal institutional politics remains low, with a mere 7 percent of the legislative branch in 1997, and only 5.5 percent of mayorships.[78] In the judiciary and the executive branch, the situation is no better. In order to address these inequities, especially in the legislative branch, a politics of quota has been instituted, stating that all parties must strive to have at least 25 percent women candidates—or, more exactly, that no gender should have a representation of less than 30 percent or more than 70 percent of candidates in each political party. Despite this new legislation, few parties in 1998 met the required quota, given the long-term nature of the process of sensitization of the electorate and of party structures required by this policy. In fact, fewer women were elected to the House of Representatives in 1998 than in 1994.

On the other hand, São Paulo, the largest city in South America, recently elected its second woman mayor through the Workers' Party. Both of these women have been strong supporters of gender equity. But we also need to look outside of institutional structures to evaluate the level and efficacy of the involvement of women, and more precisely feminists, in politics.[79]

New spaces, such as that of nongovernmental organizations and their interaction with the state, have been essential in securing new rights for women and improving their daily lives.

Women's Rights and Feminist Movements

The struggle for women's rights goes back to the second half of the nineteenth century, when a feminist press emerged with a few journals and associations. These groups had no involvement with the abolition movement: unlike in the United States, they started organizing before abolition in Brazil and abolitionist organizations did not accept women members.

The effervescent, larger-scale movement for women's suffrage in the 1920s and 1930s, as mentioned earlier, was mostly a white, upper-middle class affair as well-educated women focused on the acquisition of legal rights and equality in their struggle to enter the professions. Nevertheless, Bertha Lutz's "middle class ideals" were also part of her struggle "for new paths towards women's economic emancipation."[80]

Feminist activities between the dawning of the authoritarian Vargas regime in 1937 and the celebration of the International Women's Year, in 1975, were seriously curtailed. A few organizations, still composed mostly of white, upper-middle class professionals, did struggle arduously and, in 1962, won changes in the Civil Code that allowed women some control over decisions affecting the family. And in 1968 legislation was enacted prohibiting discrimination against women in hiring; also, the legislation was implemented that permitted married women to take up any profession without their husbands' permission. Middle-class women, afraid of labor unrest and economic difficulties, were organized by the right in their agitation for the fall of the populist government of João Goulart, which led to the 1964 military coup.

By the late 1970s, in Brazil, as throughout Latin America, organizing around gender took another turn: women organized around their identities as mothers and wives to resist authoritarian military regimes, with the help of the Catholic Church and leftist-oriented parties. At the same time, it had become evident that the Brazilian military regime had failed to transform the "economic miracle" into a reality for all Brazilians.[81] Grassroots organizations and popular movements sprang up in a collective effort to deal with the increasing difficulties of the working masses and to oppose the repressive regime. It is now acknowledged that women were the majority of participants in many of these grassroots movements, not only in Brazil but in Latin America in general. In part, this is because women have been especially affected by these hardships.

The Brazilian feminist movement reemerged in the 1970s to question inequalities experienced on the job by educated, working- and middle-class women, as well as to the deterioration of their standard of living as a consequence of the economic crisis. Contradictions between the traditional gender ideology of the military regime, which ascribed nurturing roles to women as mothers and wives, and its strong state capitalist development strategy, which prevented women from fulfilling these ascribed roles, fueled the growth of the movement. In addition to these structural conditions, "conjunctural conditions," such as the human rights discourse; the international feminist discourse, especially after the U.N.-sponsored International Women's Year in 1975; and the discrimination suffered by women within the sexist and male-dominated political organizations of the left, brought crucial ideological and organizational support to the rebirth of an autonomous feminist movement.[82] The liberalization of the military regime after the mid-1970s, known as *abertura*, and the ensuing strengthened hope for successful protest were also favorable.

One of the dictatorship's legacies to Brazilian popular and feminist movements is their wariness of co-optation by the state. They were born outside, and in opposition to, the authoritarian state, although they recognized it as a privileged interlocutor. With the return to civilian rule and competitive elections, relations with local-level state agencies intensified and facilitated successes. The coming to power of former opposition parties, especially at the local level, provided new participatory opportunities for women. Feminists increased their presence in political parties, resulting in more gender-sensitive political platforms and translating into new institutions to monitor the implementation of these policies, when these parties came into power. São Paulo's State Council on Women's Condition, the first of its kind in the country, created in 1983, is one good example. Two years later, when José Sarney took office as the first civilian president in more than 20 years, the National Council for Women's Rights (CNDM) was instituted at the federal level.

These councils had significant participation of feminists with strong ties to women's groups and thanks to their positioning within the state, they made possible undeniable advances that the movement alone would not have been able to secure; examples are the myriad new constitutional provisions in 1988, a commission on reproductive rights within the São Paulo Ministry of Health, and special police stations to handle violence against women. In part, the councils' success was a result of pressure from feminists outside the state, which strengthened the councils' position vis-à-vis the government and helped to limit co-optation.[83]

As the political scene consolidated in this new democratic phase, and as more conservative governments took power, in 1986 in the state of São Paulo and in 1989 at the federal level (administration of F. Collor de Mello), the councils turned into partisan puppets with limited ties to the women's movement and strongly reduced political clout within the government.

In 1994, the election as president of Fernando Henrique Cardoso, seen as a progressive with long-enduring ties to civil society and the husband of a self-proclaimed feminist, brought renewed hope to important segments of the movement. Cardoso called for civil society and nongovernmental organizations (NGOs) to work in collaboration with his government. Prominent and legitimate members of the feminist movements joined the federal women's rights council. However, the neoliberal policies of the federal and most state administrations, and their emphasis on a minimum state, contributed to the loss of power of the councils. The federal council did not regain the prestige or resources necessary for its proper functioning. In 1995, the São Paulo Council was moved away from the city's main commercial artery to a building in the run-down inner city, and by 2000, its staff had been reduced to less than one-third of what it had been.[84]

Despite these difficulties, women have created other channels of interaction with the state in their efforts to achieve gender equity. Strong, professionalized NGOs, most often financed by international donor agencies, have become articulators of the demands of the movement and have been actively involved in the Latin American and transnational women's movements. Their structure has not always been most conducive to the democratic construction of these demands, given the diversity of the movement in terms of race and class, in particular. Flexible network structures, such as the RedeSáude, have been working diligently to include and represent all currents in the movement. The 1990s saw the consolidation of a black women's movement distinct from, yet with solid ties to, both the black movement and the feminist movement: black women have been working to strengthen their organizations against the sexism of the one and the racism of the other.[85] They held their third national meeting in early 2001, in preparation for the UN conference on racism held in Durban, South Africa. Indigenous women have created their own organizations but remain somewhat marginalized in the women's movement.

Lesbian Rights

A lesbian underground culture flourished in Brazil in the 1990s and is now coming out of the closet. Lesbians have been actively involved in the women's movement since its inception, some overtly working for their rights as homosexuals, others not foregrounding this part of their identity. They have also created their own vibrant organizations. The 1994 Conference on Women held in Beijing by the United Nations and its statements regarding sexual rights stimulated greater visibility and public discussion of gay and lesbian rights in Brazil. Among Latin American countries, Brazil was the only one, as of 2000, to offer a legal framework for these issues. In particular, the National Program on Human Rights includes the need to respect sexual orientation. A bill, in discussion in Congress since 1995, that would provide legal recognition for the civil union of same-sex couples, has been generating both much controversy and greater visibility of homosexuals' rights.[86] However, such rights were not included in the new

Civil Code approved by the Senate. Other legal instruments that are already on the books, such as state laws (as in Rio de Janeiro), which prohibit discrimination against individuals by commercial establishments on the basis of sexual orientation have not yet been enforced by the state government. Clearly it will take more than legal initiatives to provide full citizenship to lesbians, from protection against hate crimes to more subtle forms of everyday discrimination.

RELIGION AND SPIRITUALITY

Until the early 1970s, 95 percent of Brazilians were Roman Catholic (at least nominally so; as many also practiced another religion, often Afro-Brazilian spiritism). Nominal Catholics now represent 76 percent of the population.[87] Catholicism has shaped much of the Brazilian approach to reproductive rights, sexual rights, family issues and the gender system in general.

Women's Roles

The 1960s saw a large sector of the Brazilian Catholic Church turned toward the promotion of social justice after the Second Vatican Council (1962–1965). Following what is known as Liberation Theology, the church, in order to get closer to the faithful, used the privileged vehicle of Christian Base Communities (CEBs) to work with the working classes. The CEBs were designed to get participants to understand the social origins of their situation and to promote their mobilization and organization. Women have constituted the backbone of CEBs. Many such women, having gained greater self-esteem and politicization, joined popular movements such as those dealing with health, literacy, or sanitation, some of which had privileged ties with feminist movements. However, even the progressive church has been willing to go only so far: as women have affirmed certain feminist positions, in particular with regard to abortion or contraception, they have entered into conflict with the church and have significantly curtailed their ties to it or have been ostracized from it.

From other quarters, religious women, already attuned to social issues, started building bridges with Brazilian feminists. Maria José Rosado, for example, a nun for 20 years, founded the Brazilian arm of Catholics for Free Choice in the mid-1980s. These women understand that their discourse is counterpoint to the church's official discourse: Rosado argues that the church, due to its being based on a celibate masculine hierarchy, does not and cannot understand women's needs and their wishes for control over their sexuality.[88]

If women have been excluded from the hierarchy and formal structure of the Catholic Church, nothing could be more different than Afro-Brazilian spiritist religions, such as *candomblé*. Afro-Brazilian spiritist houses of worship are most often led by a Mother of the Saints, who has considerable (both spiritual and worldly) influence on her congregation and on its often wealthy, mostly white patrons. Afro-Brazilian religious icons provide a number of role models for girls and women, including strong, defiant women, far from the Virgin Mary's selfless and sacrificing image.

Evangelical churches mushroomed in Brazil through the 1980s and 1990s. With regard to women, they present a complex picture. Despite their admonition for women to be dutiful and obedient mothers and wives, ethnographic work reveals how devout women have been using the teachings of the church on work, alcohol and drugs, and responsibility to bring their men in line, as well as to get some degree of protection from drug-related gang violence.

VIOLENCE

Domestic Violence

Women's movements have won notable battles in their struggle against domestic violence. Legacies from the Portuguese colonial legal code, which permitted a husband to kill his wife in case of adultery in order to preserve his honor, survived in the form of the possibility for a man to claim a "legitimate defense of honor" until 1991. Since then, juries and judges have too often been swayed by arguments of "violent emotions" presented by wife murderers, still not finding husbands guilty in these circumstances.

In August 1985, the first women's police station (*delegacia*), an extremely innovative approach to domestic violence, opened its doors in São Paulo city, as a result of political opportunism and feminist activism at the end of the military dictatorship in the mid-1980s. Today there are 300 such *delegacias* throughout Brazil. The system is far from perfect, since the *delegacias* and the women staffing them have to contend with the male-dominated world of police and law enforcement within which they are embedded. Yet despite their limitations, the *delegacias* gave women greater confidence to report and denounce cases of violence; they also "have an impact on policewomen's and clients' gender identity"; the women "start to articulate a discourse on women's rights, a significant change in the consciousness of women who, until 'discovering' the *delegacias*, believed that they had no rights."[89]

The justice system, on the other hand, has not offered the necessary follow-up: in many cases, absence of punishment is still very much the rule in domestic violence cases. Most cases do not involve prison sentences; instead the perpetrator engages in some sort of community service—or even simply offers a bouquet of red roses to the victim. As early as 1995, feminist organizations such as São Paulo's Colectivo Feminista Sexualidade Esaude (CFSS), known as Colectivo, pushed for and conducted training of public health workers to be able to recognize signs of domestic and other types of physical violence against women when the victims get to their services for treatment. In 1998, the Federal District launched a media campaign on intra-family violence. Some of the most recent elements of the campaign target definitions of masculinity linked to violence.

There is, however, danger in interpreting violence against women only in terms of domestic violence, especially when this interpretation is shaped by the need to protect "honest" women and the family, as is mostly the case in the *delegacias*.[90] Other acts of violence against women, such as assaults on prostitutes and disrespect of their rights by the police, are not likely to be considered seriously. Similarly, discriminatory practices against women because of their color are not taken into consideration by the *delegacias*. The black women's movement has been struggling to get other feminists to recognize that racial discrimination against black women is indeed violence against women. The São Paulo State Council for Women's Condition has finally recognized that "racism is a crime and also a form of violence against women."[91]

Rape/Sexual Assault

In the Penal Code elaborated in 1940, rape is considered a crime against custom rather than a crime against a person. Even though Brazilian law declares the rape or kidnapping of a minor 14 years or younger as a violent moral offense with no possibility of extenuating circumstances, the new Civil Code still allows marriage for a girl who is not yet nubile in order to avoid criminal charges. This means that in case of sexual violence, marriage is given the power to repair the violence committed and to provide immunity to the perpetrator.

Trafficking in Women and Children

The boom of the global sex industry since the 1980s and the economic difficulties of the low-income population have made sex tourism an everyday life issue for many Brazilian women and (to a lesser extent) men, but particularly for minors of both sexes in numerous Brazilian resorts. The matter is so dire that the city of Fortaleza, the third Brazilian city in terms of the number of denunciations of sexual exploitation of minors, has launched a commission of inquiry on sex tourism.[92] In such cases, race and class play an essential part in who is engaging in sex work and therefore is more vulnerable to such exploitation.

OUTLOOK FOR THE TWENTY-FIRST CENTURY

The record of the Brazilian women's movements to push the Brazilian state to include some of the most progressive language and provisions in its legislation, and to support international instruments that promote gender equity, has been impressive. Nevertheless, at the start of this brand new millennium, observers and activists alike fear the impact of continued neoliberal policies, which reduce state allocation of resources to sectors such as health care, education, and others that are crucial for women to fulfill their role as family caretakers, and have led to further concentration of wealth. These policies have been encouraged by international financing agencies, such as the World Bank and the International Monetary Fund, intent on getting Brazil to repay an external debt incurred largely by the military dictatorship in the 1970s. Such policies run counter to the spirit of the 1988 constitution which identifies the State as a major player in rectifying some of the inequalities generated by colonial, postcolonial and patriarchal institutions.

NOTES

I would like to thank Eva Rocha for her valuable help with researching data for this chapter, as well as for her comments on an earlier draft. Thanks as well to Amy Lind for her editorial comments.

1. John Hemming, *Red Gold: The Conquest of the Brazilian Indians* (Cambridge, MA: Harvard University Press, 1978).

2. Alcida Rita Ramos, *Indigenism: Ethnic Politics in Brazil* (Madison: University of Wisconsin Press, 1998), 3.

3. Jeffrey Lesser, *Negotiating National Identity: Immigrants, Minorities, and the Struggle for Ethnicity in Brazil* (Durham, NC: Duke University Press, 1999).

4. Pan American Health Organization (PAHO), *Basic Country Health Profiles*, summaries 1999, www.paho.org/English/SHA/prflbra.htm 8/10/01.

5. Ibid.; Estela da Cunha and María García de Pinto, "Mortalidade infantil e raça: As diferenças da desigualdade," *Jornal da RedeSaúde* no. 23 (March 2001): 48–50.

6. Da Cunha (2001).

7. IBGE, "International Marketing Data and Statistics," in *Vital Statistics* (Chicago: Euromonitor International, 2001), table N. 0209.

8. PAHO, 1999, 3.

9. Conselho Nacional dos Direitos da Mulher, www.mj.gov.br/sedh/cndm.

10. June Hahner, *Emancipating the Female Sex: The Struggle for Women's Rights in Brazil, 1850–1940* (Durham, NC: Duke University Press, 1990).

11. UNESCO, *UNESCO Statistical Yearbook* (Paris: UNESCO, 1999).

12. IBGE, 1999.

13. IPEA with PNAD data.

14. Peggy A. Lovell, "Women and Racial Inequality at Work in Brazil," in *Racial Politics in Contemporary Brazil*, ed. Michael Hanchard (Durham, NC: Duke University Press, 1999), 143.

15. Jeannette Sutherland, "Economic Development Versus Social Exclusion: The Cost of Development in Brazil," paper presented at the 2001 meeting of the Latin American Studies Association, Washington DC, September 6–8, 6.

16. Vera Soares, Ana A.A. Costa, Cristina M. Buarque, Denise Dourado Doura, and Wania Sant'Anna, "Brazilian Feminism and Women's Movements: A Two-Way Street," in *The Challenge of Local Feminisms: Women's Movements in Global Perspective,* ed. Amrita Basu (Boulder, CO: Westview Press, 1995), 43.

17. Hahner, 1990, 12.

18. Ibid., 24.

19. Lovell, "Women and Racial Inequality," 1999, 145.

20. Ibid.

21. IBGE, *Pesquisa nacional por amostro de domicilios* (Rio de Janeiro: IBGE, 1997).

22. Cristina Bruschini, "Médicas, arquitetas, advogadas e engenheiras: Mulheres em carreiras profissionais de prestígio," *Estudos feministas* 7, no. 1–2 (1999): 9.

23. In 1991, in urban São Paulo, one of the areas where the formal sector is the most developed, 69 percent of working white women, 66 percent of brown women, and 63 percent of black women had a work card, while 80 percent of white women but only 71 percent of brown and black women benefited from Social Security (in comparison, 86 percent of white men had a work card and 90 percent of them benefited from Social Security). Peggy Lovell, "Gender, Race and the Struggle for Social Justice in Brazil," *Latin American Perspectives* 27 (November 2000): 131–48.

24. Facultad Latinoamericano de Ciencias Sociales (FLACSO), *Mulheres latinoamericanas em dados* (Santiago, Chile: FLACSO, 1993), 45.

25. Bruschini, 1999, 10.

26. Peggy A. Lovell, "Development and Persistence of Racial Inequality in Brazil: 1950–1991," *Journal of Developing Areas* 33 (spring 1999): 406.

27. Sutherland, 2001, 4.

28. Lovell, "Women and Racial Inequality," 1999, 140.

29. The gender wage gap was reduced from 35 percent to 47 percent of white men's wages for whites from 1960 to 1980, and from 36 percent to 54 percent for Afro-Brazilians. Lovell, "Women and Racial Inequality," 1994, 147.

30. For example, Afro-Brazilian women employed in white-collar occupations averaged Cr$ 3,368 less than white women in 1960; by 1980, this gap had increased to Cr$ 4,747. Lovell, "Women and Racial Inequality," 1999, 143.

31. Lovell, "Development and Persistence of Racial Inequality," 1999, 407.

32. For example: only 9.5 percent of women doctors make the highest category in terms of income (more than 20 minimum wages), versus 14.1 percent of male doctors. Bruschini, 1999, 18–22.

33. Lovell "Development and Persistence of Racial Inequality," 1999, 407.

34. Ibid., 413–14.

35. Data is for 1990. Cristina Bruschini, "O trabalho da mulher brasileira nas décadas recentes," *Estudos feministas* 2, no. 2 (1994), offprint.

36. J. Pitanguy, personal communication.

37. FLACSO, 1993, 58.

38. Centro Feminista de Estudos e Assessoria (CFEMEA) *Guia dos direitos da mulher* (Brasília: CFEMEA, 1994), 27.

39. Carmen D. Deere and Magdalena León, "Institutional Reform of Agriculture Under Neoliberalism," *Latin American Research Review* 36, no. 2 (2001): 31–64.

40. CFEMEA, 1994, 136.

41. Amaury de Souza, "Social Security Excesses Threaten Brazil's Future," *Forum for Applied Research and Public Policy* 12 (1997): 103–4.

42. Ibid.

43. Barbara Weinstein, "Unskilled Worker, Skilled Housewife: Constructing the Working-Class Woman in São Paulo, Brazil, 1900–1950," in *The Gendered Worlds of Latin American Women Workers*, eds. John French and Daniel James (Durham, NC: Duke University Press, 1997).

44. *Veja*, September 5, 2001, http://vejaonline.uol.com.br.

45. Amelia Simpson, *Xuxa: The Mega-marketing of Gender, Race and Modernity in Brazil* (Philadelphia: Temple University Press, 1994).

46. Maria Luisa Nunes, "Images of the Woman of Color in Brazilian Literature: O Cortiço, Clara dos Anjos, Gabriela Cravo e Canela, and O Qinze," in *The Black Woman Cross-Culturally*, ed. Filomena Chioma Steady (Cambridge, MA: Schenkman, 1985), 600.

47. Hahner, 1990, 8.

48. Edna Roland, "Saúde reprodutiva da população negra no Brasil: Entre Malthus e Gobineau," in *Políticas, mercado, etica: Demandas e desafios no campo da Saúde reprodutiva*, eds. Margareth Arilha and Maria Teresa Citeli (São Paulo: Comissão de Cidadania e Reprodução/ Editora 34, 1998).

49. IBGE, 2001.

50. Neuma Aguiar, "Cidadania, concubinato e patriarcado: Relações de gênero e direitos civis," in *Cidadania, justiça e violência*, eds. Dulce Chaves Pandolfi, J. M. de Carvalho, L. P. Carneiro and M. Grynszpan (São Paulo: Fundação Getúlio Vargas, 1999), 194.

51. Ibid., 204.

52. Hahner, 1990, 197.

53. FLACSO 1993, 15.

54. Soares et al., 1995; Dácia Cristina Teles Costa, "Portrait of Afro-Brazilian Craftswomen," paper presented at the 2001 meeting of the Latin American Studies Association, Washington DC, September 6–8.

55. Karen Giffin and Cristina Cavalcanti, "Homens e reprodução," *Revista estudos feministas* 7, no. 1/2 (1999): 53–71

56. Centiro Brasileiro Dean Álise e Planejamento (CEBRAP), *Comportamento sexual no Brasil* (São Paulo: CEBRAP, 1999).

57. Commissão Cidadania e Reprodução, *Boletim olhar sobre a mídia* no. 8 (October 1998): 89.

58. Abong, "Sexualidade na adolescência é tema de série da programas desenvolvidos com consultoria da ECOS," *Abong Informes* 149 (August 2001), www.abong.org.br/informes/informes149.htm.

59. Silvia Pimentel, "O novo código civil representa um avanço significativo na legislação?" *Folha de São Paulo* August 18, 2001, 2.

60. Elza Berquó, "A saúde da mulheres na 'década perdida,' " paper presented at the third National Meeting of the National Feminist Network for Health and Reproductive Rights, Rio de Janeiro, March 30–31, 1995, p. 9.

61. Hahner, 1990, 204.

62. Cadernos do Observatório, "Implementando o Cairo," *O olho no furação* 2 (March 2000): 22.

63. Alan Guttmacher Institute, *Aborto clandestino* (New York: The Institute, 1994).

64. Rede Nacional Feminista de Saúde e direitos Reprodutivos, *Dossiê adolescentes* www.redesaude.org.br/jornal/html/body_au-fecun-didade.html.

65. Health Ministry data cited in ibid.

66. The remainder was 5.5 percent in 1998, according to IBGE, *Pesquisa suplementar saúde da PNAD* (1998). Berquó, 1995, 7.

67. Cadernos do Observatório, 2000, 22.

68. Margareth Arilha, "Política pública de saúde e direitos reproductivos no Brazil," in *Políticas, mercado, ética*, ed. Margareth Arilha and Maria Teresa Citeli (São Paulo: Comissão de Cidadania e Reprodução/Editora 34, 1998), 19.

69. Health Department, cited in Rede Nacional Feminista de Saúde e Direitos Reprodutivos, *Boletim electrónico: Saúde reproductiva na imprensa* (2001), www.redesaude.org.br/html.

70. CRTDST/AIDS-SP (1998), cited in Rede Nacional Feminista de Saúde e Direitos Reprodutivos, *Dossiê mulher e AIDS* (1998), www.redesaude.org.br/html/body_aids.

71. Rede Nacional de Direitos Humanos em HIV/AIDS 1998 cited in Rede Nacional Feminista de Saúde e Direitos Reprodutivos, *Dossiê adolescentes*, www.redesaude.org.br/jornal/html/body-ad-fecundidado.html.

72. Comissã o Naciónal de Populacãoe Desenvolvimento (CNPD) (1997), cited in ibid.

73. Berquó, 1995, 23, 24.

74. Cadernos do Observatório, 2000, 22.

75. Hahner, 1990, 6.

76. Ibid., 204.

77. Pimentel, 2001, 2.

78. CFEMEA, 166.

79. Céli Pinto and Regina Jardim, "NGOs—New Public Spheres? The Presence of Feminist NGOs in Brazilian Politics," paper presented at the 2001 meeting of the Latin American Studies Association, Washington DC, September 6–8.

80. Hahner, 1990, 174.

81. Albert Fishlow, "A Tale of Two Presidents: The Political Economy of Crisis Management," in *Democratizing Brazil: Problems of Transition and Consolidation*, ed. Alfred Stepan (New York: Oxford University Press 1989).

82. Sonia Alvarez, *Engendering Democracy in Brazil* (Princeton, NJ: Princeton University Press, 1990).

83. See ibid., 37–44, for more on the creation, achievements, and limitations of these councils.

84. Cecilia MacDowell Santos, "Gender, the State and Citizenship: Women's Police Stations in São Paulo, Brazil," in *Irrumpiendo en lo público: Seis facetas de las mujeres en América Latina*, eds. Sara Poggio and Montserrat Sagot (San José: Maestría Regional en Estudios de la Mujer: Universidad de Costa Rica, 2000).

85. Matilde Ribeiro, "Mulheras negras brasileiras," *Estudos Feministas* 3, no. 2 (1995): 446–58.

86. The bill is available in English at www.marta.2000.com.br/memoria/mandato/ingles.htm.

87. Ronald M. Schneider, *Brazil: Culture and Politics in a New Industrial Powerhouse* (Boulder, CO: Westview Press, 1996), 187.

88. Maria José Rosado, "A fé no feminino," *Veja* (August–September 1994): 86.

89. Santos, 2000, 83.

90. Ibid., 86.

91. Ibid., 81.

92. Pimentel, 2001, 2.

RESOURCE GUIDE

Suggested Reading

Alvarez, Sonia E. 1990. *Engendering Democracy in Brazil: Women's Movements in Transition Politics*. Princeton, NJ: Princeton University Press. Examines the dynamics and strategies of women's movements in Brazil at the time of the transition from dictatorship to electoral democracy.

Benjamin, Medea, and Maisa Mendonça. 1997. *Benedita da Silva: An Afro-Brazilian Woman's Story of Politics and Love*. Oakland, CA: Food First. A biography of the pioneer black woman politician Benedita da Silva.

Hahner, June. 1990. *Emancipating the Female Sex: The Struggle for Women's Rights in Brazil, 1850–1940*. Durham, NC: Duke University Press. Examines the women's movement in Brazil from its early beginnings in the nineteenth-century to the 1970s.

Lovell, Peggy A. 1999. "Women and Racial Inequality at Work in Brazil." In *Racial Politics in Contemporary Brazil*, edited by Michael Hanchard. Durham, NC: Duke University Press. Focuses on the interplay of gender and racial discrimination in education and in the labor market.

Patai, Daphne. 1988. *Brazilian Women Speak: Contemporary Life Stories*. New Brunswick, NJ: Rutgers University Press. Interviews with Brazilian women from all walks of life, reflecting on everyday life, family ties, discrimination, and the economic difficulties of the 1980s.

Sheper-Hughes, Nancy. 1992. *Death Without Weeping: Everyday Violence in Northeastern Brazil*. Cambridge: Cambridge University Press. A monumental work that will pull you right into the lives of women of the impoverished rural sectors of the Northeast of the country, and the dilemmas they have to face with regard to health, motherhood, and survival.

Simpson, Amelia. 1994. *Xuxa: The Mega-marketing of Gender, Race and Modernity in Brazil*. Philadelphia: Temple University Press. An excellent analysis of the social construction of gender, race, and modernity in Brazil through the thorough study of the phenomenon of the blond, blue-eyed megastar Xuxa.

Soares, Vera, Ana A.A. Costa, Cristina M. Buarque, Denise Dourado Doura, and Wania Sant'Anna. 1995. "Brazilian Feminism and Women's Movements: A Two-Way Street." In *The Challenge of Local Feminisms: Women's Movements in Global Perspective*, edited by Amrita Basu. Boulder, CO: Westview Press. Examines the dynamics between the feminist movement and other actors in the women's movements, including during the period of consolidation of democracy and involvement of substantial segments of the movement in U.N. conferences.

Videos/Films

Black Women of Brazil. 1986. 25 mins. VHS. Directed by Silvana Afram. Distributed by Women Make Movies. A documentary that unravels the myth of racial democracy in Brazil through an upbeat and sensitive examination of how Afro-Brazilian women have dealt with racism, using their music and religion as sources of strength.

"The Hour of the Star" (A hora da estrela). Segment in Helena Solberg and David Meyer, dirs., *Carmen Miranda: Bananas Is My Business*. 1995. 92 mins. VHS. Directed by Susana Amaral. Distributed by Women Make Movies. This feature film explores the media image of Latina women in the United States through the life and career of the Brazilian artist and "Tutti-Frutti Woman" Carmen Miranda.

Ventre Livre. 1995. 45 mins. VHS. Directed by Ana Luisa Azevedo. A documentary that examines the limitations of women's reproductive choices through moving interviews and structural analysis of their health-care situation.

Web Sites and Organizations

Carlos Chagas Foundation (FCC), Gender Studies Center
Carlos Chagas Foundation
Avenida Prof. Francisco Morato, 1565
Caixa Postal 11478
São Paulo 05513
Phone: (11) 3721-4511
Fax: (11) 3721-1059
Web site: www.fcc.org.br. Offers a comprehensive data set on women and work since
  1970, and information on FCC library holdings.

The FCC is a long-time participant in gender studies and feminist research in Brazil.
  Its members have contributed to research on women and work, on women's movements, on reproductive health/rights, and on women and education. The Foundation has a comprehensive library on gender issues in Brazil.

Centro Feminista de Estudos e Assessoria (CFEMEA; Feminist Center for Research
  and Advisory Services)
CFEMEA
SCN Quadra 6, Ed. Venancio 3000 Bl. A Sala 602
CEP 70718-900 Brasília, DF
Phone: (61) 328-1664
Email: cfemea@cfemea.org.br
web site: www.cfemea.org.br

A feminist NGO based in Brasília that closely monitors women's interests in the legislative process and in the political arena. Its web site contains full texts of their
  publications, including their magazine *Femea*. An English folder provides an overview of women's situation in Brazil and a summary of CFEMEA's activities. There
  are also links to a host of other women's organizations, human rights organizations,
  and government institutions of interest. The site also hosts the page of the Articu-
  lação Brasileira de Mulheres (Concerted Action of Brazilian Women), the national
  network of women's groups and federations from the various states.

Conselho Nacional dos Direitos da Mulher (National Council for Women's Rights)
Conselho Nacional dos Direitos da Mulher
Ministério da Justiça, Edifício Sede
Esplanada dos Ministérios, Bloco T, Sala 308
70064-901 Brasília DF
Phone: (61) 429-3150
Fax: (61) 429-9179
Email: cndm@mj.gov.br
Web site: www.mj.gov.br/sedh/cndm

This official government institution is in charge of representing and voicing women's
  needs and interests at the national level. Its website offers a wealth of statistical data
  on various aspects of women's lives, including some racially disaggregated data, as
  well as information on governmental action on violence against women and other
  aspects of sexist discrimination.

Núcleo de Estudos de População/UniCamp (Population Research Center/UniCamp)
Caixa Postal 6166

Av. Albert Einstein, 1300
CEP 13.081-970 Campinas, SP Brasil
Phone: (19) 3788 5890
Fax: (19) 3788 5900
Web site: www.unicamp.br.nepo

A research center focused on population at the University of Campinas, São Pauo, with a strong component on sexuality, family, immigration and reproductive health. Its web site offers numerous publications on these topics, some with abstracts in English. One can also access its library on-line.

Rede Nacional Feminista de Saúde e Direitos Reprodutivos (National Feminist Network for Health and Reproductive Rights)
Secretaria Executiva
Rua Bartolomeu Zunega, 44
Pinheiros
São Paulo 05426-020
Phone: (11) 3813-9767 / 3814-4970
Fax: (11) 3813-8578
Email: redesaude@uol.com.br
Web site: www.redesaude.org.br

The Network, active since the early 1990s, consists of almost 200 autonomous feminist organizations and independent activists and scholars involved in reproductive health and rights issues throughout the country. It engages in advocacy work, organizes campaigns, and promotes collaborative work and exchange among its members. The website offers a wealth of statistical data and analysis organized in files on issues such as women and AIDS, abortion, and young women's health.

SELECTED BIBLIOGRAPHY

Alvarez, Sonia E. *Engendering Democracy in Brazil: Women's Movements in Transition Politics*. Princeton, NJ: Princeton University Press, 1990.

Alvarez, Sonia E. "The (Trans)formation of Feminism(s) and Gender Politics in Democratizing Brazil." In *The Women's Movement in Latin America: Participation and Democracy*, edited by Jane Jaquette. Boulder, CO: Westview Press, 1994.

Benjamin, Medea, and Maisa Mendonça. *Benedita da Silva: An Afro-Brazilian Woman's Story of Politics and Love*. Oakland, CA: Food First, 1997.

Besse, Susan E. *Restructuring Patriarchy: The Modernization of Gender Inequality in Brazil 1914–1940*. Chapel Hill: University of North Carolina Press, 1996.

Briscoe, John. *Brazil: The New Challenge of Adult Health*. Washington, DC: World Bank, 1990.

Bruneau, Thomas C., and W. E. Hewitt. "Catholicism and Political Action in Brazil: Limitations and Prospects." In *Conflict and Competition: The Latin American Church in a Changing Environment*, edited by Edward L. Cleary and H. Stewart-Gambino. Boulder, CO: Lynne Rienner, 1992.

Caldeira Pires do Rio, Teresa. "Women, Daily Life, and Politics." In *Women and Social Change in Latin America*, edited by Elizabeth Jelin. Atlantic Highlands, NJ: Zed Books, 1990.

Cardoso, Ruth Corrêa Leite. "Popular Movements in the Context of the Consolidation of Democracy in Brazil." In *The Making of Social Movements in Latin America: Identity, Strategy and Democracy*, edited by Arturo Escobar and Sonia E. Alvarez. Boulder, CO: Westview Press, 1992.

Deere, Carmen Diana, and Magdalena León. "Institutional Reform of Agriculture Under Neoliberalism: The Impact of the Women's and Indigenous Movements." *Latin American Research Review* 36, no. 2 (2001): 31–64.

Drogus, Carol Ann. "Popular Movements and the Limits of Political Mobilization of the Grassroots in Brazil." In *Conflict and Competition: The Latin American Church in a Changing Environment*, edited by Edward L. Cleary and H. Stewart-Gambino. Boulder, CO: Lynne Rienner, 1992.

Fishlow, Albert. "A Tale of Two Presidents: The Political Economy of Crisis Management." In *Democratizing Brazil: Problems of Transition and Consolidation*, edited by Alfred Stepan. New York: Oxford University Press, 1989.

Hahner, June E. *Emancipating the Female Sex: The Struggle for Women's Rights in Brazil, 1850–1940*. Durham, NC: Duke University Press, 1990.

Hemming, John. *Red Gold: The Conquest of the Brazilian Indians*. Cambridge, MA: Harvard University Press, 1978.

"International Marketing Data and Statistics, 2001." In *Vital Statistics*, table N. 0209. Chicago: Euromonitor International, 2001.

Landes, Ruth. *The City of Women*. Albuquerque: University of New Mexico Press, 1994 (1947).

Lebon, Nathalie. "Professionalization of Women's Health Groups in São Paulo: The Troublesome Road Towards Organizational Diversity." *Organization* 3, no. 4 (1996): 588–609.

Lesser, Jeffrey. *Negotiating National Identity: Immigrants, Minorities, and the Struggle for Ethnicity in Brazil*. Durham, NC: Duke University Press, 1999.

Lovell, Peggy A. "Women and Racial Inequality at Work in Brazil." In *Racial Politics in Contemporary Brazil*, edited by Michael Hanchard. Durham, NC: Duke University Press, 1999.

Lovell, Peggy A. 1999. "Development and Persistence of Racial Inequality in Brazil: 1950–1991." *Journal of Developing Areas* 33 (spring 1999): 395–418.

Lovell, Peggy A. "Gender, Race and the Struggle for Social Justice in Brazil." *Latin American Perspectives* 27 (November 2000): 85–103.

Nelson, Sara. "Constructing and Negotiating Gender in Women's Police Stations in Brazil." *Latin American Perspectives* 23, no. 1 (1996): 131–48.

Nelson, Sara. "Policing Women: Race, Class and Power in the Women's Police Stations in Brazil." Ph.D. diss. University of Washington, 1997.

Nunes, Maria Luisa. "Images of the Woman of Color in Brazilian Literature: O Cortiço, Clara dos Anjos, Gabriela Cravo e Canela, and O Qinze." In *The Black Woman Cross-Culturally*, edited by Filomena Chioma Steady. Cambridge, MA: Schenkman, 1985.

Pan American Health Organization (PAHO). *Basic Country Health Profiles*, summaries 1999. www.paho.org/English/SHA/prflbra.htm, 8/10/01.

Pinto, Céli Regina Jardim. "NGOs—New Public Spheres? The Presence of Feminist NGOs in Brazilian Politics." Paper presented at the 2001 meeting of the Latin American Studies Association, Washington DC, September 6–8, 2001.

Ramos, Alcida Rita. *Indigenism: Ethnic Politics in Brazil*. Madison: University of Wisconsin Press, 1998.

Santos, Cecilia MacDowell. "Gender, the State and Citizenship: Women's Police Stations in São Paulo, Brazil." In *Irrumpiendo en lo público: Seis facetas de las mujeres en América Latina*, edited by Sara Poggio and Montserrat Sagot. San José: Maestría Regional en Estudios de la Mujer: Universidad de Costa Rica, 2000.

Schmink, Marianne. "Women in Brazilian Abertura politics." *Signs* 7, no. 1 (1981): 115–34.

Schneider, Ronald M. *Brazil: Culture and Politics in a New Industrial Powerhouse*. Boulder, CO: Westview Press, 1996.

Sheriff, Robin. "Death in Shantytowns: Gang and Police Violence in Rio de Janeiro." Paper presented at the XXII International Congress of the Latin American Studies Association, Miami, March 16–18, 2000.

Simpson, Amelia. *Xuxa: The Mega-marketing of Gender, Race and Modernity in Brazil*. Philadelphia: Temple University Press, 1994.

Souza, Amaury de. "Social Security Excesses Threaten Brazil's Future." *Forum for Applied Research and Public Policy* 12 (1997): 103–7.

Sutherland, Jeannette. "Economic Development Versus Social Exclusion: The Cost of Development in Brazil." Paper presented at the 2001 meeting of the Latin American Studies Association, Washington, DC, September 6–8, 2001.

Teles Costa, Dácia Cristina. "Portrait of Afro-Brazilian Craftswomen." Paper presented at the 2001 meeting of the Latin American Studies Association, September 6–8. Washington, DC, September 6–8, 2001.

UNESCO. *UNESCO Statistical Yearbook*. Paris: UNESCO, 1999.

Weinstein, Barbara. "Unskilled Worker, Skilled Housewife: Constructing the Working-Class Woman in São Paulo, Brazil, 1900–1950." In *The Gendered Worlds of Latin American Women Workers*, edited by John French and Daniel James. Durham, NC: Duke University Press, 1997.

White, Renée T. "AIDS and the Sexual Surveillance of Black Women." Paper presented at the 2000 meeting of the Latin American Studies Association. Miami, March 16–18, 2000.

Spanish and Portuguese Bibliography

Abdon Cury, Christiane, and Sueli Carneiro. "O poder feminine no culto aos Orixás." In *Mulher Negra*, edited by Sueli Carneiro and Thereza Suelie Santos. Sao Paulo: Nobel Conselho Esta Dualda Condicão Feminina, 1985. Mîmeo.

Abong. "Sexualidade na adolescência é tema de série da programas desenvolvidos com consultoria da ECOS." *Abong informes* 149 (August 2001) www.abong.org.br/informes/informes149.htm.

Aguiar, Neuma. "Cidadania, concubinato e patriarcado: Relaçõe s de gênero e direitos civis." In *Cidadania, justiça e violência*, edited by Dulce Chaves Pandolfi, J. M. de Carvalho, L. P. Carneiro, and M. Grynszpan. São Paulo: Fundação Getúlio Vargas, 1999.

Alan Guttmacher Institute. *Aborto clandestino: Una realidad latinoamericana*. New York: Alan Guttmacher Institute, 1994.

Arilha, Margareth. "Política públicas de saúde e direitos reprodutivos no Brasil: Um olhar para o futuro." In *Pólíticas, mercado, ética: Demandas e Desafios no campo da saúde reprodutiva*, edited by Maragareth Arilha and Maria Teresa Citeli. São Paulo: Comissão de Cidadania e Reprodução/Editora 34, 1998.

Berquó, Elza. "A saúde das mulheres na 'década perdida.' " Paper presented at the third National Meeting of the National Feminist Network for Health and Reproductive Rights, Rio de Janeiro, March 30–31, 1995.

Bruschini, Cristina. "O trabalho da mulher brasileira nas décadas recentes." *Estudos Feministas* 2, no. 2 (1994). Offprint.

Bruschini, Cristina. "Médicas, arquitetas, advogadas e engenheiras: Mulheres em carreiras profissionais de prestígio." *Estudos Feministas* 7, no. 1–2 (1999): 9–24.

Cadernos do Observatório. "Implementando o Cairo." *O olho no furação* 2 (March 2000).

(CEBRAP). *Comportamento sexual no Brasil*. São Paulo: CEBRAP, 1999.

Centro Feminista de Estudos e Assessoria (CFEMEA). *Guia dos direitos da mulher*. Brasília: CFEMEA, 1994.

CFEMEA. "Política de presença e política de idéias." In *A política de cotas por sexo*. 1999. Downloaded from www.cfemea.org.

Comissão Cidadania e Reprodução *Boletim olhar sobre a mídia* no. 8 (October 1998).

Costa, Ana Alice Alcantara, ed. *Creche comunitaria: Uma alternativa popular*. Salvador: EGBA. 1991.

Da Cunha, Estela, and Maria García de Pinto. "Mortalidade infantil e raça: As diferenças da desigualdade." *Jornal da RedeSaúde* no. 23 (March 2001): 48–50.

Facultdad Latinoamericana de Ciencias Sociales (FLACSO). *Mulheres latinoamericanas em dados*. Santiago, Chile: FLACSO, 1993.

Giffin, Karen, and Cristina Cavalcanti. "Homens e reprodução." *Revista estudos feministas* 7, no. 2 (1999):53–71.

Gilliam, Angela, and Onik'a Gilliam. "Raça Brasil: Por quem, para quem." In *Gêneros trópicos: Leituras a partir do Brasil*. Campinas: Nucleo de Estudos de Gênero, PAGU/UNICAMP, 2001.

Gohn, Maria da Glória Marcondes. *A força da periferia: A luta das mulheres por creches em São Paulo*. Petrópolis: Vozes, 1985.

(IBGE). *Pesquisa nacional por amostra de domicilios*. Rio de Janeiro: IBGE, 1997.

Oliveira, Marta de. "Sobre a saúde da população negra brasileira." *Perspectivas* 4 (2001): 8–11.

Pimentel, Silvia. "O novo código civil representa um avanço significativo na legislação?" *Folha de São Paulo*, August 18, 2001, 2.

Rede Nacional Feminista de Saúde e Direitos Reprodutivos. *Boletim eletrónico: Saúde reproductive na impresnsa*. April 16–30, 2001. www.redesaude.org.br/html/body _ed-abro1-2.html.

Rede Nacional Feminista de Saúde e Direitos Reprodutivos. *Dossiê adolescentes—Fecundidade das adolescentes*. 2001. www.redesaude.org.br/jornal/html/body_ad-fecundidade.html.

Rede Nacional Feminista de Saúde e Direitos Reprodutivos. *Dossiê mulher e AIDS*. 2001. www.redesaude.org.br/html/body_aids.

Ribeiro, Matilde. "Mulheres negras brasileiras: De Bertioga a Beijing." *Estudos feministas* 3, no. 2 (1995): 446–58.

Rodrigues, Almira. *Construindo a perspectiva de gênero na legislação e nas políticas públicas*. 2001. www.cfemea.org.br/temasedados/politica/perspectivadegenero.htm.

Roland, Edna. "Saúde reprodutiva da população negra no Brasil: Entre malthus e Gobineau." In *Políticas, mercado, ética: Demandas e desafios no campo da saúde reprodutiva*, edited by Margareth Arilha and Maria Teresa Citeli. São Paulo: Comissão de Cidadania e Reprodução/ Editora 34, 1998.

Roland, Edna and Sueli Carneiro. "A saúde da mulher no Brasil: A perspectiva da mulher negra." *Revista de cultura vozes* 80, no. 2 (1990): 205–10.

Rosado, Maria José. "A fé no feminino." *Veja* (August–September 1994): 86.

Schumaher, Maria Aparecida, and Elisabeth Vargas. "Lugar no governo: Alibi ou conquista?" *Estudos feministas* 2 (1993): 348–64.

Soares, Vera. "Feminismo e ONGs." In *O impacto social do trabalho das ONGs no Brasil*, edited by Auriléa Abelem et al. São Paulo: Abong, 1998.

Souza, Anna Maria Nunes de. *Creche domiciliar: Solução espontânea*. Rio de Janeiro: Amais, 1994.

5

CHILE

Alvaro Vergara-Mery

PROFILE OF CHILE

Chile is in southern South America between the Andes and the Pacific Ocean. It has 6,435 km (3,681 mi.) of coastline (although the widest point is only 240 km/144 mi.) and an area of 756,946 km² (292,257 sq. mi., approximately twice the size of Montana), which includes Easter Island, and Juan Fernández and Sala y Gómez islands. From north to south the Andes form the natural border with Argentina (5,150 km/ 3,090 mi.) and Bolivia (861 km/516 mi.) to the east; Peru is to the north, and the Pacific Ocean to the west. Between the ocean and the mountains the great Central Valley extends for approximately 1,500 km (900 miles) from La Serena southward to Puerto Montt, the southern extreme of Chile's famous lake region. In the north of the country, from the border with Peru, the Atacama Desert extends its domain 1,660 km (996 mi.) to the south, and is known as the driest place on Earth. Further south, beyond the Central Valley, between the cities of Concepción and Puerto Montt, there are abundant forests, lakes, and rivers. At the southern tip of Chile's mainland and after passing through fjords, glaciers, and islands, is the southernmost city in the world: Punta Arenas. South of this city lie the Strait of Magellan and Tierra del Fuego, territory divided between Chile and Argentina, and the southernmost point of South America, Cape Horn, a 424 m (1,390 ft.) rock on Horn Island, which belongs to Chile.

Chile's population totals 15,211,300, of whom approximately 50.6 percent are women. The country's ethnicity breakdown is approximately 66 percent mestizo (mixed

Amerindian and European), 25 percent European, 7 percent Amerindian, and 2 percent other.[1] Chile is not as ethnically diverse as most other Latin American countries.[2] The official language is Spanish. The primary indigenous languages spoken are Quechua, Aymara, and Mapudungo (Mapuche).

The average annual population growth has been steady since the 1970s: 1.13 percent; the percentage of population under 18 years old was 33.5 in 1996.[3] A total of 84 percent of the population lives in urban areas, and 66 percent of the people are between 15 and 64 years of age. Santiago, the capital, and its metropolitan area have a total population of around 5.1 million. Other major cities include the twin cities of Valparaíso and Viña del Mar, Concepción, and the La Serena-Coquimbo twin cities area.

In 2001, Chile ranked 39 out of 162 countries on the Human Development Index (HDI), which measures the average quality of life. (The number 1 spot was held by Norway.) In Latin America, Chile ranked third after Argentina and Uruguay. In 1998, life expectancy was 78 years for women, and 72 years for men (one of the highest in the Americas).[4] In the same year, the infant mortality rate was 10.3 per 1,000 live births; 55 out of 10,000 women died after a live birth; and 14 out of 10,000 died after having an abortion (still illegal in Chile). Also in 1998, the percentage of women who had professionally attended births set the Latin American record of 99.7 percent.[5] In the same year, UNICEF ranked Chile number 148 (out of 189, and second only to Cuba, in Latin America) in the mortality rate for children younger than age five. In 2001, Chilean women had an average of 2.1 children, compared to 5.3 in 1960.[6]

The percentage of malnourished children declined to 1 percent in 1995. Chile has 110 doctors per 100,000 people (Norway has 416; the United States, 279). The nation's health expenditure is about 4.7 percent of the GDP (U.S.$74.3 billion in 1998). The economic growth was 7.6 percent in 1997, with 19 percent of the working population employed in agriculture, 25 percent in industry, and 56 percent in service industries.

In 1997, 15 percent of the population was living on less than $1.00 a day and in 1996, 20 percent of households (30 percent of Mapuche households) were living under the poverty line.[7] At the same time, however, the income of the richest 10 percent of the population increased 83 percent, which highlights the economic inequalities in Chile (the second worst in Latin America after Brazil).

Only about 5 percent of land in Chile is devoted to agriculture. Nevertheless, Chile is one of the largest exporters of fruit in the world and is noted for its wines. Salmon, copper, and iodine are other major exports. Chile had a U.S.$31 billion foreign debt as of 1998.[8]

Chile is a presidential republic. The president serves a six-year term and is not eligible for reelection. The legislative branch consists of a Senado (Senate) and a Cámara de Diputados (Chamber of Deputies). The judicial branch is headed by the Supreme Court.

Since the 1960s Chile, once known as a model for democracy, has undergone significant political, economic, and military changes. The government of Salvador Allende was overthrown in a coup d'état on September 11, 1973. General Augusto Pinochet Ugarte assumed the office of the president and embarked on a right-wing dictatorship that was finally defeated with the election of Patricio Aylwin Azócar in December 1989. The election of 1993 reassured Chile's return to a democracy when Eduardo Frei Ruiz-Tagle won the presidency. In a closely contested presidential election in 2000, Ricardo Lagos Escobar obtained 51 percent of the vote and assumed the presidency on March 11.

In October 1998, Augusto Pinochet was arrested in London. A long process of extradition hearings began and continued through 1999 while Pinochet remained under arrest. In March 1999, the National Organization of Former Detainees and Political Prisoners filed charges against Pinochet and others who were responsible for torture, kidnapping, illegal detention, rape, and robbery during the dictatorship. On July 1, 2002, the Second Chamber of the Chilean Supreme Court of Justice dismissed the case against him, stating that his mental problems made him mentally unfit to stand trial.

The armed forces in Chile consist of the Army, the Navy (including the Coast Guard), the Air Force, and the Carabineros (National Police). In 1996, military expenditure was 3.5 percent of GDP, equivalent to 68 percent of combined government expenditure on education and health.[9] In 1999, the expenditure reached U.S.$2.5 million. With the return of democracy, the public image of the armed forces is slowly being restored. New legislation includes sentences of up to ten years in prison for the crime of torture (previously unpunished).

OVERVIEW OF WOMEN'S ISSUES

With the return of democracy and the opening of new international markets, Chile's economy and development have flourished significantly, thus launching new possibilities for change. These changes have been directed to and by the upper class, who have always held the economic and political power in Chile. The changes have had both positive and negative effects on the status and experiences of women. With the new economic development and the internationalization of the country, doors have finally opened for women to begin accessing the all-male and homosocial economic world. Women are starting to run their own businesses and participate in the government administration. However, the majority of them either belong to the upper class or have the social and family support necessary to succeed, leaving women of other social classes exposed to unemployment, poverty, and abuse. Despite all of this new potential for women, Chilean society remains haunted by behaviors and traditions that force a high degree of sex segregation and discrimination, with a great number of women in fields that have lower pay and low social importance.

EDUCATION

In 1996, the Educational Reform went into effect in order to qualitatively improve all levels of instruction. Programs that emphasize learning rather than memorizing and learning-in-context; that teach students how to use information and practice long-term preparation; and that offer competency-oriented programs and training for a productive workforce were some of the new goals. The main purpose was to adapt the curriculum to the particular needs of each community and of the new millennium. Preference was directed to the poor sectors; the use of technology was implemented at all levels, and better resources were allotted to improve the system. School hours were raised from 800 to 1,200 hours annually. Teachers and instructors had more resources and opportunities to enhance their teaching methods. Seminars, training, and professional development became priorities.

The Educational Reform (for public schools) started in the 1990s when municipalities took the role of administering education. The process has been gradual, and now most of the schools are in the hands of municipalities or districts. It is viewed as a way for Chile to create a new image and re-emerge as a democratic, economically stable, and developing country. The reform seeks social justice, public utility, integration, and social and family participation through education and is especially aimed at women. Education must be integral and conducive to improving the quality of life, especially in the poorest sectors.

Statistics provided by the Ministry of Education for the year 2000 show that of 452,347 students accepted into institutions of higher education in Chile, 47.2 percent were women; however, they are not equally represented in all fields. In 1999, of the 34,267 higher education graduates, 50.06 percent were women. Of that 50.06 percent, the greatest number was in social sciences (22.55 percent), followed by education (17.34 percent) and administration and commerce (15.62 percent). In the area of technology, commercial engineering was the most popular career for females in 1999.

Adult literacy reached 95.5 percent in the 1990s, a testament to the success of the Educational Reform.

EMPLOYMENT AND ECONOMICS

Job/Career Opportunities

Chile is a highly urbanized country; approximately 80 percent of the population resides in urban areas. A large portion resides in the Santiago Metropolitan Region. As the result of a low rate of population growth (1.13

percent), Chile's working-age groups form approximately 65 percent of the total population. The rate of unemployment has declined steadily throughout the last decade. The rate of growth in employment has historically been 5 percent. The most dynamic sectors have been construction and industry. By late 1993, the unemployment rate had plunged to 4.9 percent, significantly lower than the rest of Latin America. Interestingly, this drastic reduction in unemployment took place at the same time real

Woman sits by her fruit stall in Los Lagos. Photo © TRIP/R. Belbin.

wages increased significantly. Regional economic upheaval, world economic crises, and the economic collapse of neighboring Argentina in July 2001 raised unemployment to 9.7 percent for the period July–August 2001.[10]

Since 1952 male labor force participation has declined in comparison with female participation. Between 1960 and 1982, women's participation in the workforce was relatively stable, fluctuating between 20.9 and 26.5 percent. At the end of 1984, women represented 30.7 percent of the total Chilean workforce. By mid-1985, their participation increased to 34.6 percent.[11] This occurred in spite of the barriers to formal education and technical training they have experienced for years.

Rural-to-urban migration, characteristic of Latin America particularly during the 1950s and 1960s, has impacted the participation of women in the urban labor market. The number of young women coming to the city to look for work, especially to Santiago, has increased dramatically. But not only young, single women from the provinces are employed in the cities; the number of married women increased 25 percent from 1960 to 1982.[12] The lower real wages and general unemployment have forced poorer married women to work while the better-off women have remained deterred from entering the workforce. Most upper-class women in Chile do not work.

During the Pinochet era, the involvement of women in formal economic activity increased, and steadily continued even after his administration. Projects like the Programa de Empleo Mínimo (PEM/Minimum Employment Program) and, later, Programa de Ocupación para Jefes de Hogar (POJH/Occupational Program for Heads of Household) showed that more than half of the workers were women. The focus of these initiatives was that all the working-age members of a family had to be employed so all of them could survive. In order to generate income, these workers had to give up their leisure time. Housewives were the most affected, since the activities and chores they have to do at home are very time-consuming and therefore compete with the allocation of time to paid work outside the home. Cultural norms in Chile assign household responsibilities such as child care, household maintenance, and food production to women; the participation of women in the labor force places more stress on them.

Management positions have been traditionally restricted to men in Chile. Only a handful of women manage big companies or sit on boards of directors of social organizations, labor organizations, and students' federations. Women account for less than 10 percent of the members of boards of directors of businesses in Chile. Women are in charge of only 6.6 percent of businesses, and in the federation of the University of Chile, women make up only 15.6 percent of student representatives.[13] Men make up approximately 70 percent of the labor force while women fight for 30 percent. Unemployment among women is persistently higher than that of men, and employed women work under more precarious conditions than men.

Pay

In terms of salary, everyone is equal before the law and arbitrary discrimination is banned, although among the priorities proposed by the current government regarding women, one is to reduce the pay gap between men and women. In 1998, according to the National Statistics Office (INE), the average monthly salary for a woman was 207,895 Chilean pesos (approx. U.S.$420). The average monthly salary for a man was 305,045 Chilean pesos (approx. U.S.$610). On average, according to National Women's Service (SERNAM) Minister Adriana Delpiano, women earn 70.3 percent of what men make—a sum greater than figures provided by other sources. The INE, for instance, cites women's income as 65.4 percent of the income earned by men in similar or equivalent jobs.[14]

Working Conditions

Sexual Harassment

Sexual harassment in the workplace is still a "we-do-not-talk-about-it" issue in Chile. According to Gustavo González, "The majority of the parliamentary commission in Chile refused to classify sexual harassment as a crime, arguing that it was too difficult to define and to prove."[15] Despite the protests of women's organizations and unions, the mixed commission of senators and representatives voted against the draft law. However there is a pending bill that, if passed, will criminalize and punish sexual harassment. This second law is sponsored by the Servicio Nacional de la Mujer (SERNAM; National Women's Service) and by the CUT, the country's leading union confederation, and identifies men as well as women as possible victims of sexual harassment. The law is seen as the only legal tool to protect women from pressure and abuse by male superiors in the workplace. It will be the only device to measure and address the issue of sexual harassment.

Until now, sexual harassment has been regarded as nonexistent by the all-male Chilean judicial system. Although few cases are reported, the secretary-general of Central Unitaria de Trabajadores (CUT; Central United Workers Organization) has stated that sexual harassment constitutes a serious labor problem. This phenomenon is more pervasive in textile factories and fruit harvesting and packing centers, where the number of women employed is high and unsafe conditions exist.[16] Cases of psychological and physical pressure for sexual favors in high schools, universities, hospitals, private companies, banks, and all public spaces have been brought to authorities. However, since most of the accusations are against private institutions, no action is taken. Although Chile has administrative statutes to punish such conduct in ministries and other state bodies, "in the legal sphere, harassment can be considered a form of perversion of the course of justice or a misdemeanor."[17]

Support for Mothers/Caretakers

Maternal Leave

Women in Chile are entitled to maternity leave for a period of 6 weeks prior to and 12 weeks following the birth of a child. The employer (or the government) pays their salary during that time, and they may not be laid off between conception and a year after the end of postnatal leave. They are authorized to leave work to breast-feed and, until the child is one year of age, when he or she is ill. The latter privilege may be given to the father as well.

Daycare

In order to mix children and work, women have to find preschools or daycare facilities. In the upper- and middle-class areas, these facilities and programs are widely established and available; in some women take their children to daycare facilities located where they work. The cost may be assumed by the employer, or there may be a copayment to access the facilities. Some families hire a female servant to take care of the children at home. For lower-income families or single mothers, the extended family provides childcare; other children provide the care; or (in extreme cases) the child is left on the streets during work hours. In the last years the influx of Peruvian and Bolivian women looking for better possibilities in Chile has inundated the market and even lower middle class families have the luxury of a Peruvian or Bolivian maid to help in the household.

Inheritance and Property Rights

According to Chilean law, in terms of the marital partnership it is still the man who administers all joint property. Article 1749 of the Chilean Civil Code reads: "The marital partnership is to be headed by the husband, who shall administer the spouses' joint property as well as the property owned by his wife, subject to the obligations and limitations set forth in this Section and those agreed to at the time of marriage." This issue became a major problem for marriages in Chile, and the prenuptial agreement (*separación de bienes*) option was (and still is) extremely popular because it allows each member of the couple to administer his/her own wealth acquired before the wedding, especially inherited property (always the independent and exclusive property of the beneficiary). On May 16, 1999, the Chilean Congress approved an amendment to the Constitution that made women equal to men before the law in all aspects.

Social/Government Programs

In May 1981 Chile replaced its government-run retirement system with a privatized investment-based system of individual retirement accounts. A retirement system is now in place that ensures workers' property rights in pension contributions and offers investment incentives. Today, more than 95 percent of Chilean workers have pension savings accounts. Workers now retire with more money and more secure pensions. By most accounts, the Chilean privatization has been a great success. Chile's GDP has been growing at nearly 7 percent annually, and Chilean workers earn an average of 12 percent on their pension investments annually. The savings rate in Chile is now 27 percent of GDP. However, women retire ten years earlier: the mandatory retirement age for women is 55, while it is 65 for men.

FAMILY AND SEXUALITY

Gender Roles

Most Chilean women are both mothers and workers, and the role they play in their families is considered crucial. Most of their partners or husbands do not acknowledge their work at home as "work," and consider it a normal chore. In many households the father is absent (almost one in four families is headed by a single mother), and women have to make all decisions and raise their children alone. Even though men are still considered the head of the house, in reality Chilean society is matriarchal. Employed women in Chile typically work an eight-to-ten-hour shift. Chilean law establishes a workday of a minimum of eight hours and it should not exceed 48 hours per week. If a worker exceeds the stipulated working hours, the employer should pay overtime, which is double the normal amount. However, when major economic events occur—as in September 2000, when the unemployment rate reached 14.4 percent from the Asian market debacle that affected markets and economic growth all over the world—the law is "adapted" to the current reality. If overtime pay is beyond the financial means of the employer, the situation for the worker (especially women) becomes "take it or leave it."

Traditional gender roles in Chile have been redefined as women have gained more access to education and the labor force. After the crisis of 1981–1984, the public view of women in Chile changed as many people understood the greater benefits for women to work outside the home. As the Pinochet dictatorship fell and democracy began to reappear, it became more acceptable for women to work outside the home. Men also became more willing to participate in the housework. However, these advances have done little to erase the notion that women reach full self-realization through motherhood and housework, a belief that pressures women into the traditional roles of mother and housewife.

Marriage

Marriage in Chile is decreasing. The number of marriages dropped dramatically between 1998 and 2002 and the number of annulments (divorce does not exist) increased. In 1998, out of 1000 marriages, 85 were annulled within the first year.[18] The drop in marriage is explained partly by the fact that women are pursuing education, achieving other goals before motherhood and family, and because Chilean society is moving toward acceptance of relationships that do not require marriage. In 1980, for example, the average age at women married was 23.8 years; in 1998 it was 26.3 years. The average years of marriage in Chile is 12 (versus 7 in the United States). In Chile today, only 50 percent of women of marriageable age are married (54 percent of men). This is because of the large number of people living together without being married (*convivir*). In 1980, 43 percent of all mothers were single mothers (compared to 17.5 percent in 1965). In 1998 the figure was 77.1 percent, the most significant number being mothers in the age group 15–19. Due to the high number of children born out of wedlock, Chile had to pass a law to end discrimination against illegitimate children. In October 1999, after studies indicated that over 40 percent of children were illegitimate, the new law (No. 19620) went into effect, and now all children have the same rights before the law regardless of their parents' marital status or their adoption status.[19]

Sexuality

In Chile, marriage is disconnected from sex. It is fairly common for teens to engage in sexual activity at age 14 or 15; young people (a majority of them raised Catholic) do not necessarily believe that they must be married in order to have sex. Premarital sex is broadly accepted, except among practicing Protestants, only 40 percent of whom approve, and among those age 59 and older, only 39 percent of whom approve. A noteworthy 63 percent of practicing Catholics in Chile openly accept premarital sex, despite the strong disapproval of the church hierarchy.[20] It is estimated by popular opinion that 60 percent of married men and 50 percent of married women will have one or more lovers while married.

Reproduction

Sex Education

The significant number of illegal abortions in Chile (one for every four pregnancies) moved different groups to promote and to provide youths with sex education. In 1996, the Catholic Bishop Carlos González, publicly supported the sex education program known as JOCAS (Jornadas de Conversación sobre Afecto y Sexualidad/Conversational Sessions About Affection and Sexuality).[21] Immediately, right-wing criticism arose against both the bishop and the government's controversial sex education program. González was the only Catholic Church official to support the program, which was a means of facilitating the discussion of sexual issues among parents, educators, and high school students (especially females). The main objective was to avert some of the 40,000 annual unwanted teenage pregnancies, an estimated 150,000-plus illegal abortions, and the increasing spread of AIDS. The program was structured by a collaborative effort between the ministries of Education and Health, the National Women's Service, and the National Youth Institute. The most vocal critics of the program were Jorge Medina Estévez (another Catholic bishop), the right-wing Renovación Nacional (RN) Party, the Federation of Private Educational Institutions (FIDE), and the conservative daily *El Mercurio*.

Among the defenders, Minister of Education Sergio Molina argued that the government wanted to establish a state policy on sexuality by providing a space for youths to voice their doubts and concerns about sexuality with the guidance of educators and parents. "It's not just a question of avoiding the negative consequences of a disordered sex life. It's a question of emancipating our bodies, which is a part of Christ and the temple of the Holy Spirit," concluded Molina.[22] In *La Época*'s September 26, 1996 edition, President Eduardo Frei Ruiz-Tagle offered his unequivocal support to the Ministry of Education's sexual education program and added that JOCAS was a voluntary, three-phase program for high schools. Frei concluded that morality could not be attained without dialogue and information.

JOCAS and other initiatives headed by the government could have served young women in Chile by teaching them the value of their body and the respect it deserves as well as by educating them in what to do in the case of pregnancy. Another possibility that Chile offers is continuing in school. Chile and Brazil are the only two countries in Latin America that have generated mechanisms to enable young women in this situation to continue their studies.[23] While the schools are trying to implement sex education, the Senate is still debating an abortion law as well as a divorce law that could overhaul the existing and easy-to-obtain annulment process.

Contraception and Reproductive Health

In Chile, the government does not offer easy access to sexual and reproductive health services, especially to poor people. The Asociación Chilena de Protección de la Familia (APROFA; Chilean Association for Family Protection) is the largest nongovernmental organization (NGO) to provide sexual and reproductive health services by promoting sexual and reproductive rights, and by offering a variety of services to a broad audience, including poor women, adolescents, secondary school teachers, and health professionals. According to APROFA, Chile (where the percent of adults infected with HIV is 0.2 percent in a male-female ratio of 4.43 to 1) had a total demand for contraception of 67 percent of women in a relationship in 2000.

The acceptance of premarital relations also fosters the use of birth control. According to *Chile: A Country Study*, an impressive 81 percent of practicing Chilean Catholics accept some method of birth control.[24] National health programs have facilitated access to birth control since the 1960s, and the use of contraceptives is widespread.

Yet a double standard exists. On August 30, 2001, the Chilean Supreme Court, in a vote of 3 to 2, declared the French "morning-after pill" illegal. The reason given was that the use of the pill would equal abortion. The very same day, the Minister of Health (to exercise his power in the public space) approved a similar German drug. In Chile, it seems that it is more important to determine who gets to direct the health policies (public space) than the benefits of the inception of a pill that will give women opportunities and access to control their private space.

Abortion

With a Civil Code dating from 1855, a Penal Code dating from 1873 (despite some significant amendments through the years), and the double standard characteristic of Chilean society, women have never had the legal right to an abortion. Pinochet passed the antiabortion law shortly before he left office (abortion had been permitted in extreme and restricted cases), and even today, with the return to a democratic government, this law has not been repealed. Chile has one of the highest rates of abortion in Latin America: "each year, almost one woman in every 20 (age 15–49) has an induced abortion. In Chile there are close to six abortions for every ten births."[25] Statistics for 1990 revealed that of the 451,800 pregnancies in Chile that year, 35 percent ended in induced abortions. Also in that year, 31,930 women were hospitalized after undergoing unsafe abortions.[26] In Chile, women are familiar with teas and infusions made from herbs and other plant products that are believed to induce abortion. In a speech before a special session of the General Assembly of the United Nations in June 2000, SERNAM Minister Adriana Delpiano reiterated "Chile's full commitment to life and its opposition to abortion," thus maintaining the precarious situation for women regarding this issue.[27]

Teen Pregnancy

Most of the programs for pregnancy prevention are aimed at women who have already had at least one child and/or can afford contraceptives. Birth control, although readily available in all pharmacies without a prescription, is therefore more difficult to obtain for younger and poorer women. Thus first pregnancies out of wedlock as well as first marriages of pregnant brides are frequent. These events reflect the double standard of Chilean society, which acts one way in public, to satisfy social needs, but in a totally different way in private.

HEALTH

Health Care Access

All Chileans have access to the public health care system offered through the Ministry of Health, the National Health Care Fund (Fondo Nacional de Salud; FONASA), and municipalities. The system is supported through Social Security taxes collected from all working citizens. Chileans with little or no income can get free treatment at public hospitals. Chileans who can afford private clinics pay up front for access to some of the finest medical facilities. Modern equipment and well-qualified medical professionals are generally available at private as well as public hospitals. In 1981, Chile created the Institución de Salud Previsional (ISAPRE; Preventive Health Agency) law, by which every employed person automatically receives health insurance from his or her employer through any privately owned ISAPRE and access to a high-quality medical system of doctors, equipment, clinics, and hospitals. Approximately 10 percent of the gross income of the worker is destined to health insurance.

Diseases and Disorders

According to the National Statistics Office, diseases of the circulatory and cardiovascular systems are the primary cause of death (30 percent) for women in Chile. Cancer constitutes the second greatest cause of death for women in Chile. In 1999, 1,024 women died of stomach cancer, 973 died of breast cancer, and 904 of tumors of the gall bladder. Although access to medical care is readily available, most of women wait until the very last moment to seek medical attention.

AIDS

In 1999, an estimated 0.2 percent of the Chilean population was infected with AIDS. As of August 1998, 2,431 cases have been reported. According to the Ministry of Health's National AIDS Commission, AIDS is becoming more and more widespread in the male population, especially in the greater Santiago area. Currently, there are 8,000 reported cases of AIDS in Chile, with estimates that 30,000 citizens are HIV-infected.[28] According to *El Mercurio*, in 2000 the number of people living with AIDS was 15,000.[29] In reports released by SERNAM and INE, the number of Chilean women living with AIDS in 2000 was 13 times higher than the 1990 figure. The lower income groups and the youth have been significantly harder hit.

In a society that does not discuss sexuality, and where the AIDS epidemic has been feminized ("it happens to women and homosexuals only"), it has been hard to implement social and medical campaigns. The situation is aggravated by the infrequent use of condoms (in a society where "real" men don't wear them), by the lack of communication between men and women, by the ever-present machismo, and by the influence of the Catholic Church, which has traditionally opposed contraception of any kind. In addition, rural areas are feeling more of the AIDS impact due to poorer people moving to urban settings in search of opportunities and then returning; the lack of proper sexual protection; fear; and, above all, ignorance. Of the women infected with HIV, nearly half are housewives (infected by their husbands) and 13 percent are prostitutes.[30]

Eating Disorders

As of 2000, approximately 70,000 women between 14 and 30 years of age suffered from anorexia nervosa and 350,000 from bulimia.[31] In 1999 the Neuro-Psychiatric Center in Santiago established a program to monitor eating disorders. A year later the center was overwhelmed by patients (mostly young women) seeking assistance. Most cases occur in women between ages 12 and 30, and present a significant public health problem. Many are high school students who eat only yogurt and apples, and drink water, to be accepted.[32] The cases were so numerous that in some schools, restrooms had to be guarded during break hours because of the number of girls with bulimia who were rushing to vomit.

Mental Health

Despite efforts to create the Unidad de Salud Mental (Mental Health Unit), the number of cases has more than doubled.[33] In 1993, 70,000 people sought help while 250,000 did the same in 1997. The majority of those were women. Most patients are older women with low educational and economic levels who exhibit various psychiatric problems. Depression, general anxiety, nervous breakdown, and alcohol abuse are the most frequent disorders. In 1994, the suicide rate for women was 1.4 percent.[34]

POLITICS AND LAW

Women in Chile are striving for change through education and participation in politics and social issues. The new role of women in Chilean public life challenges a society that is adjusting to global changes. Politics and political parties are beginning to reemerge and men are taking up the traditional roles again. The challenge for women in modern Chile is to steadily push the male paradigms forward while continuing their progress to become part of the political, economic, cultural, and social areas.

Suffrage

Chilean women's political representation and public activity is not yet fully developed. Although the electoral law stated literacy as the only requirement, the Civil Code provided that women "cannot exercise civil rights." In 1945, Amanda Labarca, representing the Federación Chilena de Instituciones Femeninas (Chilean Federation of Women's Institutions), insisted that Congress pass a suffrage bill. Since 19.8 percent of the votes in the municipal election of 1947 were cast by women,[35] men recognized the potential in women's votes. Amid anticlerical divisions and conflicts between political parties, the Senate unanimously approved a women's suffrage in January 1949, giving women the right to vote in general presidential elections. Chilean women voted in parliamentary elections for the first time in 1951. They obtained 7 percent of the seats in Parliament in the elections of 1965, 1973, and 1994.

Political Participation

Chilean women entered the political arena through charitable activities. In 1931, Adela Edwards de Salas was named national president of Acción Católica de Chile (Women's Catholic Action) and a year later she founded the first recognized women's political party, the Acción Nacional de Mujeres de Chile (ANMCH, Women's National Party of Chile). Through their participation in the political scenario women finally got the right to vote in municipal elections in 1931. In 1935, only 9 percent of women who were eligible to vote, registered. The figure grew to 11.3 percent in 1938, 13.3 percent in 1941, 14.3 percent in 1944, and 27.2 percent in 1952.[36] In the municipal elections of 1935, there were 65 women candidates from various political parties, and 25 were elected (64 percent of them from the ANMCH).

In the 1960s and 1970s, during the Frei and Allende governments, women became more politically involved. Both administrations desired a democracy in which all people participated, and thus women were propelled into involvement in national issues. It was believed that their participation would move society beyond machismo stereotypes. Though gender issues were not directly addressed, since then they have been part of all governments' agenda.

The 1973 coup and the 17-year dictatorship brought a new vitality to the Chilean women's movement. Congress and national parties, both of which were exclusively male, were abolished by General Pinochet, and politicians were forced to take lower-profile positions. Women were then able to step in to fight against human rights abuses. Men could not form political groups; those who tried to do so were exiled, jailed, killed, or disappeared. Women organized themselves and entered the workforce because so many men had been fired or killed. As torture became part of the new dictatorship's scenario, women brought issues such as gender and family violence into the open.

In terms of women's participation in decision-making positions the percentage rose from 4 percent in 1990 to 30 percent in 2000.[37] Only 12.2 percent of all the personnel working in government are women.[38] Of the 49 current senators, only 2 are women (Carmen Frei, Christian Democratic Party, and Evelyn Matthei, Independent). Of the 120 representatives, only 13 (1.2 percent) are women.[39] Access to the political power has been extremely difficult for women to attain in a country where women are strongly encouraged to be mothers and to remain in the private sphere, whereas the public and homosocial sphere is reserved for men. Of the 17 ministries in Chile, 5 are headed by women (Foreign Affairs, Defense, Education, Planning and Cooperation, and SERNAM). There are eight under-Secretariats headed by women: State, Government, Energy, Mining, Social Security, Housing, National Property, and SERNAM.

Gender-specific agendas have always been absent and that is why issues such as divorce, abortion, sexual harassment, domestic violence, and child care are still left out of the legislative debate. Possibly the political arena will change in Chile and more women will hold parliamentary positions. In 1991, about 48 percent of the nation's judges were women.[40]

Although Chile ratified the U.N. Convention on the Elimination of All Forms of Discrimination Against Women in December 1989, and SER-

NAM has made significant progress in women's rights, the government has failed to revoke laws that discriminate against women. There are still three big issues that are directly connected with the violation of the Convention articles. Abortion remains illegal, divorce does not exist, and provision of reproductive health care in Chile discriminates against women.[41]

Discrimination against women is still widespread in Chile. The language is the first element through which discrimination occurs, because Spanish favors the use of the masculine. The second element is the perpetuation of stereotypes and the belief in the existence of established and fixed social roles for women (maintained by women themselves and orchestrated by a patriarchal and homosocial society). The third element is educational, civil, and penal systems that reinforce the traditional roles of males and females and differences between men and women in terms of salary. Women are still viewed as homemakers, which is why they are overrepresented in the service area (the only area in which their presence is higher than men's, at 54 percent), which includes public services, commerce, and clerical work. The unemployment rate for women has traditionally been higher than the one for men. In 2000 it was 1.6 points higher. In 1996 the unemployment rate was 7.3 percent for women and 4.9 percent for men.[42] However, Chile is the only country that offers awareness and/or training programs in leadership for civil servants, for small businesswomen and for community leaders, and the only one that offers job training exclusively for women heads of households.

Women's Rights

Feminist Movements

In the post-Pinochet Chile, feminist movements and organizations have revived. The acceptance that power is built not only by force, but also by interaction with others and by being inclusive, has become one of the goals of the feminist cause in Chile. Feminism in Chile has redefined itself to express urgent problems in the country, problems that women have been facing alone. One is the understanding that domestic violence is not a traditionally accepted and tolerated patriarchal custom, but a crime.

Feminist movements originated in Chile in 1865 with the first initiative towards women's suffrage. Catholic upper-class women started the movement by creating charitable and philanthropic organizations, hospitals, unions for women workers, schools for girls, orphanages, and other services for women.[43] From these charitable causes, the roots of feminism arose, and women's objectives unified to advocate women's integration into the social system, and especially their education and political participation. In 1850 the Women's Charitable Society opened. Nuns followed in offering charity and opening orphanages and hospices. Among the most influential women of the time, Juana Ross de Edwards was the first (and probably the only woman in Latin America) to be received by Pope Leo XIII in 1884 for her assistance in the creation of charitable institutions for women, and for her constant and generous gifts of land and money to the Catholic Church. In 1877, the publication of the anticlerical weekly periodical *La Mujer*, "whose objective was to promote women's education and their legal and civil equality," secured more public exposure for women. The same year the Amunátegui Decree passed, and women were allowed into all university careers.[44]

The women's movement in Chile originated in the upper class and then involved all classes especially after the fall of the Pinochet dictatorship, because of the widespread abuses of human rights. Despite these efforts, the patriarchal system, a strong presence of the Catholic Church, and social customs that emphasize the subordination of women to men continue in force and gender inequalities persist.

After women gained suffrage, a new mobilization to obtain other rights started, from education to politics, from private to public sphere. In the 1960s, women's movements emerged to criticize the social discrepancies, to fight not only against traditions but also against the perpetuation of stereotypes and prejudices. With the return of democracy, feminist proposals again were focused on the public sphere. At the same time, with Chile's participation in international forums, there was a new stimulus to defend the feminist positioning in a patriarchal country.

The changes that women have achieved in the last years have improved Chilean society. Feminism oxygenated old ideas and proposed a new set of beliefs and customs. It made visible a fact that had been denied in Chile for centuries and that is part of the social reality: women are more than half of the total population of Chile (51 percent of the population).[45]

Chile has 4,530 women's organizations that are slowly moving the whole society to more changes. Universities, for example, are opening greater possibilities through the creation of gender studies programs. More women are accessing the high-ranking positions in the workplace. The first woman colonel has been named in Carabineros de Chile. Women are becoming more visible in the media (more than half), sciences, literature, and economics.

The feminist movement in Chile faces organization challenges if it is to continue promoting growth and changes. More public opportunities and public presence are needed, as well as, above all, the understanding by men that women have the same rights that they do. Tolerance, inclusiveness, and diversity are key issues.

Lesbian Rights

Another issue that has been made visible by the feminist movement in Chile is homosexuality. Although in Chile it is very rare to see public displays of affection between homosexual couples, these relationships have been declared legal. On December 23, 1998, Law 1047 went into effect. This law modified the century-old Penal Code and decriminalized same-sex sexual relations between consenting adults. (Under the old law, homosexual relations between consenting adults could be punished by up to five years in prison.) The age of consent was set at eighteen. The repeal of the so-called sodomy law in Chile represented a great victory for the gay, lesbian, bisexual, and transgender communities in Chile. Despite the implementation of the new law, gay life in Chile remains mainly underground, and lesbians are almost invisible.

Homosexuality has always been a taboo subject in Chile. Contacts with groups from other countries, access to the Internet, travel, and literary and cultural products have allowed the emergence of lesbian organizations, and have opened a significant space for the debate of this issue. *Lesbianas de Chile* is a web site with information and resources for lesbians. Movimiento de Organización y Liberación Homosexual (Homosexual Organization and Liberation Movement) appeared in 1991. Its main goals were to systematically make visible the reality of gays and lesbians as members of the community, promote changes in legislation, contact political leaders, participate in forums and debates, and create a radio program, *Triángulo abierto* (Open Triangle), that discussed homosexual issues on the air. After a few internal disagreements and divisions, the group unified its efforts with Movimiento Unificado de Minorías Sexuales (Unified Movement of Sexual Minorities), which in turn led to Movimiento de Integración y Liberación Homosexual (MOVILH; Movement for the Integration and Liberation of Homosexuals). It was through MOVILH that the first openly gay city official candidate ran for elections. Other achievements are: the first Gay Pride Day (September 4, 2000), the first Cultural Exhibition for Diversity and No Discrimination (July 2001), and the first homosexual candidate for Congress (2001). In December 2001, 13 Congress members and/or candidates (nine men, four women) signed an agreement to support a constitutional reform to end discrimination against homosexuals. Despite all the efforts made by various associations and groups, and considering the achievements, most of the reform effort has been directed at male homosexuals, whereas Chilean lesbians are further marginalized, victimized, and ridiculed.

Military Service

The Recruitment Law of the Chilean Armed Forces (No. 2.306 of September 12, 1978) regulates military service. Article 13 states that all Chileans of both sexes between 18 and 45 years of age are obliged to perform military service, though the law has never been enforced for women. Every year, all men who will be 18 on or before March 30 of the following year must register by September 30. Military service was reinstituted for women in 1999, on a voluntary basis; they do not serve in combat.

Women were accepted into the Chilean Army in 1974 when the Escuela de Servicio Femenino Militar (Military School for Women's Service) was opened. The success of the project allowed the pilot program to grow into a major school to educate military women in Chile under the same principles applied to males. Although the service continues to be voluntary, access to good education, secure salary, and professional training make it very attractive, especially for lower-income members.

Women have been admitted into various areas in the military. In 1999, the first eight women graduated from the Parachute Division of the Escuela de Suboficiales (School for Warrant Officers). This opened new fields to women, and the Army offered possibilities previously forbidden to females. They were the first female Black Berets in the Chilean military. However, even though women have been part of the military since 1974, they are still generally confined to public relations, finance, military administration, personnel, and nurse and paramedic service, and still cannot participate directly in combat.

RELIGION AND SPIRITUALITY

Slightly more than half of all Chileans who declare a religious affiliation are women. Among those who practice a religion, the proportion of women is significantly higher, particularly among Protestants. About 70 percent of Protestants who attend church services at least once a week are women. Among Roman Catholics, the proportion of practicing women is about 63 percent.[46] Not only are women more religious than men, but also more open to alternative religious forms.

In recent years, Chilean women have turned to nontraditional ways of expressing their spirituality. The tribal religion of the Mapuche people is closely linked to the land and their environment. Their spiritual leader is *machi*, a woman who communicates with the divine family and works with them to maintain harmony in nature and to combat the forces of evil. The *machi* may possess the power and knowledge to cure people. *Machis* and readers of tarot cards and palms are consulted on a regular basis in Chile, not just by low-income women but also by women from more privileged socioeconomic classes. Religious syncretism is widely practiced; most of the women satisfy their religious and spiritual needs through both Catholic and nontraditional forms of religion. Despite the negation of Indian blood among Chileans, most will resort or believe in alternative ways to satisfy their spirituality.

Women's Roles

Chile is primarily a Roman Catholic country (approximate 89 percent), and the influence of the church has marked all representations of religion and spirituality. Women's roles in organized religion are limited because the Catholic Church bars women from becoming priests. Chilean Catholicism has restricted the roles of women because they are socially viewed as pillars of family life, responsible for preserving national values and traditions. Women are valuable only if they are mothers and wives. Only then do they become part of the Catholic Church's agenda, because then they can be subordinated and persuaded to ignore their own needs to satisfy those of the other members (males) of the family. Chilean women are appreciated if they are good wives and mothers. This view represents the reality of a patriarchal society that propagates women's roles determined by the church without bearing in mind other realities, such as the fact that women today are significantly more committed to work outside the home and more likely to accept divorce and abortion.

VIOLENCE

Domestic Violence

In recent years there has been a significant increase in domestic violence in Chile, to the point that even religious communities have expressed concerns. More than 50 percent of women in Chile (and 73.6 percent of children) have been victims of domestic violence.[47] Frustration, lack of employment or discontent in the work place, disaffection, aggressiveness, and other social issues are some of the causes of this significant increment in domestic violence in Chile. Uneven distribution of wealth, social segmentation, and lack of governmental services also contribute to the problem of violence. No substantial measures have been taken by governmental or private institutions, media or other organizations to stop domestic violence.

Traditionally, Chilean men have seen infidelity and adultery as justification for violence against women. In a country where adultery committed by a woman was a criminal offense, and where only in 1994 a law protecting women from domestic violence went into effect, wife-beating and other forms of domestic violence have been the norm. Despite some legal reforms, women's abilities to protect themselves are not yet developed. One in four homes in Chile have some sort of domestic violence.[48]

After democracy was restored in Chile in 1990, the National Women's Service worked for passage of a domestic violence law and a much-needed program to create awareness of family violence through public services. In 1994 the Ley de Violencia Intrafamiliar (Intrafamily Violence Law) was passed. It included definitions of sexual and psychological abuse, and provided for protective measures such as restraining orders and mandatory therapy for batterers. Following passage of the law, a high number of complaints against men were filed. However, of the 2,619 court cases presented in 1998, 20.5 percent ended in reconciliation, 2.1 percent were dropped, 1.7 percent resulted in conviction and sentencing, and 71.9 percent were still pending in 2001.[49]

Although the statistics shocked Chileans and a TV campaign was launched to appeal to the public, what is seen as violence is different for men and women. Pushes, slaps, and punches, for example, are not seen as violent acts by most men, and most women do not report them. Psychological violence is not recognized as such by most males. In Chile, approximately 65 percent of women are exposed to some degree of psychological violence.[50]

Studies have shown that 16.3 percent of women (in the Metropolitan Region alone) are victims of psychological violence, and 34 percent are victims of physical or sexual violence. Of the latter group, 40.7 percent experience a lesser degree of violence, and 59 percent, severe violence. The largest group to suffer physical violence is women (married or *convivientes*, living together) between 40 and 49 years of age (36 percent). A close second is the group 30–39 years of age (34.5 percent). The lower their education, the more abuse women receive: 44.7 percent of the physically abused women in Chile have only basic education, whereas 28.5 percent of abused women have completed higher education or are professionals. Domestic violence in Chile does not necessarily discriminate in terms of economic status, it is a problem of all social groups.[51]

On November 25, 2001, Chile observed the Día de la No Violencia contra la Mujer (No Violence Toward Women Day) and many women's groups organized to remember all the women victims of violence and to attract people's attention to a growing problem in Chile. Nevertheless, Chile is a society that believes men are inherently violent and women should always satisfy them (if not, they are guilty of provocation). Machismo, patriarchal possession of women and children, and the consequent use of authority and control are imprinted on Chilean society. Men justify the use of violence, especially to punish infidelity and not attending to children. A remarkable 39.5 percent of battered women face greater abuse while pregnant if they do not take proper care of the coming baby (and other children).[52] While men are expected to have lovers and mistresses, women are not supposed to. As men exert their power and dominance, most abused women stop enjoying both their social and their sexual relations with their partner. Being afraid to say no is overwhelming, and sex becomes rape.

Rape/Sexual Assault

Marital rape is not counted among the estimated 20,000 rapes that occur each year in Chile.[53] Talking about sex and sexual abuse is still taboo. Many myths are maintained, and marital rape or sexual assault remains beyond the reach of statistical information. The consequences of these assaults (usually by a close relative or family member) are unwanted pregnancies, sexually transmitted diseases, induced abortion, and general danger for women. Men do not take any responsibility for the results of their actions.

While studies of rape and sexual assault in Chile are scarce, it is estimated that in the Metropolitan Region alone, a woman is victim of sexual aggression every 25 minutes.[54] Most of the time the act is not reported to authorities, and when it is, it takes years to get justice. In 81 percent of the cases the rapist is a male (the remaining 19 percent is categorized under "other"), and in 80 percent of those cases, he is a relative or someone known by the victim. Two-thirds of the victims of rape in Chile are girls under the age of 14. The document "Violence Against Women" established that 58 percent of the victims of rape in Santiago in 1997 were fifteen or younger, and 32 percent were 10 years old or younger.[55]

In 1998, according to Fundación por la Paz Ciudadana (Citizens for Peace Foundation), 1,052 cases of rape were reported. According to the statistics provided by the Civil Police: 963 cases of rape, 65 cases of incest, 1,786 cases of "dishonest abuses," and 112 cases of sodomy were reported in the same year. In Chile, any abuse that goes beyond the laws of honesty as established in the civil and penal code is "dishonest abuse." Only 35 people were convicted rape and 48 of "dishonest abuses."[56] Rape and other "dishonest abuses" have not diminished since the law that increases the penalties for sexual abuse took effect in July 1999. This law replaced the old legislation that allowed a man charged with rape to be released if he would marry the victim. However, it is very improbable that someone will actually be tried for rape, because the rape has to be a habitual act with the same person. This means that an adult has to be caught having sexual relations with the same adult or minor three or more times to be arrested. If the adult has sexual relations every day with a different minor, he is not committing a crime. It has not been acknowledged that such behavior spreads sexually transmitted diseases.

Trafficking in Women and Children

Reports of sex trafficking in Chile are nonexistent, though with the influx of women from Peru, Bolivia, and Argentina, conditions are set to traffic in women and make prostitution a lucrative business. The Chilean Penal Code does not punish prostitution unless it involves minors, and the Health Code regulates the operation of prostitution. Although prostitution is legal in Chile, sex workers complain of violence toward them, especially from police officers, whom often bully them, punch them, demand free sex, or confiscate their condoms.[57] In the streets of Santiago there are approximately 20,000 prostitutes, some of whom are children. The Servicio Nacional de Menores (SENAME; National Service for Minors) reported

4,200 cases of child prostitution in 1992. Today, estimates indicate 10,000 cases.[58] Prostitutes and other sex workers must register and get a health permit to work. Currently, it is estimated that 60,000 people engage in some form of sexual commerce in Chile. Money is what draws most women into prostitution. The *temporera* (seasonal female worker) is a new concept of "prostitution" brought by the agro-export industry. These women (approximately 200,000, according to SERNAM) work 12 to 14 hours a day in unhealthy, insecure, dangerous, and precarious conditions in rural or marginal areas.[59] Many experience low pay, sexual harassment, physical abuse, and rape.

In general, all forms of sex work occur in Chile despite the opposition of many conservative sectors. The Café con Piernas (Café with Legs) is one peculiar example. It is a regular coffee place, with no seats, that serves mostly men. Female servers (mostly foreigners) wear very little clothing and can boost their income to $1,000 a month through "tips." Among the cafés, the Barón Rojo (Red Baron) became a model. The legendary Minuto de Oro (Golden Minute) was a magnet that filled to capacity. Waitresses took off their tops for one minute while they served espressos and cappuccinos in stiletto shoes and G-strings. Many Chileans believed that "working there amounts to prostitution," but the place boomed, applications poured in, and women made a decent living.[60]

Female prostitutes now have competition from their male counterparts. Single, separated, annulled, and especially married women hire the services of these young men under the most secretive conditions.

OUTLOOK FOR THE TWENTY-FIRST CENTURY

Chile is a developing country, and there are many things left to improve. Legal equality between men and women, for example, was achieved only in May 1999. As the country redefines itself, it is building a new gender order that aims to end discrimination, subordination, violence, exclusion, and the social, political, religious, and cultural devaluation of women. Equality and opportunities for women are being sought for the new millennium. Divorce and abortion must be addressed, as is the implementation of an effective judicial system to deal with the frustrations and abuses that women suffer. The continuing participation of women in all aspects of public affairs will accelerate their inclusion in the new Chile.

NOTES

1. Library of Congress, Research Division, *Chile: A Country Study*, March 1994. http://memory.loc.gov/frd/cs/cltoc.html, accessed September 28, 2001 (Chile does not have ethnicity statistics).

2. Instituto Nacional de Estadísticas (INE), "Otras estadistica," 2000. www. ine.cl.

3. Central Intelligence Agency (CIA), *World Fact Book—Chile*, February 26, 2002, www.cia.gov/cia/publications/factbook/geos/ci.html, accessed July 1, 2002.

4. INE, 2002, 27

5. INE, 2002.

6. Latin American Bureau, *Country Profiles: Chile* (September 2001), www.lab. org.uk/countryprofiles/Chile/Chile.html, accessed September 10, 2001.

7. INE, 2002.

8. Latin American Bureau, 2001.

9. Ibid.

10. INE.

11. Eugenia Muchnick de Rubinstein, Isabel Vial de Valdés, and Lucía Pardo, *Determinants of Women's Employment in Chile: A Life-History Approach* (University of Chile and Catholic University of Chile, n.d.), www.unu.edu/unupress/unupbooks/uu10we/uu10weog.htm, accessed October 15, 2001.

12. Ibid.

13. Centro de Estudios de la Mujer (CEM), *Argumentos para el cambio* 34 (2000), www.cem.cl, accessed December 2, 2001.

14. INE, "Women 2000: Gender Equality, Development and Peace for the Twenty-First Century," Twenty-Third Special Session of the General Assembly of the United Nations (New York: United Nations, 2000), www.un.org/womenwatch/daw/followup/beijing+5stat/statments/chile5.htm, accessed October 28, 2001.

15. Gustavo Gonzalez, "Sexual Harassment Not a Crime, Say Lawmakers," *Workers World* (August 14, 1998), Inter Press World News Service, www.hartford-hwp.com/archives/42a/077.html, accessed October 20, 2001.

16. Ibid.

17. Ibid.

18. INE, 2001 www.ine.cl.

19. *Servicio Nacional de la Mujer* (SERNAM), 2001, www.sernam.gov.cl/infomujer/hijospercent20epercent20hijas/igualdad/01igualdad.htm, accessed October 2001.

20. Jone Johnson Lewis, "Chile: A Country Study," in *Encyclopedia of Women History* (Washington, DC: Research Division, Library of Congress, March 1994), womenshistory.about.com/library/ency/bl_wh_chile_contraception.htm, accessed October 22, 2001.

21. ChilNet, "Bishop of Talca Supports Sex-Ed Program, but Criticism on the Right Continues," *La Época* (September 16, 1996), www.hartford-hwp.com/archives/42a/105.html, accessed October 1, 2001.

22. Ibid.

23. María Bonino, *Social Watch on Education and Gender* (Montevideo, Uruguay: Instituto del Tercer Mundo, 2001), www.socwatch.org.uy/1999/eng/thematicreports/SWgender-educat99eng.htm#Tablepercent201, accessed October 6, 2001.

24. Associación de Protección a la Familia (APROFA/Chilean Association for Family Protection), www.aprofa.cl.

25. Center for Reproductive Law and Policy and Open Forum on Reproductive Health and Rights, *Women Behind Bars. Chile's Abortion Laws: A Human Rights Analysis* (New York, 1998), www.crlp.org/pub_bo_chilesum.html, accessed September 29, 2001.

26. Ibid.

27. Adriana Delpiano, "Women 2000. Gender Equality, Development and Peace for the Twenty-first Century," speech delivered at U.N. General Assembly, New York, June 2000, www.un.org/womenwatch/daw/followup/beijing+5stat/statements/chile5/htm, accessed October 28, 2001.

28. Jennifer Pribble, "AIDS Spreading in Chile," United Press International, August 18, 2001, www.hivdent.org/publicp/inter/ppinasic082001.htm, accessed December 2, 2001.

29. *El Mercurio* (March 14, 2000), www.emol.cl.

30. Margaret Orgill, "Latin American Women Facing Rising AIDS Risks," Reuters, November 17, 1995, www.aegis.com/news/re/1995/RE951115.html, accessed November 29, 2001.

31. "Anorexia y bulimia," July 2002, www.anorexia.cl/, accessed July 24, 2002.

32. *La Tercera* (May 26, 2000), www.tercera.cl/diario/1997/09/24/19.html.

33. Olga Madariaga de la Barra, "Enfermedades mentales en Chile: Locura en alza," *Mujer a Mujer*, n.d., http://mujer.tercera.cl/2000/01/09/enfermedades.htm, accessed November 18, 2001.

34. *Fathers for Life: Suicide Rate in Selected Countries* (December 3, 2001), http://forever.freeshell.org/who_suicide_rates.htm, accessed September 25, 2002.

35. Erika Maza Valenzuela, "Catholicism, Anticlericalism, and the Quest for Women's Suffrage in Chile" in *Working Paper Series of The Helen Kellogg Institute for International Studies*, ed. Caroline Domingo (Notre Dame, IN: University of Notre Dame/Helen Kellogg Institute for International Studies, 1995), 31–32.

36. Ibid.

37. Delpiano, June 2000.

38. *Human Development Reports*, "Human Development Indicators" (2001), http://hdr.undp.org/reports/global/2001/en/pdf/back.pdf, accessed July 20, 2002.

39. Maza Valenzuela, 1995.

40. Research Division, Library of Congress, *Chile: A Country Study* (Washington, DC: Library of Congress, 1994), http://memory.loc.gov/frd/cs/cltoc.html, accessed September 28, 2001.

41. Center for Reproductive Law and Policy, 2001.

42. Delpiano, 2000. 3.

43. Maza Valenzuela, 1995, 5.

44. Ibid., 15.

45. CEM, 2000.

46. Research Division, Library of Congress, 1994.

47. Lutheran World Information, "Religious Communities Reject Domestic Violence in Chile" (October 25, 2001), www.lutheranworld.org/News/Articles/EN/LWI, accessed November 13, 2001.

48. Lezak Shallat, "Chilean Women Seek Democracy in the Nation and at Home," in *The Intimate Enemy: Gender Violence & Reproductive Health*, Panos Briefing no. 27 (March 1998), www.oneworld.org/panos/briefing/genviol.htm, accessed October 31, 2001.

49. Ibid.

50. Servicio Nacional de la Mujer.

51. Servicio Nacional de la Mujer and Centro de Análisis de Políticas Públicas de la Universidad de Chile, "Statistics" (March 1998), www.mujereschile.cl/colaboradoras/infoteca/estadisticas/violencia/index.php, accessed September 20, 2001; SERNAM, 2001.

52. Shallat, 1998.

53. Ibid.

54. Alejandra Valdez. "Cero tolerancia a la violencia sexual contra las mujeres en Chile," *Mujeres en red* (n.d.), www.nodo50.org/mujeresred/chile-violencia.htm, accessed December 2, 2001.

55. "Violence Against Women." Document.

56. Fundación por la Paz Ciudadana (Citizens Peace Foundation) (August 1998), www.pazmundial.cl/, accessed November 7, 2001; Civil Police, www.investigaciones.cl/.

57. *Anova*, "Prostitutes Teach Police Officers Respect" (June 27, 2001), www.ananova.com/news/story/sm_339103.html?menu=news.weirdworld.sexlife, accessed December 2, 2001.

58. Ibid.

59. Patricia Guerra, "Prostitutos: Problema de sexualidad y carião. Parmalentarias, actrices y profesionales se muestran impactadas por este nuevo feñomeno de la sociedad santiaguina," *La Tercera Online* (September 24, 1997), www.tercera.cl/diario/1997/09/24/19.html, accessed December 5, 2001; SERNAM Centro de Documentación.

60. Felipe Ossa, "El Barón Rojo: In Conservative Santiago, Chile, an Uncharacteristically Leggy Trend Has Slipped Into the Puritanical Mix" (May 5, 2000), www.salon.com/travel/wlust/2000/05/05/piernas/index.html, accessed December 8, 2001.

RESOURCE GUIDE

Suggested Reading

Anova. "Prostitutes Teach Police Officers Respect" (June 27, 2001). www.ananova.com/news/story/sm_339103.html?menu=news.weirdworld.sexlife. Accessed December 2, 2001.

Center for Reproductive Law and Policy and Open Forum on Reproductive Health and Rights. *Women Behind Bars: Chile's Abortion Laws. A Human Rights Analysis*. New York: Center for Reproductive Law and Policy and Open Forum on Reproductive Health and Rights, 1998. www.crlp.org/pub_bo_chilesum.html. Accessed September 29, 2001.

Lewis, Jone Johnson. "Chile: A Country Study." In *Encyclopedia of Women History*. Washington, DC: Research Division, Library of Congress, March 1994. http://womenshistory.about.com/library/ency/bl_wh_chile_contraception.htm. Accessed October 22, 2001.

Maza Valenzuela, Erika. "Catholicism, Anticlericalism, and the Quest for Women's Suffrage in Chile." In *Working Paper Series of The Helen Kellogg Institute for International Studies*, edited by Caroline Domingo. Notre Dame, IN: University of Notre Dame and Helen Kellogg Institute for International Studies, 1995.

Shallat, Lezak. "Chilean Women Seek Democracy in the Nation and at Home." In *The Intimate Enemy: Gender Violence and Reproductive Health*. Panos Briefing no. 27. March 1998. www.oneworld.org/panos/briefing/genviol.htm, accessed October 31, 2001.

Web Sites and Organizations

Asociación de Protección a la Familia (APROFA/Chilean Association for Family Protection), www.aprofa.cl.
APROFA, the largest nongovernmental organization in Chile, fills the gap left by the government in the provision of sexual and reproductive health services, and pursues this work from a gender perspective. Using modern technology, APROFA reaches a broad audience, including poor women, adolescents, secondary school teachers and health professionals.

Carabineros de Chile (Uniformed Police), www.carabineros.cl.

Centro de Estudios de la Mujer (CEM; Women's Studies Center), www.cem.cl/.
The Women's Studies Center is involved in research, training, teaching, and consulting in the field of gender studies, especially in matters related to work and labor, citizenship and participation in politics, and public policies.

Centro de Estudios para el Desarrollo de la Mujer (CEDEM, Center for the Development of Women's Studies), www.cedem-mujerycultura.cl/.
The Center develops programs for women in all social spaces, especially those who are Amerindians, live in rural areas, and are employed in the service sector.

Centro Interdisciplinario de Estudios de Género (Interdisciplinary Center for Gender Studies), http://rehue.csociales.uchile.cl/genero/index.html.
The Center, located in the Department of Social Sciences of the University of Chile, conducts research and provides training in gender-related issues.

Chile's Higher Education Database, www.usc.edu/dept/education/globaled/wwcu/background/Chile.html.

Colegio de Abogados de Concepción (Bar Association of Concepción), http://chile.derecho.org/concepcion/~/portada/.
This web site offers access to codes and legislation.

FEMPRESS, Red de Comunicación Alternativa de la Mujer para América Latina (Alternative Network for the Communication of Women in Latin America), www.fempress.cl.
An organization and a press that offer alternative ways for women to communicate and inform the public about women's issues.

Fundación Instituto de la Mujer (Women's Institute Foundation), www.insmujer.cl/.
The Institute promotes women's participation in society through programs in the following areas: participation in politics, family and women's human rights, women's employment and economic development, sexuality, and reproductive health.

Gay Chile, www.gaychile.cl.
This is the official site for the Chilean gay and lesbian community. Two related sites are Orgullo Gay (Gay Pride), www.orgullogay.cl/, and Lesbianas de Chile (Chilean Lesbians), www.geocities.com/WestHollywood/Park/2322/.

Instituto Nacional de Estadísticas (INE, National Statistics Institute), www.ine.cl.

Isis Internacional, www.isis.cl/.
A communication and information service that helps women worldwide to learn from each other.

Movimiento Pro Emancipación de la Mujer Chilena (MEMCH, Pro-Independence Movement of Chilean Women), www.memch.cl/.
Nongovernment organization works toward equal rights for women and the strengthening of the women's movement in Chile.

Mujeres Empresarias de Chile (Businesswomen of Chile), www.finam.cl/.
The goal of this branch of the Women's World Banking Corporation in Chile is to stimulate women's participation in national and international businesses.

Portal de las ONGs. (NonGovernment Organizations Site), www.ong.cl/.
This site promotes the use of the Internet by all nongovernment, nonprofit organizations in Chile.

Servicio Nacional de la Mujer (SERNAM; National Women's Service), www.sernam. gov.cl/.
SERNAM seeks to work with the government to design and implement public policies that will promote equality of women in the family, the society, the economy, politics, and culture.

SELECTED BIBLIOGRAPHY

"AIDS in Chile." N.d. www.census.gov/ipc/hiv/chile.pdf. Accessed November 3, 2001.

Bonino, María. *Social Watch on Education and Gender*. Montevideo, Uruguay: Instituto del Tercer Mundo, 2001. www.socwatch.org.uy/1999/eng/thematicreports/SWgender-educat99eng.htm#Tablepercent201. Accessed October 6, 2001.

Bunster, Ximena. *Women's Influence in Chile: The Last 150 Years*. N.d. www.localaccess.com/chappell/chile/women.htm. Accessed November 6, 2001.

Catholic World News. "Chilean Court Declares 'Morning-After' Pill Illegal." September 6, 2001.www.lifeissues.net/birthcon/news/010910-16.html. Accessed October 26, 2001.

———. "Chilean Health Ministry Defies Supreme Court by Allowing Abortifacient Pills." September 6, 2001. www.lifeissues.net/birthcon/news/010910-16.html. Accessed October 23, 2001.

Center for Reproductive Law and Policy. "Chilean Government to Present Women's Rights Record Before the UN." June 4, 1999. www.crlp.org/pr_99_0603cedaw.html. Accessed November 29, 2001.

Central Intelligence Agency (CIA), U.S. Department of State. *The World Fact Book—Chile*. February 26, 2002. www.cia.gov/cia/publications/factbook/geos/ci.html. Accessed July 1, 2002.

Chappell, Dave. *Spotlight on Chile*. www.localaccess.com/chappell/chile/htm.

Chilean Government. *Gobiernode Chile*. December 10, 2001. www.gobiernodechile.cl/. Accessed December 10, 2001.

ChilNet. "Bishop of Talca Supports Sex-Ed Program, but Criticism on the Right Continues." *La Época*. September 16, 1996. www.hartford-hwp.com/archives/42a/105.html. Accessed October 1, 2001.

Delpiano, Adriana. "Women 2000: Gender Equality, Development and Peace for the Twentieth-first Century." Speech given at Twenty-third Special Session of the U.N. General Assembly, New York, 2000. www.un.org/womenwatch/daw/followup/beijing+5stat/statments/chile5.htm. Accessed October 28, 2001.

Fathers for Life. *Suicide Rate in Selected Countries*. September 25, 2002. http://forever.freeshell.org/who_suicide_rates.htm. Accessed December 3, 2001.

González, Gustavo. "Sexual Harassment Not a Crime, Say Lawmakers," *Workers World*, August 14, 1998. Inter Press World News Agency (IPS). www.hartford-hwp.com/archives/42a/077.html. Accessed October 20, 2001.

Human Development Reports. Human Development Indicators. 2001. http://hdr.undp.org/reports/global/2001/en/pdf/back.pdf. Accessed July 20, 2002.

Latin American Bureau. *Country Profiles: Chile*. September 2001. www.lab.org.uk/countryprofiles/Chile/Chile.html. Accessed September 10, 2001.

Lutheran World Information. *Religious Communities Reject Domestic Violence in Chile*. October 25, 2001. www.lutheranworld.org/News/Articles/EN/LWI. Accessed November 13, 2001.

Muchnik de Rubenstein, Eugenia, Isabel Vial de Valdés, and Lucía Pardo. *Determinants of Women's Employment in Chile: A Life-History Approach*. Santiago: University of Chile and Catholic University of Chile, n.d. www.unu.edu/unupress/unupbooks/uu10we/uu10weog.htm. Accessed October 15, 2001.

Orgill, Margaret. "Latin American Women Facing Rising AIDS Risks." Reuters, November 17, 1995. www.aegis.com/news/re/1995/RE951115.html. Accessed November 29, 2001.

Ossa, Felipe. *El Barón Rojo: In Conservative Santiago, Chile, an Uncharacteristically Leggy Trend Has Slipped into the Puritanical Mix*. May 5, 2000. www.salon.com/travel/wlust/2000/05/05/piernas/index.html. Accessed December 8, 2001.

Pribble, Jennifer. "AIDS Spreading in Chile." United Press International, August 18, 2001. www.hivdent.org/publicp/inter/ppinasico82001.htm. Accessed December 2, 2001.

Research Division, Library of Congress. *Chile: A Country Study*. March 1994. http://memory.loc.gov/frd/cs/cltoc.html. Accessed September 28, 2001.

———. Customized Research and Analytical Service. April 4, 2000. http://womenshistory.about.com/gi/dynamic/offsite.htm?site=http://lcweb.loc.gov/rr/frd/frdhmpg.html. Accessed November 26, 2001.

———. *Report on Religious Liberty in Chile*. March 1994. http://atheism.about.com/library/world/AJ/bl_ChileReligion.htm. Accessed September 3, 2001.

Rodríguez, Jacobo. "Chile's Private Pension System at 18: Its Current State and Future." In *Social Security Privatization*. Washington, DC: Cato Institute, July 1999. www.cato.org/pubs/ssps/ssp-17es.html. Accessed November 8, 2001.

United Nations. "Chile Ending 'Gender Order' Based on Exclusion, Violence Against Women, Women's Anti-Discrimination Committee Told." Press Release WOM 1144. June 22, 1999. www.un.org/News/Press/docs/1999/19990622.wom1144.html. Accessed November 11, 2001.

United Nations Development Program. *The 1999 Human Development Report*. New York: UNDP, 1999. www.undp.org/hdro/indicators.html. Accessed October 31, 2001.

United States Department of State, Bureau of Democracy, Human Rights, and Labor. *Chile. Country Reports on Human Rights Practices.* Washington, DC: United States Government Printing Office, February 2001. www.state.gov/g/drl/rls/ hrrpt/2000/wha/index.cfm?docid=736. Accessed November 8, 2001.

Worldvision. Chile. 2002. www.worldvision.org/worldvision/projects.nsf/35f1e3cbd05 02cbd8825669d0059a32d/7036439fd64564aa88256a24006f0183!OpenDocument. Accessed July 20, 2002.

Spanish Bibliography

"Anorexia y bulimia." July 2002. www.anorexia.cl/. Accessed July 24, 2002.

Centro de Estudios de la Mujer (CEM; Center for Women's Studies). *Argumentos para el cambio* 34 (2000). December 2001. www.cem.cl. Accessed December 2, 2001.

Código Civil de Chile (Chilean Civil Code). N.d. http://colegioabogados.org/normas/ codice/codigocivil4.html. Accessed October 20, 2001.

Ejército de Chile (Chilean Army). N.d. www.ejercito.cl/estructura/index.htm. Accessed November 30, 2001.

El Mercurio. October, November, December 2001. www.emol.cl.

Federación de Estudiantes de la Universidad de Chile. (Student Federation of the University of Chile). December 5, 2001. www.fech.uchile.cl/. Accessed December 6, 2001.

Fundación por la Paz Ciudadana (Citizens' Peace Foundation). August 1998. www. pazmundial.cl/. Accessed November 7, 2001.

Instituto Nacional de Estadísticas (INE; National Statistics Institute). November 2002. www.ine.cl/. Accessed November 27, 2001.

Junta Nacional de Auxilio Escolar y Becas (National Council for School Aid and Grants). Gobierno de Chile junaeb: Red nacional de apoyo al estudiante. August 27, 2001. 16 October 2001. www.junaeb.cl/historia.htm. Accessed October 16, 2001.

La Cuarta. Prostitución infantil, inocencia perdida. N.d. www.lacuarta.cl/sitios/vas/ 2001/11/04/reportaje5.html. Accessed December 2, 2001.

Madariaga de la Barra, Olga. "Enfermedades mentales en Chile: Locura en alza." *Mujer a Mujer* (n.d.). http://mujer.tercera.cl/2000/01/09/enfermedades.htm. Accessed November 18, 2001.

Movimiento de Organización y Liberación Homosexual (MOVILH; Homosexual Organization and Liberation Movement). *Brazo político de las minorias sexuales.* December 11, 2001. www.movilh.org/. Accessed December 11, 2001.

Mujereschile. December 10, 2001. www.mujereschile.cl. Accessed December 10, 2001.

Ojeda Lara, Patricia. *Actividades que pueden desarrollar las mujeres en el ejército.* Escuela de Suboficiales, n.d. www.escueladesuboficiales.cl/lamujer.htm. Accessed November 18, 2001.

Rusowsky, Daniela. "Bulimia y anorexia: Problemas de salud pública." May 26, 2000. www.tercera.cl/diario/2000/05/26/t-26.27.3a.CYS.BULIMIA.html. Accessed July 24, 2002.

Servicio Nacional de la Mujer (SERNAM; National Women's Service). 2001. www. sernam.gov.cl/infomujer/hijospercent20epercent20hijas/igualdad/01igualdad. htm. Accessed October 2001.

Servicio Nacional de la Mujer and Centro de Análisis de Políticas Públicas de la Universidad de Chile. "Statistics." March 1998. www.mujereschile.cl/

colaboradoras/infoteca/estadisticas/violencia/index.php. Accessed September 20, 2001.

Valdez, Alejandra. "Cero tolerancia a la violencia sexual contra las mujeres en Chile." *Mujeres en Red*. N.d. www.nodo50.org/mujeresred/chile-violencia.htm. Accessed December 2, 2001.

6

COLOMBIA

Juana Suárez

PROFILE OF COLOMBIA

Colombia is the only South American country with a coastline on both the Pacific Ocean and the Caribbean Sea. Its 440,000 square miles are divided into four major geographic regions composed of three mountain ranges and intervening valley lowlands.

Colonized by Spain in the sixteenth century, Colombia gained its independence in 1810. Despite being considered one of the most violent countries of the world, Colombia has one of the longest-standing democratic political systems in Latin America. The two traditional parties—the Liberal and the Conservative—date from the nineteenth century.

Although violence is a historic problem, since the 1950s it has been exacerbated by the presence of armed groups. The 1950s and the 1960s were the period known as La Violencia.[1] However, most contemporary problems are rooted in social issues related to the distribution of wealth, social status discrimination, government corruption, and regionalism, a result of the diverse geography of the country.[2] The present armed conflict involves military forces, two guerrilla groups, FARC (Fuerzas

Armadas Revolucionarias de Colombia, Colombian Revolutionary Armed Forces) and ELN (Ejército de Liberación Nacional; National Liberation Army), and paramilitary forces known as AUC (Autodefensas Unidas de Colombia, Colombian United Militias).[3]

The economic situation of the country is dire, and this has had repercussions even for the upper class. In recent years, people from various social classes have fled, mainly to the United States. The increasing exodus has led countries like Spain to tighten immigration measures.

The population is approximately 44,000,000, of which 20,766,704 were women in 2001. There is a wide diversity of ethnic groups: mestizo, white, black, mulatto, indigenous, and a small number of members of the Rom family (traditionally known as gypsies). The *raizal* minority lives in San Andrés y Providencia intendancy. The official language is Spanish, but more than 180 Indian languages and dialects are also spoken. About 95 percent of Colombia's population is Roman Catholic, although the number of Protestant evangelicals has been increasing in recent years.

The main populated areas in Colombia are between the mountain ranges, where the most important cities are located. Bogotá, the capital city, has a population of nearly eight million. It is a cosmopolitan city with marked differences according to social class. The influx of citizens into the city has created many problems mainly because there are not enough city police to cope with the increasing population. However, the last two administrations have made visible contributions to public transportation, public services, and rehabilitation of public spaces. Medellín, the second largest city, is an important textile center characterized by its entrepreneurial people.

Currently life expectancy is 66.5 years for women and 72.4 years for men. The infant mortality rate is declining in some areas, but problems remain in rural areas. The average infant mortality is 98.2 per 100,000 live births. Nowadays, women have an average of three children. Approximately 107 mothers die per 10,000 births.

OVERVIEW OF WOMEN'S ISSUES

Since Colombia is one of the most racially diverse countries in Latin America as well as a country of sharp contrasts in social status and deep differences between rural and urban life, there are striking differences between white women, mestizas, black women, and indigenous women. The indigenous population in Colombia is approximately 700,000, and 49 percent are women. Although the Colombian Constitution recognizes rights of indigenous peoples to cultural heritage and participation, the government neglects many of these groups. It also fails to acknowledge their contribution to the survival of Colombian ethnic diversity.[4] Afro-Colombian women face similar problems.

Political mobilization of various social classes, indigenous groups and

Afro-Colombians is increasing. The mobilization of minorities and of Afro-Colombians is encouraged by the need to reaffirm identity, diversity, difference, and cultural and social participation.[5]

Lifestyles also vary between lower-, middle-, and upper-class women. Gender, race, and generational differences have been legally and institutionally acknowledged. Radical changes since the mid-1950s have strongly affected women's issues. In the change from an agricultural settlement pattern to an urban one, big cities have been formed that are not prepared to provide a good quality of life. The expansion of capitalism, industrialization, failed attempts to consolidate the state, and globalization are occurring in the midst of periodic sociopolitical violence and social inequality that keep half of the population at the poverty level.

EDUCATION

The education system consists of five years of elementary education and six years of high school, known as *bachillerato*. Colombians receive an average of seven years of education. Elementary education is theoretically free and mandatory. Besides coed schools, there are *colegios femeninos* (women's schools) and *colegios masculinos* (men's schools). Nuns run some women's schools and priests run some men's schools. There are also schools called *normales*, where students combine high school with a preliminary career in teaching; these have traditionally been schools for women. There are also trade schools called *escuelas vocacionales*, where, in addition to the high school diploma, students acquire a certificate in a vocational technical career. The number of women entering *vocacionales* has increased, but there is still the need to encourage young women to pursue these careers.

School facilities vary from private to public and from urban to rural. Private schools have more complete, modern, and sophisticated labs and equipment.

Opportunities

Colegio La Merced, established in 1832, was the first school for women. Women were first granted access to higher education in 1933. According to the Colombian Constitution, education is a right and a public service. "The Colombian government is currently implementing a project called "Education for Equality," whose main objective is to modify the educational system so that it does not foster socialization patterns which reinforce inequality between the sexes and gender stereotypes. It also seeks to promote equal access to education for boys and girls, and to identify the factors that limit girls' access to education."[6]

As is the case in many countries, professions such as administrative assistants, educators, and nurses have traditionally been assigned to women.

Although there are more women studying careers traditionally associated with men, such as engineering, mathematics, and sciences, there is a clear perception that education reform in elementary and secondary education must encourage increased participation of women in those fields.[7]

At almost every educational level, enrollment is distributed equally by sex. In the under-24 age group, men and women have completed a similar number of years of schooling: 5.8 years for women and 6 for men. Rural women have less access to education than urban women.

The number of women students in universities or institutions that offer higher degrees has increased to the point that they constitute 60 percent of the university population. Women obtain fewer master's degrees and doctorates, except in the social sciences and education.

Literacy

The level of literacy has increased for both men and for women. The current literacy rate for women is 91.4 percent. Even in rural areas, women have challenged parents' traditional idea that women do not need to get an education, and since 1964 education possibilities have increased.[8]

EMPLOYMENT AND ECONOMICS

Job/Career Opportunities

Women make up 42.6 percent of the workforce. Their distribution by economic sector is 31.8 percent in agriculture, 18 percent in industry, and 51 percent in the service industry. Women constitute 40 percent of the economically active population. However, many women are working in traditionally female jobs, which offer lower salaries, fewer benefits, and lower status. In general terms, women have achieved the same level of education as men. However, as long as women do not have more access to scientific and technological careers, they will continue to encounter difficulties competing with men in the job market.

In rural zones, jobs are still divided by gender. Many women work in domestic activities, and contribute manual labor when crops are in season. They begin working early in the day and have extended shifts. They prepare meals for families and farm workers, clean, and take care of children. In many rural areas, the production of crafts is still the main source of income not only for women but also for the whole household.

In families that derive their income from craft production, the labor of women and children is prominent. In indigenous and Afro-Colombian groups, children engage in craft production and domestic work at very early ages. Usually, women are not distributors, but work for middlemen who subcontract with them for low wages and take advantage of their "flexible" schedules since most of them work at home. The craft market gives them a minimal return for their labor. Women earn less than men, even though women can work up to twenty hours a day, while men in agriculture work eight hours. Besides paid jobs in crafts or agriculture, women are responsible for most domestic activities.[9]

There are many women working in education, but they are concentrated at the preschool level. There are fewer women university professors than male professors. Women constitute 55 percent of office personnel and 44 percent of professional employees and technicians. Women still perform 14.2 percent of domestic service. Although good working conditions exist in some urban domestic jobs, in rural areas lax enforcement of labor regulations means that domestic workers may not receive appropriate salaries and benefits.

In contrast, there are more female presidents, vice presidents, and managers in banks and corporations. Likewise, more women are participating in political administrative positions, such as mayors, members of Parliament, and secretaries of state departments.

Guambiano Indian woman dressed in traditional clothing sells fruit in Silvia. Photo © TRIP/R. Powers.

Women are affected more than men by unemployment, although they are better able to find jobs in informal sectors of the economy. Statistics from Banco de la República show that the unemployment rate among women is double the usual rate of other Latin American countries. In the case of the migrant population, women often adapt better and faster to the cities and find jobs more easily than men.[10]

Pay

The difference in wages between men and women varies between 10 percent and 30 percent depending upon the economic sector. As of January 2002, the minimum wage was 309 Colombian pesos (U.S.$150) per month. Employees who make less than two minimum wages a month receive a transportation subsidy of 34 pesos (U.S.$17).

Working Conditions

Working conditions for women have improved. Although new laws seek to guarantee a woman's right to economic independence through credit and investment projects, there is still the need for reforms in many areas.

Sexual Harassment

Machismo jeopardizes women's possibilities to work in a friendly environment. There is increasing awareness of sexual harassment as manifested by demanding sexual favors in order to obtain a job or a promotion or to keep a job. Sexual harassment is also manifested in work environments through pejorative jokes related to women's capacity or sexuality. Many companies are taking action to protect women's rights to work in a friendly, nondiscriminatory environment through informational campaigns. However, the Ministry of Labor is responsible for taking more energetic action on the issue.

Support for Mothers/Caretakers

Maternal Leave

Legal postnatal maternity leave is 12 weeks, at the woman's regular salary. A woman may reduce maternity leave to eleven weeks so that her husband or permanent companion has a week during which he may be with her during and immediately after delivery. In the case of adoption of a child under the age of seven, the same maternal leave conditions must apply. During the first six months the employer must allow a woman who has returned from her maternity leave to take two thirty-minute breaks during the work day to breast-feed her child, without deducting from her salary. In the event of miscarriage, or death of the baby during or after premature delivery, an employee has the right to two to four weeks leave of absence at her regular salary. If a premature delivery occurs and the infant survives, regular maternity leave provisions apply.

Employer violations of these provisions are punished by several legal mechanisms that protect women's rights. However, given the fact that legal action takes an average of two or three years, it is often difficult to ensure that legal protections are guaranteed.

Daycare

Many companies provide daycare centers. There are also many private daycare institutions that are affordable for middle- or upper-class families. Daycare is also provided through institutions created by NGOs and religious communities. However, the Instituto Colombiano de Bienestar Familiar (Colombian Institute of Family Welfare, known as Bienestar) provides most daycare services in urban and rural areas, and it serves many low-income families. Bienestar has implemented the hogares comunitarios (communal homes), whose main function is to group low-income families in networks of fifteen so that they can help each other with the distribution of daycare, job responsibilities, and domestic work. Bienestar also has the hogares de Bienestar familiar (Bienestar daycare centers) that provide specific daycare shifts to parents who work part- or full-time. The hogares de Bienestar familiar are organized in four groups according to age, ranging from three months to seven years old. (The official age for children to be accepted in a public elementary school is seven.) In addition to daycare, Bienestar provides nutrition services to children, nursing mothers, and pregnant women. It also has adoption services and regulates other adoption centers.

Inheritance and Property Rights

Civil law establishes equality between spouses. A married woman has full legal capacity to manage her own property and the couple's jointly owned property, to enter into contracts, and to access the courts. In 1996, Congress passed a law that requires the signature of both spouses when transferring property pertaining to the family domicile.

In the event of widowhood, the law favors a woman who has been legally married to the deceased, even if she has not lived with him for many years. She has priority in social benefits as well as access to housing. The law also recognizes, for purposes of Social Security, a woman companion in any kind of union that can be legally recognized, particularly consensual unions of at least two years. Legitimate children from the marriage have the same rights as those who are not legitimate heirs.[11] In order to receive Social Security benefits, a widow must wait at least 270 days before marrying again in a civil ceremony. A widow must declare that she is pregnant by the deceased within thirty days of his death for the child to have inheritance and property rights, and for the mother to be assigned financial support for the child.[12]

Besides the emotional turmoil that results from losing a spouse, women have to face financial hardships; in many cases, women from rural areas move to big cities when they become widows. They face displacement issues as well as other traumas related to the difficulties of adapting to urban settings. Wearing black for a period of time, living with their children, and waiting a considerable amount of time before remarrying are expected of widows in some sectors of Colombian society. However, mourning customs are less strict nowadays, since women are a significant part of the labor force. Since women typically have lower incomes than men and education is still a privilege in many rural areas and lower income sectors of the population, many widows find themselves in financial difficulty when their husband dies.

On the other hand, one important change is that women are now entitled to receive a pension if they are on their own in their older years.[13] Also, for some women widowhood might mean a more empowered situation. Making decisions at home or receiving a pension or an inheritance can make them financially independent, and even liberated, if they have been living with someone abusive or authoritarian. In the event of widowhood related to sociopolitical causes, many women have begun political organizations to support one another or to voice their concerns.[14]

Social/Government Programs

The main goal of Consejería Presidencial para la Equidad de la Mujer (President's Advisory for Women's Equality) is to coordinate activities that enable women's participation in social programs and economic development. For example, Programa de Microempresarias y Mujeres de Cabeza (Microenterprise Program for Female Heads of Families) and Programa de Apoyo Integral para Jefes de Hogar (Integral Support Program for Heads of the Household) support *microempresas* (microcompanies), and provide financial advice and credit plans from $15,000 to $70,000. The programs target women in low income sectors.[15]

Amid violence, Colombian women have contributed substantially to solutions to social problems, to supporting and encouraging a democratic political culture, and to defending life. In the absence of social and welfare services from the state, many women have organized daycare centers, public libraries, community pharmacies, and soup kitchens. Many women create small companies, not only as a solution to individual cases but also as group projects that produce income for a whole community. The tasks of these women's groups extend to facilitating discussion groups and learning centers on women's rights, democracy, and citizenship.

FAMILY AND SEXUALITY

Some of the changes that Colombian families are facing at the beginning of the new millennium are a democratization of authority by allowing participation of members other than the husband/father; a diversification in modalities of union, including more divorced women and the increase in the number of homosexual couples; an increase in the number of widows as a result of violent death of men in aged 22 to 44; gender role change since the husband/father is no longer the only breadwinner in the family and the mother no longer has the exclusive responsibility for domestic work; the decrease in fertility; the greater number of childless couples; and greater participation of women in the social sphere.[16]

Gender Roles

The Colombian Constitution states that both members of a couple have equal rights and obligations with regard to family authority and sharing expenses. Despite constitutional familial equality, machismo is still present in many daily events, both public and private, often reinforced by women's behaviors or by the heavy weight of the Colombian Marian culture.[17] Nevertheless, gender roles are changing as women's participation in many aspects of economic and social life increases. Because of the high unemployment rate and the difficult sociopolitical times, in many cases only one member of the family has access to a job, thus favoring changes in gender roles.

Many gender role changes are linked to the level of education of the couple. For example, young professional women and men share more domestic responsibilities and child care, even if they are not married. Many young parents are educating their children into patterns of equal collaboration at home. Traditionally, domestic chores were assigned to women. Many daycare centers and elementary schools are implementing educational programs based on respect for gender difference.

As part of the agenda to promote gender awareness, Mayor Antanas Mockus of Bogotá[18] has implemented programs to determine what changes in social behaviors when gender roles are inverted in urban activities. In 2001 and 2002, Bogotá celebrated the Noche de las Mujeres, similar to the Take Back the Night marches in the United States. In Bogotá men are asked to stay home from 8 P.M. to 1 A.M. so that women can participate in the event. The event includes public forums on women's issues, public concerts, and special programs in bars and entertainment places. Seven hundred thousand women participated in the first Noche de las Mujeres on March 9, 2000. The program has also been tried in cities like Medellin. Although it has provided positive results, as demonstrated by statistics on decreasing violence, the program is questioned for its obvious exclusion of males.

Marriage

As marriage rates have changed dramatically, the number of domestic partnerships (known in Colombia as *uniones de hecho*) has increased. The number of divorces has also increased. The minimum age for marriage is 18. Men over the age of 14 and women over the age of 12 may marry with the consent of their parents. The Center for Reproductive Law and Policy notes, however, that "marriage of an underage person is not null and void if its validity has not been questioned within three months after the minors reach puberty, or when the woman, even if she is underage, is pregnant. Marriage rates among females adolescents are increasing."[19]

Adoption of the husband's surname is optional, but it is a common practice. Young women who have an established career in which they are known by their maiden name are opting not to adopt their husband's name. By law, spouses are obligated to be faithful and to aid and assist one another. They have the joint right to administer household authority, to choose their place of residence, and the joint duty of contributing to the household economy according to their ability. Parental authority over children is to be shared, and either parent can act as the legal representative of their children.

A domestic partnership is defined as a stable union between an unmarried man and an unmarried woman who form a permanent household. In order to be recognized as a legal domestic partnership, the two unmarried individuals must have lived together for at least two years and prove that there is no legal impediment for them to get married. For legal purposes, they are known as "permanent companions." Any property or capital derived from work belongs jointly to both. If the two-year requirement is fulfilled or if they have one or more children, each permanent companion is entitled to the retirement or disability pension of the other as well as to death benefits payable upon an employee's death. Likewise, the permanent companion of the employee or pensioner is also entitled to health care benefits.

The average age of Colombian women at first marriage is 21.4, and average age at first child is 22.1. It is somewhat higher in the urban areas and tends to rise with educational level.

Reproduction

There has been a decrease in women's fecundity since the 1980s.[20] Twenty-seven percent of births are to women under 20 years or older than 35, the ages of higher risk pregnancies; 12 percent are women under 20 years old.

Maternity mortality rates estimate that 107 mothers die per 100,000 live births. Prenatal care is received by 82.6 percent of pregnant women from physicians, nurses, physicians' assistants, or other health care professionals. The rate of deaths due to complications during the pregnancy is still high.

The live birth rate is 22.41 per 1,000 population (2001). The infant mortality rate is 23.96 deaths per 1,000 live births (2001). The average number of children per family is three, but the average is higher for women from rural areas and lower for women from big cities such as Medellín, Bogotá, and Cali. The difference is also influenced by a woman's access to education. In some parts of Colombia, women still have five to seven children (e.g., Afro-Colombian women on the Pacific coast).[21] Indigenous women are under great pressure to have children because they guarantee the preservation of the group, but such pressures restrain development in other social and economic areas.[22]

Sex Education

PROFAMILIA, a private, nonprofit organization that is a member of the International Planned Parenthood Federation, organizes most birth control and sex education programs. It has some 43 clinics throughout the country, and is responsible either directly or indirectly for 65 percent of Planned Parenthood activity in Colombia. One of the main goals of the organization is to promote and defend the right to family planning, and to improve reproductive and sexual health by providing information and services.[23]

The Ministry of Education provides sex education programs in preschool, primary, high school, and vocational education. By law, this is an essential component of public education, and special textbooks have been designed for each level. These programs are closely regulated through the National Plan on Sex Education, whose main objectives are "to foster changes in the value and behavior relating to sexuality, to reformulate the traditional definition of gender roles, to encourage changes in the traditional family structure with the aim of promoting greater equality in the relationship between parents and children and between spouses; and to ensure that men and women make voluntary and informed decisions about when they want to have children and that they know how to use contraceptive methods properly."[24] Even though this program has been a model for other countries, the fact that it is administered through the schools makes it difficult to reach children and adolescents who are not in school. The Ministry of Education is also working on a program of sexual and reproductive health education for adolescents. It targets adolescents both in and out of the school system as well as youth organizations.

Contraception and Abortion

Information on contraceptive methods is more readily available these days. Spousal consent is not needed to obtain contraceptives. However, physicians do have the obligation to abide by the Code of Medical Ethics and to obtain the patient's consent before administering any treatment or performing any procedure related to contraception or to fertilization. Sterilization is the most common family planning method among Colombian women. Government hospitals and PROFAMILIA perform the greatest number of female sterilization procedures, IUD insertions, and vasectomies. The Ministry of Health and PROFAMILIA have clear guidelines for sterilization procedures related to age and number of children. Voluntary request for the procedure and a signed consent form describing the irreversible character of sterilization are required.

PROFAMILIA offers a program to transport women to the clinic and back to their homes. In the clinic, the procedure is very similar to that for patients who go to the clinic on their own. The difference is that it follows a series of educational discussions held in the community by PROFAM-ILIA's instructors, who motivate the patient to seek services. Private entities that contract PROFAMILIA for these purposes provide poststerilization counseling. Other commonly practiced methods of contraception used in Colombia are the birth control pill, the condom, and the IUD. Many of the women who use traditional practices, such as the rhythm method, do not fully understand how it works and are unaware of the specific times within the menstrual cycle that represent the highest risk of pregnancy.[25]

Chief among the goals of the Ministry of Health is to expand family planning counseling. Since family planning services are a component of the primary health program, every health center and hospital must provide them to low-income individuals. Nevertheless, PROFAMILIA continues to be the major provider of family planning services and contraceptive methods, supplying 70 percent of the demand for modern methods. Colombia has legalized the use of emergency contraceptives (the "morning-after" pill). It is classified as a method of birth control and not an abortifacient.

Contraceptive use is at 70 percent. Women under 30 use contraceptives mainly to space pregnancies, while women older than 30 use them to limit pregnancies. In recent years, there has been an increase in the number of women who are using contraceptives and sterilization. The use of condoms has increased, but there is still a need to create awareness that pregnancy prevention is not exclusively a woman's responsibility.

The Penal Code categorizes abortion as a crime against life and personal integrity, punishable by imprisonment from three to ten years. Criminal law penalizes a woman who induces her own abortion, as well as a person who performs the abortion with the woman's consent. The law also applies to any person who induces an abortion without the woman's consent or in a woman under 14. If an abortion is related to pregnancy resulting from rape, incest, or nonconsensual artificial insemination, the penalty is less severe; the prison sentence may be four months to one year.

Despite the illegality of abortion and its severe condemnation by the Colombian population, clandestine abortions performed in nonclinical settings present both social problems and serious health problems of unknown magnitude. Most abortions are the result of not using contraceptives. Approximately 450,000 abortions are performed every year, and it is estimated that they are the second highest cause of maternal mortality. Women of all ages and social classes obtain abortions, although the highest incidence is among women ages 16 to 27. Of every 100 female university students, 26 have had an abortion; one in three women who have ever been pregnant has had one; for every 100 women who have had an abortion, 29 suffer complications and 18 are hospitalized.[26]

Teen Pregnancy

In Colombia, a woman's first sexual encounter usually happens between the ages of 14 and 18. Eleven percent of women between 14 and 19 use contraceptive methods. Of this group, 14 percent are mothers. Women with low levels of education average 19 years of age at their first birth, while women with secondary level of education average 23. An average of 35 percent of live births among adolescent women result from premarital sexual relations.

There is a high relation between the number of single mothers and teen pregnancy. In many cases the father of the child is also a teen, and the young mother is abandoned or left without support. Many of these pregnancies end in clandestine abortions performed in inadequate conditions. Abortion is the third leading cause of maternal mortality among adolescents.

There is great need for programs to provide more accurate information regarding family planning and contraceptives, given the early age at which first sexual encounters occur. Such programs would need to challenge moralistic points of view that refrain from addressing sexual activity issues with adolescents. Reproductive health care and contraceptives are too expensive for many adolescents. At the moment, only PROFAMILIA offers these services on a sliding fee scale to adolescents. And educational institutions violate the rights of adolescent students who become pregnant, in many cases, expelling them from school.

HEALTH

The average Colombian woman's life expectancy is 74.55 years. The total fertility rate is 2.66 children per woman. More than a quarter of the death rate is from violence. Heart disease is the main cause of women's death, and it would be the same for men if the rate of death due to violence were not so high for the male population.[27] Cancer constitutes the second leading cause of death for women. Thirty-two out of every hundred women who die of cancer have shown evidence of cervical tumors, and bone, tissue, or breast cancer. Other frequent problems among women are varicose veins, cataracts, and obesity.

Health Care Access

The Colombian Constitution states that all individuals are to have equal access to health services. The government is required to provide health insurance to all its citizens. The health system is divided into a compulsory health plan, a primary health plan, and a subsidized plan. The compulsory plan provides health services, particularly maternal health care, to all families. In addition to these standard services, pregnant women and mothers of children under one year of age are covered by the compulsory plan which provides a food subsidy. The compulsory plan also mandates the creation of programs dealing with health and sex education, with special emphasis on women in rural areas and adolescents. The Ministry of Health also provides coverage for family planning services and the treatment of communicable diseases like HIV/AIDS. Primary health provision under this program is free of charge and mandatory. The subsidized plan includes health care services for those who cannot afford the fees but are entitled to coverage by the compulsory plan. It also includes programs promoting health for women of childbearing age through family planning services, reproductive health counseling, Pap smear testing, breast examination, and programs to treat sexually transmitted infections.[28]

Despite government laws regarding mandatory health care provisions, statistics show that only 97 percent of Colombians have access to primary health care. In general, most plans have severe deficiencies in coverage for medicine, preexisting conditions, and patient referrals. Most rural areas lack health care access and quality service. Problems related to management, decentralization of programs, delays, and unrealistic budgetary allocations make it difficult to implement health reforms. Among rural migrants to the cities, women constitute the majority of those in need of health services.

Since 1992, the government has been creating more policies that focus on the role of women as central decision-makers and the primary providers of health care. Thus programs like "Health for Women, Women for Health" and "Participation and Equality Policy for Women" seek to "foster autonomy and self-care for women in terms of their bodies, their sexuality and their overall health."[29] These programs also seek to improve women's quality of life, decrease the unequal access of men and women to health care, create programs of prevention, detection and treatment of preventable sexually transmitted diseases, and to implement educational programs that foster greater male participation in issues of sexual and reproductive health.

The decrease in the number of deaths related to pregnancy and labor complications indicates positive changes in maternity services. However, the death rate of children under one year as a result of birth complications shows that there are still deficiencies in adequate and timely attention to mothers giving birth. Seventy-one percent of women in labor are assisted by a doctor; almost 10% by a nurse; and 13% by a midwife. Medical assistance is more common for young mothers (minors), women with a high level of education, and women in urban areas.

Diseases and Disorders

AIDS

The total number of individuals infected with HIV/AIDS in Colombia in 1994 was 85 per million inhabitants. Deficiencies in health plans, particularly in the compulsory plan, create problems of access to services. The plan does not consider services for preexisting conditions. Consequently access for patients with conditions like cancer and HIV/AIDS is limited. In order to receive medical attention for AIDS within the Social Security system, people must pay into the system for two years, so many people are not covered.

The Ministry of Health is responsible for promoting HIV/AIDS research. It has also created laws mandating health establishments to promote and implement activities aiming to provide public health care workers with training and education that will keep them updated on scientific advances regarding the treatment of HIV/AIDS. The law also requires that public and private health establishments must provide comprehensive treatment to persons with HIV/AIDS. Treatments must consider the patients' dignity, must not discriminate, and must be in accordance with the technical and administrative regulations and the standards of the epidemiological control issued by the Ministry of Health. Employees are under no obligation to report to their employers that they are HIV-positive. Criminal charges may be brought against a person who, after being informed that he or she is infected with HIV, deliberately engages in practices that might expose other people to the infection.

In 1993, Colombia issued the Interministerial Medium-Term Plan to Control and Prevent STIs [sexually transmitted infections] and HIV/AIDS. The plan's specific objectives are "to promote greater awareness among the population of issues related to STIs and HIV/AIDS; to reduce morbidity and mortality due to STIs and HIV/AIDS; to decrease the risk of infection with HIV and other STIs; to guarantee respect for persons who are infected with HIV/AIDS or other STIs and to protect their rights; and to strengthen services such as treatment and counseling for persons infected with STIs and HIV/AIDS."[30]

There are many cases of discrimination against people, whether male or female, suffering from HIV/AIDS or STIs. Most of the discrimination is linked to social prejudice, and to the misconception that HIV/AIDS and STIs only affect the homosexual population. Many women are infected as a result of their husband's or partner's bisexual activities outside of the marriage. HIV/AIDS and STIs cases related to female couples are less discussed mainly because lesbians still have little visibility in Colombia.

The Ministry of Health has increased educational and informative campaigns, such as "Men Make the Difference." This particular campaign has good coverage and dissemination through the Internet by including chatrooms, official documents, and global links to NGOs and other organizations that provide information about fighting and/or living with HIV/AIDS. "Men Make the Difference" is creating forums in places of entertainment in cities and creating links to academic institutions. Similar programs that specifically address women's concerns need promotion as well. Although the Internet is an efficient method of spreading information, access to it is limited.

Eating Disorders

Eating disorders such as anorexia have increased among female teens but not at a high rate. This phenomenon is more common in metropolitan areas where adolescents are exposed to consumerism and fashion. Many women, particularly adolescents, idealize images that they see on TV and in the media as the standard for beauty. In poor areas and among the rural migrants to cities, many eating disorders are related to malnutrition and gastric infections.

Cancer

Women's deaths from cancer breakdown as 80.6 percent due to genito-urinary cancer and 61.2 percent due to breast, tissue, or bone cancer. La Liga Colombia de Lucha contra el Cáncer (Colombian Union Against Cancer) sponsors most preventive and educational campaigns to fight cancer. The Instituto Colombiano de Cancerología (Colombian Institute for the Study of Cancer) shares most of those responsibilities. Breast self-examination is becoming routine among Colombian women. The government is also increasing services, and extending programs to migrant women, who are in need of much medical attention upon arrival in the city. The Compulsory Health Plan includes an annual breast examination and a mammogram every two years for women older than 50.

Recently, the Consejería Presidencial para la Equidad de la Mujer (President's Advisory for Women's Equality) signed an agreement with the National Institute of Cancerology in order to develop joint activities to improve and increase cancer control. The plan "Health for Women, Women for Health" has as one of its main objectives to help the government take the necessary steps to reduce diseases that affect women, including breast and cervical cancer.

Depression

There has been an increase in depression among both males and females as a result of the violent sociopolitical situation of the country, the high rate of violent deaths, the number of kidnappings, and the repercussions of violence on the economy. Depression and anxiety levels have increased as a result of unemployment. A report on mental health from the Ministry of Health states that 90,000 Colombians seek mental health help, in only ten hospitals, in the cities.[31]

Depression exists in every sector of the population. The political situation and crime related to robberies, assaults, and reduced safety in the cities increase the anxiety and stress in urban areas. For the migrant population, abandoning their land and other property to guerrilla or paramilitary groups, and all the corresponding problems related to their forced move add to the financial hardships and problems that they experience in adapting to the city.

The rate of depression for women is about 30 percent. In addition to the causes stated above, women's depression is also associated with traditional gender roles that promote self-denial and feelings of helplessness, or the inability to free themselves from traditional patterns of male domination regardless of their economic productivity. Women in abusive and problematic relationships show major depressive symptoms.

Women in Colombia are currently more likely to seek psychiatric help for depression. Access to health care for depression and other mental health problems is not widely available. Individual sessions with a psychiatrist or a psychologist or group therapy is more affordable for the high-income population or for middle-class workers whose company offers such a benefit. As a consequence of depression and other mental health disorders, alcoholism has increased among female adolescents.[32]

POLITICS AND LAW

Suffrage

Colombian women gained the right to vote in 1954, fairly late compared to other countries in the area, and voted for the first time in 1957 elections. The right to vote only came after a tenacious process led by lawyer Esmeralda Arboleda.

Political Participation

The voting age in Colombia is 18. The rate of women voters has always been lower than the rate of men. Abstention in women is as high as 64 percent of the voting population, but in general the level of abstention in Colombia is very high. Political apathy results from the bad reputation of public corporations, lack of trust in the government, and lack of information to promote political awareness. In addition, women refrain from voting because of the low representation they have in the important decision-making processes, although the number of women elected to the Senate and the House of Representatives and serving in ministerial positions has increased in recent years.

The Colombian Constitution was revised and reformed in 1991 in response to differing political circumstances and the need to broaden civil participation. Although it considered important changes, including more guarantees for women, the model of economic distribution based on private property and capital concentration remained for the most part similar to the original document. At the same time, neoliberal economic policies were intensified. Thus, the Plan Nacional de Desarrollo (National Development Plan) created two offices—Dirección Nacional de Equidad para Mujeres (National Office of Women's Equity) and Consejo Nacional de Política Económica y Social/CONPES (National Council of Economic and Social Policy) in order to formulate the institutional framework for women's participation and to design egalitarian programs for women. Although these offices manifest state interest and constitutional commitment, international processes have also been relevant to increasing the political participation of women in Colombia. There is resistance, however, from many national and regional entities to putting women into political positions. Investment in programs for women is second on the agenda in many regional and national sectors.[33]

As a consequence of the revision of the Constitution, there has been more organized political participation among women, but the greater part of this achievement is a result of mobilization of women's groups seeking social, political, and economic visibility. There are still obvious contrasts in the way women participate in political positions. Women are a main component of the economically active population and they hold important positions in the executive branch and in the secretariats, but their presence in the Senate, the House of Representatives, and municipal councils is not in proportion to the population of women in Colombia. Women's action at the local level does not translate into high participation in the directive boards, at the national level.[34]

Unsuccessful political peace negotiations with the FARC-EP lasted approximately four years, coinciding with Andrés Pastrana's presidential period (1998–2002). Women were not conspicuously present at these meetings,[35] and there was no gender-based perspective to consider the role of women in the negotiation of the political conflict, and in the construction of a more egalitarian and peaceful country.

In contrast to the lack of inclusion of women in peace negotiations, there were major attempts to include women in the democratic processes of the 1980s. For example, feminist groups from Bogotá were active participants in the Diálogo Nacional y la Apertura Democrática (National Dialogue and Democratic Opening) in 1984. This event enabled the creation of the Colectivo de Mujeres de Bogotá (Bogotá Women's Collective), which voices women's concerns and positions on national conciliation and the peace process. Political participation in the 1980s also favored the creation of *redes* (networks) at the local and national levels.

Colombian women have been active in labor unions. One of the early Colombian labor union leaders was María Cano, in the 1920s and 1930s. Women also participate in community cooperatives and neighborhood organizations called *juntas comunales*, which were created in 1958 to encourage social and political participation in popular sectors. However, women usually participate only as secretaries because of their lack of available time.

In general terms, women's political participation is closely linked to the search for long-term solutions to problems related to unequal distribution of wealth, the consequences of war, and demands for equality in private and public affairs.

Women's Rights

Feminist Movements

Women have been active in political organizations since 1872, and feminist organizations have become stronger since the 1970s. Feminist groups have been working on issues such as sexual division of work, equal opportunity, health rights, and sexuality. Since the 1980s, feminist movements in Colombia have been greatly influenced and informed by international organizations. Women also are forming associations or coalitions whose main agenda is to mobilize participation in conflict resolution. Various women's organizations strongly denounce violence and seek to eradicate it by democratic means. In Colombia, women have become aware that they must become agents of peace for the society at large. Groups of women from every ethnic background and social status have formed associations throughout the country. A governing principle for all of them is that violence cannot be met with more violence.

For example, Ruta Pacífica de Mujeres (Women's Pacifist Route) "acts as an important national referee in the conflict zone, ensuring that women's alternative plans for peace and co-existence reach the ears of national and international political, economic and social policy-makers."[36] Ruta has bases in several cities and is one of the strongest civil associations. The organization's basic strategy is to march peacefully into the most violent regions of the country in order to create awareness that violence is not the only way to resolve social and political conflict. By the same token, "The group organizes women's forums, national and regional conferences, and training sessions with peasant and professional women working to design and implement co-existent strategies in their towns and neighborhoods during war and peace. To ensure that women's voices are heard and taken into account, both within and outside the borders of Colombia, it circulates information to the government, the media and the international community about human rights violations and threats to women's security."[37]

El Colectivo de Mujeres de Bogotá (Women's Collective of Bogotá) proposed a project oriented toward facilitating a respect for difference. It also seeks the inclusion of multiple subjects and categories, such as age, race, gender, political and religious orientation, and region. Mujeres Rompiendo el Silencio (Women Breaking the Silence) is an organization that has been advocating against violence since 1991. Since 1981, Colombia, like other Latin American countries, has celebrated the International Day Against Violence Against Women on November 25.

Other women's political associations are Asociación Juana de Arco, Asociación Nacional de Mujeres Campesinas e Indígenas de Colombia (AN-

MUCIC, National Association of Women Farmers and Indigenous Women), Colectivo de Mujeres Excombatientes (Collective of Former Guerrilla Women), Colectivo María María, Liga de Mujeres por la Paz y la Libertad (LIMPAL, Union of Women for Peace and Freedom), Liga de Mujeres Desplazadas de Bolívar (Union of Displaced Women from Bolívar), Organización Femenina Popular (Feminine Popular Association), and Red Nacional de Mujeres (National Network of Women).

Academic programs also have made substantial contributions to the dissemination of information regarding women's issues by creating women's studies programs or by sponsoring discussion groups. Academic circles also play an important role in supporting women's organizations. Publications and debates sponsored by women's studies programs and universities have been crucial in helping the administrative institutions to design better programs for women, and to create awareness of the need for equal opportunity.

Lesbian Rights

The number of associations of homosexuals in Colombia is increasing, and homosexuals are acquiring more visibility and political representation. The Asociación Colombiana de Lesbianas y Homosexuales (Colombian Association of Lesbians and Homosexuals) was founded in 1994, and is in the process of becoming a nonprofit organization. By law, Colombian citizens cannot be discriminated against on the basis of gender orientation in the military and in teaching. They have legal protection to hold public demonstrations. Gay pride parades have been held in Bogotá since 1982. Same-gender marriages are legal in civil courts. Some universities have student associations to defend the rights of homosexual students as well as to promote educational and informative campaigns.

Nevertheless, lesbian issues are still on the margin of discussions. An article in the now out-of-print gay magazine *Revista acénto* points out that there is a need for Colombian lesbians to organize politically in order to have their rights acknowledged. In it, Colombian gay rights activist Manuel Velandia points out that a main cause for lesbians' invisibility in Colombia is due to societal moral condemnation and the fact that they only become important if they occupy any important power position.[38] There is the need for educational and informative campaigns as well as for lesbian women to get organized. Many informational sources and health campaigns, and much journalistic coverage, target the male gay population.

Colombian feminist Florence Thomas[39] suggests the need to create departments of queer studies in Colombian universities. However, based on her experience in the creation of the gender studies program at the Universidad Nacional, the issue will be polemical.[40] In most of her books and articles, Thomas addresses topics related to lesbianism by applying French feminist theories.

Military Service

Military service is not mandatory for women in Colombia. However, they are accepted into military universities and into the armed forces either through ROTC programs or in order to pursue a military career. There are also many policewomen. The number of women in the armed forces and their level of achievement are increasing. For example, the Colombian Air Force is a pioneer in Latin America in training women pilots. The first group graduated in 2000 with a degree in aeronautical administration. Nonetheless, the presence and visibility of women in decision-making positions during the current political conflict is not conspicuous.

RELIGION AND SPIRITUALITY

The Law of Religious Freedom, mandating complete religious freedom, was passed in 1995. Roman Catholic instruction in state schools is no longer mandatory. New groups can be recognized as religious entities: there have been more than 80 religious communities for women.[41] Many religious women's congregations have specialized in education and in social and charitable service.

Ninety-three percent of Colombians claim to be Roman Catholic. In general, Catholic Colombians are very attentive to the formalities of the religion as presented in baptism, first Communion, and marriage ceremonies. The tradition of considering church attendance the responsibility of women is changing. The Catholic religion is practiced in the traditional way, and women are not allowed to serve as priests.

Rituals and Religious Practices

Although Catholicism is the dominant religion in the country, it is no longer the official one. According to Williams and Guerrieri, "A small minority of Colombians, mostly European immigrants who have settled in Colombia this century, have discreetly attended Protestant churches, such as the Anglican Church or Lutheran Church . . . There is also a relatively small Jewish population in Colombia that still practices Judaism. . . . Evangelical religious missions from the United States have also arrived in Colombia over recent decades. In general, they have been significantly less successful with the populace than in some other Latin American countries."[42] There is also a small group of nonreligious individuals.

In many indigenous and Afro-Colombian groups, women continue to play a central role in the practice of rituals or ceremonies related to domestic activities or labor. Many of their social customs are rooted in their religious beliefs. Some indigenous groups, such as the Kogis, refer to the earth as Mother Earth, the originator. For the Kogis, possessions were traditionally in the hands of women, and they were inherited matrilinealy.

The Emberá group asks permission from Mother Earth for activities such as hunting and fishing. The Guambianos regard menstruation as pollution that affects other spirits, and they practice a cleansing ritual known as *pishimaruk*. In this group, women participate in domestic work under the supervision of the mother in-law and sisters-in-law. The Uwa group has a rite of passage for women known as *suruwa*. Another Uwa ritual involves only women and it intended to avoid catastrophes. The Wayúus practice a rigorous rite of passage for women. Although many indigenous tribes have gone through the process of acculturation, they keep their laws and traditions relating to marriage decisions.

VIOLENCE

Colombia is undergoing one of the worst periods of violence in its history. Although death resulting from violence greatly affects the adult and young male population, the rate of violent death among women is also very high. Violence, accidents, and homicides are the leading cause of death for women between the ages of 15 and 24. Women are victims of both family and sociopolitical violence. Victims of the latter include not only women who live in places where the military forces, guerrillas and paramilitary groups are fighting each other, but also women who are harassed, kidnapped, persecuted, and killed because they hold political and administrative positions.

Domestic Violence

Most cases of domestic violence involve women in the 25–34 age group, but the data reflect only those cases that have been reported. A great many women have been victims of verbal abuse from their partner. Many cases involve abuse of minors, the greatest number of victims, both male and female, in the 5–14 age group.[43] There is a high rate of female homicides related to domestic violence.

Family or civil court judges can issue protective orders to address domestic violence but sometimes do not issue these orders with the necessary speed. The police also have mechanisms for assisting victims of abuse and preventing repetition of the behavior, but are not well trained in their use.[44]

Additional temporary shelters or halfway houses to protect domestic violence victims are desperately needed. It is important that domestic violence remain under the jurisdiction without being transferred to administrative courts such as the *comisarias de familia*. If administrative courts handle domestic violence, the issue will be considered a private matter and there will be no criminal sanctions.

Rape/Sexual Assault

It has been reported that in Colombia "one third of women living in couples have been victims of verbal abuse. One in five women has suffered physical abuse while 6 percent have suffered sexual violence. 5.3 percent of women of child-bearing age report that they have been forced to have sexual relations. In most cases, the woman knows the person responsible."[45]

The difference in sexual assault statistics by region is slight: 6 percent in urban areas, 4 percent in rural areas. Furthermore, "for adolescent rape victims, the average age at the time of the first rape lowers in direct relation to educational levels. Specifically, the average age for women without education is 13, while the average for those with several years of secondary education is 17."[46] Studies show that there is a high rate of cases where the alleged aggressor is the father or the stepfather.

Trafficking in Women and Children

Colombia is rated second among Latin American countries in terms of providing women for international networks that traffic in women. In Colombia, trafficking in women dates back to the Spanish conquest and has been regulated since colonial times. It became more visible in the 1940s with the employment of Colombian women in a prostitution center (Le Mirage) in Curaçao that served German marines, U.S. military personnel, and multinational migrant workers. Since the mid-1980s, there has been an increase in the number of Colombian women who work as prostitutes in Western Europe (Spain, Germany, Greece, Italy, and Switzerland) as well as in Japan, Hong Kong, Singapore, and Thailand.

To respond to the problem of human trafficking, the Ministry of Justice has created the Inter-Institutional Committee to Combat the Trafficking of Women, Girls and Boys. Trafficking in women is not associated only with prostitution; it includes women intended for domestic service, submissive marriages, and various jobs in the informal economy. However the Fundación Esperanza (Hope Foundation) conducted interviews with 127 governmental organizations and NGOs in which most related the issue solely to prostitution and not other areas. At the international level, trafficking in women has been considered a violation of human rights since 1993.[47] Since human rights violations are often associated with political cases in Colombia, only 18 institutions identified the problem as a human rights issue.

Internal cases of trafficking are intended to supply demands at the local, regional and national levels. Many recruited women are minors, referred by friends or relatives. They are offered jobs as waitresses in clubs or domestic jobs with families, and are then taken to prostitution centers in midsize or big cities. Many times, they are told that they will be providing financial support for their families. Many networks also operate at city bus terminals where displaced women who arrive every day, fleeing the socio-political problems in rural areas.

Newspaper advertisements offer study opportunities, secure jobs, high and fast income, and help in getting visas and other travel documents. Others refer to escort services for visiting foreign professionals or to European and American men looking for Colombian women to wed. There is no explicit mention of prostitution. Job offers include waitressing, baby-sitting, au pair, domestic service, caring for the elderly, and even modeling, always suggesting the possibility of making a lot of money in a short period of time. In general, women are informed of the real nature of the job only right before leaving the country, in the plane, or once they have arrived at their destination. Even if women suspect the nature of the job, many of them stay in the situation because they have signed a contract, and/or their families have acquired debts and financial expectations have been placed on them. In order to leave, many of them sign contracts that promise a payback of up to $5,000, a debt that increases once they reach home. The Internet has become a new way to promote sex tourism and women trafficking, and is very difficult to control.

A profile of trafficked women reveals a range of ages between 18 and 30, with an age average of 23. Many women come from a low or lower-middle income status and may have completed high school or a few years of secondary education, though there are even professional women. Most of them are single mothers or the head of the family, responsible for most of the financial income, and have never worked in prostitution before. The proliferation of these networks is strongly related to the economic hardships that Colombia faces: unequal economy, unemployment, and lack of opportunities for upward social mobility. Most victims come from cities with high rates of unemployment.

It is estimated that an average of 15 minors disappear every day in Colombia. Approximately 30,000 minors work in prostitution in Colombia, many of them the victims of internal trafficking. The number of minors is related to the apparent demand for young people as well as the high level of domestic violence. Many adolescent women who live on the streets or work in prostitution cite harassment from a stepfather as the main reason for leaving home. Once on the streets, they become easy targets for traffickers.

The Colombian Caribbean, particularly the city of Cartagena, has a pattern of prostitution similar to that of Caribbean countries such as the Dominican Republic and Cuba. Many tourism promoters present Cartagena as a part of the Caribbean, not as part of Colombia per se. The violence of the country is associated with the interior, thus isolating the image of Cartagena.[48] Tourism concentrates on the historical downtown and the beach zone of Boca Grande, an area well known for prostitution. Sex tourism is prevalent in Boca Grande, where beaches, hotels, and casinos lure foreigners, particularly Europeans and Americans.[49]

There is an obvious need to create more jobs and equal working conditions for women, as well as to design programs to help prostitutes leave the sex trade. Young women need to be informed about deceptive advertisements and fake promises, as well as information on migration laws and international support organizations for victims of trafficking.[50]

War and Military Repression

Sociopolitical turmoil is the principal cause of both direct and indirect violence against women and girls. Victims of direct violence live in an area affected by the conflict, have family members who are actively participating in the conflict; or who are social activists and /or community leaders. According to a 2001 report prepared by ACNUR, human rights reports have not properly documented the specific situation of women and girls affected by sociopolitical violence in the country. The document states that female kidnapping increased by 300 percent between October 1996 and September 1999. From a total of 38 kidnapped women in 1996, the number increased to 162 in 1999. The statistics show that guerrilla groups abducted 272 women during that period, including 19 by the Autodefensas Unidas de Colombia (AUC; United Self Defence Groups of Colombia).[51]

One of the most notorious effects of the violence is the exodus from rural areas to the cities. Since there are no centers to host the displaced, families quietly move to the cities in search of refuge on their own. Two and a half percent of the Colombian population have been victims of geographical displacement. According to Meertens, "Political violence in Colombia has gender-differentiated impact on social life. During the last two decades, one of the most dramatic social consequences of the armed conflict among guerrillas, paramilitary groups and the army has been the forced internal migration of more than a million and a half people who, individually or in small groups, flee to provincial cities and to the national capital, Bogota. Women and men experience the uprooting, displacement and reconstruction of life in different ways."[52]

Geographical displacement is already preceded by an emotional one.[53] These emotions are expressed, by men as well as by women, in feelings of poverty, sorrow, and nostalgia. The increase in the number of widows and orphans has reshaped families. According to statistics from 1998, victims of forced displacement numbered more than a million people. It is estimated that 58 percent are women, 75 percent of whom are younger than age 25. Women are the head of the family in 30.8 percent of displaced families; 40 percent of those women are widows and 18 percent have been abandoned by their husbands upon arrival in the city. These numbers do not include widows whose husbands died in the military and guerrilla conflicts and who later become refugees, nor do they take into account civilians involved in the armed conflict or those who have been victims of narco-terrorism. In order to avoid further association with guerrilla or paramilitary groups, women are forbidden to show any visible sign of mourning or to claim the bodies of their husbands because such acts may associate them with the armed conflict.[54] Women whose husbands have been disappeared or kidnapped cannot begin to recover from the trauma of loss.[55]

In many cases, women are harassed, raped, and at risk of contracting sexually transmitted diseases. For many of them, prostitution is the only outlet. Women from indigenous communities as well as Afro-Colombian groups have been harassed both individually and as a community. From April to May 2001, 60,623 people were registered as displaced. Of that number, 29,683 were women: 24,392 mestizas, 4,666 Afro-Colombians, and 625 indigenous. Of the total, 51.59 percent were children (52 percent boys and 48 percent girls).[56] Most of the geographical displacement is due to the violence and threats of violence used by the armed actors (*actores armados*) in order to control land and people: general threats, acts of combat, massacres, specific threats, and municipal siege-takeovers (*toma de municipios*). The paramilitary groups and guerrilla groups share the responsibility for these crimes. Women are also participating in the armed conflict. The FARC proudly claims in its web site that 30 percent of its members are "FARC women" (*mujeres farianas*). The ELN and paramilitary groups also have women enlisted. In the army, women work in logistics.

Mujeres en la guerra (Women at War), a collection of testimonials compiled by Colombian journalist Patricia Lara, provides a perspective on women's participation in recent political upheavals in the country. The book consists of a series of narratives that describe the involvement of women in war and a recounting of the reasons that have led them to be active participants (or, if they are victims, the reasons for getting organized and advocating problem-solving).

One of the questions that displacement poses is the possibility for people to return to their place of origin. Men often feel that displacement is a temporary stage, whereas women are more ready to establish themselves in the city. Women "may develop more autonomous behaviour and become rooted sooner than men, precisely because of their survival responsibilities. Men dream of refinding their political discourse. They demand solutions from the state, but paradoxically become dependent on public institutions. The gender balance of the displacement process thus mirrors traditional dichotomies between the public and private, political and social, but their content is daily reconfigured in the daily construction of the future."[57]

OUTLOOK FOR THE TWENTY-FIRST CENTURY

There have been significant changes in many issues related to women's participation and in the achievement of more social and political visibility for women. Although women's participation in the Asamblea Constitu-yente (Constituent Assembly, which assessed the Colombian Constitution in 1991) was not representative of the role played by women in Colombian political and economic life, most current processes that benefit women originated in discussions at that time. Women's organized political activism will continue to be central to the shaping of Colombia in the twenty-first century. Women from various income levels, professions, and ethnic back-grounds are beginning to organize, to question authority, and to seek so-lutions to the armed conflict. It is likely that the number of these organizations will increase.

Women's organizations will need to continue to take specific action ori-ented to improving women's position in society, at the same time seeking to establish political paths and nonmilitary dialogue to end the political struggles of the country. Their achievements must be extended to the so-ciety at large and into the culture, in order to create strong bonds with other groups.

Social programs must be created for displaced women. Although there are already programs for women who have been forced into prostitution or into participation in guerrilla and/or paramilitary groups, more pro-grams are needed in order to reach all parts of the country and socioeco-nomic classes. These programs must address issues such as education, possibilities for participation in the job market, and alternatives for secure income. There is also a need for programs to include women in the political process and to root out the corruption that has permeated every sector of the government. Merteens suggests that programs favoring displaced women and other sectors of the population "should not collapse after three months of relief," as has been the case in the past.

In general, Colombian women will continue to be resilient citizens. Their contribution to the political processes and their ability will undoubt-edly be crucial forces in the economic rebuilding of the nation and for the healing of Colombia after the war.

NOTES

Special thanks to Nikki M. Wilson for research assistance and to Paula Widmer for proofreading.

1. *La Violencia* was a bloody dispute for political control. For over two decades, peasants disputed the interests of Liberal and Conservative elites. The first guerrilla groups were formed during those years. They began receiving support from drug traffickers in the 1980s. Guerrilla groups operate in isolated rural areas, and the presence of drug traffickers is more visible in urban spaces.

2. Although people often refer to Colombian violence, there is a difference be-tween violence related to political causes (the armed conflict) and violence related to social problems that translates into robbery, assaults, and other criminal activities.

3. Hereafter guerrilla groups will be referred by their acronyms.

4. Olga Luz Restrepo Forero, "Mujer indígena: en la encrucijada de la cultura," www.indigenascolombia.org/mujer.asp.

5. Libia Grueso, Rosero Carlos, and Arturo Escobar, "The Process of Black Community Organizing in the Southern Pacific Coast Region of Colombia," in *Cultures of Politics, Politics of Cultures: Re-visioning Latin American Social Movements*, eds. Sonia Alvarez, Evelina Dagnino, and Arturo Escobar (Boulder, CO: Westview Press, 1998), 196–219), see 214.

6. *Women's Reproductive Rights in Colombia: A Shadow Report* (New York: Center for Reproductive Law and Policy and Corporación Casa de la Mujer, 1998), www.crlp.org/ww_sbr_colombia.html, 21.

7. Francisco Cajiao Restrepo. "ATLANTIDA: Una aproximación al adolescente escolar Colombiano," *Revista nómadas* no. 4 (March 1996): 13–23.

8. Yolanda Puyana Villamizar, "Quiero para mis hijos una infancia feliz," *Nómadas* no. 11 (Bogotá: Fundación Universidad Central, 1999): 138–45.

9. Ronald J. Duncan. *Crafts, Capitalism, and Women. The Potters of La Chamba, Colombia* (Gainesville: University of Florida Press, 2000), 8.

10. Donny Meertens, "The Nostalgic Future: Terror, Displacement and Gender in Colombia," in *Victims, Perpetrators or Actors?: Gender, Armed Conflict and Political Violence*, eds. Caroline Moser and Fiona Clark (London: Zed Books, 2001), 142–43.

11. Patricia Tovar, "Más allá del matrimonio, un territorio llamado viudez," *Nómadas* no. 11 (Bogota: Fundación Universidad Central, 1999): 180.

12. Ibid., 182.

13. Ibid., 179.

14. Tovar, 1999, 183.

15. Presidencia de Colombia, www.presidencia.gov.co.

16. Ana Rico, "Formas, cambios y tendencias en la organización familiar en Colombia," *Nómadas* no. 11 (Bogota: Fundación Universidad Central, 1999): 110–17.

17. The Catholic conception that women's lives should be modeled on virtue, resignation, generosity, and chastity exemplified by the Virgin Mary.

18. Antanas Mockus is currently serving his second term as mayor.

19. *Women's Reproductive Rights in Colombia*, 1998, 15.

20. Collin Harding. *Colombia in Focus* (London: Latin American Bureau, 1996).

21. María Isabel Plata, "El ejercicio de tres derechos reproductivos en Colombia," *En otras palabras* no. 1 (July–December 1996): 88.

22. Cajiao Restrepo, 1996.

23. Plata, 1996.

24. *Women's Reproductive Rights in Colombia*, 1998, 22.

25. Ibid., 7.

26. Ibid., 8–9.

27. Harding, 1996.

28. *Women's Reproductive Rights in Colombia*, 1998, 2.

29. Ibid., 4.

30. Ibid., 29.

31. *Mental Health in Colombia: A Cause for Concern*, trans. Hernando Ayala, www.disabilityworld.org/05.06_01.news/colombia.shtml.

32. Angela Constanza Jerez, "Menores, más alcohol, más droga," *Lecturas dominicales El Tiempo*, December 23, 2001, 1.

33. Elizabeth Quiñónez Toro, "Con equidad nuevos sujetos instituyentes para la democracia," *En otras palabras* no. 2 (January–June 1997): 105.

34. Harding, 1996.

35. Magdala Velásquez Toro, "Reflexiones sobre el conflicto armado colombiano desde una mirada feminista," *En otras palabras* no. 8 (January–July 2001): 23.

36. *Ruta Pacífica de las Mujeres, Women at the Peace Table. The Millennium Peace Prize for Women.* http://www.unifem.undp.org/mpprize/colombiabio.html.

37. Ibid.

38. Manuel Velandia, "Tras el velo del anonimato," *Revista Acénto* 1, no. 2 (December 1997), 27.

39. Born in France, Thomas now lives in Colombia and has conducted reseach on Colombian feminism and other women's issues.

40. Florence Thomas, *Homosexualismos y fin de siglo,* www.revistanumero.com/19gay.htm.

41. Raymond Williams and Kevin Guerrieri, *Culture and Customs of Colombia* (Westport, CT: Greenwood Press, 1999), 22–23.

42. Ibid.

43. *Women's Reproductive Rights in Colombia,* 1998, 19.

44. Ibid., 20.

45. Ibid.

46. Ibid., 17.

47. Sandra Claassen and Fanny Polanía Molina. *Tráfico de mujeres en Colombia: Diágnostico, análisis y propuestas* (Bogota: Fundación Esperanza, 1998), 19–22.

48. Laura Mayorga and Pilar Velásquez, "Bleak Pasts, Bleak Futures: Life Paths of Thirteen Young Prostitutes in Cartagena, Colombia," in *Sex, Sun and Gold: Tourism and Sex Work in the Caribbean,* ed. Kamala Kempadoo (Lanham, MD: Rowman and Littlefield, 1999), 159–60.

49. Ibid., 160–66.

50. Claassen and Polanía Molina, 1998, 90–96.

51. ACNUR, *"Consulta con mujeres desplazadas sobre principios rectores del desplazamiento* (Bogotá: ACNUR-OCHO, 2001).

52. Donny Meertens, "The Nostalgic Future: Terror, Displacement and Gender in Colombia," in *Victims, Perpetrators or Actors?: Gender, Armed Conflict and Political Violence,* eds. Caroline Moser and Fiona Clark (London: Zed Books, 2001), 133.

53. Ibid., 137.

54. Ibid.

55. Tovar, 1999, 182–83.

56. Merteens, 2001, 134.

57. Based on interviews by the researcher. Merteens, 2001, 146.

RESOURCE GUIDE

Suggested Reading

Harding, Collin. *Colombia in Focus.* London: Latin American Bureau, 1996. General introduction to Colombia.

Meertens, Donny. "The Nostalgic Future: Terror, Displacement and Gender in Colombia." In *Victims, Perpetrators or Actors?: Gender, Armed Conflict and Political Violence,* ed. Caroline Moser and Fiona Clark, 133–48. London: Zed Books, 2001.

Paternostro, Silvana. *In the Land of God and Men: Confronting Our Sexual Culture.* New York: Dutton, 1998.

Women's Reproductive Rights in Colombia. A Shadow Report. New York: Center for Reproductive Law and Policy and Corporación Casa de la Mujer, 1998. PDF version available at www.crlp.org/ww_sbr_colombia.html.

Videos/Films

The Courageous Women of Colombia. 1997. Directed by Robert Lloyd. A report on an investigation of whether the U.S. government uses the "drug war" as a smokescreen to justify arms sales to Colombia. It also exposes the human rights abuses of the Colombian army and how women have responded to this.

Love, Women and Flowers. 1988. Directed by Marta Rodriguez and Jorge Silva. This documentary tells the horror story of hazardous working conditions for thousands of women who labor in the flower industry. It denounces the use of pesticides and fungicides, some banned in the developed countries that export them, and the drastic health and environmental consequences in Colombia.

Never Again. 2001. Directed by Marta Rodriguez and Fernando Restrepo. This documentary follows the survivors of a series of massacres that displaced communities of Antioquia and Choco.

The Rose Seller. 1998. Directed by Víctor Gaviria. A combination of testimonial and fiction in the cinema verité style tells of the hardships of street kids in Medellín, particularly female children and teenagers.

Web Sites

Casa de Nariño, www.presidencia.gov.co.
Web site of Colombia's presidency.

Center for Reproductive Law and Policy, www.crlp.org/ww_sbr_colombia.html.
Contains *Shadow Report on Women's Reproductive Rights in Colombia*.

Consejería Presidencial para la Equidad de la Mujer, www.presidencia.gov.co/equidad/index.htm.
Describes official Colombian government programs focused on women. In Spanish.

Etnias de Colombia, www.indigenascolombia.org.

FARC-EP, www.farc-ep.org.
Web site of Mujeres Farianas, the Women of the Fuerzas Armadas Revolucionarias de Colombia-Ejército de pueblo, or FARC-EP (Armed Revolutionary Forces of Colombia-People's Army).

Mujeres Latinomaricans en Cifras, Colombia, www.eurosur.org/FLACSO/mujeres/colombia.
General statistics depicting the situation of Colombian women. In Spanish.

School of General Studies, National University of Colombia, www.humanas.unal.edu.co/genero/.
Web site for the Programa de Estudios en Género, Mujer y Desarrollo (women's studies program) at Universidad Nacional de Colombia. Very useful virtual library and summary of publications by the program in the Publications link. In Spanish.

Organizations

Corporación Casa de la Mujer
Phone: (57-1) 312-5078/312-5071
Fax: (57-4) 310-3261
Email: casmujer@colnodo.apc.org

Fundación Esperanza Colombia
Apartado Aéreo 075174
Bogotá 2 Colombia
Phone: (57-1) 526-1121/526-1080
Fax: (57-1) 671-5400
Email: esperanz@col1.telecom.com.co

Grupo Mujer y Sociedad
Programa de Estudios y Género
Universidad Nacional de Colombia
Edificio Manuel Ancízar 2003–2007
Ciudad Universitaria
Bogotá, Colombia
Phone: (57-1) 316-5000 Ext. 20010
Fax: (57-1) 316-5142
Email: fdmujgen@bacata.usc.unal.edu.co

Ruta Pacífica de las Mujeres
Fax: (57-4) 292-0902
Email: rutapacifica@epm.net.co

SELECTED BIBLIOGRAPHY

Duncan, Ronald J. *Crafts, Capitalism, and Women: The Potters of La Chamba, Colombia*. Gainesville: University of Florida Press, 2000.

Grueso, Libia, Rosero Carlos, and Escobar Arturo. "The Process of Black Community Organizing in the Southern Pacific Coast Region of Colombia." In *Cultures of Politics, Politics of Cultures: Re-visioning Latin American Social Movements*, edited by Sonia Alvarez, Evelina Dagnino and Arturo Escobar, 196–219. Boulder, CO: Westview Press, 1998.

Harding, Collin. *Colombia in Focus*. London: Latin American Bureau, 1996.

Mayorga, Laura, and Pilar Velásquez. "Bleak Pasts, Bleak Futures: Life Paths of Thirteen Young Prostitutes in Cartagena, Colombia." In *Sex, Sun and Gold: Tourism and Sex Work in the Caribbean*, edited by Kamala Kempadoo, 157–82. Lanham, MD: Rowman and Littlefield, 1999.

Meertens, Donny. "The Nostalgic Future: Terror, Displacement and Gender in Colombia." In *Victims, Perpetrators or Actors?: Gender, Armed Conflict and Political Violence*, edited by Caroline Moser and Fiona Clark, 133–48. London: Zed Books, 2001.

Mental Health in Colombia: A Cause for Concern, Hernando Ayala, trans. http://www.disabilityworld.org/05.06_01.news/colombia.shtml.

November 25. International Day Against Violence Against Women. www.redesaludweb.cl.

Paternostro, Silvana. *In the Land of God and Men: Confronting Our Sexual Culture*. New York: Dutton, 1998.

Ruta Pacífica de las Mujeres. *Women at the Peace Table. The Millennium Peace Prize for Women*. www.unifem.undp.org/mpprize/colombiabio.html.

Williams, Raymond, and Kevin Guerrieri. *Culture and Customs of Colombia*. Westport, CT: Greenwood Press, 1999.

Women's Reproductive Rights in Colombia. A Shadow Report. New York: Center for Reproductive Law and Policy and Corporación Casa de la Mujer, 1998. www.crlp.org/ww_sbr_colombia.html.

Spanish Bibliography

ACNUR. *Consulta con mujeres desplazadas sobre principios rectores del desplazamiento. Bogotá 16–18 de mayo 2001*. Bogota: ACNUR-OCHA, 2001.

Aljure, Luis. "Las carreras del futuro." *Revista Diners* (December 2000): 88–95.

Cajiao Restrepo, Francisco. "ATLANTIDA: Una aproximación al adolescente escolar Colombiano." *Revista nómadas* no. 4 (March 1996): 53–64.

Claassen, Sandra, and Fanny Polanía Molina. *Tráfico de mujeres en Colombia: Diagnóstico, análisis y propuestas*. Bogota: Fundación Esperanza, 1998.

"En Bogotá, noche del viernes para mujeres y con ley seca." *El Tiempo* (Bogotá), March 5, 2002. Instituto Colombiano de Bienestar Familiar. www.icbf.org.co.

Jerez, Angela Constanza. "Menores, más alcohol, más droga." *Lecturas dominicales El Tiempo*, December 23, 2001, 1–2.

Lara, Patricia. *Las mujeres en la guerra*. Bogotá: Planeta, 2000.

"Mujer y conflicto armado. Reporte de la Mesa de Trabajo." ACNUR, 2001. Unpublished manuscript.

Plata, María Isabel. "El ejercicio de tres derechos reproductivos en Colombia." *En otras palabras*. no. 1. Bogotá: Grupo Mujer y Sociedad. July–December, 1996.

Puyana Villamizar, Yolanda. " 'Quiero para mis hijos una infancia feliz': Socialización y cambio en torno a las representaciones sociales sobre la infancia." *Nómadas* no. 11 (Bogotá: Fundación Universidad Central, 1999): 138–45.

Quiñónez Toro, Elizabeth. "Con equidad nuevos sujetos instituyentes para la democracia." *En otras palabras* no. 2 (Bogotá: Grupo Mujer y Sociedad, January–June 1997): 99–108.

Restrepo Forero, Olga Luz. "Mujer indígena: en la encrucijada de la cultura." www.indigenascolombia.org/mujer.asp.

Rico, Ana. "Formas, cambios y tendencias en la organización familiar en Colombia." *Nómadas* no. 11 (Bogotá: Fundación Universidad Central, 1999): 110–17.

Serrano, José Fernando. "Entre negación y reconocimiento: Estudios sobre 'homosexualidad' en Colombia." *Nómadas* no. 6 (1997): 67–79.

Thomas, Florence. *Homosexualismos y fin de siglo*. www.revistanumero.com/19gay.htm.

Tovar, Patricia. "Más allá del matrimonio, un territorio llamado viudez." *Nómadas* no. 11 (1999): 178–84.

"Tras el velo del anonimato." *Revista acento* 1, no. 2 (December 1997): 24–28.

Velásquez Toro, Magdala. "Reflexiones sobre el conflicto armado colombiano desde una mirada feminista." *En otras palabras* no. 8 (January–July 2001): 20–31.

7

COSTA RICA

Ilse Agshagen Leitinger

PROFILE OF COSTA RICA

Costa Rica ("Rich Coast") is not rich in gold, as the Spaniards originally assumed, but does contain countless riches. It boasts diverse flora, fauna, topography, landscapes, and climate zones. It has a variety of people and cultures, including original indigenous tribes, subsequent Spanish colonizers, and, since its independence in the nineteenth-century, Caribbean, Asian, European, and North American immigrants. It has carried on diverse survival activities from earlier subsistence agriculture to today's complex agricultural and industrial export production, and is strongly committed to international tourism, environmental protection, and sustainable development.

Located in Central America, between Nicaragua to the north and Panama to the south, Costa Rica is roughly 51,000 square kilometers (20,000 square miles) in size, slightly larger than Switzerland and about the size of West Virginia. Costa Ricans, "Ticos" in local parlance, take pride in their long-established democracy, in which peaceful elections feel like public festivals. They adhere to a gentle style of gradual change *a la Tica*, with a persistent preference (they call it "idiosyncrasy")

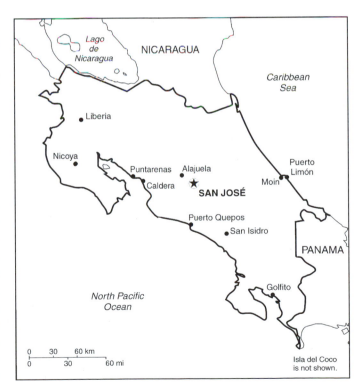

for protecting social stability. In 1949, Costa Rica eliminated its military, and has since been able to spend resources thus saved on social services and education.

In 1999, Costa Rica's population was close to 4 million, with about 30,000 more men than women. Women had a life expectancy of 79.8 yrs. compared to 74.1 yrs. for men. Infant mortality was 11.8 per 1,000 live births,[1] and female fertility was 2.43.

OVERVIEW OF WOMEN'S ISSUES

Assessing the situation of Costa Rican women requires noting positive and negative issues affecting their lives. Historically, women's position was based on traditional patriarchy. As is typical in Latin American culture, each gender had a distinct role. In recent years this pattern has been changing as a result of accelerating worldwide economic, political, and cultural globalization, and women's increasing self-confidence about their capacity to make decisions and take on responsibilities outside the family. Also, men are slowly accepting that Costa Rica cannot meet current challenges without women's active involvement. Consciousness about and demand for gender equity have increased. Of course, details of gender issues vary according to socioeconomic and ethnic conditions, but overall improvement is undeniable and substantial.

The most relevant questions about Costa Rican women are their educational opportunities, family and economic roles, health options, exposure to violence, role in religion, legal changes, and political participation While statistical data from different sources often do not agree, they always give good approximations. Over time, changes in approach to gender issues nationally and internationally have created a new understanding of human rights: Analysts now differentiate between *gender equality*, legal systems that protect women and men equally, and *gender equity*, the actual practical achievement of women's legally proposed gender equality.[2]

EDUCATION

Since 1949, education in Costa Rica has had the use of more tax resources than education in other Central American countries. As President Pepe Figueres stated in the 1940s, Costa Rica is proud to have more teachers than policemen.

Opportunities

School attendance is obligatory and free, though many students drop out before finishing. A nine-year elementary and junior high-school sequence, for ages six to fourteen, provides basic education. Students can add two years of high school and also obtain university admission. A three-year vocational cycle, for ages 15–17, offers training in agriculture, animal husbandry, industrial arts, secretarial work, accounting, mechanics, electronics, and computers.

Yet profound differences exist between public and private, or urban and rural schools. Private schools are expensive, but offer more resources, teaching materials, and qualified personnel. Frequently, they are bilingual. In public schools, students must still memorize, instead of learning to think independently. All sources agree that the Costa Rican educational system must develop more creativity, critical thinking, conflict resolution, and teamwork. At the same time, education has become "a virtual civil religion," and brought "socialization of citizens, democratization, and social mobility."[3] Nevertheless, much of the system still uses "invisible gender pedagogy." Norms, values, and beliefs promote inequality of gender and pass on to students traditional gender roles through class discussions and social relations.[4]

More girls than boys participate in basic education. In 1999, the figures for grades 1–6 were 96.0 percent and 95.6 percent respectively. The dropout rate was 4.1 percent for girls and 4.6 percent for boys. In grades 7–11, girls' enrollment was 58.5 percent and boys', 56.4 percent, with a yearly girls' dropout rate of 9.6 percent, and 13.0 percent for boys. Thus, 112 girls attended school for each 100 boys.[5] Among workers, women up to age 29 ranked higher than men in average years of education, older women ranked lower.[6]

The state university system consists of four institutions. The University of Costa Rica (UCR) was created in 1940. In 1973, the National Autonomous University (UNA) was established, followed by the Technological Institute (IT) and, in 1978, the State Extension University (UNED). The private Autonomous University of Central America (UACA), founded in 1976, initiated a private university proliferation. Some private universities are small and have been criticized for their limited course offerings. Today, many universities register more female than male students, though women are not equally represented in all fields. Fewer women study engineering or natural sciences, more study health or social sciences. Fewer women hold administrative posts.[7]

Literacy

The adult literacy rate in 1999 was 95.5 percent for both genders.[8] It is not unusual, though, that literacy data include people who can sign their name, but are functionally illiterate because of lack of practice.

EMPLOYMENT AND ECONOMICS

Job/Career Opportunities

Costa Rican women's participation in the workforce is undergoing profound changes. Their traditional roles as homemakers, domestic workers, nurses, or teachers are less popular than in the past, particularly in urban areas. However, that does not mean women have achieved gender equity in the labor market, especially in rural areas. Many women are without Social Security or insurance; 20 percent of female-headed households are among the poorest of the poor. Working conditions for female domestic servants are bad, with low salaries, long hours, and insufficient benefits such as maternal leave.

Tourist and shopkeeper and her family in Palma. Photo © Erwin Nielsen/Painet.

Recent statistics indicate that women's share of the economically active population is 34.6 percent.[9] Among professionals/technicians it is 47.1 percent, and of directors or managers, 30.6 percent. Women participate in more than 30 percent of scientific research, but their participation varies by research focus, from above 50 percent in health-related and nearly 50 percent in social-science research, to less than 30 percent in engineering and less than 20 percent in agriculture.[10] An interesting additional factor is the recent increase in women small business owners. In the late 1990s, women represented about one-fourth of all small business owners.[11]

Costa Rica has a relatively strong cooperative movement that includes about 30 percent of all economically active people. Most cooperatives are located in the Central Valley. Frequently, coop workers are also managers and owners. Women's membership in cooperatives approaches 30 percent, with slowly increasing participation in cooperative management. Less than 10 percent of all Costa Rican cooperatives are exclusively women's enterprises.[12]

Pay

Women always earn less than men. In 1999, in the private sector women earned 80.4 percent of what male professionals/technicians earned, 84.3

percent of male managers' salaries, 75.8 percent of salesmen's, and 77.8 percent of workers' or artisans' wages. Though the public sector pays equal wages to men and women, men are in higher positions.[13] Feminization of poverty is one of the many challenges that remain. Self-employed women have lower incomes, especially in rural areas or if they are single mothers. Housework and invisible self-employment are not considered "work," and do not offer sufficient income.

Working Conditions

Sexual Harassment

Working women face violence on the job. Sexual harassment at work or in education is a concern. Legal protection in the public sector is obligatory, though at times it is poorly administrated. Private employers must establish rules for their enterprises.

Support for Mothers/Caretakers

Maternal Leave

Women are entitled to four months of leave, one before childbirth and three afterward, without loss of salary or retirement benefits. Thereafter, women may take an hour a day off from work for breast-feeding for six more months.

Social/Government Programs

In 1999, through Law 7769 on Attention to Women Living in Poverty, the government initiated a program to offer poor women special assistance for education, occupational training, integration into the labor force, and support for housing.

Overall, the Costa Rican women's movement, financial government support, new institutions responding to women's needs, many nongovernmental organizations, and international agreements concerning women's struggles are having a notable effect upon Costa Rican society. Beyond support for mothers, a new approach to gender equity has arisen, with a new vocabulary. Formerly ignored problems are openly acknowledged: for example, women more frequently bring court charges of harassment and violence, or turn to self-help organizations. Moreover, the National Women's Institute (INAMU), the government agency in charge of women's issues, has initiated an effort indicating the government's commitment to gender equity in the labor market. INAMU is creating a Seal of Gender Equity, to be attached to products of enterprises whose labor practices observe true gender equity. This will raise consciousness among consumers and help Costa Rica export to countries where gender equity is valued.

FAMILY AND SEXUALITY

Gender Roles

For most women in Costa Rica, the family is still the primary focus, even though families have become smaller and many women work outside the home at least part-time. Men were power holders and decision makers in public; women were restricted to the private, vital tasks of mothers or homemakers. This system produced gender inequality that gave women no options for developing initiatives or making decisions about their lives. Men's power often led them to machismo, the overexertion of power (e.g., through domestic violence), whereas women's submission inspired them to achieve goals diplomatically with patient persistence, practicing what in Latin America has been called *marianismo*, submissive behavior patterned after that ascribed to the Virgin Mary.[14]

In overall human well-being, Costa Rica has consistently been among the nearly fifty nations in the world with the highest Human Development Index (HDI) of 0.8 or above, a measure rating human well-being on a scale from 0.1 to 1.0, and also has a high Gender-related Development Index (GDI), rating women's well-being the same way.[15] For Costa Rica, the index for women's well-being is lower than that of overall human well-being, a sign of still imperfect gender equity. But women are better off in Costa Rica than in many countries of the world.

Marriage

Marriage and stable common-law marriage are highly respected, and legally protected, and rights to Social Security services and pensions similar to those of nuclear families, which form the majority of Costa Rican households.

Reproduction

Family size varies according to location; urban mothers averaged two children, and rural mothers, four to six, in the early 1990s.[16] Yet, in rural areas we still find elderly women who have given birth to more than 20 children. In 2000, more than half of the 78,178 births registered were to single mothers, and half of these children did not receive financial support from their father.[17] The 2001 Law of Responsible Paternity may help these children, given that after the law's passage, half of those named as fathers accepted financial responsibility without DNA testing.[18]

Sex Education, Contraception, and Abortion

As for family planning, knowledge about reproduction is expanding. Costa Rican schools and communities are developing programs of sex education. A recent survey indicates that 96 percent of women in common-law marriages had used some form of contraceptives, whereas in 1976 only 83 percent had done so. Most interviewees had used condoms (62 percent) or oral contraceptives (73 percent). Birth control through rhythm was at 32 percent; some 20 percent had experience with IUDs, injections, or sterilization. The 1999 Costa Rican Social Security Service (CCSS) Executive Decree 27913-S gives individuals the right to decide about reproductive health, allowing individuals to be sterilized without their partner's approval.[19] To spread information on family planning methods, CCSS publishes popular descriptive guides, such as the *Guía de métodos anticonceptivos*, with simple text in large type, accompanied by clear illustrations of biological facts and cartoons illustrating human relationships.

Given that abortion is illegal in Costa Rica, except to save a mother's life, little is known about abortion statistics and attitudes, especially women's attitudes. The annual State of the Nation report gives a figure of approximately 8,000–9,000 abortions per year probably representing the number of legal abortions (spontaneous, medically induced, or self-induced abortions requiring medical care).[20] Abortions are available in private clinics, if the patient can afford to pay, and also are available from "less hygienic practitioners." Maternal mortality in 1998 was 0.2 per 1,000 births.[21] Abortions are available in neighboring Nicaragua, and women often travel there if they cannot afford private doctors in Costa Rica. A study on reproductive health reports that 55.1 percent of 857 interviewees opposed abortion and 37.3 percent opposed it somewhat (thus, 7.6 percent must have been in favor of it).[22]

Teen Pregnancy

Of the 2000 birth count of 78,178, 16,652 or (21.3 percent), were to mothers under 18 years of age. Two INAMU programs, Young Love, offering sex education for young people, and Constructing Opportunities, aiding adolescent mothers, help adolescents to manage their sexuality. These are only two of many governmental policies for educating the public on issues important for women.

HEALTH

Data on health are one component of the Human Development Index (HDI). In 1997, 94.5 percent of Costa Ricans had access to basic potable water service (99.6 percent in urban areas and 90.5 percent in rural areas). Access to a sewer system was 89.8 percent (98 percent in urban areas and 82.5 percent in rural ones).[23]

Information on childbirth and population growth also indicates a population's health. For 1998, the birth rate was 20.4, the mortality rate was 3.9 per 1,000 inhabitants, the population growth rate was 2.6 percent, and the birthrate was 2.43.[24] Average maternal mortality for 1980–1999 was 29 per 100,000 live births.[25] In 1998, it had fallen to 16, a significant improvement. Infant mortality for 1999, listed as 13 per 1,000 live births, placed Costa Rica in forty-second place in the world.[26]

Health Care Access

The CCSS provides wide access to health care facilities, covering about 90 percent of all Costa Ricans, though efficiency is not always exemplary. Waits of weeks for medical appointments with specialists or surgeons are common. Those who can afford it, seek private doctors. Yet, in March 2001, 747 Teams for Basic Attention to Health Needs (EBAIS), some in mobile units, were covering the needs of 80 percent of the population.[27] Also, a basic change in health care is that the CCSS is now focusing on prevention as a vital part of health care. A CCSS pamphlet, *Promoción de salud: Estilos de vida saludables* (2002) stresses diet, physical exercise, a healthy environment, good human relations, and avoidance of smoking and drugs. Also, a special Women's Hospital was created in 1999, to improve health care for women.

Medical Concerns

A concern for local professionals has been the high rate of cesarean sections. Of the 74,928 births in CCSS maternity wards in 1999, cesarean sections accounted for nearly 22 percent.[28] For private doctors, the rate was higher. In comparison, the rate set in 1989 by the World Health Organization for medically justifiable cesarean sections was 15 percent.[29]

POLITICS AND LAW

Suffrage, Political Participation, and Women's Rights

Costa Rican women have had the right to vote since June 20, 1949, though they did not vote until 1950 in local rural elections, and 1953 in a national election. The 1996 Law to Reform the Electoral Code established a minimum quota of 40 percent for women's participation on the ballot and in elected positions.[30] In the 2002 national election, when this regulation was fully implemented, women candidates won in many places, particularly in municipal elections, with a success rate in some areas of over 50 percent.[31] No doubt, women's active participation in policymaking and public administration will rise further.

Since the 1970s there have been steady improvements in women's legal rights and their participation in politics. Beginning in 1973, the Costa Rican Legislative Assembly has passed 22 decrees or laws concerning women. Ten represent issues regarding the family, four address labor problems, three deal with sexual harassment and violence, and three refer to discrimination and equality. One created the autonomous National Women's Institute (INAMU). Earlier, as the Center for the Development of Women and the Family, it had been part of the Ministry of Culture, Youth, and Sports. Finally, a 1984 decree confirmed the ratification of CEDAW, the 1979 U.N. Convention on the Elimination of All Forms of Discrimination Against Women. Topics covered by these laws are marriage, mothers' rights, protection against domestic violence, rights and protection of children and adolescents, the Law of Responsible Paternity, the ensurance of gender equity in political, organizational, and labor participation, and women's earnings.

Since 1974, 16 pieces of legislation have established or modified government institutions in support of women's concerns, six of them related to INAMU.[32] Moreover, many ministries and municipalities have added special offices for women's affairs. There is a Women's Permanent Commission in the Legislative Assembly, Costa Rica's Parliament; there will always be at least one woman vice president (of two) in the government; and many women ministers and vice ministers have been nominated. One of six women ministers, who represent 25 percent of all ministers, is the Minister for Women's Affairs, who is director of INAMU. Also, the Office of the Ombudsman has a separate section for women.[33]

In the 2002 vote, with 35.08 percent women members elected to its Legislative Assembly, Costa Rica was in sixth place among all countries of the world for its percentage of women legislators. This placed Costa Rica behind Sweden, Denmark, Finland, the Netherlands, and Norway, but ahead of Iceland, Germany, New Zealand, and Argentina. Moreover, Costa Rica is first in the Western Hemisphere, far ahead of the United States, which is in fifty-third place.[34]

Lesbian Rights

Costa Rica is home to a vibrant lesbian community that increasingly has "come out of the closet." Societal understandings of women's sexual identities and roles are still traditional, although attitudes toward homosexuality have become more positive in recent decades. Lesbians have participated actively in women's movements and in various public and private contexts. Groups such as San José–based Las Entendidas have played important roles in supporting lesbians and educating Costa Rican society about issues of homophobia and sexual identity.

Military Service

There has been no military in Costa Rica since its abolition in 1949.

RELIGION AND SPIRITUALITY

Roman Catholicism is the official religion in Costa Rica, and after the State, the Catholic Church is the strongest traditional institution. It still treats women in a patriarchal style. Women are expected to be submissive and self-denying. Divorce and abortion are forbidden. Nevertheless, women participate more actively than men in religious activities. They have found diverse ways of being religious, some accepting submission as God's will and others seeking more dignity and liberty. In recent years, the Church has expressed growing concern with women's rights and needs, particularly with regard to violence against women.

Many other religions are accepted in Costa Rica, more than 10 percent of Costa Ricans belong to non-Catholic sects and denominations.[35] Probably the strongest is fundamentalist Protestantism, but Judaism and various Asian religions are also practiced. Many private schools are connected with fundamentalist Protestantism, and there are numerous Catholic schools as well.

VIOLENCE

Violence against women is also a question of public health and safety. In that context, violence categories have literally exploded, and so have policies addressing them. The expanded vocabulary includes sexual harassment or rape; incest; sexual harassment at work; violence in a couple relationship; sexual violence in the media; forced pregnancy (through assault or rape); unsafe abortion; abuse by police officers; institutional violence; repeated victimization of mistreated women, girls, or adolescents; violence against indigenous women, migrants, lesbians, Afro–Costa Ricans, elderly women, prostitutes, handicapped women, domestic servants, women prisoners; the killing of women; and trafficking in children and adolescents for commercial sex.

Domestic Violence

Domestic violence has affected Costa Rican women for centuries. It is encouraging that basic perceptions of violence have undergone changes and definitions have expanded significantly. Formerly, domestic violence against women was simply physical aggression. Now, it is being defined as including physical, psychological, and sexual abuse, and in some cases includes a patrimonial dimension (i.e., the attack against possessions that rightfully belong to women). However, one must ask whether public attention to violence has grown through awareness of this social problem or through an increase in violence. The 1996 Law against Domestic Violence may have caused the remarkable rise in public accusations from 5,023 in 1996 to 32,643 in 2000.[36] Also, though women of all classes report violence, poor women do so more often.[37]

The search for help by women threatened by violence has led to the development of government programs, such as emergency phone lines and shelters for women administrated by INAMU's Women's Delegation, or legal advice, offered by the Women's Section in the Ombudsman's Office. Many community-action groups or women's self-help organizations are also participating. Two examples are the Alliance of Costa Rican Women and the Feminist Center for Information and Action. The latter's program, Woman, You Are Not Alone, arose in response to domestic violence in 1988.

Trafficking in Women and Children

Despite Costa Rican efforts to protect women and children, the U.S. Department of State in its Country Reports on Human Rights Practices still identifies Costa Rica as a "transit and destination country for trafficked persons."[38]

OUTLOOK FOR THE TWENTY-FIRST CENTURY

The outlook for Costa Rican women is promising. Their self-confidence is rising, as is their awareness of their right to political participation and their capacity for decision-making. Better education gives them better qualifications in the labor market. Improved health care and prevention allow them more options. Also, men are beginning to value women's contribution to national and family survival, enjoying collaboration in tasks that formerly were exclusively women's.

Of course, it will take time before conditions improve for all women. More challenges will arise, but the traditional Costa Rican openness and human warmth will help. Costa Rican women are better off than they were in the 1990s, and they can advance more rapidly than women in many developed countries, particularly if they obtain an education.

NOTES

Thanks to Aixa Ansorena, Rocío Chaves and her INAMU colleagues, Patricia Jiménez, and CEMUCA participants Lindsey Hagglund and Jane Lynch for their contributions.

1. National and international data disagree at times. For example, infant mortality is given as 12.6 for 1998 in Ministerio de Salud de Costa Rica (MSBI), *Indicadores básicos: Situación de salud en Costa Rica* (San José, Costa Rica: Ministerio de Salud, 1999), 3; as 13 for 1999 in United Nations Development Programme (UNDP), *Human Development Report 2001* (New York: Oxford University Press, 2001), 166; and as 11.8 for 1999 in Estado de la Nación (EN), *Estado de la nación en desarrollo humano sostenible* (San José, Costa Rica: Proyecto Estado de la Nación, 2001), 319.

2. EN, 2001.

3. Instituto Nacional de las Mujeres (INAMU), *Gender and Education* (San José, Costa Rica: INAMU, 2001), 1.

4. INAMU ID, "Education, 2002," 9–10, Table 1.3.

5. EN, 2001, 260.

6. Ibid.

7. (UNDP), 2001, 218.

8. John A. Booth, *Costa Rica: Quest for Democracy* (Boulder, CO: Westview Press, 1998), 94.

9. INAMU ID, *Work and Gender* (San José, Costa Rica: INAMU, 2001), 2.

10. EN, 2001, 260.

11. INAMU, *Women Owners of Small Businesses* (San José, Costa Rica: INAMU, 2000), 5.

12. Mireya G. Jiménez and Marta M. Campos, *Diagnóstico de la participación de la mujer en el movimiento cooperativo costarricense* (San José, Costa Rica: APROMUJER, 1999), 19–23, 74–75.

13. INAMU ID, *Work and Gender*, 2001, 2.

14. Evelyn P. Stevens, "Marianismo: The Other Face of Machismo in Latin America," *Female and Male in Latin America*, ed. Ann Pescatello (Pittsburgh, PA: University of Pittsburgh Press, 1973), 89–101.

15. UNDP, 2001, 141, 210; EN, 2001, 65.

16. Mavis Hiltunen Biesanz, Richard Biesanz, and Karen Zubris Biesanz, *The Ticos: Culture and Social Change in Costa Rica* (Boulder, CO: Lynne Rienner, 1999), 1, 71–73.

17. EN, 2001, 87.

18. Rocío Chaves Jiménez, personal communication, 2002.

19. Programa Centroamericano de Población de la Escuela de Estadística and Instituto de Investigaciones en Salud, *Reproductive Health* (San José, Costa Rica: PCP and INISA, 2001), 45.

20. EN, 2001, 323.

21. INAMU ID, *Gender and Health* (San José, Costa Rica: INAMU, 2001), 1.

22. M. Chen Mok et al., *Salud reproductiva y migración nicaragüense en Costa Rica 1999–2000: Resultados de una encuesta nacional de salud reproductiva* (San José, Costa Rica: 2001), 85, 94.

23. MSBI, 1999, 3.

24. MSBI, 1999, 2.

25. UNDP, 2001, 166.

26. Ibid.

27. CCSS, *Modernización*, no. 43 (March 2002).

28. EN, 2001, 326.

29. Jennifer Kozlow-Rodriguez, "The Predictability of Cesarian-Section Births. A Case Study of Students in Costa Rican Childbirth Classes," in *The Costa Rican Women's Movement: A Reader*, ed. and trans. Ilse Abshagen Leitinger (Pittsburgh, PA: University of Pittsburgh Press, 1997), 316.

30. EN, 2001, 291.

31. INAMU ID, *Political Participation* (San José, Costa Rica: INAMU, 2002).

32. EN 2001, 296.

33. C. Soto, in Leitinger, *The Costa Rican Women's Movement: A Reader*, 103–110.

34. INAMU ID, *Women's Representation in Popular Elections and Nominations: Women in National Parliaments* (San José, Costa Rica: INAMU, 2002); Herrera, personal communication, February 4, 2002.

35. Biesanz et al., 1999, 246.

36. EN, 2001, 278.

37. Biesanz et al., 1999, 190; EN, 2001, 278.

38. U.S. Department of State, *Costa Rica — Country Reports on Human Rights Practices*, www.state.gov/g/drl/rls/hrrpt/2001wha/8329.htm, accessed March 4, 2002.

RESOURCES

Suggested Reading

Biesanz, Mavis Hiltunen, Karen Zubris Biesanz, and Richard Biesanz. *The Ticos: Culture and Social Change in Costa Rica*. Boulder, CO: Lynne Rienner, 1999. This work, an update of Biesanz's 1982 *The Costa Ricans*, offers an in-depth introduction to Costa Rican culture.

Booth, John A. *Costa Rica: Quest for Democracy*. Boulder, CO: Westview Press, 1998. A Costa Rican political history with much relevant information. Helpful index.

Helmuth, Chalene. *Culture and Customs of Costa Rica*. Westport, CT: Greenwood Press, 2000.

Leitinger, Ilse Abshagen, ed. and trans. *The Costa Rican Women's Movement: A Reader*. Pittsburgh, PA: University of Pittsburgh Press. A collection of 34 articles on issues relevant to Costa Rican women in the 1990s.

Stevens, Evelyn P. "Marianismo: The Other Face of Machismo in Latin America." In *Female and Male in Latin America*, edited by Ann Pescatello, 89–101. Pittsburgh, PA: University of Pittsburgh Press, 1973. The article provides insight into gender aspects of the Latin American culture.

United Nations Development Programme (UNDP). *Human Development Report 2001: Making New Technologies Work for Human Development*. New York: Oxford University Press. This UNDP report, which appears annually, offers excellent information on all countries of the world.

Web Sites

Alianza de Mujeres Costarricenses, www.ccmrrhh.org/amc.html.
Oldest Costa Rican women's self-help organization.

CEFEMINA, www.cefemina.or.cr.
Feminist women's self-help organization.

INAMU (National Women's Institute), www.inamu.go.cr.
Government institution responsible for women's issues

Red de Mujeres para el Desarrollo, www.redmujeres.org.
Women's self-help network.

Organizations

Nongovernmental

Agenda Política de Mujeres
10032-1000
San José, Costa Rica, América Central
Contact Person: Marisel Salas
Phone: (506) 220-6026
Contact Person: Ivannia Madrigal, Area of Capacitación

Phone: (506) 220-6766, (506) 220-7563
Fax: (506) 272-5775
Email: imadrigal@ice.co.cr

Alianza de Mujeres Costarricenses (AMC)
Ana Hernández, Director
6851-1000
San José, Costa Rica, América Central
Phone: (506) 233-5769
Fax: (506) 233-0151
Email: amccpalm@racsa.co.cr

Asociación de Mujeres en Salud (AMES)
Anna Arroba, Director
583-2050 San Pedro de Montes de Oca
San José, Costa Rica, América Central
Phone: (506) 283-0161
Fax: (506) 224-3678
Email: ames@racsa.co.cr

Asociación Programa Nacional de Asesoría y Capacitación para la Mujer (APRO-
   MUJER)
Marta Campos Méndez, President
50m oeste de la Panadería Los Reyes
Los Lagos, Heredia, Costa Rica, América Central
Phone: (506) 238-3455
Fax: (508) 260-2079
Email: martacampos@costarricense.cr

Centro Feminista de Información y Acción and Mujer No Estás Sola (CEFEMINA)
Ana Carcedo, Director
5355-1000
San José, Costa Rica, América Central
Phone/Fax: (506) 224-3986
Email: acarcedo@cariari.co.cr

Red de Mujeres para el Desarrollo
Nancy Boye, Kirstin Catola, Olga Parrado, Loida Sardinias, Equipo Corrdinador
Apdo. 692-2070, Sabanilla
San José, Costa Rica, América Central
Phone: (506) 225-0248, (506) 253-9003
Fax: (506) 253-9128
Email: redmujer@racsa.co.cr

Governmental

Defensoría de los Habitantes
Ligia Martín, Defensoría de la Mujer
686-1005 Barrio México

San José, Costa Rica, América Central
Phone: (506) 258-8585
Fax: (506) 248-2371
Email: dhr@dhr.go.cr

Instituto Nacional de las Mujeres (INAMU)
Apdo. 59-2015
San José, Costa Rica, América Central
Rocío Chaves Jiménez
Phone: (506) 283-5725, (506) 253-9624, (506) 253-9836, (506) 253-7841, (506) 224-3470
Fax: (506) 283-5725, (506) 253-8825
Email: politicas-publicas@inamu.go.cr

SELECTED BIBLIOGRAPHY

Biesanz, Mavis Hiltunen, Richard Biesanz, and Karen Zubris Biesanz. *The Ticos: Culture and Social Change in Costa Rica.* Boulder, CO: Lynne Rienner, 1999.

Molina, Iván, and Steven Palmer. *The History of Costa Rica.* San José: Editorial de la Universidad de Costa Rica, 1998.

United Nations Development Programme (UNDP). *Human Development Report 2001: Making New Technologies Work for Human Development.* New York: Oxford University Press, 2001.

U.S. Department of State. *Costa Rica—Country Reports on Human Rights.* March 4, 2002. www.state.gov/g/drl/rls/hrrpt/2001/wha/8329.htm.

Spanish Bibliography

Carcedo Cabañas, Ana. 2001. "Grupos de autoayuda de 'Mujer No Estás Sola': Una propuesta exitosa para detener el maltrato contra las mujeres." In Sara Poggio et al., *Mujeres en América Latina transformando la vida.* San José, Costa Rica: Universidad de Costa Rica, Universidad Nacional, 2001.

Casa Costarricense de Seguidad Social (CCSS). *Guía de métodos anticonceptivos.* San José, Costa Rica: CCSS, Sección Salud de la Mujer, n.d. Pamphlet.

———. *Modernización* no. 43 (March 2002).

———. *Promoción de la salud: Estilos de vida saludables.* San José, Costa Rica: Dirección Técnica de Servicios de Salud, 2002. Pamphlet.

———. *La salud sexual y reproductiva es un derecho nuestro.* Decreto Ejecutivo 27913-S. San José, Costa Rica: CCSS, 1999. Pamphlet.

Chaves Jiménez, Rocío. "La perspectiva de género y la salud de las mujeres." San José, Costa Rica: Instituto Nacional de las Mujeres (INAMU), Area de Gestión de Políticas Pública para la Equidad, 2001. Internal document.

Chen Mok, M., et al. *Salud reproductiva y migración nicaragüense en Costa Rica 1999–2000: Resultados de una encuesta nacional de salud reproductiva.* San José, Costa Rica, 2001.

Estado de la Nación. (EN). *Estado de la nación en desarrollo humano sostenible.* San José, Costa Rica: Proyecto Estado de la Nación, 2001.

Ferro Calabrese, Cora, and Ana María Quirós Rojas. *Mujer y religión.* San José, Costa Rica: Universidad Nacional, Consejo Editorial IEM, 1994.

Hernández Barrantes, Anamaría. "Rebelión o sumisión—Género, religión y patriarcado." 2002.

Ibarra Cerdas, Martha. "Género y Educación." San José, Costa Rica: Instituto Nacional de las Mujeres. Area Gestión de Políticas Públicas para la Equidad, 2001. Internal document.

Instituto Mixto de Ayuda Social (IMAS). *Ley 7769—Atención a las mujeres en condiciones de pobreza*. San José, Costa Rica: IMAS, 1999.

Jiménez G., Mireya, and Marta Campos M. *Diagnóstico de la participación de la mujer en el movimiento cooperativo costarricense*. San José, Costa Rica: APROMUJER, 1999.

Ministerio de Educación Pública. "Indicadores de equidad de género." San José, Costa Rica: Departamento Estadísticas Educativas, 2001. Internal document.

Ministerio de Salud de Costa Rica. (MSBI) *Indicadores básicos: Situación de salud en Costa Rica*. San José, Costa Rica: Ministerio de Salud, 1999.

Programa Centroamericano de Población de la Escuela de Estadística (PCP), Instituto de Investigaciones en Salud (INISA). *Reproductive Health*. San José: Universidad de Costa Rica, 2001.

8

ECUADOR

Gioconda Herrera

PROFILE OF ECUADOR

Ecuador is located in South America, between Colombia to the north and Peru to the south and east. Its area of 283,600 square kilometers (113,440 square miles), is divided into three continental regions—the Andean highlands, whose major cities include the capital city of Quito and the commercial centers of Cuenca and Ambato; the coastal area, with the major port city of Guayaquil, and the Amazon region—and the Galapagos Islands located 1,000 kilometers (600 miles) west of continental Ecuador, in the Pacific Ocean.

Ecuador has been a republic since 1830. Although its formal political regime has been a democracy, since the 1980s the country has undergone several periods of political instability due to the fragility of its political institutions, which prevents accurate political representation of and participation by minority and subaltern groups. The vulnerability of political institutions is accompanied by high levels of income concentration among small groups and the regional concentration of economic and social development in two cities (Quito and Guayaquil), to the detriment of rural areas and small provincial cities. Since the 1990s,

new social movements have changed the political landscape by introducing the voices of indigenous people into the political system and compelling the state to assume the political and social responsibility for an important citizen group that has been marginalized for decades. Women's movements also have become very active since the 1990s, and although they have not reached the same levels of social mobilization as indigenous movements, they have obtained important political reforms, a major presence in public opinion regarding gender inequality, and some changes in cultural representations.

According to the national census of 2001, Ecuador has 12,090,804 inhabitants, 50.4 percent of whom are women. The population is characterized by great ethnic diversity that includes thirteen indigenous groups, mainly located in the Andean highlands and the Amazon region, small Afro-Ecuadorian groups living on the coast and in the Andean highlands, and mestizo people distributed in both urban and rural areas.

The Inter-American Development Bank estimates that 25 percent of the population is black or indigenous. Of this, 80 percent are estimated to be indigenous, and 20 percent black.[1] Ninety-four percent of the Ecuadorean population identifies itself as Roman Catholic, although there has been an important increase of evangelical groups.

The national fertility rate has declined substantially, from 6.9 in 1969 to 5.3 in 1982, and 3.4 for the period 1994–1999.[2] Education is the cause for the largest discrepancy: the fertility rate among women with a college education is 2.1, compared to 6.2 among women with no formal education. The fertility rate in rural versus urban residents is 2.8 in urban areas and 4.4 in rural ones. Women's life expectancy increased from 65 years in 1980 to 70 years in 1999; men's life expectancy was 67 years in 1999. The infant mortality rate is 28 per 1000 live births.[3]

OVERVIEW OF WOMEN'S ISSUES

Ecuadorean women have experienced important changes in their lives since the 1970s. The urbanization resulting from rural immigration to the cities; the expansion of the service sector; and the implementation of structural adjustment policies since the 1980s have combined to produce a rapid incorporation of women into the labor market. However, the jobs are mostly in economic areas characterized by their vulnerability: instable, unprotected, and badly paid. Incorporation into the labor force has occurred along with the decline of the fertility rate and increases in the use of contraceptives and access to education. These changes have transformed family structures and modified the cultural scope of gender representations. New images have intertwined with traditional representations of women in society, mostly under the influence of the predominant Catholic culture, forming complex social and cultural identities. The multiethnic character of the country and high levels of income concentration among a small group make class, ethnicity, and race important inequality markers between women and men and among women. As a product of inequality, increasing poverty affects more and more Ecuadorian women.

Since 1980, the development of women's organizations, and of a small but effective feminist movement, have produced important changes in legislation and public policies by making discrimination against women a matter for state intervention. During the 1990s, the further development of women's organizations led them to include diverse ethnic, regional, and class identities. This multiplied the voices of the women's movement and increased its demands for cultural recognition and political participation at the local level. Among the most important institutional and legal reforms have been the creation of Consejo Nacional de la Mujeres (CONAMU; National Women's Council) in 1997, as an autonomous entity under the presidency; the approval of the Equal Opportunity Plan in 1996; the enactment of the Law on Violence Against Women and the Family in 1995; and the new Constitution of 1998 that provides a legal framework to facilitate the enforcement of public policies and guarantees women's rights in work, health, education, and social and political participation.[4]

However, these gains came in an environment of high political instability and acute economic crisis that threatened democracy. Ecuador had five presidents between 1996 and 2002; two of them were withdrawn from power one year after being elected. In 1999, the country underwent an unprecedented macroeconomic and financial crisis: real GDP declined more than 7 percent, consumer prices rose 60.7 percent, and unemployment increased drastically.[5] In January 2000, following several weeks of severe exchange rate depreciation, the government dollarized the economy. Macroeconomic recovery has come at a very high cost: dollarization has provoked high levels of inflation, the collapse of real wages, massive poverty, and an unprecedented emigration of men and, increasingly, of women.

EDUCATION

Opportunities

Ecuadorean women have had formal access to public education since the nineteenth century, when the Conservative government of Gabriel García Moreno established a public educational system. But it was not until the Liberal Revolution of 1895 that women started to gain access to nonreligious education and were allowed to work in the public sector, primarily in education. In fact, the first nucleus of women activists was formed by female schoolteachers.[6]

Ecuador's educational system is organized such that after completion of ten years of basic schooling, a student has two educational options: tech-

Table 8.1
1995 Enrollment Rates (Percent enrolled of total population)

Education Level	Male	Female
Primary	88.0	90.2
Secondary	46.4	52.9
University	9.4	11.2

Source: CONAMU, 2001.

nical or secondary school. Both options lead to a secondary diploma. Although there is no formal gender discrimination in the access to vocational careers, men and women tend to maintain traditional gender roles when choosing their training area. Men concentrate in mechanics, construction, and electronics, whereas women prefer administration, garment manufacturing, commerce, and information technology.[7]

National data on school enrollment show no large disparity between male and female. Moreover, women's enrollment is slightly higher in primary, secondary, and university education (see table 8.1). However there was still a small gap in 1998 in the total years of education between women (8.6 years) and men (9.1 years). Important gender gaps also arise in terms of urban–rural differences: urban men have 9.1 years of schooling, whereas rural women have an average of 4.1.[8] Ecuador has one of the lowest education attainment rates in South America. However, women represent 46 percent of repeats and only 38 percent of dropouts.[9] Ethnicity is an important marker of inequality in education. In 1995, only 35 percent of indigenous women had completed six years of primary school and only 10 percent had entered secondary school. Dropout rates among indigenous people are particularly high.

Several studies confirm that, through textbooks and teachings practices, the school system emphasizes gender representations linking men to public life and women to the household. Male hierarchies are also illustrated by the positions occupied by women in the educational system as teachers. Although there has been a progressive feminization of education during the twentieth century (58 percent of the total), 90 percent of preschool, 65 percent of primary school, and 44 percent of secondary school teachers are women. The higher the position in the hierarchy, the lower the presence of women, which affects both income and status.[10] In addition, women are in power positions in teachers unions or school boards. Most of the directing positions are held by males.

Illiteracy

Illiteracy is still an important gender issue, particularly for rural and indigenous women. As table 8.2 shows, rural women represent 21.1 percent of illiterates, compared to 3.6 percent for urban men.

Table 8.2
1998 Illiteracy Rates (Percentages)

Area	Male	Female
Urban	3.6	6.3
Rural	14.8	21.1
National	8.3	12.2

Source: CONAMU/INEC, 1999.

EMPLOYMENT AND ECONOMICS

Job/Career Opportunities

Since the 1970s the labor market has been one of the areas of structural transformation in the lives of women. Women's participation in the labor market increased from 16 percent in 1970 to 20.5 percent in 1982 and 39 percent in 1995.[11] Moreover, since the 1990s more women have been incorporated into the labor market than men.[12] However, 12 percent to 16 percent of women were unemployed between 1993 and 1998, whereas men's rate of unemployment ranged from 6 percent to 8 percent in the same period. Of unemployed women, 56 percent have a secondary education and 24 percent have a higher education; 48 percent of unemployed women are in the 25–54 age group.[13]

The current economic crisis has particularly affected women's employment. Data for the year 2001 indicates that women's unemployment reached 17.9 percent, whereas men's rose to 10.2 percent. Working women composed the major part of the informal economy; underemployment reached 51.6 percent for females and 43.7 percent for males. In addition, 30.5 percent of women had a job considered "adequate" as compared to 46.1 percent of men.[14]

The largest proportion of economically active women works in the service sector, particularly in commerce, hotels, and restaurants (33 percent), followed by personal and social services (29 percent), then agriculture (23 percent) and industry (12 percent). Women comprise 47.8 percent of workers in the financial sector, 53 percent of personal and social services workers, and 41.8 percent of industrial workers.[15]

Weaver. Photo © Leo Meyer/Painet.

Pay

Article 36 of the CEDAW (Convention on the Elimination of Discrimination Against Women), ratified by Ecuador in 1995, guarantees women equal pay for equal work. This article also prohibits any sort of labor discrimination against women, including sexual harassment in the workplace. However, occupational segregation is accompanied by important gender wage gaps in every kind of occupation. In 1998, women earned 32.5 percent less than men, though this gap is more pronounced in rural (54 percent of what men earned) than in urban areas (66 percent). Women received 77 percent of men's average income in the formal sector, 63 percent in the informal sector, and only 48 percent in agricultural activities and domestic services.[16] These gaps are maintained even after removing educational differences. Women are less affected by wage gaps in the public sector and the teaching profession, whereas the more unequal areas are domestic work and industrial work, particularly those feminized activities such as clothing and textile production and medical and food services.[17]

Wages differences also exist among heads of households. In 1998, 19 percent of Ecuadorean households had a female head: 21 percent of households in urban areas and 15 percent in rural areas. Households headed by females received 23 percent less income than those headed by males.[18]

Differences in income are linked to inequality of status. According to a 1996 survey of large and middle-size business enterprises, women occupied 22 percent of executive positions: 32 percent in the financial sector, 29 percent in industries, 21 percent in commerce, and 18 percent in services. In 60 percent of the firms, the average income for women was less than men's.[19] At the national level, women comprise 35 percent of managers, 49 percent of professionals/scientists, and 42 percent of professional and technical workers.[20] Despite significant progress, differences in wages still exist.

Working Conditions

Sexual Harassment

Sexual harassment in the workplace is widely practiced but hardly punished and largely ignored. Ecuador has had legislation on sexual harassment since 1998 but it is very little known and almost never applied. This has not been an issue in which the women's movement has been involved.

Support for Mothers/Caretakers

Maternal Leave

Paid maternity leave is guaranteed for 12 weeks, with 25 percent of the salary paid by the employer and 75 percent by Social Security funds. However, recent changes in legislation promoting the flexibility of the labor force and budget cuts in social services due to structural adjustment policies jeopardize this support for working mothers.

Daycare

There are three main public child care programs run by the Ministry of Social Welfare and the Institute of Children and the Family (INNFA), an institution overseen by the president's wife. Although these programs facilitate women's participation in the labor force by employing female caretakers for the children of working mothers, they provide very low coverage and are in danger of being eliminated by budget cuts. According to labor laws, firms with more than 25 employees are required to provide child care facilities, although there are no enforcement mechanisms in place. In 1994 less than 10 percent of children under the age of five attended a day care facility.[21]

Inheritance and Property Rights

Article 34 of CEDAW, passed in 1995, guarantees equal rights and opportunities to men and women and equal access to productive assets. There are no male privileges, either legal or cultural, regarding inheritance, but property is usually the male's. Although joint spousal property ownership is legally approved, by custom only men register property. Only 12.7 percent of women heads of household own real property.

Social/Government Programs

Very few Ecuadoreans have retirement benefits because access to Social Security is limited. In 1998, only 18 percent of the total population was covered by Social Security, of whom 56 percent were men and 44 percent were women.[22] Most of the social programs launched by the state are not synchronized with the labor market but respond to antipoverty policies. These programs are not universal in coverage, generally targeting poor women and children, and "the low level of benefits constrains their overall antipoverty impact."[23] Ecuador does not have Social Security or welfare programs for unemployed people.

FAMILY AND SEXUALITY

Gender Roles

Despite economic and social transformations that affect the lives of women, cultural values regarding the family, sexuality, and the sexual division of labor still present a a dichotomy. Women are assigned reproduction activities of care and domestic work and have little control of their sexuality, as opposed to the greater sexual freedom of men, their participation in public life, and little expectation of their involvement in domestic activities.

Cultural values regarding the division of labor vary according to ethnicity and rural or urban residence, but overall, domestic work and child care in Ecuador are carried out mainly, although not exclusively, by women.[24] Statistical data on gender perceptions regarding family and gender roles show that 37.4 percent of women still believe that "important household decisions must be taken by males." This opinion is less acceptable among young, educated, and/or professional women, and female heads of households. In regard to marriage and home, 43.6 percent of women thought that a married woman should stay at home even if she does not want to. These percentages are higher among older and illiterate women but lower (17 percent) among women with university education.[25]

Sociological and anthropological studies have shown that there are important cultural differences among ethnicities and classes. For example, indigenous groups from the highlands tend to have a more flexible sexual division of labor: men participate in domestic tasks and women have significant responsibilities in activities related to agricultural production and natural resource management. The reasons vary: some studies maintain that this is an important cultural difference between urban mestizo people and indigenous groups which derives from a more equal-gender situation for indigenous than for mestizo women.[26] Other studies, however, maintain that gender flexibility in the division of labor represents a household coping strategy in the face of poverty and masculine migration, and that this does not necessarily mean greater participation for women in decision-making processes in the household and in their communities.[27] A study of a rural population showed that women spent an average of seven hours per day in productive activities (e.g., paid labor) and eight hours in reproductive activities such as child care, house cleaning, and preparing food.[28] A study of the urban poor in the city of Guayaquil confirms that situation, showing how poverty has pushed women into the labor market (from 32 percent to 46 percent) and has increased the time spent per day on work related to their reproductive, productive, and community responsibilities. The same study found that 96 percent of men participate in some kind of leisure activity after work, compared to 54 percent of women. However, the time that women spent watching TV was in fact simultaneously occupied by child care, ironing, or sewing activities.[29]

Information on the middle and upper classes reveals a similar situation. A survey of upper executives shows that women spend only 30 minutes on domestic tasks but manage all activities related to child care and reproduction, including the allocation of resources, decision-making, and daily follow-up of these activities. Middle- and upper-class women usually assign these activities to female domestic workers.[30] This is the main barrier that prevents a greater involvement of men in domestic tasks among these social sectors.

Several studies on gender identity argue that the traditional concept of the family and sexual control is dominant in Ecuador. However, these studies usually have not paid enough attention to ethnic, racial, and age differences. In that sense, inequality in gender representations and perceptions of the family and sexuality are well documented, but studies more attentive to the ambiguities, resistance, and contradictions of gender oppression among different generations, ethnic and racial groups, and social classes are still needed. We still know little about the cultural changes that modern economic and social structures have brought to women's concept of the family, but despite regional and ethnic differences, women are seen occupying the key role in the family. Catholic culture continues to provide the main gender representations of what a man and a woman ought to be, but its influence on women's daily practices and activities remains to be explored.

Recent massive international emigration of both men and women is bringing new family alignments and a large number of children who are cared for by other family members. Since 1998 approximately 200,000 people left Ecuador, primarily for Spain and the United States.[31] Although international migration has been traditionally masculine, new immigrants to Spain tend to be females working in domestic service. International migration is a rural as well as an urban phenomenon, and affects all three regions of the country: for instance, 10 percent of households in the Andean highlands have lost one or more family members, and 5 percent of households from the Coastal region have a family member who has emigrated. Recent data on the impact of migration on families shows that in 2000, over 150,000 children were living without one of their parents.[32] Although historically men migrate more than women, there has been an increase in women's migration, particularly among the young. The consequences of this phenomenon for family structures and families' values are yet to be analyzed at the national level. In the southern region of the country, traditional family values tend to be maintained despite significant changes in roles and family structure, thus creating a gap between ideal and reality that contributes to the stigmatization of emigrants' families and their children as unstructured and potentially deviant, and of female migrants as "bad" mothers. A study on youths' perception of the family in five cities shows that young people still value the family as the most important social structure and see it as a source of well-being; this is particularly true among families with one or more emigrants.[33]

Marriage

Marriage is still highly valued by Ecuadorians of all ages and social classes. More than 50 percent of women marry before the age of 24: 30 percent before 19 years old and 24 between 20 and 24 years old. Percentages for men are 12.4 and 36, respectively.[34]

Ecuador has had a divorce law since 1910, but it is only since the 1960s that the divorce rate has increased considerably. By 1997, the divorce rate was particularly high among women under 35: 41 percent of women 30–34 years old and 35 percent of women between 25 and 29 years old.[35] The number of divorces diminishes among women after age 35.

The separation of families due to the emigration of one or more members is provoking an increase in the breakdown of couples. Although there are no national data on marriage satisfaction, the study on migration conducted in the southern part of the country found that one of the reasons that helps women decide to emigrate is marriage conflicts.[36]

Reproduction

Sex Education

A surprising 40.7 percent of women between the ages of 20 and 24 report not wanting any more children; 70 percent of low-educated women reported the same wish.[37] The "desired" fertility rate was 2.9 children per family, 20 percent below the actual national fertility rate. Only 60 percent of women reported having seen or heard about family planning messages. Of that group, 54 percent lived in rural areas, 53 percent had a primary education, and 28 percent were illiterate.[38] The educational system includes sex education in its curriculum, but actual programs in schools do not necessarily provide information on birth control methods; rather, they offer a discourse on sexual control.

Contraception and Abortion

In Ecuador, men and women become sexually active and have children at an early age. Awareness and knowledge of birth control methods contrast with its actual use. In 1998, 87.7 percent of urban women and 78 percent of rural ones knew about birth control but only 35.6 and 31.1 percent used some kind of contraceptive. The most popular forms of birth control are the tying of the tubes (32 percent), IUD (24 percent), and the pill (22 percent), which shows that women are mainly responsible for contraception; only 3.0 percent of men use condoms and 0.3 percent have been sterilized.[39] Interestingly, reasons for not using contraceptives do not include religious factors or a partner's opposition, but mainly cite lack of information.

Private doctors and clinics are the main providers of contraceptives to 38.5 percent of the public sector.[40] The state has not been very active in providing contraceptives but depends on external organizations, such as the United States Agency for International Development or the United

Nations Fund for Population Advancement, that have established programs to provide this service.

As in most of the countries in Latin America, abortion is illegal in Ecuador, which results in major underreporting for fear of sanctions. It is estimated that 8 percent of maternal deaths are from abortions. Of these, 85 percent are spontaneous abortions, and 15 percent are induced. Older women from the coast and urban areas, as well as educated women, have the highest rates of induced abortions.[41] Youth representatives of the women's movement proposed abortion as a public health issue and launched a national campaign that has led to several debates in the media. Their continued lobbying may bring about a stronger debate about the legalization of abortion in the years to come.

Teen Pregnancy

Another indicator that may show problems in the availability of contraceptives in the country is the high percentage of teenage births. In 1994, 18 percent of women aged 15 to 19 were pregnant or had a child. Adolescents with a secondary education are four times less likely to become pregnant than those with little or no education.[42]

HEALTH

Health Care Access

In 1998 only 18 percent of Ecuadoreans were part of the Social Security System (56 percent were men and 44 percent, women). Health insurance coverage at the national level is very low: 2.7 percent of women and 3 percent of men had private coverage; 17 percent of women and 19 percent of men were covered though Social Security; 80 percent of women and 76 percent of men did not have any health coverage.[43]

Health care in Ecuador is far from universal and free of charge, even though all citizens have the legal right to free health care. Health care is one of the areas most affected by government budget cuts. Public spending on health rose slightly from 1.4 percent of the national budget in 1991, to 1.8 percent in 1995. Per capita spending on health in Ecuador was $29 in 1994. There are 13 doctors and 4 nurses per 10,000 inhabitants.[44]

There are important regional and ethnic differences regarding the quality of health service. In general, indigenous women wait more than an hour in health establishments, more than double the time that nonindigenous women and indigenous and nonindigenous men wait.[45]

Women's access to reproductive health care during pregnancy is still very low. About 20 percent of pregnant women do not receive prenatal care, and less educated and rural women have the least access to maternal health care. The average number of prenatal checkups is five (the Ministry of

Health recommends twelve). Nineteen percent of rural women receive no professional attention at delivery. At the national level, in the period 1994–1999, 69.2 percent of all deliveries were attended by a physician or an obstetrician, and 29 percent by a midwife or a family member, with important regional and rural urban differences. Half of rural women were attended by nonprofessionals. Only 39 percent of women receive postnatal care.[46] Additionally, 56.5 percent of women of childbearing age have never been screened for cervical cancer.[47]

This situation partly explains the high rates of maternal mortality despite its decline from 320 per 100,000 live births for 1981–1987 to 159 per 100,000 during 1988–1994. This rate is higher in the Andean highlands and among adolescent women.[48]

In 1999, Ecuador passed the Law of Free Maternity Care, which guarantees all women free access to prenatal care and professional attention during delivery. The implementation of this law is one of the main programs launched by the National Council on Women (CONAMU), in alliance with the public health care system. It is expected that this program will improve prenatal and maternity care, and contribute to a decrease in the high rates of preventable maternal mortality. The main causes of maternal mortality that could had been avoided were toxemia (37.6 percent), hemorrhages (23.1 percent), and abortions (5.6 percent).[49]

Diseases and Disorders

In 1997, according to the National Statistical Institute (INEC), the leading cause of illness among women was obstetric infections (20.5 percent). The main causes of female mortality were pneumonia, strokes, diabetes, and high blood pressure. According to the Social Security system, in 1998 more women (58 percent) than men accessed health care services (42 percent). Among women, the second and third reasons for seeking medical attention were disorders of the nervous system and mental health issues.[50]

AIDS

The incidence of HIV/AIDS is on the rise in Ecuador but is relatively low compared to other countries in Latin America. Reported cases are higher for males than females, but the rate of increase presents a contradiction. From 1995 to 1998 reported male cases increased from 149 to 265, and reported female cases doubled, from 36 to 70. A survey on general knowledge about AIDS/HIV shows an alarming lack of information among a vast group of women: 20 percent of women do not know that AIDS/HIV is a fatal disease; 43 percent said they had done nothing to avoid infection; and only 1.9 percent used condoms as a form of protection.[51] The state does not provide any serious prevention programs, but several nongovernment organizations are working with at-risk groups.

Workers in the sex industry are one of the target groups, although it is important to note that they are quick to adopt forms of protection on their own as a means of survival.

Depression

Few studies have addressed depression among women in Ecuador. Women commit suicide at a rate of 3.2 per 100,000 inhabitants.[52]

POLITICS AND LAW

Suffrage

In 1929 women won the right to vote. Ecuador was the first Latin American country to enfranchise women.

Political Participation

The first woman to occupy a seat in Congress was Matilde Hidalgo de Procel, in 1941. In recent years, female representation in governmental ministries has been very low. In 1998, it was 20 percent (three ministries), in 1999 26.7 percent (four ministries), and in 2002 14 percent (two ministries). The current government has appointed women as ministers of the Ministry of Tourism, Ministry of Education, Ministry of Commerce and the Ministry of Foreign Relations. The Foreign Relations Minister, Nina Pacari, is the first indigenous woman to serve as minister and in general it is the first time women have held such high offices in the country.[53] The first female Attorney General was not elected until 1999. The Ley de Amparo Laboral, passed in 1997, guarantees a minimum of 20 percent women as candidates in every election and legalizes affirmative action in employment and in access to the judicial system. In 2000, following reforms of the Election Law, the minimum percentage of women candidates was changed to 30 percent on every electoral ballot, and will increase by 5 percent in every election until attaining 50 percent. Additionally, female candidates must occupy alternate positions on the ballots in order to guarantee seats, and political parties must include policies of gender equality in their programs.

Women fare better in local and municipal elections than in national and provincial parliamentary representation. In 1996 there was no female representative in the national congress, but in 1998 4 out of 20 deputies were women. At the provincial level, in 1996 4 out of 70 provincial representatives were women (5.7 percent), and in 1996, 12 out of 101 (11.9 percent) representatives were women.[54] In the 2002 election, 18 out of 100 women were elected, marking a significant increase in participation.

The 2000 local elections show the first positive results of affirmative action. Women elected as Provincial Council members increased from 6 percent in 1996 to 18 percent in 2000 (40 percent were candidates), and Local Council members increased from 8 percent to 30 percent (45 percent were candidates).[55] However, women still account for only 6 percent of municipal government members and none of the provincial government. The legislative elections of October 2002 should mark a significant increase in women's representation. In the judiciary women's representation is not significant. As of 1999, 1 of 31 Supreme Court judges was a woman, all fiscal judges were men, and 14 percent of civil judges were women.[56]

Women's Rights

Women in Ecuador gained certain rights very early compared to other Latin American countries. The Liberal reforms of the turn of the twentieth century were meant to confront religious power not only in politics but also in culture. Although women's education and ideals continue to be based on Catholic principles, several civil and political rights have been gained. In 1895 women were allowed and encouraged to work in the public sector (mainly as educators); in 1901 the first secondary school to train female schoolteachers was founded; in 1910 the Law of Divorce was passed. Among the most important women leaders were Dolores Cacuango and Transito Amaguaña, two indigenous women who promoted the rights of indigenous people to education in the 1940s and 1950s. Their demands were framed within the struggle of the Federación Ecuatoriana de Indios, a peasant movement active in the 1940s and 1950s that was the ancestor of the 1960s movement for agrarian reform. During the same period socialist women such as Nella Martínez were pioneers in defending the place of women in politics.

Ecuador ratified the Convention on the Elimination of All Forms of Discrimination Against Women in 1995, and it became the basis for many of the proposals that the women's movement made to the Constitutional Assembly in 1998. The new Constitution of 1998 included important civil, economic, social, and political rights for women that provide a framework within which to derive significant new legislation for women.

Among the laws enacted in the 1990s that favorably affect women are the Law Against Women and Family Violence (1995), the Free Maternity Law (1999), and the reforms to the Election Law (2000.) Women's organizations were key social actors in the passing of the Law Against Violence, which permits women to report spousal abuse and to obtain protection. Twenty-one women's police stations (*comisarías*) were created, throughout the country. The Free Maternity Law ensures that women will receive necessary and timely medical attention during their pregnancy, including prenatal checkups, and medical attention at time of delivery, as well as care for sexually transmitted diseases. This law also promotes sexual and reproductive health programs.

The 1990s witnessed the creation of public organizations that further women's causes. The National Council on Women (CONAMU), created in 1997, is in charge of placing gender-specific public policies within state plans and projects, and promoting women's participation in the development processes. Other institutions include the Comisión Permanente de la Mujer, el Niño y la Familia (Permanent Commission for Women, Children and the Family), under the Congress, and the National Women's Council, under the Defensoría del Pueblo (Ombudsman). These organizations are designed to introduce gender-specific legislation and to ensure that laws related to gender are observed. At the local level, CONAMU and other institutions are stimulating local governments to implement gender equality policies.

Feminist Movements

Feminist movements emerged primarily in the late 1970s and early 1980s, when several small groups of women decided to organize to address sexism and discrimination in society and in the social movements in which they participated at the time. There are three main women's national umbrella organizations, all of which comprise smaller women's and feminist NGOs, community organizations, and other local political groups and institutions. Of these, two define themselves as feminist: the Feministas por la Autonomía (Feminists for Autonomy), who are mainly in Cuenca and Quito, and the Foro Permanente de la Mujer Ecuatoriana (Ecuadorian Women's Permanent Forum), which has representatives in other provinces of the country. The third and largest women's organization is the Coordinadora Política de Mujeres Ecuatorianas (Political Network of Ecuadorian Women). This group includes feminists and nonfeminists, and has representatives in every province.

Lesbian Rights

Homosexuality has been legal in Ecuador since 1997, when earlier sex laws were repealed. The 1998 Constitution provides explicit nondiscrimination guarantees for sexual minorities, making Ecuador one of the few countries in the world to have this type of legislation. Both of these legal advances can be attributed to the effort of grassroots activists and to changing public opinions about highly publicized acts of systemic violence against homosexuals. Despite these advances, systematic violence still occurs including bar raids and routine arrests. Sometimes, arrests are followed by further mistreatment by the police. In 2000, police thwarted a gay pride march in Guayaquil with tear gas. Some NGOs are addressing lesbian rights, including Fundación Amigos por la Vida (Friends for Life Foundation) in Guayaquil, the NGO that organized the march.[57]

RELIGION AND SPIRITUALITY

Roman Catholicism is the majority religion in Ecuador, and women have an important role in it. At the beginning of the twentieth century Catholic women's organizations were very active in defending church interests, religious education, and charity institutions. By the end of the century, women still held an important role in maintaining religious values, but were absent from decision-making processes. The church hierarchy is all male. Evangelical Protestant groups are drawing more and more followers. Here again women play a secondary role because all of the authorities are males. In addition, a small percentage of people practice indigenous forms of spirituality (often mixed with Catholicism), Judaism, and other religions.

VIOLENCE

Domestic Violence

Violence against women has been one of the most important mobilizing issues for the women's movement. Article 23 #2 of CEDAW, ratified in 1995, prohibits physical and psychological violence, sexual violence, and moral coercion. It establishes that the state will take necessary measures to prevent, sanction, and eliminate violence against children, women, and the elderly. Social legitimation and the enforcement that this law has mandated makes the problem much more visible but does not yet prevent it or decrease its frequency. Domestic violence is a problem in all social classes and ethnic groups. Some 23.6 percent of women report having been hit, 18.1 percent have been threatened, and 15.8 percent have been hit with an object. One third of women reported having seen or heard a parent being physically abused. Violence increases with age; more victims are in the age range of 30–39 years old.[58] Reports to the authorities increased from 6,101 in 1995 to 16,397 in 1999; in 93.2 percent of the cases the victim was a woman.[59]

OUTLOOK FOR THE TWENTY-FIRST CENTURY

Women gained important social and political rights in the 1990s, mainly due to the political action of the women's movement. Economic crises, increased poverty, globalization, and migration have placed economic rights as the most important agenda for women in the twenty-first century. Sexual and reproductive rights have been acquired, and increasingly they are accepted by society. However, they still need to be accompanied by broader cultural changes in order to be fully understood and integrated into people's daily lives.

NOTES

1. World Bank, *Ecuador Gender Review: Issues and Recommendations* (Washington, DC: World Bank, 2000), 10–11. The national census of 2001 included questions on ethnic and racial self-identification, but these data are not yet available.

2. Centro de Estudial de Población y Desarrollo Social (CEPAR), *Encuesta demográfica de salud materna e infantil (EDEMAIN, 1999)*: *Informe Preliminar* (Quito: CEPAR, 2000).

3. CEPAR, *Encuesta demográfica y de salud materna e infantil—1994* (Quito: CEPAR, 1995).

4. World Bank, 2000.

5. Faculted Latinoamericano de Ciencias Sociales (FLACSO) and United Nations Children's Fund (UNICEF), "El nuevo modelo monetario y el sector social: Memorandum sobre política y estrategia," Report (Quito: FLACSO, 2000).

6. Florencia Campana, *Las revistas escritas por mujeres: Espacios donde se procesó el sujeto feminista, 1905–1937* (Quito: Abya Yala, 2001).

7. World Bank, 2000, 29.

8. United Nations Development Fund for Women (SIISE and UNIFEM), *Retrato de Mujeres. Indicadores sociales sobre la situación de las indígenas y campesinas del Ecuador rural* (Quito: SIISE and UNIFEM, 1998).

9. Living Standards Measurement Survey (LSMS) (Quito: Banco Central del Ecuador, 1998).

10. Fundación Mujer y Sociedad, *La otra mitad: Las mujeres en la seguridad social* (Quito: Fundación Mujer y Sociedad, June 1999), 8.

11. Instituto Nacional de Estadística y Censos (INEC), 1997 and 1985; Consejo Nacional de la Mujer (CONAMU–INEC), *Mujeres y hombres del Ecuador en cifras* (Quito: CONAMU–INEC, 1999).

12. CONAMU–INEC, 1999.

13. World Bank, 2000, 29.

14. Carlos Larrea and Jeannette Sánchez, *Pobreza, empleo e inequidad social: Una propuesta para el desarrollo sostenible* (Quito: PNUD, 2002).

15. CONAMU-INEC, 1999.

16. Pablo Samaniego, Vanesa Brito, and Gabriela Fernández, "Mujeres y hombres en el mercado laboral ecuatoriano," in *Género, empleo e ingresos* (Quito: CONAMU, 1999), 32.

17. World Bank, 2000, 35.

18. CONAMU-INEC, 1999.

19. Fundación Mujer y Sociedad, "Tendencias del empleo y los ingresos de las mujeres en el Ecuador," *Boletín La Otra Mitad* no. 3 (Quito: Fundación Mujer y Sociedad, 1998), 9.

20. World Bank, 2000, 32.

21. Fundación Mujer y Sociedad, *La otra mitad: Tendencias del empleo y los ingresos de las mujeres en el Ecuador*, 1998, 10.

22. Fundación Mujer y Sociedad, "Las mujeres en la Seguridad Social," *Boletín La Otra Mitad*, no. 6 (1999).

23. For instance, the Solidarity Bond Bono de Solidaridad provides direct cash transfers to poor women (U.S.$15 per month) and the elderly; it reaches 1.3 million people, and there is no employment or training program related to it. World Bank, 2000, 39.

24. Anthropological studies reveal that domestic work may constitute a significant

space of power for indigenous women, as well as an important source of cultural reproduction and resistance. Mary Weismantel, *Alimentación, género y pobreza en los Andes ecuatorianos* (Quito: Abya Yala, 1995).

25. CEPAR, 2000, 53–54.

26. Sarah Hamilton, *The Two-Headed Household: Gender and Agricultural Development in the Ecuadorian Andes* (Pittsburgh, PA: University of Pittsburgh Press, 1995); Weismantel, 1995.

27. Mercedes Prieto, "Introducción" in *Mujeres contracorriente* (Quito: [ACDI-CEPLAES] Agencìa Canadiense de Desarrollo Internaciónal-Centro de Planificación y Estudios Sociales 1999).

28. Instituto Interamericano de Cooperación para la Agricultura-Banco Inter-Americano del Desarrollo (IICA-BID), "La situación de las mujeres rurales en Ecuador" (Quito: IICA-BID, 1996), working paper.

29. Moser, quoted in Fundación Mujer y Sociedad, 1998, 11.

30. Fundación Mujer y Sociedad, *Boletín La Otra Mitad* no. 3 (Quito: Fundación Mujer y Sociedad, 1998): 9.

31. INEC and Ministerio de Bienestar Social, *Encuesta de medición de indicadores de hagard y niñol des Ecuador* (Quito: 2001).

32. Ibid.

33. Gioconda Herrera and Alexandra Martínez, *Género y migración en la región sur* (Quito: [FLACSO/Netherlands Embassy] Facultad latinoamericano de Ciencias Sociales, 2002); FLACSO–Ecuador, *Informe sobre niños/as y adolescentes en Riesgo* (Quito: FLACSO/BID/Ministerio de Bienestar Social, May 2002).

34. INEC, 1997.

35. CONAMU-INEC, 1999.

36. Herrera and Martínez, 2002.

37. CEPAR, 2000.

38. World Bank, 2000, 15.

39. CONAMU–INEC, 1999, 52.

40. CEPAR, 2000.

41. CONAMU–INEC, 1999, 52.

42. World Bank, 2000, 11.

43. World Bank, 2000.

44. Sistema Integrado de Indicadores Sociales del Ecuador (SIISE), *Pobreza y Capital Humano en el Ecuador* (Quito: SIISE, 1997).

45. SIISE-UNIFEM, 1998.

46. CEPAR, 2000.

47. CONAMU–INEC, 1999, 50–51.

48. CONAMU–INEC, 1999, 48.

49. Ibid.

50. Fundación Mujer y Sociedad, *La otra mitad*, June 1999.

51. CEPAR, 2000.

52. Carlos Racos, Fernando Carrión, and Edison Palomeque, *Seguridad ciudadana y violencia* (Quito: FLACSO, 2003).

53. CONAMU-INEC, 1999, 58.

54. Ibid.

55. Ibid.

56. CONAMU–INEC, 1999, 48.

57. International Gay and Lesbian Human Rights Commission, "Police Thwart

Gay and Lesbian Pride March," Emergency Response Network, San Francisco, www.iglhrc/org/world/southamerica/ecuador2000aug.html.

58. CEPAR, 2000.

59. World Bank, 2000, 22.

RESOURCE GUIDE

Suggested Reading

Blumberg, Rae Lesser. *Gender and Development in Ecuador*. Quito: USAID, 1990.

Cuvi, María. "Making the Link Between Gender and Environment in Ecuador." In *Gender and Sustainable Development: A New Paradigm. Reflecting an Experience in Latin America and the Caribbean*, edited by María Brasileiro. New York: U.N. Development Fund for Women, 1996.

Hamilton, Sarah. *The Two Headed Household: Gender and Agricultural Development in the Ecuadorian Andes*. Pittsburgh, PA: University of Pittsburgh Press, 1995.

Handelsman, Michael. *Culture and Customs of Ecuador*. Westport, CT: Greenwood Press, 2000.

Lind, Amy. "Power, Gender and Development: Popular Women's Organizations and the Politics of Needs in Ecuador." In *The Making of Social Movements in Latin America*, edited by Arturo Escobar and Sonia Alvarez. Boulder, CO: Westview Press, 1992.

Lind, Amy. "Gender and Neoliberal States: Feminists Remake the Nation in Ecuador." *Latin American Perspectives* 30, no. 1 (2003): 182–207.

Mauro, Amalia. *Gender, Industrialization and the Labor Force in Ecuador*. Washington, DC: GENESYS PROJECT-AID, 1993.

McKee, Lauris. "Men's Rights—Women's Wrongs: Domestic Violence In Ecuador." In *Sanctions and Santuary: Cultural Perspectives on the Beating of Wives*, edited by Dorothy Ayers de Counts. Boulder, CO: Westview Press, 1992.

Moser, Caroline. "Adjustment from Below: Low Income Women, Time and the Triple Role in Guayaquil, Ecuador." In *VIVA: Women and Popular Protest in Latin America*, edited by Sarah Radcliffe and Sallie Westwood, 73–196. London: Routledge, 1993.

Radcliffe, Sarah, and Sallie Westwood. *Remaking the Nation: Place, Identity and Politics in Latin America*. New York: Routledge, 1996.

Weismantel, Mary. *Food, Gender and Poverty in the Ecuadorian Andes*. Philadelphia: University of Pennsylvania Press, 1988.

World Bank. *Ecuador Gender Review: Issues and Recommendations*. Washington, DC: World Bank, 2000.

Film

Time of Women. 1988. 20 minutes. Directed by Monica Vásquez. This film portrays women's lives in a southern Ecuadorian village populated primarily by women. As many men from this region have migrated elsewhere for work and are often gone for years, women have been forced to survive on their own.

Web Sites

Ecuadorian Women's Political Network (Coordinadora Política de Mujeres Ecuatorianas), www.cpme.org.ec/ingles/indice_ingles.html.
Contains information on the organization history, goals and areas of work. Focuses on women's political participation and legal rights.

Latin American Information Agency, Women@ALAI (Agencia Latinoamericana de Información), alainet.org/mujeres.
Provides news information on women's issues in Ecuador and throughout Latin America. Based in Quito, Ecuador. Contains web database on women's issues.

Organizations

Coordinadora Política de Mujeres Ecuatorianas
Email: cpme@andinanet.net

National women's organization that works mainly to promote women's political participation and the defense of women's rights.

Foro Nacional Permanente de la Mujer Ecuatoriana
Email: formujer@andinanet.net

A national organization concerned with violence against women and political participation.

Feministas por la Autonomía
Email: cpmujer@uio.satnet.net

A small group of activists in Quito and Cuenca that concentrates on sexual rights.

SELECTED BIBLIOGRAPHY

Chávez, María Eugenia. "Slave Women's Strategies for Freedom and the Late Spanish Colonial State." In *Hidden Histories of Gender and the State in Latin América*, edited by Elizabeth Dore and Maxine Molineux. Durham, NC: Duke University Press, 2000.
Crain, Mary M. "The Gendering of Ethnicity in the Ecuadorian Andes: Native Women's Self Fashioning in the Urban Market." In *Machios, Mistresses and Madonnas*, edited by Kristi Ann Stolen and Marit Melhus. New York: Routledge, 1995.
———. "Poetics and Politics in the Ecuadorean Andes: Women's Narratives of Death and Devil Possession." *American Ethnologist* 18, no. 1 (1991).
Cuvi, María. "Making the Link Between Gender and Environment in Ecuador." In *Gender and Sustainable Development: A New Paradigm. Reflecting an Experience in Latin America and the Caribbean*, edited by María Brasileiro. New York: U.N. Development Fund for Women, 1996.
Faulkner, Anne H., and Victoria A. Lawson. "Employment Versus Empowerment: A Case Study of Women's Work in Ecuador." *Journal of Development Studies* 27, no. 3 (July 1991): 16–47.

Garret, Patricia, and William Waters. *Incorporating Gender into Agricultural Development and Natural Resource Management in Ecuador*. Quito: USAID, 1990.

Hamilton, Sarah. "Visible Partners: Women's Labor and Management of Agricultural Capital on Small Farms in the Highlands of Central Ecuador." *Urban Anthropology and Studies of Cultural Systems and World Economic Development* 21, no. 4 (winter 1992): 353–83.

Hamilton, Sarah. *The Two Headed Household: Gender and Agricultural Development in the Ecuadorian Andes*. Pittsburgh, PA: University of Pittsburgh Press, 1995.

International Gay and Lesbian Human Rights Commission. "Police Thwart Gay and Lesbian Pride March," Emergency Response Network, San Francisco, www.iglhrc/org/world/southamerica/ecuador2000aug.html.

Lind, Amy. "Power, Gender and Development: Popular Women's Organizations and the Politics of Needs in Ecuador." In *The Making of Social Movements in Latin America*, edited by Arturo Escobar and Sonia Alvarez. Boulder, CO: Westview Press, 1992.

Lind, Amy. "Gender, Development and Urban Social Change: Women's Comunity Action in Global Cities." *World Development* 25, no. 8 (August 1997): 1205–24.

Mauro, Amalia. *Gender, Industrialization and the Labor Force in Ecuador*. Washington, DC: GENESYS PROJECT-AID, 1993.

McKee, Lauris. "Men's Rights—Women's Wrongs: Domestic Violence in Ecuador." In *Sanctions and Santuary: Cultural Perspectives on the Beating of Wives*, edited by Dorothy Ayers de Counts. Boulder, CO: Westview Press, 1992.

Moser, Caroline. "Adjustment from Below: Low Income Women, Time and the Triple Role in Guayaquil, Ecuador." In *VIVA: Women and Popular Protest in Ecuador* edited by Sarah Radciffe and Sallie Westwood, 73–196. London: Routledge, 1993.

Moser, Caroline. *Household Responses to Poverty and Vulnerability*. 2 vols. Washington, DC: Urban Management Program, World Bank, 1997.

Phillips, Lynne P. "Women, Development, and the State in Rural Ecuador." In *Rural Women and State Policy: Feminist Perspectives on Latin American Agricultural Development*, edited by Carmen Diana Deere and Magdalena León. Boulder, CO: Westview Press, 1987.

Phillips, Lynne P. "The Power of Representation: Agrarian Politics and Rural Women's Interpretation of the Household in Coastal Ecuador." *Dialectical Anthropology* 15 (1990): 271–83.

Phillips, Lynne P. "Gender Dynamics and Rural Household Strategies." *Canadian Review of Sociology and Anthropology* 26, no. 2 (1987): 294–310.

Weismantel, Mary. *Food, Gender and Poverty in the Ecuadorian Andes*. Philadelphia: University of Pennsylvania Press, 1988.

Weiss, Wendy. "The Social Organization of Property and Work: A Study of Migrants from Rural Ecuadorian Sierra." *American Ethnologist* 12 (August 1985): 468–88.

9

EL SALVADOR

Kelley Ready

PROFILE OF EL SALVADOR

The nickname given to El Salvador is El Pulgarcito, the thumb of Central America. The smallest of the Central American countries, it is also the most densely populated and the only country without access to the Atlantic Coast. Bordered by Guatemala, Honduras, Nicaragua, and the Pacific Ocean, it is a land of lakes and volcanoes. El Salvador is also a land that has been traumatized by a twelve-year civil war (1980 to 1992) and devastated by several natural disasters at the dawn of the new millennium. However this era has also witnessed the emergence of a multifaceted, dynamic women's movement that has become a prominent actor in Salvadoran civil society as the country has gone through its "democratic transition" from a government dominated by a few to one where the election process is internationally recognized as being fair.

El Salvador is a poor country, and like many poor countries, it has a small but powerful elite. The population of El Salvador in 1999 was 6,272,353 with an increasing population density of 297.[1] The GNP per capita was $1900 as of February 2002.[2] Forty-one percent of the population lives in poverty (32.8 percent in urban areas and 55.4 percent in rural). Almost 17 percent of Salvadoran households live in extreme poverty.[3] The gap between the large number of poor people and the few wealthy has been a source of violent conflict in El Salvador's history.

In the sixteenth century, when the Spanish conquistadors arrived in the territory that eventually became El Salvador, it was occupied by a number of different indige-

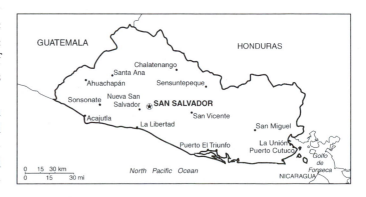

nous tribes, predominantly the Pipiles, who fiercely but unsuccessfully resisted colonization. During the early years of colonization the indigenous population was devastated by diseases brought by the Spaniards and the harsh conditions under which they were forced to work. Lacking the mineral wealth, Central America's most valuable resources were its land and the human labor to work it. The Spaniards and their descendants used a variety of methods to force the native peoples to supply their needs and the needs of the Spanish Empire. Roman Catholicism was imposed upon the new subjects of the Spanish crown, who adapted it to correspond to their own beliefs and practices. Resistance of the indigenous peoples continued—for example, the unsuccessful Indian uprising led by Anastasio Aquino in 1833.

The movement for independence from Spain was promoted primarily by the descendants of the Spanish immigrants, and so little changed for the indigenous peoples when the Central American Federation declared its independence in 1821 or when El Salvador became a separate country in 1841. Throughout the colonial period and continuing into independence, the elite tried to identify a product that could be a source of wealth. Cochineal, cacao, and indigo each succeeded temporarily, but coffee became "king" in El Salvador in the late nineteenth century.

The coffee economy increased the concentration of land in the hands of a few, an oligarchy known as El Catorce (The Fourteen), the powerful families who were believed to control the economic, social, and political life of the country. Coffee changed the composition of the elite as some large landowners failed to adopt its cultivation and were supplanted by the coffee planters, many of whom were recent European immigrants. These families were rapidly absorbed into the upper strata of Salvadoran society through marriage.

Laws were passed that required small farmers and landless laborers to work on the coffee plantations or be jailed. The Guardia Nacional (National Guard) was a security force created to force reluctant *campesinos* (or peasants) to abandon their own fields to pick coffee. Plots of land held in common by Indian communities were outlawed, and peasants were forced to sell small landholdings when they could not afford to invest in coffee cultivation.

When world coffee prices dropped in the 1930s, the Salvadoran economy was devastated and the *campesinos* suffered greatly. An uprising was planned in 1932 by a coalition of indigenous peasants, radical students, and military reformers. Their plans were discovered, however, and the military brutally repressed all suspected sympathizers in what came to be known as La Matanza (the Massacre). The intensity of the government's repression and the succession of military dictators who headed the government kept a lid on dissent for most of the next fifty years. Augustín Farabundo Martí, one of the organizers of the uprising (who was executed by a firing squad), later gave his name to a political coalition, the Farabundo Martí National Liberation Front (known by its Spanish acronym as the FMLN), which challenged the oligarchy in the civil war that began in 1980.

Pressure for economic and political reform in El Salvador grew in the 1960s. Increasing economic competition between El Salvador and Honduras led to the "Soccer War" in 1969. While El Salvador economically dominated the Central American Common Market (CACM), hundreds of thousands of landless Salvadoran peasants had migrated to Honduras and occupied uncultivated lands. Tensions broke out when the Honduran government forced the migrants to return to El Salvador. The CACM collapsed and El Salvador lost important markets. The flood of refugees returning from Honduras increased the pressure for land reform in El Salvador.

When the political party advocating reforms was denied the presidency by electoral fraud in 1972, many Salvadorans decided that electoral politics would never bring the kind of change that was needed. Active support for radical leftist groups grew rapidly, supported by a movement in the Roman Catholic Church known as liberation theology. The government's response was to increase repression and human rights abuses, often through the use of paramilitary groups known as ORDEN in rural areas, or "death squads" made up of police or military in civilian clothing.

The Salvadoran left was strongly encouraged by the success of the 1979 Nicaraguan revolution. Led by the Sandinista National Liberation Front (Frente Sandinista de Liberación Nacional, FSLN), it ousted a longtime dictator and installed a coalition government of business leaders, moderate politicians, and leftist guerrillas. But the coalition did not last, and the increasingly socialist policies of the FSLN and its close ties with Cuba and the Soviet Union made the U.S. government suspicious. After Ronald Reagan assumed the U.S. presidency, he mounted a campaign to oust the Sandinistas from power in Nicaragua. In addition, despite evidence of human rights abuses, he committed the United States to supporting the Salvadoran government.

The U.S. government provided enormous quantities of military and economic aid during the civil war that raged from 1980 until 1992. Over 80,000 people died in the war and 8,000 were "disappeared," taken away and never seen again. Many American citizens challenged the Reagan administration's support for the Salvadoran government, and Congress required regular certification of progress on human rights. A report by a Truth Commission that was compiled after the war attributed the vast majority of human rights abuses to the government. In 1990 the FMLN and the ARENA party, which controlled the government, began peace negotiations under the auspices of the United Nations. A cease-fire was declared in 1991, and a comprehensive peace agreement was signed in January 1992. The FMLN was legalized as a political party. In the midst of the war, a daring new women's movement emerged.

Women made up 52 percent of the Salvadoran population in 2001, but the ratio of women to men depends upon age. Up to the age of 19, boys outnumber girls, with males making up 51 percent of the population. But for the population over the age of 20, women are 55 percent of the population.[4] The civil war is the major reason for the lower number of males because they were the majority of those killed during the war. In addition, they have constituted the majority of those who have migrated.

Total fertility rate has dropped significantly. At 3.1, it is the third lowest in Central America after Costa Rica and Panama, but the figure is still high compared to the Latin American average of 2.7.[5] The figure is considerably higher for rural women and lower in urban areas. In addition, women with less education have more children. In 1998, the rate for women with only primary school education was 6.0, compared with 2.4 for women with secondary or postsecondary education.[6] Whether a woman has paid employment and her socioeconomic level also affect fertility levels.

At 120 deaths for every 100,000 live births, the maternal mortality rate in El Salvador is relatively high.[7] Women who do not receive prenatal care are at highest risk. It is estimated that 40 percent of Salvadoran women do not receive prenatal care. Infant mortality is 35 per 100,000 live births.[8]

Fifty-eight percent of the population lives in urban areas, and almost one third resides in the capital, San Salvador.[9] The urban population growth rate is double that of rural areas, primarily because of internal migration. The Salvadoran population is young; those under 25 make up 60 percent of the population. Life expectancy was 69.7 in 2000, with the figure for women 72.5 and that for men 65.6.[10]

The population is primarily ladino (of mixed Spanish and indigenous descent but having abandoned indigenous cultural practices). While the original indigenous population of El Salvador was "ladinoized" earlier and more extensively than other Central American peoples, it was La Matanza that drove indigenous practices completely underground in El Salvador.[11] The indigenous population abandoned their language, native dress, religious practices, and other visible signs of their culture in the ensuing years in order to avoid harassment by the authorities. Today indigenous people make up only 11 percent of the population and are located primarily in rural areas.[12]

Internal migration has had a major impact in shaping the nature of the Salvadoran population. Seasonal migration, based on the harvesting of export crops such as coffee, has been historically important El Salvador. The instability of the Salvadoran family has been attributed to the demands of this type of work.[13] A second common form of migration is the move from the countryside to the city. The decline of agriculture as a viable source of income has led to the increased urbanization of El Salvador.

OVERVIEW OF WOMEN'S ISSUES

Women's issues in El Salvador are deeply marked by the condition of poverty in which the majority of the population lives, a condition that ignited the civil war fought from 1980 to 1992. Because of the war and economic changes in the last half of the twentieth century, women's roles in El Salvador have changed dramatically. But one must be cautious in generalizing about women in El Salvador because there are dramatic differences among diverse social sectors, especially in terms of economic class and place of residence.

EDUCATION

Opportunities

The level of one's education in El Salvador is determined primarily by socioeconomic status, age, and area of residence; older rural women are the most likely to be illiterate. However, more Salvadoran women than men have a postgraduate education (51 percent according to the 2000 census).[14] Those from low-income groups and those who live in rural areas have much less access to education. Although gender is not the principal determinant of educational access, there are important differences in the educational experiences of females and males.

The formal education system consists of one year of preschool, nine years of basic education, three years of secondary education, and higher education with courses of two to six years. Basic education starts at age seven. It is followed by secondary education that prepares students for the *bachillerato* (bachelor's) diploma in specialized programs such as arts and sciences, business administration, home economics, industrial or vocational arts, and agriculture. Higher education may be either technical/vocational or academic.

The percentage of El Salvador's budget allocated to education has been one of the lowest of any country in the world. Schooling was inefficient and inadequate before the civil war, but the educational system was further devastated by the conflict, and in some regions the government completely abandoned any effort to provide education. The FMLN provided "popular education" in some of the areas it controlled in "schools" that were often held under trees and staffed with committed volunteer teachers. Though these schools had few resources, they were very effective, considering the conditions under which they were operating. After the war many of these teachers were recruited by

Salvadoran girls at military school. Photo © Reuters New-Media Inc./CORBIS.

NGOs and women's organizations to provide literacy education, particularly to rural women.

Educational reform was seen as key to economic recovery following the signing of the peace agreement. The World Bank, UNICEF, USAID and the Spanish government provided funds to finance a new decentralized model of service provision in rural areas, the Community-Managed Schools Program that was known by its Spanish acronym, EDUCO. As a result, more children are in school, educational levels have been steadily rising, and the dropout rate is declining.[15]

There are small differences between the percentages of boys and girls that attend school, but the dropout rate is high for both sexes, especially in rural areas. Many rural areas do not have schools that go beyond the third grade. If children are to continue their studies, they must find someone to live with near schools that offer more advanced education.

The primary reasons that adolescent girls drop out of school are domestic work and pregnancy. While no exact number is available, it is estimated that one third of all pregnancies are among girls who are under 20. Girls who become pregnant are forced to quit school because of school policy and/or family or social pressure. Females with less education tend to have more children. The use of birth control is much higher among females who have had at least some secondary education.

The books used in the Salvadoran educational system reinforce gender inequalities. The images and examples employ gender stereotypes that channel boys and girls into traditional careers. A study by UNICEF and UNIFEM in 1991 reported that half of all Salvadoran textbooks showed men as strong and in charge, while women were portrayed as more passive and domestic. Women were represented mostly as mothers or wives. Even after USAID provided funding for new textbooks that would eliminate stereotypes, the new edition of a textbook produced by the Salvadoran Ministry of Education was still dominated by male images, and when females appeared, it was often in conventional situations.

Literacy

Illiteracy is still higher among women (24.4 percent) than men (18.7 percent).[16] However, the difference in literacy rates between the genders is diminishing in younger populations, and these differences may soon disappear. The 2000 census indicates that over 1 million Salvadorans are illiterate (about 21 percent of the population over 6). But over 50 percent of women over 34 who live in rural areas are illiterate.[17]

EMPLOYMENT AND ECONOMICS

The economy of El Salvador has traditionally been an agricultural one. But today agriculture only contributes 12 percent to the gross domestic product (GDP). However with 35 percent of the population still employed in agriculture, it remains the country's largest source of employment. The war set the Salvadoran economy back; it had been the most industrialized country in Central America before the conflict erupted into full-fledged civil war. But with the end of the war, El Salvador, its labor force reputedly one of the most industrious in the world, has experienced dramatic changes that disproportionately affect women.

After the signing of the peace agreement, the economy improved steadily with a reduction in inflation for several years. Throughout the 1990s Presidents Cristiani, Calderón Sol, and Flores pursued policies of structural adjustment, privatizing national industries like the electric company and reducing the public sector. By the middle of the decade, the growth slowed, and since the impact of Hurricane Mitch and two earthquakes in 2001, the economy has faltered.

One of the driving forces behind the growth after the war was the dollars sent home by Salvadorans working in other countries, particularly in the United States and Canada. These remittances brought in U.S.$1.751 million in 2000, compared to the U.S.$298 million that was generated by coffee exports, the country's other primary source of foreign exchange.[18]

Job/Career Opportunities

Maquilas, factories that assemble products for export under special rules that exempt them from paying taxes, have become a major source of income and employment since the end of the war. This is especially true for women, who make up 88 percent of the *maquiladoras*, the workers in the maquilas. But the kind of work these assembly plants provide is often accompanied by working conditions that exploit women's disadvantaged position in the labor market and violate the labor laws.

Salvadoran women began to enter the wage labor market in significant numbers in the 1960s and 1970s, in both absolute terms, and relative to men.[19] This trend continued during the later decades of the century. However, while there was a demonstrated increase in female wage labor, there was no corresponding rise in male participation in domestic work.[20]

Urban men and women have almost the same rates of employment, but the differences in rural areas are dramatic. Eighty-three percent of the agricultural workforce is male. Also, 73 percent of the economically active population in rural areas is male, and only 27 percent is female. However, official statistics on rural employment are notorious for underestimating the level of women's participation. Rural women may be seen as housewives and listed as part of the economically inactive rural population when they are actually making concrete contributions to the household income.

As is true in many countries in Latin America and the Caribbean, Salvadoran women are found in higher percentages in the public sector than in the private. This may be because the working conditions in the public sector are more attractive to women. Legislation that protects women's rights is more likely to be respected in public institutions. However, the salaries for these jobs are lower than are those in the private sector.

In recent years, El Salvador has adopted neoliberal policies of structural adjustment. The theory behind these policies is that previously public services such as electrical and phone companies should be privatized in order to increase efficiency and reduce government spending. Because women are concentrated in the public sector, the resulting layoffs may impact them disproportionately. In the private sector, Salvadoran women are heavily concentrated in the service industry. They are often self-employed or in domestic work, both sectors that are low-paid and insecure.

Women are much more likely to be found in the informal sector. Seventy-nine percent of the employees in the formal sector are male, while 64 percent of the workers in the urban informal sector are female. The flexibility of the informal sector has certain advantages for women, particularly those with children. Street vendors sell their products with their babies asleep in cardboard boxes in their stalls. But the work is not secure, it pays badly, there are no benefits, working conditions are bad, and there is little opportunity for advancement.

Pay

Equal pay and access to work are protected by both the Civil Code and the Work Code, but since few workers know their rights, and even those who do have few resources with which to assert them, the laws are generally ineffective. Salvadoran women earn 72 percent of what Salvadoran men make. The difference is relatively small compared to other Latin American countries, but it is not because the gender inequality is less. Rather, it can be attributed to the fact that so many men work in the agricultural sector, where the pay is very low. If comparisons are made between men and women working in better-paying fields, the difference is much greater. Women earn only 57 percent of what men receive in industry and commerce.

Unpaid domestic work takes up a considerable amount of Salvadoran women's time — up to 13 hours a day, even for urban women.[21] Because of the lack of services such as running water and electricity in marginal communities, domestic chores such as cooking, laundry, and caring for children can be extremely time-consuming.

Another economic issue for Salvadoran women is the availability of credit. Formal sources of credit are limited to large and midsize enterprises. Small businesses and the informal sector, where more women are concentrated, are most likely to use nongovernmental organizations or informal sources of credit, such as loan sharks. The former are limited and often accompanied by significant restrictions, and the latter can be very expensive.

Working Conditions

Sexual Discrimination

The degree to which sex discrimination is accepted is illustrated in the classified ads of the national newspapers, where the employment section is divided into distinct lists of jobs for women and men. Ads for women often stipulate that they must be under 25 years of age. Women who have been trained in nontraditional careers, such as carpentry and auto mechanics, through programs developed by Salvadoran women's organizations such as Mujeres por la Dignidad y la Vida (Women for Dignity and Life, the Dignas) have found it almost impossible to obtain employment in their field.

Support for Mothers/Caretakers

Once Salvadoran women enter the labor market, they tend to remain and do not withdraw in order to have children. The profiles of women's age of participation in the workforce show that women enter the workforce after school. They arrive in the highest numbers between the ages of 20 and 23, and their participation continues at that level until between the ages of 30 and 33 when it begins to decline.[22] This trajectory is very similar to that of males, and indicates that women do not leave the workforce during their reproductive years. However, it suggests that they may be leaving the paid workforce during their daughters' reproductive years.

Maternal Leave and Daycare

Women are fired when they become pregnant, and many employers require women to provide medical certification that they are not pregnant, even though both practices are illegal. By law employers with more than 20 female employees are supposed to provide daycare, but this is not enforced. The laws that prohibit women from dangerous or unhealthy work make it more difficult for women to get into nontraditional jobs, and leave them limited to occupations with low salaries and other types of occupational hazards.

Inheritance and Property Rights

For rural women, access to land is a major problem. Men are seen as the heads of household and the ones who cultivate the land. Neither the war nor various attempts at land reform nor the peace agreement of 1992 has adequately addressed the problem. Until the Family Code was passed in 1994, there was no mention of gender in legislation on land or property rights. The Family Code, which regulates the economic relations of spouses, recognized the rights of common-law marriages and children born to them for the first time. The law also permits couples to decide how they are going to divide their property.

Most of the data on land tenancy are not disaggregated by sex, but the information indicates that after more than two decades of land reform, land continues to be heavily concentrated in the hands and names of men. Women were between 5 percent and 12 percent of beneficiaries in the first phase of the 1980 agrarian reforms. If a woman was considered a "head of a household," she was more likely to receive land, although still less likely than a male would be. In phase three (phase two was skipped for political reasons), there was no difference in the percentages of male and female heads of households who received land. Even though these programs did not stipulate that the land had to be allocated to the heads of households, in practice it was interpreted as if that were the case, and if a man was present in a household, he was defined as the head.[23]

For women who owned land, gender discrimination functioned in other ways. When land was taken by the government to be distributed in land reform programs, these women had their land expropriated proportionally more often than men.

By the end of the land reform that was part of the peace agreement of 1992, the percentage of women estimated to have received land had reached between 25 percent and 35 percent. However, women who asserted their right to land during the agrarian reforms often encountered strong opposition from the agrarian institutions. They were assigned smaller parcels that were less productive and were located in the most isolated areas. Women were often not accepted as members of the cooperatives that were formed as part of the reforms or they were subject to different eligibility requirements. They also were less likely to be on the committees that governed the cooperatives. Often the committees were more willing to accept the son of a deceased member than his widow.

Social/Government Programs

There is no welfare system in El Salvador. Women without resources must rely on their families or beg. The state does assist women in securing child support from the fathers of their children, but this can be a very long, frustrating, and futile process. Because so many children are born outside of formal marriages, there is often no documentation that links children to their fathers, and consequently many men refuse to support their children. If fathers abandon their children, Salvadoran women often have little redress except through the Procuraduría General de la República (PGR), the Office of the Attorney General. The Attorney General's Office can legally require men to pay child support, and if the men have formal employment, the PGR can have the child support payments deducted from their salaries. More and more women sought this assistance as the devastation of the war, the huge waves of migration, and the profound changes in gender relations created tremendous strains on the Salvadoran social structure, unleashing an epidemic of irresponsible fatherhood by the 1990s.

One group that took note and acted on this development was Women for Dignity and Life. In 1994 they began to organize the women who were trying to get child support, the *madres demandantes*. These women were profoundly dissatisfied with the services that they were getting from the Attorney General's Office: they were treated with disrespect, many cases were never resolved, the amount of money the mothers were awarded was extremely low, the payments were processed very slowly, and the PGR failed to pursue deadbeat dads. Within a year, the Asociación de Madres Demandantes (AMD) opened its offices and was able to get several critical pieces of legislation passed that improved the situation for *madres demandantes*.[24]

FAMILY AND SEXUALITY

Gender Roles

In rural areas of El Salvador, as in many places in the world, women's lives are also shaped by the availability, or lack, of the natural resources that are necessary to carry out their gendered roles. Problems associated with water and energy affect women and girls in the rural areas of El Salvador quite differently than they affect men, and further illustrate the gendered division of labor.

Wood, which provides most of the energy used for cooking in rural El Salvador, is a scare commodity. Everyone in the family collects wood, but women spend the most time in this activity, usually doing it daily. Because women do the cooking over the fires, they are more affected by such health consequences as respiratory infections and eye irritation. In areas without running water, the entire family participates in collecting water, but men often haul water for their own consumption, whereas women are more likely to carry it for the domestic family supply.

Census data on Salvadoran women in the 1980s depicted "a female population that is particularly young, living in a densely populated county, and for the most part poor, half urban and half rural. They have a tendency to form couples early and to still have a large number of children. Women are the heads of 30 percent of the households, in the majority of cases without a stable relationship."[25] The 2000 census indicates that this characterization is still accurate, with women heading 29 percent of the households in the country.

The figures for female-headed households in rural areas are lower; only 26 percent of rural households are identified as being headed by a female. While this looks positive, it may only reflect the particular challenges faced by women who do not have access to male labor in rural areas. It is much more difficult for women to survive without the support of a male. In addition, in rural areas women's roles as heads of households are notoriously undercounted.

Marriage

Since the 1960s, at least, the number of domestic partnerships[26] (*uniones de hecho*) among Salvadoran couples has equaled the number of formal marriages.[27] This pattern, however, varies by class and area of residence. According to the 2000 census, the number of women who are married in rural areas is virtually equal to the number of those who are "accompanied." In urban areas, particularly metropolitan San Salvador, the percentage of formal marriages is 160 percent higher than the number of informal unions.[28]

As a result, it is not uncommon for young women, particularly low-income women, to have their first child before they are formally married. When marriage does occur, it is often not "forever," and marriages have been becoming less permanent since 1975. In that year, one of every 13 marriages ended in divorce; by 1984, it was one of every 10.[29] The average marriage in El Salvador lasts between three and five years.[30] The effects of the civil war and migration, as well as high levels of teenage pregnancy and male desertion, have contributed to the "weakness of the marital bonds." This characteristic of Salvadoran family structure can be attributed to the lack of property ownership. Because Salvadoran women can earn almost as much (or as little, to be more precise) as their male partners, women prefer domestic partnerships to marriage because of the independence that it provides them.[31]

As a result, Salvadoran families take many diverse forms. According to a 1985 survey, of one million households "in almost 800,000, there were persons who were either not head of the family, their partner or their child, that is to say, that there were other family members or persons who lived with the primary couple."[32]

Reproduction

If the bond between couples in El Salvador is weak, that between mother and child is extremely strong. El Salvador is considered by demographers to be in an incipient or moderate stage of fertility decline, with the birthrate dropping from 6.5 in 1950–1955 to 4.0 in 1990–1995.[33] For many Salvadoran women, motherhood is the ultimate achievement of their womanhood and their life. Despite the hardships that they must overcome to provide for their children, and the rapidly changing conditions women have been confronted with since the mid-1970s, motherhood is a role that Salvadoran women approach with eagerness and, often, without much deliberation.

Breast-feeding is a common practice among Salvadoran mothers; 94 percent of all women breast-feed.[34] Given the levels of poverty it is not surprising that malnutrition is a problem for pregnant women, especially in rural areas.

Contraception and Abortion

The average age at which women have their first sexual relationship is 18.5; 74 percent of sexually active teenagers are not familiar with methods of birth control.[35] According to the International Planned Parenthood Federation, though many women of childbearing age know of a method of family planning, only half use some kind of contraception. The figure drops to one third in rural areas. Between the 1993 and 1998 National Family Health Surveys, contraceptive use in urban areas increased 6.5 percent, and 5.6 percent in rural areas, to 68 percent and 51 percent, respectively. The largest increase was among women under 25.[36]

With a young population, there is concern about teenage pregnancy; Salvadoran women between the ages of 15 and 19 have one of the highest fertility rates in Latin America. In general, women who have partners start using contraception at an average age of 23, when they already have two living children. The number of children a woman has before she uses contraception and the age at which she will begin is higher for rural women and women with less education.[37] There is a saying in El Salvador that "to be a woman is to be a mother." What this has meant for Salvadoran women in that their sexuality is intimately tied to their reproductive capacity. In the late 1970s the primary reason that women cited for not using birth control was the attitude of their spouse.[38] But today women often say that men's objections to their use of contraception do not necessarily come from a desire to have more children. Rather, men's suspicion that their wives want to use contraceptives to hide the consequences of illicit affairs forces many women to choose methods of birth control that cannot be detected. These methods, such as injections of Depo-Provera, also often carry serious health risks.

The most widely used method of contraception is female sterilization (32.4 percent). Drugs administered by injection are the next most popular method, followed by oral contraceptives (9 percent and 8 percent, respectively). According to the National Family Health Survey, the rate of contraceptive use varied from 38 percent in one rural state to 71 percent in San Salvador and, with one exception, was higher in urban than in rural areas. The rate increased with age, education, and socioeconomic level but "did not differ significantly with respect to religious affiliation."[39]

The government provides less than half of the contraceptives used in El Salvador. Most of the other half comes from the Salvadoran Demographic Association (Asociación Demográfica Salvadoreña; ADS), a nongovernment organization that has clinics throughout the country. ADS also has

1,100 rural workers who promote birth control and distribute contraceptives. According to ADS, Norplant is the most popular form of birth control.[40]

El Salvador has one of the most restrictive abortion laws in the world. Abortion is illegal under any circumstances. Until 1997, abortions could be performed if childbirth presented a risk to the life of the mother, if the fetus was deformed, or in the case of rape. But these exemptions were rarely used because the legal mechanisms to implement them were never clearly defined, and doctors feared repercussions if it was learned that they had performed an abortion. However, women who came to the hospital with abortion-related complications were rarely persecuted. The Catholic Church and the pro-life organization Sí a la Vida (Yes to Life) worked to create a climate that made legal abortions unacceptable. When leftist parties won a majority in the legislature in 1997, the right wing carried out a political maneuver eliminating the exemptions that theoretically allowed women to obtain abortions. Despite protests from Salvadoran feminists, the new law went into effect in 1998. A team from the state prosecutor's office was constituted to prosecute women suspected of having had an abortion. In 1999 a constitutional amendment recognizing the fetus as a human being from the moment of conception was approved, effectively blocking any possibility of decriminalizing abortion in El Salvador in the near future.

Illegal abortions were performed before the changes in the law, and they continue to occur, often with serious consequences for women who seek them. Periodically the government and police mount campaigns to close the clinics where abortions are performed, but the continuing need for this service means that the clinics soon reappear. In 1996, a newspaper article reported that 8 percent of the patients treated at the public maternity hospital show signs of abortion, many the result of using risky homemade techniques. The article further reported that the heath system reported 10,000 *abortos* annually, a figure that did not reflect the true dimensions of the practice because these included only women who were treated for complications.[41]

Teen Pregnancy

The fertility rate for adolescents in El Salvador is 137 per 1000, a rate that is exceeded in Central America only by Guatemala. Thirty percent of all births in El Salvador are to women under the age of 20, and 34.7 percent of those are to girls under the age of 15.[42] Considering the high incidence of maternal morbidity and mortality among mothers from 15 to 19 years of age, and the strong tendency for girls to abandon their studies when they become pregnant, these figures are disturbing. Almost three-quarters of the women interviewed who were in school at the time of their first pregnancy did not return to their studies.[43]

The median age at first childbirth has been 20.5 since the mid-1980s. The median age of first sexual union is 19.1 to 20.3. Women with ten or more years of schooling were 5.3 years older in median age at first sexual relations, 6.1 years older at first marital union, and 5.4 years older at first childbirth.[44]

HEALTH

Health Care Access

The Salvadoran Constitution guarantees the right to medical care for all citizens. As a result all citizens have access to the medical and hospital services of the Ministry of Public Health and Social Assistance (MSPAS), which is financed by the public treasury. Nonetheless, health care is deficient for the Salvadoran population in general. In addition to MSPAS, the Salvadoran Institute of Social Security (ISSS), an autonomous agency, provides public health care. ISSS primarily benefits state workers, retirees, and their dependents in urban areas. Most of the services of MSPAS are concentrated in San Salvador, even though half of the population is rural. Neither system pays particular attention to women's issues that are not directly related to childbearing. Private for-profit clinics and hospitals are in the capital and other urban concentrations. Private nonprofit groups also offer medical care through nongovernmental organizations (NGOs). For every 10,000 inhabitants in 1999, there were 12.11 doctors, 5.4 midwives, 6.56 nurses, and 4.94 dentists.[45]

Midwives commonly attend births, especially in rural areas. Between 1993 and 1998 only 58 percent of live births took place in hospitals. In urban areas this figure was 78 percent; it was 43 percent in rural areas. In the department of Chalatenango, only 36 percent of live births took place in hospitals.[46] Women cite a number of reasons for preferring midwives: they can give birth at home without having to find someone to care for their children, they fear cesareans sections, they are mistreated by doctors, midwives cost less.

Their fears about the medical treatment they might receive are not unfounded. In Rosales Hospital, the primary hospital in San Salvador, the most common surgical procedure is a hysterectomy. The rate of cesarean section between 1996 and 1998 increased from 13.4 per 100 live births (1991–1993) to 15.7 (1996–1998). The rate is as high as 41.5 percent for private hospitals and clinics.[47]

Diseases and Disorders

For women, the most common problems are associated with reproductive and sexual health, uterine cancer, anxiety, and poor nutrition.

Vector-born diseases such as dengue fever and malaria are prevalent, with dengue reaching epidemic proportions in 1995 (almost 10,000 cases). Cholera, an intestinal infection, was introduced into the country in 1991, and in 1994 reached a high of 15,280 cases. In 1996 parasitic intestinal diseases were the second leading cause of morbidity, followed by diarrhea.[48]

AIDS

The Salvadoran Ministry of Health recognized HIV/AIDS as an "epidemic" in June 1999. There were 2,990 cases of HIV infection and 6,016 cases of AIDS reported between 1984 and 2000.[49] The annual incidence has increased steadily since 1991, from 2.5 to 7.6 per 100,000. The ratio of men to women is 3:2, and 88.5 percent of the cases were attributed to sexual transmission. While only less than 6 percent of the cases were identified as being from nonheterosexual activities, that figure is probably low for men because of fear of reporting homosexual activity.[50]

The Law for the Prevention and Control of Infection Caused by the Human Immunodeficiency Virus (HIV) was passed in 2001. Under Article 16 of this legislation employers could require workers and job applicants to test for HIV. Because this law facilitates discrimination against workers with HIV, women's organizations, human rights groups, gay and lesbian organizations, and HIV/AIDS organizations opposed it. The Supreme Judicial Court has ruled that this article of the law is unconstitutional.

Cancer

The level of uterine cancer in El Salvador is one of the highest in Latin America: 84 per 100,000 women between the ages of 35 and 60. Half of the women who are diagnosed with this cancer die within five years. MSPAS is the primary administrator of the tests for this condition, and although the coverage has increased, the services are often faulty. It often takes excessive amounts of time for the results to be obtained, and there are few trained personnel to administer the tests in rural areas. Rural women who take the tests often fail to return for the results because of the time and expense of traveling from their remote villages or farms to the clinics. Breast cancer seems to be less common, although its prevalence is difficult to assess because neither mammography nor breast exams are widely promoted.

Depression

Little is known about mental illness in El Salvador, though it is recognized that women suffer from it more than men do. Depression, anxiety syndromes, and alcoholism are considered to be the most common mental health problems.[51] The causes of women's mental illness include sexual abuse, domestic violence, postpartum depression, and stress. Many still suffer the effects of living through a war, of having been forced to flee their homes and live in refugee camps, of having lost members of their family, or of being tortured. The difficulties of assisting ex-combatants to reintegrate into civilian society have also been a source of anxiety and depression for many women. Suicides make up 20 percent of the deaths due to external causes in adolescents, and females are the majority of those who commit suicide.[52]

POLITICS AND LAW

The Republic of El Salvador is a representative democracy in which election fraud and political repression have often undermined the legitimacy of the government. The civil war that was fought between 1980 and 1992 was a result of the government's failure to respond to the needs and demands of the poorest and most marginalized members of the society. Over 80,000 people were killed and 8,000 "disappeared" in a conflict that assumed Cold War proportions when Ronald Reagan made El Salvador his bulwark in the fight against communism in the Western Hemisphere. The victory of the Sandinistas in Nicaragua and the ongoing conflict in Guatemala led to increasing U.S. military and economic aid to El Salvador in the 1980s, reaching to over $1 million per day at its height.

But even with the U.S. military assistance the government of El Salvador (GOES) could not defeat the Frente Farabundo Martí para la Liberación Nacional (Farabundo Marti National Liberation Front, FMLN), the guerrilla army that challenged the government. Supported by an array of organizations representing peasants, students, workers, earthquake victims, Christian-based communities and human rights organizations, the FMLN fought to reform a government dominated by a wealthy elite and the military that had historically protected their interests.

With the fall of the Berlin Wall, the defeat of the Sandinistas in Nicaragua, and Reagan's departure from office, the war reached a stalemate. While the GOES claimed that the FMLN was defeated, a 1989 offensive demonstrated the FMLN's continued capacity to wreak havoc on the Salvadoran economy. But the failure of the offensive to spark an uprising, as the FMLN had hoped, also demonstrated the need to seek a negotiated settlement. A peace process was pursued under the auspices of the United Nations, and the FMLN and GOES signed a preliminary agreement in December 1991. The final agreement, known as the Accords of Chapultepec or the Peace Accords, was signed in Mexico City on January 16, 1992. By December, the FMLN had become a legal political party.

Suffrage and Political Participation

Women won the right to vote in 1939 but were not allowed to be candidates for political office until 1961.

The Salvadoran government consists of three branches: executive, legislative, and judicial. The president of El Salvador is both the chief of state and the head of the government. Elected for a five-year term, the president is not allowed to run for a second term. The executive branch includes a vice president and the cabinet ministers. Francisco Flores Perez was elected president in June 1999 along with his vice president, Carlos Quintanilla Schmidt. The president's wife automatically becomes the head of the Instituto Salvadoreño de Desarrollo de la Mujer (Salvadoran Institute for the Development of Women, ISDEMU), a government agency whose purpose is to develop and implement a national policy on women. El Salvador has not had a female president.

The legislative branch consists of a unicameral assembly with 84 members who are elected for three-year terms. In 2002, there were eight women in the assembly but this figure has fluctuated. In the 1991–1994 there were 7, in 1994–1997 there were 9, and in 1997–2000, 14 women were elected to the assembly.[53] In March 2000, the FMLN won a majority of seats in the Legislative Assembly for the first time. However, the right-wing bloc of parties, including ARENA (Alianza Republicana Nacional, National Republican Alliance) and PCN (Partido de Conciliación Nacional, National Conciliation Party) are still able to retain control. The FMLN also won 77 mayoral positions in 2000. This includes the mayor of San Salvador, Hector Silva, who was reelected that year and is a serious contender for the presidency. His city council includes Morena Herrera, one of the founders the Dignas, the Salvadoran feminist organization, and they have incorporated a gender perspective into the local plans for the city.

Of the 262 mayors in the country, only 24 are female.[54] This is a significantly lower number than in 1991–1994, when women were 30 percent of the mayors. In the next two elections, the percentages dropped to 12 percent in 1994–1997 and 8 percent in 1997–2000. On the other hand, women's participation in city councils rose steadily in the same period, going from 2 percent in 1991 to 16 percent in 1997.[55]

This increase can be attributed to the work of several women's organizations that have developed women's political platforms in the municipalities and have used them to teach women how to better participate in political processes. The first national women's platform was developed in 1993, prior to "the election of the century." This was the first election following the signing of the peace agreement and was also the first time that the FMLN could legally run candidates as a political party. In addition, candidates were being elected for local, state, and national offices at the same time. A coalition of women's organizations joined together to develop an electoral platform, Mujeres 94 (Women 94), that reflected women's interests. They used it to lobby all the political parties and to organize women. One of their demands was that the political parties establish a quota of seats to be filled by women. In 1998 the FMLN adopted a requirement that 35 percent of its candidates for legislative and municipal elections had to be women. The following year several of the women's groups replicated the efforts to develop women's platforms in local communities.

The third branch of the government is the judiciary. El Salvador has a Supreme Court, two levels of lower courts, and justices of the peace. This is an area where women have made significant progress, particularly at the lower levels. Forty percent of the judges are female, but there are only two women in the Supreme Court. Nevertheless, the Supreme Court has recognized the importance of reformulating the law so that it does not discriminate against women, and has allocated resources to develop new legislation to eliminate gender inequalities in the law.

Women's Rights

Feminist Movements

Salvadoran women were active participants in political mobilization throughout the twentieth century but no women's organization existed prior to 1947. Groups such as the Liga Feminina (Feminine League) and the Fraternidad de Mujeres (Women's Fraternity) subsequently formed to advocate for social reforms and to fight for women's right to hold office. The Salvadoran women's movement emerged in the 1970s with two organizations, The Association of Salvadoran Women (Asociación de Mujeres de El Salvador, AMES) and the Association of Progressive Women of El Salvador (Asociación de Mujeres Progresistas de El Salvador, AMPES). Both organizations were linked with groups that later formed the FMLN. They saw themselves as vehicles for channeling women into the struggle against the government, the military, and the elite. Consequently they were identified as subversive, and driven underground and into exile by the early 1980s.

This kind of repression was common during the 1970s and 1980s in El Salvador. People were "disappeared," taken away by the military or by heavily armed men in civilian clothing, never to be seen again. Others were tortured, mutilated, and killed, then left in the streets or buried in clandestine cemeteries. Union activists, neighborhood organizers, members of Christian base communities, peasants, and people who happened to be in the wrong place at the wrong time were victims of these atrocities. At the height of this terror in the 1980s, few groups were willing to come out into the streets to demonstrate against what was going on.

One group that did protest against human rights abuses during this time was the Committee of Mothers of Political Prisoners, the Assassinated and Disappeared of El Salvador (CoMadres). The CoMadres was formed in 1977 with the support of the Catholic Archbishop of El Salvador, Oscar Romero, who was later assassinated. By combining the powerful image of motherhood with the discourse on human rights and democracy, the CoMadres used traditional gender roles to challenge state repression and to draw international attention to the plight of the Salvadoran people.

Resistance to the government was waged on two levels. The first level was a guerrilla war fought by the FMLN. The other was "popular organizations," nonviolent groups like unions, churches, human rights groups, and neighborhood committees that organized to challenge poverty, government policies, and the lack of democracy in the political process. In order to be more effective, these groups recognized the need to recruit women. By the mid-1980s, there were numerous women's committees that joined to form the National Coordinating Committee of Salvadoran Women (CONAMUS), a coalition that was founded in 1986. There were nine organizations of women by 1989 as well as groups that represented specific social sectors, such as the Association of Indigenous Women. But with the growing visibility of the women's movement came increased repression. Their demonstrations were fired upon, the homes of their leaders were bombed, and members of their groups were the victims of death squads.

As the women's organizations grew, many of their leaders began to chafe under the restraints imposed upon them by the male leadership of their organizations. When the peace negotiations began in the late 1980s, Salvadoran women, in both the FMLN and the popular movement, began to assert their autonomy. With increasing support from and contact with transnational feminism, they began to challenge the sexism in their organizations and to redefine their struggle as women.

The signing of the peace agreement created the conditions that generated the "third wave" of Salvadoran feminism, the struggle for autonomy from the FMLN and subsequent political parties.[56] When the women's groups attempted to break away from party control, they often found themselves isolated from their previous constituency, without funds, and with their reputations slandered. Some of the women's organizations chose to expel more militant feminists from their ranks. Debates about the nature of autonomy raged among the groups as some organizations remained associated with the FMLN. Ultimately most of the women's organizations have remained connected to the FMLN, although the relationships are still often antagonistic. For instance, in the period leading to the elections of 2000, the women's organizations promoted a female for the FMLN's presidential candidate. In an extremely contentious convention, the party chose to reject her candidacy in favor of a male's.

Among some of the women's organizations that are currently active are Women for Dignity and Life (Dignas; Mujeres por la Dignidad y la Vida); the Women's Movement Mélida Anaya Montes (Movimiento de Mujeres "Mélida Anaya Montes"; MAM/las Mélidas); the Norma Virginia Guirola de Herrera Women's Studies Center (Centro de Estudios de la Mujer "Norma Virginia Guirola de Herrera"; CEMUJER).

The Dignas was founded by a group of women from the FMLN in 1990. In subsequent years they have come to be known as the most radically feminist of the Salvadoran women's organizations. They are also one of the most successful at gaining international financial support. Based in San Salvador, they have ties to groups in small rural towns where they have roots dating back to the war. The Dignas sponsor five programs: Political Participation and Local Development, Eradication of Gender Violence, Women and the Economy, Nonsexist Education, and Institutional Development (the administrative area of the organization).

The Political Participation and Local Development program works to increase the participation of women in politics and civil society. Eradication of Gender Violence provides treatment to women who have experienced violence and participates in various public arenas to prevent violence and improve the treatment of women who have experienced gender violence. Fighting against sexism by promoting feminist theories and proposals, particularly in the educational system, is the goal of the Nonsexist Education program, which holds a national conference on nonsexist education and organizes the Escuela de Debate Feminista (School of Feminist Debate). The Dignas' Documentation Center, also part of the Nonsexist Education program, has made information on gender issues available to thousands of individuals (including this author), especially secondary and high school students. The program on Women and the Economy promotes the participation of women in nontraditional careers and the access of girls to the training they need to pursue those careers. In the process it advocates for increased access to, and inclusion of, information on labor rights for women in technical training programs and in general. It also works to incorporate a gender perspective into the analysis of economic measures and to evaluate the impact of labor trends on women's lives.

The approach of the Mélidas, founded in 1992, differs from that of the Dignas in several ways. They operate a "mass organization" by actively building a base of women supporters, making them most probably (there is no documentation) the largest Salvadoran women's organization. While they define themselves as autonomous of the FMLN, they remain committed to working within the party. The president of the Mélidas in 1996, Lorena Peña (known as Rebecca Palacio while a guerrilla *comandante*), was also an FMLN legislator in the National Assembly. Several other key members of the organization ran as FMLN candidates in the 1997 election.

The Mélidas promote economic projects and micro enterprises. In 2001 they began a relationship with the Grameen Bank, whose work with micro enterprise lending in Asia has been renowned. In addition, the Mélidas organize women as workers, particularly in the free trade zones (*zonas francas*). Their Legislative Initiative (Iniciativa Legislativa) is a committee of lawyers and legislators that has been instrumental in the passage of several pieces of legislation, including a law regulating the free trade zones.

While the Mélidas take their name from a woman leader of one branch of the FMLN who was killed by one of her own comrades, CEMUJER is named after Norma Virginia Guirola de Herrera, a former militant of the Communist Party who was killed during the 1989 offensive. CEMUJER is recognized for its work in *capacitación* (training). It has carried out *capacitaciones* with a wide variety of groups, including many government institutions and even the military, and in 2001 began to promote gender training in the trade unions. Their approach is to attempt to work within the system in order to effect change. CEMUJER has an active research program and a library, and provides legal, medical, and emotional services for women.

While these groups were the most visible, numerous other women's organizations educate, organize, and provide services to women throughout El Salvador: ORMUSA (Organización de Mujeres Salvadoreñas por la Paz; Organization of Salvadoran Women for Peace), the Institute for Research, Training, and Development of Women (Instituto para la Investigación, Capacitación y Desarrollo de la Mujer; IMU); MSM (Movimiento Salvadoreño de Mujeres; Salvadoran Women's Movement), AMS (Asociación de Mujeres Salvadoreñas, Salvadoran Women's Association), and ADEMUSA (Asociación de Mujeres Salvadoreñas). In addition there are coalitions such as COM (Coordinadora de Organizaciones de Mujeres; Coordinating Council of Women's Organizations), which was formed during the war to bring together the women's organizations from the various tendencies of the FMLN; the Asociación de Madres Demandantes and the Red de Mujeres por la Unidad y Desarrollo (the Women's Network for Unity and Development). One final organization is Flor de Piedra (Flower of Stone), a prostitutes' group. Started in 1990, this group has had a difficult time finding funding for its clinic that provides women with birth control, condoms, and testing for HIV and other sexually transmitted diseases.

Many of these groups collaborated in 1993 when the Sixth Latin American and Caribbean Feminist Encuentro (Conference) took place in El Salvador. The Encuentros, which have been held in a different Latin American country roughly every three years since 1981, have become "critical forums for movement debates about evolving feminist politics and the movement's relationship to the overall struggle for social justice in Latin America."[57] Central Americans began to participate in the Encuentros in significant numbers only in 1987, when the Encuentro was held in Mexico. The meeting at San Bernardo, Argentina, in 1990 recognized the importance of the growth of the feminist movement in Central America by designating El Salvador as the site of the next Encuentro.

In the wake of Hurricane Mitch in 1998 and two major earthquakes (and thousands of aftershocks) in 2001, the work of many of these groups shifted. Particularly after the earthquakes, many of the women's organizations diverted their labor and resources into disaster relief. Their experiences during the war, the relationships they have with the most vulnerable rural communities, their contacts with international funding agencies, and their knowledge that gender would be a critical factor in the responses to the crisis drove these women to respond immediately with material aid and emotional support. The impact of the disasters is still evident in the plans that the groups have elaborated for their work, such as supporting the construction of new housing or providing mental health services to those traumatized by their losses.

Lesbian Rights

The first Salvadoran lesbian organization, La Coletiva Lésbica-Feminista Salvadoreña de la Media Luna (Salvadoran Lesbian Feminist Collective of the Half Moon; La Media Luna) began meeting in 1992. Lesbianism was not new to El Salvador, but affirming it as a social identity and challenging *lesbofobia* was a new political and cultural practice. Some feminists and women's organization were supportive of lesbians' efforts to organize, but that support was tempered by a profound concern that explicit support for gay rights would lead to a backlash that would threaten the existence of the feminist movement. It was not an unfounded fear, for political parties, on both the left and the right, often used charges of lesbianism to undermine the work of women's organizations. Women who had previously been in the FMLN but had resigned to build autonomous women's organizations were often accused of being lesbians by their former comrades. Particularly in rural communities, where the work of most women's groups was based, rumors of this nature often made it impossible for them to continue working. Nonetheless, the right to *el libre opción sexual*, or the freedom to exercise one's sexuality, was included in the political platform Mujeres 94.

While La Media Luna has ceased to function, women's groups associated with Entre Amigos (Between Friends), a gay male organization, continue to provide lesbian and bisexual women and their friends a safe place to gather.

RELIGION AND SPIRITUALITY

The majority of Salvadorans are Roman Catholics, a religion that was imposed up them by the Spanish. For most of its history, the Catholic Church was aligned with the upper classes, those who owned vast tracts of land and, later, the industrialists and commercial interests. In doing so, it served to uphold the status quo and justify the vast inequalities of wealth.

The Second Vatican Council put into motion changes that would challenge those practices. It proposed a new model for the church, one with "a preferential option for the poor." This phrase refers to a new concept of faith that sees it as being realized in practical actions to defend the interests of the oppressed. When Latin American bishops met in 1968 at

Medellín, Colombia, they reiterated the need for the church to respond to the social injustice that existed in Latin America. The alliance between the church and the poor was reaffirmed in 1979 in Puebla, Mexico, but not without resistance from some sectors of the Church hierarchy. Nonetheless change had begun, and what came to be known as liberation theology provoked profound realignments in the church and society, and of women's place in both.

Women's Roles

Two of the practices that emerged within liberation theology and had profound implications for women's participation in the church were the use of *delegados de la palabra* (delegates of the Word) and the rise of Christian base communities. Delegates of the word (catechists) were laypeople, both male and female, who were trained to read and preach the Scriptures according to the egalitarian principles of liberation theology. The message that they brought to the countryside was that in God's eyes, all his children are equal, and that none should suffer. The struggle for justice was seen as a religious imperative and a reflection of God's will.

Christian base communities began with nightly meetings of small groups, including many women, reflecting on their lives in terms of the Bible. But within a short time these groups were faced with the question of what to do with their insights. By the mid-1970s, events were compelling Salvadorans to respond. Eventually the lines dividing the popular movements and the Christian base communities evaporated. In part this was due to the military's response to the movement. They attacked Christian base communities, accusing them of harboring guerrillas. Catechists became targets of the death squads, as did priests and nuns who advocated liberation theology. Ultimately the highest religious officer in the church in El Salvador, Archbishop Oscar Romero, was assassinated after calling for the United States to cut off funding to the military.

These attacks created conditions that propelled women into leadership roles. When the men were forced to flee the communities because of government invasions, women were the ones who stepped in. Vatican II had allowed nuns to assume new roles in the church and to exchange their habits for normal clothing. But it was not just nuns who were affected by the changes. Laywomen became catechists and began to teach literacy and liberation theology; to promote health; to form cooperatives; and to start projects to improve their living conditions. Like men, the women were identified as guerrillas by the military and were killed. Their communities were attacked, bombed, and massacred. The women led their people in *guindas* (forced flights), and they became leaders in refugee camps in Honduras, where they continued to learn new skills

During the latter half of the 1980s, the Catholic Church began moving away from its commitment to liberation theology. An office for the Christian base communities was closed, and the priests and nuns who worked with the guerrillas received less support. The Lutheran Church, under Bishop Medardo Gómez, moved into the vacuum left by the departure of the Catholic Church. He became the religious leader who spoke out in support of human rights.

Another development is the growing popularity of more conservative *iglesias evangélicas* (evangelical Protestant churches). While some of these churches provide women with opportunities to play significant leadership roles, others, such as the Mormon Church, promote very traditional roles for women. El Salvador has not seen the kinds of conflict generated by the growth of evangelism that has erupted in southern Mexico and Guatemala.

VIOLENCE

In 1995 the Pan American Health organization listed El Salvador as having the second highest murder rate in Latin America. The extremely high levels of violent crime are a legacy of the war and of the inequality in wealth that continue to characterize the Salvadoran economy.

Domestic Violence and Rape/Sexual Assault

It is estimated that only 16 percent of the women who are the victim of sexual attacks report the crime.[58] But despite this low number, the reports of sexual crimes against women have been increasing steadily, going from five per day in 1996 to almost nine per day in 1999.[59] The majority of the victims were women, and girls and boys under the age of 19; almost 99 percent of the perpetrators were men. One third of the crimes were committed by family members, and more than three-quarters of the victims knew their aggressors. Almost 6 percent of the women between the ages of 15 and 49 interviewed for a FESAL (Federation of Southern Academic Libraries) study reported having been forced to have sexual relations, a figure that represents 91,673 women. The number of women who reported being raped was relatively high among those with a high socioeconomic level, those living in urban areas and those with seven to nine years of schooling.[60]

For many young women, their first sexual experience was violent (66 percent) and took place when they were under 15 (53 percent). A high incidence of a history of sexual abuse was found in women working as prostitutes. Sixty percent reported being raped by a stepfather and 20 percent by their biological father.[61] While many more violent crimes against women are reported in urban areas, this is probably not simply because of the higher levels of violence in the cities. It is also probably due in part to the fact that it is easier to report the crimes in the city, and urban women are more likely to be aware of the option to do so than are rural women.

The women's movement has contributed to a significant part of this rise in the number of cases reported by increasing awareness about the existence and extent of violence against Salvadoran women. One of the first studies of domestic violence in El Salvador surveyed elementary school children in the capital. Fifty-seven percent of the children answered affirmatively when asked if their father physically abused their mother, documenting for the first time that domestic violence was a widespread phenomenon.[62] The signing of the peace agreements in 1992 opened important new political spaces for women to participate in the creation of public policy. Almost all of the women's organizations had already begun to address the issue of domestic or intrafamily violence (*violencia intrafamiliar*), but the peace agreement created the conditions that allowed them to deal with it politically as well as socially.

Using international conventions such as Convention to End All Forms of Discrimination Against Women and the Convention of Belem do Pará from the First Interamerican Convention for the Prevention, Sanction, and Eradication of Violence Against Women, Salvadoran women's organizations worked to make violence against women more visible. Changes to the Penal Code in 1997 included important advances such as allowing the victim to testify as a witness. The Law Against Intra-family Violence was introduced in 1996 at the initiative of the women's movement. It simplified the procedures women had to go through to get restraining orders and created public policies to deal with domestic violence. But despite these achievements, the attitudes of many police officials and judges revictimize the women who come to them seeking support and protection.

For this reason, a coalition of women's groups and independent activists continues to work together in the 25th of November Committee, named for the day on which violence against women is internationally recognized. This committee organizes marches and educational events on that day and monitors the policies on gender violence throughout the year.

OUTLOOK FOR THE TWENTY-FIRST CENTURY

The first months of the new millennium treated El Salvador extremely harshly. In addition to two earthquakes a month apart, followed by thousands of aftershocks, the government issued its own shock with a new fiscal policy that included the dollarization of the economy. This was part of the neoliberal reforms that privatized many national industries and services, and reduced the size of the government with massive layoffs. As the price of coffee, the country's prime export, continued to fall, the government's response was to encourage the growth of the *maquila* sector. While this meant more jobs for women, the government did not commit itself to ensuring that these employers respect their workers and provide them with dignified working conditions that correspond to the country's labor laws.

But the women's organizations do have that commitment. They are fighting for women's rights in the *maquilas*; for the rights of *madres demandantes* to receive their share of the severance pay of laid-off workers; for the rights of women to participate politically on the local, national, and international levels; to end violence against women; and to gain access to nonsexist education, land, credit, and reproductive and sexual health rights. The question is whether they will continue to receive financial support from the international community to carry on these struggles.

Although the tenth anniversary of the peace agreement was celebrated in 2002, there are still significant gaps between the aspirations of the Salvadoran people and the daily conditions with which Salvadoran women must contend. The lack of significant political, economic, and social progress in the postwar period has led to a serious demoralization of the population and a corresponding apathy reflected in low levels of political participation. The perception that the justice system and police are tainted by corruption has contributed to a lack of credibility and a sense of impotence, particularly in the face of a continuing high level of crime. But the ability of the Salvadoran people to exercise their political rights has been expanded since the end of the war, and women are active participants in the political process at many levels.

During the 1980s El Salvador's civil war preoccupied international Cold War warriors. But in the twenty-first century, that focus has shifted to terrorist movements, and Central America only briefly reappears in the newspaper photos of the victims of "natural" disasters like Hurricane Mitch or earthquakes. What is not recognized all too often is that the terrible social impact of these tragedies is intensified by the faceless processes of globalization. These processes are heightening the tensions that led to earlier conflict, widening the gap between the rich and poor, and undermining the social fabric that served as a safety net. Because it is women who bear the brunt of such changes, it is not surprising that Salvadoran women's groups have challenged both the government and multilateral organizations that are promoting these policies. While it is clear that Salvadoran women will have a greater impact than ever on shaping those policies, how profound that impact will be is yet to be seen.

NOTES

1. World Bank, *Country Brief*, 1999, http://lnweb18.worldbank.org/external/lac/lac.nsf/b4clef74407031c4852567d60006b1558/83 . . . e, accessed November 3, 2001; Ministerio de Economía, Dirección General de Estadística y Censos, "Encuesta de propósitos hogares múltiples 2000" (San Salvador, El Salvador: Ministerio de Economía, Dirección General de Estadística y Censos, 2001), diskette.

2. UNICEF, *Statistics—Latin America and the Caribbean: El Salvador*, 2000, www.unicef.org/statis/Country_1page54.html, accessed November 3, 2001.

3. Organization of Management and Health Systems and Services, Division of Health Systems and Services Development, Pan American Health Organization

(OMHSS), *El Salvador: Profile of Health Systems and Services*, 2000, www.americas. health-sector-reform.org/English/elspren.pdf, accessed November 2, 2001.

4. Ministerio de Economía, 2001.

5. UNICEF, 2000, 2.

6. Federation of Southern Academic Libraries (FESAL), General Summary, n.d., www.fesal.org.sv/english/Cont_resumen.htm, 1.

7. UNICEF, 2000, 2.

8. Ibid., 1.

9. OMHSS, 2000, 1; Pan American Health Organization (PAHO), "El Salvador: Demographic Indicators," in *Basic Country Health Profiles, Summaries*, 1999, www. paho.org/English/SHA/prflels.htm, accessed November 3, 2001.

10. OMHSS, 2000, 1.

11. P. Thomas, *Matanza: El Salvador's Communist Revolt of 1932* (Lincoln: University of Nebraska Press, 1971); Roque Dalton, *Miguel Mármol* (Willimantic, CT: Curbstone Press, 1987).

12. OMHSS, 2000, 1.

13. Victor Lagos Pizatti and Maria Teresa de Mejía, *La situación de la familia y del menor en El Salvador* (San Salvador, El Salvador: Secretaría Nacional de la Familia, 1994), 22; Alastair White, *El Salvador* (New York: Praeger, 1973), 245.

14. Ministerio de Economía, 2001.

15. Jack Spence, Mike Lanchin, and Geoff Thale, *From Elections to Earthquakes: Reform and Participation in Post-War El Salvador* (Cambridge, MA: Hemisphere Initiatives, 2001).

16. UNICEF, 2000, 2.

17. Ministerio de Economía, 2001.

18. Spence et al., 2001, 13.

19. The decrease in the male PEA is attributed to their higher levels of international migration, the incorporation of males into the military during the war, and the high number of male casualties in the conflict.

20. Ana Isabel García and Enrique Gomáriz, *Mujeres centroamericanas: Ante la crisis, la guerra y el proceso de paz* (San José, Costa Rica: FLACSO, 1989), and *Mujeres centroamericanas: Efectos del conflicto* (San José, Costa Rica: FLACSO, 1989), 117.

21. Sonia Baires, Dilcia Marroquín, Clara Murguialday, Ruth Polanco, and Norma Vázquez, *Mami, mami, demanda la cuota . . . la necesitamos: Un análisis feminista sobre la demanda de cuota alimenticia a la Procuraduría* (San Salvador: Mujeres por la Dignidad y la Vida, 1996), 18.

22. Ministerio de Planificación y Coordinación de Desarrollo Económico y Social (MIPLAN), *Encuesta de hogares de propósitos múltiples urbano y rural, octubre 1993–marzo 1994* (San Salvador: MIPLAN, 1994).

23. Proyecto de Planificación y Evaluación de la Reforma Agraria (PERA), "*Décima evaluación del proceso de la Reforma Agraria*" (San Salvador: PERA).

24. They did it with the help of other women's groups such as the Dignas and the Mélida Anaya Montes Women's Movement (Movimiento de Mujeres "Mélida Anaya Montes"; the Mélidas).

25. García and Gomáriz, 1989, 105.

26. These partnerships, which are not legalized, are also referred to as common-law marriages, informal unions, and free unions.

27. White, 1973, 246; Baires et al., 1996, 30.

28. Ministerio de Economía, 2001.

29. García and Gomáriz, 1989, 110.

30. Baires et al., 1996, 30.

31. White, 1973, 245.

32. Teresa Valdés E. and Enrique Gomáriz M., *Latin American Women: Compared Figures* (Madrid: Instituto de la Mujer, 1995), 113.

33. These figures vary significantly based on education, age, and place of residence (urban or rural), but the decline has been across the board.

34. FESAL, n.d., 6.

35. FESAL, n.d., 1; Francisco Lazo, *El Salvador en cifras y trazos* (San Salvador: Equipo Maiz, 1996), 92.

36. FESAL, n.d., 2.

37. International Planned Parenthood Federation, *Country Fact Sheets—Family Planning in the Western Hemisphere* (part 4 of 9), no. 01630617, 1996, http://First Search.oclc.org, accessed October 31, 2001.

38. FESAL-78, *Eneuesta nacional de salud familiar* (San Salvador: Asociación Demográfica Salvadoreña, 1979).

39. FESAL n.d., 2.

40. Interview with Maria Elizabeth Argueta (San Salvador), October 16, 1996.

41. The Spanish word *aborto* is used for both miscarriages and induced abortions. The data, however, are usually not disaggregated. Consequently, it is difficult to accurately assess the exact impact of abortion on maternal morbidity and mortality.

42. Las Dignas, 2001.

43. FESAL, n.d., 4.

44. FESAL, n.d., 2.

45. PAHO, 2000, 7; OMHSS, 2000, 15.

46. FESAL, n.d., 4–5.

47. Ibid., 5.

48. PAHO, 1998, 262.

49. OMHSS, 2000, iv.

50. Since there is no protection against discrimination against homosexuality or HIV infection, these figures are extremely unreliable.

51. PAHO, 1999, 110.

52. PAHO, 2000, 6.

53. Miriam Zamora Rivas and Rosalía Soley Reyes, *Análisis del presupuesto general del estado desde la perspectiva de género* (San Salvador: Movimiento de Mujeres "Melidas Anaya Montes," 2000), 16.

54. Sandra Moreno, "Hombres y mujeres a la escena pública por igual," *El Diario de Hoy*, November 12, 2001.

55. Las Dignas, 2001, 101.

56. Las Dignas, *Hacer la política desde las mujeres* (San Salvador: Las Dignas, 1993), 86–93.

57. Nancy Saporta Sternbach, Marysa Navarro-Aranguren, Patricia Chuchryk, and Sonia Alvarez, "Feminisms in Latin America: Bogotá to San Bernadino," *Signs: A Journal of Women and Culture* 17 (1992): 393–434.

58. IUDOP and Las Dignas 1999 cited in Margarita Velado, *Violencia intrafamiliar y delitos contra la libertad sexual: Area metropolitano y municipio de San Salvador* (2001).

59. Velado, 2001, 1.

60. FESAL, n.d., 4.

61. Lagos Pizatti and de Mejía, 1994, 2.

62. Mercedes Cañas, "Maltrato físico a la mujer salvadoreña," licentiate thesis (San Salvador: Universidad Centroamericana, 1989).

RESOURCE GUIDE

Suggested Reading

Boland, Roy C. *Culture and Customs of El Salvador*. Westport, CT: Greenwood Press, 2000.

Golden, Renny. *The Hour of the Poor, the Hour of Women: Salvadoran Women Speak*. New York: Crossroad, 1991.

Luciak, Ilja A. "Gender Equality in the Salvadoran Transition." *Latin American Perspectives* 105 (March): 43.

Mahler, Sarah J. *Salvadorans in Suburbia: Symbiosis and Conflict*. Needham Heights, MA: Allyn and Bacon, 1995.

New Americas Press, ed. *A Dream Compels Us: Voices of Salvadoran Women*. Boston: South End Press, 1989.

Ready, Carol. "Between Transnational Feminism, Political Parties, and Popular Movements: 'Mujeres por la Dignidad y la Vida' in Post War El Salvador," Ph.D. dissertation. City University of New York, 1999.

———. "Contradicting Demands: Local and Transnational Feminisms in Post Reconstruction El Salvador." In *Rethinking Feminisms in the Americas*, ed. Debra Castillo, Mary Jo Dudley, and Breny Mendoza. Ithaca, NY: Cornell University Latin American Studies Program, 2000.

———. "Reconstructing Fatherhood from a Feminist Perspective Within Neoliberal Constraints: *La Asociación de Madres Demandantes* in El Salvador." In *Radical Women in Latin America: Left and Right*, edited by Victoria Gonzalez and Karen Kampwirth. University Park: Pennsylvania State University Press, 2001.

———. "Women's Organizations in El Salvador: History, Accomplishments, and International Support." In *Women and Civil War: Impact, Organization and Action*, edited by Krishna Kumar. Boulder, CO: Lynn Rienner, 2001.

Schirmer, Jennifer. "The Seeking of Truth and the Gendering of Consciousness: The CoMadres of El Salvador and the CONAVIGUA Widows of Guatemala." In *Women and Popular Protest in Latin America*, edited by Sara Radcliffe and Sallie Westwood. New York: Routledge, 1992.

Stephen, Lynn. *Women and Social Movements in Latin America: Power from Below*. Austin: University of Texas Press, 1997.

Stephen, Lynn, ed. *Hear My Testimony, Maria Teresa Tula, Human Rights Activist in El Salvador*. Boston: South End Press, 1994.

Thomson, Marilyn. *Women of El Salvador: Price of Freedom*. Philadelphia: ISHI, 1986.

White, Alastair. *El Salvador*. New York: Praeger, 1973.

Videos/Films

Dreams, Desires, and Lunacies. 1994. Distributed by Women Make Movies, (212) 925–0606, ext. 360, or www.wmm.com. A documentary of the Sixth Latin American Feminist Conference that took place in El Salvador in 1993. It provides a fascinating view of the vitality and breadth of the Latin American feminist movement as well as the complex issues and controversies that they face, particularly regarding race and class.

Enemies of War. 2000. 57 mins. Directed by Esther Cassidy. Distributed by New Day Films, (201) 652–6590 or http.www.newday.com. The film explores El Salvador's civil war through the investigation carried out by the late Joseph Moakley, Congressman from Massachusetts, of the assassination of six Jesuits priests in 1989.

Enough Crying of Tears. 1987. 28 mins. Directed by Catherine Russo and Jack Fahey. Distributed by Women Make Movies, (212) 925–0606 ext. 360, or www. wmm.com. An extremely powerful video about the Committee of Mothers of the Disappeared of El Salvador, the CoMadres. Features the chilling testimony of three women and footage of a prison takeover by women prisoners.

Fedefam. 1990. 40 mins. Directed by Catherine Russo and Carlota Chartier. Distributed by Women Make Movies, (212) 925–0606 ext. 360, or www.wmm.com. This film features interviews from the CoMadres and other Latin American groups of families of the disappeared. Made during FEDEFAM conference in El Salvador.

Maria's Story. 1990. 58 mins. Distributed by the Latin American Video Archives, http://lavavideo.org. An intimate portrait of a 39-year-old guerrilla leader, Maria Serrano. Born into extreme rural poverty, Maria developed a commitment to social justice that, like many Salvadoran women, compelled her to take up arms during the civil war. Filmed in guerrilla territory and under fire, this film documents her struggle.

Web Sites

Centro de Intercambio y Solidaridad (CIS), www.cis-elsalvador.org.
The Centro de Intercambio y Solidaridad (Center for Exchange and Solidarity), in San Salvador, provides language training to both Salvadorans and North Americans (in English and Spanish), sponsors delegations, raises funds, and sells Salvadoran crafts.

Committee in Solidarity with the People of El Salvador (CISPES), www.cispes.org. CISPES is a solidarity organization that provides support to the Salvadoran popular movement and alternative sources of information to North Americans.

Mujeres por la Dignidad y la Vida (Women for Dignity and Life, the Dignas), www. lasdignas.org.sv.
Mujeres por la Dignidad y la Vida is one of El Salvador's largest women's organizations.

Share Foundation, www.share-elsalvador.org.
The Share Foundation provides funds to Salvadoran nongovernmental organizations.

U.S. El Salvador Sister Cities, www.us-elsalvador-sisters.org.
During the civil war, the Sister City movement developed relationships between villages in El Salvador and cities in the United States. Many of these relationships are still strong.

SELECTED BIBLIOGRAPHY

Anderson, Thomas P. *Matanza: El Salvador's Communist Revolt of 1932.* Lincoln: University of Nebraska Press, 1971.
Argueta, Maria Elizabeth, Interview, San Salvador, October 16, 1996.

Armstrong, Robert, and Janet Shenk. *El Salvador: The Face of Revolution*. Boston: South End Press, 1982.

Federation of Southern Academic Libraries (FESAL). *General Summary*. N.d. www.fesal.org.sv/english/Cont_resumen.htm.

International Planned Parenthood Federation. *Country Fact Sheets—Family Planning in the Western Hemisphere*. Part 4 of 9. No. 01030617. 1996. http://FirstSearch.oclc.org. Accessed October 31, 2001.

Organization of Management and Health Systems and Services, Division of Health Systems and Services Development, Panamerican Health Organization (OMHSS). *El Salvador: Profile of Health Systems and Services*. 2000, www.americas.health-sector-reform.org/English/elspren.pdf. Accessed November 2, 2001.

Pan American Health Organization (PAHO). "El Salvador." In *Health in the Americas*, vol. 2. 1998. www.paho.org/english/HIA1998/ElSalvador.pdf. Accessed November 3, 2001.

———. "El Salvador: Demographic Indicators." In *Basic Country Health Profiles, Summaries*. 1999. www.paho.org/English/SHA/prflels.htm. Accessed November 3, 2001.

Saporta Sternbach, Nancy, Marysa Navarro-Aranguren, Patricia Chuchryk, and Sonia Alvarez. "Feminisms in Latin America: Bogotá to San Bernadino." *Signs: A Journal of Women and Culture* 17 (1992): 393–434.

Spence, Jack, Mike Lanchin, and Geoff Thale. *From Elections to Earthquakes: Reform and Participation in Post-War El Salvador*. Cambridge, MA: Hemisphere Initiatives, 2001.

Torres Rivas, Edelberto. *History and Society in Central America*. Austin: University of Texas Press, 1993.

UNICEF. *Statistics—Latin America and the Caribbean: El Salvador*. 2000. www.unicef.org/statis/Country_1page54.html. Accessed November 3, 2001.

Valdés E., Teresa, and Enrique Gomáriz M. *Latin American Women: Compared Figures*. Madrid: Instituto de la Mujer, 1995.

White, Alastair. *El Salvador*. New York: Praeger, 1973.

World Bank. *Country Brief*. 1999. http://lnweb18.worldbank.org/external/lac/lac.nsf. Accessed November 3, 2001.

Spanish Bibliography

Baires, Sonia, Dilcia Marroquín, Clara Murguialday, Ruth Polanco, and Norma Vázquez. *Mami, mami, demanda la cuota . . . la necesitamos: Un análisis feminista sobre la demanda de cuota alimenticia a la Procuraduría*. San Salvador: Mujeres por la Dignidad y la Vida, 1996.

Cañas, Mercedes. "Maltrato físico a la mujer salvadoreña." Licentiate thesis. San Salvador: Universidad Centroamericana, 1989.

Dalton, Roque. *Miguel Mármol*. Willimantic, CT: Curbstone Press, 1987.

FESAL-78. *Encuesta nacional de salud familiar*. San Salvador: Asociación Demográfica Salvadoreña, 1979.

García, Ana Isabel, and Enrique Gomáriz. *Mujeres centroamericanas: Ante la crisis, la guerra y el proceso de paz*. San José: Facultad Latinoamericano de Ciencias Sociales (FLACSO), 1989.

———. *Mujeres centroamericanas: Efectos del conflicto*. San José: FLACSO, 1989.

Lagos Pizatti, Victor, and Maria Teresa de Mejía. *La situación de la familia y del menor en El Salvador*. San Salvador: Secretaría Nacional de la Familia, 1994.

Lazo, Francisco. *El Salvador en cifras y trazos*. San Salvador: Equipo Maiz, 1996.

Media Luna. *Luna de Miel* no. 1 (October 1993). Newsletter.

Ministerio de Planificación y Coordinación de Desarrollo Económico y Social (MIP-LAN). *Encuesta de hogares de propósitos múltiples urbano y rural, octubre 1993–marzo 1994*. San Salvador: MIPLAN, 1994.

Ministerio de Economía, Dirección General de Estadística y Censos. "Encuesta de propósitos hogares múltiples 2000." San Salvador, 2000. Diskette.

Montes, Segundo. *El Compadrazgo: Una estructura de poder en El Salvador*. San Salvador: UCA Editores, 1987.

Moreno, Sandra. "Hombres y mujers a la escena pública por igual." *El Diario de Hoy*, November 12, 2001.

Mujeres por la Dignidad y la Vida (Dignas). *Beijing +5: Informe alternativo. Elementos sobre la situación de las mujeres salvadoreñas ante el siglo XXI*. San Salvador: Las Dignas, 2001.

———. *Hacer la política desde las mujeres*. San Salvador: Mujeres por la Dignidad y la Vida, 1993.

———. *¿Yo sexista? Material de apoyo para una educación no sexista*. San Salvador: Mujeres por la Dignidad y la Vida, 1998.

Proyecto de Planificación y Evaluación de la Reforma Agraria (PERA). *Décima evaluación del proceso de la reforma agraria*. San Salvador: PERA.

Velado, Margarita. *Violencia intrafamiliar y delitos contra la libertad sexual: Area metropolitano y municipio de San Salvador*. 2001.

Zamora Rivas, Miriam, and Rosalía Soley Reyes. *Análisis del presupuesto general del estado desde la perspectiva de género*. San Salvador: Movimiento de Mujeres "Melidas Anaya Montes," 2000.

10

FRENCH GUIANA

Diana H. Yoon

PROFILE OF FRENCH GUIANA

French Guiana (Guyane) is bordered by the Atlantic Ocean on the north, Suriname on the west, and Brazil on the south and east. Ninety percent of the land area is covered by tropical forest. The French first settled there in 1604, gradually displacing the indigenous population. France consolidated control over the region and established sugar plantations in early 1800s, but the local industry collapsed after the abolition of slavery in 1848.

Penal settlements were established shortly thereafter, and French Guiana remained a penal colony of France until after World War II. There was little population growth or economic development during this period.

In 1946, an overwhelming majority of the Guyanese population voted for departmentalization over independence. As an overseas department of France, the local government of French Guiana is headed by a 19-member General Council and a 31-member Regional Council. It also sends one elected representative to the French Senate and two representatives to the National Assembly. The total population in 2001 was 177,562, of whom 47 percent was female. French Guiana has experienced explosive population

growth since the 1950s; currently, the annual growth rate is 2.74 percent and the total fertility rate is 3.17 children born per woman. Life expectancy is 79.8 years for women and 73 years for men, and the infant mortality rate—highest among the three French overseas departments—is 13.61 per 1,000 live births. The majority of the French Guianese population is Creole (66 percent), and white Europeans constitute 12 percent.[1] Indigenous Amerindian and Maroon (descendants of enslaved Africans who came across from Suriname in the eighteenth century) communities constitute a small portion of the population, and the number of immigrants from Haiti, Brazil, Suriname, and Asia is on the rise.

OVERVIEW OF WOMEN'S ISSUES

Women in French Guiana, despite their educational success, have limited economic opportunities. Women's representation in politics seems to be improving, but their participation in decision-making roles and leadership positions is severely limited. French Guiana has not experienced the political instability and poverty of its neighbors due to its status as a department and an economy that is largely dependent on imports and subsidies from France. However, there are problems arising from an underdeveloped economy and lack of infrastructure—particularly in rural and interior areas—and women are disproportionately affected by those conditions.

EDUCATION

Opportunities

Access to education is uneven; until recently, most children in rural areas did not attend school. In general, enrollment at preschool and elementary levels is approximately equal for both sexes, but female students constitute a clear majority in private schools.[2]

At every stage of the education system, female students tend to do better than their male counterparts. In 1992–1993, a higher percentage of girls (74.3 percent) completed their age-level grade on time, compared to 69 percent of boys.[3] Also, more male students were held back in one or more grades. The gender disparity in educational success becomes more pronounced at each level of secondary and higher education. Baccalaureate (exams taken before graduating from high school) results provide a telling illustration: 71 percent of female students earned their general baccalaureates and 57 percent succeeded in receiving a technical baccalaureate, while the figures for male students were 63 percent and 48 percent, respectively.[4]

The high rate of female participation in education is not distributed evenly among the fields of study, and strong patterns of gender segregation are visible. For example, a higher portion of female students take exams for technical diplomas (CAP, BEP),[5] but an overwhelming majority of them are concentrated in business and service-oriented fields. In 1992, 221 out of 371 female students receiving a CAP diploma specialized in business and administration, while only 6 received a diploma in construction. Among those receiving BEP diplomas between 1985 and 1992, 81 percent of candidates for service-related diplomas were female.[6] During the same period, there was little or no representation of women in traditionally male-dominated fields, such as construction, electronics, and general industrial technology. Considering the close relationship between education and employment, these patterns provide strong evidence that the division of labor according to traditional gender roles remains strong in French Guianese society.

At the university level, female students are concentrated in humanities — they constitute close to 80 percent of all students in the field. This concentration corresponds to their underrepresentation in the sciences. Young women make up 40 percent of students in traditional sciences and only 31 percent of those pursuing advanced technical studies.[7]

Literacy

Adult literacy rate is approximately equal between the sexes. In 1982, 82 percent of females and 84 percent of males over the age of 15 were literate.[8]

EMPLOYMENT AND ECONOMICS

French Guiana is heavily dependent on imports and subsidies from France. The Green Plan (Plan Vert), adopted in the late 1970s to increase agricultural and forestry production, has had limited success. Development in gold and bauxite mining are hindered by a lack of infrastructure and labor. The city of Kourou has housed the European Space Agency's base for launching communication satellites since 1968. Despite the importance of this base, it is segregated from the rest of French Guiana and has not contributed to its economic activity as a whole.

Job Opportunities

Women's economic participation in French Guiana has been slow to grow. The percentage of women in the workforce increased only slightly between 1961 and 1993, from 30.6 percent to 38.5 percent. The result is that while more than half of all women over the age of 15 are active in the economy, men constitute a higher percentage of the labor force in all age groups. Evidence suggests that unemployment is a problem that disproportionately affects women. In 1990, 29.4 percent of women and 21 percent of men were unemployed, with the biggest difference in the age group of 25–49 years.[9] According to 1998 data, the overall unemployment rate

Creole woman in her back yard in French Guiana. Photo © Francois Laborde/Painet.

in French Guiana is 21.4 percent.[10] Furthermore, women are significantly more likely than men to have part-time employment, a pattern that can be attributed to their responsibilities at home as well as barriers to women seeking employment.

The biggest share of the female labor force (22.3 percent) works in civil service and other public administrative positions. In general, women are more likely than men to find jobs in the public sector, and this gap has expanded over the years. Women hold the smallest portion of industrial jobs. In professional positions, the majority of females are in intermediate-level positions such as primary school teachers and nurses. There are few female employers and business owners in French Guiana. Between 1982 and 1990, the percentage of women employers increased from 0.8 percent (of total active women) to 1.4 percent.[11]

Compared to the rest of Latin America, French Guiana stands out as an exception in terms of female participation in the agricultural labor force. In 1990, 10.9 percent of working women were employed as agricultural workers, approximately double the percentage of men.[12]

Social/Government Programs

The Social Security system of France is used in French Guiana. It provides payments for work injury, unemployment, disability, and maternity leaves. Households with children and the elderly may also receive allowances.

FAMILY AND SEXUALITY

Gender Roles

French Guiana has a relatively low number of female-headed households. According to 1990 census data, only 14.5 percent of all households consisted of a single mother and her children. Among families headed by a couple (71.3 percent of total households), slightly more than half had both parents working, 34.4 percent had only the male partner working outside the home, and 10.4 percent had the only the female partner working.[13]

Marriage

The growth in French Guianese population is reflected in the number of marriages, which increased from 240 in 1983 to 716 in 1992. Women marry at a younger age than men—4.6 percent of women between the ages of 15 and 24 were reported to be married, compared to 1.7 percent of males in the same age group. The rise in the number of marriages has not resulted in a similar pattern in divorces; the number of divorces in 1992 was only 11 more than the number in 1983.[14]

Reproduction

The number of births is highest among women between the ages of 25 and 39: approximately double the number among women 20–24 years of age. The rate of extramarital births is extremely high in French Guiana. In 1992, 72.5 percent of births among women 25–39 occurred outside marriage; for women 20 years old or younger, the figure was 94.4 percent.[15] However, the percentage of extramarital births has not increased at the same rate as the explosive growth in the total number of births.

Teen Pregnancy

Early pregnancy is among the leading issues of teens' health. Approximately 8 percent of all mothers since 1990 were under 18 years old, and in 1992, one-third of young women in this group showed signs of pathology during pregnancy.[16]

HEALTH

Health Care Access

Since 1992, all residents of France and its departments have been legally entitled to financial assistance for medical care in case of need. Health care and disease prevention centers in French Guiana provide compulsory vaccination (for polio, yellow fever, BCG, DTP) at no cost, and the General Council provides immunization against measles, mumps, and rubella for groups at high risk of infection.[17] In rural areas without private doctors or hospitals, the General Council provides free medical treatment through public health clinics.

Diseases and Disorders

Serious health problems in French Guiana include a high prevalence of sexually transmitted viral infections and epidemic outbreaks of dengue. Malaria continues to pose a danger to the population, particularly in rural and interior areas. The incidence of AIDS in French Guiana is among the highest in the Caribbean and Latin America, with the prevalence of HIV in pregnant women increasing from 0.9 percent in 1993 to 1.3 percent in 1995, and cases of mother-to-fetus transmission account for an alarming 9.9 percent of all infections.[18] Approximately 38.4 percent of the 588 AIDS cases reported since the beginning of the epidemic have been female.[19] Women between 30 and 39 years old are disproportionately affected by the AIDS problem.

Data collected during the period 1988–1990 indicated that suicide was the leading cause of death among women between the ages of 15 and 34, occurring in 20 percent of female deaths. Traffic accidents accounted for 10 percent of deaths in the same group of women. AIDS was the cause of 10 percent of deaths. During the same time period, leading causes of death among women ages 35–64 were malignant tumors (30 percent, most frequently tumors of the digestive system and the uterus) and cerebrovascular diseases (16 percent). Deaths caused by strokes were more frequent among elderly women (23 percent), and elderly women were also more likely to suffer from severe hypertension.[20]

POLITICS AND LAW

The political agenda of French Guiana has largely been shaped by its status as a department of France. Despite demonstrations and widespread discontent with economic and social conditions in French Guiana, there is little support for independence, and any change to the departmental status is unlikely.

Political Participation

On March 28, 1993, Christiane Taubira-Delannon became the first French Guianese woman to be elected to the French legislature. Her victory marked a milestone in French Guiana's politics, illustrating the potential strength of a coalition among women, young intellectuals, former activists in the small movement for independence from France, and the unemployed.[21] Taubira-Delannon's successful campaign signaled the entry of women into positions of power that were historically dominated exclusively by men. However, she stands as an exception to the general status of women in the political arena; while all adults over the age of 18 have the vote and women constitute approximately half of French Guiana's electorate, there are few female elected officials. After the 1993 elections, there were no female mayors, there was a single female member in the General Council, and only 5 out of 31 Regional Council members were female.[22]

RELIGION AND SPIRITUALITY

Roman Catholicism is the dominant religion in French Guiana. With nearly 90 percent of the population identified as Roman Catholic, its presence is significant in Guianese cultural norms and social practices affecting women.

OUTLOOK FOR THE TWENTY-FIRST CENTURY

French Guiana's status as a department of France has been a significant force in shaping its social, political, and economic reality, and structural changes affecting women's lives are largely contingent on that relationship. High unemployment is a persisting problem due to limited development in industry and manufacturing, and economic opportunities for women are further limited because of discrimination and cultural norms. Women continue to face barriers to political participation and positions of leadership due to societal norms, and the limited improvements in this area suggest that substantive changes in gender relations and women's social status will be slow in coming. Given the disparity between cities and rural areas, women in the interior remain particularly vulnerable to the problems that may arise from rapid population growth and limited economic capacity.

NOTES

1. Central Intelligence Agency (CIA), *The World Factbook* (Washington, DC: CIA, 2001), 176.
2. Institut National de la Statistique et des Études Économiques (INSEE), *Femmes de Guyane* (Cayenne: INSEE, 1995), 31.
3. Ibid.
4. Ibid., 30.
5. The CAP is a certificate of qualification in a trade or profession. The BEP diploma encompasses a broader field of qualification—a range of activities common to a professional sector, not just a given trade.
6. INSEE, 1995, 34–35.
7. Ibid., 30.
8. CIA, 2001, 176.
9. INSEE, 1995, 41, 45.
10. CIA, 2001, 177.
11. INSEE, 1995, 42, 44.
12. Ibid., 42.

13. Ibid., 26, 27.

14. Ibid., 20, 21.

15. Ibid., 22.

16. Pan American Health Organization (PAHO), *Health in the Americas* (Washington, DC: World Health Organization, 1998), 274.

17. Ibid., 276.

18. M. Sobesky et al., "HIV/AIDS Epidemic in French Guiana: 1979–1997," *Journal of Acquired Immune Deficiency Syndromes* no. 2 (2000): 178; PAHO, 1998, 274.

19. PAHO, 1998, 274.

20. Ibid.

21. Jean-Claude Artigalas, "French Guiana: Socialists Bow to Leftist Coalition," Inter Press Service, March 30, 1993.

22. INSEE, 1995, 50.

RESOURCE GUIDE

Suggested Reading

Crane, Janet. *French Guiana*. Oxford: Clio Press, 1998. Background information about the history of French Guiana and contemporary social, political, and economic condition. Provides a bibliography organized by subject.

Pan American Health Organization (PAHO). *Health in the Americas*. Washington, DC: World Health Organization, 1998. Presents a detailed analysis of health conditions and related issues in French Guiana.

Web Site

Pan American Health Organization, www.paho.org/English/SHA/prflFRG.htm. Provides background information and statistics related to social, economic, and health conditions in French Guiana.

SELECTED BIBLIOGRAPHY

Artigalas, Jean-Claude. "French Guiana: Socialists Bow to Leftist Coalition." Inter Press Service. March 30, 1993.

Bureau of Democracy, Human Rights, and Labor, U.S. Department of State. *Country Reports on Human Rights Practices—2001*. March 4, 2002. www.state.gov/g/drl/rls/hrrpt/2001/wha/8235.htm.

Central Intelligence Agency (CIA). *The World Factbook*. Washington, DC: CIA, 2001.

Crane, Janet. *French Guiana*. Oxford: Clio Press, 1998.

Institut National de la Statistique et des Études Économiques (INSEE). *Femmes de Guyane*. Cayenne: INSEE, 1995.

Pan American Health Organization (PAHO). *Health in the Americas*. Washington, DC: World Health Organization, 1998.

Sobesky, M., et al. "HIV/AIDS Epidemic in French Guiana: 1979–1997." *Journal of Acquired Immune Deficiency Syndromes* 24, no. 2 (2000): 178–81.

II

GUATEMALA

Lisa-Marí Centeno

PROFILE OF GUATEMALA

Guatemala, the "land of eternal spring," is bordered by Mexico to the north and west, by El Salvador and Honduras to the south, and by Belize to the northeast. Despite the springlike climate, however, the country might be more appropriately named the land of eternal conflict. Extreme social polarization and violence characterize Guatemala's history, from the brutal Spanish conquest, to the postindependence period of liberal dictatorship, to the bloody civil war that left the country in crisis. Currently Guatemala is in transition toward democracy and neoliberal integration into the global economy. Women have emerged at the forefront of this transition, mobilizing around the enormous challenges the country faces in the twenty-first century.

Guatemala has a population of 11.4 million, 49.7 percent of which is female. Fifty-five percent of Guatemalans are ladinos, people of mixed indigenous and European blood. Indigenous peoples, descendants of the Maya, comprise 43 percent of the population.[1] Guatemala is a historically Roman Catholic country, and 60 percent of people identify themselves as members of that religion. In recent years, however, Protes-

tant, particularly evangelical, denominations have spread across the country, and 40 percent of the population now identifies itself as Protestant.[2] The average life expectancy is 69 years for women and 63 years for men, though it must be pointed out that the numbers are much lower in rural indigenous areas of the country that experience high levels of poverty.[3] Guatemala has the lowest life expectancy in Central America and the highest infant mortality rate, at 190 per 1000 live births.[4] The fertility rate in urban areas is 3.8 children per woman and 6.8 in rural areas.[5]

OVERVIEW OF WOMEN'S ISSUES

The social polarization of Guatemala includes sharp divisions between men and women. A United Nations report notes that "women suffer from the highest rates of poverty, exclusion and discrimination at all levels."[6] The U.N. Gender-Related Development Index, which measures levels of female poverty, education, and access to health care, ranks Guatemala 100th of 174 countries.[7] Though there have been some improvements in women's legal status, traditional attitudes about gender pervade indigenous and ladino cultures, and women remain underrepresented in every sector of society.

The historical division of labor that relegated women to the private domestic sphere is changing as economic liberalization brings more and more women into the waged labor force. The feminization of labor ostensibly increases women's economic power, but low-skill, low-wage employment opportunities for women have done little to diminish female poverty. The restructuring of the economy to include women has thus far meant a restructuring of the patriarchal system, not the destruction of patriarchy itself. Guatemalan women now work harder than ever, yet they have few rights regarding their bodies and their lives. In response, women have become actors in the movements toward political, social, and economic justice in Guatemala, and offer hope for the country at a critical time in history.

EDUCATION

Opportunites

The state of education in Guatemala is dismal, but communities throughout the country have begun to form their own schools at the grassroots level. Unfortunately, women remain less educated. The primary school enrollment rate is 79 percent for girls and 90 percent for boys. At higher educational levels the numbers drop dramatically for both. Only 55 percent of women and 61 percent of men are enrolled at the secondary school level.[8] In 1999, 122,232 students were enrolled in the country's five universities.[9] Though it is difficult to find consistent statistics on female enrollment, it is estimated that only 4 percent of adult women attend university.[10]

Official numbers, however, fail to account for ethnic disparities. At best, the Guatemalan government has ignored the highlands and failed to build schools where much of the indigenous population resides. Where schools were built, classes were conducted in Spanish, a language unfamiliar to many indigenous people. At worst, the military regimes targeted the Maya as subversives, destroying villages and forcing hundreds of thousands into refugee camps where education was largely inaccessible. Returning refugees now face new problems. Children born in Mexican camps or hidden jungle settlements lack the documentation necessary to claim services such as education.[11] On a positive note, the government, with aid from international donors, has recently begun to implement bilingual education programs throughout the country in order to comply with the peace process.

According to the Peace Accords, the government further committed to increase the proportion of the GDP spent on education by 50 percent by the year 2000.[12] In fact, expenditures did rise from 1.6 percent of the GDP in 1996 to 2.46 percent in 2000, though there are concerns about how this money has been invested.[13] The current government's education strategy involves decentralization. Under this plan, the federal government distributes grants to local governments, which become responsible for building schools, hiring teachers, and establishing curricula. Federal funding is also earmarked for training more teachers across the country.

The positive potential of decentralization is for greater community involvement in education. In many rural areas, women-run community schools could benefit from the promise of funding. For example, the Women's Committee of the Community of Populations in Resistance (CPR), in the department of Petén, raises funds to send women to the city to train as teachers. In return, the teachers are expected to work for the community.[14] Federal funds could support programs such as these, as well as books and other supplies that community schools lack. Unfortunately, grants have been slow to reach most areas. Some critics suggest that the government has given up its responsibility for education without properly preparing local governments to take over.[15]

Women are legally granted equality of access to education, but economic and cultural factors often prohibit girls from attending school. According to a report by the U.N. Verification Mission, "more than a third of Guatemalan children work, the highest rate in the Americas." Moreover, the number of children between the ages of 7 and 14 has increased 5.5 percent since 1994.[16] In addition to working for wages, girls are expected to help their mothers with daily tasks that often include walking miles for water and firewood, cooking, child care, subsistence farming, and laundry. Such tasks leave little time for schoolwork. Machismo plays a large role as well. Since girls are expected to marry and remain in the home, education is deemed an unnecessary expense. Moreover, most employment opportunities for women involve low-skill work that doesn't require much education. Improving education for all, and especially for women, will require not only a better educational system but also a resolution of major economic obstacles.

Literacy

The national illiteracy rate has decreased significantly since the 1980s. As of 1999, 58 percent of Guatemalan women were literate, compared with 73 percent of men. Illiteracy among Mayan women is estimated as high as 70 percent, and can be attributed to historical discrimination and the long civil war.[17]

EMPLOYMENT AND ECONOMICS

Until recently, Guatemala was controlled by an oligarchy of wealthy, white landowners that used the military to defend its interests. This is the legacy of the current Guatemalan right, which continues to hold power and stands on a platform of free market economics and the rule of law.

Economic disparity in Guatemala is pronounced. As of 1999, 57.9 percent of the population lived below the poverty line and the richest 20 percent had a 60 percent income share, compared with a 3.8 percent share by the poorest 20 percent.[18] The gross domestic product (GDP), a measure of a country's wealth, has steadily risen since the 1990s, but the lack of redistribution policies means that increased wealth does not necessarily benefit the majority of the population. In fact, human development, measured by levels of poverty, education, and health, has steadily worsened. Between 1990 and 2001 Guatemala's human development ranking fell from 76 to 108 out of 174 countries.[19]

Current restructuring of the economy includes decreased state planning and the privatization of formerly state-owned industries. The country has signed several free trade agreements with other Latin American countries, and has declared itself committed to globalization.

Job/Career Opportunities

The promotion of foreign investment and rapid industrialization has led to the construction of many factories and export processing zones (EPZs) that are subject to very little regulation by the government. EPZs actively recruit women workers, who now constitute about 80 percent of all factory workers.[20]

Three commonly held perceptions about "third world" women encourage EPZ investors to actively seek female labor. First, the notion that these women are inherently apolitical and submissive makes them ideal as workers in substandard conditions. Second, much EPZ work, such as textile production and food processing, incorporates traditional gender roles. Third, the widely held concept that female labor is supplementary justifies low wages.[21] Proponents of the EPZs suggest that factory work provides viable economic opportunities to women. However, low wages, the rise of single motherhood, and the lack of basic services help maintain female wage laborers in a situation of economic hardship.

Pay

In Guatemala, the legal minimum wage, at U.S.$3.09 per day, falls well below the most basic cost of living for a family of four, estimated at U.S.$10 per day.[22] Women continue to have very little economic power despite the fact that they have moved into the wage labor force. They contribute 35 percent of the country's economic activity but take home less than 30 percent of the economic pie.[23] Currently 70 percent of Guatemalan women live in poverty.[24]

Because low wages limit the ability of most women to provide for even the most basic survival of their families, they must seek supplemental sources of money, largely in the informal sector. Taking in laundry, selling small commodities from the home or local market, and/or prostitution compound the demands on women's time. It is estimated that women constitute upward of 50 percent of all informal sector workers in Guatemala. Conversely, the informal economy provides a constant potential labor pool that keeps factory wages low and production high because employers can dismiss workers who are less productive than expected or who threaten to unionize.

Working Conditions

In addition to low wages for long hours of work, women often endure verbal and physical abuse, sexual harassment, unpaid overtime, and the fear of layoffs.[25] The lack of job security is omnipresent, and is evidenced in the practice of firing women workers who take just one day off from work to attend to a sick child or other family emergency.[26] More extreme evidence lies in the phenomenon known as the *maquila fantasma* (ghost factory)—factories that simply disappear over a weekend, leaving workers unemployed and, often, unpaid.[27]

Inheritance and Property Rights

In rural areas, women's unpaid agricultural work is crucial to family survival. Though by law women can own, inherit, and manage property, they are not likely to own the land they work. Another problem is that industrialization strategies have shifted attention to urban areas as the future locus of economic development. This has meant a steady decline in resources directed to rural development and a further increase in single motherhood as men leave for the cities in search of work.

Social/Government Programs

Stabilization and restructuring of the Guatemalan economy has led the government to procure loans from international financial institutions such as the World Bank and International Monetary Fund. Such loans often come with conditions known as structural adjustment programs, designed to streamline federal budgets to help ensure repayment. In Guatemala, structural adjustment has reduced public spending and privatized many public services. Consequently, fewer resources are directed to education, health care, housing, Social Security, and infrastructure. The privatization of basic services complicates women's attempts to provide for themselves and their families. The reasoning behind privatization—efficiency and better service—means little because most people cannot afford the new and improved for-profit services. The result is "a real tension between the state, which reduces more and more its space of action, and women, who demand collective services and the resolution of their basic needs."[28]

Decreased price subsidies on basic goods, for example, mean higher food prices, which puts additional pressure on women, who are traditionally responsible for buying and preparing food in the household. In addition, privatization of health care and education has limited access by women, who are responsible for the well-being of their children. To compensate for rising prices of food and services, women are forced to supplement their incomes. However, employment opportunities for women are often limited to low-wage EPZ work or informal sector work, which are both insecure and yield insufficient earnings.

FAMILY AND SEXUALITY

Gender Roles

Given the social, legal, and economic systems of Guatemala, women have few rights within the family and little legal control over their own bodies. The Civil Code enforces different roles for men and women within the family. Men owe their wives protection and assistance; women have the duty to care for the home and children, and can pursue activities outside the home only if such activities do not interfere with domestic duties.

Marriage

Twenty-four percent of women marry between the ages of 15 and 19. Only 8 percent of men between these ages are married, which suggests that young women tend to marry older men.[29] These rates, however, do not account for the number of young women who live with male partners, especially in rural areas where bureaucratic institutions are largely inaccessible. Legal marriages in Guatemala are civil ceremonies. Religious weddings are not legal in and of themselves.

A 1994 case brought before the Organization of American States challenged the constitutionality of several Civil Code decrees that discriminate against women. The results of this case and of lobbying by women's and human rights organizations recently led to the repeal of articles 109, granting men nearly exclusive right to marital property, and 114, which allowed husbands to prohibit wives' activities outside the home.[30] Changes to article 232 of the Penal Code mean that married women can no longer be punished for infidelity. However, more revision of both codes is necessary. Though a man can seek divorce if his wife bears a child fathered by another man, women cannot if the circumstances are reversed.

Reproduction

Sixty-five percent of women give birth at home, and in rural areas, more than 85 percent of all births are attended by traditional midwives known as *comadronas*.[31] The poor state of public health care and the inaccessibility of private care do not necessarily make hospital births a better option than home delivery. A quarter of hospital births are by cesarean section, many of which are unnecessary, and create undue risk for women.[32]

Midwifery is an important part of indigenous culture, in which birth signifies a spiritual connection with the earth rather than simply a clinical act. Though the Guatemalan health system has programs to train midwives, the training generally discourages traditional methods in favor of economically impractical clinical methods. Ultimately, improving maternal health involves improving women's economic and educational well-being.

Sex Education

Sex education is not widely offered in schools, and only at higher grade levels. Unfortunately, because many children do not stay in school for very long, they do not gain this information. Of all births, 11.9 percent are to girls between the ages of 15 and 19.[33]

Contraception and Abortion

Though the use of modern contraceptive methods is on the rise, only 38.2 percent of women who do not want more children use contraception.[34] Abortion is illegal unless necessary to save the mother's life. It is estimated that for every three pregnancies there are three abortions, and complications from abortion are the second most common cause of death among women in the country.[35]

Organized religion contributes to societal attitudes about sexuality and reproduction, and helps discourage family planning policies. In 1998, the National Policy on Safe Sex and the Formation of Responsible Family Life, 1998–2008 was removed from the legislative agenda.. Some suggest this was due to the strong religious fundamentalist element within the government.

The prohibitive cost of private health care has led to community health programs funded by national and international nongovernmental organizations (NGOs). Unrestrained by the politics of public funding, these organizations are taking the initiative toward improving women's reproductive health and education. For example, the nonprofit Guatemalan Association for the Well-Being of the Family (APROFAM) distributes approximately 36 percent of the contraceptives used in Guatemala. The public health system disburses only 25 percent, and rarely outside of the major cities.[36]

Women-directed community programs have the potential to become one of the most positive responses to poor public health facilities and for-profit medical services. Such programs, however, must consider local women's needs and desires as primary, because Western concerns and programs about reproduction may be misguided, given the socioeconomic circumstances of most Guatemalans. In the midst of dire poverty, children can provide necessary labor and help increase the family's future income. Moreover, indigenous women express important concerns about family planning. In the context of historical violence against the indigenous population, plans to limit women's fertility can be perceived as a threat to cultural survival.[37] Consequently, international NGOs and Western feminists must take care to avoid replacing one form of dogma about women's sexuality with another.

HEALTH

Health Care Access

The Guatemalan Constitution guarantees free public health services to all citizens who cannot afford to pay. Nonetheless, 42 percent of the population does not have access to such services. The health care sector is divided into three service providers: the Ministry of Public Health, which covers the poor; the Institute of Social Security, which serves the urban employed; and private providers, which cover the wealthy. One third of the poor population lives two hours from the nearest public health facility—37 percent of those facilities are in very poor condition, and 28 percent are closed. The Social Security system provides only 1.4 beds for every 1,000 beneficiaries, and one clinic for every 4,703 beneficiaries. The private, for-profit sector provides superior services but covers only about 10 percent of the population.[38]

Guatemalan women's health is among the worst in the Americas. The leading causes of death among women are pneumonia and intestinal infections, both of which could be prevented if more and improved health care services were available to women.[39] The 1996 Peace Accords specifically refer to women and commit the government to implement "nationwide comprehensive health programs for women, which involves giving women access to appropriate information, prevention and health care services."[40] The government has thus far complied with its agreement to increase public spending on health care by 50 percent of the GDP by the year 2000.[41] Current plans to reform the health care system include decentralization and modernization, with special priority given to improving maternal health. Decentralization involves subcontracting services to the private nonprofit and for-profit sectors, and may produce positive results as federal funds are channeled to NGOs that focus on women's health. As it stands, community clinics are understaffed and underfunded, and focus primarily on preventive care.

Genuine reform must include improving clinical care and expanding the reach of services to rural areas. The haphazard nature of reform often means that services are farmed out to private providers with little coordination or regulation. Modernization of the health care system is taking place largely within the for-profit sector, which can afford such changes. In practical terms, the health of most Guatemalans is either subject to the poverty of the public system or dependent upon the whims and/or beneficence of private care.

Diseases and Disorders

Severe poverty, particularly among the indigenous population, is a major cause of malnutrition, one of the most serious health concerns in Guatemala. It is estimated that 42 percent of children aged five and under suffer from malnutrition, the highest rate in Latin America.[42] The patriarchal structure of most families is a factor in the prevalence of malnutrition among girls and women. Though female family members are responsible for food preparation, male "breadwinners" are given priority when it comes to eating. Many women are expected to eat only after their families are finished doing so; and given the limited resources of most families, little is left over for women.

Unfortunately, the most recent statistics available on many diseases and disorders come from as long ago as 1994. Moreover, the relative inaccessibility of the health care system means that official numbers may not accurately represent disease rates, especially in rural areas. According the Pan American Health Organization, death from malignant tumors accounted for 3.6 percent of all deaths in 1994. Among women between 15 and 49 years of age, the most common sites of tumors were the cervix (40 percent), stomach (27.5 percent), liver (14.0 percent), breast (10.9 percent), and bronchi (3.7). Pneumonia is the single largest cause of death for women of the above age group (12 percent of all deaths).[43] Internal parasitic diseases are second only to respiratory diseases as the leading cause of mortality in the country.

AIDS

Approximately 400,000 Guatemalans live with HIV, and as of 2001, there have been 4,086 reported cases of AIDS. Though a significant number of female sex workers are infected with HIV (about 10 percent in some areas), 75 percent of the cases are among men.[44] The government has done little to address the growing epidemic; most prevention and treatment programs are sponsored by international aid organizations.

Mental Health

Mental health concerns have never been a priority for the Guatemalan health care system, although some measures are now being taken to address the issue. The public system maintains one 350-bed psychiatric hospital and one 25-bed psychiatric unit at the Social Security Hospital.[45] Both are in Guatemala City. State-provided services outside of the capital city are rare, however, community mental health projects, sponsored by local and international non-governmental organizations, are now appearing in rural areas. No data is currently available on the mental health services provided by the for-profit sector. The Pan American Health Organization estimates that one-fourth of the population may have some kind of mental health disorder. This number is likely to be higher in the regions affected by the civil war.

Though no official studies have been conducted on a national level, interviews with women throughout Guatemala indicate that many continue to live with the fear and insecurity caused by the armed conflict. Women's organizations have created their own community mental health projects to care for those left with the scars of physical and psychological torture. Dozens of widow's organizations, such as the Grupo de Apoyo Mutuo (Mutual Support Group; GAM), provide counseling and legal support to help bring closure to women whose family members were murdered in the war.[46] Puentes de Paz (Bridges of Peace) specializes in trauma recovery and trains women as mental health facilitators in their own communities. The Asociacion de la Mujer Maya Ixil (Association of Maya Women of Ixil) gauges the impact of civil war on indigenous women in order to assess and provide for mental health needs. As is often the case in Guatemala, when the official sociopolitical structure fails, women provide for themselves.

POLITICS AND LAW

The Guatemalan Constitution of 1985 grants that "All human beings are free and equal in dignity and rights. Men and women, independent of their civil status, have equal opportunities and responsibilities. Life, liberty, property and other rights considered basic by the various articles of the Constitution enjoy equal protection with respect to men and women." These provisions are particularly interesting because, unlike many other constitutions, including that of the United States, they mention the rights of both men and women, not simply those implied by the universal use of "man."[47] Despite the literal attention to gender equality, however, political conflicts, civil codes, and social norms have historically prohibited women from exercising their constitutional guarantees.

Suffrage

Guatemalan women gained the right to vote in 1945, during the democratic period known as the "ten years of spring." This right, however, meant very little in the years between 1954 and 1995, since elections were either fraudulent or nonexistent. Low voter turnout remains a persistent trend; a mere 14.6 percent of the population voted in the 1999 presidential and parliamentary elections.[48] Women throughout the country attribute the lack of participation in institutional politics to high levels of illiteracy and lack of information, especially in rural areas. Many indigenous people express continued distrust of the government and refuse to participate in a system they perceive as repressive and violent.[49]

Political Participation

In the realm of government, Guatemala ranks seventy-sixth of 173 countries in terms of women in parliament. As of 2001, female deputies occupied ten seats—down from 13 in 1995—and constituted 8.8 percent of the unicameral legislature.[50] Eight of the deputies come from the ruling right-wing Guatemalan Republican Front (Frente Republicano de Guatemala, FRG), one from the leftist coalition New Nation Alliance (Alianza Nueva Nación, ANN), and one is an independent. Two women have served as president of the Congress, and as of 1999, 11 women hold high-ranking positions in the ministries, the highest number in Guatemala's history. In 1999, Raquel Blandón Sandoval became the first female vice presidential candidate, running on the center-right National Advancement Party (Partido para el Avance Nacional, PAN) ticket.

In a 1999 interview, Nineth Montenegro, congressional deputy of the ANN party, stated that Guatemala would begin to change when "women are permitted to become protagonists in every sector, including political parties."[51] Most female politicians are white and represent the right wing of the political spectrum. Yet, the surge of women's political activism that began in 1985 largely derives from left-of-center popular movements. Though more research is necessary to understand this phenomenon, it likely has to do with education, class, and ideological affiliation. The upper class is historically associated with the right wing of Guatemalan politics, and women of the upper class have better access to the education and connections necessary for a career in politics. Likewise, the institutionalized left has always been marginalized as a political force, and poor, less educated women (most of the female population) have largely been excluded from the political realm. Indigenous women are grossly underrepresented in government, though Rosalina Tuyuc, a Kakchiquel Congresswoman, has become one of the most prominent politicians in Guatemala due to prolific legislation in favor of human rights.

Women's Rights

Though women remain a small minority in government, their presence has had an impact on the direction of Guatemalan politics. The 1996 Peace Accords make specific reference to women's concerns in education, health care, labor, and land rights. The creation of the Women's Forum has brought even greater attention to gender issues. The main objectives of the intercultural forum are to influence policymaking toward more integral economic development and to monitor the implementation of the Peace Accords.[52] The Forum also focuses on improving the economic conditions and legal rights of indigenous women through the newly created Indigenous Women's Defense Office. Policy directives include the right to wear indigenous clothing at school and in the workplace, bilingual education, and landownership.

Events at the institutional level may also offer some hope for women. In 1999 Parliament passed the Law to Further the Dignity and the Integral Promotion of Women, "to propose, formulate, negotiate, further and coordinate national policies of integral development from a perspective of equality between men and women." However, implementation of this law remains vague. In 2000, President Alfonso Portillo created the Secretariat for Women, which seeks to "mainstream public policies for the development of women and will function as the Government focal point for the maintenance of a permanent dialogue with the rest of civil society."[53]

The 1998 revisions of the Civil Code eliminated legal terms that discriminated against women. Spouses now have equal rights regarding responsibility for children and the administration of community property. Additionally, article 114, which allowed husbands to prohibit their wives' activity outside the home, was eliminated. Social norms, however, designate men as heads of the household. It may be some time before cultural attitudes and legal doctrine coincide.

Women's and Feminist Movements

Women have a long history of mobilization. They participated in the struggle for independence, rallied for the right to vote, and fought in guerrilla movements. The expanded women's mobilization seen today grew out of the Central American popular movements of the 1980s, when civil socicty rose up against authoritarianism, poverty, and injustice. Women's secretariats, committees, and commissions arose within the popular movement.

Women's organizations tend toward collective action that transcends individual issues and often encompasses every aspect of women's lives. The collectivization of women's traditional work and economic activity, for example, creates a communal network of interdependence among women that often extends to political action. For example, women in agricultural cooperatives and rural communities coordinate their work in this manner, and use the time saved to organize around land rights, health care, education, and/or Indigenous rights. This form of collective action also extends beyond individual goals to benefit larger communities as women organize schools, clinics, and communal landholdings.

Women's community organizations often form independently and remain autonomous, but in many cases they are coordinated by larger organizations from major cities. In Central America, *personaria jurídica* (legal recognition) grants organizations better access to international donors, grants, and legal information. Women's organizations with such recognition redistribute their resources by sponsoring smaller community organizations. For example, the women's secretariat of the Guillermo Toriello Foundation and the women's committee of the Communities of Populations in Resistance both sponsor literacy campaigns and help fund women's committees in agricultural cooperatives.

A recent trend in women's activism corresponds to women's changing societal roles that bring them into formerly male organizations. Female factory workers, for example, now identify with the labor movement because they share many issues with their male counterparts. Women's committees form within the organizations to tackle specific women's issues such as sexual harassment and discrimination. The larger cause, however, is seen as shared by men and women. Though they organize primarily among factory workers, women also organize within service sector and agricultural labor unions.

Most women's organizations in Guatemala do not identify themselves as feminist because of the pejorative connotations carried by the term. Many women consider feminism as anti-male, and therefore an obstacle to developing complementary and cooperative relationships between men and women. Moreover, indigenous women's organizations, unlike Western feminists, believe that women's subordination is a consequence of the conquest by Spain.[54]

Despite differing perceptions, as nonfeminist women's organizations negotiate power and as feminists recognize the economic facet of women's rights, they sometimes find common ground. Though class remains a significant barrier, feminists, with a larger resource base, have begun to broaden their scope and make overtures to poor women's organizations. In Guatemala, the large organizations with a feminist platform fund training workshops, literacy campaigns, and small businesses among community women. Tierra Viva (Live Earth) supports a wide variety of projects throughout the country and is committed to ecological sustainable development while remaining politically neutral. The Guillermo Toriello Foundation (FTG), an outgrowth of the Guatemalan National Revolutionary Unity (Unidad Revolucionaria Nacional Guatemalteca, URNG) guerrilla movement, however, has successfully made inroads into poor communities, including indigenous villages, precisely because of its defined leftist ideology, which coincides with that of most popular movements. In this way the FTG appeals to both men and women as comrades in arms in a way that integrates gender with economic and political equality.

Despite the similar economic context of resource mobilization, ethnicity may be the single most divisive factor among women's organizations in Guatemala. Although there is evidence of slow change and integration, the lack of understanding between indigenous and ladina women is based on vastly different worldviews and goals.

Organized indigenous women reflect ethnic and historical differences in the processes of gender consciousness-raising. Indigenous women's self-valorization derives largely from a strong ethnic identity and from locating the disregard for women's work within the context of Western imperialism. In this way, discrimination against indigenous women is perceived as part of the larger disrespect for all indigenous peoples and cultures. One member of the Indigenous Women's Defense explains: "Our struggle is not just about women, it's also about Indigenous people. Gender, our culture, you can't separate them; they go hand in hand. They compl[e]ment one another; it's an equilibrium."[55]

The common symbol of the Maya women's struggle is the traditional *traje* woven skirt and blouse. Gaining the previously denied right to wear the *traje* in public represents a bridge between the Western world and women's cultural/historical gender values. In other words, the perception of primordial equality represented in traditional dress extends to the struggle for indigenous women's rights in the larger Westernized environment. The *traje*, however, also constitutes a symbolic barrier against the homogenizing forces of globalization; a statement that even as indigenous women enter the Western world they will not necessarily conform to Western values regarding gender and community.

The women's movement has no single cohesive focus but comprises diverse currents from various sectors. Ethnicity remains the primary obstacle to genuine interorganizational solidarity, even though bridges of communication are forming within and across borders as Guatemalan women begin a dialogue with organized women from other countries in the region.

Lesbian Rights

Homosexuality is not illegal, but social norms strongly discourage same-sex relationships. Some women's organizations refuse to identify themselves as feminists because of the term's association with lesbianism. Currently there are three major Gay and Lesbian organizations that work openly in Guatemala: the Organization in Support of Integral Sexuality in the Face of HIV (Organicación de Apoyo a una Sexualidad Integral frente al SIDA, OASIS), the Liberated Lesbian and Bisexual Women's Collective (Colectiva de Lesbianas y Mujeres Bisexuales Liberadas, LESBIRADAS), and the Boundary Breaking Group (Grupo Rompiendo Fronteras, GRF). All three groups have faced harassment, particularly by the National Police.[56] Lesbian and bisexual women are relatively less confined in urban areas; however, the repression of women's sexuality in rural areas, where most people live, severely restricts lesbian relationships.

RELIGION AND SPIRITUALITY

Guatemala is a traditionally Roman Catholic country, and 60 percent of the population identifies itself as belonging to the faith.[57] The church played an important role in the subjugation of the indigenous population during the conquest and helped keep the colonial order. In the nineteenth century, the liberal victory over conservative forces effectively ended the clergy's power within the state, but the church has a defined presence in politics and society.

Conventional Catholic doctrine has been a significant force in maintaining the patriarchal family structure and restricting women's reproductive rights. However, the rise of liberation theology in the 1960s introduced an alternative vision of Catholicism and church practice. During the civil war, clerics of the liberation church became important figures in the popular movements by preaching social justice. Catholic base communities organized the poor around economic and ethnic equality, formed literacy campaigns, and built homes for those in need. Consequently, the government's counterinsurgency campaign often targeted priests, nuns, and laypeople for violence. The 1998 murder of Monsignor Gerardi, a leading bishop of Guatemala, reputedly perpetrated by the military, occurred two days after the publication of his work on human rights. Despite repression, however, progressive churches remain an important locus of popular mobilization.

Rome has never recognized the virtual division between the traditional and liberation churches, and probably will never accept the third branch of

Women take part in a religious procession. Photo © TRIP/T. Bognar.

the Guatemalan Catholic Church that blends Catholicism with indigenous spirituality. During the forced conversions of the conquest, the Maya often had to choose between accepting the European church and death. There are some notable similarities between the Catholic and Maya cosmologies, and the compromise between the two created a distinct religion that is still practiced today.[58]

The most recent religious trend is the unprecedented movement toward Protestant churches. Approximately 40 percent of the population are affiliated with the various denominations, the largest of which is the Assembly of God.[59] Protestantism in its evangelical form provides an attractive alternative to more traditional segments of society because it preaches order in the midst of the perceived chaos of Guatemalan society. In a 1999 interview, one woman praised her church for saving her family: "Before, we were in a bad situation. My husband would drink so much; he was violent. Sometimes he wouldn't come home. But since he was born again he doesn't drink, he doesn't smoke, he isn't a womanizer anymore."[60] This testimony reflects a common sentiment among evangelical women who organize around church principles.

Protestant women's organizations are quite different from Catholic or secular women's organizations. Though they may mobilize around economic needs, human rights, or domestic violence, they are more likely to identify themselves as apolitical.[61] Guatemalan evangelicalism is associated with the political right wing and often teaches its followers to avoid criticizing the government. A former guerrilla recounted how she had to become a biblical scholar during the civil war in order to counteract the "reactionary" theology of rural evangelical churches.[62] When asked how she felt about the current president, another woman, a member of the Assembly of God, replied, "I don't get involved. God makes rulers and He can unmake them. It's not for me to say."[63]

VIOLENCE

Domestic Violence

Domestic violence remains a serious problem in Guatemala. In 1997, 49 percent of women were abused in their homes, and the lack of recent statistics demonstrates the prevailing attitudes about gender and violence.[64] Social isolation and economic dependence on male family members keep many women in dangerous situations. According to some activists, women's mobilization has created a disturbing backlash. Male family members who feel threatened by women's attempts to renegotiate power in the home or community can react violently. Some leaders have resorted to seeking permission from men so that wives and daughters may attend meetings.[65]

Human rights organizations dedicated to challenging state violence and impunity now include violence against women as part of their campaigns, and the heightened awareness seems to be having a positive effect. In 1999, the government passed the Law to Prevent, Punish and Eradicate Inter-Family Violence. Though the government has invested few resources to implement and enforce this law, private women's agencies have taken the initiative by creating hot lines and counseling centers. Only three such agencies exist, and they report having received over 7,000 calls between 1999 and 2001.[66] Most women, especially in rural areas, do not have access to such services. Nevertheless, the fact that more and more women are responding to domestic violence offers hope in a country where abuse has long been a regular part of daily life.

Rape/Sexual Assault

As women claim a space in this changing society, they face a violent backlash from outside the home as well. Charges of rape nearly doubled between 1997 and 1999, though it is unclear if these figures reflect the growth of actual offenses or increased willingness to press charges or both.[67] More women than ever are entering the public realm of waged labor, yet societal attitudes about gender roles continue to suggest that a woman alone on the street deserves what she gets. Moreover, a rapist can escape prison if his victim agrees to marry him.

War and Military Repression

The 36-year civil war had a devastating effect on Guatemala: 200,000 people were killed or disappeared between 1960 and 1996, and thousands more were subjected to arbitrary arrest and torture.[68] In a 1999 report Comisión para el Esclaracimiento Histórico (CEH; the Commission for Historical Clarification) determined that 93 percent of the human rights violations during the armed conflict were committed by the state and by paramilitary forces that operated with impunity.[69] The CEH estimates that between 500,000 and 1.5 million people were displaced at the height of the conflict, 150,000 of whom fled to refugee camps in southern Mexico; 83 percent of the victims were indigenous.[70] Though war is often considered in masculine terms—involving generals and male combatants—Guatemalan women bear an equal share of the physical and psychological scars left by the violence. Today women are at the forefront of the human rights crusade to bring truth and reconciliation to Guatemala.

Many of the tactics employed by military and paramilitary organizations were gender-specific. Women were raped in front of their families in order to demonstrate the strength and will of the state to punish potential subversive activity. During the 1980s in many Maya highland communities it was difficult to find girls between the ages of 11 and 15 who had not been sexually abused by the army. When women were suspected of subversive behavior, they were subject to sexually specific forms of interrogation and torture, including rape and cigarette burns on the breasts and genitals.[71] Women accounted for 15 percent of those killed in the civil war; however, during the government's scorched earth campaign of the early 1980s, 21 percent of known victims were women.[72]

Though the majority of those killed in the war were men, women were victimized by psychological terrorism when they were forced to witness the murders of their husbands and sons during village raids by the military or paramilitary groups. When men were disappeared or murdered by the military, women were left with the economic responsibility of maintaining the family. Approximately 120,000 women were widowed by the war, and in rural areas of the country one can find entire villages without men.[73]

Women who escaped to Mexican refugee camps are perhaps the most fortunate victims of the war. Many female refugees had access to social services and gender empowerment workshops developed to prepare them for their eventual return to Guatemala. More than 40,000 have returned to their country since 1996.[74]

Thousands of women responded to the repressive government by joining guerrilla organizations. According to one woman revolutionary, two women for every 17 men participated in the military units.[75] More often women participated as cooks, nurses, and companions. Former guerrilla women say that they experienced the same type of gender discrimination by guerrilla men as they did before they joined the organization.[76]

Several women's organizations arose during the war to demand respect for human rights and an end to the violence. CONAVIGUA (National Coordinator of Guatemalan Widows), GAM (Mutual Support Group), and FAMDEGUA (Relatives of the Detained and Disappeared of Guatemala) are the three most prominent human rights organizations created by war widows. Since the signing of the Peace Accords in 1996, these organizations continue to struggle for resolution and justice for those involved in the conflict. The end of the war has not resulted in lasting peace. In challenging the postwar governments to investigate human rights violations and punish those responsible, women activists have once again become targets of intimidation and violence.[77] However, these women show no signs of ceasing their quest for truth.

OUTLOOK FOR THE TWENTY-FIRST CENTURY

In many respects these past years have raised incredible hopes for women, the poor, the oppressed, and above all for those women who are indigenous. For the first time we have achieved something: We have been heard. We are respected. At times, being heard is enough for us because as a rule we have been the object of study but we weren't listened to. Now, we are no longer the objects of study. We are the ones making history.[78]

Guatemala is at a crossroad, and the future, at this point, is difficult to determine. The primary obstacles the country faces are pervasive poverty and ethnic marginalization, two issues that gave rise to the civil war. The poor state of women's health, education, political representation, and economic well-being is particularly disturbing, considering the government's relative unresponsiveness. Unfortunately, if state leaders do not address these issues, the fledgling democracy may be in for continued violence and a return of political repression. The country's greatest hope lies in the rebirth of social movements that challenge the present course of direction. Change is a slow process, but women are moving and forming local alternatives to politics that will affect, if not transform, the future of Guatemala.

NOTES

1. World Bank, *Genderstats: Guatemala*, 2001, http://genderstats.world bank.org/SummaryGender.asp?Which Rpt=education&Ctry=GTM, Guatemala.

2. U.S. Department of State (USDS), *Annual Report on International Religious Freedom: Guatemala*, 1999, www.state.gov/www/global/human_rights/irf/irf_rpt/1999/irf_guatema/199.html.

3. Ibid.

4. United Nations Population Fund (UNPF), *The State of World Population*, 1999, www.unpfa.org; Pan American Health Organization (PAHO), *Guatemala: General Situation and Trends*, 1998, www.paho.org/english/HIA1998/Guatemala.pdf.

5. Instituto Nacional de Estadísticas (INE), *Encuesta nacional de salud materno e infantil*, 1999, www.ine.gob.gt/index_fla.htm.

6. United Nations, *Report of the Secretary General*, 1998, www.hri.ca/forthe record1998/vol4/guatema/aga.htm.

7. U.N. Population Division, Department of Economic and Social Affairs, *World Marriage Patterns*, 2000, www.un.org/popin/wdtrends/worldmarriagepatterns2000.pdf.

8. UNICEF, *Guatemala*, 2000, www.unicef.org/statis/Country_1Page69.html.

9. Ministerio de Educación, *Informative Bulletin No. 1*, 2000, www.mineduc.gob.gt/index.htm.

10. World Bank, 2001.

11. Many returning refugees had been gone for as long as 20 years. Most lost their papers when villages were burned or while they were in hiding. Children born to refugees rarely have birth certificates and cannot be legally registered for school. From interviews by author with members of the Communities of Populations in Resistance (Comunidades de Poblaciónes de Resistencia), Peten, Guatemala, July 1999.

12. *The Guatemalan Peace Accords*, 1996, www.c-r.org/acc_guat/socio.htm.

13. USAID, *Activity Data Sheet: Guatemala*, 2000, www.usaid.gov/country/lac/gt/520-002.html.

14. From interviews by author, 1999.

15. United Nations, 1998.

16. United Nations Foundation, 2001.

17. USAID, 2000.

18. UNDP, 2000.

19. UNDP, 1990, 2001.

20. Organizacion Internacional del Trabajo (OIT), *La situacion sociolaboral en las zonas francas y empresas maquiladoras del Istmo Centroamericano y República Dominicana* (San José, Costa Rica, OIT, 1996).

21. Maria Mies, *Patriarchy and Accumulation on a World Scale* (London: Zed Books, 1986); Valentine Moghadam, "Gender and Globalization: Female Labor and Women's Mobilization," *Journal of World-Systems Research* 2 (1999): 367–88, also at http://csf.colorado.edu/jwsr; June Nash, "Latin American Women in the World Capitalist Crisis," *Gender and Society* 4, no. 3 (September 1990): 338–53; Diane L. Wolf, "Linking Women's Labor with the Global Economy: Factory Workers and Their Families in Rural Java," in *Women Workers and Global Restructuring*, ed. Kathryn Ward (Ithaca, NY: Cornell University Press, 1990).

22. INE, 1999.

23. UNDP, *Human Development Report*, 2000, www.undp.org/hdr2000/english/presskit/gdi.pdf.

24. Christian Munduate, *Statement by Mrs. Christian Munduate, Minister of Social Welfare Secretariat of the Presidency of Guatemala*, 2000, www.un.org/womenwatch/daw/followup/beijing+5stat/statements/guatemala5.htm.

25. OIT, 1996.

26. From interviews by author, 1999.

27. From interview with "Amanda," Director of the Women's Committee of the Fundación Guillermo Toriello Organization, Guatemala City, June 8, 1999.

28. Ana Leticia Aguilar et al., *Movimiento de mujeres en Centroamérica* (Managua, Nicaragua: Programa Regional La Corriente, 1997).

29. UNDP, 2000.

30. Valerie MacNabb and the Central American Analysis Group, "Women's Role in Guatemala's Political Opening," *Focus* 1, no. 11 (October 12, 1998), also at www.iadialog.org/womengua.html; U.S. Department of State, *Guatemala Country Report on Human Rights Practices for 1998*, 1999, www.state.gov/www/global/human_rights/1998_hrp_report/guatemal.html.

31. Center for Reproductive Law and Policy (CRLP), *An Unfulfilled Human Right: Family Planning in Guatemala*, 2000, www.crlp.org/pdf/guatemala.pdf; JHPIEGO Corporation, *Guatemala: Improved Clinical Care Reduces Costs at Amatitlán Hospital*, 2001, www.mnh.jhpiego.org/updates/mnhaug01.htm#Guatemala.

32. CRLP, 2000.

33. UNDP, 1999.

34. INE, 1999.

35. CRLP, 2000.

36. Ibid.

37. From interviews by author, 1999.

38. Latin America and Caribbean Health Sector Reform Initiative, *Guatemala Country Profile*, 1999, www.americas.health-sector-reform.org/english/clhmgutpr.htm.

39. Pan American Health Organization, *Guatemala: General Situation and Trends*, 1998, www.paho.org/english/HIA1998/Guatemala.pdf.

40. Guatemalan Peace Accords, 1996.

41. Ibid.; UNDP, 1999; PAHO, 1998.

42. INE, 1999.

43. PAHO, 1998.

44. USAID, *Leading the Global Fight Against HIV/AIDS: Guatemala*, 2001, www.usaid.gov/pop_health/aids/country_guatemala.html.

45. PAHO, 1998.

46. Interviews by author, Guatemala City, June–August 1999.

47. Facultad Latinoamericano de Ciencias Sociales (FLACSO), *Guatemala*, 1998, www.eurosur.org/FLACSO/mujeres/guatemala/portada.htm.

48. International Institute for Democracy and Electoral Assistance, 2001. www.idea.int/.

49. From interviews by author, 1999.

50. Interparliamentary Union, *Women in National Parliaments*, 2001, www.ipu.org/wmn-e/classif.htm.

51. From interviews by author, 1999.

52. United Nations, 1998.

53. Munduate, 2000.

54. Aguilar, 1997.

55. Guatemala Human Rights Commission/USA, *Human Rights Update #14/99*, 1999, www.eecs.umich.edu/~pavr/harbury/archive/1999/19990806c.html.

56. International Gay and Lesbian Human Rights Commission (IGLHRC), *Demand an End to Harassment of Gays, Lesbians, Bisexuals, and Transgender People* (San Francisco: IGLHRC, 2001), www.iglhrc.org/php/section.php?id=5&detail=210.

57. USDS, *Annual Report on International Religious Freedom: Guatemala*, 1999.

58. Maud Oakes, *The Two Crosses of Todos Santos: Survivals of Mayan Religious Ritual* (New York: Bollingen Foundation, 1951).

59. USDS, *Annual Report on International Religious Freedom: Guatemala*, 1999.

60. From interviews by author, 1999.

61. From interviews by author, 1999.

62. From interviews by author, 1999.

63. From interviews by author, 1999.

64. USDS, *Annual Report on International Religious Freedom: Guatemala*, 1999.

65. From interviews by author, 1999.

66. Women's Justice Center, Tertulia, "Guatemala: Each Day Twenty Women Report Family Violence," 2001, www.justicewomen.com/tertulia_8_18_01.html.

67. USDS, *Annual Report on International Religious Freedom: Guatemala*, 1999.

68. Patrick Ball, Paul Kobrak, and Herbert F. Spirer, *State Violence in Guatemala, 1960–1996* (Washington, DC: American Association for the Advancement of Science, 1999), Conclusions.

69. Comisión para el Esclaracimiento Histórico (CEH), *Memoria del Silencio* (Guatemala City: CEH, 1999), 15.

70. Ibid.

71. Adrianne Aron, Shawn Corne, Anhea Fursland, and Barbara Zewler, "The

Gender-Specific Terror of El Salvador and Guatemala," *Women's Studies International Forum* 14, no. 2 (1991), 37–47.

72. Ball et al., 1999, chap. 15.

73. Malinda Leonard, *Post Conflict Situation in Guatemala*, 2001, www.womenscommission.org/reports/gbvsplit/gbv/america.pdf, 9.

74. Ibid., 8.

75. Hooks, Margaret, *We Guatemalan Women Speak* (Washington, DC: Ecumenical Program on Central America and the Caribbean, 1991), 118–22.

76. Interviews conducted by the author, Guatemala City, July 1999.

77. Christian Task Force on Central America (CTFCA), 2000; Religions Task Force (RTF), 2002.

78. Rigoberta Menchu, *I, Rigoberta Menchu* (London: Verso, 1984).

RESOURCE GUIDE

Suggested Reading

Anderson, Thomas P. *Politics in Central America*. Westport, CT: Praeger, 1988.

Barry, Tom. *Central America Inside Out*. New York: Grove Weidenfeld, 1991.

Booth, John A., and Thomas W. Walker. *Understanding Central America*. Boulder, CO: Westview Press, 1993.

Carmack, Robert M., ed. *Harvest of Violence: The Maya Indians and the Guatemalan Crisis*. Norman: University of Oklahoma Press, 1998.

Jonas, Susan. *The Battle for Guatemala*. Boulder, CO: Westview Press, 1991.

Menchu, Rigoberta, and Elisabeth Burgos-Debray. *I, Rigoberta Menchu: An Indian Woman in Guatemala*. London: Verso, 1984.

Perrera, Victor. *Unfinished Conquest: The Guatemalan Tragedy*. Berkeley: University of California Press, 1993.

Schlesinger, Stephen, and Stephen Kinzer. *Bitter Fruit: The Untold Story of the American Coup in Guatemala*. New York: Doubleday, 1982.

Shea, Maureen E. *Culture and Customs of Guatemala*. Westport, CT: Greenwood Press, 2000.

Videos/Films

Approach of Dawn. 1998. 52 minutes. Directed by Gayla Jamison Film, Produced by Lightfoot Films. Three women's struggles for human rights in war-torn Guatemala.

Broken Silence. 1993. 25 minutes. Produced by Films for the Humanities. A profile of Rigoberta Menchu, the first indigenous woman to be awarded the Nobel Peace Prize.

Daughters of Ixel: Maya Threads of Change. 1993. 29 minutes. Produced by Dakota Productions. A documentary about Maya women weavers in a changing society.

Web Sites

Center for Reproductive Law and Policy, *An Unfulfilled Human Right: Family Planning in Guatemala*, www.crlp.org/pdf/guatemala.pdf.
An excellent, detailed report on reproductive rights in Guatemala.

Central American Analysis Group, *Women's Role in Guatemala's Political Opening*, www.iadialog.org/womengua.html.

Centro de Estudios de Guatemala, *Documentos*, www.c.net.gt/ceg/doctos/.
A wonderful site that provides the text of legislation passed by the Guatemalan Congress (in Spanish only).

Committee on the Elimination of Discrimination Against Women, *Concluding Observations: Guatemala, U.N. Doc. A/49/38*, paras. 38–87. 1994, www1.umn.edu/humanrts/cedaw-Guatemala.htm.
This is a good report on Guatemala's compliance (or lack thereof) with the U.N. resolution.

Guatemalan Peace Accords, summary, www.personal.engin.umich.edu/~pavr/harbury/archive/guatemala/PeaceAccordsSummary.html.

Guatemalan peace process, chronological summary, *The Guatemalan Peace Accords*, 1996, www.c-r.org/acc_guat/socio.htm.

Inter-American Development Bank, *Guatemala Country Report*, www.iadb.org/regions/re2/gu/cpgueng.pdf.
Provides fairly detailed information on the current political and economic situation in Guatemala.

Mujeres en Red, *Informe sobre los derechos humanos de las mujeres en Guatemala*, www.nodo50.org/mujeresred/guatemala-ddhh.html.
Discusses the current situation of women's human rights in Guatemala (in Spanish only).

SOCWATCH, www.socwatch.org.uy/2000/eng/nationalreports/guatemala_eng.htm.
These national reports provide comprehensive social analyses by year and country.

World Bank, Genderstats, http://genderstats.worldbank.org/menu.asp.
This database on women allows searches for information on women's education, health, and labor by country.

Organizations

For more organizations (in Spanish only), see Ceiba Base de Datos, *Organizaciones de la Sociedad Civil*, www.arias.or.cr/ceiba/.

Comisión de Derechos Humanos de Guatemala (CDHG; Guatemalan Commission for Human Rights)
12 calle "A" 0-28, Zona 1
Ciudad de Guatemala
Phone: (502) 232-8747
Fax: (502) 232-8747
Email: cdhg@c.net.gt

Objectives: The defense and promotion of an integral concept of human rights.

Consejo Nacional de Mujeres de Guatemala (CNMG; National Council of Guatemalan Women)
1ᵃ Calle 6-19, Zona 9
Ciudad de Guatemala
Phone: (502) 332-5912
Fax: (502) 332-5912

Objectives: To promote solidarity and cultural, social, and economic development among all Guatemalan women.

Defensoría de la Mujer Indígena (Indigenous Women's Defense)
Majawil Qij, 32 Av. 1-40
Zona 7, Residenciales Acuario
Ulatlán
Phone: (502) 599-4155
Fax: (502) 599-6296
Email: qmajawil@c.net.gt

Objectives: The struggle for indigenous women's rights

Mujeres en Acción (Women in Action)
4ta. Calle 4-39, Zona 3
Chimaltenango
Phone: (502) 849-0326
Fax: (502) 849-0326
Email: mujeresenaccion@conexion.com.gt

Objectives: To promote the strengthening of communal organizations via the incorporation of women in productive activities.

Organización de Mujeres Guatemaltecas Mamá Maquín (Mamá Maquín Organization of Guatemalan Women)
8ᵃ calle 0-76 Zona 3
Ciudad de Guatemala
Phone: (502) 220-5173
Fax: (502) 251-4896
Email: mmqu@intelnet.net.gt

Objectives: To promote the emancipation of women through the struggle for gender, ethnic, and class equality.

SELECTED BIBLIOGRAPHY

Acosta-Belen, Edna, and Christine E. Bose. "From Structural Subordination to Empowerment: Women and Development in Third World Contexts." *Gender and Society* 4, no. 3 (September 1990): 299–320.

The Advocacy Project. "Portillo Casts a Shadow over Activism." *Guatemala News* 11, no. 6 (July 14, 2000). Also at www.nisgua.org/articles/GN-2.html.

Afshar, Haleh, and Stephanie Barrientos, eds. *Women, Globalization and Fragmentation in Developing Countries*. New York: St. Martin's Press, 1999.

Anderson, Thomas P. *Politics in Central America*. New York: Praeger, 1988.

Aron, Adrianne, Shawn Corne, Anhea Fursland, and Barbara Zewler. "The Gender-

Specific Terror of El Salvador and Guatemala." *Women's Studies International Forum* 14, no. 2 (1991): 37–47.

Ball, Patrick, Paul Kobrak, and Herbert F. Spirer. *State Violence in Guatemala, 1960–1996: A Quantitative Reflection*. Washington, DC: American Association for the Advancement of Science, 1999.

Barry, Tom. *Central America Inside Out*. New York: Grove Weidenfeld, 1991.

Booth, John A., and Thomas W. Walker. *Understanding Central America*. Boulder, CO: Westview Press, 1993.

Carmack, Robert M., ed. *Harvest of Violence: The Maya Indians and the Guatemalan Crisis*. Norman: University of Oklahoma Press, 1998.

Center for Reproductive Law and Policy. 2000. *An Unfulfilled Human Right: Family Planning in Guatemala*. www.crlp.org/pdf/guatemala.pdf.

Central Intelligence Agency. *World Factbook*. 2000. www.cia.gov/cia/publications/factbook/geos/gt.html.

Committee on the Elimination of Discrimination Against Women. *Concluding Observations: Guatemala, U.N. Doc. A/49/38*. www1.umn.edu/humanrts/cedaw/cedaw-Guatemala.htm.

Facultad Latinoamericano de Ciencias Sociales. *Guatemala*. 1998. www.eurosur.org/FLACSO/mujeres/guatemala/portada.htm.

Goldman, Noreen, and Dana A. Glei. *Evaluation of Midwifery Care: Case Study of Rural Guatemala*. Carolina Population Center, University of North Carolina. www.cpc.unc.edu/measure/publications/workingpapers/wp0129ab.html.

Guatemala Human Rights Commission/USA. *Human Rights Update #14/99*. 1999. www.eecs.umich.edu/~pavr/harbury/archive/1999/19990806c.html.

The Guatemalan Peace Accords. 1996. www.c-r.org/acc_guat/socio.htm.

Gutierrez, Gustavo. *A Theology of Liberation*. New York: Maryknoll, 1988.

Hadjicostandi, Joanna. "Facon: Women's Formal and Informal Work in the Garment Industry in Kavala, Greece." In *Women Workers and Global Restructuring*, edited by Kathryn Ward. Ithaca, NY: Cornell University Press, 1990.

Human Rights Watch. *Country Reports: Guatemala*. 2002. www.hrw.org/wr2k2/americas6.html.

Ignacio Martin-Baro Fund for Mental Health and Human Rights. *2001 Grants: Asociación de la Mujer Maya Ixil*. 2001. www.martinbarofund.org/projects/2001.htm/ixil.

Inter-American Development Bank. *Guatemala Country Paper*. 2001. www.iadb.org/regions/re2/gu/cpgueng.pdf.

International Institute for Democracy and Electoral Assistance, "Guatemala." 2001. www.idea.int/.

Interparliamentary Union. *Women in National Parliaments*. 2001. www.ipu.org/wmn-e/classif.htm.

Jelin, Elizabeth, ed. *Women and Social Change in Latin America*. London: Zed Books, 1990.

JHPIEGO Corporation. *Guatemala: Improved Clinical Care Reduces Costs at Amatitlán Hospital*. 2001. www.mnh.jhpiego.org/updates/mnhaug01.htm#Guatemala.

Jonas, Susan. *The Battle for Guatemala*. Boulder, CO: Westview Press, 1991.

Latin America and Caribbean Health Sector Reform Initiative. *Guatemala Country Profile*. 1999. www.americas.health-sector-reform.org/english/clhmgutpr.htm.

Leonard, Malinda. *Post Conflict Situation in Guatemala*. 2001. www.womenscommission.org/reports/gbvsplit/gbvlamerica.pdf.

MacNabb, Valerie, and the Central American Analysis Group. "Women's Role in Guatemala's Political Opening." *Focus* 1, no. 11 (October 12, 1998). Also at www.iadialog.org/womengua.html.

Mies, Maria. *Patriarchy and Accumulation on a World Scale*. London: Zed Books, 1986.

Ministerio de Educación. *Informative Bulletin No. 1*. 2000. www.mineduc.gob.gt/index.htm.

Moghadam, Valentine. "Gender and Globalization: Female Labor and Women's Mobilization." *Journal of World-Systems Research* 5, no. 2 (1999): 367–88. Also at http://csf.colorado.edu/jwsr.

Mohanty, Chandra, "Cartographies of Struggle: Third World Women and the Politics of Feminism." In *Third World Women and the Politics of Feminism*, edited by Chandra Mohanty, Ann Russo, and Lourdes Torres. Bloomington: Indiana University Press, 1991.

Munduate, Christian. *Statement by Mrs. Christian Munduate, Minister of Social Welfare, Secretariat of the Presidency of Guatemala*. 2000. www.un.org/womenwatch/daw/followup/beijing+5stat/statments/guatemala5.htm.

Nash, June. "Latin American Women in the World Capitalist Crisis." *Gender and Society* 4, no. 3 (September 1990): 338–53.

Oakes, Maud. *The Two Crosses of Todos Santos: Survivals of Mayan Religious Ritual*. New York: Bollingen Foundation, 1951.

Organization of American States, Inter-American Commission on Human Rights. *Report No. 4/01. Case 11.625. Maria Eugenia Morales de Sierra*. 2001. www.cidh.oas.org/annualrep/2000eng/ChapterIII/Merits/Guatemala11.625.htm.

Organization of American States, Inter-Amerian Commission on Women. *Congressional Decree 7-99: Law for the Dignity and Integral Promotion of Women*. March 1999. http://www.oas.org/cim/English/LawsViolence.htm.

———. *Law 97-96 to Prevent, Punish and Eradicate Family Violence*. 1999. www.oas.org/cim/English/LawsViolence.htm.

Pan American Health Organization. *Guatemala: General Situation and Trends*. 1998. www.paho.org/english/HIA1998/Guatemala.pdf.

Perrera, Victor. *Unfinished Conquest: The Guatemalan Tragedy*. Berkeley: University of California Press, 1993.

Plant, Roger. *Indigenous Peoples and Poverty Reduction: A Case Study of Guatemala*. Inter-American Development Bank, 1998. www.iadb.org/sds/doc/IND-RPlantE.PDF.

Religious Task Force on Central America and Mexico. *Action Alert*. 2002. www.rtfcam.org/take_action/CONAVIGUA.htm.

Rodas Melgar, Haroldo. *Lecture to the US-Central America Forum*. 1997. http://lanic.utexas.edu/~sela/eng_capitulos/rcapin495.htm.

Safa, Helen Icken. "Women's Movements in Latin America." *Gender and Society* 4, no. 3 (September 1990): 354–69.

Schlesinger, Stephen, and Stephen Kinzer. *Bitter Fruit: The Untold Story of the American Coup in Guatemala*. New York: Doubleday, 1982.

Social Watch. *National Reports: Guatemala*. 2000. www.socwatch.org.uy/2000/eng/nationalreports/guatemala_eng.htm.

Tiano, Susan. "Maquiladora Women: A New Category of Workers?" In *Women Workers and Global Restructuring*, edited by Kathryn Ward. Ithaca, NY: Cornell University Press, 1990.

United Nations. *Indigenous People: Challenges Facing the International Community*. 1997. www.un.org/rights/50/people.

United Nations. *Report of the Secretary General*. 1998. www.hri.ca/fortherecord1998/vol4/guatemalaga.htm.

United Nations Childrens Fund (UNICEF). *Guatemala*. 2000, www.unicef.org/statis/Country_1Page69.html.

United Nations Development Program. (UNDP). *Human Development Report*. 2000. www.undp.org/hdr2000/english/presskit/gdi.pdf; United Nations Foundation. "Child Labor: Guatemala Has Highest Rate in Americas." www.unfoundation.org/unwire/archives/UNWIRE001213.asp.

UN Population Division, Department of Economic and Social Affairs. *World Marriage Patterns*. 2000. www.un.org/popin/wdtrends/worldmarriagepatterns2000.pdf.

UN Population Fund. *The State of the World Population*. 1999. www.unfpa.org/.

UN Wire. *Thousands of Children Work in High Risk Conditions*. 2001. www.unwire.org/unwire/2001/10/02/current.asp#18907.

USAID. *Activity Data Sheet: Guatemala*. 2000, www.usaid.gov/country/lac/gt/520-002.html.

———. *Leading the Global Fight Against HIV/AIDS: Guatemala*. 2001. www.usaid.gov/pop_health/aids/country_guatemala.html.

U.S. Department of State. *Annual Report on International Religious Freedom: Guatemala*. 1999. www.state.gov/www/global/human_rights/irf/irf_rpt/1999/irf_guatemal99.html.

———. *Guatemala Country Report on Human Rights Practices for 1998*. 1999. www.state.gov/www/global/human_rights/1998_hrp_report/guatemal.html.

Wolf, Diane L. "Linking Women's Labor with the Global Economy: Factory Workers and Their Families in Rural Java." In *Women Workers and Global Restructuring*, edited by Kathryn Ward. Ithaca, NY: Cornell University Press, 1990.

Women Members of Government by Country. 2001. http://hjem.get2net.dk/Womenin governments/Ministers_by_Country.htm.

Women's Justice Center, Tertulia. *Guatemala: Each Day Twenty Women Report Family Violence*. 2001. www.justicewomen.com/tertulia_8_18_01.html.

World Bank. *GENDERSTATS: Guatemala*. http://genderstats.worldbank.org/SummaryGender.asp?WhichRpt=education&Ctr=GTM.Guatemala.

Spanish Bibliography

Aguilar, Ana Leticia, et al. *Movimiento de mujeres en Centroamérica*. Managua, Nicaragua: Programa Regional La Corriente, 1997.

Comision para el Esclaracimiento. *Memoria del silencio*. Guatemala City: CEH, 1999.

Constitución de la República de Guatemala. 1985. www.georgetown.edu/pdba/Constitutions/Guate/guate85.html.

Instituto Nacional de Estadísticas. *Encuesta Nacional de Salud Materno e Infantil*. 1999. www.ine.gob.gt/index_fla.htm.

Ministerio de Salud Pública. *Plan Nacional de Salud 2000–2004*. 2000. www.mspas.gob.gt/.

Organización Internacional del Trabajo. *La situación sociolaboral en las zonas francas y empresas maquiladoras del Istmo Centroamericano y Republica Dominicana*. San Jose, Costa Rica: OIT, 1996.

WorldWatch. *Exija el fin al hostigamiento contra las lesbianas, gays, personas bisexuales y travestis/transexuales*. 2001. www.iglhrc.org/world/mex_centam_carib/Guatemala2001May_es.html.

12

GUYANA

Kalowatie Deonandan

PROFILE OF GUYANA

Graced by splendid natural wonders and famed as the land where sixteenth-century explorers sought El Dorado, the legendary city of gold, the Co-operative Republic of Guyana is located on the northern seaboard of South America. Also known as the Land of Six Peoples, it comprises a diverse, multiethnic population: 49 percent East Indians (or Indo-Guyanese); 32 percent African-Guyanese (or Afro-Guyanese); 12 percent mixed race; 6 percent Amerindian; and 1 percent Chinese and white.[1] The political history of the nation has been marked by racial conflicts, slavery, the indentured labor system, colonialism, racial conflicts, and authoritarianism. Only in 1992 did the Guyanese people succeed in overcoming thirty years of authoritarian rule and in implementing a political democracy.

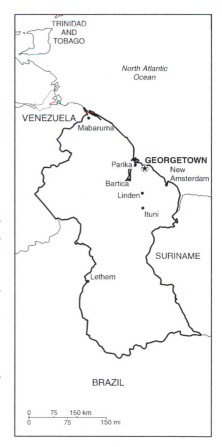

Though rich in natural resources (gold, bauxite, and timber), Guyana is among the poorest nations in the Western Hemisphere. Figures from 1996 revealed a national debt of U.S.$1.5 billion, a per capita debt of U.S.$1,947, and a debt servicing rate of 61.2 percent of national revenue, among the highest in the world.[2] During this same period, GDP stood at U.S.$577 million, and *per capita* GDP was U.S.$840.[3] After decades of adhering to a planned economy model, it was compelled in 1988 to embark on a process of economic liberalization through the adoption of structural adjustment policies that included privatizing state enterprises and reducing social expenditures. Initiated at the behest of the International Monetary Fund and the World Bank, this transformation was aimed at countering the nation's dramatically deteriorating economic status. In return,

Guyana was promised debt reduction support and other forms of financial aid, very little of which has materialized despite the continuation of market reforms by all subsequent administrations. While this economic program indeed resulted in some macroeconomic gains, overall, it has been particularly detrimental to women, children, and the poor because they rely heavily on public sector social programs.

Estimates for 2001 placed Guyana's population at approximately 700,000 and population growth rate, which has been steadily declining, at 0.7 percent.[4] Women were expected to be in the majority.[5] Fertility rate was projected at 2.11 children per woman with infant mortality at 38.72 deaths per 1000 live births, an increase from 27.8 deaths in 1995.[6] Data from 1999 showed maternal mortality at 172 per 100,000 births, one of the highest in the region. Life expectancy at birth averaged 64.04 years—61.08 years for men and 67.15 years for women—a dramatic decline from the 1986 average of 70 years.[7]

OVERVIEW OF WOMEN'S ISSUES

Guyanese women made great strides economically and politically in the twentieth century, but nevertheless they remain on the margins of the nation's development priorities. Research on the status of women in Guyana confronts an immediate handicap—a paucity of data. Complicating the process is the fact that significant variations exist among women in the various ethnic groups, and while this does not mean that overarching conclusions cannot be derived, it does alert the researcher to the dangers of generalizations.

Many of the problems facing Guyanese women are rooted in the nation's gender-biased cultural traditions, its socialization processes, its ongoing political tensions, and its deep and enduring poverty. Among the specific challenges women confront, according to the government's own analysis, are the absence of legal recognition of women's reproductive work as a social function; the lack of gender consciousness in national planning; inappropriate or inadequate policy mechanisms; gender inequalities in education, health, and employment; increased burden of nonremunerated work; and lack of adequate training, especially in business practices and marketing. While there is growing official recognition of the problems, and legislation has been enacted to address some of them, the de facto reality has not kept pace with the de jure changes.

EDUCATION

Opportunities

Historically, education has been deemed critical in Guyanese society because it was viewed as the ticket to upward mobility. Theoretically, the right to education at all levels is granted equally to both sexes and it is one of the few areas where women have attained some degree of parity with men, even outnumbering them at most educational levels.[8] In 1992–1993, as a percentage of the school age population, enrollment at the primary level for females was 41.1 percent and for males it was 42.6 percent; at the secondary level it was 29.4 percent and 25.2 percent, respectively; at the tertiary level, total female enrollment was 53.4 percent, whereas in 1980/ 1981 it was 31.9 percent.[9]

In terms of educational attainment, there is a fair degree of parity between the sexes. In 1992, 20.8 percent of males and 20.3 percent of females had education below the primary level; the percents for those with primary education were 55.4 percent and 54.2 percent, respectively; the secondary level distribution was 22.5 percent and 24.2 percent; and university level education for both groups stood at 1.3 percent (a significant increase from 1970, when only 0.3 percent of women were this category, compared to 1.3 percent of males).[10]

However, in terms of areas of study, the traditional dichotomies still apply: women concentrate in the liberal arts and men in the sciences, despite a common curriculum until form 3 (approximately grade 9 in the American system). Men outnumber women in science and technology, and in technical and vocational training (accounting, for example, for 75.6 percent of enrollment in technical schools).[11] This imbalance is exacerbated by gender stereotyping practices within the education system: in teaching style, where instructors unconsciously encourage male participation, leaving females to observe; in textbooks, where women are underrepresented in the science and technology materials and where sex stereotyping often still exists; in the absence of gender-sensitive career guidance programs; and in the lack of female and male role models in nontraditional occupations.[12]

Literacy

The importance accorded education is reflected in the relatively high levels of literacy, 98.1 percent of the population (98.6 percent for males and 97.5 percent for females).[13] That education is free from nursery to university is a not insignificant element in contributing to this positive situation (though admittedly families are compelled to subsidize the system by having to purchase textbooks and uniforms, and to pay examination fees). However, for Amerindian women, a different situation prevails: 56.2 percent of them are illiterate.[14] To ameliorate this situation, adult distance education programs are being expanded, particularly to the rural areas, and indications are that the service is being accessed primarily by women.

While literacy has been improving, Guyana's education system ranks among the lowest in the Caribbean (in the 1960s it was second only to Barbados), and further deterioration is looming due to the government's commitment to reducing public expenditures, including spending on education, as part of its debt reduction strategy.

EMPLOYMENT AND ECONOMICS

Job/Career Opportunities

As with education, labor participation rates for women have been growing, from 20.5 percent in 1980 to 32.2 percent in 1992, though this figure has since declined to 26 percent.[15] Employment patterns, however, are not uniform, but vary by ethnicity and location. Only 29 percent of Indo-Guyanese women, compared to 50 percent of their Afro-Guyanese counterparts, were reported as economically active in 1992; as for location, while urban employment for women grew to 47 percent in 1992, up from 28 percent in 1970, the figures were 36 percent and 14 percent, respectively, for rural areas.[16]

Overall, women comprise barely one-third of the employed population and form the majority of the unemployed: 53 percent in 1992 (with Indo-Guyanese women reporting 21 percent unemployment and Afro-Guyanese women 18 percent).[17] Gender stereotyping of their roles may have influenced some of these women's classification of their employment status. Generally, Afro-Guyanese women, historically more active on labor issues, are more likely to consider "their informal endeavours as work or to offer their status as unemployed . . . [while] Indo-Guyanese women may define the same activities as secondary to their main roles as housewife and [are] less likely to consider themselves unemployed."[18]

As for women's employment choices, they remain the traditionally low-paying, low-status jobs—teachers, nurses, typists, garment workers, domestic help, and vendors. To supplement their income, many women are forced to hold two jobs, one formal and the other informal, with market vending being one of the most frequent options of the latter type.[19] A growth area for women, and one that takes advantage of them as cheap labor, is piecework, a trend that is deepening as production becomes more global and as corporations seek ever cheaper labor.[20]

Where women are present in managerial ranks, they occupy the middle or lower level, though admittedly their numbers in these categories have been improving, from 14.9 percent in 1985 to 25.4 percent in 1993; at the executive level, the picture is far bleaker, for women's presence declined from 25.5 percent to 12.4 percent during the same period.[21]

Women pursuing self-employment face an array of financial obstacles. Legally no barriers exist to their seeking bank loans and credit. However, the need for substantial collateral, combined with high interest rates and women's low income-earning power, have made formal credit inaccessible to many. Consequently, women have resorted to organizing their own informal systems of credit. In addition, the Women's Affairs Bureau

(WAB) within the Ministry of Labour has organized small business management training programs and has established a revolving fund to provide loans for micro projects. However, the organization's effectiveness is hindered by its limited resources.[22]

Pay

In Guyana income data are typically collected for households, and are not gender-specific; however, it is estimated that men receive 78.8 percent of the earned income in the nation.[23] Where specific data are available, they confirm women's inferior earnings status. Public-sector wages illustrate the point. Women accounted for almost 60 percent of public sector employees in 1993, but there were "47.3 percent more women than men in the bottom seven salary scales, while there [were] 79 percent more men than women in the top seven."[24] Additionally, while civil service employment offered women better protection in terms of social benefits, it also placed them at the forefront of those immediately affected by the economic crisis and the accompanying downsizing of the public sector. Real income in this area fell by an estimated one-sixth between 1986 and 1991.[25]

With respect to wage determination, there is no legally set minimum wage for the private sector, though there is one for the public sector. The 1990 Equal Rights (Amendment) Act guarantees women protection from discrimination in hiring or promotion and advocates equal pay for equal work. Employer compliance is limited, however for though enforcement mechanisms exist (the Chief Labour Officer can bring criminal charges), the combination of inadequate resources and the more weighty evidence requirements associated with criminal suits (as opposed to civil) has resulted in their nonimplementation.[26]

To supplement the wages of low-income earners, the government increased the minimum threshold for payment of personal income tax, a move beneficial to women because their wages generally fall below the threshold. Additionally, the earnings of civil servants were increased (from U.S.$52 per month in 1992 to U.S.$129 per month in 1997, an increase of 148 percent in five years), and again women were the group most advantaged by this, given their high numbers in this sector.[27] Critics charged, however, that the increase was still not enough to ensure a decent standard of living for a worker and her/his family.[28]

Working Conditions

Working conditions are regulated by the Shops Act and the Factories Act, but the guarantees offered by these pieces of legislation are undermined by the government's weak enforcement of them. Since the female labor force is largely unorganized, it relies greatly on governmental protection, and thus it is the group most harmed by the inadequate enforcement of legal guarantees.

The Shops Act determines the hours of employment—which can vary across industries or sectors. Nevertheless, the general standard is an 8-hour day or 44-hour week, and work in excess of this must be reimbursed with overtime wages. However, if a contract stipulates differently, such as requiring a 48-hour week, then overtime rates are only applicable for work in excess of this. Furthermore, no provisions have been made in the Shops Act for rest periods.[29] This longer workweek can be particularly burdensome to women, who must also make time for their household and child care responsibilities, and lack of legally sanctioned rest periods could prove detrimental to their health, especially if they are pregnant. In this way, contracts that stipulate hours and conditions outside the norm can exclude women from seeking certain types of employment.

Health and safety standards fall under the purview of the Factories Act, which was altered to allow women to work in factories at night. Under this act, the Ministry of Labour is responsible for inspecting workplaces for health and safety violations, and for following up on complaints regarding substandard working environments. Here again, however, insufficient resources have translated into limited implementation. Workers, especially women, who face more limited employment options, are therefore rendered vulnerable because fears of unemployment may preclude their filing formal complaints against their employers or their removing themselves from unsafe workplaces.[30]

Sexual Harassment

Legal silence prevails when it comes to the issue of sexual harassment in the workplace, leaving those who suffer such abuse no formal recourse.[31] Even on the subject of sexual discrimination there is a void, because no legal definition of what constitutes such conduct has been established. While the ERA and the Prevention of Discrimination Act ban discrimination based on sex, skeptics note that thus far no judicial challenges have been brought under their auspices. As with other protections afforded women, enforcement falls under the jurisdiction of the Chief Labour Officer and has not occurred because the department is understaffed and over-extended.

Support for Mothers/Caretakers

Maternal Leave

Maternity leave is protected under the National Insurance Act, which provides for leave and pay for six weeks before childbirth and six weeks after. The act also requires both employers and employees to pay into a fund to ensure fulfillment of the provisions. However, in practice, these guarantees are enjoyed only by government employees. For women in the private sector there are no legal or administrative mechanisms to ensure employer compliance, and thus they are generally denied maternity benefits. Furthermore, they have no safeguards ensuring their right to return to their employment after pregnancy, despite constitutional guarantees against sexual discrimination. The Guyanese Minister of Labour reported that employers "circumvent . . . [the legislation] through contractual provisions" or other covert mechanisms.[32] Aggravating women's employment hardships is the dearth of child care services; these exist to a limited extent only in the capital and are accessible only to those who can afford the costs.[33]

The absence of a national mandatory maternity leave policy has been interpreted as an infringement on women's employment rights and as confirmation of the claim that policymakers' location of women within the domestic sphere remains unchallenged.[34]

Inheritance and Property Rights

Women's rights to property are entrenched in two pieces of legislation, both passed in 1990: the Married Persons (Amendment) Act and the Family and Dependent Act. The latter accorded widows, whether they had been legally married or in a common law union (of seven or more years immediately prior to the partner's death), the right to seek support from the estate of their deceased partner. The former stipulates that in case of separation or divorce, a spouse's contribution to the marriage (legal or common law) and to the family's welfare can be part of the calculations to determine property rights, providing the couple were together for less than five years. For unions of longer duration, the claimant is entitled to one-third of the couple's property if he/she did not work outside the home, and to one-half if she/he did.[35]

FAMILY AND SEXUALITY

Gender Roles

Cultural norms combined with legislation have relegated Guyanese women largely to the private sphere, as mothers and wives. However, there are significant differences as to how these roles are manifested within the two dominant ethnic groups. Within Afro-Guyanese society, family structures are defined as matrifocal—households are organized and administered by females (and males may or may not be present).[36] The converse applies to Indo-Guyanese society, classified as patrifocal, where "stringent paternal authority" prevails, though the women are considered "mistresses of their own households and are responsible . . . for housework . . . [and] decision making within that realm."[37]

Despite this difference, there is evidence of a growing trend across ethnic groups toward female household headship, from 24.4 percent in 1980 to 29.5 percent in 1992.[38] The percentages, though, vary dramatically within each group. Among Afro-Guyanese households, 51 percent are female-headed; among Indo-Guyanese 32.5 percent are thus organized; and among Amerindians the figure is 2.6 percent.[39] Such households are generally in the lower economic stratum, thus accentuating the feminization of poverty.

Marriage

Ethnic variations also prevail in attitudes toward marriage. For the Afro-Guyanese woman, while motherhood is intricately linked to her femininity and identity, marriage is not a priority. She may participate in a series of relationships and even common-law marriages before (if at all) choosing marriage. The same does not hold true for her Indo-Guyanese counterpart, for whom marriage and motherhood, in that order, are intrinsic to her identity. To be of a certain age and unmarried brings with it a certain degree of stigma for both the Indo-Guyanese woman and her family, as does being married and childless. Being an unwed mother carries even greater disgrace. This difference in the importance attributed to marriage is confirmed by the statistics. In 1992, only 23 percent of Afro-Guyanese women were living in marital arrangements, compared to 41 percent of Indo-Guyanese women. However, there is evidence that this trend is shifting as more and more Indo-Guyanese women are opting for common-law unions: 5 percent in 1975 and 17 percent in 1992.[40]

Arranged marriages within the Indo-Guyanese community are relatively common (though this pattern, too, is changing). Also changing is the age at which women are getting married, a fact aided by legislation (which raised the marriageable age from 14 to 16 years). For Indo-Guyanese women, marriage in their late teens or early twenties is generally the norm. However, it is becoming increasingly acceptable for women to postpone marriage in order to pursue employment or education options, or to facilitate their chances of successful emigration in their search for better economic opportunities.[41]

Reproduction

In a 1999 survey on women's reproductive health conducted by the NGO Red Thread, it was found that approximately half (45.1 percent) of the women who have been pregnant have had multiple pregnancies (defined as more than four) and that the average age of the mother at the time of the first pregnancy was between 17 and 21 years (56.6 percent), though some (15.1 percent) were under 16 years; less than one-third of the women had their first pregnancy over the age of 22 years, and no pregnancies were reported among those over 35 years.[42]

Sex Education

In this same survey, over 50 percent of the women admitted to having acquired their knowledge of reproductive health largely from television, books or friends. As sources of information, parents and teachers rated extremely low, between 7 and 8 percent, pointing to a need for more education to inform not only women but also parents and teachers about their obligations with respect to conveying information.[43]

Contraception and Abortion

A majority of the women in the poll indicated having some knowledge of contraceptives. However, of those who had been or currently were in a relationship, a significant majority (63.7 percent) confessed that their partners did not use protection, a finding not surprising, given the dominant perception that birth control is the woman's responsibility.[44] Use of contraception by the women themselves was quite low. Of those who acknowledged having used them, the majority (71.2 percent) said were no longer doing so.[45] It should be noted that the subjects of this study were women in the capital city. Among rural women and those in the hinterland, the numbers would be even more disturbing, given their lower educational levels, greater poverty, and poorer access to information.

Abortion remains a dominant method of birth control, with many women endangering their lives by resorting to untrained abortion practitioners. To protect women's health, the Medical Termination of Pregnancy Act, passed in 1995, legalized abortions under prescribed conditions, making Guyana the first South American country to have adopted such measures. The bill's effects reportedly were immediate, for within six months hospital admissions for septic and incomplete abortions fell by 41 percent.[46] Still, Red Thread's survey revealed that a huge percentage of women were still not aware of their rights; 66.3 percent had not heard of the act and a comparable number, 61 percent, were unaware of the legal status of abortion.[47] The rate of repeat abortions remained quite high, indicating the need for still greater educational efforts. Red Thread's study, done four years after passage of the bill, found that of the women who had had abortions, 55 percent had between one and two; 24.4 percent had three or four; 8.9 percent had between five and seven; and 11.1 percent had more than seven.[48]

HEALTH

Health Care Access

Medical care is free in Guyana but access is limited, particularly for those in remote areas. Spending cutbacks on health services (almost 50 percent in 1994) have resulted in a steady deterioration of the system and in the health of the almost 86 percent of the population living below the poverty line, especially women and children.[49] While the government has been trying to reverse this trend by increasing health sector investments, its efforts are far below what is required to ensure the well-being of Guyanese. In 1992, of the pregnant women visiting health clinics, the majority (65 percent) suffered from anemia (and the rate of severe cases of the illness was increasing), and nutrition-related sicknesses in general accounted "for five out of ten leading causes of deaths in both sexes and all age groups."[50]

Diseases and Disorders

AIDS

One of Guyana's most challenging health problems is HIV/AIDS. With an infection rate between 3.5 and 5 percent of the population,[51] it is the second most highly infected country in the Caribbean, and women represent 45 percent of those diagnosed with the disease.[52] Women also show an infection rate higher than that of men.[53] Among prostitutes, the infection rate is 47 percent, and many display little knowledge of the seriousness of the disease or that they are at risk of infection.[54]

To care for those with the illness, the government began purchasing generic anti-AIDS drugs from an Indian pharmaceutical company at a fraction of what it would have had to pay Western multinationals, and since April 2002 it has also been trying to manufacture some domestically.[55] The drugs are provided free of cost to patients, but limited state resources have restricted availability.

POLITICS AND LAW

Formerly a colony of Great Britain, the Co-operative Republic of Guyana (called British Guiana until 1970, when it proclaimed itself a republic within the British Commonwealth) won its independence in 1966, and women such as Janet Jagan—later the nation's President—played a prominent role in this struggle. Politics in Guyana has been dominated by two political parties, the People's National Congress (PNC) and the People's Progressive Party (PPP, now PPP/Civic). Political loyalty is delineated along ethnic lines, with Afro-Guyanese supporting the PNC and Indo-Guyanese the PPP/Civic. Through electoral manipulation the PNC held power from 1964 to 1992. However, in 1992, under the supervision of international observers, electoral democracy was restored and the PPP/Civic has since been successful in all subsequent national elections.

Suffrage and Political Participation

Universal suffrage was granted in 1953 to all qualified persons 18 years and over. If participation in national plebiscites is any indication, Guyanese are politically mobilized. In the 2001 presidential elections, won by the PPP's Bharrat Jagdeo, voter turnout was approximately 90 percent.[56] Yet in the higher echelons of power women are still significantly underrepresented (in comparison to their numbers in the population), although no legal obstacles preclude their presence. Nevertheless, their presence has been increasing. In the 2002 cabinet, women hold 4 of the 20 ministerial posts (20 percent; up from 11 percent in 1994), and for the first time an Amerindian woman is among them. Of the 65 elected parliamentarians (the National Assembly has 76 members—the Speaker, 65 elected members, and 10 presidential appointees), 20 are women, up 15 percent from 1997.[57] Facilitating this increase were the 2002 constitutional amendments legislating a mandatory representation of 33.3 percent of women candidates for all political parties contesting the national and regional elections.

Female presence has also been improving in other high level political positions such as permanent secretaries, with the number climbing from 21.4 percent in 1987 to 33.3 percent in 1993.[58] Guyana remains one of the few countries in the world that has had a woman at the helm; Janet Jagan held the office of President of the Republic from 1997 to 1999 (she was also the first woman to serve as Prime Minister and as Vice President of the country). As of 2002, Guyana had a woman serving as the Chancellor of the Judiciary (her previous position was the nation's Chief Justice).

In regional political structures, 30 percent of council members in 2001 were women,[59] up from 22 percent for the period 1990–1994. There was a decline in the percentage of female mayors, however, to 17 percent in 1994 from 40 percent in 1980.[60]

To address the overall problem of women's underrepresentation in leadership positions, the Women's Leadership Institute was established in 1999 and tasked with promoting women's participation in government and industry. It also was made responsible for training approximately 350 women annually on matters dealing with women's rights, with the objective of both increasing women's participation in various sectors and making them more cognizant of their legal and political entitlements.

Women's Rights

Legally, women's rights are significantly advanced in Guyana. For example, Article 29(1) of the nation's constitution guarantees women and men equal status. It proclaims that "Women and men have equal rights and the same legal status in all spheres of political, economic and social life." Strengthening these protections are the 1990 Equal Rights Act (ERA) and the 1997 Prevention of Discrimination Act (PDA) which entitle women to seek compensation for discrimination based on sex. Enforcement of these guarantees falls largely to the Women's Affairs Bureau (WAB), established in 1981. However, as critics note, thus far no cases have been brought under the ERA or the PDA, a fact attributed to the inadequate resources available to WAB. Other important enforcement mechanisms include the Women and Gender Equality Commission, approved by Parliament in 2001 and tasked with ensuring that gender is integrated into all policies and planning processes across the various ministries. However, the commission's authority is restricted in that it neither reports directly to Parliament nor has status in initiating legislative changes.[61]

Feminist Movements

Strong influences on the women's movement in Guyana are the two political parties, both male-dominated.[62] Not surprisingly then, the movement reflects party politics and duplicates the divisiveness of the racial politics that has dominated the nation, with Afro-Guyanese women belonging to the women's organization linked to the PNC and Indo-Guyanese women to that associated with the PPP/Civic.

The Women's Auxiliary of the PNC was an organization active primarily during electoral campaigns and devoted to mobilizing support for the party. Despite having undergone several changes of name (at one time declaring itself an NGO—the Women's Revolutionary Socialist Movement—while still being officially listed as a government department under the PNC), it has generally endorsed the party's policies, even when these were detrimental to the interests of women. In 1994, two years after the PNC's electoral defeat, the organization again transformed itself, this time into the National Congress of Women (NCW), and since then it has been trying to articulate a more independent stance, "though technically the PNC still speaks for the NCW."[63]

The Women's Progressive Organization (WPO) of the PPP/Civic also is strongly tied to the party. Unlike the NCW, however, the WPO has remained fully committed to the PPP/Civic, though it has been active in raising issues of poverty and gender equity, and in pushing for legislation on abortion and domestic violence. Since the PPP/Civic has regained power, several of the WPO's most prominent members have held senior governmental offices. In sum, "It seems fair to say that neither the WPO nor the WRSM . . . linked the . . . disruption in women's lives to existing development policies and practices; neither has . . . spoken out against the implementation, by both the PNC and the PPP, of structural adjustment measures."[64]

Among the groups seeking to fill the need for an independent women's organization are Red Thread and Women Across Difference, both NGOs. While they have had many successes in education programs and in advocacy work, their existence is precarious in that they are largely dependent on external funding and are encumbered by the racial politics which dominate the political debate.

Lesbian Rights

Lesbian rights have thus far been neglected in the human rights and public policy debates within the nation: "There continues to be a deafening silence around issues of women's sexuality. The reproduction of families, children and future citizens is normalized through state and legal discourses. . . . [and] it is male homosexuality that is explicitly criminalized under the Offences against Morality Act."[65] Though in 2001 the National Assembly did approve legislation rendering discrimination based on sexual orientation illegal, the bill was put on hold by President Jagdeo. Facing a national election and widespread opposition to the legislation (spearheaded by religious leaders), he delayed signing the bill by returning it to Parliament, ostensibly for reconsideration of its broader implications.

RELIGION AND SPIRITUALITY

Religion has played an important role in defining women's identities in Guyana. Christianity, Hinduism, and Islam are the dominant religions practiced by 50 percent, 33 percent, and 9 percent of the population, respectively, and while within each of these faiths there are significant variations in the degrees of orthodoxy prescribed (within each are progressive and conservative variants), they have all contributed to women's cultural subordination to varying degrees.[66] Hinduism and Islam, for example, are practiced primarily by Indo-Guyanese and traditionally have been interpreted to favor a strongly patriarchal family structure where a woman's value is determined by her fidelity (for wives), dutifulness, obedience, modesty and chastity (for the unwed). This construction of the female identity has in turn influenced official policies affecting women in such areas as domestic violence and rape.

Guyanese women from the African Mystical Apostolic Community Church participate in an ancient African ritual during the Emancipation Day festivities at the National Park in Georgetown, Guyana, 2002. AP/Wide World Photos.

VIOLENCE

Domestic Violence

Gender-based violence, especially domestic violence, is prevalent across ethnic and socioeconomic lines, with between 33 and 50 percent of all women reportedly having suffered some form of verbal, physical, or sexual violence.[67] Yet it was only in 1999 that legal protections became available with the passage of the Domestic Violence Law, though one study revealed that a majority of women (65 percent) were not aware of its existence.[68] Aggravating the situation has been the lack of enforcement of the bill's protections, a fact no doubt rooted in societal perceptions of domestic violence as being a private issue or as secondary to other personal crimes. Reflecting this attitude are the law enforcement officials who show reluctance to interfere in cases of such violence, viewing them as private concerns. To alter perceptions and to promote awareness, in 2002 the government organized a 14-week domestic intervention training program for police and social workers.

Rape/Sexual Assault

Rape and incest are significant problems, though they are rarely reported and even more rarely prosecuted, due in large part to the stigma attached to the victim. Rape within marriage still remains legally unrecognized. According to Help and Shelter, the first local NGO dedicated to combat domestic violence, 62 percent of its counseling cases involve victims of spousal abuse, 10 percent involve child abuse, and another 10 percent involve rape, with the majority of the victims age 16 and under.[69]

OUTLOOK FOR THE TWENTY-FIRST CENTURY

The legal guarantees available to Guyanese women promise to expand in the twenty-first century, if current trends persist. However, the full realization of these rights remains a dubious proposition in light of the nation's deepening poverty and the pressures on the state by organizations such as the International Monetary Fund and World Bank to reduce social spending in order to reduce the debt. Nevertheless, women's rights promise to become more central in national planning policies in light of the objectives laid out in the National Development Strategy (NDS), the comprehensive six-volume study, unveiled in 1999, outlining the future direction of the nation. According to the country's late President, Dr. Cheddi Jagan, under whose leadership the study was undertaken, the NDS represents the government's commitment to promoting "people-centred development" by focusing on the country's "most basic social problems, including health, education, housing, poverty . . . [and] the role of women."[70]

NOTES

1. Central Intelligence Agency (CIA), *The World Factbook*, 2000, www.cia.gov/cia/publications/Factbook/geos/gy/html.

2. Pan American Health Organization (PAHO), *Guyana*, 1999, www.paho.org/prflguy.htm, accessed August 10, 2002.

3. U.S. Department of State, Bureau of Democracy, Human Rights and Labor, *Country Reports on Human Rights Practices 2001: Guyana*, March 4, 2002, www.state.gov/g/drl/rls/hrrpt/2001/wha/8337.htm, accessed August 8, 2002.

4. CIA, 2000.

5. Red Thread Women's Development Programme, *Women Researching Women: Methodology Report and Research Projects on the Study of Domestic Violence and Reproductive Health in Guyana* (Georgetown, Guyana: Inter-American Development Bank, 2000), www.sndp.org.gy/hands/wom_surv.htm.

6. CIA, 2000; PAHO, 1999.

7. International Women's Rights Action Watch (IWRAW), *Country Reports: Guyana*, 1999, www.igc/org/iwraw/publications/countries/guyana.html; Red Thread, (2000).

8. IWRAW, 1999.

9. Ministry of Finance, National Development Secretariat (NDS), "Women, Gender and Development," *National Development Strategy* (April 17, 1996), www.guyana.org/NDS/chap21.htm.

10. NDS, 1996.

11. IWRAW, 1999.

12. NDS, 1996.

13. CIA, 2000.

14. NDS, 1996.

15. Ibid.; Committee on the Elimination on All Forms of Discrimination Against Women (CEDAW), *Concluding Observations: Guyana*, U.N. Doc./A/49/38, paras. 88–125, 1994, www1.umn.edu/humanrts/cedaw/cedaw-Guyana.htm.

16. D. Alissa Trotz and Linda Peake, "Work, Family and Organising: An Overview of the Contemporary Economic, Social and Political Roles of Women in Guyana," *Social and Economic Studies* 50, no. 2 (2002): 74.

17. Ibid.

18. Ibid., 76.

19. NDS, 1996.

20. Ibid.

21. CEDAW, 1994.

22. CEDAW, *Press Release, WOM/1297*, July 18, 2001, www.un.org/NewsPress/docs/2001/wom1297.doc.htm.

23. NDS, 1996.

24. Ibid.

25. Ibid.

26. CEDAW, 2001.

27. PAHO, 1999.

28. U.S. Department of State, Bureau of Western Hemisphere Affairs, *Background Notes: Guyana*, April 2001, www.cia.gov/r/pa/ei/bgn/1984.htm.

29. International Labor Organization (ILO), *The Shops Act: Guyana Policy for Women*, June 2002, http://ilo.org/public/english/employment/gems/eeo/law/guyana/eeo_sag.htm.

30. USDS, 2001.

31. Ibid.

32. CEDAW, 2001.

33. Trotz and Peake, 2001, 95.

34. CEDAW, 2001.

35. IWRAW, 1999.

36. Matrifocality implies neither female-headed households nor matriarchal family systems, "but . . . a social process in which the woman is prominent in her role as mother within the domestic domain" Kimberley Nettles, "Homework: An Examination of the Sexual Division of Labor in the Urban Households of East Indian and African Guyanese," *Journal of Comparative Family Studies* 26, no. 3 (1995): 3.

37. Ibid., 3–4.

38. Trotz and Peake, 2001, 85.

39. Ministry of Labour, *Statement on the Situation Affecting Women in Guyana*, www.guyana.org/woman_situation.htm.

40. Ibid., 84.

41. Ibid., 85.

42. Red Thread, 2000.

43. Ibid.

44. Ibid.

45. Ibid.

46. IWRAW, 1999.

47. Red Thread, 2000.

48. Ibid.

49. CEDAW, 1994.

50. NDS, 1996.

51. "Guyana in Line for Major Support in HIV/AIDS Fight," *Stabroek News*, July 10, 2001, www.landofsixpeoples.com.gynewsjs.htm.

52. CEDAW, 2001.

53. CEDAW, 1994.

54. IWRAW, 1999.

55. *Stabroek News*, July 10, 2001.

56. IWRAW, 1999.

57. CEDAW, 2001.

58. CEDAW, 1994.

59. CEDAW, 2001.

60. CEDAW, 2001; NDS, 1996.

61. IWRAW, 1999.

62. Trotz and Peake, 2001, 87.

63. Ibid., 88.

64. Ibid., 89.

65. Ibid., 91–92.

66. CIA, 2000.

67. IWRAW, 1999.

68. Red Thread, 1999.

69. USDS, 2001.

70. Cheddi Jagan, *Guyana's National Development Strategy*, speech delivered at the

Carter Centre's Global Development Initiative Advisory Group Meeting, June 6, 1996, http://jagan.org/articles3b.htm.

RESOURCE GUIDE

Suggested Readings

Peake, L., and A. Trotz. *Gender, Ethnicity and Place: Women and Identities in Guyana*. London: Routledge, 1999.

Rodney, Walter. *A History of the Guyanese Working People, 1881–1905*. Baltimore: Johns Hopkins University Press, 1981.

Thomas, Clive Y. *The Rise of the Authoritarian State in Peripheral Societies*. New York: Monthly Review Press, 1984.

Williams, B. *Stains on My Name, War in My Veins: Guyana and the Politics of Cultural Struggle*. Durham, NC: Duke University Press, 1991.

Web Sites

Caribbean Association for Feminist Research and Action, www.cafra.org/English_CAFRA/links.htm.

Guyana: Academic Research Resources, http://lanic.utexas.edu/la/sa/guyana/.

Guyana News and Information, www.guyana.org/GuyNews/guynews.html.

NGO Forum: Association of Guyanese NGOs, www.sdnp.org.gy/ngo.

Sustainable Development Networking Programme Guyana, www.sdnp.org.gy/guylink.html.

Organizations

Help and Shelter
Homestretch Avenue
Georgetown, Guyana
Phone: (592) 2-254731
Fax: (592) 2-278353
Email: hands@sdnp.org.gy

Red Thread Women's Development Project
173 Charlotte Street
Lacytown, Georgetown, Guyana
Phone: (592) 2-73952
Fax: (592) 2-74232
Email: thread@sdnp.org.gy

Women Across Differences
Homestretch Avenue
Georgetown, Guyana

Phone: (592) 2-73974
Email: wad@sdnp.org.gy

Women's Affairs Bureau
Ministry of Labour
Water and Cornhill Streets
Georgetown, Guyana
Phone: (592) 2-54362
Fax: (592) 2-73497

SELECTED BIBLIOGRAPHY

Central Intelligence Agency (CIA). *The World Factbook*. 2000. www.cia.gov/cia/publications/factbook/geos/gy/html. Accessed August 6, 2002.

Committee on the Elimination of All Forms of Discrimination Against Women (CEDAW). *Concluding Observations: Guyana*. U.N. Doc./A/49/38, paras. 88–125. 1994. www1.umn.edu/humanrts/cedaw/cedaw-Guyana.htm. Accessed August 30, 2001.

Committee on the Elimination of All Forms of Discrimination Against Women (CEDAW). *Press Release, WOM/1297*. July 18, 2001. www.un.org/NewsPress/docs/2001/wom1297.doc.htm. Accessed August 25, 2002.

Constitution of the Cooperative Republic of Guyana Act 1980 (20 February 1980) with 1996 Reforms. www.georgetown.edu/LatAmeriPolitical/Constitutions/Guyana/guyana96/html. Accessed June 19, 2002.

Denny, Patrick. "The 'Sexual Orientation' Bill Going Back to Parliament." *Stabroek News*. January 25, 2001. www.landofsixpeoples.com.gynewsjs.htm.

"Guyana in Line for Major Support in HIV/AIDS Fight." *Stabroek News*. July 10, 2001. www.landofsixpeoples.com.gynewsjs.htm.

International Labor Organization (ILO). *The Shops Act—Guyana Policy for Women*. June 2002. http://ilo.org/public/english/employment/gems/eeo/law/guyana/eeo sag.htm. Accessed August 6, 2002.

International Women's Rights Action Watch (IWRAW). *Country Reports: Guyana*. 1999. www.igc,/org/iwraw/publications/countries/guyana.html. Accessed June 18, 2002.

Jagan, Cheddi. *Guyana's National Development Strategy*. Speech delivered at the Carter Centre's Global Development Initiative Advisory Group Meeting, June 6, 1996. http://jagan.org/articles3b.htm. Accessed February 2, 2001.

Ministry of Finance (Guyana), National Development Secretariat. "Women, Gender and Development." *National Development Strategy* (April 17, 1996). www.guyana.org/NDS/chap21.htm. Accessed February 18, 2001.

Ministry of Labour (Guyana). *Statement on the Situation Affecting Women in Guyana*. www.guyana.org/woman_situation.htm. Accessed June 18, 2002.

Nettles, Kimberley. "Homework: An Examination of the Sexual Division of Labor in the Urban Households of the East Indian and African Guyanese." *Journal of Comparative Family Studies* 26, no. 3 (1995).

Pan American Health Organization (PAHO). *Guyana*. 1999. www.paho.org/prflguy.htm. Accessed August 10, 2002.

Red Thread Women's Development Programme. *Women Researching Women: Methodology Report and Research Projects on the Study of Domestic Violence and Repro-*

ductive Health in Guyana. Georgetown, Guyana: Inter-American Development Bank, 2000. www.sndp.org.gy/hands/wom_surv.htm. Accessed June 26, 2002.

Trotz, D. Alissa, and Linda Peake. "Work, Family and Organising: An Overview of the Contemporary Economic, Social and Political Roles of Women in Guyana." *Social and Economic Studies* 50, no. 2 (2002).

U.S. Department of State, Bureau of Democracy, Human Rights and Labor. *Country Reports on Human Rights Practices 2001: Guyana*. March 4, 2002. www.state.gov/g/drl/rls/hrrpt/2001/wha/8337.htm. Accessed August 8, 2002.

U.S. Department of State, Bureau of Western Hemisphere Affairs. *Background Notes: Guyana*. April 2001. www.cia.gov/r/pa/ei/bgn/1984.htm. Accessed August 14, 2002.

13

HONDURAS

Julie Cupples

PROFILE OF HONDURAS

Honduras is located in Central America, between Guatemala to the northwest and El Salvador and Nicaragua to the south. It has a total land area of 112,087 square kilometers (43,277 square miles). Its land is mostly mountainous in the interior with narrow coastal plains. It has a very short Pacific coastline and a long Caribbean coastline that includes the largely uninhabited Mosquito Coast. Honduras gained its independence from Spain as a member of the Central American Federation in 1821 and became an independent republic in 1839. The postindependence period was marked by frequent civil wars and changes of presidents. For most of the twentieth century Honduras was seen as a classic "banana republic" because its economy has been dependent on the export of bananas and its political life has been manipulated by foreign-owned fruit companies. The foreign control of Honduras's most important export crop and the late development of coffee for export meant that, unlike the other Central American republics, Honduras did not develop a strong national elite tied to agricultural exports.

Its twentieth-century history was marked by long periods of

military rule and ongoing political intervention by banana companies. In 1945 Honduras was the most economically vulnerable of the Central American countries, dominated by foreign banana plantations in the north and an underdeveloped agrarian sector in the rest of the country.[1] The 1950s were marked by incipient economic modernization, ongoing political infighting by elites, and the growing militancy of the labor movement. This situation created a political vacuum that was filled by the military, which quickly became the most important political institution in the country.

The political and economic situation deteriorated markedly in the 1980s, which were dominated by increasing unemployment and poverty and by the institution of a reign of terror. Although a civilian government was elected in 1982, the military continued to play a significant role in Honduran politics, and the 1980s were marked by frequent abuses of human rights, including the disappearance and torture of social activists.

At this stage, Honduras played an important strategic military role for the United States. The United States built a number of military bases in the country, and between 1980 and 1989 provided more than $4 billion in military aid.[2] Honduras became a base for the U.S.-sponsored Nicaraguan Contras who were fighting against Nicaragua's revolutionary government, and provided military support to the Salvadoran government's counterinsurgency campaign.

Honduras suffers from deep-seated economic inequality: the poorest 20 percent of the population controls 1.6 percent of national wealth while the richest 20 percent controls 61.8 percent.[3] It is estimated that more than half of the population lives below the national poverty line, and malnutrition, poor housing, crime, and infant diseases are extremely common.[4] Economic inequalities increased in the 1990s as a result of the implementation of structural adjustment policies and attempts to service Honduras's large external debt. The fragility of Honduras's economic and social system was revealed in 1998 when the country was hit by Hurricane Mitch, which left more than 5,000 dead and 1.5 million homeless. The hurricane also destroyed 70 percent of the country's harvests and caused $3.79 billion worth of damage. Small producers, street children, and female-headed households were hardest hit by the disaster. Before Honduras had a chance to recover from the hurricane, further losses were caused in 1999 by floods, and entire harvests were wiped out in 2001 by droughts.

The current president and chief of state is Ricardo Maduro of the National Party. Maduro came to power after elections in November 2001, promising to crack down on crime. The Honduran National Congress has 128 members, elected for a four-year term by proportional representation.

Honduras has a population of 6.3 million, 50.3 percent of whom are women.[5] Mestizos (people of mixed indigenous and European descent) make up 90 percent of the population; 7 percent are Amerindians; 2 percent are black; and 1 percent is white. The population is predominantly

Roman Catholic (97 percent), with a growing minority of Protestants. As of 2001, life expectancy is 63.2 years for men and 68.8 years for women.[6] The infant mortality rate is 33 deaths per 1,000 live births, and the reported maternal mortality rate is 110 per 100,000 births. The total fertility (average number of births per woman) is 4.3, down from 7.1 in the early 1970s.[7]

OVERVIEW OF WOMEN'S ISSUES

In many ways, Honduras continues to be a conservative, Catholic, and *machista* society in which daily life is shaped by its historical dependence on foreign powers and economic vulnerability. Machismo is a cult of virility expressed through the dominance of men over women.

The restructuring of the Honduran economy since the 1980s and the implementation of structural adjustment by the Callejas government in the 1990s had a devastating impact on women. Structural adjustment consists of economic measures, implemented under the guidance of the International Monetary Fund (IMF), that are designed to cut public spending and boost exports in order to stabilize the economy and enable governments to keep up with debt service payments. Under structural adjustment, many women have seen their roles as caregivers made more difficult by the rise in prices of basic goods and services and declining access to health and education. Whereas some employment for women has been generated by the establishment of free trade zones and *maquila* industries, in which textiles or other goods are assembled for export, these jobs tend to have an emphasis on low-paid, nonunionized labor. Many Honduran women are sole income earners in their households, owing to the fluidity of family structures and widespread lack of paternal responsibility.

Women also continue to be deeply affected by the legacies of militarization that are demonstrated in Honduras's exceptionally high levels of violent crime and HIV infection. Violence permeates society on many levels, in street crime and also in the high levels of domestic violence experienced by many Honduran women.

According to the United Nations, the gender gap is being closed in Honduras as a result of women's greater access to education and their growing participation in the labor market.[8] Legal changes favoring women's rights have also made significant progress in recent years, but moves toward greater gender equality are hampered by economic hardship, cultural understandings of gender roles, and a lack of awareness of their rights among many women. These factors perpetuate the subordinate position of women in spite of legislative advances. Honduran women continue to do the bulk of child care and domestic work, and many suffer from poor health and malnutrition. The research and campaigning conducted by the women's movement have brought about favorable changes in government policies.

EDUCATION

Opportunities and Literacy

Literacy rates and school enrollment rates have improved significantly, with both rates for women now surpassing those of men. Women now have better rates of enrollment at primary, secondary and tertiary levels. The female adult literacy rate for women was 85 percent, compared with 78 percent for men.[9] However, more than a half of all Honduran women receive less than three years of formal education, a figure that increases to two-thirds in rural areas. While Honduran women and girls have a primary school enrollment rate of 78 percent, only 35 percent go on to secondary education and only 12 percent to tertiary.[10]

EMPLOYMENT AND ECONOMICS

Job/Career Opportunities and Working Conditions

The Honduran population is still predominately rural and engaged in agriculture, although there has been quite significant rural–urban migration since the 1980s. The mountainous territory and the concentration of the most fertile land in banana plantations mean there is considerable pressure on fertile cultivable land. While traditional crops such as coffee and sugar, and nontraditional ones such as seafood, melons and pineapples, have become more important agricultural exports, the Honduran economy is still dependent on bananas, which generate a third of all export earnings. Female participation in and contribution to the economy tend not to be accurately reflected in official statistics because of methodological and conceptual limitations that fail to recognize the contribution of women's unpaid labor and reproductive work to the national economy.[11]

Woman at work on a traditional loom in Honduras. Photo © TRIP/I. Genut.

Employment opportunities for women are restricted by Honduras's dependent positioning within the global economy and by cultural understandings of masculinity and femininity. There is little paid work for women outside of the urban centers. Though women make up 34.8 percent of the economically active population (EAP) in urban areas, they make up only 17 percent of the EAP in rural areas.[12]

When women do engage in paid employment, they tend to be concentrated in the feminized sectors of the economy, such as domestic service, export assembly factories (*maquilas*) or prostitution. Paid work in agriculture for women is concentrated in coffee harvesting and banana packing. While many Honduran women lack formal employment, most of them are economically active in the informal sector (and are therefore excluded from official statistics). Many Honduran women work in subsistence agriculture, prepare and sell tortillas and other food items, make clothes, and take in washing and ironing. The Honduran armed forces and the National Police accepted female recruits for the first time in 1998.

Honduras is the largest *maquila* producer in Central America and the second largest in Latin America and the Caribbean. Seventy percent of all *maquila* workers are women, working mostly in textiles and clothing assembly in the north of the country.[13] Women are now migrating in greater numbers than men in search of employment in export processing factories. This rapid migration has pushed up rents and daily living costs in areas close to the manufacturing plants, and many migrants are forced to live in overpriced and crowded conditions. Others, who are unable to meet the high rents charged by landlords, set up home on unserviced land where they live with the constant threat of eviction, flooding, or illness from unsanitary living conditions.[14] Working conditions in the Honduras *maquilas* tend to be characterized by low wages, job insecurity, sexual harassment of women, and the systematic repression of trade unions. Only 10 percent of Honduran *maquila* workers are unionized.[15] A number of *maquila* companies have closed as a result of the economic slowdown in the United States, and this has resulted in job losses for a number of women.

The number of women working in prostitution increased significantly in the 1980s as a result of the establishment of U.S. military bases.[16] There are large numbers of Honduran women working in prostitution, with more than 4,000 prostitutes in San Pedro Sula alone.[17] The pressure on women to engage in prostitution as a source of income increased after Hurricane Mitch. A number of temporary shelters in rural areas reported coerced prostitution, particularly among teenage girls.

Pay

Not only is access to employment more limited for many women, but women's average earnings are only 35 percent of men's.[18] Most *maquila* workers earn between $62 and $182 a month.[19] *Maquila* salaries are higher than the legal minimum wage, but they are still insufficient to meet basic needs. While male and female unemployment were negatively affected by Hurricane Mitch, research conducted after the hurricane suggested that women seemed to be reentering the waged labor market much more slowly than men. Women working in the banana industry had yet to return to work, while men had received paid employment in construction and rehabilitation activities.

Support for Mothers/Caretakers

Maternal Leave and Daycare

The minority of Honduran women who are fortunate enough to have paid work in the formal sector of the economy are entitled to ten weeks' maternity leave at full pay. A third of this is provided by the employer and two thirds by the government.[20] Honduran women who work in the informal sector do not have these benefits.

There is little formal public or private daycare provision for children in Honduras. Most working women rely on extended family and kinship networks, and children tend to be cared for by grandmothers, older siblings, or other family members. In many cases, children are left alone to fend for themselves, either at home or on the streets. Many women combine work and childcare by engaging in productive activities from their home or on the street.

Inheritance and Property Rights

Under the Agrarian Reform Law of 1984, women were not permitted to own land unless they were widowed and had no male children. This provision was changed in the Agricultural Modernization Law passed in 1993, but landownership patterns are slow to change. When women do gain access to land, it is often the least fertile land or is taken over by male family members once it becomes productive.[21]

Social/Government Programs and Welfare

In response to the first United Nations Decade for Women, the Honduran government established a National Policy for Women in 1989 to comply with international commitments. In the 1990s the government created the Honduran Social Investment Fund in recognition of the hardships caused by structural adjustment. This fund created a number of employment projects and provided welfare payments for single mothers.[22] Since then other government initiatives aimed at achieving greater gender equality have been passed that aim at the agricultural sector and the environment (Policy of Gender Equity in Agriculture [Política de Equidad de Género en el Agro] and the Policy of Gender Equity in Natural Resources and the Environment [Política de Equidad de Género en Recursos Naturales y Ambiente]). As a result of Hurricane Mitch, the Honduran government is committed to increasing poverty-related spending by implementing the IMF- and World Bank-approved Poverty Reduction Strategy Paper (PRSP). It is too early to say to what extent women will benefit from this initiative. Spending on health and education continues to be inadequate, and Honduras is still a profoundly unequal society. Economic inequalities—in particular the wealth of the minority and the poverty of the majority—are one of the major obstacles to sustainable development in Honduras.

FAMILY AND SEXUALITY

Gender Roles

Boys and girls in Honduras are socialized early into differentiated gender roles. Men are expected to head the family household and to be family providers, while women are to become mothers who are self-sacrificing and who pass spiritual values on to children. Men are also expected to father many children and there is little social stigma attached to men's premarital and extramarital sexual relationships. Honduran culture, as in much of Latin America, tends to place a strong emphasis on notions of romantic love, which for many young women become conflated with eroticism and lead to early sexual relationships. Women take on the bulk of child care and reproductive work, but their productive activities tend to be undervalued. Constructions of appropriate masculinities and femininities are informed by both machismo and its female counterpart *marianismo*, based on the cult of the Virgin Mary.[23] *Marianismo* is based on notions of self-sacrificing motherhood, and consequently motherhood is elevated to a high status. The coexistence of *marianismo* and machismo means that paradoxically, while women are respected as mothers, they are degraded as women.

Marriage

Despite the influence of the Catholic Church and the circulation of discourses that idealize Eurocentric understandings of marriage and the family, formal marriage is uncommon in Honduras. Women often refer to the man with whom they have had sexual relations as *mi esposo* or (my husband) without being legally married. Both informal cohabitation and serial polygamy are widespread and socially accepted. Nonresidential unions, where couples do not live together, also are fairly commonplace. Sexual relations and pregnancy tend to start at an early age, and many Honduran women are single mothers. According to official statistics, more than 20 percent of Honduran households are headed by women.[24] Forty percent of urban households are headed by females, and 16 percent of rural-area households are female headed.[25] Formal marriage, more common in rural areas than in urban areas, appears to reduce the chance of separation.[26]

As in other Central American countries, lack of paternal responsibility is endemic in Honduras. It is common for Honduran men to have polygamous unions and children with several different partners. There is a high level of abandonment of women by men, particularly in urban areas, which is often at least partly the result of economic constraints, such as the need to migrate to another part of the country in search of work, and was intensified after Hurricane Mitch. Some statistics suggest that female-headed households in Honduras increased after Mitch from 20 percent to over 50 percent, as a result of male desertion and migration.[27]

Reproduction

Sex Education

The spread of the HIV/AIDS epidemic along with Honduras's high rate of teenage pregnancy has forced sex education onto the development and political agenda. A number of local and international NGOs, such as the Red Cross and the Honduran Association of Family Planning, are promoting sex education to young people. Formal sex education was not part of the education system in Honduras until 1999, when it was made compulsory as part of the Special Law on HIV/AIDS passed in that year. However, the amount and quality of sex education received by Honduran girls is still patchy because religious prejudices and church-led concerns that sex education promotes the use of contraception mean that teachers are often reluctant to fully implement the law.

Contraception and Abortion

While U.N. statistics suggest that Honduran women have contraception use rates of 50 percent, it is believed that official contraceptive use rates are misleading as a result of the high rate of de facto partnerships such as common marriages, which are not accounted for in statistics.[28]

Honduran women display a high awareness of contraception, yet the use rates are very low.[29] This gap between knowledge and use can be explained by dominant cultural patterns and expressions of masculinity. Many men do not like their wife or partner to use contraception because of the cult of virility that encourages men to father as many children as possible. There is a deep-seated cultural resistance to the use of condoms. Many Honduran men say "they would rather be shot in the head than have a relationship using condoms."[30]

Fertility rates, while still relatively high, have fallen sharply since the 1970s. There are, however, quite significant rural–urban differences. Rural women continue to have higher rates of fertility, possibly as a result of both more entrenched cultural attitudes regarding the desirability of large families and lack of access to contraceptive services.

Abortion has always been illegal in Honduras and the "right to life" is enshrined in the Honduran Constitution. While the Honduran Penal Code makes no exception to the prohibition of abortion, the Code of Medical Ethics allows therapeutic abortions if the life of the pregnant woman is in danger. The Honduran government amended the Penal Code in 1996 so that the penalties were increased for those found seeking or performing abortion, and abortion was redefined as the murder of a human being during pregnancy. Women convicted of having had an abortion face between three and six years' imprisonment, and health professionals or others found performing abortions face between three and eight years.[31]

Though legal abortion is basically outlawed, clandestine abortion is common. No accurate figures exist as a result of an unwillingness to report an illegal abortion, but many low-income women turn to unqualified abortion providers, and botched abortions undoubtedly contribute to the high rate of maternal mortality in Honduras.

Teenage Pregnancy

Sexual relations tend to start at an early age in Honduras, and many women have their first child at around 15 or 16 years of age. The extent of teenage pregnancy is a significant contributing factor to the existence of nonresidential and de facto unions, since many women give birth before they have formed a family unit with the child's father.

HEALTH

Health Care Access

There is no doubt that the Honduran health system is both inadequate and overburdened, and the lack of access to decent health care impacts more severely on women because of their caregiving roles. The health of many women is compromised by multiple births with inadequate spacing and continuous breast-feeding.[32] While the Honduran government recognizes that women's health is one of the major problem areas, there is a lack of financial resources to make visible improvements. Per capita government expenditure on health in Honduras is only $210, compared with $4180 in the United States.[33] Many pregnant women have no access to prenatal care, and only one-fifth of Honduran women aged between 30 and 60 have received Pap smears.[34] Only 40 percent of all Hondurans have access to essential drugs, and 25 percent of all children under age five are underweight as a result of malnutrition.[35] Malnutrition leads to ill health, and consequently Honduran women spend much time caring for sick children without access to essential foods and medicines. Honduran women often present at health centers with high levels of malnutrition, vitamin A and iodine deficiency, and anemia.

In Honduran households, most cooking is done indoors over open wood fires. Consequently, women who are responsible for cooking in the household are exposed to smoke for long periods. This exposure creates high levels of respiratory illness in both women and children.

Diseases and Disorders

AIDS

The northern Honduran city of San Pedro Sula has become known as the AIDS capital of Latin America. Honduran HIV/AIDS infection rates far outstrip those of other Latin American countries, including Brazil, and the disease has virtually reached the scale of an epidemic: 1.92 percent of the Honduran population is suffering from AIDS, compared with 0.2 percent in Nicaragua and 0.57 percent in Brazil.[36] More than half of all Central American AIDS cases are reported in Honduras, and three-quarters of these are in the city of San Pedro Sula.[37] Factors that have contributed to the rate of HIV infection in Honduras include the establishment of foreign military bases on Honduran territory, the extent of the sex trade, lack of paternal responsibility, serial polygamy, early sexual relations, and the cultural resistance to condom use.

Unlike many other Latin American countries, where HIV infection spreads largely through drug use and sex between men, AIDS in Honduras is an overwhelmingly heterosexual disease, with roughly equal numbers of men and women infected. AIDS has recently overtaken maternal mortality as the main cause of death in women of reproductive age.[38] The extent of the epidemic—it is not uncommon to meet Hondurans with full-blown AIDS in their late teens or early twenties—is severely testing the already overstretched health system. Hondurans suffering from AIDS are extremely unlikely to gain access to essential antiretroviral drugs that can help to control the disease. Despite these distressing circumstances, AIDS is slow to occupy a high priority on the political agenda.

POLITICS AND LAW

Suffrage

Honduras was the last country in Latin America to grant women the vote. Universal suffrage was not granted until January 25, 1955. To mark this event, January 25 has been designated a national holiday in celebration of women's rights.

Political Participation

Women are represented at all levels of government but not in large numbers. Increasing numbers of women are occupying public office, and while Honduras has never had a female president, women have occupied the position of vice president, have headed several ministries, and have held several mayoralties, including that of the capital, Tegucigalpa. In the last elections in 2001, women gained 9.4 percent of the total seats in the National Congress, and women occupy a third of all ministerial positions.[39] A woman ran for president for the first time in the 1997 elections. Nora Gunera de Melgar stood as the presidential candidate for the National Party but was beaten by the Liberal candidate, Carlos Roberto Flores.

Women's Rights

Feminist Movements

Women's organizations have been in existence since the 1920s, when the Women's Cultural Society (Sociedad Cultural Feminina Hondureña) was formed and began to fight for women's rights. One leader, Visitación Padilla, actively opposed U.S. intervention in Honduras in 1924. Women also played important roles in the development of the labor movement, which became particularly active in the 1950s. According to Gladys Lanza, a trade union activist, women were extremely active in the 1954 national strike of banana workers. They controlled the entrances to towns and markets, closed the bars so men could not get drunk, and ran collective kitchens. Despite the extent of this logistical work, there was not a single woman on the strike committee.[40] In the 1950s women also became active in the fight for women's suffrage.

In the 1970s a number of rural organizations were formed, including the Federación Hondureña de Mujeres Campesinas (FEHMUC, Honduran Federation of Rural Women), which grew rapidly over the next few years. The Consejo de Desarrollo Integral de Mujeres Campesinas (CODIMCA, Council for the Integrated Development of Rural Women) was formed in the late 1980s.

Women's movements became politically important in the 1980s when many Honduran women began to organize in response to the political disappearances and human rights abuses. A number of organizations were formed, including the Comité de Familiares Detenidos y Desaparecidos en Honduras (COFADEH, Committee of Families of the Detained and Disappeared in Honduras) and the Comité Hondureño de Mujeres por la Paz "Visitación Padilla" (Visitación Padilla Honduran Committee of Women for Peace). Both of these groups were objects of political repression by the police and the military.

In 1986, a group of professional women formed a research institute known as Centro de Estudios de la Mujer—Honduras (CEM—H, Honduran Center for Women's Studies). Its main aim is to use a feminist analysis to contribute to the democratization of Honduran society. It operates a documentation center, conducts research on Honduran women, and offers support and counseling to battered women. In 1989, the Colectiva de Mujeres Hondureñas (CODEMUH, Honduran Women's Collective), a feminist NGO aimed at popular education for women, was formed. Since 1995 a number of women's organizations have united to develop a national campaign against domestic violence.

Women were politically active after Hurricane Mitch on a number of levels. They were involved in rescue operations, in administering first aid to survivors, in collecting and distributing food and clothing, in organizing and supplying emergency shelters, in formulating housing projects and rebuilding communities and infrastructure.[41] The hurricane caused widespread hardship and devastation, but paradoxically enhanced the visibility of women in the political sphere. Some Honduran women stated that their public involvement in disaster response teams increased their self-esteem and is strengthening political demands for greater gender equality.[42]

Lesbian Rights

As in other parts of Central and South America, lesbians and gays in Honduras face tremendous discrimination as a result of machismo and institutionalized homophobia. This discrimination has intensified as a result of the AIDS epidemic, and in 1985 the army and police forcibly closed all the gay bars and clubs in the country.[43] Although not many Honduran lesbians are out in their families and workplaces, there are a number of politically visible gay and lesbian groups in existence that seek to increase AIDS/HIV awareness and to create safe social spaces. These include the Gay Community of San Pedro Sula (Comunidad Gay de San Pedro Sula), the Colectivo Violeta (Violet Collective), and Prisma (Prism). Lesbian organizing is still in its infancy. A lesbian discussion group made up of women from Prisma has formed, and is focusing on issues of concern to lesbians, such as violence, lesbian communities and building links with organizations in other countries.[44]

Military Service

Between 1982 and 1994, all able-bodied men aged between 18 and 30 were required to complete two years of compulsory military service. Young men were often forcibly recruited in their workplaces, restaurants, and bars, or on public transport. Constitutional reforms in 1994 brought an end to compulsory military service, which was widely seen by human rights groups as a key step in ending the militarization of Honduras. The Honduran armed forces and the National Police accepted female recruits for the first time in 1998.

RELIGION AND SPIRITUALITY

Although religious freedom and the separation of church and state are guaranteed by the Honduran Constitution, the Catholic Church remains a powerful political institution that has a considerable impact on gender roles, relations, and identities. Saints play an important role in people's sense of spirituality, and many Honduran homes contains statues or pictures of the Virgin Mary or the Virgin of Suyapa, the patron saint of Honduras, who is believed to have special powers. The *marianismo* paradigm means that gender imagery pertaining to the Madonna is potent and informs local discourses of good mothering. Consequently, women are considered to be spiritually superior to men.

Many Hondurans have linked religious faith with political organization, particularly in rural areas, where Christian base communities use the Bible to analyze political and social conditions.

VIOLENCE

Domestic Violence and Sexual Assault

There is no doubt that the physical, sexual, and psychological abuse of women by men is an endemic social problem in Honduras. A study by the Pan American Health Organization reported that 60 percent of Honduran women have been victims of domestic violence, and the U.N. Population Fund estimates that 80 percent of women experience domestic violence.[45] The Municipality of Comayagua reported that domestic violence accounted for 60 percent of all police cases in 1996.[46] The main causes of domestic violence are seen to lie in cultural understandings of male dominance, alcoholism, and the tendency to see domestic violence as a private problem rather than a social or human rights issue. There has been a tendency among Honduran women to tolerate domestic violence as a normal part of gender relations. These attitudes are beginning to change, and in 1997 the National Congress approved the Law Against Domestic Violence after substantial campaigning on the issue by the women's movement. Organizations like CEM—H and CODEMUH have for many years been providing shelter and counseling for battered women, conducting research on domestic violence, and lobbying for changes in the law. In 1998, the year after the law came into force, cases of domestic violence reported in the capital, Tegucigalpa, quintupled.[47]

After Hurricane Mitch, many NGOs reported increases in domestic violence and sexual assault. Familial and sexual violence appeared to increase during the reconstruction phase.[48] While there is no doubt that Mitch substantially increased violence against women, for some women it provided them with an opportunity to leave violent partners.

Trafficking in Women and Children

The problem of child trafficking and the sexual exploitation of minors is a serious problem in Honduras, but no government policy has been created to address this. Hundreds of Honduran children go missing every year, and there has been mounting evidence that they are being sold into illegal adoption, or being used as prostitutes or drug dealers. A scandal uncovered in the early 1990s revealed the widespread illegal adoption of Honduran children by North American couples. Children were abducted and housed in one of 22 *casas de engorde* (literally "fattening houses") in the capital before being illegally adopted in the United States. Senior members of the government and some 60 lawyers were found to be implicated in the adoption racket, as well as a number of National Registry employees who were selling false identity cards and birth certificates.[49]

More recently, it was revealed that up to 250 Honduran children were being used as street dealers by drug trafficking gangs in Canada.[50] Many more have ended up working as prostitutes in Guatemala, El Salvador, Mexico, and the United States. Girls as young as 13 and 14 have been offered jobs and scholarships by organized crime groups and are then sold to brothels in neighboring countries.[51] In 2002, raids on a number of bars in Fort Worth, Texas, discovered 60 Honduran women and children working as prostitutes for sex traffickers. The Honduran women and girls were forced to work as prostitutes in order to pay off up to $10,000 in smuggling fees.[52] This case has forced the issue of human trafficking onto the national political agenda.

War and Military Repression

Honduras continues to be a militarized and violent society, although the political situation has improved considerably since the early 1990s. While the military has played an important role in national politics for a long time, the situation in Honduras worsened in the 1980s as a result of civil wars in neighboring Central American countries that led to the establishment of U.S. military bases, sustained U.S. military aid, and the abuse of human rights by the Honduran government, which included extrajudicial killings and kidnappings.

The Honduran government did not create an official and effective human rights monitoring body until 1992, when the Comisión Nacional para la Protección de Derechos Humanos (CONAPRODEH, National Commission for the Protection of Human Rights) was created by the Callejas government. Until then this role was carried out by the Comité de Defensa de Derechos Humanos (CODEH, Committee for the Defense of Human Rights) and COFADEH. These organizations protested against the militarization of Honduran society and the concomitant human rights abuses, and both involved significant participation by women.

Many Honduran families were displaced during the 1980s by the expanding U.S. military presence and by the Nicaraguan Contras. This military policy particularly affected thousands of small-scale coffee producers living close to the Nicaraguan border.

While the government has tried to limit its role, the military is still one of the most powerful political institutions in Honduras. It owns several major companies and has a monopoly on arms sales.[53]

OUTLOOK FOR THE TWENTY-FIRST CENTURY

Honduras's problems—in particular its economic crisis, its legacy of militarization, and its foreign debt—were overwhelming before Hurricane Mitch. Women especially have been struggling to cope in the context of structural adjustment policies that have taken a toll on living standards. Since Mitch, all of these problems have been intensified because the hurricane set development back a number of decades. The loss of harvests and the destruction of infrastructure further undermined Honduras's internal food security and its ability to service its foreign debt. Some advances have been made in education, and while its provision remains inadequate, the gender gap has been closed. Legislation to promote gender equality has been strengthened, and as a result of lobbying by the women's movement, attitudes toward domestic violence are beginning to change. However, significant challenges lie ahead. The domestic security situation continues to worsen; there are serious inadequacies in the protection of both maternal and child health; and women's lives continue to be devastated by constant environmental uncertainty, the lack of employment opportunities, high fertility, and the AIDS epidemic.

NOTES

1. Richard Lapper, *Honduras: State for Sale* (London: Latin America Bureau, 1984).

2. Economic Intelligence Unit, *Country Profile 1994–5* (London: The Economist, 1994), quoted in Jo Rowlands, *Questioning Empowerment: Working with Women in Honduras* (Oxford: OXFAM, 1997).

3. UNDP, *Human Development Report 2001: Making New Technologies Work for Human Development* (New York: Oxford University Press, 2001).

4. Ibid.

5. Ibid.; Blanca Estela Dole, "Honduras: Un movimiento de mujeres naciente," in *Movimiento de mujeres en Centroamérica*, edited by Ana Leticia Aguilar, Blanca Dole Duran, Morena Herrera, Sofia Montenegro, Lorena Camacho, and Lorena Flores (Managua, Nicaragua: Programa Regional La Corriente, 1997).

6. UNDP, *Human Development Report*, 2001.

7. Ibid.

8. UNDP, *Informe sobre el desarrollo humano en Honduras: Por un crecimiento con equidad*, 2001, available at www.undp.un.hn/idh2000.htm.

9. UNICEF, *UNICEF Statistics—Honduras*, 2002. www.unicef.org/statis/Country_1Page74.htm.

10. Dole, 1997; Rowlands, 1997.

11. Dole, 1997.

12. Patricia L. Delaney and Elizabeth Schrader, *Gender and Post-Disaster Reconstruction: The Case of Hurricane Mitch in Honduras and Nicaragua* (Washington, DC: LCSPG/LAC Gender Team, The World Bank, 2000).

13. Christian Aid, *Honduras: Background Information*, 2002, www.christian-aid.org.uk/caweek02/infopacks/honduras.htm.

14. CODEMUH, *El camino de la maquila en Honduras* (San Pedro Sula: Colectiva de Mujeres Hondureñas, 1998), available at http://codemuh.globalnet.hn/hnmaquila.htm.

15. Jane Turner, "Strategies for Change in the Maquila Sector," *Central America Report* (spring 1998): 13.

16. Cynthia Enloe, *Maneuvers: The International Politics of Militarizing Women's Lives* (Berkeley: University of California Press, 2000).

17. Douglas Farah, "Rampant AIDS Overwhelms Medical Facilities in Honduras," *Washington Post*, 31 May 1997.

18. UNDP, *Human Development Report*, 2001.

19. Ana María Ferrer, *Honduras: Nuevo gobierno, viejos problemas por resolver* (Instituto del Tercer Mundo, 2002), Available at www.socwatch.org.uy/2002/esp/informespercent20nacionales/honduras2002_esp.htm.

20. United Nations, *The World's Women 2000: Trends and Statistics* (New York: United Nations, 2000).

21. Rowlands, 1997.

22. Ibid.

23. Evelyn P. Stevens, "Marianismo: The Other Face of Machismo in Latin America," in *Female and Male in Latin America*, edited by A. Pescatello (Pittsburgh, PA: University of Pittsburgh Press, 1973), 89–101.

24. Dole, 1997.

25. Sarah Bradshaw, "Female-Headed Households in Honduras," *Third World Planning Review* 17, no. 2 (1995): 117–131.

26. Ibid.

27. Delaney and Schrader, 2000.

28. UNDP, *Human Development Report*, 2001; Rowlands, 1997.

29. Dole, 1997.

30. Dan Thomas, "Honduras Uses Soccer . . . ," Reuters, 1998, www.ilga.org.Information/americas/cleaning_up_the_streets.htm.

31. Population Division, United Nations Secretariat, *World Abortion Policies*, www.un.org/esa/populationpublications/abt/fabt.htm.

32. Susan Fleck, *Extension "Woman-to-Woman" in Honduras: Experiences of a FAO Project*, Food and Agriculture Organization of the United Nations, Sustainable Development Department, 1996. www.fao.org/WAICENT/FAOINFO/SUSTDEV/Wpdirect/Wpan0005.htm.

33. UNDP, *Human Development Report*, 2001.

34. *Washington Times*, "National Holiday Honors Women," *Washington Times*, 24 March 2000. www.internationalspecialreports.com/theamericas/00/honduras/19.htm.

35. UNDP, *Human Development Report*, 2001.

36. Ibid.

37. Secretariat of Health, *HIV/AIDS Communication Strategy*, 2001, http://pcs.aed.

org/HIVAIDSHonduras.htm; Douglas Farah, "Rampant AIDS Overwhelms Medical Facilities in Honduras," *Washington Post*, 31 May 1997.

38. Secretariat of Health, 2001.

39. UNDP, *Human Development Report*, 2001.

40. HHRC, *Honduras: A People's Struggle for Change* (London: Honduras Human Rights Committee, n.d.).

41. Mirta Kennedy, *Civic Participation of Women in the Reconstruction Process* (Tegucigalpa: Centro de Estudios de la Mujer—Honduras, 1999), available at www.oneworldaction.org/download/CEMHwomenrecon.rtf.

42. Delaney and Schrader, 2000.

43. Juan Pablo Ordóñez and Richard Elliot, *Cleaning Up the Streets: Human Rights Violations in Colombia and Honduras* (Brussels: ILGA, 1999), available at www.ilga.org/Information/americas/cleaning_up_the_streets.htm.

44. Ibid.

45. US Department of State, *Country Reports . . . Honduras* (Washington, DC: U.S. Department of State, 2001).

46. Municipality of Comayagua, Regional Commission for Human Rights, and the Ministry of Health, *Communities Working to End Domestic Violence in Honduras* (Comayagua: Municipality of Comayagua, 2000), available at www.unifem.undp.org/beijing+5/pressroom/honduraspro.pdf.

47. CEM—H, *National Report . . . Women* (Tegucigalpa: CEM—H, 2000).

48. Delaney and Schrader, 2000.

49. Ana Ramírez, "Honduras: The Traffic in Children," *Central America Report* 55 (Autumn 1992): 5.

50. Thelma Mejía, "Minors Smuggled into Canada to Deal Drugs," *Interpress Service*, 1999, www.casa-alianza.org/EN/human-rights/other-exploit/990407.shtm.

51. Donna M. Hughes, Laura Joy Sporcic, Nadine Z. Mendelsohn, and Vanessa Chirgwin, *The Factbook on Global Sexual Exploitation* (Amherst, MA: Coalition Against Trafficking in Women, 1999), available at www.catwinternational.org/fb/Honduras.html.

52. Catherine Elton, "Coyotes' Offer Evil Deal," *Washington Times*, 23 July 2002.

53. Christian Aid, 2002.

RESOURCE GUIDE

Suggested Reading

Alvarado, Elvia. *Don't Be Afraid, Gringo: A Honduran Woman Speaks from the Heart*. New York: HarperCollins, 1987. A useful autobiography of a female *campesina* and labor leader in Honduras.

Central America Report. A biannual publication of the U.K. solidarity movement that usually contains an article on Honduras. For subscription information, contact CAR, Red Rose Club, 129 Seven Sisters Rd, London, N7 7QG, UK.

Delaney, Patricia L., and Elizabeth Schrader. *Gender and Post-Disaster Reconstruction: The Case of Hurricane Mitch in Honduras and Nicaragua*. Washington DC: LCSPG/LAC Gender Team, The World Bank, 2000. A report commissioned by the World Bank that looks at the gender dimensions of Hurricane Mitch in Honduras and Nicaragua.

De Mejía, Alba. "Demanding Women's Rights in the Shadow of the Military." In *Compañeras: Voices from the Latin American Women's Movement*, edited by G.

Küppers. London: Latin America Bureau, 1994. Based on an interview with a member of Visitación Padilla Committee of Women for Peace on how women have fought against the militarization of Honduras.

Green, Duncan. *Hidden Lives: Voices of Children in Latin America and the Caribbean*. London: Latin America Bureau, 1998. This book explores the lives of children in Honduras, Nicaragua, Brazil, Jamaica, Peru, and Colombia, based on interviews with children, teachers, and welfare workers.

Norsworthy, Kent, and Tom Barry. *Inside Honduras*. London: Latin America Bureau, 1994. This book provides an overview of politics, the military, the economy, and the environment in Honduras, but does not explicitly consider the gendered dimensions of these processes.

Rowlands, Jo. *Questioning Empowerment: Working with Women in Honduras*. Oxford: OXFAM, 1997. This book focuses on two development projects in Honduras and assesses the extent to which the women involved were empowered as a result of their experiences. It also examines the various meanings attached to the concept of empowerment.

Video

Elvia: The Fight for Land and Liberty. 27 min, PBS, 1988. This film tells the story of the landless poor through the life of Elvia Alvarado, a 49-year-old activist.

Web Sites

Colectivo de Mujeres Hondureñas (Collective of Honduran Women), http://codemuh.global.net.
It contains information in English and Spanish on their work and publications.

Latin American Network Information Center (LANIC), Honduras, http://lanic.utexas.edu/la/ca/honduras/
One of the Latin American pages operated by the University of Texas, this site contains links to a wealth of Honduran media and organizations.

United Nations Development Programme, Honduras, www.undp.un.hn/idh2000.htm
Online version of the 2001 development report on Honduras (in Spanish).

Organizations

Centro de Estudios de la Mujer—Honduras (CEM—H)
Apartado postal 3543
Tegucigalpa
Phone: 504-232-6310
Fax: 504-232-6301
Email: cemh@sdnhon.org.hn

CEM—H is a feminist NGO established in 1986 to promote women's rights through political organization, training, communication, research, and provision of services for women.

Colectiva de Mujeres Hondureñas (CODEMUH)
Barrio El Guayabal, 6ta Calle 2 Ave, N.E.
Casa 612
Choloma, Cortes
Apartado Postal 696
San Pedro Sula, Honduras
Phone: 504-669-1180
Email: codemuh@globalnet.hn

CODEMUH is a feminist organization aimed at the exchange of ideas and promotion of education. It focuses in particular on violence, sexuality, self-esteem, and friendship between women.

Colectivo Violeta
Apartado 4053
Tegucigalpa, Honduras
Phone: 504-237-6398
Email: alfredo@optinet.hn

A gay/lesbian organization working on AIDS awareness and ending discrimination toward gays and lesbians.

Comité Hondureño de Mujeres por la Paz "Visitación Padilla"
Apartado postal 1796
Tegucigalpa, Honduras
Phone: 504-38-3704
Fax: 504-38-3704

Created in 1984, this organization has lobbied extensively against the abuse of human rights and the militarization of Honduran society. It promotes women's rights and is working toward ending violence against women.

Federación Hondureña de Mujeres Campesinas (FEHMUC)
Apartado Postal 804
Tegucigalpa, Honduras
Phone: 504-37-0613

The Honduran Federation of Rural Women provides economic and financial support and training in health issues for rural woman.

SELECTED BIBLIOGRAPHY

Bradshaw, Sarah. "Female-Headed Households in Honduras." *Third World Planning Review* 17, no. 2 (1995): 117–31.

Centro de Estudios de la Mujer—Honduras (CEM—H) *National Report on Gender Violence Against Women*. Tegucigalpa: CEM—H, 2000.

Christian Aid. *Honduras: Background Information*. 2002. www.christian-aid.org.uk/caweek02/infopacks/honduras.htm.

Delaney, Patricia L., and Elizabeth Schrader. *Gender and Post-Disaster Reconstruction: The Case of Hurricane Mitch in Honduras and Nicaragua*. Washington DC: LCSPG/LAC Gender Team, The World Bank, 2000.

Economic Intelligence Unit. *Country Profile 1994–5: Honduras, Nicaragua*. London: The Economist, 1994.

Elton, Catherine. " 'Coyotes' Offer Evil Deal." *Washington Times*, 23 July 2002.

Enloe, Cynthia. *Maneuvers: The International Politics of Militarizing Women's Lives*. Berkeley: University of California Press, 2000.

Farah, Douglas. "Rampant AIDS Overwhelms Medical Facilities in Honduras." *Washington Post*, 31 May 1997.

Fleck, Susan. *"Extension 'Woman-to-Woman' in Honduras: Experiences of a FAO Project*. Food and Agriculture Organization of the United Nations, Sustainable Development Department, 1996. www.fao.org/WAICENT/FAOINFO/SUSTDEV/Wpdirect/Wpan0005.htm.

Honduras Human Rights Committee (HHRC). *Honduras: A People's Struggle for Change*. London: HHRC, n.d.

Hughes, Donna M., Laura Joy Sporcic, Nadine Z. Mendelsohn, and Vanessa Chirgwin. *The Factbook on Global Sexual Exploitation*. Amherst, MA: Coalition Against Trafficking in Women, 1999. Available at www.catwinternational.org/fb/Honduras.html.

International Labour Organisation (ILO). "IPEC Action Against Child Trafficking." *World of Work* 41 (2001). Available at www.ilo.org/public/english/bureau/inf/magazine/41/traffic.htm.

Kennedy, Mirta. *Civic Participation of Women in the Reconstruction Process*. Tegucigalpa: CEM–H, 1999. Available at www.oneworldaction.org/download/CEMHwomenrecon.rtf.

Lapper, Richard. *Honduras: State for Sale*. London: Latin America Bureau, 1984.

Mejía, Thelma. "Minors Smuggled into Canada to Deal Drugs." Interpress Service. www.casa-alianza.org/EN/human-rights/other-exploit/990407.shtm.

Municipality of Comayagua, Regional Commission for Human Rights, and the Ministry of Health. *Communities Working to End Domestic Violence in Honduras*. Comayagua: Municipality of Comayagua, 2000. Available at www.unifem.undp.org/beijing+5/pressroom/honduraspro.pdf.

"National holiday honors women." *Washington Times*, 24 March 2000. www.internationalspecialreports.com/theamericas/00/honduras/19.htm.

Ordóñez, Juan Pablo, and Richard Elliot. *Cleaning Up the Streets: Human Rights Violations in Colombia and Honduras*. Brussels: ILGA, 1999. Available at www.ilga.org/Information/americas/cleaning_up_the_streets.htm.

Population Division, United Nations Secretariat. *World Abortion Policies*. 1999. www.un.org/esa/population/publications/abt/fabt.htm.

Ramírez, Ana. "Honduras: The Traffic in Children." *Central America Report* 55 (autumn 1992): 5.

Rowlands, Jo. *Questioning Empowerment: Working with Women in Honduras*. Oxford: OXFAM, 1997.

Secretariat of Health. *HIV/AIDS Communication Strategy*. 2001. http://pcs.aed.org/HIVAIDSHonduras.htm.

Stevens, Evelyn P. "Marianismo: The Other Face of Machismo in Latin America." In *Female and Male in Latin America*, edited by A. Pescatello. Pittsburgh, PA: University of Pittsburgh Press, 1973.

Thomas, Dan. "Honduras Uses Soccer in War Against AIDS." Reuters. 1998. www.aegis.com/news/re/1998/RE980110.htm.

Turner, Jane. "Strategies for Change in the Maquila Sector." *Central America Report* (spring 1998): 13.

United Nations. *The World's Women 2000: Trends and Statistics*. New York: United Nations, 2000.

United Nations Development Programme (UNDP). *Human Development Report 2001: Making New Technologies Work for Human Development.* New York: Oxford University Press, 2001.

United Nations Children's Fund (UNICEF). *UNICEF Statistics—Honduras.* 2002. www.unicef.org/statis/Country_1Page74.htm.

U.S. Department of State. *Country Reports on Human Rights Practices: Honduras.* Washington, DC: U.S. Department of State, 2001. Available at www.state.gov/g/drl/rls/hrrpt/2000/wha/801.htm.

Spanish Bibliography

Colectiva de Mujeres Hondureñas (CODEMUH). *El camino de la maquila en Honduras.* San Pedro Sula: CODEMUH, 1998. Available at http://codemuh.globalnet.hn/hnmaquila.htm.

Dole, Blanca Estela. "Honduras: Un movimiento de mujeres naciente." In *Movimiento de Mujeres en Centroamérica,* edited by Ana Leticia Aguilar, Blanca Dole Duran, Morena Herrera, Sofia Montenegro, Lorena Camacho, and Lorena Flores. Managua, Nicaragua: Programa Regional La Corriente, 1997.

Ferrer, Ana María. *Honduras: Nuevo gobierno, viejos problemas por resolver.* Montevideo, Uruguay: Instituto del Tercer Mundo, 2002. Available at www.socwatch.org.uy/2002/esp/informespercent20nacionales/honduras2002_esp.htm.

United Nations Development Programme (UNDP). *Informe sobre el desarrollo humano Honduras: Por un crecimiento con equidad.* 2001. Available at www.undp.un.hn/idh2000.htm.

14

NICARAGUA

Florence E. Babb

PROFILE OF NICARAGUA

Located in the middle of Central America, between Honduras to the north and Costa Rica to the south, Nicaragua is about the size of the state of Iowa, and its terrain ranges from tropical coast to mountainous areas and forest in the interior. Known as "the land of lakes and volcanoes" and rich in resources, the country has suffered a series of natural disasters through its history, most recently Hurricane Mitch in 1998. The population has grown to nearly 5 million, most of whom are Spanish-speaking; indigenous groups and African-Nicaraguan Creoles make up significant numbers in the Atlantic coast region, where English as well as indigenous languages are spoken. Nicaragua has the dubious distinction of being one of the poorest countries in the Western Hemisphere, second only to Haiti, and in recent years has contended with harsh austerity programs intended to stabilize the economy. As elsewhere, women and children, along with nonelite groups in general, have borne a disproportionate burden of the social and economic cost of such programs.

The Pacific area of western Nicaragua, which was colonized by the Spanish in the sixteenth century, is the most heavily pop-

ulated, and its residents are generally referred to as mestizos, Spanish speakers of mixed European and Indian descent. British rule in the Atlantic coast region applied to diverse indigenous groups as well as to those who came from Africa under conditions of slavery. Nicaragua gained its independence as a nation in 1838 and has struggled to achieve political stability since that time. The colonial cities of León and Granada vied for power during the nineteenth century as Liberals and Conservatives represented the interests of merchants and professionals on the one side, and the landed aristocracy and rural workers on the other. In 1852, the young city of Managua was declared the capital in order to quell the rivalry. A few years later, the American adventurer William Walker declared himself president of the country until he was routed in 1857. Through the end of the nineteenth century the Liberals and Conservatives were still in contention, and again U.S. intervention altered the course of Nicaraguan history. The U.S. Marines occupied the country, with only a brief departure, between 1912 and 1933. By the time of their formal withdrawal, the Marines had trained the National Guard, which subdued a national uprising led by Augusto César Sandino. Between 1936 and 1979, the Somoza family controlled the country under a repressive dictatorship.

In 1979, Nicaragua received wide international attention when the Sandinista Revolution successfully uprooted the 43-year Somoza family dictatorship and brought about a process of political, economic, and social transformation. Among the vast changes undertaken were land reform and the redistribution of such key resources as national industry, health care, and education, all of which brought significant benefits to women. The positive gains of the revolution were slowed, however, as a result of the Contra war (a national conflict that the United States had a hand in promoting), which endured through much of the 1980s. A democratic election in 1990 saw the removal of the Sandinistas from leadership, though their party, the Frente Sandinista de Liberación Nacional (FSLN; Sandinista National Liberation Front) remained one of the two strongest contenders in subsequent national elections in 1996 and 2001. Moreover, the current mayor of Managua, who holds an elected position second in importance to that of the president, is a member of the FSLN.

A coalition of opposition parties, the Unidad Nacional de Oposición (UNO; United National Opposition), elected the nation's first woman president, Violeta Barrios de Chamorro, in 1990, and in the two most recent elections, Liberal Party candidates gained power. The hallmark of these more moderate governments has been to dismantle reforms brought about by the revolutionary government, to introduce measures to control high inflation, and to develop a more competitive market economy. But rising unemployment, reduced social services, diminished health care, and lower levels of education are some of the adverse effects of rolling back state support and relying on the market, an orientation known as neoliberalism. Women have often been the first to lose jobs, and they have had to struggle to maintain their families in the face of harsh conditions and minimal state support.[1]

Recent data from Nicaragua show that the infant mortality rate (children under one year) is 39 per 1,000 live births.[2] Maternal mortality has been estimated at around 155 per 100,000 live births, as a result of high fertility and other risk factors.[3] The total fertility rate is 4.4, and life expectancy at birth is 68 years.[4]

OVERVIEW OF WOMEN'S ISSUES

Few nations have undergone such fundamental changes as Nicaragua has since the early 1900s, and this has had a pronounced effect on women. Statistics tracing these changes during the past century are not always reliable or even available, but a number of observers have described the dramatic shifts in political, economic, legal, and social conditions that bear on women's lives. Some of the changes and their gendered effects as the country moved from dictatorship to revolutionary government, and then to the neoliberal governments of the 1990s, will be discussed here. The difficult current situation will be shown to have an impact on many areas, including education, employment, family and sexuality, health, politics and law, religion, violence, and the outlook for the future. Although Nicaraguan women are challenged by their social conditions, they are addressing gender inequalities and other issues in innovative ways through social mobilization. Diverse groups of women in nongovernmental organizations (NGOs) and social movements are seeking to redress past and present problems in Nicaragua.[5]

EDUCATION

Opportunities

Education was the privilege of the elite through much of Nicaraguan history, especially for men, but during the years of the Sandinista government (1979–1990) it became a high priority for the general population. A literacy campaign in 1980 was said to have reduced the national illiteracy rate from 50 percent to 12 percent by sending brigades into the countryside.[6] Schooling was made a universal right, and new school materials were produced as part of a broad effort to create a more egalitarian society. After 1990, however, those efforts were deemed counter to traditional social values, and the United States Agency for International Development put millions of dollars into the production and distribution of socially conservative curriculum materials that would reestablish values shaken by the revolutionary government. Among the traditional values that were brought back into the classroom were those reflecting conventional nuclear families—images showed women as wives and mothers in the home, while men were shown in professions or relaxing after work at home—which in fact were not those typical of a majority of working-class and poor Nicaraguans.

In contrast to the popular participation of teachers in the 1980s through the National Association of Educators of Nicaragua, the 1990s saw the exclusion of teachers from policymaking and the hierarchical emphasis of the Ministry of Education. Teachers' strikes protested the Ministry's centralized authority, low pay, and the new materials and new costs to families for children's education. University students also have protested the changes in government policy since 1990, particularly as governments have not respected the constitutional guarantee that 6 percent of the national budget would go to public education.

Literacy

Female literacy currently stands at 67 percent, compared to male literacy of 65 percent. While 85 percent of girls and 82 percent of boys are enrolled in primary school, far fewer attend secondary school and university.[7] Women's education has been linked specifically to their level of self-esteem and their ability to mobilize resources for themselves and their families; regardless of their social class, women as mothers are linked closely to infant and child survival, and their education is instrumental in improving family well-being.

EMPLOYMENT AND ECONOMICS

Throughout its history, Nicaragua has depended on agriculture as the mainstay of its economy. Yet, from the time of the Somoza dictatorship through the Sandinista government and the neoliberal governments of the 1990s, the Nicaraguan economy has undergone substantial changes.[8] By the 1950s, the agro-export economy that had developed in the nineteenth century was turned toward cotton production, and less food was produced for the nation's consumption. The Somoza family fortune grew exponentially while per capita income was below average even by Latin American standards.[9] Harsh conditions in the rural areas drew many to the cities, especially Managua, where employment was scarce and many residents lived in crowded dwellings. An earthquake in 1972 had destroyed much of Managua, and the Somoza government's lack of concern for rebuilding the urban area contributed to a climate of hardship and despair that prompted the revolutionary insurrection a few years later.

In 1994, 30 percent of Nicaraguan women 15 or older were counted in the economically active population.[10] Also in 1994, the economically active population was distributed by gender and sector as follows: in agriculture, 8 percent of women and 52 percent of men; in industry, 14 percent of women and 17 percent of men; and in services, 79 percent of women and 31 percent of men.[11] To put these figures in perspective, it is instructive to note that recent documentation puts the gross national product (GNP) per capita in Nicaragua at U.S.$410, the annual rate of inflation at 68 percent, and the percentage of the population living on less than a dollar per day at a startling 44 percent.[12]

Job/Career Opportunities

Since the 1990s, the gendered effects of changing economic policies may be seen, particularly for women in formal and informal work in Managua's small industries and commerce. Take the example of a study of four urban cooperatives that were a legacy of the Sandinista period, when more egalitarian work organization was favored.[13] These cooperatives included seamstresses, bakers, welders, and jewelry artisans, traditional as well as nontraditional areas of women's employment. Like rural cooperatives, urban cooperatives benefited from the state's distribution of low-cost materials and its assistance in marketing their products. Over time, however, the dramatic transition in the national political economy produced equally dramatic changes in small industries. The cooperatives that survived during this period needed to refashion themselves along the lines of the micro enterprises preferred by neoliberal governments. While the changes were often fairly superficial, they signaled a willingness to compete under radically new economic terms. Unfortunately, while the post-Sandinista leadership declared its support for small and energetic businesses, the challenge to become competitive was nearly insurmountable for the majority insofar as the support they formerly received was eliminated and incentives went instead to larger national industries and multinationals. The welders disbanded and the seamstresses sold their shop and worked out of their homes; the bakers saw a vast decline in production and sales, and the artisans struggled to obtain loans that would keep them afloat as a reorganized micro enterprise.

The author of a study of small industries in Nicaragua, then the director of an NGO assisting micro enterprises, reported that of the 10,000 or 11,000 small industries in the country in 1985, only about 5,000 survived by 1992.[14] He noted that women were experiencing higher rates of failure than men, since they were located in the more vulnerable areas, such as garment production. As many women in cooperatives and other formal employment lost ground after 1990, they turned to a precarious livelihood in the urban informal sector. There, small-scale production and commerce, often based in the home, do not benefit from protective legislation or the representation of a trade union. Earnings are typically quite low, and there is great diversity within the informal sector in terms of economic activities and the individuals who perform them.[15] The preponderance of women in the sector is particularly striking, as are the added burdens they experience as a result of the gender division of labor.[16]

The urban informal sector has for some time included about half of Managua's economically active population, but there has been significant growth in recent years. Under the Sandinista government, some informal workers were "formalized" when they joined cooperatives and state enterprises. The early efforts became more aggressive, and those who did not leave informal work were scrutinized, licensed, and taxed, and consumers were cautioned to report instances of hoarding and speculation. Yet while a few informal sector merchants were growing rich, the majority subsisted at best.[17] Since 1990, neoliberal measures have had the effect of promoting the growth of a small, formal economic elite, on the one hand, and a vast and impoverished, if often hidden, informal workforce, on the other. The free market has driven many Nicaraguans to the economic margins, and a disproportionate number of them are women.

Social/Government Programs

When the Sandinistas rose to power, they quickly brought about a series of economic reforms that served to redistribute access to the country's resources. A broad-based agrarian reform was the first in Latin America to include women as beneficiaries on the same basis as men, at least on paper. Rural women were encouraged to participate in agricultural and artisan cooperatives, although men sometimes expressed resentment at their new activities.[18] In the urban areas, both women and men benefited from a restructuring of urban employment, and women heads of households were especially aided by a safety net of price subsidies and a guarantee of basic foods available to all. Although inspired by the example of socialist societies and desiring to bring about a thoroughgoing process of state-led change, the Sandinistas tolerated private enterprise in the new "mixed economy." The development project was stalled, however, when the Contra war required that attention and resources be turned toward defense. By the late 1980s, the Sandinistas sought to control hyperinflation by cutting back the state sector, which meant rising unemployment and poverty conditions. The loss of the FSLN in the 1990 elections has been attributed to weariness of war and a desire to see an end to a U.S. embargo that had been imposed as an economic sanction. There was a notable gender gap in the vote, with more women supporting the opposition candidate, Violeta Chamorro, whose campaign emphasized the family, peace, and economic security.[19]

The Sandinista government introduced economic measures mandated by the International Monetary Fund that were intended to stabilize the economy but were crushing for the majority of Nicaraguans and particularly for women.[20] Further cuts in the public sector and a major devaluation of the currency were meant to favor the market economy, but the new measures produced unemployment and underemployment nearing 60 percent, and the prices of newly available goods were out of reach for all but a small elite. A more conservative social ideology encouraged working women to return home, where many set up small, informal enterprises that were destined to fail in neighborhoods saturated with front-room stores.[21]

FAMILY AND SEXUALITY

Historically, the family as an institution has been highly important in Nicaragua, often influencing politics and society at the national level. Today, families can take many forms and a large number are female-headed, without an adult male present, or extended, with several generations living under a single roof. Poverty and a culture of machismo can account for both arrangements, since unemployment besets many households and contributes to instability, and expectations that women will serve as the principal caregivers for families are widespread. In a small but evidently growing number of cases, young adults remain single or form same-sex relationships. Whatever the living arrangements, families of origin tend to be of enduring importance in a society that reveres motherhood and depends on personal networks of support as a coping strategy. This is not to overlook

Nicaraguan women extract milk for their newborns at a milk bank in the women's state hospital in Managua, July 1998. The Nicaraguan legislature had passed a law requiring all Nicaraguan mothers to breastfeed their babies until they were six months of age. AP/Wide World Photos.

the serious problems of domestic violence, paternal abandonment, and conflict that are present in many families.

Gender Roles

The frequently invoked injunction that women belong *en la casa* (in the house) and men *en la calle* (in the street) reinforces traditional gender roles. The media and advertising lend weight to conservative thinking, even when that thinking finds little basis in reality, as in notions of conventional middle-class nuclear families with the husband out working and the wife remaining home with the children. Although sexism in advertising was banned during the revolutionary period, it is back in force as women are once again linked to the products men desire to consume—most notoriously in ads for beer and luxury goods. Representations of women as homemakers and sex objects serve to trivialize women's lives, which are often difficult and far more complex than their portrayal in popular culture.[22]

Marriage

In Nicaragua, families are more often than not headed by women, and even when men are present, couples generally do not marry legally but cohabit informally. While the statistics are inconsistent, most studies show a large majority of female-headed families in both the rural (82 percent) and the urban (65 percent) areas.[23] This means that substantial burdens are carried by women, who have lower incomes than men, experience higher unemployment, and suffer the consequences when they have inadequate resources to provide for their children. Under the Sandinistas more jobs were created and a basic food basket, comprised of basic food items such as flour and sugar, along with health care and education, was provided at little or no cost.

The reversals in policy in the 1990s have meant that women must try to provide what the state no longer offers, and when they fail, they often have nowhere to turn. The FSLN made paternal responsibility a moral principle that was not always effective but did give women a right to seek legal redress. In a society in which even stable unions were rarely sanctified by marriage and many men had relationships with more than one woman, the Sandinistas recognized that gender inequality in heterosexual unions needed to be addressed by empowering women and calling on men to assume responsibility for their children. Following their electoral loss in 1990, the social ideology shifted in a significantly more conservative direction, and regardless of their marital and work status, women were encouraged to devote themselves first and foremost to home and family — giving men more latitude to pursue their own interests.

Reproduction

Despite some rethinking of gender roles during the Sandinista period, reproductive rights were a tense subject due to beliefs that dominated the Catholic Church as well as resistance within the popular sector and the FSLN itself.[24] Since 1990, there has been more criticism of the revolutionary government's unwillingness to engage in discussion of reproductive rights and of the widespread double standard of Nicaraguans who often sought contraception and abortion, but would not make access to reproductive control a matter of public importance.[25] Recently, more conservative governments have tried to take another step back by establishing even more barriers to gender equality and reproductive choice. Overall, Nicaraguan women have an average of 4.6 children, the highest rate in Latin America.[26]

Contraception and Abortion

The 1990s saw the emergence of a more autonomous women's movement that was less dependent on party politics and raised issues deemed too politically sensitive in the past.[27] A women's health network was established, and a number of women's health clinics gave special attention to contraception and reproductive health. Abortion has remained illegal in

Nicaragua, and although it is performed—often self-induced and contributing to high maternal mortality—it is a clandestine procedure. Feminists discuss the subject but need to avoid any appearance of advocating wide availability of abortion. Indeed, under President Arnoldo Alemán, elected in 1996, social and moral intolerance was manifested most clearly in the fast erosion of women's rights. His administration sought to replace the Nicaraguan Institute of Women with the Ministry of the Family, representing a turn toward the political Right, and to eliminate the legal right to therapeutic abortion in the case of rape or incest. Therefore, activists have been forced to establish alternative centers to provide medical, legal, and other services no longer provided by the Ministry of Health.

Teen Pregnancy

Despite the morally conservative climate, in Managua teenage girls have a 30 percent probability of becoming pregnant, and among teenagers in the rural area the figure is 41 percent.

HEALTH

In a nation in which only 78 percent of the population has access to safe water and 85 percent has access to adequate sanitation in their homes,[28] health problems are notably widespread. Among women, maternal mortality, or death associated with pregnancy, is a major problem due to poor living conditions, health conditions, and lack of access to care and services. According to one estimate, of 900,000 women between 14 and 45 (childbearing age), almost 200,000 will become pregnant in a given year, and many of them will be at risk.[29]

The Pan American Health Organization maintains a close connection with Nicaragua through its Women, Health, and Development division. This serves to reinforce the importance of women's health and to help establish priorities within the Ministry of Health. Officials from international agencies as well as women's movement activists have attended conferences on women's health at the regional and continental levels, and this has served to direct greater attention to improving women's condition. Networking and exchanging ideas at such conferences has led to international funding and other support to feminist groups and NGOs in the country.[30]

Health Care Access

The Sandinista government made health care a high priority, and to that end health brigades and immunization campaigns were initiated that brought about better conditions for many Nicaraguans. The number of health clinics in the country rose from 43 in 1978 to 532 in 1983, and polio and other infectious diseases were nearly eradicated.[31] But cutbacks in state services and privatization of health care in the 1990s have meant worsening levels of health for a majority. Close to 3,000 health workers left the public sector because of low wages, lack of equipment and supplies, and government incentives to turn to the private sector. Some hospitals saw the departure of up to 25 percent of health workers. What little sex education there was in the schools has been curtailed in the conservative moral climate. At the same time, the heavy sexualization of women's bodies in the media suggests a double standard.[32]

Diseases and Disorders

The health of average Nicaraguans deteriorated in the 1990s, as health workers attempted to meet the needs of an ever-growing population. Dengue fever, malaria, and cholera were on the rise, and infant mortality, which had declined in the 1980s, also was increasing.[33] At times like these, when resources are scarce, research shows that women are frequently the ones to suffer most.[34] They are at a disadvantage in the labor force as well as in the home, and they tend to meet other family members' needs before their own. This contributes to their malnutrition and general lack of well-being, and has further implications for their families and the society. Difficulties are felt disproportionately by poor, less-educated, and rural women.

Since contraception is not widely available and public health services are of poor quality, women have more children and experience more complications. In addition, they are susceptible to cervical cancer and stress-related psychological problems. Not surprisingly, the women's movement in Nicaragua has made empowerment through better health education and services a fundamental objective, and a means to address broad concerns about overcoming gender inequality. The emphasis is on integral health for women—that is, the total well-being of women rather than the more usual, exclusive focus on maternal and reproductive health. Independent women's health centers served over 125,000 women in 1992 and had a positive influence on government policy—until Alemán's administration began dismantling programs directed to women.[35]

AIDS

By the early 1990s, AIDS was becoming better known as a health risk in Nicaragua, and international activists lent support to local men and women who sought to increase awareness through popular education. Although the community centers and NGOs did not identify publicly as gay organizations, their leadership was generally composed of lesbians and gay men who came together out of solidarity and found AIDS work to be a venue for an emergent movement. It is now known that gay organizing had its beginnings in the 1980s, but was suppressed within the Sandinista

Party and did not make a public appearance until several years later. Today, a number of groups have formed to address gay rights issues, including Nicaragua's repressive sodomy law that declares intimacy between members of the same sex to be scandalous and illegal. Gay pride is celebrated annually, and while many gay men and lesbians do not have the support of their families, self-esteem and satisfaction among those who depart from the heterosexual norm appear to be increasing.[36]

POLITICS AND LAW

Suffrage and Early Feminist Activism

Nicaraguan women's campaigns for suffrage began during the nineteenth century, and by the 1920s some women, mainly of the middle class, began to call themselves feminists. New research is bringing to light the vibrant feminism of the early decades of the twentieth century, which was later replaced by a nonfeminist pro-Somoza women's movement.[37] When women first exercised the right to vote, in 1957, the Somoza family received the credit. Although right-wing and paternalistic, the dictatorship government of the Partido Liberal Nacional (PLN, National Liberal Party) managed to garner the support of many women by espousing the cause of women's rights and by offering legal and social support in exchange for political loyalty. While middle-class women found new opportunities for gaining higher education and professional employment, working-class and poor women placed their hopes on the protection of the state. Of course, many other women were joining the opposition to the dictatorship during the years leading up to the Sandinista victory in 1979.

Political Participation and Women's Rights

Nicaragua has undergone two major political transitions since the mid-1970s. The first was the revolutionary upheaval that ended the Somoza dictatorship and introduced broad changes in political organization, based on popular participation in the political process and in the redistribution of resources. Democratic elections were held in 1984, when Daniel Ortega won the vote to retain leadership, and again in 1990, when he lost to Violeta Chamorro, ushering in the neoliberal era and the second major transition. Though the period has been a turbulent one, Nicaraguans appear to be committed to a democratic process and to be willing to make compromises in order to achieve national reconciliation.[38]

Under the Sandinistas, a new Constitution was approved in 1987 that gave women certain rights in the family and society for the first time. Women were consulted in the Constitution's formulation, and the result was the inclusion of ten articles specifically concerning women's rights. The Constitution established the right to equality of women and men, recognized both common-law and legal unions, and laid the groundwork for further legislation benefiting women. However, recent governments have sought to overturn certain gains of the revolutionary period. The Ministry of the Family was established in 1998 after the National Assembly passed a bill sponsored by the ruling Liberal Party that was intended to shore up traditional family values at a time when families were perceived to be in a state of chaos. The bill established nuclear families based on legal marriage and procreation as the single acceptable family form, and this has been reinforced in schoolbooks that are used throughout the country.[39]

Feminists were quick to condemn the Ministry of the Family as intended to confine women to domesticity and to disregard the reality of women's lives. They pointed out that the legislation sponsoring the Ministry violates articles of the Nicaraguan Constitution which recognize the legality of de facto unions, as well as international agreements on women's rights that the nation ratified, including the Convention on the Elimination of All Forms of Discrimination Against Women. Yet despite feminists' opposition to the Ministry, they have nonetheless sought opportunities to use the conservative government's orientation to their advantage by challenging some of the harsh effects of neoliberalism and machismo. Thus, they have called for the creation of more jobs and for more enforcement of paternal responsibility for children to contribute toward family stability. By drawing attention to problems faced by families, feminists are politicizing the private sphere.[40]

During the Sandinista period, women held more government positions than ever before, including 40 percent of the seats in the National Assembly, Nicaragua's Parliament. However, they held only a few high-level positions as ministers, and the nine members of the FSLN Directorate remained all male, despite the availability of women who had distinguished themselves as combatants in the revolution and possessed strong leadership abilities. The 1990 election, which resulted in the unseating of the FSLN to Violeta Barrios de Chamorro's coalition government, represented an abrupt political shift to the Right under the country's first woman president. Chamorro had used her status as the widow of a slain and celebrated opponent of the Somoza government, launching a campaign in which she appeared as a motherly symbol of national peace. Her term in office was successful in reconciling differences, but she also turned back gains made by women and other nonelite sectors. This process of rolling back earlier gains was deepened under the Alemán administration, which rivaled the Somoza dictatorship in its reputation for corruption and opportunism. It is too soon to say what the recently elected President Enrique Bolaños will do to stay or alter the course.

Women's Movements

The Sandinista revolution sparked the organization of the broad-based Asociación de Mujeres Nicaragüenses "Luisa Amanda Espinosa" (AMN-

LAE, Nicaraguan Women's Association "Luisa Amanda Espinosa") in recognition of the importance of women in supporting the FSLN government and in defending its interests. Women of the working class and popular sectors in particular were encouraged to participate and to form a commitment to revolutionary politics. Women's centers were founded to offer vocational, medical, and legal assistance, but when some women desired to embrace a more conscious feminism, they were reined in by the party. Therefore, after 1990, a more autonomous feminist movement emerged as an alternative to AMNLAE's party-based loyalty.[41]

What has been notable about the women's movement since the 1990s has been its diversity: it ranges from a small but influential intellectual current and a strong NGO presence to a popular base in a variety of women's organizations. This diversity has been both a strength and, at times, a cause for consternation because social class and other differences have been pronounced. Middle-class feminist collectives such as the Partido de la Izquierda Erótica (PIE, Party of the Erotic Left), and later the Malinches (named after the legendary Indian woman in Mexican history), along with such NGOs as CENZONTLE (named for a bird) and Mujer y Cambio (Women and Change), have taken the lead in theorizing women's position and formulating strategies for change. Women's health and legal clinics, including Servicios Integrales Mujer (Women's Integral Services) and Ixchen (named after a Mayan fertility goddess), have been established to meet immediate needs of the popular classes and also to enable women to become better informed on gender issues. In addition, the Central American University has offered one of the first gender studies programs in Central America, and Puntos de Encuentro (Meeting Points) offers courses to more diverse groups of women through what it calls Women's University, focusing especially on gender and economic development. Such differences in the women's movement, typified by the Malinches' vanguardist politics, on the one hand, and Puntos' strategy of appealing to a broad base of Nicaraguans (including men, youth, and people of different racial and class backgrounds), on the other, are still apparent at the beginning of the twenty-first century.

A number of women's groups came together to form the Comité Nacional de Feministas (CNF; National Feminist Committee) after a well-attended conference in 1992. The CNF experienced a rupture two years later over internal differences concerning orientation and leadership—marked also by differences of social class and education—but was reconstituted by a number of the former groups. Although there is sometimes competition for scarce resources, feminists continue to work together effectively through networks on a range of issues, notably domestic violence, health, and other matters that concern women's fundamental rights to personhood and citizenship. Nicaraguan women have become significant players in regional feminist politics, and Managua is now the location of the program office of the Central American feminist organization El Corriente (The Current).

Lesbian Rights

In the early 1990s lesbians and gay men organizing to identify common interests and concerns in Nicaragua were not publicly visible. AIDS activism in the late 1980s inspired about 50 gay and lesbian Sandinistas to come out in public for the first time during the tenth anniversary celebration of the revolution's victory. They wore black T-shirts with pink triangles as they marched together, empowering them for further political activity. In 1991, lesbians had another public and well-received "coming out" at the Festival of the 52 Percent in Managua, a pivotal weekend of feminist activity, when their organizations staffed a resource and information booth. Since then, a number of groups have formed, centers have opened, and magazines have begun publication. Each year, gay pride offers an opportunity for women and men to come together for panels and other events that are open to the public, devoted to increasing awareness and calling for "a sexuality free of prejudice."

However, the 1992 revision of the Penal Code included Law 150, which regulated sexual behavior and defined what was moral and legal in terms of procreation, so that nonprocreative and nonheterosexual sex was defined as immoral and illegal. Significantly, the call for justice and equality includes the private sphere as well as the public sphere, the integrity of the body and the person as well as of the society. Feminists, gay men, and lesbians are contributing in this way to the remaking of a national political culture of opposition.

RELIGION AND SPIRITUALITY

About 80 percent of Nicaraguans are at least nominally Roman Catholic and the rest of the population is largely Protestant, but religious beliefs and practices vary considerably on the basis of socioeconomic differences.[42] On the one side are those identified with the middle class and elite who have sought to uphold the traditional, hierarchical Catholic Church, and on the other are those, more commonly of the working class and poor, who have challenged official church practices and supported a Church of the Poor and liberation theology. The head of the Nicaraguan Catholic Church, Cardinal Miguel Obando y Bravo, had opposed the Somoza dictatorship but became a particularly strong opponent of the Sandinista revolutionary government. He remained influential in the 1990s as an outspoken and conservative voice, often supporting traditional cultural values and opposing movements for gender and sexual equality and reproductive rights.

Following the historic Latin American bishops' conference held in 1968 at Medellín, Colombia, where there was a call for ordinary people to make a "preferential option for the poor," Christian base communities (CEBs) were established as a popular organization in Nicaragua. The CEBs were active in supporting the Sandinista revolution and the FSLN government, and have remained committed to progressive, grassroots activity. Many devout Catholics became convinced that struggle was necessary to bring about justice, but like other popular organizations, this one became divided over political differences after 1990. Nevertheless, the CEBs—particularly women members, who make up the majority in the Nicaraguan popular church—continued to have an active presence in Managua.

Along with other mass organizations, CEBs have adopted an oppositional stance in relation to the state and have attempted to offer low-income Nicaraguans social services no longer provided by the government. A number of women involved in Managua's CEBs have organized neighborhood communal kitchens to provide meals and supplemental nutrition to pregnant and nursing women and young children.[43] Women in the more progressive Protestant traditions (which also include Christian fundamentalists, at the other end of the political spectrum) also have worked to bring about positive changes for women and their families. One well-known organization, the Council of Protestant Churches (Consejo de Iglesias Evangélicas Pro-Alianza, or CEPAD), assists in community development programs including some directed to women. To be sure, the powerful Catholic Church hierarchy often stands in the way of such initiatives—recently by supporting the state's conservatism and campaigning to strengthen the heterosexual nuclear family and to prohibit birth control and abortion. However, CEBs and CEPAD are religious-based organizations that have had some success as they involve women in developing and sharing critically needed resources.

VIOLENCE

The rising crime rate and gang activity in Managua, which clearly are related to the economic crisis and social disaffection, have made the capital city still less hospitable, especially for women and children. Although prostitution was made illegal under the Sandinistas and documentation of its occurrence remains scant, a growing number of women and girls (and, sometimes, young men) appear to have turned to this precarious means of gaining a livelihood, taking significant personal risks.

Domestic Violence

In recent years, the Nicaraguan women's movement has made domestic violence a key area of concern and activism. The government's Demography and Health Survey, which included interviews with more than 13,600 Nicaraguan women, found that one in three women had experienced sexual abuse or physical mistreatment.[44] Many more women suffer the emotional abuse of men who control their activities, threaten, or demean them. Increasing reports of domestic violence may be attributed to continued patterns of male dominance and to the women's movement's support of women who report domestic abuse, and there appears to be a correlation with worsening economic conditions as well.[45] An encouraging development is that several men's groups have begun to address the problem, including one group that is organized through the feminist NGO Puntos de Encuentro. In addition, special police stations devoted to addressing violence against women and children have been established in some parts of the country and have met a warm response.

The 1987 Constitution laid the groundwork for laws to criminalize violence against women: all citizens were guaranteed the right to physical, psychological, and moral integrity, and degrading behavior was declared a crime punishable by law. Soon after its implementation, a policy statement issued by the FSLN Directorate, known as the *Proclama*, was the first to officially recognize the problem of male violence against women.[46]

Rape/Sexual Assault

Nicaragua has confronted the problem of sexual abuse and violence from the neighborhood level to the national level, with varying results. The country was in shock when, in 1998, allegations were made against the former president and celebrated FSLN leader, Daniel Ortega, by his adopted stepdaughter, who charged that he had sexually abused her from the age of eleven through her adulthood. Until recently, Ortega was protected by parliamentary immunity and by a pact with President Alemán that shielded each political leader from close legal scrutiny. Nevertheless, public discussions of the highly visible case, along with popular education undertaken by feminists, have at the least demanded that serious attention be directed to what in the past was regarded as a private, family matter.[47]

The legal system underwent a reform in 1992 with the revision of the Penal Code, which served to reestablish traditional gender roles and impede women's rights. Furthermore, although rape became a public crime for the first time, under the new legal concept of rape a man could not be charged with raping his wife or common-law partner, and women who were raped and became pregnant were not allowed an abortion; rather, they were forced to have contact with the rapist if they wished to receive child support. Also, for the first time, legal punishment of doctors and midwives performing abortions was required.[48]

National Conflict

Given Nicaragua's politically tumultuous history, it is not surprising that there have long been appeals for an end to national conflict and a peaceful resolution of differences. Most recently, following the Sandinista victory in 1979, the Contra war divided members of society during the 1980s; the outcome of the 1990 election was determined in significant part by voters' desire for an end to civil war, forced military conscription, and social division. Since then, the nation has engaged in a discussion of reconciliation and sustainable human development.

Inspired by the United Nations' emphasis on peace, human rights, environment, and development, the ideal of a "culture of peace" has become part of a national discourse. Creating a culture of peace is the central concept of a new university program, the Martin Luther King Institute, whose director has praised feminists in Nicaragua for their political work against violence and for advocating ways of interacting with mutual respect. Notably, the Peace Studies program seeks to find ways to end many forms of violence in society, from warfare and armed conflict to domestic violence. It is innovative in its attention to the social and psychological foundations of violence and to social class and gender differences in the experience of violence. Poverty and gender inequality are thus recognized both as forms of violence and as serving to reproduce violence. If successful, a culture of peace would offer dignity, justice, and tolerance to a society weary from social conflict and factionalism. For women, it would offer democracy in the home as well as in the society. Clearly, Nicaragua is far from achieving such a social ideal, but what is striking is the level of seriousness and commitment in the discussion.

OUTLOOK FOR THE TWENTY-FIRST CENTURY

Nicaraguan history has been marked by conflict and abrupt transitions. The dramatically shifting experiences of recent decades have resulted in advances and setbacks for women. The revolutionary movement in the country that so rapidly ushered in reforms was just as quickly displaced following the 1990 elections. New economic measures and social policies have had a profound effect, presenting opportunities for a minority and growing hardship for a large majority of the population. Women, particularly among the working class and the poor, have had to absorb the harsh impact on families of rising unemployment, higher prices, and declining social services. Yet despite economic problems and a socially conservative climate, a growing women's movement has emerged as part of a wider political culture, working to safeguard gains made earlier and calling for a more inclusive, democratic nation. The neoliberal orientation of the 1990s favored a small elite, but the conditions are present for women of different social classes to join with men in asserting their claim for a more just society.

NOTES

1. For further discussion of Nicaraguan history through the contemporary period, see John A. Booth, *The End and the Beginning* (Boulder, CO: Westview Press, 1985); Rose J. Spalding, ed., *The Political Economy of Revolutionary Nicaragua* (Boulder, CO:

Westview Press, 1987); Thomas W. Walker, *Nicaragua* (Boulder, CO: Westview Press, 1986), *Revolution and Counterrevolution in Nicaragua* (Boulder, CO: Westview Press, 1991), and *Nicaragua Without Illusions* (Wilmington, DE: SR Books, 1997); David Close, *Nicaragua* (Boulder, CO: Lynne Rienner, 1999).

2. UNICEF, *The State of the World's Children*, 2001, http://www.unicef.org/sowc00/stat9.htm.

3. Pan American Health Organization (PAHO), *Health in the Americas*, http://www.paho.org/english/country.htm.

4. Ibid.

5. A number of authors have written on Nicaraguan women during the revolutionary era. Margaret Randall, *Sandino's Daughters* (Vancouver, BC: New Star Books, 1981), *Gathering Rage* (New York: Monthly Review Press, 1992), and *Sandino's Daughters Revisited* (New Brunswick, NJ: Rutgers University Press, 1994); Maxine Molyneux, "Mobilization Without Emancipation? Women's Interests, State, and Revolution," in *Transition and Development*, eds. Richard R. Fagen, Carmen Diane Deere, & José Lius Coraggio (New York: Monthly Review Press, 1986); Clara Marguialday, *Nicaragua, revolución y feminismo* (Managua, Nicaragua: Editorial Vanguardia, 1990); Helen Collinson et al., *Women & Revolution in Nicaragua* (London: Zed Books, 1990); Aria Julia Brenes, Ivania Lovo, Olga Luz Restrepo, Sylvia Soakes, & Flor de María Zuniga, *La mujer nicaragüense en los años 80* (Managua, Nicaragua: Nicaras, 1991); Norma Chinchilla, "Feminism, Revolution & Democratic Transitions in Nicaragua," in *The Women's Movement in Latin America*, 2nd ed., ed. Jane Jacquette (Boulder, CO: Westview Press, 1994). More recent work examines women's experience during the post-Sandinista decade of the 1990s: Florence E. Babb, *After Revolution* (Austin: UTXP, 2001); Lorraine Bayard de Volo, *Mothers of Heroes & Martyrs* (Baltimore: JHUP, 2001); Cynthia Chávez Metoyer, *Women & the State in Post-Sandinista Nicaragua* (Boulder, CO: Lynne Rienner, 2000).

6. Karen Kampwirth, "Social Policy," in *Nicaragua Without Illusions*, ed. Thomas W. Walker (Wilmington, DE: SR Books, 1997), 120.

7. UNICEF, 2000.

8. Mario Arana, "General Economic Policy," in *Nicaragua Without Illusions: Regime Transition and Structural Adjustment in the 1990s*, ed. Thomas W. Walker (Wilmington, DE: SR Books, 1997).

9. Thomas W. Walker, ed., *Nicaragua Without Illusions: Regime Transition and Structural Adjustment in the 1990s* (Wilmington, DE: SR Books, 1997), 4.

10. Women in Development Network (WIDNET), 2001, www.focusintl.com/statangl.htm.

11. Ibid.

12. UNICEF, 2000.

13. Babb, *After Revolution*, 2001.

14. Arie Laenen, *Dinámica y transformación de la pequeña industria en Nicaragua* (Amsterdam: CEDLA, 1988).

15. Amalia Chamorro, Mario Chávez, and Marcos Membreño, "El debate sobre el sector informal urbano en Nicaragua (1979–1989)," in *Informalidad urbana en Centroamérica: Evidencias e interrogantes*, eds. R. Menjívar Larín and J.P. Pérez Sáinz (Guatemala City: Fundación Friedrich Ebert, 1989).

16. Fundación Internacional para el Desafío Económico Global (FIDEG), *Seminario regional: El impacto de las políticas de ajuste sobre la mujer en Centroamérica y Panamá* (Managua, Nicaragua: FIDEG, 1991); J.P. Pérez Sáinz, and Menjívar Larín, "Central American Men and Women in the Urban Informal Sector," *Journal of Latin American Studies* 26 (1994): 431–47.

17. John G. Speer, "The Urban Informal Economic Sector," in *Nicaragua Without Illusions: Regime Transition and Structural Adjustment in the 1990s*, ed. Thomas W. Walker (Wilmington, DE: SR Books, 1997).

18. Laura J. Enríquez, *Harvesting Change* (Chapel Hill: UNCP, 1991), considers agrarian change broadly. Rural women's experience is discussed in Martha Luz Padilla, Clara Murguialday, and Ana Criquillon, "Impact of the Sandinista Agrarian Reform on Rural Women's Subordination," in *Rural Women & State Policy*, eds. Carmen Diane Deere and Magdalena León (Boulder, CO: Westview Press, 1987); and Paola Pérez Alemán, *Organización, identidad y cambio* (Managua: Nicaragua Editorial Vanguardia, 1990).

19. Karen Kampwirth, "The Mother of the Nicaraguans: Doña Violeta and the UNO's Gender Agenda," *Latin American Perspectives* 23, no. 1 (1996): 67–86.

20. Paola Pérez Alemán et al., *Industria, género y mujer en Nicaragua* (Managua, Nicaragua: Instituto Nicaragüense de la Mujer, 1989); Anna M. Fernández Poncela, "The Disruptions of Adjustment: Women in Nicaragua," *Latin American Perspectives* 23, no. 1 (1996): 49–66; Florence E. Babb, "After the Revolution: Neoliberal Policy and Gender in Nicaragua," *Latin American Perspectives* 23, no. 1 (1996): 27–48.

21. Babb, *After Revolution*, 2001.

22. David E. Whisnant, *Rascally Signs in Sacred Places: The Politics of Culture in Nicaragua* (Chapel Hill: University of North Carolina Press, 1995); Katherine Borland, "The India Bonita of Monimbó: The Politics of Ethnic Identity in the New Nicaragua," in *Beauty Queens on the Global Stage: Gender, Contexts, and Power*, eds. C. Ballerino Cohen, R. Wilk, and B. Stoeltje (New York: Routledge, 1994).

23. Fernández Poncela, 1996, 55.

24. Lois Wessel, "Reproductive Rights in Nicaragua: From the Sandinistas to the Government of Violeta Chamorro," *Feminist Studies* 17, no. 3 (1991): 537–50.

25. The use of contraception among "married women in age of procreation" was found to be 49 percent in 1990. UNICEF, 2000.

26. Julie Cupples, "Families and Feminism," *Hemisphere: A Magazine of the Americas* 9, no. 1 (1999): 22–25.

27. For discussion of the women's movement since 1990, see Florence Babb, "Women's Movements & Feminism," in *Cross-Cultural Research for Social Science*, eds. Carol R. Ember & Melvin Ember (Englewood Cliffs, NJ: Prentice-Hall, 1997), and *After Revolution* (2001); Bayard de Volo, 2001; Ana Criquillon, "The Nicaraguan Women's Movement," in *The New Politics of Survival*, ed. Minor Sinclair (New York: Monthly Review Press, 1995); Les Field, *The Grimace of Macho Ratón* (Durham, NC: DUP, 1999); Katherine Isbester, *Still Fighting* (Pittsburgh, PA: University of Pittsburgh Press, 2001); Karen Kampwirth, "Confronting Adversity with Experience," *Social Politics* (summer/fall 1996); 136–58, and "The Mother of the Nicaraguans," 1996; Gaby Küppers, *Compañeras* (London: Lat Am Bureau, 1994).

28. UNICEF, 2000. A study in 1985 found domestic violence to be widespread in all socioeconomic sectors, and to affect 44 percent of women between the ages of 25 and 34.

29. Ana Quiros, "Women's Health and Status in Nicaragua," *Women's International Network News* 17, no. 4 (1991): 27–28.

30. Christina Ewig, "The Strengths and Limits of the NGO Women's Movement Model," *Latin American Research Review* 34, no. 3 (1999): 75–102.

31. Kampwirth, "Social Policy," 124.

32. Quiros, 1991.

33. Kampwirth, "Social Policy," 125.

34. Rae Lesser Blumberg, "Income Under Female Versus Male Control: Hypotheses from a Theory of Gender Stratification and Data from the Third World," in *Gender, Family, and Economy: The Triple Overlap*, ed. Rae Lesser Blumberg (Newbury Park, CA: Sage, 1991).

35. Ewig, 1999.

36. Mary Bolt González, *Sencillamente diferentes* (Managua, Nicaragua: Centro Editorial de la Mujer, 1996). For accounts of gay men's and lesbians' experiences during the past two decades, see Roger N. Lancaster, "Subject Honor & Shame," *Ethnology* 27, no. 2 (1988): 111–25, and *Life Is Hard* (Berkeley: University of California Press, 1992); Ann Ferguson, "Lesbianism, Feminism, & Empowerment in Nicaragua," *Socialist Review* 21, no. 3/4 (1991): 75–97; Margaret Randall, "To Change Our Own Reality & the World," *Signs* 18, no. 4 (1993): 907–24; Millie Thayer, "Identity, Revolution & Democracy," *Social Problems* 44, no. 3 (1997): 386–407; Babb, *After Revolution*, 2001.

37. Victoria González, "Somocista Women, Right-Wing Politics, and Feminism in Nicaragua, 1936–1979," in *Radical Women in Latin America: Left and Right*, eds. Victoria González and Karen Kampwirth (University Park: Pennsylvania State University Press, 2001).

38. Katherine Hoyt, *The Many Faces of Sandinista Democracy* (Athens: Ohio University Press, 1997).

39. Cynthia Chávez Metoyer, "Nicaragua's Transition of State Power," in *The Undermining of the Sandinista Revolution*, eds. Gary Prevost and Harry Vanden (New York: St. Martin's Press, 1997), and *Women and the State in Post-Sandinista Nicaragua* (Boulder, CO: Lynne Rienner, 2000).

40. Cupples, 1999.

41. Babb, *After Revolution*, 2001.

42. Roger N. Lancaster, *Thanks to God and the Revolution: Popular Religion and Class Consciousness in the New Nicaragua* (New York: Columbia University Press, 1988); Collinson et al., 1990, 83.

43. Stephanie Linkogle, *Gender, Practice and Faith in Nicaragua* (Aldershot, UK: Avebury, 1996).

44. "Domestic Violence on the Rise," *Envío*, 18, no. 212 (1999): 25.

45. "Women in Nicaragua," *Envío*, 1991, 31.

46. Collinson et al., 1990, 17.

47. "The Zoilamérica Case," *Envío*, 18, no. 215 (1999): 30, and "The Pact's Roots Go Deep and Its Fruits Are Rotten," 18, no. 216 (1999): 311.

48. Isbester, 2001.

RESOURCE GUIDE

Suggested Reading

Babb, Florence E. *After Revolution: Mapping Gender and Cultural Politics in Neoliberal Nicaragua*. Austin: University of Texas Press, 2001.

Bayard de Volo, Lorraine. *Mothers of Heroes and Martyrs: Gender Identity Politics in Nicaragua, 1979–1999*. Baltimore: Johns Hopkins University Press, 2001.

Chinchilla, Norma. "Feminism, Revolution and Democratic Transitions in Nicaragua." In *The Women's Movement in Latin America*, 2nd ed., edited by Jane Jaquette, 177–97. Boulder, CO: Westview Press, 1994.

Collinson, Helen, et al. *Women and Revolution in Nicaragua*. London: Zed Books, 1990.

Criquillon, Ana. "The Nicaraguan Women's Movement: Feminist Reflections from

Within." In *The New Politics of Survival: Grassroots Movements in Central America*, edited by Minor Sinclair, 209–237. New York: Monthly Review Press, 1995.

Ewig, Christina. "The Strengths and Limits of the NGO Women's Movement Model: Shaping Nicaragua's Democratic Institutions." *Latin American Research Review* 34, no. 3 (1999): 75–102.

Fernández Poncela, Anna M. "The Disruptions of Adjustment: Women in Nicaragua." *Latin American Perspectives* 23, no. 1 (1996): 49–66.

Isbester, Katherine. *Still Fighting: The Nicaraguan Women's Movement, 1977–2000*. Pittsburgh, PA: University of Pittsburgh Press, 2001.

Kampwirth, Karen. "Legislating Personal Politics in Sandinista Nicaragua, 1979–1992." *Women's Studies International Forum* 21, no. 1 (1998): 53–64.

Lancaster, Roger. *Life Is Hard: Machismo, Danger, and the Intimacy of Power in Nicaragua*. Berkeley: University of California Press, 1992.

Metoyer, Cynthia Chávez. *Women and the State in Post-Sandinista Nicaragua*. Boulder, CO: Lynne Rienner, 2000.

Molyneux, Maxine. "Mobilization Without Emancipation? Women's Interests, State, and Revolution." In *Transition and Development: Problems of Third World Socialism*, edited by Richard R. Fagen, Carmen Diana Deere, and José-Luis Coraggio, 280–302. New York: Monthly Review Press, 1986.

Pérez Alemán, Paola. "Economic Crisis and Women in Nicaragua." In *Unequal Burden: Economic Crises, Persistent Poverty, and Women's Work*, edited by Lourdes Benería and Shelley Feldman, 239–58. Boulder, CO: Westview Press, 1992.

Randall, Margaret. *Sandino's Daughters Revisited: Feminism in Nicaragua*. New Brunswick, NJ: Rutgers University Press, 1994.

Videos/Films

Nicaragua: From Red to Violet. 1997. Directed by Carmen Sarmiento García. Series on Women of Latin America. Films for the Humanities & Sciences, Princeton, NJ. Considers the transition from the Sandinista government of Daniel Ortega to that of Violeta Barrios de Chamorro.

Pictures from a Revolution: A Memoir of the Nicaraguan Conflict. 1991. Directed by Susan Meiselas. GMR Films. A noted photojournalist returns to Nicaragua to look for and reinterview individuals she photographed during the revolutionary insurrection more than a decade earlier.

Sex and the Sandinistas 1991. Directed by Lucinda Broadbent. Women Make Movies, New York, New York. Interviews with Nicaraguan lesbians and gay men regarding their lives and emergent social movement.

Web Sites

Nicaragua Network, www.infoshop.org/nicanet.
Web site of the Nicaragua Network, a project of the Alliance for Global Justice, which publishes the *Nicaragua Monitor* to educate Americans about the effects of U.S. policy on the people of Nicaragua and to build ties of friendship between the two peoples.

La Prensa, www.laprensa.com.ni.
Nicaragua's leading daily newspaper, and a source of current information about events in the country.

Puntos de Encuentro, www.puntos.org.ni/boletina/.
An NGO based in Managua, Nicaragua, that is dedicated to addressing matters of importance to women in the country.

UNICEF, www.unicef.org/sowco0/stat12.html.
Web site where current statistics on the status of women and children, including education, health, fertility, and other information, may be found.

Witness for Peace, www.witnessforpeace.org.
A United States–based organization that has a long-standing relationship with Nicaragua; one of its three international offices is in Managua, Nicaragua.

Organizations

La Corriente
Apartado Postal 18-33
Managua, Nicaragua
Phone/fax: 22253555
Email: corrient@ibw.com.ni

Regional office of the Central American feminist organization. It publishes *Malabares*, has a feminist documentation center, and coordinates activities.

Nicaragua Network
1247 "E" Street, SE
Washington, DC 20003
Phone: (202) 544-9355
Email: nicanet@afgi.org

A U.S.-based solidarity organization that disseminates current news and information about Nicaragua to U.S. readers through its publication, *Nicaragua Monitor*.

Puntos de Encuentro
Apartado Postal RP-39
Managua, Nicaragua
Phone: (505) 266-6233
Email: puntos@puntos.org.ni

Feminist NGO in Managua, Nicaragua; publishes *La boletina* and offers classes through Universidad de la Mujer.

Witness for Peace
1229 15th St., NW
Washington, DC 20005
Phone: (202) 588-1471
Email: witness@witnessforpeace.org

Witness for Peace is an independent grassroots organization that supports peace, justice, and sustainable economies in the Americas, and has a special commitment to working in Nicaragua.

SELECTED BIBLIOGRAPHY

Arana, Mario. "General Economic Policy." In *Nicaragua Without Illusions: Regime Transition and Structural Adjustment in the 1990s*, edited by Thomas W. Walker. Wilmington, DE: SR Books, 1997.

Babb, Florence E. *After Revolution: Mapping Gender and Cultural Politics in Neoliberal Nicaragua*. Austin: University of Texas Press, 2001.

———. "After the Revolution: Neoliberal Policy and Gender in Nicaragua." *Latin American Perspectives* 23, no.1 (1996): 27–48.

———. "Women's Movements and Feminism." In *Cross-Cultural Research for Social Science*, edited by Carol R. Ember and Melvin Ember. Englewood Cliffs, NJ: Prentice-Hall, 1997.

Bayard de Volo, Lorraine. *Mothers of Heroes and Martyrs: Gender Identity Politics in Nicaragua, 1979–1999*. Baltimore: Johns Hopkins University Press, 2001.

Blumberg, Rae Lesser. "Income under Female Versus Male Control: Hypotheses from a Theory of Gender Stratification and Data from the Third World." In *Gender, Family, and Economy: The Triple Overlap*, edited by Rae Lesser Blumberg, 97–127. Newbury Park, CA: Sage, 1991.

Booth, John A. *The End and the Beginning: The Nicaraguan Revolution*. Boulder, CO: Westview Press, 1985.

Borland, Katherine. "The India Bonita of Monimbó: The Politics of Ethnic Identity in the New Nicaragua." In *Beauty Queens on the Global Stage: Gender, Contexts, and Power*, edited by C. Ballerino Cohen, R. Wilk, and B. Stoeltje, 75–88. New York: Routledge, 1994.

Chinchilla, Norma. "Feminism, Revolution and Democratic Transitions in Nicaragua." In *The Women's Movement in Latin America*, 2nd ed., edited by Jane Jaquette, 177–97. Boulder, CO: Westview Press, 1994.

Close, David. *Nicaragua: The Chamorro Years*. Boulder, CO: Lynn Rienner, 1999.

Collinson, Helen, et al. *Women and Revolution in Nicaragua*. London: Zed Books, 1990.

Criquillon, Ana. "The Nicaraguan Women's Movement: Feminist Reflections from Within." In *The New Politics of Survival: Grassroots Movements in Central America*, edited by Minor Sinclair, 209–37. New York: Monthly Review Press, 1995.

Cupples, Julie. "Families and Feminism," *Hemisphere: A Magazine of the Americas* 9, no. 1 (1999): 22–25.

"Domestic Violence on the Rise." *Envío* 18, no. 212 (1999): 25.

Enríquez, Laura J. *Harvesting Change: Labor and Agrarian Reform in Nicaragua, 1979–90*. Chapel Hill: University of North Carolina Press, 1991.

Ewig, Christina. "The Strengths and Limits of the NGO Women's Movement Model: Shaping Nicaragua's Democratic Institutions." *Latin American Research Review* 34, no. 3 (1999): 75–102.

Ferguson, Ann. "Lesbianism, Feminism, and Empowerment in Nicaragua." *Socialist Review* 21, no. 3/4 (1991): 75–97.

Fernández Poncela, Anna M. "The Disruptions of Adjustment: Women in Nicaragua." *Latin American Perspectives* 23, no. 1 (1996): 49–66.

Field, Les. *The Grimace of Macho Ratón: Artisans, Identity, and Nation in Late-Twentieth-Century Western Nicaragua*. Durham, NC: Duke University Press, 1999.

González, Victoria. "Somocista Women, Right-Wing Politics, and Feminism in Nicaragua, 1936–1979." In *Radical Women in Latin America: Left and Right*, edited by Victoria González and Karen Kampwirth, 41–78. University Park: Pennsylvania State University Press, 2001.

Hoyt, Katherine. *The Many Faces of Sandinista Democracy*. Athens: Ohio University Press, 1997.

Isbester, Katherine. *Still Fighting: The Nicaraguan Women's Movement, 1977–2000*. Pittsburgh, PA: University of Pittsburgh Press, 2001.

Kampwirth, Karen. "Confronting Adversity with Experience: The Emergence of Feminism in Nicaragua." *Social Politics* 3, no. 2/3 (1996): 136–58.

———. "The Mother of the Nicaraguans: Doña Violeta and the UNO's Gender Agenda." *Latin American Perspectives* 23, no. 1 (1996): 67–86.

———. "Social Policy." In *Nicaragua Without Illusions: Regime Transition and Structural Adjustment in the 1990s*, edited by Thomas W. Walker, 115–29. Wilmington, DE: SR Books.

Küppers, Gaby. *Compañeras: Voices from the Latin American Women's Movement*. London, England: Latin America Bureau, 1994.

Lancaster, Roger N. *Life Is Hard: Machismo, Danger, and the Intimacy of Power in Nicaragua*. Berkeley: University of California Press, 1992.

———. "Subject Honor and Object Shame: The Construction of Male Homosexuality and Stigma in Nicaragua." *Ethnology* 27, no. 2 (1988): 111–25.

———. *Thanks to God and the Revolution: Popular Religion and Class Consciousness in the New Nicaragua*. New York: Columbia University Press, 1988.

Linkogle, Stephanie. *Gender, Practice and Faith in Nicaragua: Constructing the Popular and Making "Common Sense."* Aldershot, UK: Avebury, 1996.

Metoyer, Cynthia Chávez. "Nicaragua's Transition of State Power: Through Feminist Lenses." In *The Undermining of the Sandinista Revolution*, edited by Gary Prevost and Harry Vanden, 114–40. New York: St. Martin's Press, 1997.

———. *Women and the State in Post-Sandinista Nicaragua*. Boulder, CO: Lynne Rienner, 2000.

Molyneux, Maxine. "Mobilization Without Emancipation? Women's Interests, State, and Revolution." In *Transition and Development: Problems of Third World Socialism*, edited by Richard R. Fagen, Carmen Diana Deere, and José-Luis Coraggio, 280–302. New York: Monthly Review Press, 1986.

"The Pact's Roots Go Deep and Its Fruits Are Rotten." *Envío* 18, no. 216 (1999): 3–11.

Padilla, Martha Luz, Clara Murguialday, and Ana Criquillon. "Impact of the Sandinista Agrarian Reform on Rural Women's Subordination." In *Rural Women and State Policy: Feminist Perspectives on Latin American Agricultural Development*, edited by Carmen Diana Deere and Magdalena León, 124–41. Boulder, CO: Westview Press, 1987.

Pan American Health Organization (PAHO). "Economic Crisis and Women in Nicaragua." In *Unequal Burden: Economic Crises, Persistent Poverty, and Women's Work*, edited by Lourdes Beneria and Shelley Feldman, 239–58. Boulder, CO: Westview Press, 1992.

———. *Health in the Americas*. www.paho.org/english/country.htm.

Pérez Sáinz, J.P., and Menjívar Larín. "Central American Men and Women in the Urban Informal Sector." *Journal of Latin American Studies* 26 (1994): 431–47.

Quiros, Ana. "Women's Health and Status in Nicaragua." *Women's International Network News* 17, no. 4 (1991): 27–28.

Randall, Margaret. *Sandino's Daughters: Testimonies of Nicaraguan Women in Struggle*. Vancouver, BC: New Star Books, 1981.

Randall, Margaret. *Gathering Rage: The Failure of 20th Century Revolutions to Develop a Feminist Agenda*. New York: Monthly Review Press, 1992.

Randall, Margaret. "To Change Our Own Reality and the World: A Conversation with Lesbians in Nicaragua." *Signs* 18, no. 4 (1993): 907–24.

Randall, Margaret. *Sandino's Daughters Revisited: Feminism in Nicaragua*. New Brunswick, NJ: Rutgers University Press, 1994.

Spalding, Rose J., ed. *The Political Economy of Revolutionary Nicaragua*. Boulder, CO: Westview Press, 1987.

Speer, John G. "The Urban Informal Economic Sector." In *Nicaragua Without Illusions: Regime Transition and Structural Adjustment in the 1990s*, edited by Thomas W. Walker. Wilmington, DE: SR Books, 1997.

Thayer, Millie. "Identity, Revolution, and Democracy: Lesbian Movements in Central America." *Social Problems* 44, no. 3 (1997): 386–407.

UNICEF. *The State of the World's Children*. 2000. www.unicef.org/sowco0/stat9.htm.

Walker, Thomas W. *Nicaragua: The Land of Sandino*. Boulder, CO: Westview Press, 1986.

Walker, Thomas W., ed. *Revolution and Counterrevolution in Nicaragua*. Boulder, CO: Westview Press, 1991.

Walker, Thomas W., ed. *Nicaragua Without Illusions: Regime Transition and Structural Adjustment in the 1990s*. Wilmington, DE: SR Books, 1997.

Wessel, Lois. "Reproductive Rights in Nicaragua: From the Sandinistas to the Government of Violeta Chamorro." *Feminist Studies* 17, no. 3 (1991): 537–50.

Whisnant, David E. *Rascally Signs in Sacred Places: The Politics of Culture in Nicaragua*. Chapel Hill: University of North Carolina Press, 1995.

Women in Development Network (WIDNET). www.focusintl.com/statangl.htm.

"Women in Nicaragua: The Revolution on Hold." *Envío* 10 (June 1991): 30–41.

"The Zoilamérica Case." *Envío* 18, no. 215 (1999): 30.

Spanish Bibliography

Bolt González, Mary. *Sencillamente diferentes . . . : La autoestima de las mujeres lesbianas en los sectores urbanos de Nicaragua*. Managua, Nicaragua: Centro Editorial de la Mujer, 1996.

Brenes, Aria Julia, Ivania Lovo, Olga Luz Restrepo, Sylvia Saakes, and Flor de Maria Zuniga. *La mujer nicaragüense en los años 80*. Managua, Nicaragua: Nicarao, 1991.

Chamorro, Amalia, Mario Chávez, and Marcos Membreño. "El debate sobre el sector informal urbano en Nicaragua (1979–1989)." In *Informalidad urbana en Centroamérica: Evidencias e interrogantes*, edited by R. Menjívar Larín and J.P. Pérez Sáinz, 153–86. Guatemala City: Fundación Friedrich Ebert, 1989.

Chamorro, Amalia, Mario Chávez, and Marcos Membreño. "El sector informal en Nicaragua." In *Informalidad urbana en Centroamérica: Entre la acumulación y la subsistencia*, edited by J.P. Pérez Sáinz and R. Menjívar Larín, 217–57. Caracas, Venezuela: Editorial Nueva Sociedad, 1991.

Fundación Internacional para el Desafío Económico Global. (FIDEG). *Seminario regional: El impacto de las políticas de ajuste sobre la mujer en Centroamérica y Panamá*. Managua, Nicaragua: FIDEG, 1991.

Fundación Internacional para el Desafío Económico Global. *Situación del sector informal en la ciudad de Managua*. Managua, Nicaragua: FIDEG, 1991.

Laenen, Arie. *Dinámica y transformación de la pequeña industria en Nicaragua*. Amsterdam: CEDLA, 1988.

Murguialday, Clara. *Nicaragua, revolución y feminismo (1977–89)*. Madrid: Editorial Revolución, 1990.

Pérez Alemán, Paola. *Organización, identidad y cambio*. Managua, Nicaragua: Editorial Vanguardia, 1990.

Pérez Alemán, Paola, et al. *Industria, género y mujer en Nicaragua*. Managua, Nicaragua: Instituto Nicaragüense de la Mujer, 1989.

15

PANAMA

Elida Guardia Bonet

PROFILE OF PANAMA

Panama, a narrow country connecting Central and South America, has Colombia on its east and Costa Rica on its west. Its history has mainly been shaped by its role as an international crossroads and a business and banking center. Since colonial times, Panama has been a trading center, a necessary stop on the merchant routes taking riches from the New World to Europe. Its being a narrow strip of land less than 50 miles wide in one area made it the ideal spot to build a railroad that allowed those wishing to reach California during the gold rush of the 1840s to do so more quickly. A canal, the next step, was opened in 1914, making the transit from east to west easier for world commerce. The building and operation of the Panama Canal and the establishment of the Canal Zone, used, occupied, and controlled by the United States, has shaped the political and economic history of the whole nation. After much political unrest, and the Torrijos-Carter treaties, which were signed on September 7, 1977, the Panama Canal returned to the hands of Panama at midnight on December 31, 1999, and all U.S. soldiers left the national territories. The military dictatorships that had controlled the nation since 1968 came to an end when U.S. troops invaded Panama on December 20, 1989, to arrest General Manuel Antonio Noriega, who was under U.S. federal indictment on drug charges. The influence of the United States is still strongly felt but other international players are becoming active in the business arena, especially China.

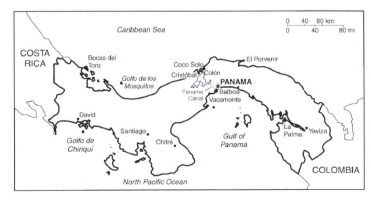

According to the 2000 census, Panama's population has reached 2.8 million, with 48.9 percent residing in the province of Panama, mainly in the capital, Panama City. Women comprise 49.5 percent of the total population. The ethnic population of Panama is 70 percent mestizo, 14 percent West Indian, 10 percent white, and 6 percent Amerindian of six different ethnic groups. The official language is Spanish, but English is also spoken, especially in the business sector. About 85 percent of the population is Roman Catholic, with Protestant sects increasing their membership to 15 percent. The life expectancy is 72.94 years for males, and 78.53 years for females. Infant mortality is 20.18 per 1,000 live births. The total fertility (average number of births per woman) is 2.4, slightly lower than in 1990, when it was 2.8, and even lower than in the 1960s, when the average was around 6.

OVERVIEW OF WOMEN'S ISSUES

The status of women has improved since the 1980s as a result of the changes called for by international organizations such as the United Nations, the Instituto de la Mujer (Women's Institute) in Spain, and Panamanian women's and feminist organizations such as the Centro para el Desarrollo (Center for the Development of Women; an NGO), the Departamento de la Mujer (Women's Department) in the Ministry of Labor, and the Instituto Nacional de Mujeres (National Institute of Women) at the University of Panama. These organizations have brought awareness to the government and the general public of women's problems and issues. Their programs have empowered women through gains in education and in the business and political sectors.

Many laws acknowledge the equality of women in the workforce and the political arena, which is a positive step, but discrimination still persists. Indeed, equality is more prevalent on paper than in real life. The advances that have taken place tend to empower mostly women in the urban centers and those with higher educational levels. Rural women (46.9 percent of the rural population) and indigenous women (48.77 percent of the indigenous population), as well as those with lower educational levels, are still at a disadvantage.[1] The concentration of women workers in the service economy, especially those employed as domestic servants, is testimony to the fact that women have far to go in terms of gaining entry into full-paying, more stable forms of employment. Diversification in the workforce and in rural areas is needed for economic reforms to reach all Panamanian women.

EDUCATION

Opportunities

Article 91 of the Constitution of the Republic grants free public education to all children at the elementary and secondary levels. Education at the elementary level, first through sixth grades, is mandatory. Education is optional at the secondary level. Some of the secondary-level schools offer vocational programs, but more men than women attend the vocational centers and the women who enroll tend to concentrate on sewing, cooking, and beauty courses. There are two state universities, Universidad Nacional de Panamá (National University) and Universidad Tecnológica (Technological University). At both universities, tuition is affordable to the majority of the population. Besides the state universities, which have campuses in major cities throughout the country, there is the Catholic University and several smaller universities that serve the postsecondary population. Among those who have completed their secondary education, a higher percentage of women than of men enter the university. The 2000 census reported that 56.79 percent of university students were women. In 1990, 70 percent of the graduating students at the University of Panama were women. However, at the postgraduate level women accounted for only 35 percent of total enrollment. At the Technological University, women comprise one third of the student body.[2]

Women who attend the universities tend to cluster in the fields of nursing, education, and public administration. The 1990s showed an increase in women's enrollment in the schools of dentistry, social communications, humanities, pharmacy, business administration, economics, and accounting, and in some of these schools women numbered over 50 percent of all students.[3]

Most teachers at the primary and secondary levels are women. In contrast, women are only 35 percent of the faculty at the university level, and tend to teach at the same schools where women have a higher enrollment as students.[4]

Literacy

According to the 2000 census, the 7.8 percent level of illiteracy in the country is lower than in 1990 (10.7 percent), and much lower than in the 1960s (21.7 percent). Among women, the percentage is greater (8.2 percent) than among men (7.1 percent). Higher levels of illiteracy are found among the women in rural areas and the indigenous populations, where the percentages range from 34.5 percent to 45.9 percent.

There is a strong effort to bring literacy to all areas of the country, not only through the public school system but also through other means. Radio Hogar, a radio station owned and operated by the Society of Jesus (Jesuits), implemented a study program *Maestro en casa* (Teacher at Home) in 2001 that is broadcast throughout the country. Approved by the Ministry of Education, it was anticipated that by the end of 2002 the program would help approximately 400 people complete their primary education through sixth grade. The average educational level of the population increased from 6.7 years of schooling in 1990 to 7.5 years in 2000.

EMPLOYMENT AND ECONOMICS

Job/Career Opportunities

According to the 2000 census, women constituted 35 percent of the labor force in the country, an increase from 28 percent in 1990, but the majority were household maids, retail clerks, hotel staff, receptionists, and secretaries. Only one third of the female workforce was in technical and professional fields.

Sewing inseams for jeans to be exported to the United States in the processing plant of Geomi Industries, Colón. AP/Wide World Photos.

In technical and professional fields, women generally occupy positions that are more service-oriented (nurses and teachers), and men tend to occupy the positions of engineers, architects, and doctors. Even though women in Panama tend to have more years of schooling than men, it is difficult for them to enter management in careers that are not service-oriented.

Women and children can legally work in agriculture or in the domestic sector as early as twelve years of age. This increases the number of young girls who abandon their studies and migrate to the bigger towns and cities to take jobs as domestic workers. Many rural parents send their daughters to the city as soon as they can because they need the additional income for the family to be able to subsist. Many more girls than boys migrate to the bigger towns and cities because employers usually prefer girls as domestic workers.

Pay

Article 63 of the Constitution of the Republic calls for equality of pay in cases in which the job responsibilities and conditions are the same, regardless of sex, nationality, age, race, social class, and political or religious ideas. In the majority of situations, women tend to be underpaid and underemployed, reflecting the cultural norms that place them in subordinate positions.[5]

Women receive lower pay than men in the majority of occupations that have the same responsibilities and conditions, the only exception apparently in finance and insurance, according to a study conducted by the Instituto de la Mujer (Women's Institute) in Spain in 1993.[6] Women seem to hold many management positions, and they are also better paid than men. Once again, however, these are professional positions that have to do with service. Women seem to be accepted in areas in which the cultural norms that view women as service providers, as caretakers, are emphasized.

The situation of the domestic worker, in which the greater percentage of women workers falls, is one of long hours and low wages. At wages that vary between U.S.$100 and U.S.$200, they do not make enough to cover what are considered the basic necessities. In addition to their wages, they receive room and board because the majority of domestic help lives in the family home and has only a day off per week.

Working Conditions

Women not only are paid less than their male counterparts, but are also discriminated against because of their age and fertility status. It is not always a subtle discrimination; some newspaper ads openly state that women should apply only if they are in a specific age range, and supervisors openly ask during interviews about a woman's fertility status and plans to have children. Application forms ask for age and a photo. Race and appearance are taken into consideration. The laws on maternity leave are very protective of women, but the monetary expense incurred by the company while following these laws makes management prefer men or women who are not in their reproductive years.

Sexual Harassment

There are few statistics available on sexual harassment cases. Women do not tend to make accusations for fear of losing their jobs in a very dire economy.[7] There is an awareness that sexual harassment occurs, but some of it is seen as acceptable because of the cultural norm of machismo, the belief that men will be men and will assert their sexual power in all spheres.

The practice of having domestic workers live with the family and away from their own families brings problems of discrimination, and in some cases sexual, physical, and psychological abuse.[8] There is no organization of domestic workers that can monitor the social and labor conditions in their workplace. Afraid of losing their employment and being left homeless in the city, many domestic workers do not speak out against the abuses.

Support for Mothers/Caretakers

Maternal Leave

Maternal leave is prescribed by Article 68 of the Constitution and explained in detail in the Family Code and Labor Legal Code. Women who are pregnant have the right to leave with full pay and all benefits for six weeks before their due date and for eight weeks after the birth of the child.

Breast-feeding mothers must be allowed 15 minutes every 3 hours to lactate their children or 30 minutes twice a day. The employer must provide a safe and clean place for the mother to breast-feed or must allow her to go home to do so.[9]

The May 2001 amendment of the Labor Code in regard to adoptions grants maternity leave with pay and benefits of four weeks to the mother, from the moment the child has been placed in her home.

The job is secure, and women return to the same position at the end of the maternal leave. Their jobs are secure up to a year after the birth of the child, with the exception of special cases designated by the law.

Daycare

The availability of domestic workers and extended families that can care for children cut back on the need for government-subsidized or other types of daycare. Article 115 of the Labor Code (1972) states that the executive branch and the Social Security Administration would establish daycare centers in industrial and commercial centers where there is a high concentration of workers. There are no free daycare facilities in the countryside. The economic situation in the country has not allowed for government-subsidized or private daycare centers to flourish. The weak economy is not the only reason for this lack of child care centers: Patriarchal cultural norms contribute to a business environment that has done little to address the daycare needs of working mothers.

Inheritance and Property Rights

Women have the right to inheritance and to the financial gains and possessions accumulated during their marriage, taking into account any legally registered prenuptial agreements. Children born in and out of wedlock have the same rights of inheritance as long as the parents acknowledge them as their biological children.

Social/Government Programs

Welfare Reform

With the rise of Omar Torrijos to power in the early 1970s there were major welfare reforms in Panama, many of which were important for women. His populist military dictatorship implemented agrarian reforms, a progressive labor code, health reforms, and educational reforms. After years of oligarchic governments, Torrijos, a man of humble beginnings, addressed the needs of poor women and men in the cities and the rural areas. By implementing a new Labor Code in 1972, Torrijos increased employee rights and facilitated union organizing, but alienated many business leaders and made union leaders and activists dependent on the government. The pressure from the private sector brought about the revision of the Labor Code in 1976, and a change in the political direction of the regime took place.[10] The health centers established throughout the country improved health conditions in rural areas where no medical and basic-needs services had been available. These reforms directly affected poor women by contributing to a drop in mortality rates as well as an increase in life expectancy in the 1970s. The agrarian reform implemented some land-distribution projects and it also sponsored colonization projects, giving legal recognition to squatters in some areas. But only 5 percent of the peasant population benefited from the land distribution and landownership remained much the same.[11] As a result, urban poor women gained more from Torrijo's welfare reforms than did peasant women.

Many of the reforms implemented during Torrijos's populist military dictatorship were opposed by the business sector and the higher social classes, who claimed the economic decline was in response to these reforms, and demanded changes in the laws. After Torrijos's death in 1981 and the ascent to power of General Manuel Antonio Noriega, welfare reforms were not the priority of the new military dictatorship. During this period any welfare benefits to the nation were outweighed by the censorship, restrictions, and repressions the military government imposed to be able to remain in power.

FAMILY AND SEXUALITY

Gender Roles

Gender roles in Panama are still very traditional: the man is seen as the head of the home and the provider for the family, and the woman as the heart and keeper of the home. This view establishes privileges for men and calls for subordination and discrimination for women.[12] In the major cities, among the more educated women, those roles are being challenged by women who are more educated, one part of the workforce, and make sizable incomes, but that is not the case in the majority of the population. Men usually earn more than women, and women who work outside of the home are still held responsible for running the home and caring for the children.

Marriage

Fifty-five percent of the Panamanian population over fifteen years of age is in some kind of relationship, the majority of which are not legal or religious marriages.[13] Conjugal relationships that are consensual but not legalized comprise 29.4 percent of the population, whereas legal or religious marriages comprise 26.4 percent of the population over 15 years of age. The divorce rate is low at 1.2 percent, but may not reflect the reality of the situation. Members of consensual relations are not considered divorced when the relationship comes to an end because they were never legally registered.

There seems to be a cultural norm of acceptance of mistresses and male promiscuity. Women seem to be inculcated that male infidelity is to be expected and accepted. Male infidelity is openly discussed, and most of the time the female partners are aware of it. Female infidelity, on the other hand, is strongly condemned and the reputation of the woman is greatly affected. Machismo, the exaggerated sense of masculine sexual, physical, and emotional power and strength, has detrimental effects on female–male relationships. Machismo seems to be accepted and encouraged by the women.[14]

The law states that males under 16 years of age and females under 14 years of age cannot legally marry.[15] Those under 18 years of age must have the consent of their parents or guardians. Consensual unions between two persons legally capable to be in a relationship are considered legally bound if the partners have been together for five years, if the relationship has been stable and consistent during those five years, it has been exclusive, and has been registered in court.

Until 1990 it was mandatory that a married woman adopt her husband's last name: this was done by adding to her maiden name her husband's last name preceded by the article *de* (of), declaring that she belonged to her husband. With the implementation of Law No. 22 of December 7, 1990, name change is now optional.

A divorce cannot be granted until two years after the marriage.[16] Men can marry immediately after the divorce has been registered, but women must wait 300 days after the registration of the divorce. To be able to marry before the allotted time, women must present proof that they are not pregnant, or that the child that they are carrying is not the child of the former husband.

Legal or religious marriages or consensual relations that have been legally registered are treated the same in regard to the division of wealth, property, and possessions when a divorce takes place. Each spouse is to get half of all the wealth, property, and possessions acquired by either one during the period of their union.[17]

Reproduction

Even though about 85 percent of the population is Roman Catholic and the Protestant sects have increased their membership to close to 15 percent, the teachings of Christian religions calling for sex within marriage are not heeded by the greater part of the population. The majority of children are born to parents who are not married or in legally sanctioned unions. Only

26.3 percent of children born in 1990 had parents who were married or in legally sanctioned unions.[18]

The average number of children per woman has declined from 6 in the 1960s to 2.4 in 2000. But there are correlations between location and reproduction rate; rural women have more children than urban women.[19] The 2000 census shows that the average number of children per women ranges from 3.1 to 3.4 among indigenous women.

Sex Education

Article 671 of the Family Code states that the Ministry of Education will include sex and family education in the official education programs that all public and private schools must follow. But education does not reach the majority of women at the time when it is needed. Education is mandatory only up to the sixth grade, and in many rural areas, girls stop going to school even before that, or do not attend school at all because of the distance to the schools or the need to work.

Contraception and Abortion

Contraception methods are widely used by 70 percent of women who want to avoid having children,[20] but by only 28 percent of indigenous women.[21] Even though the majority of the population is Catholic, the church's doctrines on family planning are not popular, and the majority of the people do not follow them. The Ministry of Health has led public education campaigns in urban and rural areas—at times even using billboards beside major thoroughfares—and has made contraceptives available to the population. Sterilization has been used as a method of family planning; one out of every three women in her fertile years has been sterilized. Studies done by the Asociación para la Planificación Familiar (Association for Family Planning) show that younger women seem to resort to abortion as a birth control device.[22]

Abortion is not legal in Panama. The Penal Code states that a woman who causes her own abortion or allows someone to cause the abortion of her fetus will be imprisoned for one to three years (Article 141). A person performing the abortion with the consent of the woman will be subject to three to six years in prison (Article 142), and a person who performs an abortion against the wishes of the woman will be subject to four to eight years. If in the process the of abortion, the woman dies, the sentence will be five to ten years (Article 143).

The only exceptions are when the abortion is done with the consent of the woman in cases of rape, or when the life of the mother or the child is in danger. Illegal abortions are performed in Panama, but are done clandestinely and do not reach any statistical reports. Some physicians offer abortion services, but the fees are so high that only women who can afford them or who can afford to go abroad to countries in which abortion is legal can dispose of unwanted pregnancies. Rural and lower-income women procure clandestine abortions, at great risk to their health.[23]

Teen Pregnancy

In 1990 there were 1,200 pregnancies of girls between 13 and 15 years of age.[24] The 2000 census shows that there were 611 births to women younger than 15 years of age, and 23,018 births to women between 15 and 19 years of age. Studies done by students in the School of Nursing show that the high pregnancy rate among teenagers reflects a lack of sex education and knowledge about their bodies, lack of use of contraception, low social economic status and dysfunctional families, and the tragic fact that 20 percent of them had been sexually abused.[25]

HEALTH

Health conditions in Panama are very favorable compared to other Central American countries. Since the beginning of the Republic, and because of the construction of the Panama Canal and the U.S. presence in Panama, the U.S. government played a very important role in health conditions. It fought to eradicate malaria and yellow fever, and helped the Panamanian government to improve its public health system, running water, sewage facilities, and road system. With the ascent of Torrijos to power in 1968 there was a renewed commitment to health care. The Ministry of Health was established, and it sponsored latrine, water, popular education, and communal farming projects. The Social Security system expanded in the 1970s, and more doctors were accessible to the general population.[26]

Health Care Access

Government-operated clinics all throughout the country serve the general population free of charge. Doctors and dentists must serve a two-year internship for the government when they complete their education. The majority of these internships are in small towns and remote areas of the country. In this manner the government is able to offer services to the majority of the population, and the doctors and dentists are assured of a job and an income as soon as they graduate. Many of these clinics lack sufficient supplies and facilities, but basic services are offered.

All workers and their employers must contribute to the Social Security system, which pays for hospitals and clinics that offer full services to those who contribute. But the Social Security system has had many financial difficulties because of corruption and misuse of funds that have adversely affected health services.[27] Many employers of domestic workers do not contribute to the system, so a large portion of women workers are not covered, and have fewer options for good health care services.

By law the government must offer free services to all women during pregnancy, delivery, and the period after birth, if she is not able to afford them. It must also give a food subsidy if the woman is unemployed or abandoned.[28] To be able to receive these services, women must visit government-operated clinics, which is a problem for many rural and indigenous women, so many times they do not receive the medical care needed.

Diseases and Disorders

The major causes of death among women are heart disease, and cervical, uterine, and breast cancer. Since the 1980s there has been an increase in the malnutrition of women, mainly in the rural areas because of the level of poverty there. Poverty is also to blame for respiratory and gastrointestinal ailments caused by inadequate and crowded housing and lack of electricity and potable water.[29] In the rural areas, distance is a problem for those who are sick and must travel to the health centers; in many cases they do not seek help until it is too late.

AIDS

AIDS has been a problem mainly among men, but it has also affected women due to promiscuous males who infect their spouses or partners.[30] The problem of AIDS and HIV has been present since the 1980s, but it was not until January 2000 that General Law No. 3 went into effect; it delineates prevention, education, and other measures dealing with AIDS/HIV. The Ministry of Education and the Ministry of Health are responsible for educating the public through the public schools and universities, as well as other methods of communicating methods of prevention and the dangers of AIDS/HIV.

Depression

Poverty and the prevalence of the *machista* attitude are seen as the major causes of women's depression, low self-esteem, prostitution, drug abuse, and self-destruction. The *machista* attitude encourages a domination of women that is reflected in irresponsible fatherhood and domestic violence. The additional stress placed on women who must head their households and be the sole caretakers of their children is reflected in the neurotic problems, anxiety, hysteria, depression, and compulsive and obsessive behaviors prevalent among women who seek psychiatric help.[31]

POLITICS AND LAW

Since the beginnings of the republic, Panama has enacted laws that have benefited women, especially in the social realm. The reforms during the Torrijos military populist dictatorship improved women's health, educational opportunities, and labor conditions, and provided maternity leave with pay and benefits. Following the United Nations proclamation of the International Year of Women and the Decade of Women (1975–1985), Panama created a commission to look at the restructuring of family programs. This commission proposed the creation of the Family Institute and a special legal code dealing with family issues. However, the political unrest and economic crisis of the 1980s brought women's rights and integration into the nation's development to a halt. But in the 1990s changes began once again, and the Civil Code was amended regarding divorce, marriage, and a woman's option to keep her maiden name or add her husband's last name in identity documents. The Judicial Code and the Penal Code also were modified to protect women in cases of domestic violence or when women who are pregnant or nursing are detained. The Family Code, created in 1995, promotes the development and protection of families.

Suffrage

Women obtained the right to vote in 1941, but only educated women were allowed to vote. The right to vote for all women was granted in 1946.

Political Participation

As a constitutional republic, Panama has three branches of government: executive, legislative, and judicial. The executive branch consists of the president and two vice presidents elected by popular vote for a five-year period. The legislative branch consists of a National Assembly composed of 72 legislators elected by popular vote for a five-year period, and the judicial branch consists of a Supreme Court of Justice, lower tribunals, and other courts. In 1997, women's participation in these higher government positions was very low; only 7 legislators out of 72 were women, only two women were part of the Supreme Court, and only two others were in lower courts.[32]

The first free elections took place in 1994, after the military regime was deposed in 1989. At that time there were 16 political parties running 14,072 candidates for the 1,695 positions decided by popular vote. Women made up 10 percent of those candidates, and 123 were elected. Women were named heads of the Ministry of Education and the Ministry of Commerce and Industry, 2 of the 12 ministries in the national government. Among the 46 autonomous or semi-autonomous institutions, a woman led only one. Eleven women were elected as mayors, out of 67 districts, and 40 were elected as representatives, out of 510 *corregimientos* — an administrative division of the country.[33]

The 1999 elections brought into power the first woman president of the Republic, Mireya Elisa Moscoso, widow of former President Arnulfo Arias, who had been deposed by the military three times. The most recent ousting of Arias, a democratically elected president, had taken place in 1968 and led to over 20 years of military dictatorship in Panama.

The military dictatorships of Torrijos and Noriega came to an end in 1989 when the United States invaded Panama and took Noriega into custody. During the years of military rule the role of the United States was questioned by the Human Rights Watch and the Lawyers Committee for Human Rights. The United States was charged with supporting the military governments and dismissing their human rights violations because Panama served the needs of the United States in running guns for and training Nicaraguan Contras, providing intelligence, laundering money, and offering a safe haven to deposed dictators.[34] It was believed by many Panamanians that the United States had created a monster by supporting Noriega, and it was therefore the United States' responsibility to dispose of him.

Women's Rights

Feminist Movements

The first feminist movement was established in 1922 by the first woman lawyer in Panama, Clara González de Behringer, who was not able to practice law until 1926 because of discriminatory laws. Under her leadership, the first feminist political party was created, the Partido Feminista Nacional (National Feminist Party). In 1923 the first feminist association — the Asociación (National Feminist Association for the Progress of Panamanian Women) — was founded by the teacher and writer Esther Neira Calvo, with hopes to improve the education opportunities for women. In 1945, the Liga Patriótica Femenina (Patriotic Feminine League) was established, and helped in the election of the first two congresswomen of the Republic. In 1985, the executive branch created the Consejo Nacional para la Promoción de Mujeres (National Commission for the Promotion of Women), and in 1988 the first nongovernmental organization for women was created, the Centro para el Desarollo de la Mujer (CEDEM, Center for the Development of Women). In 1995, a new department was created in the Ministry of Labor: the Departamento de la Mujer (Women's Department). This department focuses on the economic, cultural, and social development of women. Also in 1995 the University of Panama created the Instituto Nacional de Mujeres (National Institute of Women), which has been a catalyst in the development of studies, legal reforms, and educational programs that have led to the advancement of women in all areas of society.

Lesbian Rights

There are no laws in Panama that specifically address the issue of homosexuality or the rights of homosexuals. The studies of women in Panama do not consider the issues of lesbian women. Article 34 of the Family Code states that persons of the same sex cannot marry. The May 2001 amendment to the Family Code regarding adoption does not specifically ban homosexuals from adopting. In practice, however, when the sociopsychological studies of the prospective adoptive parents are done, those who are homosexual may be denied, based on the belief that they do not offer the best family environment for the child. The nuclear family consisting of a heterosexual couple is considered the ideal for adoptive parents.

The Asociación de Hombres y Mujeres Nuevos de Panamá (AHMNP, Association of New Men and Women of Panama) is a nongovernmental, nonprofit association organized in 1996 to unite gays, lesbians, bisexuals, and transvestites/transgenders (GLBTs). AHMNP was registered with the Ministry of Government and Justice in September 2001, the first step in its recognition as part of Panamanian society but a small step in the long struggle ahead.

There are no "out" gays/lesbians/bisexuals/transgenders in positions of power in the government or in the private sector who are fighting for the rights of the GLBT population. The Catholic Church, the official religion of the nation, shows little tolerance toward homosexuals. Schools avoid the subject as much as possible. The societal norms foment a homophobic culture that prefers to deny or ignore the existence of GLBTs, despite the fact that there is a small but significant community.

Military Service

There is no obligatory military service in Panama. After years under military rule (1968–1989), the Panama Defense Forces (PDF) ceased to exist. Prior to the PDF, the National Guard was responsible for both police and military issues. Both the PDF and the National Guard were composed of men and women who were mostly trained and funded by the United States. With the U.S. invasion of 1989, a realignment of the forces took place and, trying to dissociate itself from the military regime, the Panamanian Public Force was formed mainly as a security force.[35]

RELIGION AND SPIRITUALITY

About 85 percent of the population defines themselves as Roman Catholic, and Protestant sects have increased their membership to 15 percent of the population. The Constitution of the Republic states that Catholicism is to be taught in all public schools, but attendance at the religious classes or services is not mandatory. Regardless of the large number of the population who identify themselves as Catholic, the Catholic Church is a weak institution that does not wield much influence in the everyday life of the people. Religious marriages accounted for only 16 percent of all legal marriages in the 1980s, and even though the Catholic religion calls for complete fidelity, there are no indications that Catholic marriages fare better than other unions in terms of faithfulness of the spouses, especially the males. The Catholic Church's negative position on divorce may be one of the factors that allow male promiscuity and encourage women to accept it.

Since women are in charge of the care and education of the children, they also are in charge of the religious life of the family. They are generally "looked on as the family's representative before the church for it is generally the women who attend mass and participate in religious functions."[36]

Until the 1960s, the Catholic Church served mostly the oligarchy, and it was not until after Vatican II that it began to promote the interests of the poor. In the 1970s, the church became involved in other social issues, such as the canal treaties. Amid the fraud of the 1989 elections, the church hierarchy openly aligned itself with the opposition forces against General Noriega and was a strong voice calling for his ouster.[37] Even though the church has become an active participant in social reform and in education, it has not taken a strong stand in relation to the situation of women in Panama, and its silence allows the *machista* attitude and the oppression of women to continue.

VIOLENCE

Domestic Violence

It was not until the 1980s that domestic violence was brought into public debates.[38] Institutions and the general public were not willing to face the physical, sexual, and psychological violence in homes that was directed against female partners and children. In some instances, incest was registered as physical child abuse, and spousal abuse was not investigated because it was considered a "private" family matter. It was not until nongovernmental organizations, feminist organizations, and the Public Ministry cooperated in the proposal of legislation that changes began to occur.

There were no laws that dealt directly and forcefully with domestic violence until Law No. 27 was passed on June 16, 1995. This law defines domestic violence and child abuse; orders the establishment of specialized organizations to offer assistance to victims; and creates and reforms articles of the Penal Code and Judicial Code. Since the passage of Law No. 27 there has been an increase of domestic violence denunciations and more social awareness of the problem, but the specialized organizations to assist victims have not been implemented because of lack of funds in the national budget.

There is still a great need for educating the officials who encounter and deal directly with the victims. The law also must be amended to recognize as domestic units those consensual relations which are not legally registered, and to provide preventive and security measures in cases of possible future assaults, such as the eviction of the aggressor.[39]

War and Military Repression

Panama has not been involved in any major wars, but during the late 1980s, in face of the opposition from the majority of the population, the military repression grew under the leadership of General Manuel Antonio Noriega. The repression was directed toward all opposition members, including women. It consisted of "violent suppression of demonstrations, arbitrary short-term detentions, sexual abuses of detainees, and sharp limitation of freedom of press and expression."[40]

OUTLOOK FOR THE TWENTY-FIRST CENTURY

The 1990s brought many changes for women in Panama, especially in legal reforms. The influence of feminist governmental and nongovernmental organizations, as well as of feminist leaders and career women, has made possible the many legal changes that are bringing about reform, expurgating laws that discriminate against women, and implementing new laws that protect and provide equal rights to women in all aspects of the political, economic, and social realms. Without legal changes, no other changes can take place, but they have little impact without active support.

Profound and lasting changes benefiting Panamanian women in the twenty-first century will require a rethinking of the cultural norms that form the basis of the values and expectations taught to girls. School textbooks, educational materials, and study programs must be revised so that they do not reaffirm the traditional roles for women and men. The vocational programs at the secondary educational level that offer opportunities in technical areas previously dominated by men need to incorporate more women. At the university level women should be encouraged to enter areas of study other than those which are service-oriented. Unless women develop other areas of expertise, they will continue to work in areas that are low-paying and not well regarded.

The most important change that must occur regards the mentality of machismo and the acceptance of male promiscuity. The eradication of machismo is one of the greatest challenges facing Panamanian women, for how can something that is so intangible, and yet so profound that it permeates the soul and mind of society, be eradicated?

NOTES

1. Mariela Arce and Julia Leonel Fukuda, *Políticas públicas desde las mujeres: Una propuesta concertada en Panamá* (Panama City: Centro de Estudios y Acción Social Panameño, 1996), 14.

2. Aida Libia Moreno de Rivera, Amelia Márquez de Pérez, and Aracelly de León de Bernal, *Perfil de la situación de la mujer en Panamá y lineamientos de acciones prioritarias* (Panama City: Centro para el Desarrollo de la Mujer, 1992), 33.

3. Moreno de Rivera et al., 1992, 35.

4. Ibid.

5. Vielka Bolaños Moreno, "Mujer y mundo laboral en Panamá," *Revista cultural lotería* 417 (March–April 1998): 51–52.

6. Marco A. Gandásegui, Jr., "La Segmentación de mercado de trabajo y la discriminación de la mujer," *Revista cultural lotería* 417 (March–April 1997): 103.

7. Claude Verges de López, "Salud de la mujer. Situación actual y proyección hacia el siglo XXI," in *Mujeres panameñas frente al siglo XXI*, eds. César Picón and Ileana Gólcher (Panama City: Universidad de Panamá, 1996), 81.

8. Luz Aleyda Terán, "Mujeres rurales, prioridad nacional," *Revista cultural lotería* 417 (March–April 1998): 89.

9. Labor Code, Article 114.

10. Tom Barry, *Panama: A Country Guide* (Albuquerque, NM: Inter-Hemispheric Education Resource Center, 1990), 63.

11. Barry, 1990, 56.

12. Moreno de Rivera et al., 1992, 23.

13. 2000 Census.

14. Richard F. Nyrop, *Panama: A Country Study* (Washington, DC: American University Press, 1980), 69–71.

15. Family Code, Article 33.

16. Family Code, Article 212.

17. Constitution, Articles 128 and 133.

18. María Jose Marín Martín, *Panamá: Género y cooperación* (Panama City: Universidad de Panamá, Instituto de la Mujer, 2000), 11.

19. Barry, 1990, 74.

20. Ibid.

21. Arce and Fukuda, 1996.

22. Ibid., 17.

23. Moreno de Rivera et al., 1992, 48.

24. Arce and Fukuda, 1996.

25. Verges de López, 1996, 77.

26. Barry, 1990, 73–75.

27. Ibid., 75.

28. Family Code, Article 699.

29. Verges de López, 1996, 56.

30. Arce and Fukuda, 1996.

31. Verges de López, 1996, 63.

32. Mariablanca Staff Wilson, "La situación de la mujer panameña y los avances en su condición jurídica," *Revista cultural lotería* 411 (March–April 1997): 59.

33. Staff Wilson, 1997, 59–60.

34. Barry, 1990, 27.

35. Ibid., 29–30.

36. Nyrop, 1980, 71.

37. Barry, 1990, 78.

38. Moreno de Rivera et al., 1992, 53.

39. Rosina Pérez Bermúdez, "Violencia contra la mujer: Pasos a su erradicación en Panamá," *Revista cultural lotería* 417 (March–April 1998): 120.

40. Barry, 1990, 25.

RESOURCE GUIDE

Suggested Reading

Barry, Tom. *Panama: A Country Guide*. Albuquerque, NM: Inter-Hemispheric Education Resource Center, 1990. Describes and analyzes the economic, national security, political, and social systems and institutions of the country.

James, Joy. "Hunting Prey: The U.S. Invasion of Panama." In *Resisting State Violence*, 63–83. Minneapolis: University of Minnesota Press, 1996. A cultural and political analysis of the 1989 U.S. invasion of Panama, with special emphasis on Panamanian feminist and antiracist resistance to U.S. military, economic, and political control of the country.

Nyrop, Richard F. *Panama: A Country Study*. Washington, DC: American University Press, 1980. Describes and analyzes the economic, national security, political, and social systems and institutions of the country.

Web Sites

Asociación de Hombres y Mujeres Nuevos de Panamá (Association of New Panamanian Men and Women), www.chemibel.com.
An association for gays, lesbians, bisexuals, and transgender/transvestites, with information about its history and activities. In Spanish.

LegalInfo Panama, www.legalinfo-panama.com/leyes.htm.
A legal information site with the constitution and many of the legal codes of Panamá. There is an abbreviated English version of the site.

Programa de Formación en Cooperación Internacional "Mujeres y Desarrollo" ("Women and Development" Educational Program for International Cooperation), www.eurosur.org/MyD/myd.htm.
This organization was founded by the Instituto de la Mujer (Women's Institute) and the Instituto de Estudios Políticos para América Latina y Africa (Latin American and Africa Political Studies Institute) in Spain. Has information about its programs in all of Latin America and Africa, including the Panamá CEASPA and FUNDAMUJER organizations. In Spanish.

Organizations

Centro de Estudios y Acción Social Panameño (CEASPA, Center for Panamanian Social Action Studies)
Phone: (507) 226-6602
Nongovernmental organization that works for the education and promotion of the poor, especially in rural areas.

Centro para el Desarrollo de la Mujer (CEDEM, Center for the Development of Women)
Apartado 6339
Panamá 5, República de Panamá
Phone: (507) 227-2061
Fax: (507) 227-0579

Fundación para la Promoción de la Mujer (FUNDAMUJER, Foundation for the Promotion of Women)
Apartado 8926
Panamá 5, República de Panamá
Phone: (507) 262-1800
Fax: (507) 262-1855

Instituto de la Mujer, Universidad de Panamá (Women's Institute, University of Panama)
Estafeta Universitaria
Universidad de Panamá, República de Panamá
Phone: (507) 223-4787
Fax: (507) 264-9951
E-mail: imup1@ancon.up.ac.pa
Research center that investigates and proposes new directives in regard to the problems of women.

SELECTED SPANISH BIBLIOGRAPHY

Arce, Mariela, and Julia Leonel Fukuda. *Políticas públicas desde las mujeres: Una propuesta concertada en Panamá*. Panama City: Centro de Estudios y Acción Social Panameño, 1996.

Bolaños Moreno, Vielka. "Mujer y mundo laboral en Panamá." *Revista cultural lotería* 417 (March–April 1998): 34–54.

Contraloría General de la República, Dirección de Estadística y Censo. *Censos nacionales*. Vol. 6, *Censo de Vivénda*. Vol. 10, *Censo de poblacion*. 2001.

Gandásegui, Marco A., Jr. "La segmentación del mercado de trabajo y la discriminación de la mujer." *Revista cultural lotería* 411 (March–April 1997): 81–105.

Marín Martín, María José. *Panamá: Género y cooperación*. Panama City: Universidad de Panamá, Instituto de la Mujer, 2000.

Miller R., Gladys. "Violencia contra la mujer." *Revista cultural lotería* 417 (March–April 1998): 106–14.

Moreno de Rivera, Aida Libia, Amelia Márquez de Pérez, and Aracelly De León de Bernal. *Perfil de la situación de la mujer en Panamá y lineamientos de acciones prioritarias*. Panama City: Centro para el Desarrollo de la Mujer, 1992.

Pérez Bermúdez, Rosina. "Violencia contra la mujer: Pasos a su eradicación en Panamá." *Revista cultural lotería* 417 (March–April 1998): 115–21.

Picón, César, and Ileana Gólcher, eds. *Mujeres panameñas frente al siglo XXI*. Panama City: Universidad de Panamá, Instituto de la Mujer, 1996.

Staff Wilson, Mariablanca. "La situación de la mujer panameña y los avances en su condición jurídica." *Revista cultural lotería* 411 (March–April 1997): 55–69.

Staff Wilson, Mariablanca. "Mujer y derechos humanos." *Revista cultural lotería* 417 (March–April 1998): 6–33.

Terán, Luz Aleyda. "Mujeres rurales, prioridad nacional." *Revista cultural lotería* 417 (March–April 1998): 88–96.

Verges de López, Claude. "Salud de la mujer. Situación actual y proyección hacia el siglo XXI." In *Mujeres panameñas frente al siglo XXI*, edited by César Picón and Ileana Gólcher. Panama City: Universidad de Panamá, 1996.

16

PARAGUAY

*Jane Clough-Riquelme and
María Molinas Cabrera*

PROFILE OF PARAGUAY

Paraguay is a landlocked country in the heart of South America whose political, economic, social, and cultural history as a nation-state has been framed and influenced by its attempts to maintain sovereignty amid its larger and more powerful neighbors — Brazil, Argentina, and Bolivia. Unlike its neighbors, the country's colonial history was characterized by a set of political alliances between the Spaniards and the Guaraní Indians who inhabited the region. The alliance resulted in a mestizo, Guaraní-speaking population who formed the social base for the independence movement in the early 1800s. Since the 1989 overthrow of the 35-year-long dictatorship of General Alfredo Stroessner, the country has been engaged in a slow and complex process of creating democratic institutions and the rule of law amid constant threats of economic instability, increasing poverty, rampant corruption, and the specter of a new military strongman, Lino Oviedo who fashions himself the country's savior.[1]

The country is divided in two by the Paraguay and Pilcomayo river systems, which flow out of the Brazilian Gran Pantanal. Ninety-eight percent of its pre-

dominantly rural, mestizo population of 5.5 million people lives in the eastern half of the country. Half of Paraguayans speak both the indigenous Guaraní language and Spanish, and 37 percent are monolingual in Guaraní, despite the fact that less than 1 percent of the population is indigenous.[2] Despite its favorable population density, Paraguay today has the most severely inequitable distribution of wealth and land in the region: 40 percent of the poorest people earn only 10 percent of the total Gross National Product (GNP), while the richest 10 percent receive 40 percent of the GNP.[3] It also has an extremely young population, with 40 percent of Paraguayans under 15 years old.[4] Paraguay has one of the highest fertility rates in the region (2.8 percent to 4 percent).[5] Women between the ages of 15 and 44 have an average of four children; those with less than three years of formal education have six children on average.[6] The crude death rate was 5.4 per 1,000 population between 1995 and 2000. Life expectancy rates have risen substantially since the 1950s; that of men has gone from 60 to 67.5 years old, while that of women has gone from 69 to 72 years old.[7] According to the 1999 Integrated Household Survey conducted by the General Office of Statistics, Surveys, and Census (DGEEC), more than a million people live in extreme poverty, the majority of them women and children.[8]

OVERVIEW OF WOMEN'S ISSUES

The current situation of women in Paraguay is influenced both negatively and positively by three intertwining factors: the transition from authoritarian rule to democracy, the economic crisis, and the country's position in relation to its neighbors in the Southern Cone; and shifting cultural norms brought on by the legacy of colonialism, modernization, and integration.

The military revolt that overthrew the Stroessner regime was the result of power conflicts within his inner circle of political allies. Even so, many social groups were able to capitalize on international expectations for democracy and institutional changes to advocate for their political, social, economic, and culture rights over the course of the transition. Women's groups were particularly well prepared to take advantage of this opportunity, forming broad coalitions, developing a systematic legislative agenda, and engaging the international community for financial, technical, and political support. Gender equality was a significant issue at the Constitutional Assembly in 1991. Women's groups were able to form caucuses that put forward critical articles, thus the new Constitution ratified in 1992 explicitly mandates the equal treatment of men and women under the law. Throughout the transition period the women's movement has pursued and passed several precedent-setting laws based on the new Constitution. In 1993, through a concerted effort from academics and advocates in nongovernmental organizations (NGO), women in political parties, and congresswomen, the Secretaria de la Mujer (Secretariat of Women) with cabinet status was created, structured, financed, and activated. In 1997 the National Equal Opportunities Plan for Women was developed as a regulatory document for creating public policy to comply with the commitments signed by Paraguay in the Declaration of Beijing and the Fourth United Nations World Conference on Women.

Despite advances in legal reforms that support equal rights and access to education, the material conditions of most women have deteriorated due to the failing economy, the persistence of patriarchal norms and behaviors, and the twin specters of mismanagement and corruption undermining public policy reform efforts. The most critical sector is health care, especially reproductive health. A recent survey on reproductive health shows that maternal morbidity rates have actually *risen* in recent years. A 1996 National Household Survey revealed that 85 percent of the households had no Social Security and 53 percent had no medical insurance.[9] In other spheres, such as participation in the labor force, women's presence has increased, but at a distinct disadvantage. Women are entering low-paid jobs with few, if any, benefits, working longer hours, and having less flexibility in thier jobs. Despite legal reforms, there is a significant cultural lag that differs by class. On the one hand, educated, urban women have more freedom to access education and work, and marry later, despite the fact that traditional sexual stereotypes continue to be the norm. On the other hand, poor rural women's lives are still dictated to a large extent by the male members of their families and their continued isolation from society at large. Now that a legal framework is in place, the challenge for women in Paraguay is to transform these gains on paper into reality in terms of health and well-being, as well as to change patriarchal norms and values.

EDUCATION

Education is the basis of women's emancipation. The first Paraguayan woman to voice this argument publicly was Serafina Dávalos, considered Paraguay's first feminist, who wrote in 1907 a treatise titled *Humanism*, on the situation of women in Paraguay from a gender perspective, for her doctoral degree in law and social sciences.[10] Her central argument turned on the importance of education as the source of economic independence and political emancipation for women.

Reform of the public education system in Paraguay has been at the core of political debates over how to achieve social change during the transition. In 1996 the Ministry of Education published the strategic plan for educational reform, titled "Paraguay 2020: Confronting the Educational Challenge." This strategic plan embodies an inclusive consensus-forming process involving all of the major stakeholders, and marks a fundamental shift in thinking regarding the structure and functioning of education. Two themes dominate the document: gender equity and bilingual education.

Opportunities

Opportunities for access to basic education are now the same for girls and boys; there are currently no legal restrictions of any kind. Table 16.1 summarizes a UNICEF report on the educational situation of women and men in Paraguay.[11]

Since the 1980s, girls' access to education has improved dramatically. In 1995 a specific national program was initiated with international financial and technical support, Programa de Igualdad de Oportunidades y Resultados para las Mujeres en la Educación (PRIOME, Program for Equal Opportunities and Results for Women in Education). Its objective was to incorporate a gender perspective in the training of teachers. In 1998 Congress passed the General Law of Education, which laid out the principles of equality and mandated an end to sexual discrimination.

Whether people live in urban or rural areas bears considerably on levels of access to education. In 1997, the overall female enrollment for grades 1–6 was lower than for boys (female, 47.4 percent; male, 52.6 percent), though in the urban areas girls had higher rates of enrollment (female, 51 percent; male, 48 percent).[12] The situation for indigenous women is the most critical, for poverty, language, and gender discrimination affect them; according to the 1992 census, 59 percent of the indigenous women recorded not having any formal education at all.

Opportunities for women in higher education have improved dramatically since the 1990s. In fact, at one of the two principal universities of the country, the National University, female (52 percent) enrollment exceeded male (48 percent) enrollment in 1997. Although there are still few women in traditionally male-dominated fields such as engineering (12 percent), women are close to parity in others such as medicine (46 percent), and have exceeded male enrollment in still others, such as law (55 percent). A surprising result from a survey of the National University campuses in the countryside was that female enrollment accounted for 57 percent of the total.[13]

These advances must be tempered by three facts. One is that the quality of the educational system is extremely poor. Despite the new constitutional mandate to spend at least 20 percent of the national budget on education, Paraguayan children have the fewest contact hours in all of Latin America,

Table 16.1
Educational Situations of Men and Women

Indicator	Situation of women compared to men
Educational coverage	Equal
Reasons for dropping out	Equal with slight variation
Matriculated	Equal or superior
Dropout rate	Higher (rural areas)
Performance rate	Higher

and the mandate has yet to be fulfilled. Second, despite major relative advances in university education, only 3 percent of the population reach the university level.[14] Third, there have been few reforms to accommodate marginal populations such as the indigenous peoples who speak neither Guaraní nor Spanish, poor migrant populations, and children with special needs. These issues have yet to be addressed.

Literacy

Illiteracy rates differ markedly, depending on whether we are talking about urban or rural populations, or whether we are discussing women or men. According to the 1992 census, of the total illiterate population over the age of 15, 14.2 percent were women, and 13.4 percent were men, although there is variation based on sector and regional differences. Seventeen percent of women living in rural areas were illiterate, while only 11.8 percent of the men were illiterate. There are significant differences among women, depending on whether they live in urban or rural areas; the absolute illiteracy rate for urban women is 63 percent, while it is 55 percent for rural women.[15]

Literacy rates in the country are intimately connected to Paraguay's being a bilingual nation.[16] Data from the 1992 census show the pattern of social exclusion based on language; only 2.4 percent of the population living in Asunción is monolingual in Guaraní, while 80 percent of the population in the northern state of San Pedro is monolingual in Guaraní. Although the 1992 Constitution declares the two national languages to be Spanish and Guaraní and mandates that all public institutions use both languages, the process of creating educational materials in Guaraní has been very controversial, difficult, and slow. Since it originated as a Spanish colony, education in Paraguay has always been in Spanish. Under some regimes, the speaking of Guaraní was prohibited, reflecting the state's devaluation of the indigenous language and its role in social identity. Yet despite state efforts to suppress Guaraní, it has been used by a significant portion of the population throughout the nation's history. One of the fundamental tenets of the 1992 Constitution is its acknowledgment of Paraguay as a multiethnic, multicultural, bilingual nation. In 1993 the National Program for Bilingual Education was established to adapt the primary education system to meet the 1992 constitutional mandate.

EMPLOYMENT AND ECONOMICS

Job/Career Opportunities

One of the areas where there is significant inequality between men and women is in the labor market, as evidenced in marked differences in wage levels, access to wage labor, and the segmentation of the labor market.

Female police officers on guard in Ascunción. Photo © TRIP/M. Barlow.

Although their participation in the labor market has increased sharply because of the economic crisis, women enter under disadvantageous conditions. Some economists have estimated that, depending on the econometric model utilized, the economic participation of women could be anywhere from 22 percent to 77 percent. The two principal activities that can influence this are unpaid domestic labor and unpaid labor for a family business.[17] Unemployment rates are higher for women than for men; the national unemployment rate for men is 11.8 percent, while it is 20.5 percent for women. In the urban areas the rate for men is 15.3 percent and for women it is 18.9 percent, while in the rural areas it is 22.9 percent for women and only 8 percent for men.[18]

The majority of women are domestic workers or rural workers. Domestic work in private homes, performed almost exclusively by women, is not valued and is one of the worst-paid jobs. In fact, this discrimination is still inscribed in the Labor Code; employers are permitted to pay only 40 percent of the legal minimum wage for up to 12 hours of work a day for this type of job. Moreover, the practice of *criadazgo* continues. This is a traditional social practice based on informal arrangements between families that involves the transfer of young girls and boys from poor households to richer households to work as domestics or apprentices in exchange for room and board, clothes, and basic education. This and other common practices of child labor place children and adolescents in situations of extreme vulnerability. In recent years there has been a growing concern about this, and an active network of nongovernmental organizations, national agencies, and projects funded by international development agencies is finally beginning to research this critical problem and develop policies and programs to deal with it.

In the sectors that are traditionally considered to be for men, women are expected to have more training and education to do the same job. For example, in plumbing and electricity, as well as for transportation and communications, women with vocational training constitute 64 percent and 51 percent, respectively, while the proportions for men are 46 percent and 18 percent.[19]

Pay

Wage levels for men and women differ considerably between areas of residence. Although a woman earns 76 percent of what a man earns nationwide, the average wage earned by a woman as a percentage of a man's wage is higher in urban areas than in the rural areas. It differs by type of activity also. For example, in agriculture women only receive 53 percent of the male wage, while in the service sector they earn 64 percent of the male wage.[20] Regardless of the average level of education, the average income of men is higher, regardless of place of residence or type of work. Women also occupy the jobs with the lowest wages overall.[21]

The law requires every worker to be registered for Social Security, but compliance is very irregular and there are no systematic forms of control. Only 10.9 percent of the population have Social Security, and the effective coverage is severely compromised by the lack of resources and services.

Working Conditions

According to a report prepared for the Congressional Commission on Equity, Gender, and Social Development, a significant proportion of women are in especially vulnerable working conditions, including rural workers, migrants, domestic workers and women in the informal economy.[22] Moreover, there is an increase in the number of women who are the only breadwinner in the household, reaching 27 percent in urban areas. According to the 1997–1998 Integral Household Survey (Encuesta de Hogares), the percentage of women working in the informal sector in urban areas is 38 percent, while it is only 29 percent for men.[23] More than half of the women in urban areas fall into three occupational categories: self-employed (34 percent), domestic worker (21 percent), and unpaid family employee (7.2 percent). Men, however, have higher rates of participation in the other categories. The informal sector in Asuncion absorbs more than 50 percent of women workers and 75 percent of the women in urban areas of the Department of Central.[24]

Sexual Harassment

The Labor Code was modified in 1995 to include sexual harassment as a justified cause for termination by the employer (Article 81) and a justified cause of rescinding a contract by a worker (Article 84). In 1997, the Paraguayan Penal Code incorporated the notion of sexual harassment as a crime in Article 133, establishing a penalty of two years' imprisonment. Despite this major advance, there are still many obstacles to seeing this become a substantive reform, including the difficulty of proving the commission of this type of crime; the stigma that it represents for the victim; and the threat of losing one's job as a result of sexual harassment because the woman may choose to quit her job or get fired because she filed a complaint.

Support for Mothers/Caretakers

Despite the current inequalities in labor participation and remuneration, since 1993 there have been major advances in protecting women through reforms to the Labor Code. According to the new Labor Code (Article 128), "women have the same labor rights and obligations as men." In addition, there is now a special section which covers issues specifically related to protecting the rights of women before and after they give birth and while nursing the child. Articles mandate and establish such important issues as the length of maternity leave, nursing breaks during work, job security during maternity leave, and prohibition of dismissal. In addition, industrial or commercial enterprises in which there are more than 50 workers of either sex are now obligated to provide a child care facility for children under two years of age (Article 134). Although these legal landmarks were introduced into the Labor Code between 1993 and 1995, they are still not a practical reality.[25]

FAMILY AND SEXUALITY

Women's groups who participated in the writing of the 1992 Constitution contributed to laying the legal foundation for fundamental social change in gender relations in the family unit. The Constitution establishes specific protections for the family and reproductive rights, including guaranteeing the protection of paternity and maternity as state responsibilities. It recognizes that every citizen has the right to make decisions freely and responsibly regarding reproductive health, as well as to receive education, scientific counseling, and adequate services. In addition, it mandates the establishment of special programs for populations with limited resources.

Gender Roles

Despite the fact that women have had to reconstruct the country after two major wars during the nineteenth and twentieth centuries (Triple Alliance War, 1860s; Chaco War, 1930s) that devastated the male population, gender roles are consistent with a predominantly Catholic country. In their report for Beijing+5, Paraguayan feminist intellectuals expressed a sentiment common among Paraguayan women: "We are for others."[26] The patriarchal notion of the woman sacrificing everything, including her health, for the good of the rest of the family is embedded in the social relations of daily life. In public discourse women are revered, while in reality they are often subjected to domestic violence and many types of discrimination at home, in their communities, and in the workplace. This is slowly changing as women and the lives they lead are becoming more and more visible in the democratic context through studies, more accurate census data, and better media coverage.[27]

The focus of the women's movement during the last years of Stroessner's rule was the Civil Code, which was abruptly changed in 1986 to essentially negate the rights of autonomy of women in marriage. The passage of this modification spurred diverse women's groups to overcome differences and band together. Thus, they were prepared after the overthrow of Stroessner with a strategic plan not only to regain their rights but also to push for substantive changes in the Civil Code to reflect modern gender relations and roles.[28] Substantive changes to the Civil Code in 1992 were intended to improve gender equity through, at the very least, definitions and statuses.

According to the partially reformed Civil Code, "Women and men have equal capacity to enjoy and exercise their civil rights, regardless of their marital status." Within the family unit, the equality of the partners and the welfare and protection of underage children are now considered fundamental principles of the application and interpretation of the law. According to the Civil Code, these principals are public mandates and cannot be modified by conventions or agreements except when the law expressly authorizes it (Article 2). This is in essence the legal equality within marriage for which Serafina Dávalos fought throughout her career as a justice of the Supreme Court, in the early twentieth century.

Marriage

The reformed Civil Code also protects women in relationships outside of marriage. Partners living together in a common-law marriage are now regulated by Law 1/92 (Articles 83–94), Law 1183/86 (Article 217), and Article 51 of the Constitution, which states, "Common-law marriages between a man and a woman, without legal obstacles to enter into a formal marriage, that fulfill the conditions of stability and monogamy, produce the same effect as marriage, within the conditions established by law."[29] Again, this is a precedent-setting law, which provides much-needed protection to women in the most common type of relationship—common law marriage.

The passage of the Divorce Law in 1991 was a major victory for women living in a predominantly Catholic society. Despite the protests of the church, Congress passed a law, that includes no-fault divorce. Among the justifications for divorce are immoral conduct by either partner; prostitution or other crimes; abuse, either physical or psychological; and voluntary abandonment. In addition, divorce may be sought in cases in which either partner abandons his/her responsibilities of child care for more than four consecutive months without just cause. There is also a provision for the judge to order the provisional separation of the couple, securing the necessary resources for a partner who is being abused to be justly compensated while the divorce is being processed (Article 18). Before the passage of the Domestic Violence Law, this was a critical mechanism for protecting women in cases of domestic violence.

Reproduction, Sex Education, and Contraception

The fertility rate in Paraguay is one of the highest in the region with a national rate of 4.1 and of 5.6 in rural areas, according to a 1998 national study on women's reproductive health.[30] According to the National Survey on Demographics and Reproductive Health, the rate of unwanted pregnancies reached 25 percent.[31] The survey reported that 74.3 percent of women surveyed claimed unsatisfactory access to contraception, as well as an increased desire by younger and less educated women to have access to contraception.[32] The use of contraception has a direct relationship to levels of education; the women who have at least two years of primary education use contraceptive methods 37 percent of the time, while 72 percent of women who have completed secondary education or have higher education use it.[33] Despite a lack of support from the public health system and pressures from the Catholic Church, nongovernmental organizations have focused their attention on sex education.

Fertility rates have shifted since the 1970s, according to the DGEEC, from young women in their twenties having the highest rates to teens between the ages of 15 and 19.[34] The relationship between fecundity in adolescents and young adults who have completed their secondary education and those who have only had one or two years of schooling is three to eight times higher among those with less education.[35] Fifteen percent of mothers in the country are between the ages of 15 and 19, the second highest rate in South America.[36]

Abortion

Abortion is a serious but unspoken health risk for women in Paraguay. Despite the fact that it constitutes the principal cause of maternal mortality in the country, the public health system has not incorporated any plans or programs to change the situation. Women's groups have been unable to get the Penal Code modified to decriminalize abortion. This has been the major area in which the lobby groups supported by the Catholic Church have been able to maintain dominance. Paradoxically, the pressure to maintain abortion as a crime has served to lead to the deaths of hundreds of women each year due to a flourishing unsafe and clandestine industry to support their needs.

HEALTH

Although the 1992 Constitution recognizes health care as a fundamental right of all citizens, the distance between the law and its implementation, especially for women, is significant. The National Census Institute (Direc-ción General de Estadística, Encuestas y Censos, DGEEC) conducted a study in collaboration with the United Nations Population Programme on the sociodemographic profile of Paraguay in the twenty-first century. Their findings state the following:

> The data collected from various surveys and studies show that reproductive health does not have the necessary support from either the state or the private sector to curb the high percent of maternal mortality, the unsatisfied demand for family planning, teen pregnancy, and domestic violence.[37]

The study concluded that the mortality rate for women in their initial reproductive years was expected to increase.

Health Care Access

In 1996 the Paraguayan Congress adopted the National Health System (Law 1032), which expressly mandates equal access, quality, efficiency, and social participation as central elements. Yet statistics show another story. It is estimated that there are seven doctors for every 10,000 people and one hospital bed for every 1,204. Of these, 25 percent are located in the capital city, and 19 percent are in the Central department, the state surrounding the capital, in which the majority of the population lives. According to a 1999 document published by the Ministry of Public Health and Welfare, Paraguay is among the five countries worldwide with the highest rate of maternal mortality.[38]

During the 1990s policies and specific plans were developed and implemented to focus on women's health issues, including the Integrated Health Plan for Women, the National Plan for Reproductive Health (1997–2001), and the National Plan for the Prevention and Sanction Against Violence Toward Women (1994). Despite these interventions, the leading causes of death in women between the ages of 25 and 29 are those related to childbirth. They are the second leading causes of death in women under 25 years of age.[39]

The Congressional Commission on Equity, Gender, and Social Development drew attention to the fact that between 1996 and 1999 more than 90 percent of the cases of maternal mortality were attributable to medical conditions which are all preventable at a low cost: hemorrhaging (25.4 percent), abortions (24.6 percent), and toxemia (20.6 percent).[40] Other related factors are low educational levels, cultural barriers that prevent women from seeking assistance in clinics, and inadequate attention from health professionals. In the rural areas, there is an inadequate coverage of institutional births; 60 percent of births in rural areas are attended to by midwives outside of the public health care system.[41]

Diseases and Disorders

In recent years, diseases and disorders typically associated with industrial countries have become more prevalent in Paraguay, due in part to lack of regulations in various industries and increasing environmental degradation. The mortality rate for cancer of the uterus in 1997 was 22.4 per 100,000 women, 20 years old or older; the breast cancer rate for the same year was 11.3 per 100,000 in the same cohort. According to a national survey on demographics and reproductive health conducted by CEPEP in 1997, 63 percent of women between the ages of 15 and 19 had ever had a Pap smear, and 44.8 percent had had at least one performed in the last two years.[42]

AIDS

Although it is still a taboo subject, the health threat of HIV/AIDS is strong and growing stronger. Rates of adolescent sexual activity, and unprotected sex make this disease a growing epidemic. These behaviors are prevalent, yet they are not accepted culturally in public discourse, so providing appropriate sexual education and information to avoid contracting HIV is not possible. One of the most concerning tendencies in the data is that the proportion of women to men is increasing. In 1992 the ratio was one woman for every 28 men; in 1999 it was one woman for every three men.[43]

Despite this profile, there is an active community of nongovernmental organizations (NGOs) that have been advocating for progressive health rights and have made some headway. In 1993–1997 a consortium of NGOs focusing on gender issues participated in a project with the Ministry of Health, Strengthening of Reproductive Health and Family Planning in Paraguay. NGOs such as CEPEP conduct applied research on health issues, operate health clinics for family planning and preventive medicine, and provide data to support legislative bills to improve health care.

POLITICS AND LAW

The most significant advances for women during the transition have been in legal reforms that have created the platform for attaining gender equity and equal opportunities in society. According to the new Constitution, it is the state's responsibility to create the conditions and mechanisms for making equality real and effective, and to remove obstacles that impede implementation. Article 46 states: "The protective measures established against unjust inequalities will not be considered as discriminatory, but rather equalizing." Nevertheless, there is still no sanction for discrimination, except for those established in the Electoral Code.

Suffrage

Women in Paraguay were the last in the Western Hemisphere to obtain the right to vote (in 1961, during the Stroessner regime). Although they technically had their first opportunity to vote in 1963, they were not able to exercise that right in a democratic context until almost thirty years later. Within the current judicial regime, the Constitution (Article 117) explicitly establishes the bases for women's equality in the context of political participation:

> Citizens, regardless of sex, have the right to participate in public affairs, either directly, or through their representatives, in the manner set out in the Constitution and the laws. Moreover, women's access to public office will be promoted.

Political Participation

Two traditional, multiclass parties—the Asociación Nacional Republicana (ANR, National Republican Association) and the Partido Liberal Radical Auténtico (PLRA, Authentic Radical Liberal Party commonly known as the "Liberal Party")—that have existed for more than 100 years dominate the political landscape in Paraguay.[44] Their combined membership accounts for over 95 percent of the affiliated registered voters. Most resources and influence are distributed through this two-party structure. Since political parties are so central to Paraguay's political system, advances for women in this area have been high on the feminist agenda.

Women constitute approximately half of the affiliated members of each party, yet their participation in decision-making roles is extremely limited. The political parties have been slow to make structural changes to encourage female representation, but there have been some significant advances, including the establishment of a quota law in the Electoral Code. The new Electoral Code (835/96) mandates that political parties include a minimum of 20 percent of women and alternate male and female candidates on their internal lists and that a "significant" number of women hold decision-making posts in the party structure.

Numerically, women continue to be extremely underrepresented in all areas of formal leadership, both elected and appointed. In 1997, the Centro de Documentación y Estudios (CDE, Center of Documentation and Studies), a private, nonprofit research and advocacy institute, collaborated with the Secretaria de la Mujer to create a database on women in formal positions of leadership in the state, political parties, and social organizations, with the hope of being able to do periodic updates. In the executive branch there has never been a female president or vice president, and only a few women have held ministerial positions. However, this study found that the percentages become important at the third level of the Executive branch;

women represent 31 percent of the departmental directors. In Congress, during the 1993–1998 congressional period women made up 5.6 percent, and grew to 8 percent in the following congressional period, which ends in 2003. The effects of the 20 percent quota law in the Electoral Code are now evident in the Senate, with an increase of women members in those same periods from 11.1 percent to 17.8 percent. However, membership in the House of Representatives is not even 3 percent.[45]

At the level of regional government, there has yet to be a female governor elected. Where women are beginning to be seen is at the local level. Although the electoral record for women as mayors is not very encouraging (6 percent in 1991; 3 percent in 1996), women are becoming more prevalent in city councils (10 percent in 1991; 15 percent in 1996). This success has to be tempered with the fact that there is an inverse relationship between the size of the city and the presence of women in elected positions; the majority of those women elected were in small municipalities with equally small budgets.[46]

Women's Rights

Since the ratification of the Constitution in 1992, the women's movement has been the most systematic in following a legislative agenda to pass laws that uphold the constitutional mandates. The women's movement was well represented in the Constitutional Assembly and was able, through strategic coalitions, to include articles that guarantee equality for women and men under the law. The challenge, then, was to follow through with the legal reforms necessary to make the laws comply with the constitutional mandate. Between 1992 and 2001, various women's groups and coalitions gained passage of the following legal reforms: the Divorce Law (1991); the Penal Code in which adultery is no longer a crime (1991) and additional reforms in favor of gender equality (1995); the Constitution, making women and men equal under the law; the Civil Code (1992), giving partners in both legal and common-law marriages equal rights and obligations to the family; the Labor Code (1993), which provides for maternity leave and other protections, including against sexual discrimination; and the Electoral Code (1996) with a 20 percent quota.[47]

Feminist Movements

Although there were recognized feminists in the early part of the century, such as Serafina Dávalos, the feminist movement did not gain momentum until the 1980s. Even then, as with all types of activity in a civil society under an authoritarian regime, their work was clandestine and piecemeal, focusing on developing networks of solidarity both at home and abroad. Under the Stroessner regime, there was no freedom of association; three people meeting together constituted grounds for arrest, as it was seen as subversive behavior. Feminists formed part of a subculture of "society despite the state"; the focus of their activities was advocating for the most basic human rights for everyone within a repressive regime. The Paraguayan feminists became more systematic in their efforts in the last years of the dictatorship as their ties to international networks and the Latin American feminist community became stronger. The global movement for women's rights through the United Nations system had a strong and lasting influence on the women's movement in Paraguay to garner support for gender equity. In 1993, for the first time in history, the United Nations appointed a woman as Chief of Mission to coordinate the U.N. system in Paraguay. Thus the U.N. mission in Paraguay during this period encouraged and supported a series of groundbreaking studies on the situation of women in Paraguay, as well as state reforms informed by a gender perspective.

A critical element of the success of the feminist movement in Paraguay has been its ability to facilitate collaborative efforts among a diverse array of women's groups with very different ideologies and beliefs about the role of women in society. This was so from the very beginning, and is largely attributable to the personal philosophy of several of its principal leaders. This philosophy of inclusiveness enabled coalitions to form, such as: the Coordinadora de Mujeres Paraguayas (CMP, Paraguayan Women's Coalition), the Coordinadora Interpartidaria de Mujeres de Paraguay (Paraguayan Women's Interparty Coalition), the Red de Mujeres Munícipes (Network of Women Elected City Officials), and the Coordinadora de Mujeres Campesinas y Indígenas (Coalition of Rural and Indigenous Women). Where other social movements have not been able to secure coalitions to push policy reforms, women have succeeded.

Lesbian Rights

With regard to freedom to express one's sexual orientation, the report prepared by the Grupo de Acción Gay Lésbico (GAG-L, Gay-Lesbian Action Group) for the 1999 Human Rights Report for Paraguay, highlights some key legal issues.[48] First, the 1992 Constitution recognizes the right to equality in dignity and nondiscrimination in Article 46, but in Chapter IV, which refers to the rights of the family, it refers to "a stable union between a man and a woman" (Article 49). Second, the Civil Code in Article 140 states that "marriage cannot be contracted between persons of the same sex." Third, Article 179 of the Civil Code refers to the nullifying of a marriage if it involves persons of the same sex. Finally, in the Penal Code there are different punishments for the crime of sex with a minor: if it occurs between a man over 18 and a girl between the ages of 14 and 16, there is a fine. If it occurs between an adult male in a homosexual relationship with a minor under 16, the punishment is two years of incarceration (Article 138).

Military Service

Obligatory military service has been an issue around which young people, both men and women, have rallied to fight against the violation of human rights and the excessive role of the military in society. The Constitution requires military service, but this requirement has often been abused by the military hierarchy to gain access to indentured servants. Since the rich and well-connected can usually buy their way out of the service requirement, the rank-and-file tend to be poor young boys from the countryside who either enlist or are volunteered by their families, in the hopes of their receiving food and clothing and, perhaps, some vocational training. But the Constitution also guarantees the right to conscientious objection. In the early 1990s the Movement for Conscientious Objection was born from this serious social issue, which affects many youths. Young women have played a significant role in this movement, which has been monitoring abuses, assisting families in locating their children, and preparing human rights cases against the military establishment. They have championed the elimination of obligatory military service for youth and have publicized the systematic violations of the recruits' human rights, both nationally and internationally.

RELIGION AND SPIRITUALITY

Until 1992, there was no separation of church and state in Paraguay; Roman Catholicism was the official religion of the nation-state. Although Paraguay legally is no longer a Catholic country, the vast majority of the population still claims that faith. Religiosity, especially among women, is a unique mixture of the Guaraní belief system and Catholicism. The latter still permeates public life; public events continue to involve the celebration of a special mass, and celebrations of Catholic religious traditions continue to be public holidays. Its saints have given their names to towns and cities. The church's festivals and religious processions form an important part of traditional folklore with many enthusiastic participants. The church forms part of the basis for the social identity of each region of the country in its process of melding the influences of Guaraní and Spanish heritage into a regional identity. Throughout its history in Paraguay, the Catholic Church has played an important part in reinforcing traditional patriarchal relations between men and women.

Women's Roles, Rituals, and Religious Laws

The role of women in different religions is distinct, although their lack of participation in the hierarchy is a common denominator.[49] In the Catholic Church only men are permitted to be priests. There is a clear sexual division of labor, with the majority of women in service positions such as teaching catechism, maintenance, and cleaning of the church buildings; the decision-making is reserved for the men.

In Paraguay there are 32 male religious congregations with 532 priests and 82 congregations for women with a total of 1,500 nuns.[50] To become a priest, one must have a university degree in theology, but to become a nun only a high school education is required. In general, nuns continue to wear the tradition habit, although in recent years, rules about dress have become more relaxed. In religious ceremonies such as the mass there is no special dress for men and women, although tradition suggests that women should avoid wearing pants or miniskirts and men should not wear shorts.

The evangelical movement has taken hold in Paraguay in recent years. There is a Consortium of Evangelical Churches with 16 Christian churches scattered throughout the country. They have 600,000 followers nation-wide and 600 pastors. Although women can be named as pastors, there is only one woman who heads a church. Only 30 percent of these churches allow women in decision-making positions. Again, women are principally in service roles. A university degree in theology is required to be a minister in these churches. The selection process for the position of minister or pastor is the responsibility of the association of pastors, who are all men. The religious community democratically elects the church authorities. There is no particular religious attire for either men or women, although it is prohibited for women to wear pants in a religious building.

In terms of gender, the pressure exerted principally by the Catholic Church to avoid public policy issues related to sexual health and re-production is notorious. A similar pressure is evident in relation to sex education as part of the educational reform movement. The religious lobby, especially the Catholic Church, also pushed hard against the Divorce Law, but was unsuccessful. Slowly the church's influence in shaping public opinion is being challenged by access to information and alternative views offered by nongovernmental organizations and other interest groups.

VIOLENCE

Violence against women in its distinct manifestations, even by the state, is one of the cruelest expressions of inequality for women. However, since there is no system for registering cases, it is impossible to establish the magnitude of the problem. In an analysis derived from newspaper accounts of violence, Centro de Documentación y Estudias estimates that crimes against sexual autonomy account for 63 percent of the crimes reported, and murders of women account for 29 percent. In 100 percent of the rape cases, the perpetrator was a man, and in 87 percent of the cases the victim was a woman.[51]

Major victories have been won for women in recent years with regard to various forms of violence. Again, most of the triumphs have been within the legislative realm, increasing public awareness, and improving the methods and extent of documentation, rather than in the reduction of actual cases. Still, these constitute the first steps to addressing this issue; violence cannot be curbed until there are more data to show that it exists, its nature, and whom it impacts most. According to a report by the Secretariat of Women, between 1994 and 1998 there were 19,436 reported cases of violence against a woman. A national survey on demographics and reproductive health conducted by the CEPEP in 1997 indicated that almost 14 percent of all adult women have experienced some type of physical abuse. The report indicated further that the percentages drop slightly with age and education.[52]

Domestic Violence

In Paraguay, one of the most prevalent forms of violence against women is conjugal violence. According to newspaper data, in 1998 the average mention of a woman being killed was every twelve days; of those cases, 70 percent of the cases involved a man killing his partner.[53] However, in the same period, according to the Paraguayan Statistical Almanac, only one man was imprisoned for killing his wife.[54]

The section on "justifiable femicide" based on questions of honor was removed from the revised Penal Code that became effective in 1998.

The 1992 Constitution expressly states in Article 60: "The State will promote policies whose objective is the elimination of violence in the family environment." In 1995 Paraguay signed the International Convention on the Prevention, Sanction, and Eradication of Violence against Women. These two documents served as the framework and basis upon which to develop a legislative agenda against violence toward women. In 2000 the Domestic Violence Law (*Ley*/Law 1.600) was enacted. This was the result of a long and arduous battle led principally by feminist NGOs to document and publicize cases, work with the police during the transition period, and work with various members of Congress to develop the legislative proposals that began in 1998. However, this is only the beginning. With legal instruments in place, the work of NGOs and the state will be facilitated. But there is more work to be done in investigating cases, registering cases of violence adequately, and making sure that the new laws in place are applied and that aggressors are processed and punished by the law in an appropriate manner.

Rape/Sexual Assault

Sexual crimes are now considered punishable crimes. Sexual abuse has now been added, as well as incest and sexual harassment. Although the prison terms for sexual crimes have been reduced, the relationship of the victim to the perpetrator is now considered in sentencing. Despite major advances in the Penal Code, the punishment for stealing a cow is still harsher than for a sexual violation.

Victim Assistance

Within the framework of the National Strategic Plan for Health, several clinics and assistance centers have been set up, including the Department of Family Affairs at the National Police, which was specifically designed to receive victims of domestic or sexual violence. However, they have limited resources and are all located in the capital city. In 1999 the Secretary of Women, in partnership with the European Community, initiated a program to decentralize integral assistance to women throughout the country by setting up Centers for Initiatives and Development of Women. It is still too soon to evaluate how well this will work, but its objective is to offer integral support to women—including, legal, psychological, and social assistance to women suffering from violence. There is still no place in the entire country where women who are suffering from violence can seek temporary refuge.

Trafficking in Women and Children

For first few years of the transition, Paraguay was one of the top ten exporters of children to the United States. Although most of the cases of international adoption were legitimate, during the first years after the fall of Stroessner there was a rapid increase in the industry due to high demand and lack of state regulation. According to State Department statistics on the granting of citizenship to orphans adopted by U.S. citizens, Paraguay was consistently in the top six in volume by country of origin. Between 1992 and 1993 the number of cases doubled from 212 to 412.[55] As the number of cases that involved girls being duped, kidnapped, and even mutilated in order to meet the international demand gained public attention, the issue of the state's role as protector of children's rights was raised.

Under the leadership of a coalition of NGOs and the Technical Secretariat of Planning, in 1996 a moratorium was placed on international adoptions. A coalition of organizations concerned with children's rights developed a legislative project, lobbied Congress successfully, and in 1998 the Child Protection Law was passed. One of the components of the law is the creation of a state-run agency to oversee all adoptions, whether national or international. Within the guidelines for adopting orphans absolute priority is given to finding relatives or Paraguayan adoptive parents, which has all but stopped the international adoption trade in the country.

War and Military Repression

Very little is known about the social history of war in Paraguay and its impact on women and their roles in the family. Although its history is punctuated by several major wars in the nineteenth and twentieth centuries that decimated the male population, Paraguay has been free of armed conflict with its neighbors since the Chaco War with Bolivia in the 1930s. The civil war of 1947 pitted family members against each other over party politics. The extensive loss of life in the Triple Alliance War in the mid-nineteenth century left many women de facto heads of household, a phenomenon that continues today.

From the mid-1950s to the end of the 1980s, the authoritarian regime of General Alfredo Stroessner perpetrated a form of state terrorism that is just beginning to be understood. During the 1970s, at the height of the presence of authoritarian regimes in the Southern Cone, Paraguay participated in a scheme of regional state-sponsored espionage, repression, and exchange of political prisoners, the evidence of which is now coming to light through the Archivos del Terror.[56] This is a collection of documents and artifacts housed in the Department of Investigations of the Paraguayan Police that "disappeared" right after Stroessner was overthrown, and was recovered in 1992. It was microfiched by the United Nations and is now available for public viewing at the Ministry of Justice in Asunción. This is a critical source of information about the differential impact of state terrorism on men and women, which has yet to be explored.

OUTLOOK FOR THE TWENTY-FIRST CENTURY

The democratic environment that Paraguay is currently experiencing has opened up many opportunities for advancing the well-being of women and girls. At the same time, the patriarchal norms of Paraguayan society, the fragility of democratic institutions, and the deteriorating economic climate in the region have combined to make the struggle for women's equality, especially in their material conditions, a very difficult fight. Maintenance of the most minimum democratic guarantees is critical to the future of women's rights. Freedom of speech and association enable women to meet and to voice their opinions on policies and norms that discriminate against them. Slowly patriarchal norms are being questioned, and little by little change is taking place. Gains in the legislative realm, however, will not be enjoyed if the economic situation does not improve dramatically; the annual per capita income (U.S.$1,506) has fallen steadily and is lower now than ten years ago.[57] Women continue to bear the burden of economic reforms and a shrinking economy based on agriculture and primary products. So far government strategies for integration into the regional economy have left Paraguay as a major exporter of cheap labor and primary products with little value-added. But the women of Paraguay are strong and change is inevitable. As leading Paraguayan feminist intellectuals Line Bareiro and Clyde Soto reflect, "Perhaps the greatest success of the transition for women is a female population who are able not only to respond to situations that threaten their rights, but who are also able to propose alternatives."[58]

NOTES

1. Paraguay was one of the top three countries in the world in terms of the people's perceptions about their leaders and levels of corruption in society, with a score of 1.7 on a scale of 10 (0 being highly corrupt), according to the Transparency International Corruption Perception Index for 2002.

2. Dirección General de Estadística, Encuestas y Censos (DGEEC), *Población en el Paraguay—Año 1999* (Asunción: DGEEC/FNUAP, 1999).

3. United Nations Development Programme (UNDP)/Programa de Desarrollo de Naciones Unidas (PNUD), *Visión conjunta de la situación del Paraguay*, 2001, http://enalianza.org.py/vision/html/introduccion.html; www.undp.un.hn/idh2000.htm; www.undp.org.

4. Dirección General de Estadísticas, Encuestas y Censos (DGEEC), 1992.

5. Centro de Estudios de Población del Paraguay (CEPEP), *Encuesta nacional de salud materno infantil 1998 (informe preliminar)* (Asunción: CEPEP/USAID/CDC, 1999).

6. DGEEC, *Visión conjunta*, 1999.

7. Panamerican Health Organization (PAHO), "Paraguay," *Health in the Americas*, vol. II (2002): 441.

8. Comisión de Equidad, Género y Desarrollo Social, *Informe anual 2001: Componente de género y participación de la mujer* (Asunción: Banco interamericano de Desarollo 2001).

9. Federico Barrios and Luis Galeano, *Pobreza y vulnerabilidad social* (Asunción: DGEEC/BID/BM/STP, 1999), 39.

10. The discovery of Dávalos's thesis by the feminist community in 1986 was a revelation that inspired a group of feminist researchers to search for other evidence of the social history of women in Paraguay. Their initial findings are published in Line Bareiro, Clyde Soto, and Mary Monte, *Alquimistas. Documentos para otra historia de las mujeres* (Asunción: CDE, 1993). CDE also produced a documentary based on the book.

11. Graziela Corvalán, "Educación y capitación de la mujer," in Coordinación de Mujeres del Paraguay, *Implementación de la plataforma de Beijing en Paraguay 1995–2000. Informe no gubernamental*, ed. Line Bareiro and Mirtha Rivarola (Asunción: CMP and Sistema de Naciones Unidas, 2001), 69.

12. Ibid., 37.

13. Graziella Corvalán, *Patrones sexistas en la educación paraguaya* (Asunción: CPES/GEMPA/BID, 1993).

14. Esther Prieto, *Paraguay: Mujer y desarrollo en síntesis 1988–1998* (Asunción: Secretaría de la Mujer de la Presidencia de la República, Fondo de Desarrollo de las Naciones Unidas para la Mujer, Coordinación de Mujeres del Paraguay, Sistema de las Naciones Unidas en Paraguay, 1999).

15. Corvalán, *Patrones sexistas*, 1993.

16. Corvalán, "Educación y capitación de la mujer," 2001.

17. In 1997, for the first time, the Integrated National Household Survey included information on time dedicated to domestic work.

18. Comisión de Equidad, Género y Desarrollo Social, 2001.

19. Ibid.

20. The classification of economic sectors includes the following activities: (a) primary: agriculture, livestock, and hunting and fishing; (b) secondary: mining, industry, manufacturing, and construction; and (c) tertiary: electricity, water, sanitary services, tourism, transportation, finance, security and exchange, and real estate; Verónica Serafini Geoghegan, "La mujer, la pobreza, y la economia," in *Coordinación de mujeres del*

Paraguay (CMP): Implementación de la plataforma de Beijing en Paraguay 1995–2000. Informe no gubernamental, ed. Line Bareiro y Mirtha Rivarola (Asunción: CMP and United Nations System, 2001).

21. Serafini, 2001.

22. María Victoria Heikel, *La mujer jefe* (Asunción: BASE Investigaciones Sociales, 1989), cited in Comisión de Equidad, Género y Desarrollo Social, 2001.

23. DGEEC, 1999.

24. Serafini, 2001, 2.

25. María Molinas Cabrera, "Los derechos humanos de la mujer," in *Coordinación de mujeres del Paraguay (CMP): Implementación de la Plataforma de Beijing en Paraguay 1995–2000. Informe no gubernamental*, ed. Line Bareiro and Mirtha Rivarola (Asunción: CMP/FNUAP/PNUD/UNIFEM, 2001).

26. Bareiro and Rivarola, eds., 2001.

27. Olga Caballero Aquino and Marina Díaz de Vivar Prieto, *Mujer paraguaya, jefa de familia* (Asunción: CIDSEP-Universidad Católica, 1992); María Lilian Román, *Tengo que luchar: Mujeres jefas de hogar en ocupaciones de tierras urbanas* (Asunción: Universidad Nacional de Asunción/FNUAP, 1996).

28. Encuentro Nacional de Mujeres (ENM), *Por nuestra igualdad ante la ley* (Asunción: RPEdiciones, 1987).

29. Translation by Jane Clough-Riquelme.

30. CEPEP, 1999.

31. CEPEP, *Encuesta nacional de demografía y salud reproductiva* (Asunción: CEPEP/USAID/CDC, 1997).

32. María Molinas Cabrerea, "Mujeres," in *Informe de derechos humanos en Paraguay 1999*, ed. Marín et al. (Asunción: Coordinación de Derechos Humanos, 1999), 75.

33. CEPEP, 1999.

34. E. Prieto, 1999, 15.

35. Cynthia Prieto, "La mujer y la salud," in *Coordinación de mujeres del Paraguay (CMP)*, ed. Line Bareiro and Mirtha Rivarola (Asunción: CMP and United Nations System in Paraguay, 2001).

36. *Ultima Hora*, Suplemento Femenino (January 5, 1999): 4–5.

37. DGEEC, 1999, 31.

38. Ministerio de Salud Pública y Bienestar Social (MSPBS), *Política nacional de atención a la salud integral de la mujer* (Asunción: MSPBS, 1999).

39. Ibid.

40. PAHO, 2002; Comisión de Equidad, Género y Desarrollo Social, 2001.

41. Comisión de Equidad, Género y Desarrollo Social, 2001, 59.

42. CEPEP, 1997.

43. C. Prieto, 2001.

44. The Liberal party splintered several times during the course of the dictatorship as factions disagreed on whether or not to comply with Stroessner's maintenance of the "formal" vestiges of democracy, such as a Congress. The Liberal Party today, which participates in the new elected Congress, is the Partido Liberal Radical Auténtico (Authentic Radical Liberal Party), known as the PLRA.

45. Line Bareiro and Clyde Soto, *Liderazgo femenino en Paraguay* (Asunción: Secretaría de la Mujer, 1997).

46. Ibid.

47. Molinas Cabrera, 2001.

48. Grupo de Acción Gay-Lésbico, "Derecho a la libre orientación sexual," in *Derechos humanos en Paraguay 1999*, ed. Coordinadora de Derechos Humanos del Paraguay (Asunción: CODEHUPY, 1999), 95–108.

49. Interviews by Fátima Figari with Gregorio Fernández, Ecumenical Council, August 2002; interviews with Cristina Vila, Executive Secretary of Comité de la Iglesia para la Ayuda en Emergencias (CIPAE) and Manuel Molinas by María Molinas, August 2002. Asunción.

50. Ibid.

51. Helena Martínez and Verónica Villalba, "Mujeres," in *Informe de derechos humanos en Paraguay 2001*, ed. González et al. (Asunción: CODEHUPY, 2001).

52. CEPEP, 1997.

53. Coordinación de Mujeres del Paraguay, *Implementación de la plataforma de Beijing en Paraguay 1995–2000. Informe no gubernamental,* ed. Line Bareiro and Mirtha Rivarola (Asunción: CMP and Sistema de Naciones Unidas en Paraguay, 2001).

54. Molinas Cabrera, 2001, 124.

55. http://travel.state.gov/orphan_numbers.html.

56. R.A. Nickson, "Paraguay's *Archivo del Terror,*" *Latin American Research Review* 30, no. 1 (1995): 125–29.

57. U.S. State Department, "Paraguay," Country Reports on Human Rights Practices, Bureau of Democracy, Human Rights, and Labor, 2001, www.state.gov/g/drl/rls/hrrpt/2001/what8297pf.htm.

58. Bareiro and Soto, 1997, 94.

RESOURCE GUIDE

Suggested Reading

Bareiro, Line, and Clyde Soto. *Liderazgo femenino en Paraguay: El poder formal en cifras*, part 1. Asunción: Secretaría de la Mujer de la Presidencia de la República/CDE-Área Mujer, 1997. CDE in conjunction with the Secretariat of Women developed a database on women in formal leadership positions in government, political parties, and social organizations. They hope to update it periodically.

Bareiro, Line, and Clyde Soto. *Vencer la adversidad: Historias de mujeres líderes*. Asunción: Secretaría de la Mujer/CDE-Área Mujer, 1999. This is a qualitative analysis of a cross section of thirty-five female national leaders from all sectors. The findings show that these women share several common characteristics, including the influence of their fathers on their career trajectory, and their leadership experience in various types of organizations from an early age.

Heikel, María Victoria. *La mujer jefe: Un concepto revisado para explicar nuevas relaciones sociales en sectores populares*. Asunción: BASE Investigaciones Sociales, 1989. Using census data, Paraguay's leading demographer analyzes the growing phenomenon of female-headed households.

Lambert, P.W. "Mechanisms of Control: The Stroessner Regime in Paraguay." In *Authoritarianism in Latin America Since Independence*, edited by W. Fowler. Westport, CT: Greenwood Press, 1996. A clearly written analysis of the Stroessner regime for those who want to understand more about that period and state repression in general.

Lambert, Peter, and Andrew Nickson, eds. *The Transition to Democracy in Paraguay*. New York: St. Martin's Press, 1997. The volume contains a chapter on women by Line Bareiro and Clyde Soto. In general, this is an excellent overview of the transition process in Paraguay since 1989, written mostly by leading Paraguayan academics.

Nickson, R.A. "Paraguay's *Archivo del Terror*." *Latin American Research Review* 30, no. 1 (1995): 125–29.

Ocampos, Genoveva. *Mujeres campesinas y estrategias de vida*. Asunción: RPEdiciones/ BASE-ECTA, 1992. This is an excellent, theoretically informed empirical study on rural women and survival strategies written from a gender perspective. The study compares women in established settlements and in state-sponsored land reform settlements, based on a household survey.

Prieto, Esther. *Paraguay: Mujer y desarrollo en síntesis 1988–1999*. Asunción: Sistema de las Naciones Unidas en Paraguay, 1999. Synthesized data on a range of issues with brief commentary. This document may be available through the United Nations publications system.

Programa de las Naciones Unidas de Paraguay. *Informe nacional de desarrollo humano desde la perspectiva de género 1995*. Asunción: PNUD, 1995. The first U.N. National Human Development Report from a gendered perspective. The chief of mission in Paraguay at the time of publication was a woman.

Whigham, Thomas L. "Rosa Dominga Ocampos: A Matter of Honor in Paraguay." In *The Human Tradition in Latin América. The Nineteenth Century*, edited by Judith Ewell and William H. Beezley, 73–81. Latin American Silhouettes. Studies in History and Culture. Wilmington, DE: Scholarly Resources, 1989. An interesting story of gender and citizenship at the end of the nineteenth century. This article demonstrates the wealth of data on social history in the National Archives that few historians have taken advantage of.

Zarza, Olga Maria, ed. *Mujeres latinoamericanas en cifras. Paraguay*. Santiago de Chile: FLACSO, 1993. This is the Paraguay volume of a Latin America–wide project to collect compatible statistics on the situation of women in each country. A team of more than ten Paraguayan researchers contributed to this volume.

Videos/Films

Alquimistas. Otra historia de las mujeres. Documentary produced by the Centro de Documentación y Estudios that draws on its book of the same title. In a beautifully artistic manner this film reveals what is known to date about the first feminists of Paraguay in the early twentieth century and their struggle for equal rights as citizens. Contact CDE for more information at cde@cde.org.py.

One Man's War. 1991. 91 minutes. Distributed by HBO Canada. A drama based on the famous Filártiga case—an international human rights case regarding the murder of the son of Joél Filártiga, a prominent doctor and outspoken opponent of the regime, by a police officer while in custody. The officer fled to the United States, setting in motion the events that led to a precedent in international law for charging human rights violators outside of their own country as Filártiga's daughter succeeds in getting the Paraguayan officer tried in a U.S. court.

Web Sites

CIDEM (Centros de Iniciativas y Desarrollo de la Mujer), www.cidem.org.py/.
The Red CIDEM (Network of Women's Centers for Initiatives and Development of Women) project is a collaboration between the European Community and the Sec-

retariat of Women to create a social infrastructure to empower rural women across the country through the creation of a network of centers in each state.

DGEEC (Dirección General de Estadísticas, Encuestas, y Censos) www.dgeec.gov.py/
This is the semiautonomous state agency responsible for the design and implementation of the national population census, as well as intercensal surveys. It works with researchers, international agencies, and public institutions to provide the most accurate data to the public.

United Nations Development Programme, Paraguay (PNUD) www.undp.org.py/
The UNDP in Paraguay has formed a tripartite commission between the N60 sector, government, and the United Nations to monitor the Beijing agreements.

University of Wurzburg, www.uni-wuerzburg.de/law/paoot_.html.
For an English translation of the 1992 Paraguayan Constitution, see this site.

Organizations

For a complete directory of nongovernmental and governmental development organizations in Paraguay online in PDF, see www.devdir.org/files/Paraguay.PDF. Key organizations whose principal mission is to empower women through research, capacity building, and development assistance are listed below.

Alter Vida (Centro de Estudios y Formación para el Ecodesarrollo)
Itapua 1372 e/Primer Presidente y Rio Monday
Barrio Trinidad
Asunción, Paraguay
Contact Person: Margarita Ma. Molinas
Phone: (595-21) 298-842/3
Fax: (595-21) 298-845
Email: info@altervida.org.py
Web site: www.altervida.org.py

This private, nonprofit educational and community development organization focuses on sustainable development. The gender perspective is apparent throughout its programs. In Spanish.

BASE-ECTA (Educación, Comunicación, Tecnologia Adecuada)
Aviadores del Chaco 350, piso 1
San Lorenzo, Paraguay
Email: baserural@mmail.com.py

A research and advocacy NGO that focuses on rural populations. It has an excellent resource library that is open to the public.

CDE (Centro de Documentación y Estudios)
Cerro Cora 1426 e/Pai Perez y Peru
Asunción, Paraguay
Contact: Line Bareiro, Clyde Soto (Area Mujer)
Phone: (595-21) 204-295
Fax: (595-21) 213-246
Email: cde@cde.org.py

A private, nonprofit research and advocacy organization that focuses on gender, rural populations, and labor unions. It runs the Serafina Dávalos Library on Gender, one of the most complete collections on gender in the country, and collaborates on public policy studies with the Secretariat on Women. CDE/Area Mujer conducts research and advocacy for legislative reforms related to gender equity, and has contributed significantly to global and regional understanding of the situation of women and gender issues in Paraguay.

CEPEP (Centro de Estudios de Población de Paraguay)
Web site: www.ippfwhr.org/profiles/paraguay.html, in English, through Planned Parenthood; www.cepep.org.py/default.htm, in Spanish

CEPEP is a research and health advocacy organization with clinics in various parts of the country.

CIRD (Centro de Información y Recursos para el Desarrollo)
Padre Cardozo 569 e/Juan de Salazar y Tte. Núñez
Asunción, Paraguay
Phone: (595-21) 207-373
Fax: (595-21) 212-540
Email: cird@cird.org.py
Web site: www.cird.org.py

A resource center for nongovernmental organizations, CIRD produces a directory of development organizations that is updated every few years.

CPES (Centro Paraguayo de Estudios Sociológicos)
Eligio Ayala 973 entre EEUU y Tacuary
Asunción, Paraguay
Phone: (595) (21) 440-885, 493-737
Fax: (595) (21) 446-617
Email: cpes@sce.cnc.una.py
Web site: www.cpes.org.py
Contact Person: Graziella Corvalán or Mirtha Rivarola

CPES is one of the most established independent research centers in Paraguay, having functioned throughout the dictatorship. It produces an academic journal, *Revista Sociológico de Paraguay*, which is widely available throughout Latin America. One of its cofounders, Graziella Corvalán, heads the Gender Research Unit called GEMPA (Grupo de Estudios de la Mujer Paraguaya).

SEFEM (Servicios de Formación y Estudios de la Mujer)
Defensa Nacional 699 y Tte. Morales ·
Barrio las Mercedes
Asunción, Paraguay
Phone/Fax (595-21) 22-3081
E-mail: Sefem@sce.cnc.una.py
Contact Person: María Victoria Heikel or Cynthia Fernandez

This private, nonprofit research, educational, and community development organization focuses exclusively on the empowerment of women. It analyzes census data on a variety of topics from a gender perspective; develops educational programs on gender sensitivity for local and state governments as well as the central government; and supports popular women's organizations in advocating for their rights.

Secretaría de la Mujer—Presidencia de la República de Paraguay
Edificio AYFRA, bloque B, piso 13
Presidente Franco y Ayolas
Asunción, Paraguay
Phone: (595-21) 450-036; 450-037, 450-038, 450-039
Fax: (595-21) 450-041
Email: secmujer-sec@sce.cnc.una.py

This government ministry is responsible for assuring that the constitutional mandates for equal rights and opportunities for women and men are fulfilled, and that the government actually promotes gender equity through affirmative action policies.

UNICEF
Mcal. López y Saraví, 1er piso
Edificio Sede de las Naciones Unidas
UNICEF—Paraguay
Asunción, Paraguay
Phone: (595-21) 611-007/8
Fax: (595-21) 611-015
Email: asuncion@unicef.org.py
Web site: www.unicef.org/paraguay/

The United Nations Children's Fund has an office in Asunción from which it supports the national government, as well as local governments and NGOs, in protecting children's rights and nurturing their development through a variety of outreach and educational programs.

SELECTED SPANISH BIBLIOGRAPHY

Arditi, Benjamin, and J.C. Rodríguez de Alcalá. *La sociedad a pesar del estado. Movimientos sociales y recuperación democrática en el Paraguay*. Asunción: Editorial El Lector, 1987.

Bareiro, Line, and Clyde Soto. *Liderazgo femenino en Paraguay: El poder formal en cifras*. Asunción: Secretaría de la Mujer de la Presidencia de la República/CDE-Área Mujer, 1997.

Bareiro, Line, and Clyde Soto. *Vencer la adversidad: Historias de mujeres líderes*. Asunción: Secretaria de la Mujer/CDE-Área Mujer, 1999.

Barrios, Federico, and Luis Galeano. *Pobreza y vulnerabilidad social*. Asunción: DGEEC/BID/BM/STP, 1999.

Caballero Aquino, Olga, and Marina Díaz de Vivar Prieto. *Mujer paraguaya, jefa de familia*. Asunción: CIDSEP-Universidad Católica, 1992.

Centro de Estudios de Población de Paraguay (CEPEP). *Encuesta nacional de demografía y salud reproductiva*. Asunción: CEPEP/USAID/CDC, 1997.

Centro de Estudios de Población de Paraguay. *Encuesta nacional de salud materno infantil 1998 (informe preliminar)*. Asunción: CEPEP/USAID/CDC, 1999.

Coordinadora de Derechos Humanos (CODEHUPHY). *Informe de derechos humanos en Paraguay 1999*, edited by Marín et al. Asunción: CODEHUPY, 1999.

Coordinadora de Derechos Humanos. *Informe de derechos humanos en Paraguay 2001*. Edited by González et al. Asunción: CODEHUPY, 2001.

Comisión de Equidad, Género y Desarrollo Social. *Informe anual 2001: Componente de género y participación de la mujer*. Programa de Fortalecimiento de las Instituciones Democráticas II. Asunción: Banco Interamericano de Desarrollo, Congreso Nacional, 2001.

Coordinación de Mujeres del Paraguay (CMP). *Implementación de la plataforma de Beijing en Paraguay 1995–2000. Informe no gubernamental*, edited by Line Bareiro and Mirtha Rivarola. Asunción: CMP/Sistema de Naciones Unidas en Paraguay, 2001.

Corvalán, Graziella. *Patrones sexistas en la educación paraguaya*. Asunción: CPES/GEMPA/BID, 1993.

Corvalán, Graziella. "Educación y capacitación de la mujer." In *Coordinación de Mujeres del Paraguay (CMP): Implementación de la plataforma de Beijing en Paraguay 1995–2000. Informe no gubernamental*, edited by Line Bareiro and Mirtha Rivaroles. Asunción: CMP and United Nations System, 2001.

Corvalán, Graziella, ed. *Entre el silencio y la voz. Mujeres: Actoras y autoras de una sociedad en cambio*. Asunción: GEMPA/CPES, 1989.

Dávalo, Serafina. *Humanismo. Serafina: Feminista paraguaya desde comienzos de siglo*. Asunción: RPEdiciones/Edicion Facsimilar/Instituto de la Mujer-Solidaridad Internacional, 1990 [1907].

Dirección General de Estadística, Encuestas y Censos (DGEEC). *Ser mujer en Paraguay: Situación socio-demográfica y cambios registrados en el periódo intercensal 1982–1992*, by María Victoria Heikel. Fernando de la Mora: DGEEC, 1996.

DGEEC. *Población en el Paraguay—año 1999*. Asunción: DGEEC/FNUAP, 1999.

DGEEC. *Encuesta integrada de hogares 2000/01*. Asunción: STP/DGEEC/World Bank/IDB, 2002.

Elias, Margarita. "Mecanismos institucionales para el adelanto de la mujer." In *Coordinación de Mujeres del Paraguay (CMP): Implementación de la Plataforma de Beijing en Paraguay 1995–2000. Informe no gubernamental*, edited by Line Bareiro and Mirtha Rivarola. Asunción: CMP/ Sistema de Naciones Unidas, 2001.

Encuentro Nacional de Mujeres. *Por nuestra igualdad ante la ley*. Asunción: RPEdiciones, 1987.

Galeano, Luis A., and Federico Barrios. "El rol de los actores sociales en la superación de la exclusión social: El caso del Paraguay." *Revista paraguaya de sociología* 36, no. 105 (1999): 29–90.

Grupo de Acción Gay-Lésbico. "Derecho a la libre orientación sexual." In *Derechos humanos en Paraguay 1999*. Asunción: CODEHUPY, 1999.

Martínez, Helena, and Verónica Villalba. "Mujeres." In *Informe de derechos humanos en Paraguay 2001*, Edited by González, et al. Asunción: CODEHUPY, 2001.

Ministerio de Salud Pública y Bienestar Social. *Política nacional de atención a la salud integral de la mujer*. Asunción: MSPBS, 1999.

Molinas Cabrera, María. "Mujeres." In *Informe de derechos humanos en Paraguay 1999*, edited by Marin et al. Asunción: CODEHUPY, 1999.

Molinas Cabrera, María. "Los derechos humanos de la mujer." In *Coordinación de Mujeres del Paraguay (CMP): Implementación de la plataforma de Beijing en Paraguay 1995–2000. Informe no gubernamental*, edited by Line Bareiro and Mirtha Rivarola. Asunción: CMP/FNUAP/PNUD/UNIFEM, 2001.

Prieto, Cynthia. "La mujer y la salud." In *Coordinación de Mujeres del Paraguay (CMP): Implementación de la plataforma de Beijing en Paraguay 1995–2000. Informe no gubernamental*, edited by Line Bareiro y Mirtha Rivarola. Asunción: CMP and Coordinadora de Mujeres, FNUAP/PNUD/UNIFEM, 2001.

Prieto, Esther. *Paraguay. Mujer y Desarrollo en Síntesis 1988–1998*. Asunción: Secretaría de la Mujer de la Presidencia de la República, Fondo de Desarrollo de las

Naciones Unidas para la Mujer, Coordinación de Mujeres del Paraguay, Sistema de las Naciones Unidas en Paraguay, 1999.

Programa de Desarrollo de Naciones Unidas (PNUD). *Visión conjunta de la situación de Paraguay.* 2001. http://enalianza.org.py/vision/html/introduccion.html.

PNUD. *Informe de desarrollo humano 2002.* New York: Ediciones Mundi-Prensa, 2002. Web version: www.undp.org.

Román, María Lilian. *Tengo que luchar: Mujeres jefas de hogar en ocupaciones de tierras urbanas.* Asunción: Universidad Nacional de Asunción/FNUAP, 1996.

Serafini Geoghegan, Verónica. "La mujer, la pobreza, y la economia." In *Coordinación de Mujeres del Paraguay (CMP): Implementación de la plataforma de Beijing en Paraguay 1995–2000. Informe no gubernamental,* edited by Line Bareiro and Mirtha Rivarola. Asunción: CMP and FNUAP/PNUD/UNIFEM, 2001.

Soto, Clyde. "La mujer en el ejercicio del poder y la adopción de decisiones." In *Coordinación de Mujeres del Paraguay (CMP): Implementación de la plataforma de Beijing en Paraguay 1995–2000. Informe no gubernamental,* edited by Line Bareiro and Mirtha Rivarola. Asunción: CMP and FNUAP/PNUD/UNIFEM, 2001.

17

PERU

Amy Lind and Emi McLaughlin

PROFILE OF PERU

Peru is located in the Andean region, on the Pacific coast of South America. Approximately twice the size of Texas, it shares borders with Ecuador and Colombia to the north, Brazil and Bolivia to the east, and Chile to the south. Peru is a country full of natural beauty, rich cultures, and a diverse topography. It is composed of three principal regions: the *costa*, the *sierra* and the *selva*. The coastal region (*costa*), which is dry and arid, makes up 10 percent of the territory and is home to more than 60 percent of the population.[1] The *sierra*, the snow-peaked, rugged mountains of the Andes runs through the middle of the country and contains the city of Cuzco, the ancient capital of the Incan empire. It accounts for 26 percent of the territory and is home to 35 percent of the population, mostly of indigenous descent. The lush rain forests of the jungle region (*selva*), including the Amazon River, comprise 60 percent of the territory but are home to only 5 percent of the population. Peru's total population is almost 26 million; 70 percent live in urban areas, 8 million of them in the capital city of

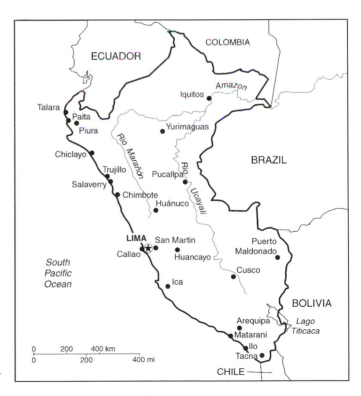

Lima. More than half of Lima's residents live in *pueblos jovenes* (young towns), the urban shantytowns scattered around Lima's core.

At the time of conquest by the Spanish in the sixteenth century, the Incan empire controlled much of the region and hundreds of indigenous groups lived throughout Peru. Machu Picchu, the largest remaining ruins of an abandoned Incan village, and Cuzco, the former center of the Incan empire, provide a glimpse into the lives of these early inhabitants. Today, while there are no longer racial classifications in the census, approximately 35 percent of the population is indigenous, 33 percent mestizo, and 10 percent white (of Spanish/European descent). A significant Chinese community (200,000+ people) resides primarily on the coast, the descendents of Chinese brought to Peru as indentured servants in the mid-nineteenth century. Japanese began migrating to Peru as early as 1899; today, the Japanese-Peruvian community includes 100,000 people. Afro-Peruvians, the descendants of slaves, play an important role in Peru's culture and development. In particular, coastal Afro-Peruvian music has a long tradition and has produced internationally acclaimed female musicians such as Chabuca Granda, Eva Ayllón, and Susana Baca.[2]

Women constitute 50.4 percent of the population. Average life expectancy is 69 years. The total fertility rate is 2.8. The infant mortality rate (per 1,000 live births) is 31.8, and the mortality rate under five years old (per 1,000 births) is 41.4.[3] The population growth rate is 1.3 percent. In 2000, 54 percent of the population lived below the national poverty line.[4] According to one study, 60 percent of Peruvian women are poor.[5]

The Incas' elaborate political and economic systems allowed them to rule over several cultures. Today, it is difficult to document the vastly diverse cultures that existed before the period of Incan rule. To a large extent, we have to rely upon the writings of Spanish conquerors and soldiers, who were focused on establishing rule over indigenous communities rather than understanding their cultural, political, and economic contributions. The legacies of pre-Incan cultures such as the Chavín, the Tiahanuco, the Wari, and the Moche are only partially understood, although many contemporary Peruvians, themselves descendants of these cultures, have attempted to study their histories and preserve their cultural artifacts. Colonial Spanish rule greatly influenced the region's growth during the eighteenth and early nineteenth centuries. Peru gained independence from Spain in 1821, during the same period that most South American colonial territories gained their independence as autonomous nation-states.

Spanish and Quechua are the official languages of Peru. Quechua is the most widely spoken indigenous language in Peru. Aymara is spoken in southern Andean provinces, and several other indigenous languages are spoken in the Amazon region. There are approximately 300,000 people living in the Amazon region who belong to 65 distinct ethnic groups. The largest groups include the Aguarunas, with around 45,000 people, and the Ashaninka, with around 40,000.[6]

Historically, Peru's economy has been largely dependent upon its relations with wealthy countries of the North, including Europe and the United States. Its natural resources include oil, guano, copper, fish meal, rubber, cocoa, and bananas. Sugar, cotton, and wool were important products in earlier periods. The economy faces serious challenges because of a persistent economic crisis that originated in the early 1980s. In addition, Peru has experienced periods of military rule followed by redemocratization. Women have been active in shaping the national political environment and in supporting the economy, particularly since the 1950s.

OVERVIEW OF WOMEN'S ISSUES

Because Peruvian women are from diverse socioeconomic, ethnic, racial, and geographic backgrounds, it is difficult to generalize about their lives. Women in rural areas, including the Andes and the Amazon region, often rely upon subsistence agriculture. Poor women in Lima may have more access to basic amenities, but face the challenging circumstances of economic crisis, unemployment, and poverty that the rapidly growing city offers. Middle-to-upper-class women have made many gains professionally and politically, yet still face gender barriers. Since the 1960s, many women have benefited from legal and political reforms regarding gender issues. Women's status has improved over the years: they are living longer, have increased control over their fertility, have entered the formal workforce in higher numbers, and have become important public figures in economic, cultural, and political sectors. Yet despite these advances, there are still many challenges: women's economic situation has deteriorated, not improved, due to two decades of war and poverty; more women are living in poverty than ever before, and jobs are few and far between; and indigenous women and new urban settlers in Lima still experience major racial, gender, and class-based discrimination. In the twentieth century, in the country's so-called modernization process, in which the state attempted to become welfare-oriented and promoted urbanization and economic development, women made gains through their political activism. The Peruvian women's movement is one of the strongest and largest in the region—and indeed, in the world. At the same time, inequalities among rich and poor women make their experiences of the country's modernization process during this period very different.

EDUCATION

Opportunities

The Peruvian Constitution states that no one shall be prevented from receiving an adequate education for financial reasons or because of physical

Peruvian women at the School of Hairdressing in Lima. Photo © TRIP/M. Jelliffe.

or mental limitations.[7] Public education is free to all citizens. Nevertheless, many women are illiterate, particularly in rural areas.

During the early colonial period, the Catholic Church promoted and managed educational programs that focused on European notions of literacy and citizenship. Women who had access to education typically were from upper-class, Spanish backgrounds, although a handful of indigenous women were provided access to education as part of Spain's strategy to "civilize" the original inhabitants of the area. Today, Peru's educational system is based on the Spanish model, although the state has undergone a series of reforms to address illiteracy and to make education more accessible to all Peruvians. In the Amazon region, many elementary students reach their schools by canoe; in the Andes, small schoolhouses dot the landscape of relatively remote villages. In Lima, schoolchildren attend school en masse, all wearing the uniforms that are required by the state for public schools throughout the country.

In the early twentieth century, growing discontent from peasant, indigenous, and labor sectors concerning their disenfranchisement contributed to the state's push to reform the educational system, including making education accessible to Quechua-speaking Peruvians and others who spoke an indigenous language. It was not until the 1960s and 1970s, however, that the state first recognized Quechua as an official language in Quechua-speaking regions of the country.

Literacy

In 2000, 14.7 percent of Peruvian women were illiterate, a sharp decline from 29.3 percent in 1980,[8] 5.3 percent of all men were illiterate in 2000, down from 11.7 percent in 1980. A 1993 survey shows that of the total number of illiterate people (1,784,282), 72.7 percent were women.[9] Of this percentage, two-thirds live in rural regions. In general, women's illiteracy rates have always been higher than men's, a result of gender relations and social stereotypes about men's and women's roles in the family and economy. Often, if poor parents have both boys and girls and can send only some of them to school, they will send the boys and ask the girls to stay home and help with the household. These figures account primarily for literacy in Spanish, not in Quechua or other indigenous languages. Poor female Quechua-speakers face additional barriers because many teachers do not speak their language or dialect;[10] yet other teachers do not want to move to rural areas to teach, leaving the countryside and the Amazon region with a limited supply of teachers. Over the decades, governments have offered higher salaries, free housing, and/or moving benefits, but this has not been enough to encourage teachers to work outside Peru's cities.

Many women's organizations have established literacy and educational programs for illiterate women. Some middle-class feminist organizations in Lima offer literacy classes to women in poor neighborhoods and in rural zones. Movimiento Manuela Ramos, for example, has offered classes in poor neighborhoods since its inception in the 1970s. In addition, promoters of liberation theology traditionally have focused on educating the poor, including women. Some women have benefited from this, even if they have not attended formal schools.

EMPLOYMENT AND ECONOMICS

Peru's economy can be characterized by its dependence on a few exports. Oil is an important source of revenue, as are copper and other minerals, fish meal, guano (a type of fertilizer), and agricultural products. The country's colonial legacy continues to shape Peru's economy: it relies upon the export of natural resources for its revenue, seeks foreign investment, and receives aid from institutions such as the World Bank, the International Monetary Fund, and private banks. Today, Peru's foreign debt exceeds U.S.$28 billion, and the government spends just under 50 percent of its annual gross domestic product (GDP) on debt service alone.[11] In practice, this translates into harsh living circumstances for most Peruvians: the cost of daily lives rises,[12] wages stay the same or decrease, and the Peruvian currency is devalued. Women's experiences are greatly affected by these economic forces.

Job/Career Opportunities

Women constitute 31 percent of Peru's total labor force. This figure accounts only for women's participation in the formal sector of the economy, in jobs where they are paid salaries or hourly wages and receive benefits. In 2000, the total unemployment rate was 8 percent, and 8.6 percent of the female labor force was unemployed.[13] Informal sector laborers, who comprise the majority of the economic population, typically are excluded from statistics because it is difficult to account for their work. For a variety of reasons, many women seek employment in this sector. Particularly during the past few decades, recent women migrants in Lima have created their own businesses to survive. Many poor women, for example, work as street vendors or domestic servants. Although it is difficult to assess, some scholars have pointed out that domestic service would account for a significant percentage of Peru's national income, if it were to be officially counted.[14] Women work in the streets, selling everything from food to clothing to imported goods, while they simultaneously care for their children. Many times, their children learn how to vend at an early age as a way to help their parents survive economically.

A well-known Peruvian economist, Hernando de Soto, writes about Peru's large informal sector in his widely acclaimed book *The Other Path* (1989). Unlike many economists of industrialized, wealthy countries, who believe that the informal sector is a hindrance to formal economic growth, De Soto was the first to argue that poor countries' economies—and, indeed, those of countries throughout the world—benefit from the informal sector, including women's work. Following this idea, many women workers in the informal sector have attempted to organize themselves and address issues such as fair salaries and discrimination in the workplace. Paid domestic laborers have organized events and planned holidays in honor of domestic work, bringing awareness to Peruvian society about this largely "invisible" form of labor.

Pay

Although there are few data on women's wages and the gender gap in wages, many women's organizations have addressed these issues. Peruvian laws provide women with job protection in terms of gender discrimination. However, in practice many women continue to receive salaries that are less than their male counterparts, and some places of employment do not hire women if the labor is considered "male." Social and cultural values placed on men's and women's work determines, to a large degree, what jobs men and women decide to seek and obtain. Some women's NGOs offer training courses in areas not considered traditionally female, with the idea that women's increased knowledge and skill formation will facilitate their increased entry into traditionally male sectors of the economy. Despite this, much remains to be done to change societal values about women's work, and comparable worth measures have not been adopted by the Peruvian government.

Working Conditions

Peru has ratified several international instruments adopted by the International Labour Organisation (ILO) that protect women's labor rights. According to Peruvian law, men and women have equal opportunities in the workplace, including the right to equal pay. Women are protected against discrimination in employment on grounds of pregnancy. The Law for the Promotion of Employment states that a dismissal on grounds of pregnancy within ninety days before or after a birth is null and void.[15] In practice, these laws are difficult to enforce, given persistent conceptions about the value of women workers and their labor.

The state recognizes the work of domestic servants by giving them the right to vacations, pensions, and a nightly leave at their workplace. In general, however, their labor rights are minimal compared to other workers. Because the informal sector remains largely unregulated, most female workers in this sector do not receive benefits or regular pay. Rather, the amount of time they spend at work determines their daily living wage.

Sexual Harassment

Peru's labor legislation treats sexual harassment as an act of hostility by the employer. The time limit for taking legal action in relation to sexual harassment in the workplace is 30 days following the incident. A worker may either take action to end the harassment or terminate her employment contract. In cases where the worker opts to terminate her contract, she is entitled to demand compensation for arbitrary dismissal as established by law, apart from any fines imposed on the employer for sexual harassment. Legislation that seeks to prevent and punish sexual harassment is under consideration by Congress, thanks to the efforts of women's organizations. Despite the legal protection that does exist, many Peruvian women continue to face sexual harassment in the workplace. Most cases are unreported, due to social stigmas and to the complicated and often unfriendly legal system.

Support for Mothers/Caretakers

Maternal Leave and Daycare

According to law, Peruvian women are entitled to 45 days' leave before and 45 days' leave after birth. In the public administration and education, sectors, female employees and teachers are entitled to breast-feeding leave of an hour each day during the child's first year. Businesses that have more than 25 employees are required to provide areas for child care.[16] In practice, much has to be done to raise awareness in the business sector about maternity leave, and many firms do not comply with the laws.

Inheritance and Property Rights

In Peru, there are no legal restrictions on women's property rights. The Constitution establishes equal rights to own property and to inherit. More important, perhaps, is the sharp contrast among rural and urban, poor and rich women. Poor peasant women have participated in struggles for access to land. As elsewhere in Central and South America, peasant families have lived largely as tenants on large parcels of land owned by Peru's oligarchic elite.

Social/Government Programs

Peruvian governments have a long history of addressing the needs of the poor and disenfranchised through state-sponsored welfare programs. Like other countries in the region, the Peruvian state was developed as a welfare state in the early twentieth century, when social and educational reformers argued that the state should be responsible for those in need — a direct result of European influences and the process of modernization in Peru, whereby governments attempted to improve the standard of living of the population. Unlike other countries in the region, some of Peru's most interesting experiments with welfare reform stem from a period of military rule. The leftist military government of General Juan Velasco (1968–1975) changed the lives of many Peruvians. During the late 1960s and early 1970s, General Velasco, who became leader through a military coup d'état, maintained support for his regime by mobilizing poor communities.

Among others, the Velasco regime gave legal status to several *pueblos jóvenes* that until then were considered illegal. This was an important turning point in the history of the urban poor, for prior to that time, inhabitants of *pueblos jóvenes* were driven out by private landowners and politically repressed by governments. This was due in part to the history of Lima's shantytowns: as migrants from the countryside made their way to Lima, they relied upon social networks that had established informal housing on large areas of unused land owned by wealthy landowners. In a process sometimes referred to as "land invasions" (*invasiones*), to this day many migrants establish their first homes and acquire land through this process. The Velasco regime was the first to acknowledge the economic and political contributions of *pueblos jóvenes*, thereby extending new citizen rights to settlers previously seen as second-class citizens. Thus, while Lima's urban poor continue to be extremely marginalized, some of the older communities are now established municipalities, and are self-governed and planned.

Villa El Salvador is the shining example of General Velasco's populist strategies: once a newly settled area of poor migrants from the countryside, it now boasts a population of over 1 million and a semisocialist political structure. Many residents of Villa El Salvador still speak of General Velasco with great fondness, since it was his government that established the communal block system which characterizes the city and has made it famous as a model of development for poor communities throughout the world. Critics of Villa El Salvador contend that while the model emphasizes socialist planning, including fair distribution of resources among the population, it is still organized in a top-down manner reminiscent of Velasco's regime. Indeed, while some admire Velasco's approach to social welfare, many others are critical of his authoritarianism and top-down approach.

Importantly, the Velasco regime set the stage for extending certain rights to women. First, women were further incorporated into the educational system at this time, as teachers and students, as never before. Second, new labor laws gave women and men workers more rights, particularly those in the working class. Third, in 1974 the regime established the first state agency that specifically addressed women's issues: the Technical Committee to Revalue Women (Comité Técnico de Revaloración de la Mujer). This was a precursor of the later women's movement.

Since the early 1980s, Peru's economic crisis has led to new strategies for development, including cutting social spending on welfare programs. What was once seen as a growing welfare state in the early-to-mid-twentieth century is now a shrinking welfare state. Women, in particular, have suffered from and experienced the contradictions of this historical process. As the government has ended some welfare programs that focus on child development and family issues, it has encouraged private (for-profit and nonprofit) organizations to take over. The Catholic Church, Christian organizations, political parties, NGOs, and community-based groups have all helped during the crisis. This has contributed to the growth of local women's organizations, particularly those which address resource distribution (e.g., food) and community development (e.g., land, housing, water, electricity, gas).

Lima's communal kitchens are perhaps the best-known example of women's mobilization at the grassroots level. During the 1980s, every morning some 40,000 women belonging to the Federation of Self-Managed Popular Kitchens (Federacíon de Comedores Populares Auto-gestionarios) gathered at 2,000 sites in Lima's poor neighborhoods, pooling their family resources to serve over 200,000 persons.[17] Twenty to 30 female friends, fellow church members, neighbors, and family members work together at each kitchen. Although the kitchens are not as numerous now, they continue to provide an important service to poor communities. Women have gained valuable skills from their participation in these move-ments. Critics contend, however, that because women typically participate on a volunteer basis and often work long hours, they are not necessarily becoming empowered. Some studies have shown that their workloads have increased, rather than decreased, as a result of the new welfare strategies—something that feminists and development advocates did not anticipate when they first helped to organize poor women.[18]

FAMILY AND SEXUALITY

Gender Roles

Women's and men's gender roles are influenced by a variety of factors, including colonialism, indigenous belief systems, the educational system, and the Catholic Church. One dominant view is that women's primary responsibility lies with her family, children, and household. Men, on the other hand, are viewed as the primary breadwinners. This model of gender relations, although it has changed over time, continues to predominate throughout the society. Cultural expectations of gender and family roles are sanctioned by the church and sometimes by political parties, international organizations, community associations, and the media. Women who do not fit within this notion of gender relations, including single mothers and unmarried women, often face social stigmas, despite the fact that 18 percent of all Peruvian households are headed by a woman (19.2 percent in urban areas and 15.7 percent in rural areas).[19]

Marriage

A recent survey shows that 24 percent of Peruvian women between the ages of 15 and 59 are living in domestic partnerships (*uniones de hecho*). The Constitution supports domestic partnerships, or common-law marriages, and the Civil Code states that such unions will be recognized legally in cases where they have existed for at least two consecutive years.[20] The minimum age for marriage without parental consent is 18 years. Divorce is legally permissible only under certain circumstances.

Reproduction

Women often face severe discrimination in terms of their reproductive rights. Social attitudes among health care professionals are the basis for much of this discrimination. Some women report that health care professionals believe suffering is the lot of women, especially in terms of reproduction, and that it is women's duty to make it easier on the staff by not complaining about pain or asking questions about diagnoses or prescriptions. Lack of knowledge about their rights, lack of education about contraceptive options, and discriminatory attitudes and practices among health care professionals result in human rights violations and dangerous health care experiences for women.[21]

The Peruvian government declared that the 1990s would be the Decade of Family Planning. In Peruvian national policy the family is paramount, and one way to ensure its well-being, President Fujimori argued, is through family planning. Peru's state policy on reproduction is contained in the National Policy on Population (the Population Law), as set forth in the Constitution. The controversial Population Law, established by the Fujimori administration in the early 1990s, is framed as a state campaign to end poverty through increased population control. The Law outlines three objectives: "to promote a stable and harmonious equilibrium between the growth, structure, and territorial distribution of the inhabitants of the country; to encourage and ensure free, informed, and responsible choice by individuals and couples regarding the number and spacing of children; and to reduce the number of deaths caused by disease, particularly among mothers and children."[22]

The aim of national policy is to ensure that all Peruvians have access to information with which to make informed decisions regarding responsible parenthood, the number of children desired, and appropriate forms of contraception. In practice, however, this freedom of information is often not the case, and health care professionals often demonstrate socioeconomic and age bias that results in discrimination, verbal and sexual abuse, and even rape against young, poor, and unmarried women and girls.[23] Such denigrating practices are evident in the case of 200,000 indigenous Andean villagers who were forced or coerced by health care professionals to undergo sterilization procedures in the 1980s; procedures that often took place without anesthesia and/or under unhygienic conditions.[24] These occurrences demonstrated extreme disregard for patients' rights to physical integrity and personal dignity.

Contraception and Abortion

Peruvian national policy encourages responsible parenthood and the use of contraception, and the Constitution affirms the individual's right to freely choose a preferred method of contraception. Indeed, the only reproductive service that is guaranteed by law to be entirely free is contraception. However, the Center for Reproductive Law and Policy found that many women, especially young, unmarried, and poor women, are denied their basic legal right to information regarding contraception as well as their right to a full range of contraceptive methods. When seeking family planning services, some young, unmarried, and poor women are met with verbal abuse concerning their sexual lives from nursing staff and doctors, and even sexual abuse from doctors. So although the government would like to control poverty through family planning, health care providers often belittle and abuse women who seek those services.[25]

In spite of the many obstacles and abuses that women seeking contraception face, one report showed that 64 percent of Peruvian women use contraception: 41 percent use modern family planning methods, and 23 percent use traditional methods. Twelve percent of women in stable cohabiting relationships use intrauterine devices, 10 percent have been sterilized, and 8 percent rely on hormone injections. The pill, condoms, and vaginal spermicides are preferred by 6.2 percent, 4.4 percent, and 0.7 percent respectively. The Population Law endorses breast-feeding due to its nutritional benefits to the child and its birth spacing effects. Emergency postcoital contraception can be obtained in cases of unprotected sexual relations, rape, or failure of barrier contraceptive methods, although its use is regulated.[26] Whether or not women are made aware of emergency contraceptives is unknown.

In light of the discouraging obstacles women face in obtaining contraceptives, it is not surprising that so many pregnancies end in abortion. Although it is illegal for a woman to have an abortion except in certain cases, it is estimated that there are 270,000 abortions in Peru annually.[27] Abortion is the second leading cause of maternal death, and Peru ranks third for maternal mortality rate in the region.[28] If health care staff suspect that a woman is experiencing complications from an abortion, they are legally required to report it to authorities. Even when their suspicions are incorrect, health care staff may give her lower quality care and subject her to abuse.

There are three cases when a woman's prison sentence for an illegal abortion is reduced from a maximum of two years to a maximum of three months: "extramarital rape or nonconsensual artificial insemination outside marriage or where the fetus will be born with serious physical or mental defects."[29] It is apparent that in the eyes of the law, women's rights to physical integrity are limited in marriage.

Lack of respect for women's physical integrity also is apparent in an earlier version of the laws concerning sterilization, which required a woman to have her spouse's consent to obtain sterilization. Until 1995, sterilization was prohibited by the 1993 Population Law, but it is now legal with the patient's written consent. Once it was legal, sterilization was abused by the Fujimori administration, which took extreme measures to respond to international pressures to reduce poverty. The Ministry of Health oversaw the forced sterilizations of at least 200,000 indigenous Andean villagers between 1996 and 2000. The majority of these sterilizations were performed on poor and illiterate women from the Quechua and Aymara ethnic groups. About 16,000 vasectomies were performed among the males in this same population.[30] Today, some women still face pressure from health care workers to undergo sterilizations and, contrary to law, are often presented with sterilization as the only free contraceptive method.

Teen Pregnancy

In public hospitals 20 percent of births are to teenage mothers. Teens have legal access to reproductive health services and to contraceptives. The rhythm method of contraception is the most widely used among adolescents. Education also seems to play a factor in teen pregnancies; school or university attendance correlates with a lower incidence of unwanted pregnancies. One study shows that despite legal restriction, large percentages of adolescents—up to 86 percent in some samples—who attended school, as well as those who did not, chose to abort pregnancies. Although there is a lack of research in this area, it is not uncommon for pregnant teenagers to be kicked out of school. More than a quarter of male and female adolescents are unaware of legal restrictions on abortion. In one sample, only 6 percent of pregnant adolescents and 13 percent of their partners reported consulting their parents about their unplanned pregnancy.[31] In light of the difficulties facing the general population of women seeking reproductive and contraceptive services, one can only presume that adolescent women and students face greater challenges in having their reproductive health needs met.

HEALTH

Health Care Access

The Peruvian Constitution recommends that health care should be free and accessible to all Peruvians. In reality, women's access to health care depends upon their socioeconomic status as well as their geographic location: poor, rural women are faced with extreme barriers, while middle- and upper-class women have more access. Poor women also find their personal dignity degraded by hospital staff, such as social workers, when it comes to the cost of health care. And despite the fact that the Constitution recommends free health care for all, some women are charged for services for which they cannot pay. Flagrantly disregarding the recommendations in the Constitution, the Ministry of Health facilities began to charge fees for clinical services in 1990.[32] Some women are even denied emergency care because of a real or perceived inability to pay for service.[33] In general, women's experiences with illness or diseases tend to be less reported than men's, a result of social stigmas and cultural barriers that poor, especially indigenous, women face.

Diseases and Disorders

AIDS

In general, legislation concerning HIV/AIDS suggests support and protection of those living with HIV/AIDS. However, it is unclear how the rights of individuals play out in practice. The National Plan to Fight AIDS, passed in 1996, gives labor and medical protections to people with HIV/AIDS. It protects a worker with HIV/AIDS for as long as he or she is able to perform her or his duties, and termination based on HIV/AIDS status is prohibited. It also ensures the right to comprehensive medical treatment and to state benefits. Testing for HIV/AIDS must be voluntary and requires prior consent, "except in the case of blood or organ donors and other cases for which testing is required by law"; however, health care providers are required to notify the Ministry of Health of any AIDS diagnosis.[34]

Most HIV/AIDS cases occur in men, with transmission through heterosexual contact outpacing cases through homosexual contact. Incidence in women has not been broken down hetero-, homo-, or bisexual contacts. HIV prevalence among sex workers was found to be 5 percent in 1997, up

4.5 percent from the previous decade. The incidence of HIV/AIDS contraction was down drastically among both men and women in 2000 as compared to the previous three years. At the end of 2001, 0.4 percent of Peruvian adults were infected with HIV/AIDS. At this time it was estimated that 38,500 men, 13,000 women, and 1,500 children were living with HIV/AIDS in Peru. Estimates place the death toll during 2001 for adults and children at 3,900.[35]

Gay and lesbian organizations have been at the forefront of struggles to address the HIV/AIDS pandemic in Peru. The Homosexual Movement of Lima (Movimiento Homosexual de Lima), an NGO that addresses gay and lesbian rights, has dedicated itself to this issue for several years. It provides support for people living with HIV/AIDS, educational outreach, and a crisis hotline, as well as intellectual and policy-related scholarship on the prevalence of HIV/AIDS in the country.

Eating Disorders

There is virtually no documentation on eating disorders in Peru. This does not mean, however, that eating disorders do not exist. Although they are much less common than in other Latin American countries (such as Argentina and Venezuela), there are reported and visible cases. Generally speaking, women (and men) with eating disorders in Peru are not necessarily from upper-class backgrounds, but reflect all social classes. Reported cases include women who are victims of sexual abuse, domestic violence, racism, and classism. A variety of factors contribute to this phenomenon.

The Peruvian women's movement has addressed issues of body image, particularly how women are represented in the media. In 1982, Peruvian women of various sectors organized a protest against the Miss Universe contest, which was held that year in Peru. Plastic surgery is expensive and inaccessible to most Peruvians except the upper class. In addition to choosing plastic surgery for gender-related cosmetic reasons, some have chosen to surgically alter their appearance for ethnic/racial reasons. For example, during the government of President Fujimori, Peru maintained strong ties with Japan. Peruvians of Japanese descent were encouraged to live and work in Japan, under Japan's lenient visa program that gave foreigners of Japanese descent temporary work visas. Many Peruvians who went to Japan during this time worked long hours in factory production. Women typically made less than men in Japan's gender-biased factories. Because of the extreme economic crisis, coupled with political violence, in Peru, some indigenous and mestizo Peruvians surgically altered their eyes to appear Japanese-Peruvian and obtain documentation to go to Japan.

Cancer

Little research has been conducted to evaluate the incidence and types of cancer among women. One study conducted in 1990 shows that women experienced higher rates of colon cancer than men. A high rate of stomach and digestive tract cancers, as well as of uterine cancer, also were reported by women that year. Breast cancer constituted 9.3 percent of all reported cases of cancer among women.[36] Most of these figures are lower than the regional average. This may be because cancer is underreported in Peru. Particularly in rural and poor urban areas, many women may die from cancer but cannot afford medical support and/or the cause of their illness or death is never reported.

Depression

Studies of women's depression are few and far between in Peru. As elsewhere, women's depression arises from a wide variety of social, environmental, and physical circumstances. Women with severe depression may attribute their mental health to issues within their families (e.g., sexual abuse, drug abuse, abandonment, dysfunctionality) as well as to broader social inequalities (e.g., racism, poverty, classism, institutionalized heterosexuality, political violence).

POLITICS AND LAW

In 2002, a process is taking place by which the 1993 Constitution will be updated and amended. The government is a parliamentary democracy and consists of three branches: judicial, legislative, and executive (divided into ministries). Men and women have equal opportunities under the law. Women are protected against discrimination on the basis of sex, although, as elsewhere, this is difficult to sustain in practice. Peru ratified the United Nations–sponsored Convention to End All Forms of Discrimination Against Women in 1981, two years after it was adopted by the United Nations.

Peruvian women have made many important legal and political gains, particularly since the 1960s. Government programs and agencies have been established to address women's issues; governments have adopted United Nations resolutions regarding discrimination against women; women have gained entry into national political positions; and women from various sectors have organized independent movements based on feminist principles. A number of societal forces have contributed to women's successes and failures, including welfare reforms, political repression and violence, and a growing awareness of women's issues among many Peruvians.

Suffrage

Women gained the right to vote in 1955. Early women suffragists were influenced by and participated actively in regional suffragist movements. The Pan American Congress of Women was held in Peru in 1924. As elsewhere, Peru's suffragists were primarily from upper-class, literate, Spanish backgrounds. They were more concerned with being treated as equals of their male counterparts than with the literacy and voting rights of indigenous Peruvians. They were influenced by early feminist, anarchist, socialist, and liberal writings from Europe.[37]

Political Participation

Women have participated actively in the political process for decades, although it has only been recently that their political roles have become more acceptable. The first two women were appointed as ministers in 1987 (Minister of Health, Minister of Education). In the early 1990s, twenty women served as vice ministers. Peru is one of the few countries in the region that has a Ministry of Women and Social Development (Ministerio de la Mujer y Desarrollo Social)—which is headed by a woman. In 1990, 4 out of 60 national senators were women (6.7 percent), and 10 out of 180 legislators were women (5.6 percent). In 1994, 2 out of 24 Supreme Court judges were women (8.3 percent), and many more women held positions in lower courts. According to one study, in 1993, fourteen out of 226 mayors were women (6.2 percent)[38]; in Lima, three out of 30 city council members were women (7.7 percent).[39] Few women have held leadership positions in labor organizations. A larger percentage of women have held leadership positions in rural labor unions (30.6 percent of rural labor union leaders were women in 1993.[40] Few women have held leadership positions in business organizations, although this is slowly changing.

Women's Rights

Feminist Movements

Perhaps more important than women's participation in formal politics has been the growth of the Peruvian women's movement. Virginia Vargas, founder of the "Flora Tristan" Center for Peruvian Women (Centro de la Mujer Peruana "Flora Tristan"), a Lima-based NGO, characterizes the Peruvian women's movement as having three branches: feminist, popular, and *política* (literally, "political"). Feminists, primarily from urban, middle-class backgrounds, have emerged as important players in defining a social agenda for women's rights. They have helped draft and create gender-sensitive state policies, state-sponsored and NGO-sponsored social programs, antipoverty initiatives, and Women's Studies academic programs. In addition, they have brought great awareness of women's roles in and contributions to Peruvian society. Popular feminists tend to be from working-class and/or rural backgrounds, and focus much of their attention on daily economic survival and the specific needs of poor women. *Políticas* tend to focus on reforming the political process from within; they therefore emphasize reforming male-based political parties, creating political platforms for women's rights and female political candidates, and introducing a quota system for female candidates. Feminists who work in civic-based organizations (e.g., NGOs, community groups), on the other hand, focus more on changing views on women within civil society, rather than exclusively in the formal political process—a political sphere, they argue, that has excluded many women and continues to do so. All of these strands contribute to one of the most vibrant movements in the region. Peruvian feminists have been at the forefront of regional and global initiatives to reform discriminatory legislation at home and throughout the world.

Lesbian Rights

Peruvian lesbians have made major contributions to the broader women's movement and to the rights of lesbians, gay men, bisexuals, and transgendered (LGBT) people in Peru. Lima is home to a very large population of "out" LGBT people. In general, Peruvian lesbians are not protected by law. Homosexuality is illegal, and many gay bars continue to be raided. President Fujimori fired "out" homosexuals in his government, and many LGBT people are discriminated against primarily on the basis of their appearance. Not surprisingly, street workers, cross-dressers, drag queens, transsexuals, and transgendered people often face difficulties when seeking housing or employment.

In the 1970s, some gay and lesbian organizations were established, including the Homosexual Movement of Lima (Movimiento Homosexual de Lima, MHOL) and the Lesbian Feminist Consciousness-Raising Group (Grupo de Auto-Conciencia de Lesbianas-Feministas, GALF). Many of MHOL's and GALF's original members continue to be active participants in struggles for the rights of LGBT communities in Peru. MHOL is now a leading NGO in the country. Although GALF was not active in the 1980s and early 1990s, it reemerged in the late 1990s and continues to thrive as a collective. Most recently, seven LGBT NGOs have created a coalition called the Front for the Right to Be Different (Frente por el Derecho a Ser Diferente, FREDIF). FREDIF is promoting the inclusion of "sexual orientation" as a category protected against discrimination in the Peruvian Constitution.[41] Significantly, a coalition of women's organizations led by the Latin American and Caribbean Committee for the Defense of Women's Rights (Comité de América Latina y el Caribe para la Defensa de los Derechos de la Mujer), is a major supporter of this initiative.

RELIGION AND SPIRITUALITY

A major goal of Spanish colonial rule was to spread Catholicism throughout the region. Many indigenous people were converted to Catholicism, and over generations many of the original inhabitants of the region adopted the religion as their own. Most Peruvians today are Roman Catholic.

Increasingly, in the past few decades Mormons, Jehovah's Witnesses, Protestant, Adventist, and other evangelical Christian sects have grown in number. It has been estimated that over 1.5 million Peruvians belong to evangelical churches.[42] Poor and middle-class women have been targeted and mobilized by these sects in specific, gendered ways. Some build showy temples or churches in poor areas; others set up simple, one-room buildings. Many of these sects, along with the Catholic Church, continue to rely upon foreign clergy to staff their churches. Some Peruvians also practice Judaism or Buddhism.

Women's Roles

Traditionally, women have been limited in their roles within the church, although there are some exceptions. A small but significant percentage of Catholic women and men are participants in the liberation theology movement, a progressive faction of the Catholic Church that focuses on empowering the poor and disenfranchised. The Peruvian Gustavo Gutiérrez, one of Latin America's foremost proponents of liberation theology, has led many peasant and urban poor Peruvians in their struggles for land and civil rights.

Rituals and Religious Practices

In Peru, women have played important roles in Catholicism, the country's largest religion, and in indigenous spiritual traditions. Researchers have debated women's roles in pre-Incan and Incan religious traditions although many agree that women held higher statuses in indigenous practices than in modern Catholicism.[43] Since the colonial period, indigenous women and men have combined aspects of Catholicism with their own beliefs and rituals. Today, many women participate in processions that take place in cities, towns, and rural areas that include a combination of elements from Catholicism, with Inca and pre-Inca rituals and beliefs. In one of Cuzco's famous cathedrals, a colonial painting of the Last Supper portrays the main dish as a guinea pig, a commonly eaten meat in the Andes. This interpretation of the Last Supper contrasts sharply with European depictions of the same event.

Coca leaves continue to be an important component of indigenous rituals and social events. An exchange of coca leaves among families typically is an act of kindness, a friendly gesture that often reflects an important event, such as an engagement. Shamans and other spiritual leaders play important healing roles in their communities. Some are trained to read coca leaves, a tradition in the Andean region. Those who are able to read coca leaves believe that the surrounding mountains, water, plains, or earth (depending upon the location) is speaking through them. According to the Incas, the natural environment—whether water, sky, the land, forest, mountains, desert, or plains—is alive, and deserves to be as respected as much as we respect ourselves. Many Peruvian women adhere to these principles as well as to Catholic beliefs. Since the 1960s, liberation theology has been very strong in Peru, and women have been active in the ranks of this popular movement perhaps because of its focus on the underprivileged, including illiterate, poor and peasant women.

Religious Law

Peru's Constitution states that there is a separation between church and state. Nonetheless, the Catholic Church has influenced legislation in the areas of sexual rights, family, and education.

VIOLENCE

Peruvian scholars are among the best in the world when it comes to studying processes of violence in contemporary societies. The field of "violentology" (*violentología*), the academic study of political violence, is vibrant in Peru. Peruvian social scientists, including feminist scholars, have contributed to important debates about the effects of Peru's civil war on political institutions and on people's daily lives. Women have played roles in Peru's civil war on various levels: in the military and police forces; as *guerilleras* in the Maoist-based Shining Path and the Tupac Amaru Revolutionary Movement (Movimiento Revolucionario "Tupac Amaru"); as mothers of the "disappeared"; as new settlers in Lima, displaced by the violence in the countryside; and as human rights activists.

In addition, feminists and other female community leaders have created programs that address domestic violence, rape, and sexual assault. While these crimes traditionally are seen primarily as a form of gender violence, in Peru one cannot always distinguish between broad political violence and gender-based violence. Since the 1980s these forms of violence have been inseparable, and can be understood only in relation to one another.

Domestic Violence

Statistics on the incidence of domestic violence are difficult to obtain because it often goes unreported by the victims. However, the government gave a nod of recognition to the social problem of domestic violence by adopting the Law for Protection from Family Violence in 1993, one of the first of its kind in Latin America. Although the objectives of the law are noble and, were they attained, would hugely reform and expedite the judicial process, victims of domestic violence find that they face systemic gender bias that hinders the judicial process. Furthermore, the full weight of the law does not suppress the danger they face in their daily lives. As reported by a Human Rights Watch (HRW) memorandum, "In 1998, the National Police received nearly 28,000 reports of domestic abuse."[44] Unfortunately, however, systemic gender bias, occurring at many points in the process of serving justice, and unaddressed by the law, denies women the very protection that the law promises, and discourages women from reporting violence.

The first obstacle to justice is the definition of family violence under which the law operates. Although the law covers both married and unmarried partners, it applies only if the victim and her aggressor are cohabiting when the violence occurs. It does not classify sexual violence as a type of domestic violence, a lapse that does not help to stem marital rape. While the law recognizes psychological abuse as a form of domestic violence, it does not spell out what might constitute such abuse. The law also makes conciliation mandatory, which in effect focuses proceedings on the victim's behavior rather than the abuser's violence.[45]

The law requires that the victim attend one conciliation session with her abuser before prosecution proceeds. This requirement delays prosecution, puts undue obligations on the victim, keeps the victim in danger, and results in conciliation agreements that carry little or no legal weight and impose little or no penalty when the abuser does not comply with the agreement. While this legal victory was important to Peruvian women activists who had pushed for it for several years, critics contend that this method places emphasis not on the violence but rather on the preservation of the relationship between the victim and her abuser.[46] This same gender bias is evident in police treatment of victims. Victims often report disbelief as well as abusive treatment from the police. Some officers will not take a women's statement until after she has been seen the medical examiner and had some time to "cool off" rather than make a report in the heat of the moment. After receiving a statement from the victim, some officers will give a summons to the victim that she must then deliver to her abuser—which puts her in danger once again. Bureaucratic red tape in the form of obtaining and delivering medical examiners' certificates also delays the process.[47]

Forensic doctors show bias against women during physical exams. Some doctors do not take photographs or otherwise record the victim's injuries as evidence. They often report the victim's injuries as much less severe than they actually are, resulting in a misdemeanor classification of the violence, different judicial proceedings, and limited redress for the victim.[48]

Under pressure from the women's movement, since the late 1980s 12 women's police stations and 20 specialized sections within regular police stations have been established to deal with domestic violence, in order to circumvent some of the obstacles women face when reporting such violence. These specialized units, based on the well-known Brazilian feminist model of women's police stations, house women police officers, medical examiners, and state prosecutors to facilitate the legal process for victims of domestic violence.[49]

Women's organizations have made significant gains in legislation, but there is still room for reform. There is much work to be done in terms of addressing social attitudes concerning women's rights to physical integrity inside and outside of marriage and intimate relationships. While little research has been conducted to examine the effects of the broader political violence on rates of domestic violence in the country, it is clear in some cases that political violence exacerbates violence within intimate relationships.

Rape/Sexual Assault

Rape is a felony offense in Peru. Although many victims of rape do not make official reports, rape and sexual assault are ranked as the third most frequently committed crimes in the country. According to the National Police of Peru, 4,146 rapes were registered in 1995.[50] In 1997, the law exempting the aggressor and any accomplices from punishment if one of them married the victim was amended; however, marriage to the adolescent victim with her consent, when no violence was used in the sexual act of seduction and deception, still precludes punishment. The fact that such a provision ever existed is disturbing but perhaps to be expected, since Peruvian law does not criminalize marital rape. The law requires that any offspring resulting from rape must be financially supported by the convicted rapist. How often rape cases result in conviction is unknown. Considering the challenges many women face in having meaningful conversations regarding their sexuality and sexual health concerns with doctors and nurses, and the obstacles they face in seeking redress for domestic violence, it is doubtful that they are able to obtain support and redress in cases of rape.

War and Military Repression

Peru has experienced civil war since the early 1980s, when Shining Path gained momentum as an underground, Maoist-based guerrilla movement. Once an arm of the Communist Party of Peru, Shining Path gained international fame for its powerful attack on the Peruvian state. Peru's military responded to Shining Path with severe repression. As Shining Path took hold in the central Andes and made its way to Lima, the government imposed security measures province by province, including a night curfew and restrictions on public gatherings and on travel. In addition, military personnel and vehicles were present throughout the country. Overall, the militarization of Peruvian society contributed to an atmosphere of fear, in which many women found it increasingly difficult to work, live, and support their families for fear of political persecution or the economic deprivation that accompanied the war. In the end, tens of thousands of people lost their lives during the 1980s; most of them were killed by the military, although a significant percentage were killed by Shining Path.

Women have played an important role in Shining Path. Unlike earlier left-wing movements, Shining Path promoted its women by having them present at public executions, including at the death of María Elena Moyano in Villa El Salvador. Some of the most powerful images of Shining Path members include newspaper photographs of women with machine guns at the front of a group assembly. This image perplexed and haunted many Peruvians, since it was an abrupt rupture from traditional representations of women's gender roles in the country. At the same time, some female Shining Path members served in the ranks of the movement as secretaries or prostitutes, thus participating as second-class members.[51]

In 1995, Abimael Guzman, founder and leader of Shining Path, was caught and imprisoned by the government of President Alberto Fujimori. Fujimori gained much support for Guzman's capture, despite his authoritarian tactics since his entry into office in 1990. While Shining Path has greatly decreased its activities and presence in Peru, it continues to exist as a movement.

Women also have played roles in MRTA, a left-wing movement that originated in Peru's Amazon region, one of the most isolated regions of the country. Most notably, the MRTA took over the Japanese Embassy in Peru in 1995, a major event in world news.

Yet despite women's participation in left-wing movements, by far the majority of Peruvian women have been caught in the cross fire of the civil war. Peasant and indigenous women in the Andes, along with their families, have been displaced by the violence. Many Peruvians have migrated to Lima, and some have sought political refuge in Europe, Canada, or the United States. Poor urban women faced many challenges in the 1990s, since Shining Path infiltrated many of their organizations and communities.

Also during this period, Peru established its campaign to eradicate coca production, a process financially sponsored by the U.S. government as part of that country's proclaimed "War Against Drugs." With a growing presence of U.S. and Peruvian officials in coca-producing regions, poor families that rely upon coca production have lost their livelihoods. In addition, much debate exists as to coca's significance in indigenous communities, where it has been an integral part of local traditions. Although some international organizations have attempted to promote alternative agricultural programs as a way to replace coca production with the production of, for example, potatoes, the economic return for local families cannot compare to the amount of money they received for coca. Women in these regions have organized as *cocaleras* (female coca producers), in an attempt to maintain their economic livelihoods and cultural traditions.

OUTLOOK FOR THE TWENTY-FIRST CENTURY

Despite the persistence of poverty and political instability felt by many Peruvians during the past few decades, Peruvian women have much to celebrate. Major legal gains have been made, and women have become important political and professional figures in the country's public sphere. Women's NGOs and the feminist movement have played pivotal roles in shaping national policies concerning development and social welfare. Domestic violence and sexual abuse are now recognized by the law and increasingly the law is enforced.

What remains to be seen is how these legal reforms translate into concrete changes in women's daily lives. In most cases, indigenous, peasant, and urban poor women remain largely excluded from these legal advances. The broad issues of poverty and historical structural inequalities continue to shape how rich and poor women do or do not benefit from Peru's twentieth-century modernization project. Recent reforms in land rights and ownership have the potential to shift more economic power to traditionally marginalized sectors of women and men.

NOTES

1. Jane Holligan de Díaz-Límaco, *Peru in Focus: A Guide to the People, Politics and Culture* (London: Latin American Bureau, 1998).

2. Ibid.

3. World Bank, Gender Statistics: Peru, 2002, http://genderstats.worldbank.org/genderRpt.asp?rpt=profile&cty=PER,Peru&hm=home4.

4. World Bank, "Peru at a Glance," 2002, http://devdata.worldbank.org.

5. Center for Reproductive Law and Policy (CRLP) and Comité Latinoamericano y del Caribe para la Defensa de los Derechos de Mujeres, *Silence and Complicity: Violence Against Women in Peruvian Public Health Facilities* (New York: Center for Reproductive Law and Policy, 1999).

6. Holligan de Díaz Límaco, 1998, 17.

7. CRLP, *Women of the World: Peru* (New York: CRLP, 2001).

8. World Bank, "Gender Statistics: Peru," 2002.

9. CRLP, *Women of the World*, 2001.

10. Various dialects of Quechua are spoken throughout Peru, and often Quechua speakers in one region do not understand the dialects of other regions. Thus teachers must learn specific dialects and be assigned to specific regions in order to implement bilingual education programs.

11. Latin Focus, "Peru: External Debt, 1995–2003" (Barcelona: Latin Focus, 2003), www.latin.focus.com/countries/peru/perdcbt.htm.

12. The cost of daily living typically includes basic food items, transportation, public education, gas, electricity, and water.

13. World Bank, "Gender Statistics: Peru," 2002.

14. Elsa Chaney and Mary García Castro, eds., *Muchachas No More: Household Workers in Latin America and the Caribbean* (Philadelphia: Temple University Press, 1989).

15. CRLP, *Women of the World*, 2001.

16. Teresa Valdés et al., *Mujeres latinoamericanas en cifras: Tomo comparativo* (Santiago, Chile: Instituto de la Mujer, Ministerio de Asuntos Sociales de España, and Facultad Latinoamericana de Ciencias Sociales, 1995).

17. Amy Lind, "Gender, Development and Urban Social Change: Women's Community Action in Global Cities," *World Development* 25, no. 8 (1997): 1205–24.

18. Amy Lind, "Making Feminist Sense of Neoliberalism: The Institutionalization of Women's Struggles for Survival in Bolivia and Ecuador," *Journal of Developing Societies* no. 2/3 (fall 2002): 228–58.

19. This figure is based on a 1996 study.

20. CRLP, *Women of the World*, 2001.

21. CRLP, *Silence and Complicity*, 1999.

22. CRLP, *Women of the World*, 2001.

23. CRLP, *Silence and Complicity*, 1999.

24. Owain Johnson, *Peru Apologizes for Sterilizing Indians*, October 1, 2002. www.washtimes.com/world/2002725-98233216.htm.

25. CRLP, *Silence and Complicity*, 1999.

26. CRLP, *Women of the World*, 2001.

27. Ibid.

28. Ibid.

29. CRLP, *Women of the World*, 2001, 172.

30. Johnson, 2002.

31. I. Alarcón and G. Gonzales, "Attitudes Towards Sexuality, Sexual Knowledge, and Behaviour in Adolescents in the Cities of Lima, Cusco and Iquitos" (Lima: Cayetano Heredia Peruvian University, 1996), unpublished report.

32. CRLP, *Women of the World*, 2001.

33. CRLP, *Silence and Complicity*, 1999.

34. CRLP, *Women of the World*, 2001.

35. World Bank, "Peru at a Glance," 2002, http://devdata.worldbank.org; World Health Organization (WHO), "Sexual Relations Among Young People in Developing Countries," 29 September 2002, www.who.int/reproductive-health/adolescent/publications/RHR_01_8_Sexual_relations_among_young_people_in_developing_countries/RHR_01_08_chapter5.en.html.

36. CRLP, 2001.

37. Valdés et al., 1995.

38. Ibid, 163.

39. Ibid, 166.

40. Ibid.

41. International Gay and Lesbian Human Rights Commission, *Peru: Support Equality and Sexual Rights in Constitutional Reform*, Emergency Response Network (San Francisco: IGLHRC, September 2002).

42. Holligan de Díaz-Límaco, 1998.

43. Irene Silverblatt, *Moon, Sun, and Witches: Gender Ideologies and Class in Inca and Colonial Peru* (Princeton, NJ: Princeton University Press, 1987). Also see Olivia Harris, *To Make the Earth Bear Fruit: Ethnographic Essays on Fertility, Work and Gender in Highland Bolivia* (London: University of London, Institute of Latin American Studies, 2000).

44. Ibid.

45. Human Rights Watch, *Peru: Law of Protection from Family Violence*, October 2002, www.hrw.org/backgrounder/wrd/peru-women.htm.

46. Ibid.
47. Ibid.
48. Ibid.
49. Ibid.
50. CRLP, 2001.
51. Robin Kirk. *The Monkey's Paw: New Chronicles from Peru* (Amherst: University of Massachusetts Press, 1992).

RESOURCE GUIDE

Suggested Reading

Anderson, Jeanine. "The U.N. Decade for Women in Peru." *Women's Studies International Forum* 8, no. 2 (1985): 107–9. Anderson, a prominent feminist anthropologist who resides in Peru, addresses the role the U.N. Decade for Women played in effecting legal change for women in Peru.

Barrig, Maruja. "The Difficult Equilibrium Between Bread and Roses: Women's Organizations and Democracy in Peru." In *The Women's Movement in Latin America: Participation and Democracy*, edited by Jane Jaquette, 151–75. Boulder, CO: Westview Press, 1994. A leading feminist sociologist in Peru, Barrig addresses the contradictions organized women face as they address gender-based social change, particularly in the context of redemocratization, following Peru's military years.

De la Cadena, Marisol. " 'Women Are More Indian': Ethnicity and Gender in a Community near Cuzco." In *Ethnicity, Markets, and Migration in the Andes*, edited by Brooke Larson and Olivia Harris, 329–48. Durham, NC: Duke University Press, 1995. Explores the ways in which gender and ethnic relations have shaped one small town near Cuzco, Peru.

De Soto, Hernando. *The Other Path*. New York: Harper and Row, 1989. Peru's large informal sector as described by well-known Peruvian economist.

Kirk, Robin. *The Monkey's Paw: New Chronicles from Peru*. Amherst: University of Massachusetts Press, 1992. Journalist Kirk combines interviews and personal narratives to present a portrait of Peru in the early 1980s, just as Shining Path emerged. See especially the chapter on women's participation in Shining Path.

———. *Untold Terror: Violence Against Women in Peru's Armed Conflict*. New York: Americas Watch/Women's Rights Project, 1997. Chronicles the abuses that women faced by both the military and Shining Path during Peru's civil war.

Milosavich Tupac, Diana, ed. *The Autobiography of María Elena Moyano: The Life and Death of a Peruvian Activist*. Gainesville: University Press of Florida, 2000. This book chronicles the life of María Elena Moyano, an Afro-Peruvian community leader and feminist activist who was assassinated by Shining Path in 1992. Moyano's struggle is an example of the many human rights activists caught in the cross fire of Peru's civil war.

Silverblatt, Irene. *Moon, Sun, and Witches: Gender Ideologies and Class in Inca and Colonial Peru*. Princeton, NJ: Princeton University Press, 1987. This pioneer study in its field is based on the author's extensive historical and anthropological research on gender roles in Inca cultures prior to and during the early colonial period.

Starn, Orin, Carlos Ívan Degregori, and Robyn Kirk, eds. *The Peru Reader: History, Culture, Politics*. Durham, NC: Duke University Press, 1995. This anthology includes primary texts by historians, political activists, poets, artists, social scientists, and others who have contributed to Peru's vibrant intellectual history.

Stern, Steve J., ed. *Shining and Other Paths: War and Society in Peru, 1980–1995*. Durham, NC: Duke University Press, 1998. An excellent collection of essays on Shining Path and Peru's recent decades of violence.

Videos/Films

Miss Universe in Peru. 1982. VHS, 66 min. English subtitles. Directed by Grupo Chaski. Shot during the Miss Universe pageant held in Peru in 1982, this documentary addresses the contradictions between the glamour of a global beauty pageant and the lives of diverse sectors of women from Peru. It focuses on the role multinational corporate interests play in fashioning women's lives in poor countries such as Peru.

Mujeres de El Planeta. 1984. VHS, 30 min. Directed by María Barea. This documentary examines the difficulties and contradictions women settlers face in El Planeta, one of Lima's shantytowns. Their roles as mothers and community development activists are addressed in the context of Lima's rapid urbanization, discrimination against rural migrants, and the hardships of adapting to city life.

Web Sites and Organizations

Centro de la Mujer Peruana "Flora Tristan" (Flora Tristan Peruvian Women's Center)
Parque Hernán Velarde 42
Lima 18 Peru
Phone: (511) 433-1457, 433-2765
Fax: (511) 433-9060, 433-9500
Email: postmast@flora.org.pe

A leading nongovernmental organization (NGO) in the contemporary women's movement, this research and action center provides legal and support services, and conducts research on gender issues in various fields. It houses the largest women's studies library collection in the country.

Grupo de Auto-Conciencia de Lesbianas-Feministas (GALF, Lesbian Feminist Consciousness Raising Group)

A lesbian feminist group that was founded in the 1970s and re-emerged with renewed energy in the 1990s, GALF produces an excellent e-magazine, *Revista Labia*. To subscribe to the magazine, you may contact GALF at galf@terra.com.pe and request to be added to their mailing list.

Ministerio de la Mujer y Desarrollo Social (Ministry of Women and Social Development)

Jr. Camaná 616
Lima, Peru
Phone: (511) 428-9800

Fax: (511) 426-1665

Email: postmaster@minmimdes.gob.pe

Web site: www.promudeh.gob.pe

The state ministry responsible for overseeing national programs, projects and policies concerning women and development. The web site provides information on the ministry's philosophy, international sponsors, and current programs and services. In Spanish.

Movimiento Homosexual de Lima (MHOL, Homosexual Movement of Lima).

Mariscal Miller 828, Jesús María

Lima, Peru

Phone: (511) 433-6375

Fax: (511) 433-5519

Email: mholpe@terra.com.pe

Web site: www.mhol.tripod.com.pe/mhol

This is Peru's largest gay and lesbian organization, dedicated to addressing the human rights of gays, lesbians, bisexuals, and transgendered people, and to providing support for those with HIV/AIDS and education concerning HIV/AIDS.

Movimiento Manuela Ramos (Manuela Ramos Movement)

Av. Juan Pablo Fernandini 1550

Pueblo Libre

Lima, Peru

Phone: (511) 423-8840

Fax: (511) 332-1280

Email: postmast@manuela.org.pe

Web site: www.manuela.org.pe

Established in the 1970s, Movimiento Manuela Ramos is a leading women's NGO in Peru that has dedicated itself to improving the lives of poor and marginalized women in Lima and throughout the country.

SELECTED BIBLIOGRAPHY

Alarcón, I., and G. Gonzales. "Attitudes Towards Sexuality, Sexual Knowledge, and Behaviour in Adolescents in the Cities of Lima, Cusco and Iquitos." Lima: Cayetano Heredia Peruvian University, 1996. Unpublished report.

Center for Reproductive Law and Policy (CRLP). *Women of the World: Peru*. New York: Center for Reproductive Law and Policy, 2001.

Center for Reproductive Law and Policy (CRLP) and Comité Latinoamericano y del Caribe para la Defensa de los Derechos de Mujeres. *Silence and Complicity: Violence Against Women in Peruvian Public Health Facilities*. New York: Center for Reproductive Law and Policy, 1999.

Chaney, Elsa, and Mary García Castro, eds. 1989. *Muchachas No More: Household Workers in Latin America and the Caribbean*. Philadelphia: Temple University Press, 1989.

Holligan de Díaz-Límaco, Jane. *Peru in Focus: A Guide to the People, Politics and Culture*. London: Latin American Bureau, 1998.

Human Rights Watch. *Peru: Law of Protection from Family Violence*. 2000. www.hrw. org/backgrounder/wrd/peru-women.htm.

International Gay and Lesbian Human Rights Commission (IGLHRC). *Peru: Support Equality and Sexual Rights in Constitutional Reform*. Emergency Response Network, San Francisco: IGLHRC, September 2002.

Johnson, Owain. *Peru Apologizes for Sterilizing Indians*. October 1, 2002. www. washtimes.com/world/20020725-98233216.htm.

Kirk, Robin. *Untold Terror: Violence Against Women in Peru's Armed Conflict*. Amherst: University of Massachusetts Press, 1997.

Lind, Amy. "Gender, Development and Urban Social Change: The Institutionalization of Women's Community Action in Global Cities." *World Development* 25, no. 8 (1997): 1205–24.

———. "Making Feminist Sense of Neoliberalism: Women's Struggles for Survival in Ecuador and Bolivia." *Journal of Developing Societies* 2/3 (Fall 2002): 228–58.

Silverblatt, Irene. *Moon, Sun, and Witches: Gender Ideologies and Class in Inca and Colonial Peru*. Princeton, NJ: Princeton University Press, 1987.

Valdés, Teresa, et al. *Mujeres latinoamericanas en cifras: Tomo comparativo*. Santiago, Chile: Instituto de la Mujer, Ministerio de Asuntos Sociales de España, and Facultad Latinoamericana de Ciencias Sociales, 1995.

World Bank. *Gender Statistics: Peru*. 2002. http://genderstats.worldbank.org/genderRpt.asp?rpt=profile&cty=PER,Peru&hm=home4.

———. *Peru at a Glance*. 2002. http://devdata.worldbank.org.

World Health Organization (WHO). *Sexual Relations Among Young People in Developing Countries*. September 29, 2002. www.who.int/reproductive-health/adolescent/publications/RHR_01_8_Sexual_relations_among_young_people_in_developing_countries/RHR_01_08_chapter5.en.html.

18

SURINAME

Diana H. Yoon

PROFILE OF SURINAME

Suriname is the smallest independent nation on the South American continent, with Guyana to its west, French Guiana to its east, and Brazil on its southern border. Its northern border is the Atlantic Ocean, and most of the land is covered by forests and woodland. Prior to becoming a Dutch colony in the seventeenth century, Suriname was inhabited by indigenous tribes. The colony's plantations exploited enslaved Africans until slavery was abolished, and laborers were subsequently imported from India and Indonesia. Contemporary demographics of Suriname reflect the legacy of this mass labor migration. Suriname gained autonomy as a part of the Kingdom of the Netherlands in 1954 and became independent in 1975. The period of autonomy saw the formation of many of Suriname's political parties, most of which were organized along ethnic lines. Suriname has experienced violence and political instability since gaining independence, but a democratically elected government has been in power since 1992. Women constitute 49 percent of the total population of 433,998 people,[1] most of whom live in and around Paramaribo, which is the nation's capital and the center of its political, social,

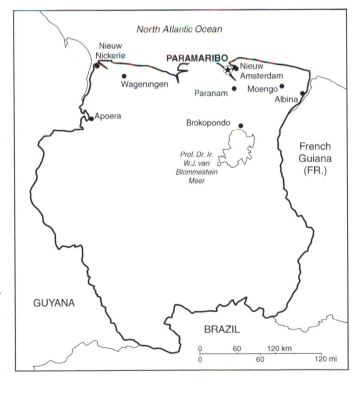

and economic life. The three largest ethnic groups consist of Hindustanis (locally known as "East Indians"), Creoles, and Javanese. The fourth largest group is the Maroons—descendants of enslaved Africans who were brought to the country in the seventeenth and eighteenth centuries, also known as "Bush Negros." The rest of the population consists of native Amerindians, other Asians, and Europeans. The total fertility rate is 2.47 children per woman and the infant mortality rate is 24.27 per 1,000 live births.[2] The maternal mortality rate was 8.7 per 10,000 live births in 1994.[3] Life expectancy is 74.4 years for women and 69 years for men.[4]

OVERVIEW OF WOMEN'S ISSUES

The struggles and opportunities of women in Suriname have been shaped by a succession of major changes in the nation's sociopolitical and economic conditions, ranging from national independence and civil war to dramatic shifts in the economy. Suriname enjoyed one of the highest standards of living in the Caribbean in the early 1980s. Since then, waves of economic crises and suspension of aid from the Netherlands during the military regime of the 1980s has led to dramatic declines in the quality of life. At the start of the twenty-first century the country is in a state of economic crisis, with high inflation and a severe shortage of foreign exchange making it difficult for the government to maintain a minimum level of economic activity.[5] Along with the elderly and children, women have been disproportionately affected by job loss, falling wages, and cutbacks in social and medical services. The situation of Amerindian and Maroon women living in the interior is particularly bleak; 91 percent of the interior's population lives below the poverty line (compared to 52 percent in urban areas), and the armed conflict of 1986–1992 has left the residents without adequate transportation, water supplies, education, and health care.[6]

Suriname ratified the U.N. Convention on the Elimination of All Forms of Discrimination Against Women in 1993.[7] However, certain provisions in the law facilitate discrimination against women. While women have made limited gains in political participation and leadership positions, gender equality is far from reality.

EDUCATION

Opportunities

The Surinamese Constitution guarantees equal access to education regardless of gender, and education is funded by the state at all levels. School attendance is compulsory until twelve years of age, but some children lack the necessary transportation or facilities. The number of school-age children attending school is considerably lower in the interior. Another barrier for some children is a strong pressure to quit school in order to work. Enrollment in primary education is nearly equal between the sexes, and the percentage of female students is higher at the secondary level.[8] Despite high levels of female enrollment, however, sex segregation is evident in secondary and tertiary education: young women are concentrated in preparation for teaching and teacher training, while young men choose more technical skills in industry and production.[9]

Literacy

Most of the adult population in Suriname can read and write. In 1995, the literacy rate was 91 percent for females and 95 percent for males.[10]

EMPLOYMENT AND ECONOMICS

Suriname's economy is largely dependent on export earnings from raw materials such as bauxite (alumina) and crude oil, and agricultural production. Vulnerable to fluctuating prices on the world market and suffering from inadequate policy measures to deal with such effects, Suriname has faced external and internal obstacles to implementing sustainable development plans.[11] Deteriorating relations with the Netherlands resulted in the freezing of development aid in 1997, and the nation's economic growth suffered from decline in the mining, construction, and utility sectors.[12]

Evidence suggests that women are increasingly bearing the financial burdens caused by the state of economic hardship. A 1999 survey of 1,000 households indicated that female-headed households account for approximately 85 percent of those living in poverty.[13] Financial needs have compelled women to seek outside employment even in families with a male head, and in low-income households, multiple jobs have become a necessity. Women face social and cultural barriers in securing employment. For example, employers believe that women are more willing to quit their jobs than men, and therefore less reliable employees. Thus, the high rate of Surinamese

Planting crops. Photo © Adam Woolfitt/CORBIS.

female participation in the education system does not correspond to a comparable rate of employment.

Job/Career Opportunities

The General Bureau of Statistics reported that during 1994–1997, women constituted 35 percent of the labor force. However, the actual number of economically active women is likely to be higher than this estimate because women's participation is underreported and informal paid labor is not reflected in formal statistics.

The government of Suriname is the nation's biggest employer and provides the most jobs for women. In civil service as well as in other fields of employment, female workers are concentrated in the lower echelon. They hold 71 percent of lower-level civil service jobs, and a recent report showed that 89 percent of working women were placed in entry-level positions, 9 percent had midlevel positions, and only 3 percent held management positions.[14] While there is a lack of data on the gender breakdown of Suriname's alarming unemployment rate (20 percent), evidence suggests that women are disproportionately affected by job loss: between 1992 and 1997, the share of women in civil service jobs fell from 40 to 28.4 percent.[15]

With the government as the nation's largest employer, job creation and entrepreneurial activity in the private sector have been limited. Women seeking employment in the private sector face challenges due to the scarcity of jobs as well as social and cultural factors. As seen in other countries, women in Suriname are more likely than their male counterparts to work part-time. In 1990–1994, women accounted for between 32 percent and 35 percent of the total labor force, but their share among those working less than fifteen hours per week was between 67 and 81 percent.[16]

In recent years, there have been signs of improvement in the share of women among business owners. Women's advocacy groups have succeeded in placing female entrepreneurship onto the national agenda, resulting in the inclusion of women trying to establish their own businesses as a target group in the country's 2001–2005 development plan. Despite these efforts, cultural and social barriers persist for women seeking loans from financial institutions, and significant improvement in women's entrepreneurial activity is not likely without substantial improvements in access to credit.

Pay

Though women are guaranteed equal access to employment and property by the constitution, they are generally paid less than men for equal or comparable work. The gender inequality in wages is compounded by the concentration of female workers in lower-level and part-time employment.

The government has yet to take specific measures to address economic discrimination against women.

Working Conditions

Sexual Harassment

In a survey conducted in a 1998 study, 50 percent of women stated that sexual harassment existed in the workplace and one third reported having experienced sexual harassment at work.[17] Despite the existence of such problems, there are no legal provisions to prohibit sexual harassment. For organizations such as the National Women's Movement, working toward securing protections and provisions for women's equal participation in the economic sector is among the primary agenda.

Support for Mothers/Caretakers

Maternal Leave and Daycare

Along with protection of the family and children, the Surinamese Constitution protects women's entitlement to paid maternity leave. However, this right fails to fully protect women because certain provisions in labor law allow employers to reduce the number of vacation days during the year in which maternity leave is taken.[18] In addition, employers in the civil sector discriminate against women who marry or become pregnant. Working mothers face challenges in securing adequate child care. While the Ministry of Labor provides support for working mothers by operating twenty-two daycare centers, there is reason to believe that adequate assistance in child care is not available for women who work outside the home—in a 1996 survey of households in a poor neighborhood of Paramaribo, a daycare center was named as the most needed social service.[19]

Inheritance and Property Rights

Article 8 of the Surinamese Constitution prohibits discrimination based on sex and guarantees equal rights in education, employment, and property. However, cultural norms and social practices inhibit women's exercise of these rights—particularly in matters of marriage and inheritance.

Social/Government Programs

The Ministry of Social Affairs provides a support system that includes cash assistance to the elderly and poor families, child allowances, and free medical care for those in need. Of the 80,000 persons receiving aid from the Ministry, 60–65 percent are women.[20] Due to current economic conditions, both government and nongovernmental programs devoted to improving welfare and social services suffer from a shortage of resources and trained personnel.

FAMILY AND SEXUALITY

Gender Roles

Traditional gender roles and gendered divisions of labor vary among communities of Suriname's ethnically heterogeneous population. However, a study focusing on forty-five women of various ethnic backgrounds suggests that the state of the economy is contributing to a "restructuring" of gender relations in household management.[21] The study illustrates the consequences of coping strategies adopted by the women in dealing with economic hardship. While some reconfigurations in gender roles can be observed, the division of labor within the household is negligible because male heads of households assume that women are responsible for child care and domestic production work, regardless of their work outside the home. The women in the study did not challenge this notion—instead, they relied on relatives and family members for assistance.

Marriage

Under the civil code, the legal age to marry without parental consent is 31 years, although a draft law has been proposed to abolish that rule.[22] The age of sexual consent is fourteen years,[23] and the legal minimum age for marriage of girls is fifteen years. The Asian Marriage Law provides a marriage age of twelve for girls of Asian descent and fifteen for Asian boys. Married women won the right to conduct legal actions without their husband's permission in 1981. However, the Surinamese legal system in general has little detail on the rights of women, unmarried women in particular, which leaves them vulnerable to social barriers and discrimination arising from cultural norms.

Reproduction

About 80 percent of childbirths take place in hospitals; the rest, in homes with traditional birth attendants and midwives. According to a national survey, Surinamese women of different ethnic background differ in their fertility rates.[24]

Sex Education, Contraception, Teen Pregnancy, and Abortion

Although they are not enforced, Suriname's Penal Code has provisions that prohibit the display and offering of contraceptives. Stichting LOBI is the only private agency providing family planning services. Founded in 1968, the foundation distributes contraceptives, offers reproductive health care services, and provides sex education in fifty-two schools in cooperation with the Ministry of Education.[25]

A contraceptive prevalence survey indicated that the pill is the most frequently used method of birth control. The country has low male condom usage, and family planning strategies primarily target females. About 40–50 percent of women between ages fifteen and forty-four use some form of contraception. The rate of contraceptive use among girls fifteen to nineteen years old, however, is only 23 percent. This pattern of contraceptive prevalence helps to explain why the overall fertility rate has decreased in recent years but adolescent girls are accounting for a higher percentage of births. It is estimated that 60 percent of first pregnancies among teenagers are unplanned.[26] Teen pregnancy contributes to another social problem, since teenage mothers frequently drop out of school.[27] Institutional practices are partially responsible for this trend—some schools view teenage mothers as having a negative influence on other female students and refuse to readmit them after they give birth.[28]

Abortion is illegal in Suriname, but an estimated 8,000–10,000 pregnancies are aborted annually.[29] Along with emigration, contraceptive prevalence and abortion are generally accepted causes for a decline in overall fertility rates.[30]

HEALTH

Health Care Access

Approximately 89 percent of households in Suriname are within five kilometers of a health clinic, and 60 percent use them on a regular basis.[31] The overall statistics do not reveal the severity of the lack of health care experienced by residents of rural and interior areas. Since the nation is unable to finance basic services, inadequate access to health care is a problem that will persist until there are improvements in the economy. Problems arising from a lack of access to health services are exacerbated by the many environmental and health hazards created by economic development (e.g., industrialization and dam construction). There are obvious human costs from poor facilities and lack of infrastructure—the Pan American Health Organization reports that the lack of blood transfusion facilities and transport results in unnecessary maternal deaths.[32]

Diseases and Disorders

AIDS

Since the first diagnosis of AIDS in Suriname, about 6,000 cases of HIV infection have been reported.[33] In the total number of HIV-infected persons diagnosed between 1983 and 1996, the male-to-female ratio was 1.7:1.[34] Although the general proportion of HIV-positive males is greater, a disproportionate number of women between the ages of fifteen and twenty-nine—the age group with the highest prevalence of HIV infection—are at risk. In addition, girls tend to become infected at a younger age. This trend is apparently due to risks that are present in other Caribbean nations—early sexual activity among adolescents and young women having sex with older men.[35]

Cancer and Other Diseases

Fifty-nine percent of malignant tumor cases diagnosed between 1991 and 1993 were females—the most frequent cases were cervical cancer,[36] followed by breast cancer. In 1993, the proportion of deaths according to causes was similar between the sexes. However, cerebrovascular accidents were more frequent among elderly women.[37] Outbreaks of malaria continue to be a major health problem in Suriname, particularly in the interior.

POLITICS AND LAW

Suffrage

Surinamese women won the right to vote in 1948. Since then, universal suffrage has been guaranteed to all adults over the age of eighteen. Article 35 of the constitution states the equality of women and men before the law.

Political Participation

From 1996 to 2000, the number of women in the fifty-one-member National Assembly increased from three to ten.[38] The share of women in government personnel went up from 10 percent in 1991 to 19.6 percent in 2000.[39] Despite the limited improvements in women's participation in national politics, social and cultural barriers persist and positions of political leadership continue to be dominated by men. In a 2001 report presented by the United Nations Development Fund for Women (UNIFEM), Suriname ranked second to last among Latin American countries according to the percentage of women in parliament.[40]

Women's Rights

The level of women's political mobilization and organizing efforts in Suriname can be seen in the presence of various institutions devoted to women's issues. The National Women's Center is a government agency that implements programs which address women's needs. The nonpartisan National Women's Movement was founded in 1982. Its organizing and advocacy efforts are devoted to strengthening women's community groups, offering training and guidance for women leaders, and supporting female micro entrepreneurs. Women's Parliamentary Forum is an umbrella organization for advocacy groups working on women's issues.

Lesbian Rights

There is little research on same-sex relationships among Surinamese women. However, sexual activity among women involved in *mati* relationships have been noted by outside observers since Dutch colonial times. *Mati* refers to a friend, either male or female. Creole women refer to these relationships as *mati* work because "it involves mutual obligations between two female partners in nurturing, social, sexual, and economic sphere."[41] *Mati* relationships are also common among teenage females and women in Saramaka Maroon groups.

RELIGION AND SPIRITUALITY

Religious practice in Suriname reflects the ethnic heterogeneity of its population; 27.4 percent is Hindu, 25.2 percent is Protestant, 22.8 percent is Roman Catholic, and 19.6 percent is Muslim.[42] The rest of the population observes indigenous beliefs. Article 18 of the constitution provides for freedom of religion and philosophy of life, and the law does not differentiate among citizens based on religion and ethnicity except in regard to ethnic marriage laws.

Due to the vast heterogeneity of spiritual practices among the various religious and indigenous groups, it is difficult to make general conclusions about Surinamese women's participation in spiritual activities. Literature on Creole culture in Suriname points to women's participation in spiritual activities, which include "leadership roles in Afro-Surinamese *Winti* religion, spiritual possession, prophecy and healing; women's oral skills; motherhood; conferring titles to women in recognition of reputation."[43] Saramaka Maroon women generally acknowledge the dominance of men in religious leadership. However, girls and women participate in important rituals and other spiritual activities within the strong matrilineal social structure.

VIOLENCE

Domestic Violence

A 1993 study based on police and hospital data reported that 54 percent of police reports involved women.[44] While these figures are taken to indicate heightened awareness of women in reporting instances of abuse, adequate response from the government has not been achieved because police have been reluctant to intervene in domestic violence. The negative consequences of this stance become highlighted when considering evidence that violent crime against women is most likely to occur in the home. The Ministry of Justice has initiated legislative change toward criminalization and effective punishment of offenders. Through its National Gender Bureau, the Ministry of Home Affairs has addressed care and counseling needs of women affected by domestic violence.[45] Nongovernmental organizations have made significant efforts in addressing this problem, providing services and working to increase awareness among the general public. A national women's group has reported that training sessions for police officers have led to improvements in police intervention in domestic violence cases.[46]

Rape/Sexual Assault

In 1995, 108 instances of rape were reported. According to hospital emergency unit data, nearly all victims of sexual assault were female, and an alarming 20 percent were girls under the age of ten.[47] Due to lack of data, it is difficult to assess the problem of marital rape. The current law does not define marital rape as a crime.

Trafficking in Women and Children

The Penal Code does not define trafficking in women and girls as a specific crime, and the general crime of trafficking in human beings is punishable by a maximum penalty of five years' imprisonment. Officials state that the police perform regular checks on brothels and other establishments that offer sexual services, to ensure that women are not abused or being held against their will. However, law enforcement officers often have informal agreements with owners of such establishments (in some cases, police officers work as their advisers), and it is unlikely that they provide strict enforcement and adequate protection. There have been reports of trafficking in women and girls for sexual exploitation within Suriname (including gold mining sites in the interior), as well as of cases where the country was used as a stop in the transportation of Brazilian women to the United States and Europe.

War and Military Repression

Suriname's relatively recent history of civil conflict and military repression emerged from its volatile political climate at the time of national independence. The system of parliamentary democracy established at the time of independence was overthrown in 1980, ushering in an oppressive military regime. In 1986, an armed group (known as the Surinamese Liberation Army or Jungle Commando) began oppositional activities against the military regime, and the armed conflict between the army and the oppositional group led to massive casualties and destruction in the southern and eastern regions of the country. This caused hundreds of Amerindian and Maroon refugees to flee to French Guiana. According to information collected by Amnesty International, there were reports of soldiers killing civilians—including women and children—as well as numerous arrests and detention without trial.[48] Military officers and supporters of the dictatorship were purged during the military reform of 1995–1996. Current human rights problems include police brutality against detainees and abuse of prisoners.

OUTLOOK FOR THE TWENTY-FIRST CENTURY

The current economic crisis is a major structural force shaping the lives of Surinamese women, in determining opportunities and challenges for earning income, in contributing to changes in family structure (regarding the division of labor at home as well as the feminization of households and poverty), and in leading to a general decline in the standard of living. Transformations in women's status and living conditions will be contingent on future economic policy and development. Legal reform to ensure gender equality has been slow, and women continue to face significant barriers to economic and political participation. However, women's political mobilization has led more women to take political leadership positions, and gender issues have become visible as an agenda in national politics. Growing bodies of organizations devoted to multifaceted strategies for improving the lives of women suggest women's potential to successfully articulate their needs and claims for social justice.

NOTES

1. Central Intelligence Agency (CIA), *The World Factbook* (2001), 477.

2. Ibid.

3. Pan American Health Organization (PAHO), *Health in the Americas* (Washington, DC: PAHO, 1998), 473.

4. CIA, 2001, 477.

5. Mayke Kromhout, "Women and Livelihood Strategies: A Case Study of Coping with Economic Crisis Through Household Management in Paramaribo, Suriname," in *Gender and Global Restructuring: Sightings, Site and Resistances*, ed. Marianne H. Marchand and Anne Sisson Runyan (London: Routledge, 2000), 143.

6. Brook Hayes, *Poverty, Health, HIV/AIDS—Suriname*, letter to The Communication Initiative, December 21, 2001. www.comminit.com/issuestrends/sld-3878.html.

7. The Convention requires a state party to ensure that the legal system incorporates gender equality.

8. Kromhout, 2000, 145.

9. Kromhout, 2000, 145.

10. CIA, 2001, 477.

11. Maggie Schmeitz, *Country Report: Suriname*, 2002, www.socwatch.org.uy/2002/eng/nationalreports/suriname2002_eng.htm.

12. CIA, 2001, 478.

13. Kromhout, 2000, 143.

14. Hayes, 2001; "Bureau of Democracy, Human Rights, and Labor," *Country Reports on Human Rights Practices—2001* (Washington, DC: U.S. Department of State, 2001), www.state.gov.g.drl.rls.hrrpt/2001/wha/8235.htm.

15. Hayes, 2001.

16. PAHO, 1998, 471.

17. Rosalyn Hazelle, "Draft Report for the Committee of the Elimination of Discrimination Against Women," 27th session, June 3–21, 2002, 6, www.un.org/womenwatch/daw/cedaw/cedaw27/ConcComments/Suriname.PDF.

18. Hazelle, 2002, 7.

19. PAHO, 1998, 471, 475.

20. PAHO, 1998, 471.

21. Kromhout, 2000, 140.

22. United Nations, "Committee Urges Suriname to Implement Announced Measures for Advancement of Women," 2002, press release, www.unhchr.ch/huricane/huricane.nsf/view01/B279ABA88FCD1BE2C1256BD80026A97B?opendocument.

23. This law is not strictly enforced.

24. PAHO, 1998, 472, 474.

25. International Planned Parenthood, "Country Profile: Suriname," 1996, http://ippfnet.ippf.org/pub/IPPF_Regions/IPPF_CountryProfile.asp?ISOCode=SR.

26. Hayes, 2001.

27. In 1989, the government initiated a student-mothers project in order to encourage teenage mothers to complete their education. The project subsequently became a part of a nongovernmental organization in 1992. Hazelle, 2002, 2.

28. Ibid., 6.

29. Hayes, 2001.

30. PAHO, 1998, 472.

31. Ibid., 480.

32. Ibid., 474.

33. Hazelle, 2002, 2.

34. PAHO, 1998, 476.

35. Hayes, 2001.

36. Stichting LOBI provides services in cervical cancer prevention, targeting young adults and communities of the interior.

37. PAHO, 1998, 474, 477.

38. The National Assembly is the highest government entity with legislative powers and elects the president and vice president.

39. Hazelle, 2002, 2.

40. Gustavo Gonzalez, "Scant Progress in Status of Women, Says Unifem." April 10, 2001, Inter Press Service, www.twnside.org.sg/title/scant.htm.

41. Gloria Wekker, "One Finger Does Not Drink Okra Soup: Afro-Surinamese Women and Critical Agency," in *Feminist Genealogies, Colonial Legacies, Democratic Futures*, ed. M. Jacqui Alexander and Chandra Talpade Mohanty (New York and London: Routledge, 1997).

42. CIA, 2001, 477.

43. Wekker, 1997, 341.

44. PAHO, 1998, 477.

45. Hazelle, 2002, 2.

46. Gonzalez, 2001.

47. PAHO, 1998, 477.
48. Amnesty International, 1987.

RESOURCE GUIDE

Suggested Reading

Hoefte, Rosemarijn. *Suriname*. Oxford: Clio Press, 1990. Overview of Suriname's economic, social, and historical background with a bibliography organized by subject.

Kromhout, Mayke. 2000. "Women and Livelihood Strategies: A Case Study of Coping with Economic Crisis Through Household Management in Paramaribo, Suriname." In *Gender and Global Restructuring: Sightings, Site and Resistances*, ed. Marianne H. Marchand and Anne Sisson Runyan. London: Routledge, 2000. An in-depth study of forty-five women and their households in Paramaribo, examining the various strategies used by women in dealing with economic hardship.

Pan American Health Organization. *Health in the Americas*. Washington DC: World Health Organization, 1998. Presents a detailed analysis of health conditions and related issues in Suriname.

Price, Sally. *Co-Wives and Calabashes*. Ann Arbor: University of Michigan Press, 1984. An extensive study of social and cultural activities of Saramaka Maroon women.

Wekker, Gloria. "One Finger Does Not Drink Okra Soup: Afro-Surinamese Women and Critical Agency." In *Feminist Genealogies, Colonial Legacies, Democratic Futures*, edited by M. Jacqui Alexander and Chandra Talpade Mohanty. New York and London: Routledge, 1997. Examines Creole women's subjectivities, sexualities and political activity.

Web Sites

www.cq-link.sr/nonprofit/nvb/informat.htm.
Provides information about the programs and activities of the National Women's Movement.

www.paho.org/English/SHA/prflSUR.htm.
Website for the Pan American Health Organization. Provides background information and statistics related to social, economic, and health conditions in Suriname.

www.socwatch.org.uy/2002/eng/nationalreports/suriname2002_eng.htm.
A report on Suriname's economic conditions with comments on women's situation.

Organizations

Johanna Schouten-Elsenhout Vrouwendocumentatiecentrum (Johanna Schouten-Elsenhout Documentation Center)
Limesgracht 80, Postbus 129
Paramaribo, Suriname
Phone: (597) 410 784
Fax: (597) 433 167
Email: knott@cq-link.sr

Founded by the National Women's Movement, the center was named after the first woman poet who wrote in the Surinamese language. The Center houses the nation's only library offering material on women, and its mission is to collect and make accessible women's literature and documentation on women and development. Languages: Dutch, English, German, Spanish.

Stichting LOBI
Fajalobistraat 13
P.O. Box 9267
Paramaribo, Suriname
Phone: (597) 400-444
Fax: (597) 400-960

The foundation provides sex education, distributes contraceptives, and offers various reproductive health services. It also conducts surveys on issues related to women's reproductive health and family planning.

Stichting Sanomaro Esa (Sanomaro Esa Foundation)
Verlengde Keizerstraat 92
Gebouw PA #5
Phone: (597) 421-262
Email: sanomaro-csa@sr.net

In 1989 this organization was founded by indigenous women seeking to address the needs of indigenous people (women and children in particular). The foundation operates a resource center, contributes to the planning and implementation of various programs, and facilitates educational programs.

SELECTED BIBLIOGRAPHY

Amnesty International. *Suriname: Violations of Human Rights*. London: Amnesty International Publications, 1987.

Bureau of Democracy, Human Rights, and Labor. *Country Reports on Human Rights Practices*—2001. Washington, DC: U.S. Department of State, 2001.www.state.gov.g.drl.rls.hrrpt/2001/wha/8235.htm.

Central Intelligence Agency (CIA). *The World Factbook*. 2001.

Gonzalez, Gustavo. "Scant Progress in Status of Women, Says Unifem." April 10, 2001. Inter Press Service. www.twnside.org.sg/title/scant.htm.

Hayes, Brook. *Poverty, Health, HIV/AIDS—Suriname*. Letter to The Communication Initiative. December 21, 2001. www.comminit.com/issuestrends/sld-3878.html.

Hazelle, Rosalyn. Draft Report for the Committee of the Elimination of Discrimination against Women. 27th session, June 3–21, 2002. www.un.org/womenwatch/daw/cedaw/cedaw27/ConcComments/Suriname.PDF.

Hoefte, Rosemarijn. *Suriname*. Oxford: Clio Press, 1990.

International Planned Parenthood (IPPF). *Country Profile: Suriname*, 1996. http://ippfnet.ippf.org/pub/IPPF_Regions/IPPF_CountryProfile.asp?ISOCode=SR.

Kromhout, Mayke. "Women and Livelihood Strategies: A Case Study of Coping with Economic Crisis Through Household Management in Paramaribo, Suriname." In *Gender and Global Restructuring: Sightings, Site and Resistances*, edited by Marianne H. Marchand and Anne Sisson Runyan. London: Routledge, 2000.

Pan American Health Organization (PAHO). 1998. *Health in the Americas*. Washington, DC: PAHO, 1998.

Price, Sally. *Co-wives and Calabashes*. Ann Arbor: Univ. of Michigan Press, 1984.

Schmeitz, Maggie. *Country Report: Suriname*. 2002. www.socwatch.org.uy/2002/eng/nationalreports/suriname2002_eng.htm.

United Nations. "Committee Urges Suriname to Implement Announced Measures for Advancement of Women." 2002. Press release. www.unhchr.ch/huricane/huricane.nsf/view01/B279ABA88FCD1BE2C1256BD80026A97B?opendocument.

Wekker, Gloria. "One Finger Does Not Drink Okra Soup: Afro-Surinamese Women and Critical Agency." In *Feminist Genealogies, Colonial Legacies, Democratic Futures*, edited by M. Jacqui Alexander and Chandra Talpade Mohanty. New York and London: Routledge, 1997.

19

URUGUAY

Susana Rostagnol

PROFILE OF URUGUAY

Uruguay is a small country located in the southern cone of South America with an area of 176,220 square kilometers (70,488 square miles). The land consists mostly of gently rolling plateaus, interrupted by low hilly ridges. The Atlantic Ocean coasts are fertile lowlands occasionally broken by lagoons. There are many streams and rivers throughout the country. The people are primarily of European descent (mostly Spanish and Italian); there is very little ethnic or linguistic diversity. Approximately 10 percent of the population is Afro-Uruguayan. The official language is Spanish. The form of government is a republic. Elections are held every five years. Voting is universal and compulsory for all citizens eighteen years of age or older. There are three main political parties: Colorado, Nacional and Encuentro Progresista. The executive branch is headed by the president; the legislative branch consists of the Senate and House of Representatives; and the judiciary branch is headed by the Justice Supreme Court. The territory is divided into nineteen departments, each with its own government. Independence was gained from the Portuguese-ruled Brazilian Empire on August 22, 1825.

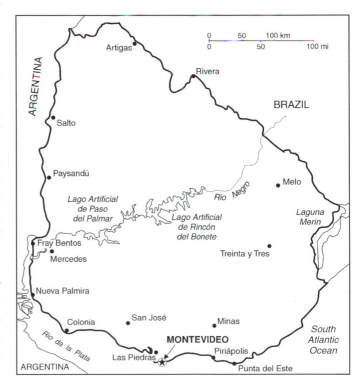

The current constitution was ratified in 1966. Main exports are beef, wool and rice; tourism is another important economic sector. Most people work in services. According to the last population census in 1996, the population is 3,322,141: 1,712,942 women and 1,609,199 men. Ninety percent of the population lives in urban areas, almost half in Montevideo, the capital. In 2001, infant mortality was 13.9 deaths per 1,000. In 1997, maternal mortality was 2.8 deaths per 10,000 live births. Average life expectancy at birth in 2001 was 71.3 years for men and 78.8 years for women. The total fertility rate is 2.2.[1]

In the late 1960s the Tupamaro urban guerrilla movement was active in Uruguay. In 1973, amid increasing economic and political turmoil, the armed forces closed the Congress and established an authoritarian civilian–military dictatorship. The taking of political prisoners, torture, and persecution became common. A new constitution drafted by the military was rejected in a November 1980 plebiscite. Following the plebiscite, the armed forces announced a plan for return to democratic rule. Political institutions were reinstalled and social movements (e.g., trade unions, student and human rights groups) were reorganized. Women took part in this process. Economic development in the country has been uneven, and while Uruguay boasts some progress in terms of growth, as a whole the country has not been very prosperous. In 1991 Uruguay was included in the Southern Cone Common Market (MERCOSUR). A few months after the 2001 Argentine financial crisis, Uruguay's most important economic crisis in the last hundred years took place.

OVERVIEW OF WOMEN'S ISSUES

Traditionally, the statuses of women and men have been fairly equal in Uruguay. This was mostly the result of advanced legislation passed in the first decades of the twentieth century and women's early entrance into all levels of education. However, the situation of women is not as good as it could be, in part because some economic standards have deteriorated. Even though more women than men are enrolled in universities, this is not reflected in job opportunities. Women's participation in economic activity has been increasing since the 1980s, and is one of the highest of the region. During the first decades of the twentieth century, Uruguay passed some of the strongest welfare legislation in the region, with important benefits extended to workers, including the eight-hour workday. However, free market economic policies in the 1990s contributed to cutbacks in state welfare programs. The new economic order 1990s does not take into account the flexible and informal sector of temporary jobs, which means they offer no guaranteed eight-hour workday, no maternity leave, no holidays, and no Social Security. A high proportion of women's jobs lack regulation and have little Social Security coverage; rather, women work longer hours and are paid lower salaries. For instance, women knitting sweaters for export work out of their homes and are paid by on a piece work basis.

EDUCATION

Opportunities

For several decades, the state educational system has achieved much in the realm of public education, particularly for women. In Uruguay, education is free from kindergarten through the university level. Although private schools are becoming more popular at the primary and secondary levels, less than 10 percent of all university students have attended private schools. Young people have a higher level of education than older people, especially among women. The average level of education among women has increased, in relative as well as in absolute terms, more than among men.[2] Girls outnumber boys in secondary school, but twice as many boys attend technological high school as do girls. It is presumed that boys are more interested in studying a subject that might help them get a job. At the university level, there are more women students (68 percent) than men (32 percent).[3] However, higher educational levels do not give women an advantage in the job market: they need more education than men to compete and achieve similar income levels.[4] At the university level, some traditionally masculine careers, such as medicine and law, have been feminized, while in others, such as psychology, which are already femininized, the participation of women has increased even more. Still other fields, such as engineering, remain basically dominated by men, though women's participation is gradually increasing.[5]

Broader access to education does not necessarily translate into less discrimination against women, who continue to enter careers associated with women's traditional gender roles, or careers that will not compete with their responsibilities as mothers.[6] Typically, universities do not provide daycare facilities for students with children. The Universidad de la República has lagged behind most universities in the region on gender studies, even though some academics have been researching in that area for a long time. In 2001 a University Gender Network was set up to gather all researchers and coordinate their work.

Outside formal education,

Students at a Montevideo university celebrate their heritage. Photo © TRIP/A. Tovy.

there are a few special courses for women. In the area of micro enterprise, in 1995 the Ministry of Livestock, Agriculture and Fishery launched a program called "Productive Training for Women." That same year the IMM (Montevideo Municipal Government) implemented leadership courses for women, for example, "Training for Political and Social Participation."

Literacy

The literacy rate is exceptionally high: 98 percent of all women and 97 percent of all men are literate, one of the highest rates in the region.[7]

EMPLOYMENT AND ECONOMICS

Job/Career Opportunities

The female labor rate has been increasing steadily since the 1980s, coinciding with the deterioration of salaries and household income, which necessitates a second salary to supplement the man's. In 1973 the rate was 31.7 percent; it increased to 42.7 percent in 1986[8] and reached 50.9 percent in 2001.[9] Married women are participating in the labor market at the same rate as single and divorced women because they no longer quit their jobs when their children are small.[10]

Pay

The average per-hour value of men's work is 80 pesos; that of women is 59.7 pesos. And even though women on average have more years of education than men, and women with more education are highly over-represented in the labor force, the most unfavorable relation between male and female earnings is in the category of professionals and management.[11]

Working Conditions

High participation of women in the labor market does not mean they are better off. Work segregation and less obvious forms of discrimination are present: part-time jobs, piecework, and seasonal and hazardous tasks are more prevalent among women than men; most of the posts they hold are low-level and they suffer higher levels of unemployment. In 2001 the unemployment rate was 19.7 percent among women and 13 percent among men; those looking for a job for the first time were not counted.[12]

The increase in women's labor force participation is related to the economic model of market liberalization, which has contributed to a new, gendered pattern of labor requiring a well-educated female workforce.[13] Labor flexibility also requires women, who are preferred for temporary and part-time jobs as well as noncontract jobs that are not backed by trade union agreements.[14] Despite changes in the labor market, important inequities in male and female labor patterns, including salaries, persist. A strong concentration of women persists in a small number of sectors and occupations labeled "women's." Women tend to be concentrated in a small number of activities. Most FEAP work in domestic service (60 percent), followed by social services (health, education) and clerical work. To this horizontal segregation, a vertical one is added: the concentration of women in the lowest tiers of the each occupation.[15]

Working Conditions

Since the 1970s, Uruguay has undergone a series of economic and political changes known as structural adjustment policies, within a World Bank and International Monetary Fund framework for developing poor economies with large foreign debts. Uruguay's foreign debt was $7.6 million (1998), representing 23.5 percent of export income. These policies, which include economic liberalization, privatization, laying off state employees, and the general "opening up" of the Uruguayan economy to the world market, are part of what many refer to as the dominant neoliberal model of development in Latin America. Changes put into practice with the new employment policies reduced the negotiating capacity of waged workers. This especially affected the female workforces employed by small firms and those with no union organization to back them up. New sources of jobs are characteristically seasonal or have poor working conditions (tourism, certain consumer services, and agro-industries), and they prefer to recruit women and young people, even women with their children, for intensive labor that demands certain skills and qualities.[16]

Since in the 1990s a high proportion of women workers have had to change their working conditions. Their new jobs lack regulation and have little Social Security coverage; they work longer hours and receive lower salaries.

Sexual Harassment

Even though sexual harassment is an issue, there is only a weak legal reference. In 1997 the Law of Equal Treatment and Opportunities in the Labor Market made sexual harassment in the workplace or as a consequence of the job a discriminatory behavior.[17]

Support for Mothers/Caretakers

There is protective legislation for mothers. A pregnant woman cannot be fired. In governmental and public administration women who are nursing an infant can work half-time for six months.

Maternity Leave

Uruguayan labor legislation provides for a maternal leave of three months. If necessary, it can be a month and a half before the probable birth date, and a month and a half after. There is a regulation giving some days of maternity leave to adoptive mothers.

Daycare

The greater participation of women in the workforce has not meant a reduction in their domestic tasks. Availability of services has not kept pace with the new demand. According to a 1992 UNICEF report, nurseries (for newborns to five-year-olds) in neighborhoods with 25 percent or more homes having unsatisfied basic needs reach only 20 percent of the children.[18] On the other hand, the public education reform implemented in the late 1990s puts a special emphasis in achieving better social equity and plans a long-term scheme to make public preschool education (from ages three to five years) universally available for the most vulnerable sectors. Many departmental administrations have started programs for needy children that offer free meals and nurseries, generally with support from UNICEF.

Family and Medical Leave

Women working in governmental offices and public administration have the right to ask for special leave to care for sick children or any other dependent relative.

Inheritance and Property Rights

Uruguayan law does not make any distinction between men and women in relation to inheritance and property rights.

Social/Government Programs

The increase of women's participation in the labor market has not been accompanied by social policies that might facilitate it (daycare centers, kindergartens, laundries, etc.). Therefore, working women, particularly those from low-income sectors, have to cope with the double burden of housework after working long hours outside the home.

However, action is being taken to facilitate the entrance of women into the labor market. In October 2001, the Program to Promote Equal Opportunity to Women for Employment and Professional Training (PRO-IMUJER) was launched. Managed by the Ministry of Labor and CINTERFOR/ILO (International Labour Organisation), its goal is to incorporate 30 percent of the women enrolled in the program into the labor market.

Welfare

Among the economically active population, 35 percent have no Social Security coverage and 60 percent of unemployed workers have no unemployment insurance.[19] This permanent and structural problem is related to the growing presence of women in the informal sector.

FAMILY AND SEXUALITY

Gender Roles

Uruguayan families usually are small, though relatives tend to live nearby and family get-togethers are part of daily life. It is common for an older couple to have their married children and grandchildren come to lunch on Sundays; pasta is usually served, a reflection of the large population of Italian heritage. Even if the household is a nuclear family, there may be a strong presence of other relatives, for instance, grandparents taking care of small children on a daily basis. Since the 1970s some important changes have taken place in family structures. Some traditional family functions are no longer performed exclusively within the family—for example, care and early socialization of children are shared more often with other social agents: schools, kindergartens, and preschools, or other family members or outsiders. Although taking care of children and going to the grocery or the street market are increasingly becoming shared activities among middle-class couples, women are still responsible for the household chores, even if a domestic service worker actually performs them.

Marriage

In recent decades there have been an increasing number of middle-class couples who live together without getting married. This has been a traditional behavior among poor classes. Marriage age differs according to socioeconomic class. Poor women tend to move in with a partner at a very young age (seventeen years old) and have many children, whereas women from middle and upper classes get married or move in with a partner at a much older age (around twenty-five) and have few children. In the population over fifteen years of age, 9.53 percent live with a partner without being married, and 48.39 percent are married.[20]

Divorce is fairly common—the divorce rate is 2.6.[21] Some people remarry, and blended families are quite common. Other people remain divorced (3.92 percent), and 2.39 percent are separated. Close to a third of the population over fifteen is single (27.96 percent), and 7.81 percent are widows or widowers.[22] These percentages are different when individual socioeconomic classes are considered.

Nuclear families decreased from 63.3 percent in 1983 to 60.9 percent in 1997, but most significant is their diversity. They include blended families, single-parent families, and families without children. Nuclear families numbered 11.9 percent in 1986 and increased to 15.9 percent in 1997; blended families were 18.6 percent in 1986 and 17.3 percent in 1997; and non-traditional households totaled 6.2 percent in 1986 and 5.7 percent in 1997.[23]

Reproduction

Reproductive practices in Uruguay are characterized by a small number of offspring. This has been the prevailing behavior among middle-class families since the beginning of the twentieth century. The fertility rate of 2.25 is not homogeneous throughout the society, but differs from one socioeconomic class to another.[24] Poor people have many children, while the tendency in the middle class is to have fewer children. In 1986, 42.1 percent of urban families' eldest children were newborn to twelve years old; in 1996 the percentage was 20.4 percent.[25] Among the poor population these percentages increased; in 1995, in Montevideo, the percentage of children under fourteen years of age living in poor homes was 65.4 percent; it was almost 80 percent in the city center, traditionally a poor area.[26]

Sex Education

For many years sex education has consisted of a lesson on the male and female reproductive organs in the framework of biology classes. Officially, in the public education system there are no sex education programs, although many private schools do teach it. In 2000, the book *Listen, Learn, Live* was issued by the AIDS Program of the Ministry of Public Health together with the Ministry of Education and Culture, following an initiative of United Nations AIDS Program (UNAIDS). It was meant to be distributed to all third- and fourth-year high school students. The contents of the book drew tremendous opposition from the most conservative sectors of the Catholic Church and other social groups. As a consequence, it was not distributed.

Contraception and Abortion

Most Uruguayan women (82 percent) have used contraception: 33 percent had started before they were eighteen years old; 42 percent, between eighteen and twenty years old. The most popular contraceptive method is "the Pill" (54 percent of women prefer oral contraception); 30 percent prefer the condom, particularly among the youngest polled; and 16 percent prefer the IUD.[27] No prescription is needed to purchase contraceptives;

they can be obtained in any drugstore, and condoms can be obtained almost anywhere.

At the national level, the Voluntary Paternity and Maternity Program, financed by the United Nations Population Fund, was implemented by the Ministry of Health from 1996 to 2000. In Montevideo, where half of all Uruguayans live, the municipality has implemented the Integral Attention Program for Women, emphasizing aspects of reproductive and sexual health. There are approximately twelve municipal clinics.

In Uruguay abortion is a common practice, despite the fact that it is illegal and considered a crime. Its being outlawed makes abortion a highly unsafe practice. In 2001, complications from illegal abortions were the main cause of maternal death.[28]

Teen Pregnancy

Since the 1970s important reproductive behavior changes have taken place, especially in the fertility distribution according to ages. There has been a noticeable increase in teen pregnancies, with an equally important percentage of children born out of wedlock among the poorest women.[29] In 1996, 16.53 percent of births were to mothers between ten and nineteen years old. If only births that occurred in public hospitals (where the poorest women go) are considered, the percentage increases to 25.1 percent.[30]

HEALTH

Health Care Access

Ninety percent of the population has some sort of access to health care, but access varies according to socioeconomic status, age, and gender: public health services (the poorest), collective health services (people become partners, pay a monthly fee for health care), Social Security health services, and private health services. Among all women, 36.2 percent go to Public Health hospitals and 46 percent go to collective health services.[31] Because of this cross-class coverage, 99 percent of births occur in hospitals. In 2001 the "company during childbirth" law was approved, giving all women in labor the right to be with the person of their choice during childbirth.

Diseases and Disorders

AIDS

Between 1983 and 2000, the National AIDS Program reported 1583 cases of AIDS, 842 of which ended in death. There is still a high prevalence among men, although the male–female gap is decreasing. In 1991, for every 8.5 cases among men there was one among women; in 2001, for every 2.4 cases among men, there was one among women. Thus, AIDS is expanding among heterosexual women.[32]

Most people know how the disease is transmitted. The increase in condom use corresponds to HIV/AIDS prevention. There is no systematic information about the incidence of AIDS among pregnant women, although some cases of children born with the disease have been registered.

Eating Disorders

Eating disorders have become more common in recent years, although they are not seen as a public health issue. Most eating disorders are bulimia and anorexia among teenagers and young women. There is also an increasing problem of obesity among children, apparently due to eating too many unhealthy foods.

Cancer

Uruguay has the highest rate of breast cancer deaths, as a proportion of all cancer-related deaths, in Latin America. In 1996, deaths in Uruguay from breast cancer as a percent of all cancer deaths reached 35.5 percent; cervical cancer, 5.5 percent.[33] After the age of forty-five, the possibility of getting breast cancer increases; among all women who died in 1996 from breast cancer, 91.46 percent were forty-five or older. Many campaigns are being launched to educate women about the importance of having preventive exams. In 2000, a law was approved declaring that all women workers have the right to a day off with pay each year to have their mammogram and Pap smear done.

Depression

Depression is a relatively new health problem in Uruguay. There are no systematic studies analyzing its gender impact upon men and women. The economic crisis and rising unemployment rates, together with the lack of opportunities in the near future, have become a major cause of depression, especially among men. Women are more likely than men to take medication following a diagnosis of depression. Uruguay has a high suicide rate, and many of the suicides are believed to be caused by depression. There are several NGOs working on these issues, one of them with a twenty-four hour phone to help people who are considering committing suicide, as well as friends and relatives of such persons.

POLITICS AND LAW

Suffrage

In 1932 Uruguayan women were granted the right to vote and to be elected to political office as a result of women's activism and a liberal government.

Political Participation

During the second half of the twentieth century, few women headed lists of candidates for the Senate or the House of Representatives, although their percentage in municipal positions was higher.[34] This is consistent with the idea that women enter the political system from the base and encounter greater obstacles as they get closer to the more powerful positions. Unlike other Latin American countries, Uruguay has no affirmative action laws that mandate a bottom-line quota for female candidates and/or politicians. During the period of military authoritarian rule women played a major role in resisting—socializing their children and using their informal networks of neighbors and friends to circulate news about political prisoners and about what was going on abroad. Many of them also were tortured in prison.

During the transition to democracy (1983–1985), the women's movement gained visibility in the public sphere. Women were called to take part in the negotiations within the framework of the Comisión Nacional de Programación (CONAPRO, National Programmatic Commission), together with representatives of political parties, trade unions, and civil society. However, since then the political representation of women in decision-making positions has remained very low (from not a single woman elected to Parliament in 1984 to just 12 percent elected in 1999). In the 1999 elections only 8.6 percent of the House of Representatives lists were headed by a woman; the Partido Encuentro Progresista (the Progressive Encounter Party, a progressive-leftist party) had the highest percenage.[35] After the election, sixteen women entered Parliament, three as senators (two from Encuentro Progresista-Frente Amplio and one from the Partido Nacional, or National Party) and thirteen as representatives (five from the Encuentro Progresista-Frente Amplio, six from the Partido Colorado, or Colorado Party, two from the National Party). Immediately following dictatorship, women politicians developed a strong network that represents their interests and concerns as women within political parties. This network is the basis of the Bancada Femenina, an association of women in the House of Representatives that carries out gender-specific agendas.

Women's Rights

The Uruguayan Constitution guarantees equal rights, irrespective of sex. However, there are many discriminatory practices in daily life. In 1989 the Law of Equal Treatment and Opportunities for Men and Women in the Labor Market was approved, but it was not implemented until 1997, showing a lack of political will to change the situation for women. In 1981 Uruguay ratified the Convention of the Elimination of All Forms of Discrimination Against Women. However, customs, traditional discriminatory behaviors, and a lack of procedures for enforcement of the Convention are reasons most commonly cited to explain the delay in the advancement of women.

In 1985, the Woman and Family Institute was created in the Ministry of Culture and Education. Although in theory the establishment of this institute was a step forward for women's rights, in reality it had little power and a small budget.

Uruguay doesn't have an Equal Opportunity Plan at the national level, but there is one in Montevideo, which was enacted in 2002.[36]

Feminist Movements

In Uruguay, feminist thought can be traced to the beginning of the twentieth century. Among the immigrants from Europe were some important groups of anarchists and sindicalists who brought socialist ideas and were somewhat concerned about women's issues. After those early years, there was a blank until the 1980s, when women began to meet and gradually formed a movement that played a remarkable role in the return to democracy. Most groups and organizations in the late 1980s devoted themselves to a reflection on their situation as women, women's work, and women's participation in trade unions and political parties. There were also some academic groups.[37] In 1991 there were eighty-nine groups with legal status.[38] In 1996, after the WWC of Beijing, women's groups and organizations gathered at the National Commission for Beijing Follow-up, which has been coordinating and centralizing actions ever since; it brings together eighty groups and national networks.[39] Feminist organizations have developed a variety of activities and actions to address the pressing issues they have identified. Some engage in political lobbying to change legislation and regulations affecting women; others provide services to women ranging from counseling for women victims of violence to job retraining. Women's movement connections in the MERCOSUR region have been strengthened since the Beijing conference. There are also several groups affiliated with international networks: REPEM, an adult women's education network; DAWN, Development Alternatives with Women for a New Era; and CLADEM, Latin American and Caribbean Committee for the Defense of Women's Rights.

Lesbian Rights

Uruguay is a rather homophobic country.[40] In recent years some small organizations of gays and lesbians have tried to organize and have held public demonstrations on Gay Pride Day in June. Some of them have gathered in the Gay, Lesbian, Transsexual and Bisexual Network to lobby for their rights. The Network has coordinated some specific actions and statements with the women's movements. Currently there is a proposal in the House of Representatives to establish legal and institutional reforms to protect sexual minorities. Its provisions include the recognition of homosexual couples and of gender identity change in transsexuals.

Military Service

Uruguay does not have compulsory military service. Though women have entered the army in recent years, their number is still very low.

RELIGION AND SPIRITUALITY

Women's Roles

In Uruguay the state has been separate from the church since the early twentieth century. All religions are allowed, and none of them can be taught in school or have a presence in a public hospital. There is a large number of atheists and agnostics. Among religions, the Roman Catholic Church is the most important one; there are also some traditional Protestant churches. The Jewish community also is quite important. Since the 1970s, Umbanda, an Afro-Brazilian cult, has been gaining importance and, more recently so have the neo-Pentecostal cults. Women attend church more often than men, and whatever the religion or cult, they seem to be more attached to religious norms. Typically, women do not have leading roles, except in Umbanda, where they can be *mãe* (the priest).

Some traditional churches and synagogues have "ladies commissions," which usually devote themselves to community work with orphans, the elderly, or the poor.

Rituals and Religious Practices

Rituals and religious practices do not play an important role in Uruguayans' daily lives, although major festivities—such as Christmas—are widely celebrated. Women tend to play leading roles in the preparation for and observance of rituals and religious practices, particularly in traditional religions.

Religious Law

Since the state is separated from all religions, there are no religious laws. However, the Catholic Church has influenced legislation in the areas of education, family, and sexual rights.

VIOLENCE

Domestic Violence

According to newspaper reports, in Uruguay a woman dies every nine days as the result of domestic violence.[41] This is a high number if one considers that Uruguay only has 3.3 million inhabitants. Only in the last several years has domestic violence become a public issue. The women's movement, including nongovernmental organizations (NGOs) that have worked with United Nations' and other international agreements, put the issue on its agenda. Since 1992, the Montevideo municipal government has run a "violence telephone line" that receives calls twenty-four hours a day. Since 2001, it has been taking calls from all over the country. The popularity of the phone line has shown the real size of the problem. There are eleven women's police stations throughout the country specializing in domestic violence problems. Recently, their personnel have received special training through the Citizen Security Program that includes topics such as sexual abuse. The Women's Commission of the Montevideo municipal government facilitates the program, "Prevention of All Forms of Gender Violence." Comuna Mujer, another program run by the municipality, develops activities in six zones of Montevideo. One of its free services is counseling in domestic violence, including psychological and legal aid. This also has allowed women to participate in advocacy and campaigning in order to put this issue on the public agenda.

The Citizen Security Program, funded by the Inter-American Development Bank (IDB), included the development of a center to take care of domestic violence victims—girls as well as women. It was established through cooperative programs involving seven NGOs and public services, allowing them to widen their coverage. They included direct care of victims as well as training for the police, members of the judiciary, and community agents. Unfortunately, the program was not self-sustaining; IDB funding ended in December 2001, and the government's severe economic problems interrupted its services.

There are no shelters for women victims of domestic violence.

In 1994, Uruguay approved the Interamerican Convention to Prevent, Sanction and Eradicate Violence against Women. In 1995, Law 16.707, containing an article on domestic violence, was approved. However, it was not clear, and violent acts remained hard to prove. Therefore, feminist groups concerned about domestic violence continued their struggle for a law that really would contemplate women. In 2002 a law on domestic violence was finally approved in Parliament, although its implementation is yet to happen because of problems arising from resistance by some members of the judiciary.

Rape/Sexual Assault

In Uruguay legislation on rape and sexual assault is out-of-date and insufficient: in both cases it is hard for women to gather the required proof. Research on news about rape and sexual assault done in 1996 shows that the aggressor is a person the victim knows—relative, neighbor, acquaintance (48.3 percent); someone unknown to the victim (31.8 percent); a parent, usually the father (17.6 percent); or the partner or ex-partner of the victim (2.2 percent).[42]

Trafficking in Women and Children

Even though prostitution is widespread, it is not seen as a major problem. It is still regulated by a law dating from 1928, and therefore a new regulation is being discussed in Parliament. Under the new regulation, sex workers will have to register and pay taxes, and will be able to retire like any other workers; areas where the sex industry will be allowed will be strictly determined; the workers will continue to have obligatory regular tests for sexually transmitted diseases. The Association of Sex Workers agrees with this regulation.[43] Some NGOs—such as El Faro—are involved in children's issues and therefore are concerned with sexual exploitation of children. The issue of trafficking came to light through research done by a journalist who showed a connection between Uruguay and Milan, Italy, in that girls were taken from one place to the other with no documents. An important chain of corruption was involved in the business, including police and travel agents.[44]

War and Military Repression

During the dictatorship years (1973–1984), repression touched everybody. Women and men endured terrible torture in prison; strong repression was exerted on ordinary people. In 2001, former women political prisoners published a book, *Memories to Put Together*, which was the result of several years of workshops in which they tried to recall and reconstruct the collective memory together, as well as a wider project in which all women were invited to write about the dictatorship years: memories, poems, and even fiction inspired in those dark days. Women have been the first group willing to remember, to talk about, and to go though the necessary process of re-creating in their memories those years of their lives and in the life of the whole country.

OUTLOOK FOR THE TWENTY-FIRST CENTURY

Uruguay is undergoing an important economic crisis, and poverty is increasing exponentially. Deeper changes in family structure and working conditions are expected. Uruguayan women's tools to face the coming events are the creativity, solidarity, and character they have already shown. It is likely that women's empowerment will continue, most probably because they will have to make decisions in areas where they are not involved at the present time. On the other hand, activists have been lobbying for some women's rights that have not yet been achieved. Whatever the legal outcome, important gender issues have been placed on the public agenda, and most women have made them their own.

NOTES

1. Instituto Nacional de Estadísticas (INE), *Uruguay en cifras* (2002).

2. Susana Dornel, "Educación," in *El estado uruguayo y las mujeres: Monitoreo de políticas públicas*, ed. CNS (Montevideo: Macondo Impresos, 1999).

3. Latin American and Caribbean Committee for the Defense of Women's Rights (CLADEM/MYSU), "Derechos sexuales y reproductivos en Uruguay (1995–2000)" (Montevideo: CLADEM/MYSU, 2000). Photocopy.

4. Nea Filgueira, "Uruguay, a Very Vulnerable 'Development,'" in *Social Watch*, 1999, www.socialwatch.org.

5. Universidad de la República, *Censo universitario* (Montevideo: UDELAR, 2002).

6. Diosma Piotti de Fortuna, "Mujer joven y educación en el Uruguay," In *La situación laboral de las mujeres jóvenes en el Uruguay: Recopilación de trabajo del seminario mujer joven en América Latina* (Montevideo, 1998); Zulema María Zulema Rodrigo, *Las mujeres uruguayas en el sistema educativo*, Working paper no. 7, Universidad de la República, Facultad de ciencias sociales, Montevideo, 1993; Dornel, 1999.

7. Comisión Nacional de Seguimiento de los Acuerdos de Beijing (CNS), 2002, www.comision.chasquenet.org.

8. Rosario Aguirre and Susana Rostagnol, "Las mujeres organizadas," *Relaciones* no. 30 (1986).

9. INE, 2002.

10. Amarante, V., and A. Espino, "La segregación laboral por sexo en el mercado de trabajo Uruguay (1986–1999)," *Documentos de trabajo*, March 1, 2001, www.iecon.ccee.edu.uy/instec/doctrab.htm.

11. Filgueira, 1999.

12. INE, 2002.

13. Paola Azar and Alma Espino, *El comercio internacional: ¿Una oportunidad para la equidad social y de género? Los procesos de integración y las políticas comerciales más importantes para américa Latina y el Caribe revisados y analizados incorporando criterios de género* (Montevideo, 2001).

14. PIT-CNT/Cuesta Duarte. *Las dimensiones del MERCOSUR y las trabajadoras*, www.chasque.net/icudu/tyu/Aın3/mujer.html.

15. Alma Espino, "El MERCOSUR y el impacto del comercio en la situación de las mujeres en el mercado laboral. Una propuesta de indicadores." In *Trabajo, género y ciudadanía en los países del Cono Sur* (Montevideo: Cinterfor, 2001).

16. Filgueira, 1999.

17. CLADEM MYSU, 2000.

18. Filgueira, 1999.

19. Banco de Previsión Social (BPS), *Informal Work and Social Security* (Montevideo: BPS, 2001). Report by the bank team representing the workers.

20. INE, 2002.

21. Instituto Nacional de la Familia y la Mujer, Ministerio Educación y Cultura (INFM), *Mujer y estadísticas. Series históricas e indicadores sobre la situación de la mujer uruguaya durante el S* (Montevideo: INFM, 1999).

22. INE, 2002.

23. Economic Commission for Latin America and the Caribbean (ECLAC), *Special Tabulations of Household Surveys of the Respective Countries*, 1998, www.un.org.htm.

24. Susana Rostagnol, "Encrucilhadas estado—Sociedade civil em saúde reprodutiva no Uruguai," in *Saúde reprodutiva na esfera pública e política Núcleo de estudos de populaçao*, ed. Maria Coleta Ferreira Albino de Oliveira and Marla Isabel Baltar da Rocha (Editora da UNICAMP, 2001).

25. ECLAC, 1998.

26. INE, *Cuantificación de la pobreza por el método de ingreso para Uruguay urbano* (INE/BIDI CEPAL, 1996).

27. Centro Latinoamericano Salud y Mujer (CELSAM), *Anticoncepción en América Latina. Reporte ejecutivo Uruguay*, 2001, uruguay@celsam.org.

28. *Iniciativas Médicas por Aborto Inseguro* (IMCAI), *Informe sobre mortalidad por aborto inseguro* (Montevideo: Centro Hospitalario Pereira Rossell, 2001).

29. Carmen Varela Petito, *Implicaciones de las políticas de población y salud en el embarazo adolescente en el Uruguay*, Documento de Trabajo, 38 (Montevideo: Unidad Multidisciplinaria, Facultad de Ciencias Sociales, Universidad de la República, 1997).

30. A. Lopez and Susana Rostagnol, "Salud sexual y reproductiva," in *El estado uruguayo y las mujeres: Monitoreo de políticas públicas*, ed. CNS (Montevideo: Macondo Impesos, 1999).

31. Rostagnol, 2001.

32. INE, 2002.

33. Ministry of Health Statistics, 2000.

34. Alicia Lissidini, *Mujer y cargos de representación política en el Uruguay (1950–1989)*; Graciela Sapriza, "Participación política," in *El estado uruguayo y las mujeres, Monitoreo de políticas públicas*, ed. CNS (Montevideo: Impresos Macondo, 1999).

35. CNS, www.comision.chasquenet.org, 2002.

36. CNS, www.comision.chasquenet.org, 2002; CLADEM-UY, *CEDAW Shadow Report*, 2002, www.cladem.org.

37. Rosarío Aguirre, "Las mujeres uruguayas en el mercado de trabajo urbano: Cambios y problemas," in *Uruguay hoy*, no. 1, in series Mujer y Trabajo (Montevideo: CIEDUR, 1988).

38. Teresa Valdes, ed., *Mujeres latinoamericanas en cifras. Tomo comparativo* (Santiago de Chile: FLACSO, 1995).

39. CNS, 2002, www.comision.chasquenet.org.

40. Carlos Basilio Muñoz, *Uruguay homosexual: Culturas, minorías y discriminaicón desde una sociología de la homosexualidad* (Montevideo: Trilce, 1996).

41. CLADEM, 2000.

42. Nea Filgueira, *Violencia sistémica contra las mujeres* (Montevideo: Gremcu, 1997).

43. Susana Rostagnol, "Regulamentação: Controle social ou dignidade do/no trabalho?," in *Na batalha, identidade, sexualidade e poder no universo da prostituição*, eds. Ana I. Fabregas-Martinez and Marcas R. Benedetti (Porto Alegre, Brazil: Da Casa/GAPA, 2000).

44. María Urruzola, *El huevo de la serpiente* (Montevideo, 1995).

RESOURCE GUIDE

Suggested Reading

Aguirre, Rosario. *Sociologia y género: Las relaciones entre hombres y mujeres bajo sospecha*. Montevideo: Editorial doble clic, 1998.

Aguirre, R. and K. Batthyány. *Trabajo, género y ciudadania en los paises del Cono Sur*. Montevideo: AUGM/Cinterfor, 2001.

Araujo, A., L. Behares, and G. Sapriza. *Género y Sexualidad en el Uruguay*. Montevideo: Trilce/FHCE/CEIU, 2001.

Colectivo Cotidiano. *Medio y medio: Los medios del futuro, el futuro de los medios*. Cotidiano, Uruguay, 1993.

Espino, Alma. "Women and Mercosur: The Gendered Dimension of Economic Integration." In *Women's Empowerment and Economic Justice: Reflecting on Experience in Latin American and the Caribbean*, edited by Liliana De Pauli, 16–26. New York: United Nations Development Fund for Women, 2000.

Grupo de Estudios sobre la Condición de la Mujer Uruguaya (GRECMU). *Mujeres e historia en el Uruguay*. Montevideo: Trilce, 1991.

Laurnaga, Maria Elena. *Uruguay adolescente: Prostitución de adolescentes y niños, Aproximación a un diagnóstico*. Montevideo: Trilce/INFM/UNIFEM, 1995.

Rodriguez Villamil, Silvia and Graciela Sapriza. *Mujer, estado y politica en el Uruguay del siglo XX*. Montevideo: Banda Oriental, 1984.

Rostagnol, Susana. "Women facing the information and communication revolution: The case of Uruguay." In *APWIN, gender equality/equity through ICT/Internet*, 102–16. Seoul, South Korea: Sookmyung Women's University Press, 2001.

Rostagnol, Susana, et al. *Las artesanas hablan: La memoria colectiva de Manos del Uruguay*. Montevideo: CIEDUR/Manos del Uruguay, Altamirano, 1988.

Sapriza, Graciela. *Memorias de rebeldía: Siete historias de vida*. Montevideo: Punto Sur/GRECMU, 1988.

Sapriza, Graciela, ed. *Mujer y Poder en los márgenes de la democracia Uruguaya*. Montevideo: GRECMU, 1991.

Video/Film

La Caja de Pandora. 1991. 43 minutes. Directed by Maida Moubayed. Produced by Imagenes associated with PLEMUU (Plenario de Mujeres Uruguayas).

Web Sites

CLADEM (Latin American and Caribbean Committee for the Defense of Women's Rights), www.cladem.org.

Cotidiano Mujer, www.chasque.apc.org/cotidian/.

Guia del Mundo/World Guide, www.eurosur.org/guiadelmundo/paises/uruguay/.

Library of Congress/Federal Research Division/Country Studies, http://memory.loc.gov/frd/cs/uytoc.html.

Political Database of the Americas, http://cfdev.georgetown.edu/pdba/Countries/countries.cfm?ID=33.

Social Watch, www.socialwatch.org.
Information on the follow-up of United Nations conferences in Beijing and Copenhagen in Uruguay.

University of Texas-Latin American Network Information Center, http://lanic.utexas.edu/la/uruguay/.

Organizations

Comisión Nacional de Seguimiento de los Acuerdos de Beijing (Post-Beijing National Commission)
Email: comision@chasque.apc.org
Web Site: www.chasque.apc.org/comision

This activist network includes over eighty Uruguayan women's organizations. It was created to follow up on the implementation of U.N. agreements signed at the 1995 post-United Nations Decade for the Advancement of Women Conference in Beijing, China.

Comité de América Latina y el Caribe para la Defensa de los Derechos de la Mujer, (CLADEM-Uruguay; Latin American and Caribbean Committee in Defense of Women's Rights)
Email: clademuy@adinet.com.uy
Web site: www.cladem.org

This activist and research group, focused on women's rights, is a member of the regional organization, CLADEM.

Grupo Multidisciplinario de Estudios de Género (GMEG; Gender Studies Multi-Disciplinary Group)
Facultad de Humanidades y Ciencias de la Educación
Magallanes 1577
Montevideo 11200 Uruguay
Phone: 598 2 409 2553
Fax: 598 2 408 4304
Email: gmeg@fhuce.edu.uy

This is an academic group dedicated to the study of gender issues in various fields.

Red de Educacion Popular Entre Mujeres de America Latina y el Caribe (REPEM; Popular Education Network for Women)
Colonia 2069
11200 Montevideo
Uruguay
Phone: (598) 2-403-0599 or (598) 2-400-6894
Fax: (598) 2-403-0599 or (598) 2-409-2343
Email: repem@chasque.apc.org

REPEM is a network of 160 NGOs active in the field of education for women with low incomes and little education. Its objective is to develop a series of activities, programs, and projects aimed at achieving equal opportunities for men and women through gender-oriented education and policy. REPEM publishes several email-distributed electronic magazines in Spanish as well as in English with diverse international information on and for women. The headquarters of REPEM is in Uruguay, but there are national groups operating in Mexico, other countries in Central America, the Caribbean, Andean countries, Brazil, and the southern countries. Languages: Spanish, Portuguese, English.

SELECTED BIBLIOGRAPHY

Arriagada, Irma. 2001. "New Families for a New Century?" *Social Watch*, 2001, www.socialwatch.org.

Banco de Previsión Social (BPS). *Informal Work and Social Security*. Report by the bank team representing the workers. Montevideo: BPS, 2001.

Cortinas, Fernanda. "Uruguay, Would the Last One to Leave Please Turn Off the Lights?" *Social Watch*, 2001, www.socialwatch.org.

Economic Commission for Latin America and the Caribbean (ECLAC). *Special Tabulations of Household Surveys of the Respective Countries*, 1998, www.un.org.htm.

Filgueira, Nea. "Uruguay, a Very Vulnerable 'Development.'" *Social Watch*, 1999, www.socialwatch.org.

Latin American and Caribbean Committee for the Defense of Women's Rights (CLADEM-UY). *CEDAW Shadow Report*. www.cladem.org.

Spanish Bibliography

Aguirre, Rosario. "Las mujeres uruguayas en el mercado de trabajo urbano: Cambios y problemas." *Uruguay Hoy*, no. 1, in series Mujer y Trabajo. Montevideo: CIEDUR, 1988

Aguirre, Rosario and Susana Rostagnol. "Las mujeres organizadas." *Relaciones*, no. 30 (1986): 5–7.

Amarante, V., and A. Espino. "La segregación laboral por sexo en el mercado de trabajo: Uruguay (1986–1999)." *Documentos de trabajo* (March 1, 2001). www.iecon.ccee.edu.uy/instec/doctrab.htm.

Azar, Paola and Alma Espino. *El comercio internacional: ¿Una oportunidad para la equidad social y de género? Los procesos de integración y las políticas comerciales más importantes para América Latina y el Caribe revisados y analizados incorporando criterios de género*. Montevideo, 2001.

Centro Latinoamericano Salud y Mujer (CELSAM). *Anticoncepción en América Latina*. Reporte Ejecutivo Uruguay. 2001. uruguay@celsam.org.

Comisión Nacional de Seguimiento de los Acuerdos de Beijing (CNS). *CEDAW Shadow Report*. Montevideo: CNS, 2002.

———. 2002. Web site, www.comision.chasquenet.org.

Documento de trabajo no. 7. Montevideo: Facultad de Ciencias Sociales, Universidad de la República.

Dornel, Susana. "Educación." In *El estado uruguayo y las mujeres: Monitoreo de políticas públicas*, edited by CNS. Montevideo: Macondo Impresos, 1999.

Dufau, Graciela, and Elena Fonseca. *Cosa juzgada: Otra forma de ver la violencia de género*. Montevideo: OEA/CIM, Cotidiano Mujer, and CLADEM/MYSU, 2002.

Espino, Alma. "El MERCOSUR y el impacto del comercio en la situación de las mujeres en el mercado laboral. Una propuesta de indicadores." In *Trabajo, género y ciudadanía en los países del Cono Sur*, 75–85. Montevideo: Cinterfor, 2001.

Filgueira, Nea. *Violencia sistémica contra las mujeres*. Montevideo: Grecmu, 1997.

Iniciativas Médicas por Aborto Inseguro (IMCAI). *Informe sobre mortalidad por aborto inseguro*. Montevideo: Centro Hospitalario Pereira Rossell, 2001.

Instituto Nacional de Estadísticas (INE). *Cuantificación de la pobreza por el método de ingreso para Uruguay urbano/Programme for the Improvement of the Systems of Socioeconomic Information in Uruguay.* Montevideo: INE/BID/CEPAL, 1996.

———. *Uruguay en cifras.* Montevideo: Instituto Nacional de Estadísticas 2002. www.ine.gub.uy/biblioteca/uruguayencifras/uruguay%20en%20cifras.htm.

Instituto Nacional de la Familia y la Mujer, Ministerio Educación y Cultura (INFM). *Mujer y estadísticas. Series históricas e indicadores sobre la situación de la mujer uruguaya durante el S.* Montevideo: 1999.

Latin American and Caribbean Committee for the Defense of Women's Rights (CLADEM/MYSU). *Derechos sexuales y reproductivos en Uruguay* (1995–2000). Montevideo: CLADEM, 2000. Photocopy.

Lissidini, Alicia. "Mujer y cargos de representación política en el Uruguay (1950–1989)." *Revista de ciencias sociales* no. 7 (1992): 53–70.

Lopez, A., and Susana Rostagnol. "Salud sexual y reproductiva." In *El estado uruguayo y las mujeres. Monitoreo de políticas públicas.* Montevideo: Macondo impresos. CNS, 1999.

Melgar, Alicia. "Pobreza y distribución del ingreso: La evolución reciente." In *Salario, pobreza y desarrollo humano en Uruguay.* Montevideo: CLAEH-PNUD (UNDP), 1995.

Muñoz, Carlos Basilio. *Uruguay homosexual: Culturas, minorías y discriminaicón desde una sociología de la homosexualidad.* Montevideo: Trilce, 1996.

Piotti de Fortuna, Diosma. "Mujer joven y educación en el Uruguay." In *La situación laboral de las mujeres jóvenes en el Uruguay.* Conference proceedings from the seminar *Mujer joven en América Latina.* Montevideo: 1988.

PIT-CNT/Cuesta Duarte, *Las dimensiones del MERCOSUR y las trabajadoras.* www.chasque.net/icudu/tyu/A1n3/mujer.html.

Rodrigo, Zulema María Zulema. *Las mujeres uruguayas en el sistema educativo.* Working paper no. 7, Universidad de la República, Facultad de ciencias sociales, Montevideo, 1993.

Rostagnol, Susana. "Encrucilhadas estado—Sociedade civil em saúde reprodutiva no Uruguai." In *Saúde reprodutiva na esfera pública e política. Núcleo de Estudos de Populaçao*, edited by Maria Coleta Ferrcira Albino de Oliveira and Isabel Baltar da Rocha. Campinas, Brazil: Editora da UNICAMP, 2001.

———. "Regulamentaçao: Controle social ou dignidade do/no trabalho?" In *Na batalha, identidade, sexualidade e poder no universo da prostituiçao*, edited by Ana I. Fabregas-Martínez and Marcos R. Benedetti. Porto Alegre, Brazil: Da Casa/GAPA, 2000.

Sapriza, Graciela. "Participación política." In *El Estado uruguayo y las mujeres. Monitoreo de políticas públicas*, edited by CNS. Montevideo: Macondo Impresos, 1999.

Universidad de la República (UDELAR). *Censo universitario.* Montevideo: UDELAR, www.rau.edu.uy/universidad/censo2000. 2002.

Urruzola, María. *El huevo de la serpiente.* Montevideo: Caballo Perdido, 1995.

Valdés, Teresa, et al., eds. *Mujeres latinoamericanas en cifras: tomo comparativo.* Santiago de Chile: Facultad Latinoamericana de Ciencias Sociales (FLACSO-Chile), 1995.

Varela Petito, Carmen. *Implicaciones de las políticas de población y salud en el embarazo adolescente en el Uruguay.* Montevideo: Unidad Multidisciplinaria, Facultad de Ciencias Sociales, Universidad de la República, 1997.

20

VENEZUELA

Elisabeth Jay Friedman

PROFILE OF VENEZUELA

Venezuela, formally known as the Bolivarian Republic of Venezuela, is located in the north of South America, bordered on the west by Colombia, on the south by Brazil, and on the east by Guyana, with which it has an ongoing border dispute. Its northern boundary is a 1,748-mile coastline on the Caribbean Sea, and it claims several nearby islands, including the large island of Margarita. The Cordillera de la Costa mountain range runs just south of the coast, and the Andes Mountain range originates in the northwest of the country. About a third of Venezuela's territory is made up of plains (*llanos*); and half is south of the Orinoco River, divided among the Amazon tropical forest, the highlands of the Gran Sabana and its table mountains (the *tepuis*), and the Orinoco Delta swamp area.

Politically, Venezuela was once considered the "model" for democratic nations in Latin America due to the stable political institutions and strong parties that arose with the transition to democracy in 1958. But by the end of the century, political upheavals, including two coup attempts in the 1990s; the splintering of the party system in the face of the nationalist movement led by a former coup plotter, Colonel Hugo Chávez Frías, now president of Venezuela; and the redrafting of its constitution in 1999, which expanded rights while centralizing authority and included an official name change to celebrate the national and regional hero, Simón Bolívar, altered the model considerably.

It is clear that not all Venezuelans supported Chávez's attempt to restructure the country. Anti-government demonstrations increased in frequency, and in April 2002, following a massive protest headed by the most prominent labor and business organizations that ended in the deaths of fourteen people, Chávez was removed from office. Although he returned to the presidency a few days later and continues to hold power, the political future of Venezuela is highly uncertain. Political polarization, undergirded by extreme class divisions, is the order of the day. Nevertheless, it remains a presidential democracy with a unicameral National Assembly and a federal system made up of 23 states.

Economically, Venezuela faces the regionwide pressures of transition from state-led to market-driven capitalism. Although its status as an oil-exporting country has brought it considerable wealth, its heavy dependence on oil has subjected it to the natural resource's boom–bust cycles, resulting in economic turmoil since the 1980s. A vast majority of the population currently live in poverty, and unemployment is a growing problem.

Venezuela has roughly 23.5 million people, over 80 percent of whom live in urban areas.[1] Although the national census does not ask about ethnic or racial origin, it is estimated that 70–80 percent of the population has a mixed background of European, Indian, and African ancestry; 15–20 percent is of European descent, around 10 percent is of African descent, and under 3 percent are of indigenous origin.[2] While over 90 percent of the population are Roman Catholic, up to 33 percent are at least "passively linked" to the Maria Leonza syncretic religion.[3] The male–female sex ratio is 1.02:1. Life expectancy is 76.5 years for women and 70.3 years for men. The total fertility rate (average number of children per woman) is 2.5, and the infant mortality rate is 25 deaths per 1,000 live births.[4] The maternal mortality rate is 60 per 100,000 live births.[5]

OVERVIEW OF WOMEN'S ISSUES

In many ways, the democratic regime that began in 1958 has been good for women. Since the 1960s, women's status in Venezuela has improved, at times dramatically: they have exerted increasing control over their fertility, entered the workforce in significant numbers, achieved more than parity in higher education, and raised their profile in the professions and political life. However, this picture is not as bright as it may seem. Most troubling, the massive expansion of poverty and the shrinking of state welfare provisions in the face of economic reform and crisis has meant that the majority of Venezuelan women, as well as men, work in badly paid, often informal or temporary jobs; have trouble making ends meet for their families; receive substandard health care; and are unable to take advantage of what educational opportunity is extended to them. Moreover, sex discrimination in education and the workplace has limited women's opportunity across economic classes. Finally, a history of gender-biased political institutions and political practices has limited their participation in public life and weakened their movement potential.

However, women have developed strategies to respond to the problems they face, from innovative women's organizations to participation in larger movements for change. It is too early to evaluate the full impact of the latest changes in government, but it is clear that women are an important part of Chávez's restructuring, holding key posts and given a certain amount of leeway in legal reform.

EDUCATION

In the early colonial era, education provided by the Roman Catholic Church served a minority of wealthy landowners. The system was designed to promote academic study among the elite, and curricula were not geared toward the basic educational and vocational needs of the majority. Free public education began in the late 1800s. However, the dictatorships of the first half of the twentieth century interrupted its growth. With the transition to democracy in 1958, the education system improved considerably. Primary education was made compulsory, and new universities and agricultural extension programs put into place. The system as a whole grew rapidly with the state expansion of the 1970s and early 1980s.

Opportunities and Literacy

Preschool and nine years of basic education are now required by law, if not always implemented in practice. For those continuing their education, academic, technical, or vocational study is offered in high school, which can be followed by junior college, university, or a technical institute. Night school is also available for adult continuing education.

Over 80 percent of educational services are provided by the state.[6] However, since nearly a third of public education monies are dedicated to higher education, primary and secondary education is chronically underfunded.[7] It is also below average in quality for the region. Teachers and professors alike are considered the among the most badly remunerated sectors of the formal labor market, and school buildings are in poor repair across the country. The state of public education has garnered a lot of attention from the current administration, which has begun rebuilding and restructuring schools and universities. Increased government control over private schools, as well as programs including premilitary instruction to instill "patriotic values and a sense of national identity in students," are some of the more controversial reforms on the table.[8]

Most women in Venezuela have access to some education, and women tend to stay in school longer than men. Only 8.2 percent of women over 15 are illiterate,[9] and they tend to be older, rural women.[10] Although boys have higher enrollment rates in first through fifth grades, in sixth through ninth girls pull ahead. A similar phenomenon has happened in higher education. Although only 31 percent of all university students in 1960, by 1990 women made up 57.4 percent.[11] This gender-based difference may be connected to the poor economic situation, in which families decide that boys and men are more valuable in the labor force than the classroom.[12] Women's headway notwithstanding, as a whole, school enrollments fall off after fifth grade, by which time 34 percent of children have withdrawn from school; dropout figures are considerably higher in public schools.[13] Moreover, only 5 percent of the population reaches the university level.[14]

Historically, women's entry into higher education has been oriented toward the "helping professions," such as nursing and teaching. Educational paths are still divided along gender lines; currently women are overrepresented in majors in the humanities, social sciences, health, and education, while men form the majority in the hard sciences, engineering, architecture, and technology.[15] Although women make up nearly 80 percent of primary school teachers, their numbers decline as the educational level increases: they make up half of secondary teachers, and 40 percent of university professors.[16]

EMPLOYMENT AND ECONOMICS

The Venezuelan economy is characterized by its extreme dependence on oil. In 2000, petroleum accounted for 86 percent of export revenues, while agricultural profits made up a scant 5 percent of the GDP. Employment is concentrated in the service sector, with industry the closest runner-up and agriculture trailing behind. Despite the often abundant profits from the oil industry, which enabled the massive expansion of the state in the 1970s, welfare benefits, and public support for industry, dependence on a natural resource with a boom-and-bust cycle has had its dark side. Venezuela has suffered from chronic economic mismanagement, including massive opportunities for cor-

Women buy groceries in a Caracas, Venezuela, supermarket on Wednesday, January 22, 2003, during the second month of a nationwide work stoppage by the opposition against the government. AP/Wide World Photos.

ruption, and despite its wealth has shared in the debt crisis of the region as a whole. Since the 1980s sporadic neoliberal economic reform has not halted the economic downturn for Venezuela's population. Although in 2000 the overall GDP was U.S.$120 billion, the GDP per capita has declined 15 percent since 1980. While inflation improved from a peak of 115 percent in 1996 to around 27 percent in 2000, unemployment 250 percent since the 1980s. Government expenditures on social services such as education have declined during the same period. Although poverty numbers are contested, it is clear that well over 50 percent of the population fall below the national poverty line, possibly up to 86 percent.[17]

Job Opportunities

Women have moved steadily into the formal labor force; in 1970 they made up 22.4 percent of the economically active population, and 35.6 percent by 2002.[18] To give another indication of the expansion of the female labor force, during the same period the number of economically active women increased by over 200 percent, while the number of men increased by just over 100 percent. Although the growth has been strongest among young women, they are also staying in the labor force during their child-rearing years. This expansion can be explained in part by the overall economic expansion of Venezuela, particularly in the 1970s and early 1980s, in tandem with women's increasing educational levels, but it is also due to women's need to remain active during periods of economic uncertainty and crisis.

In the 1990s, women made up 22.9 percent of administrators and managers and 57.1 percent of professional and technical workers.[19] Thirty-seven percent of all women with college or professional degrees are employed in the public sector, making up 40 percent of the relatively large number of state workers and about 16 percent of all workers in Venezuela.[20] Although they have advanced in professions such as medicine and law, there are few women in the higher ranks of unions and industry. The vast majority (84 percent) of women work in services, 14 percent are industrial workers, and 2 percent are employed in agriculture.[21]

Like their situation in higher education, as women's participation in the formal labor force has increased, they have been employed primarily in "feminized" occupations, such as lower-level office work, sales, teaching, nursing, and domestic work. In industry they make up a majority of textile workers and a third of food workers, but are almost absent from mechanical and electrical trades.[22] One study reveals that the variable with the largest difference among formally employed men and women is their position within the employment hierarchy, where women are significantly underrepresented among management positions.[23]

The informal labor market is expanding rapidly in Venezuela; it is estimated to be 42.4 percent of all workers, and almost 40 percent of women's employment is in this sector.[24] Concentrated among women from lower income brackets, informal work is quite varied, ranging from street peddling to casual labor to personal services. According to the Ministry of Health, 350,000 women work as prostitutes. In a recent ruling denying legal recognition to a sex workers' union, UNTRASEX, sex work has been officially declared a "social fact" (*hecho social*, part of the general social context) rather than "work."[25]

Unemployment has been estimated at between 14 percent and 20 percent across the country, and even higher for younger workers.[26] In the last years of the twentieth century, women's unemployment rate was higher than men's, with average 1997 figures 14.8 and 10.6 percent, respectively.[27] These figures affect women across classes; professional women employed by the state sector lose their jobs with state retrenchment, and unskilled workers are forced into casual employment.

Pay

Women who have training similar to men's and perform the same activities make an estimated 20 to 25 percent less salary. Women in the informal sector make an estimated 70 percent less than men.[28]

In June 2001, in response to unemployment among women, the government-funded Women's Bank was established, with longtime women's rights advocate and economist Nora Castañeda as its head. It provides micro credit loans ($420 to $7,000), often to small groups of low-income women who are unable to meet the requirements for regular bank loans.

Working Conditions

Sexual Harassment

On-the-job harassment is a common problem that can cause women to leave their jobs.[29] However, in a legal reform without precedent within the country, sexual harassment is now considered a crime subject to substantial legal action, as stipulated in the 1999 Law Against Violence Towards Women and the Family.

The law defines sexual harassment as soliciting sexual responses or favors (including for a third party); making any type of unwanted sexual insinuation; or taking advantage of a position of power in the workplace with the threat of damage to the legitimate expectations of a workplace relationship. If found guilty, the perpetrator of the crime of sexual harassment must serve a jail term of 3 to 12 months, and must pay the victim twice the amount of any economic damage caused by the crime with respect to access to positions or promotion. Moreover, the law establishes a fine for employers—national or multinational—who, although aware of the situation, fail to prevent sexual harassment by employees. Sexual harassment may be reported by victims, their blood relatives, representatives of the Justice Department, the Ombudsperson for Women's Rights, or nongovernmental organizations.

Support for Mothers/Caretakers

Maternity Leave

Pre- and postnatal leave, as well as job protection for new mothers, are specified by the Organic Labor Law. Pregnant women are exempted from work that might endanger their pregnancies, are granted 18 weeks of maternity leave, and are protected from job termination during pregnancy and the first year following birth or adoption. Working mothers are granted nursing breaks at onsite nurseries or at home.

Daycare

Employers of more than twenty workers must supply child care for all employees (male and female) with children under age six.[30] According to the Ministry of Labor and the major union confederation, leave is honored in the formal sector, though the Social Security payments that cover leave salary are often delayed. The large numbers of women in the informal sector have to resort to more makeshift arrangements that can put their children at significant risk.[31]

FAMILY AND SEXUALITY

Gender Roles

One decided theme in the development of gender relations in Venezuela is women's predominant responsibility for home and children. As in other predominantly Catholic countries, this association is strengthened by the cultural expectations based on the traditional family structure sanctioned by the church, with the mother as the central figure of the home and the father as primary income earner. The last collected statistics (1983) showed 70 percent of women's time spent in "non-market" activities, as compared to 13 percent of men's.[32] Despite women's focus on homemaking, the large number of female heads of household makes clear that men are not always willing to fulfill their traditional roles as breadwinners. About 60 percent of poor families, and a quarter of all families, are headed by women.[33] Some see this matricentric family organization as another part of the historical legacy of Spanish colonization, along with the gender mores of Catholicism: in this case, the outcome of the "conquest" of indigenous women by Spanish men, who later reject them (or keep them on the side) in favor of more "suitable" Spanish or Creole wives.[34]

Direct challenges to traditional gender relations have on the whole been rejected by society; feminists have long been assumed to be prostitutes or lesbians, indicating their transgression of cultural norms,[35] and reports of hate crimes against gay and transgender communities continue to surface.[36] Indirect or somehow mediated challenges have been more successful. For example, the 1988 United Women Leaders movement sought to promote women's political leadership as part of the process of democratization, rather than women's advancement per se. The particular role that beauty queens have played in the political development of Venezuela attests to the power of blending the nation's obsession with women's looks with women's symbolic—or at times actual—leadership.

"Beatriz I" was crowned as part of the 1928 week of student protests against authoritarianism, which were disguised as Carnival celebrations. Students behind these protests went on to form one of the most significant cohorts of Venezuelan politicians during the first decades of democratization. In 1944, the election of the Queen of the Seventh World Series of Amateur Baseball was turned into a primer for universal suffrage, in which more than 20,000 people cast ballots. The election's symbolic promotion of the power of the people was confirmed by the overwhelming victory of a poor schoolteacher, who had taken on no less than the daughter of the secretary to the president. The most famous contemporary example is Irene Saez, the Miss Universe-turned-politician who successfully governed a wealthy subdivision of Caracas before going on to become a presidential candidate in 1998. Venezuelans continue to elect beauty queens with noticeable frequency: at sports events, to celebrate holidays, in companies, and of course, during Carnival. Reportedly even women's prisons crown their most beautiful convicts.[37]

Marriage

Marriage rates reflect the uneven fulfillment of traditional gender relations. Although the vast majority Venezuelans identify as Catholic, only about a third of the population over 15 is married.[38] The number of marriages has declined from a high of 113,125 in 1988 to 81,951 in 1996, close to the numbers of the mid-1970s. After divorce laws were eased with the reform of the Civil Code in 1982, divorces shot up from 4,377 in 1975 to a high of 24,774 in 1988; they then subsided to 17,627 in 1996. Thus from 1988 to 1996 about 21 percent of all marriages ended in divorce.[39] Venezuela has had a historically high rate of out-of-wedlock births; they reached 53 percent of all births in the mid-1970s, before such statistics were discontinued following a legal reform outlawing discrimination against children whose parents are not married.[40]

Reproduction

Although there is no national policy of birth control, the average fertility rate declined from 6.7 to 2.5 children per woman between the 1960s and 1990s. A former minister of the family attributes this drop to the process of urbanization and women's entry into education and paid work, which result in their conceiving later in life. She also points to the delaying effect that the rising cost of living has on starting a family.[41] However, among women who live in rural areas, are low-income, and have little schooling, fertility rates can be as high as six or seven children per woman.[42] Twenty percent of all births are to mothers under 20.[43]

Sex Education

The government's efforts to promote family planning are so weak as to have been ranked as the lowest of 89 developing countries; moreover, its ranking has dropped steadily since 1989. It has not implemented a national program of sex education, and relies heavily on the private sector to provide services. Thus, for almost two decades organizations such as AVESA and PLAFAM, another family planning group, have been developing research and pilot programs. AVESA created a program for teen peer education in the mid-1990s that does hands-on work in high schools and develops multimedia educational materials; in 2001, PLAFAM opened a youth center in eastern Venezuela to do outreach with young people in the interior.

Contraception and Abortion

Forty-nine percent of married women between 15 and 49 use contraception.[44] In the 1980s, the most popular methods were the contraceptive pill, intrauterine devices (IUDs), and sterilization.[45] However, birth control access and use are not consistent across economic classes or generations. According to the national sex education group AVESA, though 60 percent of the Venezuelan population becomes sexually active before age 20, only 20 percent of all young people use any kind of contraception.[46] Although contraceptives are supposed to be distributed through the public health service, they are rarely given a budget line.[47] Some hospitals demand the male partner's consent for women's sterilization, regardless of the relationship between the partners.[48]

Abortion is illegal under most circumstances. The Penal Code outlaws abortion unless the life of the mother is at stake, or if a male head of household approves the procedure in cases where the pregnancy is due to the rape of a female family member. The illegality of abortion is related to a significant percentage of illness and even death among women. In 1980, 40,000 female hospitalizations were abortion-related. Abortion complications are responsible for 18 percent of all maternal deaths, and for 56 percent of deaths of pregnant women in their most fertile years.[49]

HEALTH

With the state expansion of the 1970s, public sanitary and medical facilities expanded considerably across Venezuela, although always with a concentration of services around the capital, Caracas. However, economic crisis and population growth resulted in the decline of clean water and sewer systems, as well as in the number of hospital beds, in the 1980s.

Health Care Access

In the 1990s, the government began a strategy of promoting primary health care with the participation of local communities.[50] Although the new administration has improved funding for heath care, service provision remains inadequate throughout the country; it in no way reaches the free universal coverage promised in the new constitution.

Diseases and Disorders

Women's reproductive systems, and a lack of reproductive rights, account for much of their morbidity.

AIDS

An estimated 2000 people died of AIDS in 1999, leaving 921 orphans. The overall adult rate of HIV infection is about 0.5 percent of the population, including 9,200 women. In 1999, the estimated rate among young women (15–24) ranged between 0.12 percent and 0.17 percent. In 1992 HIV was reported in 6 percent of sex workers in Caracas, and in 1994 was found in 4 percent of street sex workers on Margarita Island, a popular tourist destination.[51]

Body Image

Since the 1950s, Venezuelan women have won more titles in international beauty contests than any other country's contestants, including Miss World five times and Miss Universe four times. The emphasis on beauty—a certain kind of beauty, modeled on a Western ideal—is said to be the product of racism against the mixed-race descendants of black slaves, combined with the pressure from commercial images for women to conform to the slim-figured, large-breasted, light-skinned embodiment of this ideal.

The importance of beauty can be measured in dollar amounts; in 1999, Venezuelans spent a fifth of their personal income buying beauty and grooming products. More invasive procedures are also the norm. Plastic surgery is a booming business, with breast augmentation, liposuction, and stomach stapling topping the list of requests. Teenagers have been sent for stomach stapling to prevent their addiction to diuretics and laxatives, which many rely on to cope with the peer pressure for thinner bodies. And it is well known that Venezuelan beauty contest entrants routinely have plastic surgery to improve their chances of capturing world titles.[52]

Cancer

The leading causes of death in women are heart disease and cancer; the leading causes of cancer deaths are cancer of the breast, cervix, and stomach.[53] According to the regional office of the World Health Organization, in 1995 stomach cancer was on the decline, while lung cancer and breast cancer were rising. After decreasing until 1985, cervical cancer also began to rise again through 1995.[54]

POLITICS AND LAW

In Venezuela, the first half of the twentieth century was marked by long periods of dictatorship and liberalized authoritarian rule, accompanied by often clandestine party-building. The largest party, Democracy Action, took power with the help of the military in 1945 and began the first period of contemporary democratization, during a three-year period known as the *trienio*. This attempt was ended by a military coup that ushered in the dictatorship of Marcos Pérez Jiménez. By the end of the 1950s, however, clandestine parties and organized civil society joined with disgruntled elements in the military to force Pérez Jiménez's ouster.

Venezuelan democracy finally began in 1958 with the institution of the so-called *Punto Fijo* democracy, named after the place where the pacts for the transition to democracy was hammered out by three parties. These pacts were a series of economic and political accords that mollified the sectors most threatened by the new regime—military, church, and business—and rewarded potential (or actual) party supporters—labor, peasants, and the middle class. The distribution of power among non-Communist parties, and their political dominance, was also ensured as they agreed to coalition governing.

Whereas the policies resulting from the political pact and party-based organizing resulted in a stable foundation for the democratic regime, the degree of democracy was questionable. The sectors included in the negotiations had access to the channels of power but inhibited the mobilization of constituencies that had not participated in the pact written at Punto Fijo. This permanent exclusion of these other sectors would come back to haunt Venezuela thirty years later.

Venezuelan democracy held firm until the late 1980s, with regular elections, alternation of the party in power, and the protection of civil rights. Moreover, with the highest wages in Latin America, welfare benefits, significant subsidies for food and transportation, and public credits for private business, the majority of the population was satisfied with their situation.

By 1989 Venezuelan prosperity had succumbed to the severe indebtedness of the region and the consequences of chronic economic mismanagement. A neoliberal reform package attempted in 1989 was met with opposition, particularly from the lower income sectors. Repression of rioting over the withdrawal of transportation subsidies resulted in at least 300 deaths. Discontent with traditional politicians, also triggered by corruption scandals, led to two coup attempts in 1992, the first led by Hugo Chávez, followed by the impeachment of the president in 1993.

The rise of Hugo Chávez's Fifth Republic Movement (MVR) was mirrored by the crumbling of the traditional parties over the course of the 1990s. With well over half of the country living in poverty, class cleavages ultimately destroyed political consensus that had been forged at Punto Fijo. By April 2002, organized civil society was mainly in opposition to the government, and an attempt was made to remove Chávez from power.

Suffrage

After serious internal debate over the importance of fighting for civil versus political rights, middle-class women's rights organizations began a suffrage movement in 1941. Literate women won the right to vote in municipal elections in 1945, during a period of liberalized authoritarian rule. The movement continued its demands for full suffrage into the *trienio* period. In 1946 the Democratic Action party granted national universal suffrage of all citizens over 18, regardless of age or literacy. This right was confirmed in the Constitution of 1947.

Political Participation

Until the transformation effected by Chávez, the Democratic Action and COPEI parties formed the dominant channel of political participation in Venezuela, and were heavily involved in structuring civil society-based interest organizing as well. Women fared particularly badly under this system of "partyarchy" at both the leadership and the membership levels. Participation in the leadership ranks was based on requirements not easily fulfilled by women. The various requirements centered on the central obligation of full-time work for the party. Most women either had or were assumed to have responsibilities in the private sphere that kept their numbers perpetually low in leadership ranks.[55] As part of the 1992 Equal Opportunity Law, parties were mandated to have at least 30 percent of their electoral lists made up of women candidates; this has been thwarted to some extent with the introduction of more single-candidate races, where lists cannot be used.

Women were always active as party members, but the traditional mechanism for their inclusion resulted in little attention being paid to their interests. The women's branches of political parties did not function for women the way they did for more male-identified sectors, such as labor and the peasantry. Whereas those originally male sectors were organized in such a way as to successfully represent their interests and even include some of their leadership in high party positions, women were mainly mobilized to take on the domestic duties, generally organizational or functional, of the parties. At the founding of the parties in the 1930s, this type of inclusion was justified by the fact that the majority of women focused on domestic duties in their daily lives. Extending those responsibilities into the public sphere was a way to give women a role. But this role did not change as rapidly as women's roles changed outside of the party, leading to frustration for many members.[56] During the 1970s the Socialist party Movement Towards Socialism was somewhat more responsive to its linked women's organization, Socialist Women. But as a whole, women have had trouble convincing parties to support them or their issues. Particularly women on the far Left and from poorer sectors are an important part of Chávez's mass following and his Fifth Republic Movement party, and he has appointed a few to key leadership positions.

The first female elected representatives at the national level were the 12 women elected to the Constitutional Assembly of October 1946.[57] Those numbers would not be repeated for nearly 40 years, when 12 women were elected to the lower house of Congress in 1983. Women did not break the 10 percent barrier in that house until 1998, with 26 representatives, the year when the lower house also had its first female speaker, a long-time party operative of the Democratic Action party. However, even with the change in government, women's representation is still low: they currently hold 16 of the 165 seats (9.7 percent) of the National Assembly.[58] With the constitutional reform replacing the bicameral Congress with a National Assembly, the former Bicameral Commission for Women's Rights, established in 1989, has been subsumed into the Commission on the Family, Women, and Youth. This organizational reshuffling appears to have subordinated women's interests and linked them to their traditional role in the family and as mothers/caretakers. But the head of the Commission, Marelis Pérez Marcano, is a confirmed socialist feminist and one of the motors behind the gender-friendly reform of the constitution.

Women have been substantially underrepresented in governmental ministerial posts. The first female cabinet member was minister of development in 1968, and in 1998 women made up only 3.2 percent of the cabinet.[59] While there have been some standout appointees such as a minister of the economy in the 1990s, female ministers tend to occupy the "social" portfolios such as education and health. At first Chávez seemed no different from his predecessors, appointing no women to his cabinet. In a reshuffling in 2000, however, he offered what was termed a "gift" to women's rights advocates. He not only selected economist and longtime leftist militant and women's rights advocate Adina Bastidas as his vice president (currently an appointed post), but also named four leading women's activists to nontraditional cabinet positions: solicitor-general and ministers of the environment, production and commerce, and labor.[60]

Another positive development under Chávez has been the government's decision to grant permanent legal status to the national women's agency, the institution responsible for coordinating and promoting gender equality policy at the national level. This agency, like so many others around the world, had been established, moved, or removed depending on the whims of various presidents since its first appearance in 1974. Even after it was sanctioned by the Equal Opportunity Law of 1992, Chávez's predecessor, Rafael Caldera, refused to appoint its directors. However, the National Institute for Women is now fully operational. Moreover, unlike many of the women who were appointed to head its former incarnations, the current director, María León, is an avowed women's rights advocate. There are also regional women's councils in 16 of the 23 states, and women's centers in many municipalities.

The Ombudsperson for Women's Rights was created by the Equal Opportunities Law. Nominated by the Executive Council of the National Institute for Women, he or she is responsible for monitoring laws concerned with women as well as for raising awareness about the existence and usage of such laws. The national Ombudsperson is also responsible for nominating local ombudspeople to provide free legal assistance to women and represent them in courts or before governmental agencies.

Women have been well represented in the judicial system, a branch with relatively low political standing. In 1990, they made up 53 percent of the judges and 78 percent of the public defenders.[61] A woman was appointed to head the Supreme Court in the mid-1990s, but resigned in the face of Chávez's purge of the judiciary, which he and many citizens considered politicized and corrupt. No women currently sit on the Supreme Court.

Women's Rights

In many areas of the law, Venezuela shows considerable progress in gender equality. Most of this progress is attributable to the mobilization of women's rights advocates. For example, the new constitution includes almost all of the recommendations made by women's rights supporters. It outlaws gender discrimination and enshrines gender equality, going so far as to use both masculine and feminine endings for all references to people. Throughout, it speaks of *venezolanos y venezolanas* (male and female Venezuelans) and *cuidadanos y cuidadanas* (male and female citizens). It outlaws gender discrimination, including in legal matters. It protects maternity, including conception, pregnancy, delivery and postpartum; allows women's citizenship to be transferred to foreign spouses; and recognizes housework as an economic activity. However, gay rights advocates were not successful at including a nondiscrimination clause in the constitution.[62]

Before 1982, the Civil Code, which regulates private matters between citizens, was one of the most discriminatory in the region, giving fathers and husbands substantial control over family matters, from the disposition of community property[63] to all decisions regarding children's upbringing. It was reformed in 1982 to allow spouses equal control over property and equal sanction for adultery; to give fathers and mothers equal say in all decisions regarding their children; and to abolish any legal distinction between children born inside and outside of wedlock. It also eased and quickened divorce procedures.[64]

The 1992 Equal Opportunity Law, which was devised largely as a political vehicle for its major sponsor, repeats legislation found in the 1961 Constitution, the Civil Code, the Organic Labor Law, and the Convention for the Elimination of All Forms of Discrimination Against Women, the U.N. treaty on women's rights (known as CEDAW), that Venezuela ratified in 1982. It also establishes a Women's Defense Office as part of the Attorney general's office; legalizes party-based quotas for women candidates; and institutionalizes the national women's agency.[65]

The reform of the Organic Labor Law in 1989 equalized men's and women's rights in the workplace and also ensured the rights of working mothers. From the removal of discriminatory articles to the adoption of the newly titled chapter "Of the Labor Protection of Maternity and the Family," the reform makes clear that no provisions are to be permitted that disadvantage working women. Thus discrimination on the basis of sex in employment advertising and in work conditions (e.g., mandatory pregnancy testing) are banned, and neither spouse can now demand that the other's work be terminated on the basis of family needs. At the same time, the special maternity dispensations are explicitly labeled as nondiscriminatory.[66]

The 1999 Rules and Regulations of the 1997 Comprehensive Labor Act of 1997 reiterated the principle of employment nondiscrimination on the grounds of sex, and also included nondiscrimination on the grounds of sexual preference. And in a legal reform without precedent in the country, sexual harassment is now considered a crime subject to substantial legal action, as stipulated in the 1999 Law Against Violence Toward Women and the Family. Despite gains in other areas of legislation, the national Penal Code has proven intractable to reform. The legislation on rape still does not consider it a crime against women. It also outlaws abortion except for specific circumstances.

Feminist Movements

Venezuelan women have a history of mobilization for women's rights that extends back to the mid-1930s. Its sporadic and often limited nature has led some analysts to call it "women in movement" as opposed to a "women's movement."[67] However it is defined, unified organizing around particular issues, coordinated through civil society and state structures, has worked to promote women's leadership and certain gender-based interests. But women have also struggled with the legacy of the dominant institutional culture as well as important divisions among themselves.

Prior to the domination of interest representation through parties, middle-class and some elite women in the mid-1930s and 1940s formed organizations, debated gender interests, and mobilized to demand suffrage and legal reform. Women also participated as individuals and in women's groups as part of the clandestine opposition to the Pérez Jiménez dictatorship of the 1950s, and founded the multiparty Women's Committee of the Patriotic Union (the coordinating body of the opposition).

Women then found themselves excluded from the reconstruction of Venezuelan democracy in the 1960s and 1970s, victims of gender-biased political structures and partisan rivalries. Finding their opportunities to act through political parties limited, they soon turned to other forms of organizing.

In the 1970s both middle-class feminists and low-income women formed autonomous organizations that were constructed in opposition to the hierarchical parties. Through the Popular Women's Circles low-income women built the largest nonpartisan women's group in the country, organizing at both local and national levels for self-help and representation. Although providing trenchant political and gender-based analysis, feminists' emphasis on gender equality was too threatening to gain a large following, and feminist groups remain small to this day. In more recent times, women have organized groups devoted to environmental issues, Afro-Venezuelan identity, violence against women, and health. Women's studies departments have been formed in the major universities, and feminist faculty and students provide much of the leadership for mobilization on women's rights, both inside and outside of government. In 1985, a national umbrella organization of women's groups, the Coordinating Committee of Women's NGOs (CONG), was formed. With autonomy for its member groups and frequent change in its directorate, it offers a space for sharing information and a base for national campaigns. Women's rights advocates have also been key in the establishment of political institutions for women's representation. Since 1974, elite groups have repeatedly put pressure on national administrations to keep open a "women's space" in the state, taking the form of some sort of office or ministry for women, and beginning in 1984 women sought to establish municipal women's centers across the country.[68]

In the 1980s and 1990s, activists in the nongovernmental umbrella organization CONG, staff in the national agency for women, and certain party members developed a model of "conjunctural coalition-building" that allowed them to work together on specific issues, usually legal reform, without demanding ongoing organizational or ideological coherence. The model of nonpartisan, issue-specific coalition-building can be found as far back as the campaigns for legal reform in the 1940s. But its "state/party/ civil society" networking aspect was fully developed in the very successful 1976–1982 campaign to reform the Civil Code, the 1987–1988 United Women Leaders movement to increase the number of women in elected office, and the 1985–1990 campaign to reform the Organic Labor Law.[69] Working through the Permanent Forum for Gender Equality, a high-profile network of women's rights advocates including NGO representatives, party members, union leaders, academics, legislators, and ex-ministers, women achieved similar success with the 1994–1998 campaign to pass domestic violence legislation. And the success at "gendering" the new constitution was also due to women's networking across different political arenas, albeit more focused on women on the political Left and in the academy.

A fundamental challenge to women's organizing in Venezuela has been how to demand women's rights without transgressing socially acceptable gender norms. As a solution, women's association with the family, particularly motherhood, was used to justify their demands for equal rights for over 40 years. Another strategy, developed in the 1980s, was to deny the gender-based nature of their demands and appeal to the principles of democracy. Such principles were claimed as necessary in the family, and to women's actions. More recent campaigns have challenged traditional roles. In the campaign to reform the Labor Law, for example, a distinction was drawn between the rights of women workers and working mothers by focusing on the "social function" of maternity. But the (repeated) failure to achieve any reform of the strict abortion laws, or the recognition of the rights of homosexuals, points to the difficulty of challenging gender roles head-on.

Political culture permeates all forms of organizing, and in Venezuela both the national women's agency and the CONG suffered from an increase in centralism and clientelistic behavior as they became institutionalized. The successes of the 1990s produced many "instrumental feminists"—leaders who seek self- or party promotion through resources intended to advance women as a whole. Historically, partisan rivalries have been a major impediment to women's united action, and are never wholly absent from the different forms of organizing.

Other challenges stem from the divisions among women. One of the strongest is economic. In every historical period, women's rights advocates have struggled with class differences. As a result, those issues most salient to women from the popular classes have often been excluded from consideration. For example, because predominantly upper-class women led the Labor Law reform campaign, class-based discrimination remained in the final document. Domestic workers, pieceworkers, and home-based workers were not given health care benefits or Social Security coverage. Due to this sort of outcome, cross-class organizing is rarely successful on an ongoing basis; for example, the Popular Women's Circles chose to direct their organizing efforts around the 1995 U.N. Women's Conference through a regional network of low-income women's groups. As poverty increased dramatically in the 1990s, women became unable to offer a gender-specific critique or mobilized response to economic crisis.

International mobilization and attention to women's rights has had a crucial influence on Venezuelan women's organizing. Regional networks supported the early suffrage campaign. Academics who lived abroad in the 1970s brought back ideas from "second-wave" feminism, and participated in the early regional feminist "encounters," offering to sponsor the very first one. Elites drew on the international legitimation provided by the United Nations Decade on Women (1975–1985) to justify founding the national women's agency and other actions. In particular, the 1985 U.N. meeting in Nairobi that closed the Decade was crucial for activists in Venezuela: it inspired the creation of CONG, its cooperation with the national women's agency, and the justification for reform of the Labor Law. The first network of family planning and women's health groups, Red de Poblacion (REDPOB), was formed to follow up on the 1994 U.N. Population and Development conference in Cairo. The 1995 U.N. Fourth World Conference on Women in Beijing also provided another opportunity for studying the status of women, including the collection of data on many subjects by NGOs around the country, as well as follow-up activities uniting women's rights advocates.

But the impact of international influences has not been wholly positive. For example, the influx of foreign funding for Beijing preparations, as well as the focus on an international event at a time of intertwined social, economic, and political crises within the country, alienated some supporters and failed to generate much of a national response from women. Congresswomen's requests for funding to attend the conference were greeted by a national outcry of disapproval.[70]

Lesbian Rights

Racial prejudice began to be raised systematically as an issue only in the 1990s, and lesbian and bisexual women historically have kept a very low profile organizationally. However, this may be changing: a gay pride march has been celebrated in Caracas since 2001; the first University Conference on Sexual Diversity was held in 2002; and since 2001 a web site, Amazons of Venezuela, has included lesbianism as one of its central themes.

Military Service

All Venezuelan citizens were required to register for military conscription. But the combination of a generous set of deferments, low conscription needs, and the limited economic opportunities of low-income families has resulted in a mostly male military made up of soldiers predominantly from modest backgrounds. Since 1978, a legal reform has required women to register for the draft, but holds that military service itself is mandatory only during wartime (an unlikely event). The categories of service open to women who volunteer for the military include support, health, civil defense, police, transport, and refugee services.

VIOLENCE

Venezuela is no exception to the high rates of violence against women in the region. Police generally are not trained to deal with victims of rape or domestic violence, and courts rarely prosecute the accused. Poor women have the least knowledge of or access to laws that protect them, and often are forced to rely on neighbors for assistance and protection.[71]

Domestic Violence

It has been estimated that 60 percent of Venezuelan women have experienced mistreatment in their homes. In 1998, 14,500 cases of domestic violence against women were reported in Caracas,[72] where one report also found that in many public hospitals half of all emergency cases attended were the result of domestic violence.[73] Domestic violence is not a class-restricted phenomenon, with "higher strata" abuse "more sophisticated and dangerous, with deeply traumatized family situations."[74] In response to concerted action by women's rights advocates working inside and outside of the government, domestic violence legislation came into force in 1999.

In 1999 Venezuela became the last Latin American country to put into effect a national law against domestic violence, the Law Against Violence Toward Women and the Family. It requires the police to undergo special training on how to handle domestic violence situations and obligates hospitals to advise authorities of abuse; provides shelters for victims of violence; and mandates eight days of custody for perpetrators of minor injuries and six to 18 months for more serious cases. Moreover, there is no need for a victim to show visible signs of abuse to prove that violence took place; previously, a victim had to present injuries bigger than seven centimeters to press charges.

Rape/Sexual Assault

In 1995, 75,530 cases of sexual violence were reported nationwide; 64 percent of all rapes that took place in Caracas were perpetrated by someone known to the victim. In 1997, almost 12 women a day were raped in Venezuela. Moreover, some 40,000 children and adolescents were prostitutes in 1994.[75]

Rape is still referred to as "an attack on respectable customs" instead of as a crime against women. To prove rape, the victim must undergo a medical exam within 48 hours of the attack, and the perpetrator can avoid sentencing if he proposes marriage.

OUTLOOK FOR THE TWENTY-FIRST CENTURY

As Venezuelan women enter the twenty-first century, they confront considerable obstacles. Many of these are rooted in the burden of poverty that seems to fall disproportionately on women's shoulders. On the whole more responsible for children and paid less than their male counterparts, without the safety net of well-functioning welfare services, the majority of women struggle to make ends meet for themselves and their families on a daily basis. They take on work in the informal sector, extend their workdays, and disregard their health and well-being. Many are subject to violence at the hands of those they know as well as of strangers. In addition, they continue to be underrepresented in political leadership and in the top ranks of the professions and business management. Finally, women have been as affected as men by the current polarization over Chávez's leadership and policies, lining up as both supporters and opposition.

However, the picture is not without hope. Women's overrepresentation in education, their movement into the workforce, and their long history of creative and successful mobilization bode well for the future. Although their historical mobilization model, which relies on the coordinated action of select advocates within civil society, parties, and the state, is unlikely to extend to include the masses of women largely untouched by feminist ideas, it continues to achieve success in legal reform. And while many of the political changes wrought by Chávez are suspect, it is undeniable that he has been responsive to women's demands at a national level. This military man who exudes machismo has placed confirmed feminists in important political positions and has been responsive to some of their demands.

NOTES

1. Magally Huggins Castañeda and Diana Domínguez Nelson, *Mujeres latinoamericanas en cifras: Venezuela* (Santiago, Chile: Facultad Latinoamericano de Ciencias Sociales, 1993), 28.

2. David J. Myers, "Venezuela: The Stressing of Distributive Justice," in *Latin American Politics and Development*, eds. Howard J. Wiarda and Harvey F. Kline, 4th ed. (Boulder; CO: Westview Press, 1996), 232.

3. Ibid.; Siemon-Netto Uwe, "Bewitched by Bolivar," *Civilization: The Magazine of the Library of Congress* 7, no. 2 (April/May 2000): 78–85.

4. Central Intelligence Agency (CIA), *World Factbook — Venezuela*, 2001, www.odci.gov/cia/publications/factbook/geos/ve.html, 2.

5. United Nations Development Programme (UNDP), *Human Development Report 2001* (Oxford and New York: Oxford University Press, 2001), 167.

6. Huggins Castañeda and Dominguez Nelson, 1993, 51.

7. U.S. Department of State, *1999 Country Reports on Human Rights Practices: Venezuela* (Washington DC: U.S. Department of State, 2000), 16.

8. Nora Castañeda and María Isabel Bertone, *Education for All*, 2000, www.socwatch.org.uy/2000/eng/nationalreportsvenezuela_eng.htm.

9. UNDP, 2001, 211.

10. Huggins Castañeda and Domínguez Nelson, 1993, 53.

11. Oficina Central de Estadística e Informática (OCEI), *Censo general* (Caracas: OCEI, 1961).

12. Women's enrollment in higher education declines when they reach childbearing age, but it is still higher than men's.

13. Castañeda and Bertone, 2000.

14. Huggins Castañeda and Domínguez Nelson, 1993, 54.

15. Elisabeth J. Friedman, *Unfinished Transitions: Women and the Gendered Development of Democracy in Venezuela, 1936–1996* (University Park: Pennsylvania State University Press, 2000), 57; Nora Castañeda, "Las políticas públicas y la equidad de género en Venezuela," *Revista venezolana de estudios de la mujer* 3, no. 7 (April–June 1998): 42.

16. Carolina Coddetta, "Mujer y democracia: Reflexiones sobre una crisis," *Revista venezolana de estudios de la mujer* 3, no. 7 (April–June 1998): 84.

17. Economist Intelligence Unit (EIU), *Country Commerce: Venezuela*, October 31, 2000, www.viewswire.com; World Bank, *Venezuela, RB at a Glance*, September 13, 2001, www.worldbank.org/data, and *World Development Indicators Database*, April 2002, www.worldbank.org/data.

18. OCEI, *Censo General*. Caracas, 1961; Comisión Económica para América Latina y el Caribe (ECLAC), *UN estadísticas de género*, 2002, www.eclac.cl/mujer/proyectos/perfiles/comparados/milenio18.htm.

19. James W. Wilkie, Eduard Alemán, and José Guadalupe Ortega., eds., *Statistical Abstract of Latin America*, vol. 36 (Los Angeles: UCLA Latin American Center, University of California, 2000), 114.

20. OCEI, 1990; EIU, 2000.

21. UNDP, 2001, 223.

22. Huggins Castañeda and Domínguez Nelson, 1993, 43–44.

23. Castañeda, 1998, 38; Comunicación e Información de la Mujer (CIMAC), *Aún existe disparidad en el mercado laboral entre hombres y mujeres*, 2001, www.cimac.org.mx/noticias/01mar/01031313.html.

24. Niels-Hugo Blunch, Sudharshar Canagarajah, and Dhushyanth Raju, *The Informal Sector Revisited: A Synthesis Across Space and Time*, World Bank Social Protection Discussion Paper no. 0119, 2001, www.worldbank.org.

25. Giovanna Merola, "La prostitución es un hecho social, no un trabajo," *Fempress* no. 200 (June 1998): 5.

26. EIU, 2000.

27. Coddetta, 1998, 83.

28. EIU, *Venezuela Economy: Background*, August 8, 2001, www.viewswire.com.

29. Castañeda, 1998, 39.

30. Friedman, *Unfinished Transitions*, 2000, 228.

31. Ibid., 209–12.

32. UNDP, *Human Development Report 2000* (Oxford and New York: Oxford University Press, 2000), 263.

33. Estrella Gutierrez, "Sterilisation Workshops Spark Controversy," Interpress Service, Global Information Network, March 3, 1999.

34. Friedman, *Unfinished Transitions*, 2000, 46.

35. Ibid., 169.

36. Amnesty International, *Venezuela: Fear for the Safety of the Transgendered Community in Valencia, Carabobo State*, AI-index: AMR 53—2000, dated December 2000, www.amnesty.org.

37. Roberto Hernández Montoya, "The Cult of Venus in Venezuela," *Venezuela analítica* (January 31, 1999), www.analitica.com/bitblioteca/roberto/venus-i.asp; Friedman, *Unfinished Transitions*, 2000, chap. 2.

38. Huggins Castañeda and Domínguez Nelson, 1993, 30–31.

39. Wilkie et al., 2000, 151, 149.

40. Friedman, *Unfinished Transitions*, 2000, 170.

41. Efe News Services, "Las venezolanas tienen cada vez menos hijos," *Ete* (June 30, 1999).

42. Huggins Castañeda and Domínguez Nelson, 1993, 26.

43. UNDP, 2000, 252.

44. Wilkie et al., 2000.

45. Huggins Castañeda and Dominguez Nelson, 1993, 78.

46. Asociación Venezolana para una Educación Sexual Alternativa (AVESA), *Sexualidad adolescente en cifras* (Caracas: AVESA, 1998).

47. Castañeda, 1998, 43.

48. Gutierrez, 1999.

49. Huggins Castañeda and Domínguez Nelson, 1993, 23–24, 71.

50. Ibid., 68–69.

51. UNAIDS/Pan American Health Organization/World Health Organization (UNAIDS/PAHO/WHO), *Epidemiological Fact Sheet on HIV/AIDS and Sexually Transmitted Infections: 2000 Update* (Geneva, Switzerland: UNAIDS/WHO Working Group on Global HIV/AIDS and STI Surveillance, 2000); UNDP, 2001, 163; ECLAC, 2002.

52. Rakel Sosa, "Under the Sun, Under the Knife," *UNESCO Courier* (July/Aug. 2001), www.unesco.org/courier/2001_07/uk/doss32.htm.

53. Huggins Castañeda and Domínguez Nelson, 1993, 71.

54. PAHO, "Country Health Profile: Venezuela," 2001, www.paho.org/english/sha/prfiven.htm.

55. Friedman, *Unfinished Transitions*, 2000, 271.

56. Ibid., 274.

57. Ibid., chap. 2.

58. Inter-Parliamentary Union (IPU), *Women in National Parliaments*, 1999, www.ipu.org.

59. Wilkie et al., 2000, 105; UNDP, 2000, 265.

60. Rubin Armendriz, "Women Make Strides in Politics," Interpress Service, Global Information Network, Jan. 24, 2001.

61. Centro de Investigación Social, Formación y Estudios de la Mujer (CISFEM), *Situación de la mujer en Venezuela* (Caracas: CISFEM/UNICEF, 1994).

62. Although homosexuality is not outlawed in general, it is proscribed in the armed forces. Giocanda Espina, *Psicoanálisis y mujeres en movimiento* (Caracas: Ediciones FACES/UCV, 1997).

63. Married women were allowed control over the property they brought into a marriage under the 1945 reform of the Commercial Code. Wives are still not able to transact marital property commercially without their husband's consent, but husbands do not need their wives' consent. Huggins Castañeda and Dominguez Nelson, 1993, 83.

64. Elisabeth J. Friedman, "Democracia en la Casa: The 1982 Partial Reform of the Venezuelan Civil Code," *Americas & Latinas: A Journal of Women and Gender* 1, no. 1 (1993).

65. Friedman, *Unfinished Transitions*, 2000, 262.

66. Ibid., 228.

67. Espina, 1997.

68. Elisabeth J. Friedman, "State-Based Advocacy for Gender Equality in the Developing World: Assessing the Venezuelan National Women's Agency," *Women and Politics* 21, no. 2 (2000); *Unfinished Transitions*, 2000.

69. Friedman, *Unfinished Transitions*, 2000, chap. 5.

70. Elisabeth J. Friedman, "The Effects of 'Transnationalism Reversed' in Venezuela: Assessing the Impact of Global U.N. Conferences on the Women's Movement," *International Feminist Journal of Politics*, 1, no. 3 (1999).

71. Beatriz Rodríguez, "La cuantificación de la violencia doméstica," *Revista venezolana de estudios de la mujer* 3, no. 8 (1998): 25–42.

72. Efe News Services, "Mujeres son principales victimas de violencia y discriminación," *Efe* (March 8, 1999).

73. Estrella Gutierrez, "Finally, a Law Against Domestic Violence," Interpress Service, Global Information Network, Aug. 20, 1998.

74. Estrella Gutierrez, "Violence Against Women Rises Onward and Upward," Interpress Service, Global Information Network, Nov. 24, 1998.

75. United Nations Inter-Agency Campaign on Women's Human Rights in Latin America and the Caribbean, *Venezuela National Report*, 2000, www.undp.org/rblac/gender/venezuela.htm.

RESOURCE GUIDE

Suggested Reading

Friedman, Elisabeth J. *Unfinished Transitions: Women and the Gendered Development of Democracy in Venezuela, 1936–1996.* University Park: Pennsylvania State University Press, 2000.

Goodman, Louis W., Johanna Mendelson Forman, Moisés Naím, Joseph S. Tulchin, and Gary Bland, eds. *Lessons of the Venezuelan Experience.* Washington, DC: Woodrow Wilson Center Press; Baltimore and London: Johns Hopkins University Press, 1995.

Karl, Terry Lynn. *The Paradox of Plenty: Oil Booms and Petro-States.* Berkeley: University of California Press, 1997.

McCoy, Jennifer, Andrés Serbin, William C. Smith, and Andrés Stambouli, eds. *Venezuelan Democracy Under Stress.* New Brunswick, NJ: Transaction Publishers, 1995.

Rakowski, Cathy A. "Planned Development and Women's Relative Power: Steel and Forestry in Venezuela." *Latin American Perspectives* 22, no. 2 (1995): 51–75.

Web Sites and Organizations

Amazon Women of Venezuela (Amazonas Mujeres de Venezuela)
Final Av. Casanova. C.C.777, ofic. 16
Chacaíto
Caracas, Venezuela
Phone: 9524562
Email: amazonas@amazonasdevenezuela.com
Web site: www.amazonasdevenezuela.com

Amazon Women of Venezuela works for women's social equality and rights, respecting the free choice of how, with whom, and where they live their lives. Its objectives are the integration of women into professional and sports activities where they are underrepresented; promotion of cultural diversity; organization of workshops, meetings, cultural events, and eventually a community center to benefit women and their families; and publications on issues of relevance to women. This group has the most developed web site on women's issues in Venezuela.

Center for Social Research, Training, and Women's Studies (CISFEM)
Avenida Anauco, cruce con Roraima, Quinta Avesa
San Bernardino
Caracas, Venezuela
Phone: 518081/510212
Fax: 525410
Email: cisfem@cantv.net or cisfem@redsoc.org.ve
Web site: www.redsoc.org.ve:83/cisfem/index.html

CISFEM carries out research and takes action on behalf of the most vulnerable groups of society, with special attention to women, families, and children. Its programs are undertaken with a gender focus, from their design to their evaluation.

Central University of Venezuela's Women's Studies Center (CEM-UCV)
Office: Centro Comercial Los Chaguaramos, Piso 10, Oficina 10-4
Avenida Neveí
Los Chaguaramos
Caracas, Venezuela
Fax: 6933286
Documentation Center: Instituto "Rodolfo Quintero," Piso 1, Oficina 306
Universidad Central de Venezuela
Phone: 6053909/6053906
Mailing address: Apartado Postal 47744
Caracas, Venezuela, 1041-AA
Email: cem-ucv@yahoo.com
Web site: www.fpolar.org.ve/redsoc/cem/html

CEM is a women's studies center that promotes research, teaching, and outreach on women's issues within and outside of the university community. It offers psychosocial assistance to victims of domestic violence and consultation on gender-based research, and houses the Tecla Tofano documentation center. It also distributes the *Venezuelan Journal of Women's Studies* and coordinates a master's degree program.

Coordinating Committee of Women's Nongovernmental Organizations (CONG)
Apartado Postal 47468
Los Chaguaramos
Caracas, Venezuela, 1041-A
Phone: 6932609/6933286
Fax: 6932609/6933286

CONG is an umbrella organization of women's groups that works to increase public awareness of women's issues and coordinate actions for women's rights.

Popular Women's Circles (CFP)
San Vicente a Las Mercedes, No. 8
La Pastora
Caracas, Venezuela
Fax: 8649135
Email: cfp@redsoc.org.ve
Web site: www.redsoc.org.ve:83/cfp/index.html

CFP is an organization of women of the marginal urban and rural neighborhoods. It seeks to train and organize low-income women. It is run by them, and has 110 affiliates throughout the country.

Venezuelan Association for an Alternative Sexual Education (AVESA)
Avenida Anauco, cruce con Roraima, Quinta Avesa
San Bernardino
Caracas, Venezuela
Phone: 518081/510212
Fax: 525410
Email: avesa@reacciun.ve

AVESA promotes the study of sexuality, reproductive rights, and domestic violence through information provision, workshops, and publications.

SELECTED BIBLIOGRAPHY

Agency for International Development (AID). *Gender and Development (Latin America and the Caribbean, 1990–1999)*. Washington, DC: USAID, 1999.

———. *Labor Force Profile (Latin America and the Caribbean, 1980–1996)*. Washington, DC: USAID, 1999.

———. *Women and Education (Latin America and the Caribbean, 1980–1996)*. Washington, DC: USAID, 1999.

Amnesty International. *Venezuela: Fear for the Safety of the Transgendered Community in Valencia, Carabobo State*. AI-index: AMR 53/013/2000. Dated December 10, 2000. www.amnesty.org.

Armendriz, Rubin. "Women Make Strides in Politics." Interpress Service, Global Information Network, January 24, 2001.

Blunch, Niels-Hugo, Sudharshar Canagarajah, and Dhushyanth Raju. *The Informal Sector Revisited: A Synthesis Across Space and Time*. World Bank Social Protection Discussion Paper no. 0119. 2001. www.worldbank.org.

Canizalez, Andres. "Micro-lending to Feature at Women's Bank." Interpress Service, Global Information Network, May 25, 2001.

Castañeda, Nora, and María Isabel Bertone. *Education for All*. 2000. www.socwatch.org.uy/2000/eng/nationalreports/venezuela_eng.htm.

Central Intelligence Agency (CIA). *World Factbook—Venezuela*. 2001. www.odci.gov/cia/publications/factbook/geos/ve.html.

Economist Intelligence Unit (EIU). *Country Commerce: Venezuela*. October 31, 2000. www.viewswire.com.

———. *Venezuela Economy: Background*. Aug. 27, 2001. www.viewswire.com.

Friedman, Elisabeth J. "Democracia en la Casa: The 1982 Partial Reform of the Venezuelan Civil Code." *Americas & Latinas: A Journal of Women and Gender* 1, no. 1 (1993): 16–22.

———. "The Effects of 'Transnationalism Reversed' in Venezuela: Assessing the Impact of Global UN Conferences on the Women's Movement." *International Feminist Journal of Politics* 1, no. 3 (1999): 357–81.

———. "State-Based Advocacy for Gender Equality in the Developing World: Assessing the Venezuelan National Women's Agency." *Women and Politics* 21, no. 2 (2000): 47–80.

———. *Unfinished Transitions: Women and the Gendered Development of Democracy in Venezuela, 1936–1996*. University Park: Penn State University Press, 2000.

Gutierrez, Estrella. "Finally, a Law Against Domestic Violence." Interpress Service, Global Information Network, August 20, 1998.

———. "Violence Against Women Rises Onward and Upward." Interpress Service, Global Information Network, November 24, 1998.

———. "Sterilisation Workshops Spark Controversy." Interpress Service, Global Information Network, March 3, 1999.

Hernández Montoya, Roberto. "The Cult of Venus in Venezuela." *Venezuela Analítica* (Jan. 31, 1999). www.analitica.com/bitblioteca/roberto/venus-i.asp.

Inter-Parliamentary Union (IPU). *Women in National Parliaments*. 1999. www.ipu.org.

———. "Sudden Awakening in Venezuela: Venezuelan Women Active in Placing Controversial Issues in Parliament." *LOLApress* 13 (May 2000): 62.

———. *Women in National Parliaments*. 2001. www.ipu.org.

Myers, David J. "Venezuela: The Stressing of Distributive Justice." In *Latin American Politics and Development*, edited by Howard J. Wiarda and Harvey F. Kline, 227–269. 4th ed. Boulder, CO: Westview Press, 1996.

Ross, John, and John Stover. "The Family Planning Program Effort Index: 1999 Cycle." *International Family Planning Perspectives* 27, no. 3 (2001): 119–39.

Sosa, Rakel. "Under the Sun, Under the Knife." *UNESCO Courier* (July/Aug. 2001).www.unesco.org/courier/2001_07/uk/doss32.htm.

UNAIDS/Pan American Health Organization/World Health Organization (UNAIDS/ PAHO/WHO). *Epidemiological Fact Sheet on HIV/AIDS and Sexually Transmitted Infections: 2000 Update*. UNAIDS/WHO Working Group on Global HIV/ AIDS, and STI Surveillance, 2000.

United Nations Development Programme (UNDP). *Human Development Report 2000*. Oxford and New York: Oxford University Press, 2000.

———. *Human Development Report 2001*. Oxford and New York: Oxford University Press, 2000.

United Nations Inter-Agency Campaign on Women's Human Rights in Latin America and the Caribbean. *Venezuela National Report*. 2000. www.undp.org/rblac/ gender/venezuela.htm.

U.S. Department of State. *1999 Country Reports on Human Rights Practices—Venezuela*. Washington, DC: U.S. Department of State, 2000.

Uwe, Siemon-Netto. Bewitched by Bolivar." *Civilization* (April/May 2000).

World Bank. *Venezuela: RB at a Glance*. September 13, 2001. www.worldbank.org/ data.

———. *GenderStats: Venezuela*. 2002. www.genderstats.worldbank.org.

———. *World Development Indicators Database*. April 2002. www.worldbank.org/data.

Spanish Bibliography

Asociación Venezolana para una Educación Sexual Alternativa (AVESA). *Sexualidad adolescente en cifras*. Caracas: AVESA, 1998.

Castañeda, Nora. "Las políticas públicas y la equidad de género en Venezuela." *Revista venezolana de estudios de la mujer* 3, no. 7 (1998): 32–49.

Centro de Investigación Social, Formación y Estudios de la Mujer (CISFEM). *Situación de la mujer en Venezuela*. Caracas: CISFEM/UNICEF, 1994.

Coddetta, Carolina. "Mujer y democracia: Reflexiones sobre una crisis." *Revista venezolana de estudios de la mujer* 3, no. 7 (1998): 79–88.

Comisión Económica para América Latina y el Caribe (ECLAC). *UN estadísticas de género*. 2002. www.eclac.cl/mujer/proyectos/perfiles/comparados/milenio18.htm.

Comunicación e Información de la Mujer (CIMAC). *Aún existe disparidad en el mercado laboral entre hombres y mujeres*. 2001. www.cimac.org.mx/noticias/01mar/01031313.html.

Consejo Supremo Electoral (CSE), División de Estadística. *Elecciones 1993*. Caracas: CSE, 1993.

Efe News Services. "Las venezolanas tienen cada vez menos hijos." *Efe* (June 30, 1999).

———. "Mujeres son principales victimas de violencia y discriminación." *Efe* (March 8, 1999).

Espina, Gioconda. *Psicoanálisis y mujeres en movimiento*. Caracas: Ediciones FACES/UCV, 1997.

Merola, Giovanna. "La prostitución es un hecho social, no un trabajo." *Fempress* no. 200 (June 1998): 5.

Ministerio de Educación. *Memoria y cuenta 1998*. 123, no. 119. Caracas, 1999.

Oficina Central de Estadística e Informática (OCEI). *Censo general*. Caracas: OCEI, 1961.

———. *Censo general*. Caracas: OCEI, 1990.

———. *Encuesta de hogares por muestra*. Caracas: OCEI, 1971.

Rodríguez, Beatriz. "La cuantificación de la violencia doméstica: Mostrario de una impunidad." *Revista venezolana de estudios de la mujer* 3, no. 8 (1998): 25–42.

INDEX

SEE MAP BELOW

Isl

CENTRAL AND SOUTH AMERICA

SOUTH

PACIFIC

OCEAN

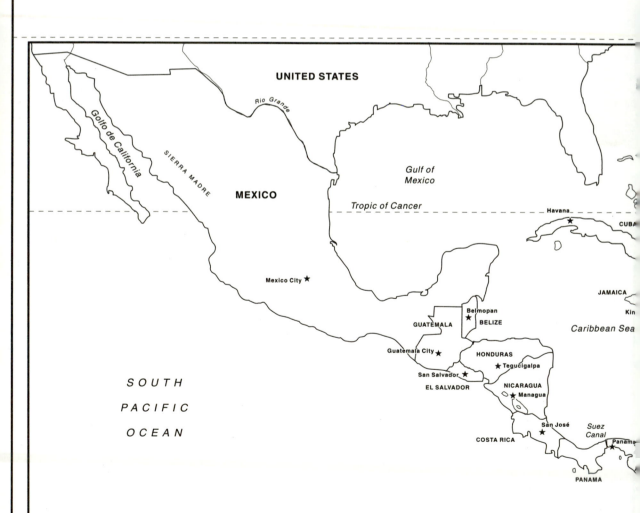

UNITED STATES

Rio Grande

Golfo de California

SIERRA MADRE

MEXICO

Gulf of Mexico

Tropic of Cancer

Havana ★

CUBA

Mexico City ★

JAMAICA

Kin

Belmopan ★

Caribbean Sea

GUATEMALA

BELIZE

Guatemala City ★

HONDURAS

★ Tegucigalpa

San Salvador ★

EL SALVADOR

NICARAGUA

★ Managua

SOUTH

PACIFIC

OCEAN

San José ★

Suez Canal

COSTA RICA

Panama ★

PANAMA